ROOTS OF
GERMAN NATIONALISM

ROOTS OF GERMAN NATIONALISM

Louis L. Snyder

Indiana University Press

BLOOMINGTON/LONDON

FOR OUR GODCHILDREN
Jessica Courtenay Wilson
AND
Victoria Paige Wilson
AND TO THE MEMORY OF
Sara Lou

MANUFACTURED IN THE UNITED STATES OF AMERICA

Library of Congress Cataloging in Publication Data

Snyder, Louis Leo, 1907–
    Roots of German nationalism.
    Bibliography:
    Includes index.
    1. Nationalism—Germany. 2. Germany—Politics and government. I. Title.
DD112.S65   320.9′43′08   77-74437
ISBN 0-253-35026-3   1 2 3 4 5 82 81 80 79 78

Contents

Introduction

Before the outbreak of World War I, British publicist Norman Angell made a significant statement about nationalism. "Political nationalism," he said, "has become for the European of our age, the most important thing in the world, more important than humanity, decency, kindness, piety; more important than life itself." Angell's conclusion was by no means exaggerated. At that time and even to the present day, nationalism has permeated every political philosophy, whether it be national, imperialistic, pannational, or international. The idea of national consciousness has become dominant in the life of every modern state, large or small, and there are few signs that it has been thrust into the background by current historical developments.

Nationalism has played a special role—and a tragic one—in the history of the German people during the lat two hundred years. From the emergence of Prussia in the late 18th century as the leading power in the Germanies to the unification of Germany in the Second Reich by Bismarck in 1871 to the overwhelming events of two World Wars, nationalism was of critical importance in German history. It follows that the study of nationalism in general and German nationalism in particular have become subjects of great concern to historians, both outside and inside Germany.

Traces of nationalism may be seen as early as the 13th century. As I pointed out in *The Meaning of Nationalism* (1954) the major turning point for the modern world was the French Revolution, when the French clearly turned from loyalty and identification with *le roi* to loyalty and identification with *la patrie*. From then on nationalism developed into one of the major ideological components of the modern world.

By the same token nationalism in Germany has been identified by some as emerging as early as the late 15th–century reform movement, or seen as the underlying cause of the 16th-century turmoil unleashed by Luther's revolt. The sense of German nationalism, however, was for the most part left unsolved by the Hapsburg dynasty. Only the octopuslike expansion of Prussia, with her Hohenzollern dynasty and her able *Junker* agricultural nobility, gave direction to the formation of what may be called Prusso-German nationalism. The root of later German national consciousness was expressed in this Prusso-German symbiosis which gave German nationalism its form and content.

It is the purpose of this book to throw light on various aspects of German nationalism by combining some of my articles and lectures with additional material written especially for this study. The chapters are grouped chronologically from the early 19th century to the present day. The theme of each chapter is one aspect of that ism which has caused so much trouble for Germans as well as for other peoples.

Any approach to the study of nationalism, as well as for any other major topic in history, must be pluralistic. Nationalism cannot be understood by stripping it to one monistic factor: it tends to combine elements which are economic, political, social, cultural, psychological, and on occasion religious. Historians today generally agree on the importance of economic factors in historical causation, although only historicists (as opposed to historians) maintain that economic factors are *exclusively* motivating in history and that other elements—political, social, cultural, and psychological—are only ideological veils which tend to obscure the true generating factor. Yet, the economic factor in early German nationalism remains of prime importance. Little attention has been paid to it outside of the studies of Theodore Hamerow, especially in his *Restoration, Revolution, Reaction, 1815–1871* (1958), and several others.

The first chapter of this book concerns the role of Friedrich List, a Württemberger economist, in the formation of the *Zollverein,* the German customs union which preceded the political unification of Germany. Originally delivered as a paper before the American Historical Association, the material in this chapter, as well as that on the brothers Grimm in the following chapter, has been published in different form elsewhere. It is included here as basic for the meaning of this collection.

The cultural side of early German nationalism is best observed in German romanticism, which passed well beyond its literary phase and became closely associated with the course of German nationalism. There are many apostles of German romanticism who could be treated here, including Fichte, Novalis, Schleiermacher, von Kleist, the Schlegel brothers, and many others. For the second chapter I have chosen again to write on the brothers Grimm and the nationalistic aspects of their famous fairy tales. The study appeared originally in the *Journal of Social Psychology* and is reproduced here in that form instead of later versions. The article created a stir at the time of its publication, especially among German historians, who refused to admit any evidence whatever of a budding national consciousness in the "cosmopolitan" fairy tales. The continued interest in these tales is revealed by the reception of Bruno Bettelheim's book, *The Uses of Enchantment* (1976), concerned with the meaning and importance of the fairy tales.

The third chapter, written for this book, traces the genesis and early development of German nationalism, with emphasis upon the impetus received from Napoleon, the gradually emerging Prussian mold, the failure of liberal nationalism in the Revolution of 1848, the leadership of Bismarck in the unification of Germany, and the establishment of the Second Reich. Where nationalism in the conglomerate Austro-Hungarian Empire acted as a force for disruption, in the Germanies it was decidedly a means to unification.

German nationalism and imperialism, as in other countries, were closely related in the latter part of the 19th century. Chapter 4 treats Bismarck's gradual conversion from Prussian to German nationalist. It examines German penetration into SouthWest Africa from 1880 to 1885. Attention is given to the role of Bismarck's son, Herbert, in the negotiations between Germany and Britain on the Angra Pequena question. Somewhat similar clashing national interests between Germany and the United States also took place in the 1880s, as described in Chapter 5. This study traces the story of importation of German pork from the United Staes into Germany, a confrontation in which Bismarck again played a leading role.

The concept of national character is interesting if controversial. Authoritarianism in family, school, and everyday relationships became a theme of the German way of life in the eras of Bismarck and William II. Well beyond a simple stereotype, this characteristic became vital in the development of the German mind. Chapter 6 treats the political implications of Herbert von Bismarck's marital affairs and reveals how the Iron Chancellor used pressure on his oldest son to prevent a politically embarrassing marriage. While not specifically concerned with important issues of German nationalism, the incident does throw some light on authoritarianism in the German family, one aspect of the German national character.

Chapter 7, devoted to Bismarck's rejection of the Lasker Resolution sent to Germany by the American Congress in 1884, also shows in microcosm an outburst of national pride, coupled with bitter political sensitiveness. Diplomatic protocol meant nothing to the hard-bitten Chancellor, not even normal courtesy, when anyone dared even in a matter of death to praise any of his especially hated political enemies.

In line with the chronological scheme, chapter 8 is concerned with the

Weimar Republic from 1919 to 1933. Researched and written with my colleague, Howard L. Adelson, who did the major share of the work, the chapter treats the older form of German nationalism with a new mythology expressed in iconographic terms during the era of the Weimar Republic. The theme of the chapter is that German satiric medallic propaganda contributed heavily to the perpetuation of old and the creation of new nationalistic myths in Germany. The chapter is included with Dr. Adelson's permission.

The next two chapters treat nationalism in the Third Reich. Chapter 9 describes Hitler's transferred nationalism, his opposition to bourgeois nationalism, and his role as innovator of racial nationalism. Chapter 10 shows how the German people reacted to the nationalism advocated by Hitler.

Chapter 11 is devoted to the career and work of Hans Kohn, the historian who gave much of his attention to German history and to the German mentality. In his *Mind of Modern Germany* (1960) and elsewhere Kohn provided a wealth of information and valuable insight on the views of individual apostles of German nationalism such as Jahn and Treitschke.

Chapter 12 treats a new trend in the study of nationalism, the controversial concept of territorial imperative transferred from animals to humans. While this chapter is geared to the general study of nationalism, it has implications for the study of German nationalism in particular, especially in explanation of German aggression before both World Wars. The account does not take sides for or against the Lorenz-Audrey-Morris (LAM) school, but it does advocate an open mind instead of denunciatory derision. Future investigation may well either destroy or bolster the thesis of territorial imperative among humans as a clarification of nationalism.

The final chapter summarizes the story of German nationalism after 1945, with emphasis upon the changing nature of German nationalism, the political and economic miracles of the present West German Federal Republic, German youth and the new nationalism, the specter of Neo-Nazism, the nationalisms of West and East Germany, and the changing German national character.

Every book is a product of driving interest, love, and hard work. In the production of this volume the assistance of Ida Mae Brown Snyder was of more than ordinary importance. Once again it is a pleasure to pay tribute to her superb work well beyond the normal help of a devoted spouse.

Princeton, N.J.   LOUIS L. SNYDER
September 1977

CHAPTER

1

Economic Nationalism: Friedrich List, Germany's Handicapped Colbert

> I would indicate, as the distinguishing characteristic of my system, *nationality*. On the nature of *nationality*, as the intermediate interest between those of *individualism* and of *entire humanity*, my whole structure is based.
>
> Friedrich List

The pioneer investigators of nationalism, Carlton J. H. Hayes and Hans Kohn, together with their apostles, have been criticized for devoting too much attention to the cultural aspects of nationalism and too little to its energizing economic motivations. The older literature is termed inadequate because it failed to take into consideration the all-important economic factor. The charge is somewhat exaggerated. Both Hayes and Kohn were well aware of the role of economics in the origins and development of nationalism.

German nationalism during the early 19th century undoubtedly had its utilitarian and functional aspects. It is unreasonable to insist that cultural influences merely legitimatized the German national state, and that German nationalism, as elsewhere, was generated among a people only by the growing awareness of economic backwardness and by the desire for a modern economy. Certainly, economics played an important role, but to denigrate the intellectual precursors in favor of exclusive economic forces is a serious error.

This chapter is a rewritten and updated version of a paper originally delivered before the American Historical Association at its annual meeting in Chicago, December 28, 1950.

I

One need only remind the economic determinists that the *philosophes* of the Enlightenment were the intellectuals who presented the ideas which led to the economic, social, and political explosion of the French Revolution.

Economic determinists also hold that once a country has been industrialized, nationalism becomes merely one of the ideologies employed to integrate a society in which traditional loyalties have been undermined. What is overlooked is the fact that a sense of German nationalism emerged long before the drive of Germany (along with the United States) to a place of leadership in the New Industrial Revolution commencing after the middle of the 19th century. Admittedly, one must take into consideration the critical role of economics in all such historical movements as nationalism, but at the same time the discerning scholar must not fall to his knees before the idol of economics.

Friedrich List took a leading role in the economic motivations of German nationalism. He successfully fixed the attention not only of theorists but also of men of action on the idea of a national economy. He was the driving force behind the *Zollverein*. He contributed much to the economic maturity of Germany, to the vigorous expansion of its manufactures and commerce, and to its status as a political power of the first rank. In a very real sense he was the Alexander Hamilton of his people. He is worthy of our attention.

On the Emergence of German Nationalism

German nationalism was born in the darkness of Napoleonic despotism. In the Germanies, as elsewhere, nationalism was a movement of resistance to the forcible internationalism promoted by the French conqueror. The Germans were not attracted by the prospect of a European continent dominated by Napoleon. Nationalist reaction took varying forms, ranging from the British preference for democratic institutions to the Spanish counterrevolutionary sentiment calling for restoration of the Bourbons and the clergy. The Germans rebelled not only against Napoleonic rule but also against the philosophy of the Enlightenment.

Ironically, as we shall see in more detail in chapter 3, Napoleon unconsciously performed an important service for the Germans by simplifying their political structure. This was by no means an altruistic gesture: he wanted a more manageable Germany to be included in his proposed United States of Europe under his own leadership. Before his time the Germanies were a crazy quilt geographical expression of some three hundred separate political units (in 1789, if the minor principalities be included, there were exactly 1,789 sovereign units). The statesmen at the Congress of Vienna in 1815 extended the process by setting up a new Germany composed of thirty-eight states ranging from the five kingdoms of Prussia, Bavaria, Saxony, Württemberg, and Hanover to such miniscule states as Lippe and such free cities as Hamburg. The era after 1815 was known as the *Biedermeier* period, a time of stability and peace in which the ordinary German was occupied not by politics but by the traditional concern for family, village, or urban community. There were political stirrings in the land, especially the new sense of nationalism which called for moral and political regeneration and which embraced the cause of national unity. Early German nationalists were intellectuals who were dissatisfied by the abstractions of the Enlightenment floating across the Rhine from the west. These litterateurs and scholars became the leaders of 19th-century German thought, much as their British and French counterparts had functioned in the late 18th century. Most German intellectuals of this era preached the virtues of the new German nationalism.

The tone was set by Johann Gottfried von Herder, who urged his fellow Germans to cease their imitation of French ways and turn instead to contemplation of their own national heritage. He called for a return to German native roots and for an accent upon the life of the *Volk,* the common people. A sound civilization, he warned, must reflect a specific national character, what he called a *Volksgeist,* or spirit of the people. Attention to the *Volksgeist* was to become an important element of German nationalism.

Other German intellectuals, fascinated by the ideas of national unity and national prestige, took up the banner of romanticism. (See chapter 3 for a more detailed discussion of romanticism.) They would work for the creation of a great new German national state reflecting the special German will and the distinctive German culture. They would thrust aside the ineffective petty princes and the half-Frenchified nobility in favor of a new national government which would protect the interests of the German *Volk* and especially of its rising bourgeoisie.

They came from all levels of the intellectual spectrum. The eccentric Turnvater Jahn organized a youth movement, invented political gymnastics on the Swedish model, and called for the unity of the German people. At the university level Johann Gottlieb Fichte, in his *Addresses to the German Nation,* declared that there existed a powerful German spirit as well as a permanent German national character which had to be kept clean of any foreign, especially French, influence. Similarly, the brothers Grimm collected their folk tales in an attempt to discover and to revive the old indigenous German Spirit. (See the following chapter.)

Even more influential in solidifying the structure of German nationalism was the philosopher Georg Friedrich Wilhelm Hegel, considered by many to be one of the greatest philosophical minds of the 19th century. There is little doubt about the eminence of this seminal thinker, but there is also little doubt about the fact that Hegel was responsible for turning German nationalism in a dangerous direction. He set the tone by presenting the state as the embodiment of reason and liberty. To him the state was the sovereign power, where to Rousseau and the *philosophes* of the Enlightenment the sovereignty of the individual human being was paramount. Hegel's dialectic (pattern of opposites) held that the very disunity of Germany, by producing the idea of unity, would result eventually in the creation of a powerful German state "corresponding to the genius of the nation." This thinking was to lead to that form of integral nationalism which had catastrophic results for the German people, for Europeans, and for the world. Hegel's influence was enormous. By the late 19th century it had become almost impossible for a school teacher to obtain a position unless he had been Hegelian-trained.

A multiplicity of political, social, and psychological motivations played a part in the formation of German nationalism. Cultural nationalism passed into political nationalism: the national culture had to be preserved and the state was sovereign. At the root was a generating economic force. Here the name of Friedrich List is of prime importance. In economics he came to the same conclusions as Herder, Jahn, Fichte, and Hegel. In defining the requirements of nationhood, he placed emphasis upon extensive territory, customs union, protective tariffs, colonies, and "adequate power on land and sea." These, he said, were to be preferred to the Enlightenment's recommendation of law and the spirit.

The Role of Prussia

It is possible to overemphasize the uniqueness of German nationalism, yet its historical development was quite different from other European nationalisms. The German nationalism which emerged in the 19th century was fixed in a Prussian matrix. Prussia took the lead in German life, openly, discreetly, or secretly. From the 18th century onward, the steady extension of Prussia was a key factor in German history. Prussia was the dominant power controlling the unification of Germany and the formation of the Second Reich by Otto von Bismarck.

There were certainly parallel movements in the history of other European nations but not on the same scale. Sardinia played a similar role in the unification of Italy; the house of Savoy was the counterpart of the Hohenzollerns. Cavour took the Bismarckian role in the building of a united Italy. In early Russian history there were three distinct centers emerging from the chaos—Galicia, Novgorod, and Moscow, but politically the Muscovite dukedom merged into the Muscovite tsardom. Modern France, too, was an extension of the *Îsle de Paris*. But in all these cases the major trend was essentially political.

In Germany the influence of Prussia was considerably more pronounced. The story of how the Prussian *Junkers* pushed to the leadership of Germany is a classic tale of piecemeal conquest. There was an important added factor to territorial expansion—the Prussian way of life was superimposed upon the Germans and gave them a unique or at least a very different quality of national life. Prussia and the *Junkers* gained not only political but also industrial and commercial control. The drive began in the early 19th century and continued on into the 20th century. First came leadership in the *Zollverein* wrested from List. Paradoxically, the *Zollverein* was originally a device used by Prussian administrators to prevent a general German economic union. In the early stages the Prussians were concerned that the economic union might react to the advantage of Austria in the confrontation between *Gross Deutschland* (a Greater Germany under Austrian control) and *Klein Deutschland* (a small Germany under Prussian leadership). Moreover, Prussian administrators at first had little desire to unify the customs of all the German states. They were interested primarily in their own economic problems. Such administrators as Karl Georg Maasen, director-general of taxation, and Friedrich Adolf von Motz, minister of finance, were more concerned by the economic amalgamation of strictly Prussian territories scattered over the map of Central Europe. Their attitude began to change as Prussia's political power was enhanced.

At this time there existed a strong sense of particularism among the German states. Both the Central German and the South German states looked forward to the benefits of their own customs unions. They had no intention of relinquishing their economic independence to Prussia or to Austria or to any other outside power. Yet, one by one the German states, on occasion against their own will, were forced into the Prussian orbit. Not the least important among the causes for this shift was an ongoing social transformation. The up-and-coming middle class, the bourgeoisie motivated by an urge for profits, began to see the desirability of Prussian leadership at precisely the time when the Prussian landholding *Junkers* had begun to think in terms of a German rather than a narrow Prussian nationalism.

Early Career

The originator of the *Zollverein* was not a Prussian but a Württemberger. Friedrich List was a battered and bruised soul, the target of industrialists and a favorite prey of the Austrian secret police. Nevertheless, he went doggedly ahead with his ideas despite slander and calumny. He was denounced by critics as "Jacobin," "demagogue," "Republican," "revolutionary," and "traitorous trader." Metternich pronounced him "an heroic swindler" and "the tool of squealing German manufacturers." During his lifetime List was a prophet with little honor in his homeland.

Yet, and here is the irony, after List's death, when it had become obvious that his idea of national economy was in reality a magnificent service to his Fatherland, the man who had been violently denounced during his life now became honored as a great German patriot-hero. The historian Heinrich von Treitschke, himself an ardent German nationalist, said that List was "a demagogue only in the noblest sense." In 1925 the List-Gesellschaft was founded in honor of the great economist. Gone were the denunciations of earlier years. List was now called "a great German without Germany," "Germany's *verhinderten* Colbert," an economic genius "who embodied the finest thinking of Cromwell, Canning, Dr. Quesnay, Robert Peel, even Aristotle." The man who was once attacked viciously now received posthumous homage from his fellow Germans.

Somewhere between the limits of denunciation and approbation appears an important figure in the development of German nationalism. List was the first economist to emphasize the critical importance of a national German railway system. He projected a number of ideas which were eventually implemented, including a program of protective tariffs, a national merchant marine, a German navy, German colonialism, the concept of a Greater Germany (beyond Austrian control), and the idea of *Mitteleuropa*. His propaganda for the *Zollverein,* which was to include all German states, fired the imagination of Germany's political leaders and administrators and turned their thoughts to political economy. He influenced Bismarck in his drive for national unification.

Friedrich List was born on August 6, 1789, just eight days before the fall of the Bastille in Paris and the beginning of the French Revolution.[1] His native city was Reutlingen in Württemberg. The youngest son of a prosperous tanner, at an early age he showed a distaste for his father's occupation. Determined to carve out a career for himself in government, he entered the civil service in Württemberg. His progress was rapid and within a decade he rose to the post of ministerial under-secretary. A voracious reader, he was interested in the writings of the French *philosophes,* and especially in anything concerned with classical economics. At this time he was convinced that the administration of Württemberg as well as other states had to accept reform which would relieve the burden of an arbitrary bureaucracy. As his reputation began to grow, List was appointed Professor of Practical Administration (*Staatspraxis*) at the University of Tübingen.

List's efforts to reform the antiquated administration of Württemberg angered the reactionary officials who disliked the French revolutionary ideas

---

[1]The life of List has attracted much attention among German scholars. The earliest biography was Ludwig Häusser, *Friedrich Lists Leben* (Stuttgart, 1850), which was appended to List's *Gesammelte Schriften.* Later biographies include Karl Jensch, *Friedrich List* (Berlin, 1901); Margaret E. Hirst, *Life of Friedrich List and Selections from His Writings* (London, 1909), which included List's *Outline of American Political Economy;* and Friedrich Lenz, *Friedrich List, Der Mann und das Werk* (Munich, 1936). In 1931 Walter von Molo wrote a novel titled *Ein Deutscher ohne Deutschland (A German without Germany),* which was based on List's career. List's career in the United States is discussed in two articles by William Notz, "Friedrich List in Amerika," in *Weltwirtschaftliches Archiv,* XXI (1925), 199–265, and XXI (1925), pp. 154–82; and "Friedrich List in America," in *American Economic Review,* XVI (1926), pp. 248–65. The eighth edition of List's *Das nationale System der politischen Ökonomie* (Stuttgart, 1925) contains a critical introduction by K. Th. Eheberg and a bibliography by Max Hoelzel. List's *National System of Political Economy* appeared in a new English translation by Sampson S. Lloyd in London in 1928. The Friedrich List-Gesellschaft issued a complete edition of List's works in 12 volumes: *Friedrich List: Schriften-Reden-Briefen* (Berlin, 1927–1936). Other works on List include the following titles arranged chronologically: H. P. Olshausen, *Friedrich List und der Deutscher Handels-und Gewerbsverein,* List Studien, no. 6 (Jena, 1935); H. Boetsch, *Einkommen und Vermögen von Friedrich List* (Lorach-Stetten, 1936); M. Bouvier-Ajam, *Frédéric List, Sa vie, son oeuvre, son influence* (Paris, 1938); K. A. Meissinger, *Friedrich List, Der Pioneer des Reichs* (Leipzig, 1943): H. Ritschl, *Friedrich List: Leben und Lehre* (Tübingen, 1948); C. Brinkmann, *Friedrich List* (Berlin, 1949); G. Fabiunke, *Zur historischen Rolle des deutschen nationalökonomen Friedrich List* (Berlin, 1955); H. Gehrig, *Friedrich List und Deutschlands politisch-ökonomische Einheit* (Leipzig, 1956); F. Bülow, *Friedrich List: Ein Volkswirt kämpft für Deutschlands Einheit* (Göttingen, c. 1959); P. Gehring, *Friedrich List: Jugend und Reisejahre, 1789–1825* (Tübingen, 1964); H. Gehrig., ed., *Friedrich List: Wegbereiter einer Wirtschaft* (Berlin, 1966); F. Lenz, *Friedrich Lists Staats-und Gesellschaftslehre* (Berlin, 1967); H. Kobayashi, *James Steuart, Adam Smith, and Friedrich List* (Tokyo, 1967); W. Strosslin, *Friedrich List: Lehre von der wirtschaftlichen Entwicklung* (Tübingen, 1968); and E. N. Roussakis, *Friedrich List, the Zollverein, and the Unity of Europe* (Bruges, 1968). The most useful articles are: E. M. Earle, "Friedrich List: Forerunner of Pan-Germanism," *The American Scholar,* XII, no. 4 (October, 1943), pp. 430–43; F. Clairmonte, "Friedrich List and the Historical Concept of Balanced Growth," *The Indian Economic Review,* IV, no. 3 (February, 1959), pp. 24–44; and W. Fischer, "The German Zollverein," *Kyklos* XIII, no. 1, pp. 65–88.

drifting in from across the Rhine. Moreover, governmental officials deplored List's association with the *Handels- und Gewerbsverein,* a group of merchants and industrialists who called for reform. The young economist could not withstand the strength of his enemies in Württemberger officialdom and eventually he was forced to resign his professorship. He now became secretary of the *Handels- und Gewerbsverein* and editor of its journal.

At this time List decided to embark upon a political career as a means of furthering his demand for change. In 1819 he was elected to the Diet of Württemberg to represent Reutlingen, his native city. He plunged into his work for reform. He called loudly for more effective local government and for publicity on judicial procedures. Again he demanded economic reforms, including more equitable taxes, changes in the budget system, and aid to industry. His activities in opposition to the reactionary state government were regarded as virtually treasonable. There was little understanding then in Württemberg and in other states of the mechanics of a viable democracy. Opposition to the ruling authorities was regarded not as parliamentary dissent but as a wild revolution which had to be countered by force. It was a serious matter. List was not only expelled from the Diet, but he was also condemned to ten months of imprisonment at hard labor. In addition, he was required to pay the costs of the proceedings initiated against him. From our viewpoint today List's activities fell well within the framework of normal political opposition, but to the hard-bitten bureaucrats of Württemberg he was a dangerous radical who had to be silenced for the good of the state and its ruling class.

The thirty-one-year-old civil servant spent the next four years in Paris i exile from Württemberg. On the advice of friends he returned in May 182 but it was a serious mistake. The authorities arrested him again and he wa sent to a fortress. He was released only when he promised to emigrate tc America. Like Carl Schurz, who later in 1848 was to leave his homeland because of "dangerous" liberal activities and make his way in the New World, List, too, decided to seek his fortune in America. He sailed for New York in 1825.

While in exile in Paris, List had met Marquis de Lafayette, who had played an important role in the American Revolution. Each was attracted to the other, and they became fast friends. When List came to New York, he was warmly welcomed by Lafayette, who introduced his German friend to Andrew Jackson, Henry Clay, James Madison, Edward Livingston, and other prominent American statesmen.

At this time List's most pressing problem was to earn a living. His first step was to purchase a small plot of land near Harrisburg, Pennsylvania, which he would cultivate for a profit. He was unlucky as a small farmer and he soon gave up the project. Instead, he became editor of the *Readinger Adler,* a small weekly newspaper designed for German immigrants. The paper soon became one of the most influential publications in Pennsylvania. In its columns List attacked the cosmopolitan system of free trade advocated by Adam Smith and instead supported a political economy based on protection of native industry. This was in line with what was then known as the "American system," which advocated high tariffs to protect native industries and subsidies for such industries. List acquired a national reputation as one of the foremost defenders of the American system.

In 1827 List was offered the presidency of Lafayette College, but he reluctantly turned down the quiet life of an academician. During the presidential campaign of 1828, he worked among the Pennsylvania Democrats to win their support for Andrew Jackson and he was influential in that task.

Most of all, List was impressed by the possibility of advancement in the young American republic by devoting his efforts to business. Careers were open to talent there. List was gifted not only as a theoretical economist but also as a practical business man. Within a comparatively short time he was able to accumulate a comfortable fortune through various successful business projects. These included the discovery and development of a new coal field in Pennsylvania, the construction of a railroad, and the formation of the Little Schuykill Navigation, Railroad & Coal Company, the forerunner of the modern Reading System.

These enterprises made List independently wealthy, but he never forgot his homeland and always looked forward to returning there some day. After becoming a naturalized American citizen, he served as United States consul at Baden, Leipzig, and Stuttgart. He then decided to make his permanent home in Augsburg. At this time he embarked on an ambitious plan to organize a German railway system. Although faced with many obstacles, he completed a railroad from Leipzig to Dresden.

Again the activities of List attracted the angered attention of Metternich and his police agents. In 1837 Metternich forced the embattled Württemberger to leave his homeland. List spent the next three years in Paris. Here he wrote an essay entitled *System naturel d'économie politique* on the most feasible method of changing from a system of protection to free trade. This work was later judged to be an *"ouvrage remarquable"* by the French Academy. In 1839 List received the crushing news that his only son, Oskar, had lost his life while serving as a lieutenant in the French Foreign Legion.

List as Political Economist

The work of Friedrich List places him historically among the leading economists of modern times. He rejected the idea of abstract validity of economic doctrines. Instead, he examined commonly accepted views and rejected whatever he felt had no practical value. He was careful to project his own ideas in terms of viable political considerations. He was opposed to the principle of cosmopolitanism in the economic system, and especially to the doctrine of free trade, which he regarded as in harmony with that principle.

Although he recognized the importance of the work of Adam Smith and the classical school of economics in assuring the industrial and commercial supremacy of England in the First Industrial Revolution, List deemed that work unsuited to Germany. He rejected the parallelism proposed by Adam Smith between the economic conduct of the individual and that of a nation, and asserted that the special interests of the individual members of the nation would not necessarily lead to the highest good of the nation as a whole. Departing from Smith's individualistic-cosmopolitan economics, List turned to productive forces as the core of his economic system. In contrast to the classical division of labor he stressed the cooperative aspects of the productive process in society. This accent on productive forces led him to advocate protective tariffs as the sure means of exploiting national resources.

Above all, List was a firm advocate of the national idea. Each nation, he said, had its own special requirements dependent upon the degree of development of its historical circumstances. What was good for England with her industrial and commercial supremacy was not necessarily the right formula for a rising country such as Germany. The national unity which is vital for all states, large or small, is necessary for every individual in the nation, and the interests of the individual must always be held secondary to the preservation of national unity. Unlike the individual, the nation has a continuous life. The wealth of nations, according to List, must consist, not in the sum total of the exchange-values which it possesses, but in the full use of its powers of production. Nations achieve their very best condition when they are able to develop to the same degree the three productive powers of manufacturing, commerce, and agriculture.

List believed that only the nations of the temperate zones are adapted for the growth of higher forms of industry. These nations normally pass through certain stages of economic development: (1) pastoral life; (2) agriculture; (3) agriculture united with manufactures; and (4) the combination of agriculture, manufactures, and commerce. It is the vital task of political leaders and economists to enact the proper legislative and administrative actions necessary for the nation to proceed through these stages. Each nation should begin by supporting its agriculture by free trade. When it reaches a point when it can provide its own manufacturing, it should change to a system of protective tariffs to nourish and support the development of home industries. When its industries attain a high plane of development, the nation can then revert to free trade. During the period of protection, the nation may for a time lose a part of its exchange values, but she will gain in the long run from her valuable productive power.

As patriot and nationalist, List was interested primarily in the economic development of his homeland. He believed that the vigorous expansion of German manufactures and commerce was possible only if German territory were extended to the seacoasts both in the north and the south. In effect this was a plea for imperialist expansion though List was careful to avoid using the word "imperialism." The idea was later translated into reality by political activists. The way to expansion, List believed, was through protective legislation emanating from a customs union of all German lands. These were the views of the spiritual father of the *Zollverein*.

List and the National Idea

Few other German economists of the time emphasized so strongly as List the nexus between economics and politics. From his point of view List saw no validity in economic doctrines unless they were considered in terms of politics. He had one consistent purpose—to present "a theoretical system which should express the interest of countries occupying second or third rank but possessing the potentialities of first-class nations." Always uppermost in his own mind was the case of his German Fatherland.

One of the best List scholars, Arnold H. Price, made this judgment about List's work: "Although List was important as a leader of public opinion and succeeded in making the governments conscious of the necessity for reform, he failed to follow consistently a sound program and exhibited an intellectual instability which was so common during that period."[2] It is a keen observation. List, indeed, highly self-confident and assured of the truth of his views, was

---

[2]Arnold H. Price, *The Evolution of the Zollverein* (Ann Arbor, Mich., 1949), p. 253.

also dogmatic in his argumentation and often arrogant toward those who differed with him. In this respect he may well be compared with Karl Marx, who was absolutely convinced that he had discovered the key to the natural laws of history and who often showered with abuse those who dared to express a contrary point of view to his materialist conception of history.[3]

List was well aware of this quality in his own personality and on occasion attempted to justify it. He was so deeply bound up in his work for economic reform that he resented any obstacles in the way and sought to brush off all of different views. "If I appear," he said, "to condemn in too strong language the opinions and the work of individual authors of entire schools, I have not done so from personal arrogance. But as I hold that the views which I have controverted are injurious to the public welfare, it is necessary to contradict them energetically. And authors of celebrity do more harm by their errors than those of less repute, therefore they must be disputed in more energetic terms."[4] List was convinced that the bureaucracies of German states were filled with mediocrities. In his view the good Lord had sent these incompetent bureaucrats to plague the German people and, incidentally, to stir men such as himself into action.

List was often vague in thought and action, but it is not difficult to discover in his work a certain uniformity of purpose. At the root of his thinking was the importance of the national idea, and he never deviated from that concept. He was one among those important leaders of German intellectual thought who were responsible for the molding of a strong sense of German national consciousness. His unique contribution was the first expression of the national concept at the economic level. Despite his denial, he may well have used personal arrogance as a tool to achieve what he deemed necessary for his fellow countrymen.

List's goal was always a strong Germany, unified economically and politically. Early in the 19th century he revealed that kind of *Realpolitik* which was

---

[3]This characteristic of Karl Marx was described by Carl Schurz, who, along with Marx and Richard Wagner, was among those who escaped from Germany after the unsuccessful Revolution of 1848. Schurz gave a fascinating picture of Marx's personality: "Marx's utterances were, indeed, full of meaning, logical and clear, but I have never seen a man whose bearing was so provoking and intolerable. To no opinion, which differed from his, he accorded the honor of even a condescending consideration. Everyone who contradicted him he treated with abject contempt; every argument he did not like he answered either with biting scorn at the unfathomable ignorance that had promoted it, or with opprobious aspersions upon the motives of him who advanced it." See *The Reminiscences of Carl Schurz* (New York, 1908), vol. 1, pp. 139–140.

[4]Friedrich List, *The National System of Political Economy*, tr. by Sampson S. Lloyd (London, 1904), p. xliii. This is List's basic work. Hereafter cited as List, *National System*.

to distinguish the work of Bismarck. When List saw that his goal of a general German customs union was impossible for the time being because of particularistic tendencies throughout the Germanies, he altered his plans by opting for regional unions in South and Central Germany. He would settle for this as a partial solution, but there was no doubt in his mind that this temporary solution was only a step toward the desired goal.

In his *National System of Political Economy* List carefully explained the genesis of the national idea in his own mind. He was not satisfied, he wrote, to present to young men the kind of political economy that existed at that time. What he wanted to teach them was "by what policy of economics the welfare, the culture, and the power of Germany might be promoted."[5] Even at this early stage of his career he had the national idea in mind.

> I was led to consider the nature of nationality. I perceived that the popular theory took no account of *nations,* but simply of the entire human race on the one hand, or of single individuals on the other. I saw clearly that free competition between two nations which are highly civilized can only be mutually beneficial in case both of them are in a nearly equal position of industrial development, and that any nation which owing to misfortunes in getting behind others in industry, commerce, and navigation, must first of all strengthen her own individual powers. In a word, I perceived the distinction between *cosmopolitical* and *political* economy. I felt that Germany must abolish her internal tariffs, and by the adoption of a common uniform policy towards foreigners, strive to attain to the same degree of commercial and industrial development to which other nations have attained by means of their commercial policy.[6]

Again, in his *National System* he pointed out that the nineteenth article of the constitution of the German *Bund* carefully left the door open for a national commercial system. According to List, the article fascinated him and provided for him the foundation on which the future prosperity of the German Fatherland might be based. "Hence the idea arose of establishing a league of German merchants and manufacturers for the abolition of our internal tariffs and the abolition of a commercial policy for the whole of Germany."[7]

List was intrigued by the term "nationality":

> I hesitated some time whether I should not term mine the *natural* system of political economy, but was dissuaded from so doing by the remark of a friend, that under

---

[5]List, *National System,* p. xxxix.
[6]*Ibid.,* p. x.
[7]*Ibid.,* pp. xl–xli.

the title superficial readers might suppose my book to be a mere revival of the physiocratic system.[8]

"My encouragement," List wrote, "lies in the thought that much will be found in my book that is new and true, and also somewhat that may serve especially to benefit my German Fatherland."[9] This became the theme of his thinking, of his career, and his life. Anything connected with the national idea became an obsession. The pages of his *magnum opus* are filled with an extraordinary number of references to the nation, nationality, and nationalism. One of the characteristics of the German language is the tendency to form new words by combination. List was influenced by this desire to present novel word forms. Again and again he used the prefix "national" and coined many words in their German form. Among the scores of such terms were: national soul, national idea, national will, national integrity, national self-sufficiency, national consciousness, national character, national liberty, national self-respect, national well-being, national security, and national envy.

Listed out of context this way the use of the term "national" seems to have been an *idée fixe* in List's mind. Certainly it expressed an unusually strong sense of national consciousness. Throughout his life he expressed again and again his deep love for his country. In 1817, when he was twenty-eight, List wrote to his fiancée: "I love my Fatherland perhaps more than my own happiness."[10] By "Fatherland," List meant not Württemberg, his native state, but his *German* Fatherland, which he saw as a united nation ("*Deutschland als Gesamtstaat*"). To the young economist his Fatherland had been crippled by its plethora of customs and excise duties. In his estimation it could be compared to "a European pasture land on which foreign herds roamed to satisfy their appetites."[11] The German people, he warned, must undergo "a total national understanding" for their own good. He pointed out that other countries which failed to take advantage of the national idea had run into difficulties. It was lack of "national leadership," he said, that had caused the Dutch much difficulty.[12] Their provincial and counting-house heads, men imbued with "a spirit of pepper-salesmanship," had selfishly looked to their own welfare, as a result of which the state had suffered economic woes.[13]

---

[8]*Ibid.*, p. xliii.
[9]*Ibid.*, p. xliv.
[10]Friedrich Lenz, *Friedrich List: Der Mann und das Werk* (Munich, 1936), p. 57.
[11]*Ibid.*
[12]Friedrich List, *Schriften-Reden-Briefe* (10 vols., Berlin, 1927–1935), vol. 1, p. 777.
[13]Lenz, *op. cit.*, p. 399.

List made a distinction between theory and practice. He regarded the romantics with their versified appeals for national unity as useful bearers of the signs for unity, but in his estimation something more than inspired verse was needed. Where the literary romantics concentrated on reviving and polishing the German language, List looked forward to the plane of economic necessity. Where others clothed their nationalism in terms of passionate romanticism, List sought a similar goal in cold economic phrases. A unified Germany could not be complete, he warned, unless "it extends over the whole coast, from the mouth of the Rhine to the frontier of Poland, including Holland and Denmark. A natural consequence of this union must be the admission of both these countries into the German nationality, whereby the latter will at once obtain that which it is now in need of, namely, fisheries, naval power, maritime commerce, and colonies. Besides, both these nations belong, as respects their decent and whole character, to the German national-ity."[14] It was typical of List's nationalism and also of his arrogance that he paid no attention whatever to the national consciousness of the Dutch and the Danes. Uppermost in his mind was the need of the forthcoming great German state, for whom a shoreline in the north as a gateway to the sea was an absolute necessity. In his view the lesser nationalism of the Dutch and Danes was unimportant in the face of German requirements.

List had no use for the *philosophes* or the rationalists of the Enlightenment. He attacked the Adam Smith-Say school of economy as suffering from three main defects: boundless cosmopolitanism, dead materialism, and a disor-ganizing particularism. According to List, Adam Smith just did not under-stand that humanity is divided into separate national societies. Between the individual and all of humanity, List said, stands the nation, with its language and literature, its special history, its peculiar traditions, customs, laws, and institutions. The nation was "a society which, united by a thousand ties of mind and of interest, combines itself into one independent whole, which recognizes the law of right for and within itself, and in its united character is still opposed to other societies of a similar kind in their national liberty, and consequently can only under the existing conditions of the world maintain self-existence and independence by its own power and resources.[15]

The nation, List warned, must be cemented by a common economic life, always by a *national* economy. This was the *sine qua non* of its very being. The people must join to break down the chains of political division.[16] At first

---

[14]List, *National System*, p. 143.
[15]*Ibid.*, p. 141.
[16]See *ibid.*, pp. 102–103.

they must think in terms of a protective tariff; then ultimately they could turn to free trade. Universal free trade in a disunited Germany, he warned, was dangerous and unacceptable. First things must come first.

Milieu: The Germanies in 1815

The Germanies of 1815 were still burdened by medieval residues. In political, intellectual, and economic life it was difficult to find a formula for the reconstruction of post-Napoleonic Germany and for the implementation of German unity.

Politically, there remained divisions between states, cities, and princes of every rank. Those German rulers who returned from Vienna in 1815 were united only in their resolve to prevent any revolutionary outbreaks and to retain their own power. The statesmen at Vienna had imposed a constitutional change from the Holy Roman Empire to the German Confederation, but there was little agreement on how the new *Bund* was to function. Each government in the *Bund* held stubbornly to its sovereignty on the ground that the German Confederation was a *Staatenbund* (federation of states) and not a ''federal state.'' Both the German Confederation and the Austrian Empire hewed to the supranational features of the Holy Roman Empire with its *Res publica Christiana* concept.

Most of all the Germanies of 1815 were burdened by a persistent dualism between Austria and Prussia. Both Prussia and Austria were not simply German, and in the case of Austria not even primarily German. Metternich and the Austrians regarded their European ambitions as taking precedence over their German elements. Indeed, Austria had grown progressively more and more multinational, with non-German nationalities outnumbering their German components. Austria in 1815 was described as *"une puissance slave, magyars, italiennes, mélangée et douteuse, au point de vue de la nationalité."*[17] Both Austria, with her multinational minorities, and Prussia, which held the two Polish provinces of Posen and West Prussia, were at this time opposed to German national unity and especially deplored any form of representative democracy which might give their non-German populations any excuse for expressing their own national sentiment.

Along with this political chaos was an intellectual life which wandered off into the clouds. In the early 19th century, German intellectualism seemed to be

---

[17]Edmond About, *La Prusse en 1860* (Paris, 1860), p. 12.

in a state of suspended animation. Many German writers were influenced by the cosmopolitanism from across the Rhine.[18] Most wrote for one another or sought the patronage of a friendly prince. Goethe, the greatest of all German writers, could not live by the sale of his books and had to seek a living at the court theater in Weimar.[19]

List recognized this backwardness of German intellectual life: "The Germans are in the position of an individual who, having been formerly deprived of the use of his limbs, first learned theoretically the arts of standing and walking, of eating and drinking, of laughing and weeping, and then only proceeded to put them into practice. Hence comes the German predilection for philosophic systems and cosmopolitan dreams."[20]

The Germanies in 1815 needed drastic economic reconstruction. The prosperity of the Hanseatic League in the north had vanished with the opening of new trade routes to the New World, and the German states were not yet fully recovered from the devastation and desolation of the Thirty Years' War. The economy remained primarily agricultural, with some three-fourths of the people engaged in farming. In the west and the south, where there were many small farms, the great baronies of the aristocrats constituted a strong conservative counterbalance.[21] The entire urban population of the Germanies was only half as much again as the population of Paris.[22] There were no important industries, little coal production, no steam engines, no large factories. There was little adequate material for an independent, prosperous middle class.

The German states at this time were burdened by a bewildering variety of water, inland, and provincial tolls. An army of 8,000 officials worked to collect duties on some 2,775 articles of commerce. List described it in 1819: "Thirty-eight customs boundaries cripple inland trade, and produce much the same effect as ligatures which prevent the circulation of the blood. The merchant trading between Hamburg and Austria, or Berlin and Switzerland, must traverse ten states, must learn ten customs-tariffs, and must pay ten successive traffic dues. Anyone who is so unfortunate as to live on the boundary line between three or four states spends his days among hostile tax gatherers and customs-house officials; he is a man without a country."[23] To List this was economic insanity.

The Prussians suffered as much as other Germans. Their officials found it

---

[18]See Friedrich Meinecke, *Weltbürgertum und Nationalstaat* (Munich, 1928), p. 164.

[19]A. J. P. Taylor, *The Course of German History* (New York, 1946), p. 54.

[20]List, *National System*, pp. 67–68.

[21]Veit Valentin, *The German People* (New York, 1946), p. 379.

[22]Taylor, *op. cit.*, p. 54.

[23]*Cf.* Price, *op. cit.*, pp. 39–41.

an almost impossible task to control active smuggling. In the late 18th century Frederick the Great had introduced a strong tariffs system as a means of stimulating manufacturing, but the unfavorable geographical location of Prussia plus its division into several noncontiguous provinces reacted unfavorably.[24] In time Prussia was burdened by 67 different tariffs with as many as 119 separate currencies. Clearly something had to be done to control this increasingly chaotic economic situation.

After the downfall of Napoleon and the end of his Continental System, the British began to flood German markets with the products of their factories. List looked on this development as an attempt to crush German industry. He was hostile and bitter: "English national economy has for its object to manufacture for the whole world, to monopolize all manufacturing power, even at the expense of the lives of her citizens, to keep the world, and especially her own colonies, in a state of infancy and vassalage by political management as well as by the superiority of her capital, her skill, and her navy."[25] It was a classic denunciation of British economic supremacy.

List was much distressed by conditions in his homeland, by the decline of trade industry, by the unwillingness of his fellow Germans to face up to their economic problems, by the lack of national sentiment, and by the weakness of Germans in dealing with foreign countries. "One thing only," he said, "the Germans had preserved: that was their aboriginal character, their love of industry, order, thrift, and moderation, their perseverance and endurance in research and in business, their honest striving after improvement, and a considerable natural measure of morality, prudence, and circumspection."[26] In other words, basically the German people possessed tremendous assets. What was necessary was an end to the interminable quarrels between the states coupled with the forging of economic unity. Then a politically united Germany could take her place as a respected power among the world's nations.

The political unification of rival states in the Germanies was achieved by a long, slow process of economic integration which subordinated the needs of the individual states to the interest of a larger empire under Prussian auspices. For centuries the Germanies had been weakened by disunity and economic weakness. The emergence of a vigorous national market began with Prussia's absorption of the *Zollverein,* a step which was to make Germany eventually the leading industrial nation of Europe. And in the story of the unfolding of the *Zollverein,* one man—Friedrich List—was to play the leading role.

---

[24]List, *National System,* p. 68.
[25]Friedrich List, *Outlines of American Political Economy* (Philadelphia, 1827), Letter II.
[26]List, *National System,* p. 66.

Genesis of the Zollverein

The formation of the *Zollverein* was a gradual process lasting from 1819 to 1835, during the course of which South German and Prussian ideas were amalgamated under Prussian auspices. Its existence, as Price pointed out, was due "to the coordination of practical and theoretical elements in the Prussian Customs Law of 1818; List's plan of economic unification, to be achieved through separate negotiations outside the framework of the Confederation; Hofmann's synthesis of particularism, with necessity of a custom's system; and Motz's integration of Prussia's fiscal and foreign policy."[27]

Among all these varying factors List's role was dominant. He was responsible for setting into motion the chain reaction which eventually led to formation of the *Zollverein*. He appeared on the scene at precisely the right psychological moment. In his own way and without much subtlety he brought attention to the central problem of national unification. He would allow nothing to remain in his way, not the recriminations of critics nor the immovability of politicians. On occasion many of his ideas were vague and inconsistent, but on one matter he remained firm and unchangeable—the absolute necessity for German economic unification. Even in the late stages of the formation of the *Zollverein,* when he was shunted aside, his one basic idea and his personality remained to give direction to the development of the *Zollverein.*

The critical early years were 1819 and 1820, when List began his campaign of propaganda to reform the increasingly intolerable economic situation. At the Spring Fair held in Frankfurt am Main in 1819 he organized a number of receptive businessmen in the *Deutsche Handels- und Gerwerbsverein* (German Commercial and Industrial League), an organization dedicated to the task of abolishing the conglomeration of tariffs in the German states and at the same time setting up a workable customhouse system for all of Germany. More than five thousand manufacturers and merchants joined this private union.

List was indefatigable in promoting this organization. He was careful to submit the articles of association for approval to the *Bund* at Frankfurt as well as to the many governments of the individual German states. He chose the old city of Nuremberg as his headquarters. As founder he was authorized to appoint a central committee to direct the business of the organization under the advice of an assessor, a critical position to which he appointed himself. He saw to it that every important German city and town had a local correspondent and that each German state had a provincial correspondent. He started a

---

[27]Price, *op. cit.,* pp. 255–256.

weekly journal to publicize all transactions of the central committee and to describe its possible transactions, including treaties, proposals, and statistics. The committee was to give an account of its stewardship at annual meetings to be held in conjunction with the Spring Fair at Frankfurt.

List put every ounce of his energy into the organizing process. He interviewed individual businessmen and industrialists and poured out to them his plans for reform; he drew up petitions and memorials; he personally organized the network of correspondents; he insisted upon giving his own approval for every local publication by League members. He traveled extensively on behalf of the League, including visits to South German courts as well as to the Vienna Ministerial Conference and the Darmstadt Trades Congress.[28]

This kind of zealous work did not go unnoticed, especially by foreign observers. A French agent reported to Paris that a "new Hanse" had been started in Frankfurt by a Tübinger professor, who, acting to meet the deficiency in political unity, had organized a national trade organization and was seeking to work on German public opinion by training the masses in the necessity for economic unification.[29] Even more interested was List's old opponent, Metternich, who from Vienna watched List's activities with scarcely concealed contempt. By June 1819 the Austrian statesman was denouncing "this cabal of a new, highly dangerous confederation which is attempting to expand its idea of the Germanies into the circle of German practical revolutionaries."[30] For Metternich anyone who attempted to lessen the authority of Austria in German affairs was little short of a wild revolutionary.

During this early phase of his career, List was functioning as a South German nationalist still conscious of his regional background, but nevertheless he was thinking in terms of a united Germany.[31] He was aware that a movement for economic reform was already under way in Prussia, and he hoped that the Prussian King Frederick William III would be willing to recognize "the German spirit" as a whole.

List's next step was to seek a broader ground for his activities. From November 1819 to June 1820 the Vienna Ministerial Conference, also called the Vienna Final Conference, met for the purpose of putting the finishing touches on the 1815 Acts of Confederation, the formation of the German

---

[28]Lenz, *op. cit.*, p. 78.
[29]*Ibid.*, p. 77.
[30]*Ibid.*
[31]Price, *op. cit.*, p. 41.

Bund. List was careful to lead a delegation of his League to this critical conference. Prime attention at the meeting was given to political matters, but it was clear that discussions would be held on the question of German economic unification. List and his colleagues arrived at Vienna on January 5, 1820, hopeful that they would obtain some recognition for their views. In a letter to his wife List spoke of "the holy cause" and said that "we are on the way to converting the Austrian regime to our way of thinking."[32] List spoke to as many Viennese bankers and businessmen as he could, always propagandizing for the right of Germans to create a national system of trade of their own. By the following March he felt that he was making progress.

List was well aware of the distaste that Metternich felt for him. He was careful in his daily conversations to flatter "the imperial savior of the German Fatherland" and "the enlightened prince of the German *Bund*." This made little impression on the hard-bitten Austrian diplomat, who made certain that his secret police watched the intruder from Württemberg. To Metternich, List's plan for a German customs union and for German economic unification was merely "a pious wish."[33] List, Metternich said, was only "a screaming German manufacturer,"[34] and what he proposed would only cause trouble for all Germans. Above all, Austria had little to gain from List's idea of German national unification. On the surface Metternich spoke glibly of "compromise," but actually he had no intention whatever of either compromise or giving in to List's "dangerous" ideas.

Gradually, it became clear to List that he had nothing to gain in Vienna. He would try a different approach. There was little support in Vienna for a general German customs union. Perhaps Metternich and the Austrians might agree to a regional union in South and Central Germany. That might be a partial answer to Germany's economic distress and at the same time it might satisfy the Austrians. List had suggested this idea as early as June 1819. When it became evident during the Vienna Ministerial Conference that little or no progress could be made on general German economic uification, the wheels were set in motion for five years of negotiations for a regional union in South and Central Germany.

Actually, despite his enormous energy, List was working under severe handicaps. His most important enemies were Metternich and the Austrian

---

[32]For a good account of the Vienna Ministerial Conference, see Adolf Suchel, *Hesse-Darmstadt und der Darmstädter Handelskongress von 1820–1823* (Darmstadt, 1922), pp. 4–23.
[33]See Ludwig Karl Aegidi, *Aus der Vorzeit des Zollvereins* (Hamburg, 1865), p. 90.
[34]Lenz, *op. cit.*, p. 102.

secret police, who were anxious to throttle any calls for German economic independence and who wanted to maintain Austrian control of German affairs. Also among his opponents were the rulers of the individual German states, who always spoke accommodatingly to List about plans for economic unity but who jealously guarded their own political and economic status. There were also small state bureaucrats in the Rhineland, dubbed "separatists" by an impatient List, individuals who alternately invoked French, Dutch, or British protection of their sovereignty.[35] Finally, there was the forbidding shadow of an aloof Prussia, which had her own plans for German economic unification under Prussian guidance and certainly not that by the professor from Tübingen. At this time the thirty-one-year-old List had his hands full with these varying and powerful opponents, all of whom resented his "interference" in their affairs and all of whom would have been considerably pleased had the Würtemberger economist decided voluntarily to silence himself.

Furthermore, in the early days of the negotiations for a *Zollverein,* List had to face some powerful historical forces as well as individual opponents. There were four major forces at work in the Germanies at this time. First was the idea of particularism, the sentiment existing in the many German states for sovereignty and independence from any other control. Second was the concept of dualism promoted by Metternich, a dualism which was supposed to cover both Austria and Germany, but which the Austrian diplomat interpreted as Austrian hegemony. Third was the idea of trialism, which added to Austrian and Prussian dualism an additional stage—a third German power in Central and South Germany to act as a balance weight against Austria and Prussia. Finally, there was the idea of a new German nationalism, which would represent all the German states outside of Austria and which would reflect the prestige of a first-rate power in Central Europe. List looked upon German nationalism as the ultimate goal. He realized, however, that this was something for the future and he would have been willing to compromise along the way with any idea or force which would ultimately lead to the desired national unification.

List's plan for a regional union in South and Central Germany was not successful. The negotiations took place from 1820 to 1825 in an atmosphere of political chaos. Expediency proved to be more durable than economic

---

[35]See Hermann Oncken, in *Vorgeschichte und Begründung des deutschen Zollvereins, 1815–1834,* edited by Hermann Oncken and F. E. M. Saemisch (Berlin, 1934), vol. 1, pp. lxiv–lxvii.

desires. Some rulers called for a common customs union, while others, fearing loss of sovereignty, insisted upon a limited system of mutual preference. List had made his proposal in a burst of enthusiasm, but thus far he seemed unable to implement his plans.

The Prussian Octopus Moves

While List was pursuing his remedies for Germany's economic backwardness, Prussian authorities were already at work on their own plans for a customs union. As early as 1818 the Prussians had introduced legal measures designed to reform their own customs system. Prussia's *Zollanschluss* (foreign territory within a customs district) was designed to incorporate neighboring territories into her own customs system.

List was well aware of the developments in Prussia. Shortly before the start of the Vienna Ministerial Conference in 1819, he led a delegation from his League to Berlin to present a petition to Frederick William III. Prussian officials were careful to give the Württemberger economist and his colleagues a warm welcome, as a result of which List believed that he would have support as "the savior of Prussia and Germany."[36] What he did not know was that Prussian administrators had no intention of cooperating with him and that they would sabotage any effort he made to lead the way to German economic unification. They had their own plans.

During the next five years, while the South German negotiations were going on, the Prussians went ahead with their goal of achieving a larger customs union of their own as a counterbalance to the proposed South German union. From 1828 to 1833 Prussia concluded a series of treaties which resulted in the formation of the *Zollverein* under Prussian auspices.[37] In the summer of 1829 Prussia wooed the Thuringian states of Saxe-Meiningen and Saxe-Coburg-Gotha from the Middle German Commercial Union by persuading them to build duty-free highways through their states to be used as a direct route between Prussia and Bavaria. That same summer Friedrich Adolf von Motz, the Prussian minister of finance, completed negotiations with Holland concerning the navigation of the Rhine. Within a few months the Reuss

---

[36]See Oncken and Saemisch, *op. cit.*, vol. 1, p. 356.
[37]See Price, *op. cit.*, pp. 106–159 and 192–255, for the steps outlining Prussia's formation of the *Zollverein*.

principalities (Reuss-Schleitz, Reuss-Lobenstein, and Reuss-Ebersdorf) concluded agreements with Prussia to join the Prussian customs system as soon as possible. The next state to desert the Middle Union was Saxe-Weimar, which agreed to join the Prussian customs system by January 1, 1835.

To these desertions were added the Electorate of Hesse-Cassel in 1831. Prussia then began negotiations with Bavaria and Württemberg to ease the way to establishment of a north-south customs union. Talks began in December 1831 and a treaty unifying the customs union of North and South Germany was signed on March 22, 1833. There followed agreements with Saxony (1833) and Thuringia (1833).

In each of these steps the Prussians were careful to provide for a common tariff system, administrative regulations, separate administrations with mutual controls, proportional sharing of revenues, and the standardization of tolls, measures, weights, and coinage.[38] The German *Zollverein,* which began its operations at the beginning of 1834, consisted of eighteen states with an area of 162,870 square miles, at least two-thirds of the territory out of which the later Second German Reich was to be formed, with a population of nearly 23.5 million people of whom some 15 million were Prussian.[39] From 1833 to 1885, when Bremen, the last of the holdouts was brought into the system, Germany was unified into an economic system strong enough to support an industrialized economy.

At long last Germany emerged as the vigorous nation which List had wanted. The credit for this transformation was taken by Prussian administrators who without any sense of shame appropriated List's ideas and then proceeded to ignore him as much as possible. Yet it is clear that List's contribution was a major one. He was the one who took the germ of an idea, nourished it, and then laid the groundwork for an enduring economic system. This is the classic case of the propagator of an idea being shunted aside by a stronger political power.

List and the American System

There has been an interesting confrontation of historians on the question of the extent of American influence on List and his ideas of economic unity. Some

---

[38]Roussakis, *op. cit.,* p. 68.
[39]*Ibid.,* pp. 70–71.

American historians claim that List imbibed his original ideas from two Americans, Daniel Raymond and Matthew Carey.[40] In 1897 Charles Patrick Neill compared Raymond's *Elements of Political Economy* (1820) and List's *National System* and in page-by-page references of parallel quotations came to the conclusion that there were some striking similarities:

> It is not too much to say that not only the germ of List's system is to be found in Raymond, but that a very considerable development is to be found scattered throughout its eight hundred and odd pages [2nd ed.]. The sum of the whole matter is this—that Raymond and List hit upon the same principles as the basis of their systems of political economy; that Raymond had given his principles to the public some months before List had shown evidences of his having conceived similar ideas; and that List only gave his system to the world after he had such opportunities for becoming acquainted with Raymond's work, that it is difficult to believe that he did not have a knowledge of it.[41]

Later American historians in the 20th century came to the same conclusion that List's agitation for the *Zollverein* was motivated by his experiences in the United States. The distinguished American historian, Merle Curti, pointed out that the United States was for a brief period the residence of the German economist Friedrich List, "whose doctrines were to play a subsequent role in the movement of the customs union of the German states.[42] The economist Joseph Dorfman presented a similar conclusion: "Not many years passed [after List's suicide] before he was worshiped in Germany as the greatest German economist, the source of the new and supposedly unique German political economy of national power."[43] Both Curti and Dorfman regarded List's experiences in the United States as vital for his future career in Germany.

There is little doubt that List was influenced by Alexander Hamilton's

---

[40]In 1820 Daniel Raymond, a native of Connecticut and an attorney in Baltimore published his *Thoughts on Political Economy,* the first systematic treatise of its kind in the United States. Raymond held that a classical economy was unsuited to the needs of his country. He supported governmental paternalism as opposed to *laissez-faire* and called for a system of high protective tariffs. Matthew Carey, an Irish immigrant and a publisher in Philadelphia advocated not only a system of protective tariffs but also internal improvements at governmental expense. A lively polemicist, he published a series of pamphlets and speeches in support of his views. As president of the Pennsylvania Society for the Promotion of Manufacturers and the Mechanic Arts, he made the acquaintance of List, who undoubtedly knew of his work.

[41]Charles Patrick Neill, *Daniel Raymond and Friedrich List* (Baltimore, 1897), pp. 46, 63.

[42]Merle Curti, *The Growth of American Thought* (New York, 1943), p. 255.

[43]Joseph Dorfman, *The Economic Mind in American Civilization, 1606–1865* (New York, 1946), vol. 2, p. 584.

celebrated *Report on German Manufactures*.[44] Issued in 1791 as a state paper, the *Report* presented the thesis that encouragement of manufacturers was a policy which was bound to increase the national wealth. Most American historians believe that the *Report* must surely have been read by List, even though he did not mention it in his major works. Margaret E. Hirst, outstanding among the early List scholars, pointed out that a comparison of Hamilton's *Report* with List's writings reveals some similar ideas, such as free trade to be beneficial must be universal; manufactures and agriculture benefit one another; protective tariffs increase the productive powers of a nation; and high prices due to tariffs would be temporary and would be lowered by domestic competition.[45]

It may well be an indication of nationalist sentiment in historiography that German historians are reluctant to accept the idea of American influences on List's work. K. Th. Eheberg, the German List scholar, denied the influence of Hamilton and attributed the resemblance merely to List's stay in the United States:

It is obvious that if List knew Hamilton's *Report* he would find in it confirmation of the accuracy of his own views; but he had no occasion to borrow Hamilton's ideas, since he had formed similar ones before his arrival in America. Besides, Hamilton could not influence the new theories which List added to the old ones in these *Letters,* for they had no similarity to those in his *Report*. The beneficial influence exerted on List by his stay in America arose from practical circumstances and not from printed books.[46]

Eheberg's judgment, written in 1853, was accepted by later German List scholars.[47] Despite the similarities of List's ideas to those of Raymond and Carey, and despite the resemblance of List's ideas to those found in the Hamilton *Report,* most German List scholars stress the originality of his thinking and deny the importance of American influences. Curt Köhler was sensitive to what he regarded as an attempt to prove List guilty of "plagiarism" in borrowing American ideas. He denied that List had taken his ideas from either Adam Müller, Raymond, or Hamilton. Köhler presented an

---

[44]See *Papers on Public Credit, Commerce, and Finance by Alexander Hamilton,* edited by Samuel McKee, Jr. (New York, 1934). See Dorfman, *op. cit.,* vol. 1, pp. 408–411, for an analysis of Hamilton's *Report*.

[45]Margaret E. Hirst, *Life of Friedrich List* (New York, 1909), pp. 114–115.

[46]K. Th. Eheberg, in the introduction of *Friedrich List: Das nationale System der politischen Oekonomie* (Stuttgart, 1853), p. 149.

[47]For example, H. Losch in *Patrie* (1906), pp. 171 ff.; and E. Meuser in *Z.f.g. Staatswissenschaft* (1913), pp. 104 ff.

extraordinary argument. Because he (Köhler) had been unable in 1908 "despite many pains" to obtain a copy of Hamilton's *Report on Domestic Manufactures,* obviously List could not possibly have seen it eighty years before! It was a strange conclusion:

> It doesn't seem possible to me that List himself ever read Hamilton's *Report.* Hamilton wrote his report for the House of Representatives as an "official opinion," and it may well be assumed that his work was not immediately published. It may well be possible that the Pennsylvania Society for the Encouragement of Manufactures informed List of the views of this report; at least I cannot show the opposite. It is sufficient, however, to say that I do not believe that this report had a decisive influence on List's system.[48]

A later German scholar, Friedrich Lenz, took the opposite view and stated flatly that "List knew and utilized Hamilton's *Report* in his *Outlines* of 1827, even the expression 'productive powers' and 'productive and political powers,' which he obviously borrowed from Hamilton."[49] This view was confirmed by British and American scholars. Margaret E. Hirst believed that Hamilton's *Report* "must surely have been read by List."[50] She pointed out that in 1820, five years before his visit to America, List wrote two addresses to the American Congress on behalf of the German Commercial and Industrial League.[51]

List's debt to the American political economy was substantiated by William Notz in his study on "Friedrich List in America." According to Notz, there is no doubt that in the writings of Raymond and Carey, List found a process of reasoning which had many points in common with his own, that he substantiated and confirmed their accuracy, and that Raymond and Carey provided an incentive for further study.[52] Notz concluded that List's first-hand knowledge of American affairs and his keen grasp of their significance, as well as his sympathetic attitude toward American institutions, made him the foremost, if not the best, interpreter of Europeans to the American people and their aspirations during the first half of the 19th century.[53]

---

[48]Curt Köhler, *Problematisches zu Friedrich List* (Leipzig, 1908), pp. 100 ff.
[49]Friedrich Lenz, *Friedrich List: Der Mann und das Werk* (Munich, 1936), p. 25.
[50]Hirst, *op. cit.,* p. 115.
[51]*Ibid.*
[52]William Notz, "Friedrich List in America," *The American Economic Review,* XVI (1926), pp. 248–265.
[53]*Ibid.,* p. 265.

Unfortunately, List himself did not mention the names of Raymond or Carey in his major or minor works. He did pay tribute to Hamilton. In Letter III of his *American Political Economy* (1827), he listed Alexander Hamilton among "the most enlightened minds of all ages," and stated that in his own early years he "not only studied the works of the masters, but also of their ablest disciples in England, Germany, and France."[54] In 1846 List wrote that he had used the period between his political fall (1821) and his journey to the United States (1825) to study all phases of American political and economic life. "I made it a point to pay attention to [American] political science and administration (and my knowledge of them was not so limited as has been said). It is self-understood that I thought about learning exactly the American constitution and all the social and economic conditions of North America."[55]

In the introduction to his *National System,* List admitted that his ideas had been strongly reinforced by his stay in the United States: "The best book in political economy which one can read in America is life itself. I read this book with eagerness and industry, and sought to bring the lessons I had learned from it into harmony with my former studies, experiences, and reflections."[56] This was in line with List's generally favorable impression of the United States and its way of life. He had left his homeland because he had lost his freedom of expression. "While exhausted by persecutions," he wrote, "I had found a great land, where heroes are sages and sages rulers—where, for the first time, a great empire was founded on industry, on equal rights, and on the moral force of its citizens—where the governments are mere committees of people, and conquests made for no other purpose than the participation in freedom, civilization, and happiness with the conquered."[57]

In his diary List wrote that in the United States it first became clear to him that nations passed through different stages of economic development. A process which in Europe would have required many centuries was taking place in the New World, the transition from a state of nature to pastoral cultivation, from that to manufacture to commerce:

Here we can observe how rent gradually grows from zero to an important sum. Here a simple father by practical experience has a better understanding of the means by which agriculture and rent can be advanced than by the keenest in-

---

[54]Friedrich List, *Outlines of American Political Economy* (Philadelphia, 1827), Letter III, July 15, 1827.
[55]List, *Schriften-Reden-Briefe,* vol. 1, pp. 72–73.
[56]List, *National System,* introduction, p. xliii.
[57]From List's Philadelphia speech of 1827, in *Schriften-Reden-Briefe,* vol. II, pp. 157–172.

tellects of the old world—he tries to attract manufacturers and artificers into the vicinity. Here the contrast between the agricultural and manufacturing nations shows itself in the clearest manner and causes the most violent agitations. Nowhere so well as here, can we learn the true value of the means of transport and their influence on the intellectual and material life of the people.[58]

There is further evidence in List's published work about his deep interest in the American economy. In his *National System* he wrote that the history of the trade and industry of North America was more instructive for his subject than any other, because in the United States the course of development proceeded rapidly, the periods of free trade and protection followed closely on one another, and the consequences stood out clearly and sharply defined. "The whole machinery of national industry moves exploded before the eye of the spectator."[59] "Americans," List wrote, "came to realize the truth that it behooves a great nation not exclusively to set its heart upon the enjoyment of proximate material advantages; that civil power, a more important and desirable possession than mere material wealth, as Adam Smith himself allows, can only be secured and retained by the creation of a manufacturing power of its own."[60]

List also learned from his American experience that the existence of a flourishing manufacturing power in the Atlantic states had an important effect on the European economy. "Population, capital, technical skill and intellectual power flow into them from all European countries; now the demand for the manufactured products of the Atlantic states increases simultaneously with their consumption of the raw materials supplied by the west."[61] List admired what he saw in the United States. "With the Americans, common sense, and the instinct of what was necessary for the nation, were more potent than a belief in theoretical propositions. The arguments of the theorists were thoroughly investigated, and strong doubts entertained of the infallibility of the doctrine which its own disciples were not willing to put into practice."[62]

It is clear then from even a rough perusal of List's works that the Württemberger economist not only admired the American economy but that he was influenced by the theoretical implications behind it and desired to extend its salient features to his own country. Certainly his ideas were very similar,

---

[58]Quoted in Notz, *op. cit.*, p. 220.
[59]List, *National System*, p. 77.
[60]*Ibid.*, p. 83.
[61]*Ibid.*, p. 85.
[62]*Ibid.*, p. 82.

indeed, to those already developed in the United States. By no means does this conclusion detract from his status as one of the most original and outstanding of German economists.

The Last Days of Friedrich List

Despite his happy experiences in the United States, List always kept his Fatherland uppermost in his mind. Even though he was treated with disdain in his homeland and persecuted by the omnipresent Metternich, he never gave up hope of returning permanently to the land of his birth. Friedrich Lenz expressed it succinctly: "In the background of all his plans lay Germany—at least he wanted his children to 'acquire a German home.'"[63] His sense of national consciousness was always strong. As early as 1828 he wrote: "I regard my Fatherland as a mother looks on her crippled children; she loves them so much more strongly, the more crippled they are. In the back of my mind was always Germany and the idea of returning to Germany."[64]

After his return to his homeland from America, List was saddened to witness the implementation of the *Zollverein* under Prussian auspices. He, above all other Germans, had prepared the path for this great step in the economic unification of his country, but he was now a prophet without honor in his own country. He was the one individual finally responsible for healing the schism between the free-trading interests of the agrarian North and the protection-inclined industrialists of the Southwest, but by this time the torch had been appropriated by other hands. Ill-health and severe financial difficulties darkened his later days. An anonymous attack by a German university professor on his sense of honor led List, in a moment of mental aberration to commit suicide on November 30, 1846. The man who had provided the economic foundation of modern Germany died by his own hand.

During his lifetime List received little recognition or encouragement from his fellow countrymen. Typical of the way he was treated were his expulsion in April 1822 from the Württemberg chamber, his sentence to ten months' imprisonment, and his release only on his promise to migrate to America. This attitude changed drastically after List's death. He was recognized belatedly and was eventually elevated to the position of a national prophet. Friedrich Bodenstedt expressed the new opinion of List when he said that the

---

[63]Friedrich Lenz, *Friedrich List und Grossdeutschland* (Leipzig, n.d.), p. 7.
[64]List, *Schriften-Reden-Briefe,* vol. II, p. 41.

economist was a leader on the road to Germany's unification and greatness and as such was the most important predecessor of Bismarck.[65] List reached the height of his fame in 1877 when Bismarck turned to a protective tariff policy. This was what List had wanted throughout his life.

There were now calls from all over Germany for monuments to be erected to the memory of the man who had been hounded into exile. On List's grave at Kufstein were placed the words: GERMANY'S FRIEDRICH LIST. At the base of the tombstone is carved this tribute:

A DEFENDER OF HIS COUNTRY WHO TOILED WITHOUT REWARD
A WARRIOR OVER WHOSE STRONG WILL GOLD CAST NO FETTERS
A HERO WHO SAW BEYOND HIS OWN AGE FAR INTO THE FUTURE
A SOWER FOR WHOM THE STARRY WORLD IS PREPARED AS A DWELLING

List and German Nationalism

As a prophet and apostle of German nationalism, List was the first German to express the national concept at the economic level. As a ceaseless advocate of the *Zollverein,* national railroads, a national merchant marine, and a national protection policy for young industries, he helped give direction to the rising German nationalism. In stressing the close interrelation between theoretical economic concepts and political factors, List had important influence on the development and nature of German nationalism. He criticized classical economists for failing to take into account the significance of the nation as the critical link between the individual and mankind. He made a careful distinction between the national economic policies of England and Germany. The economic principles of the classical school were justified in the industrial and commercial supremacy of England, but such principles, he said, were unsuited to the needs of rising countries such as Germany and the United States. The two latter countries were at the time occupying positions of second rank but possessed the potentialities of first-class nations. They needed, he concluded, a special brand of national economics.

For Germany to rise to the rank of a *Normalnation,* it was necessary, List believed, that she adopt a strong national protective tariff. Here List saw a traditional economic development in action. The first state to emerge from

---

[65]Quoted in Lenz, *Friedrich List und Grossdeutschland, op. cit.,* p. 12.

primitive conditions was the agricultural, followed by the agricultural and manufacturing state, which in turn merged into an agricultural, manufacturing, and commercial state. After normal nationhood was achieved, the necessity for a national protective tariff would cease and free trade could be introduced.

These ideas—the reality of the nation and the necessity for a protective tariff—gave direction to List's sense of German nationalism.

From the beginning of his career, List understood the effects of the internal divisions in the German states, which he regarded as a significant factor in German economic subordination to Britain. He was the first economist to call for the national integration of German states with the argument that a particularistic, fragmented Germany could not possibly reach her economic potential. His work had the effect of fixing the attention of practical men of affairs on the necessity for the general economic unification of Germany. When his initial proposals were rejected by German political leaders, he proposed a less ambitious but more realistic scheme for German economic unification. He now advocated the formation of a regional customs union between the Middle and South German states. His rational arguments in favor of this solution finally persuaded the concerned governments to act. At this point the Prussians combined their own *Zollanschluss* with List's proposals and provided the legal basis for the formation of the *Zollverein*. Thus the economic unification so ardently desired by List was established through the agency of Prussia.

As an apostle of German nationalism, List in his early career presented his views in liberal terms. His ideas of general economic unification were progressive in the sense of a move away from an antiquated and partly feudal economy. At this time he called for "an independent, free, enterprising, industrially diligent, and prosperous nation." He simply wanted for a united Germany what had already been achieved by a united and prosperous Britain.

Somewhere along the way, however, List's somewhat vague liberal ideas were cast into a mold of different quality. Hans Kohn recognized this transformation when he described List as the father of German economic nationalism but at the same time as "one of the most extreme of Pan-German imperialists."[66] The reason for this judgment may be seen in the transforma-

---

[66]Hans Kohn, *The Idea of Nationalism* (New York, 1944), p. 322. A later List scholar disputed the view of List's chauvinism. "He was, perhaps the only truly cosmopolitan German citizen of his age, a man of national and international influence, possessed in equal measure of ideas and action. List has been completely misunderstood by those critics, both foreign and domestic, who called him a nationalist. While he was a passionate protagonist of German unification, he was not the chauvinist his detractors have frequently called him. His ardent support of the cause of unity

tion of German political life from the unsuccessful liberal attempt to unify the Germanies in the Revolution of 1848 to the blood and iron policy of Junker Otto von Bismarck. In the struggle between a steadily intensifying nationalism in the Bismarckian power-mold and the weakening German liberalism, List chose the side which would eventually be led by Bismarck.

There is evidence in List's writings to support Kohn's designation of him as an extreme Pan-German imperialist. Although in the early stages of his career List expressed something akin to liberal sentiments, he was not at all attracted by Manchester liberalism. In opposing Adam Smith's "cosmopolitanism and disorganizing particularism," List in reality was expressing a decided distaste for liberalism. List regarded the State as the nodal point between the processes of the spirit, an idea which he shared with Hegel and others who gave direction to 19th and 20th century German intellectual thinking. Just as Napoleon had once set up a powerful Continental System, so did List look forward to a similar German-controlled continental system. Even further, he advocated an ambitious oceanic policy which would extend German power throughout the world. It was necessary, he contended, that Germany needed *Ergän-zungsgebiete* (supplementary territories) "as much as breath." This expressed need for "vital living space" was to be repeated later by such expansionists as William II ("Germany needs a place in the sun!") and Hitler ("We want *Lebensraum!* [living space].")

In his study, *Friedrich List, the Zollverein, and the Unity of Europe,* E. N. Roussakis objects to categorizing List in nationalistic terms: "German nationalist," "militant nationalist," and "aggressive nationalist." He rejects this picture of List as neither accurate nor complete.

If List pleaded the national cause, he did so because he wanted to see the bal kanized German states welded firmly into a national entity, into a united Germany with a vigorous national market unimpeded by the age-old barriers of its feudal past. Alongside this German Friedrich List, however, there existed another equally important and largely neglected European Friedrich List who believed that the twentieth century was destined to witness the unification of European nations into a European Union—a great United States of Europe. Economically, this

was a manifestation of his awareness of the common bonds of language, culture, and history which the fragmented German territories had. More than that, he was also conscious of the importance of the economic interests and the geographical proximity of those territories. Only nationhood, he felt, offered those territories the necessary framework for economic and political development. In his writings, List emphasized again and again the importance of the nation state and its advantages as a vehicle for furthering industry by means of moderate protective tariffs; and it is on these grounds that he generally reproached the classical school for failing to realize the significance of the nation as a link between the individual and mankind." From E. N. Roussakis, *Friedrich List, the Zollverein, and the Unity of Europe* (Bruges, 1968), p. 147.

Union would be the vehicle for economic development and growth, and politically for maintaining it as the equal of the United States of America.

There was a strong vein of internationalism in List as well. He was, in fact, an ardent advocate of world-wide free trade and universal organization. The latter he expected would be brought about by the gradual political maturing of the nation states and the development and growth of their economies to a level at which economic inequalities between them would cease to exist.[67]

This revisionist attempt to transform List from his status as the father of German economic nationalism into the precursor of the European Common Market and the proposed United States of Europe rates a bravo for an interesting thesis, but there is really little evidence to support it. Certainly List suggested the lines of a blueprint for such a union. Certainly he predicted that European communities would think in terms of the creation of larger markets as a stimulus to economic development and growth. He even foresaw that economic and political integration were linked together inextricably. But nowhere did he indicate that such a potential drive toward overall European economic unity would be the initial move toward political unification.

On the contrary, as a zealous German patriot List looked forward to European economic unification eventually under German auspices. He was, as Roussakis himself states, profoundly skeptical of the economic viability of other continental nations, especially in the face of British economic competition. If there was to be a regional European economic, and eventually political, unification, then List expected his German Fatherland to play the leading role in its implementation. He devoted his lifetime to agitation for Germany and not for Europe, and he was by no means an embryonic Jean Monnet, the French political economist who conceived the idea of the Common Market or a Robert Schuman, the French premier who worked to promote the European Community.

Subsequent German political leaders confused national greatness with national aggression. They accepted the meat of List's system of national economy and at the same time appropriated his somewhat vague Pan-German ideal and attempted to extend this kind of extremist nationalism into the life of a viable German Reich, which would succeed the British Empire as the dominant power on earth. The two World Wars which resulted in part from this kind of thinking proved to be a tragedy not only for Germany but for the entire world.

---

[67]Roussakis, *op. cit.*, p. 9.

CHAPTER

2

Cultural Nationalism:
The Grimm Brothers' Fairy Tales

All my works relate to the Fatherland, from whose soil they derive their strength.

Jakob Grimm

For generations the Grimm *Fairy Tales* have enjoyed international popularity. Children all over the world have been and are still fascinated by the stories of Cinderella, and Hansel and Gretel. Yet, paradoxically, the scholars who collected and refined these tales worked within the framework of that romanticism which became an important element of German nationalism. The Grimms regarded all their work, including the fairy tales, as deriving its strength from the soil of the Fatherland.

When this theme was presented originally, it turned out to be most controversial. It was denounced by defenders of childhood on the ground that no taint of nationalism could possibly exist in stories so popular among the world's children. Among the most vociferous critics were German scholars who had been obliged to leave Hitler's Germany as refugees: to them the idea was exaggerated and unfair. It is, perhaps, an indication of the tenacity of cultural nationalism that even refugee academicians, themselves victims of Nazi irrationalism, should regard this theme as an attack on their old homeland. Somehow, the presentation of nationalistic sentiment in the *Hausmärchen* was taken as a reflection upon "the superior cultural standards" of the old but not forgotten *Vaterland*.

Adapted from Louis L. Snyder, "Nationalistic Aspects of the Grimm Brothers' Fairy Tales," *The Journal of Social Psychology*, XXXIII (1951), pp. 209–223.

It is, therefore, a matter of some satisfaction that distinguished folklorists have come to accept the conclusions presented in this study. Richard M. Dorson, Professor of History and Folklore and Director of the Folklore Institute at Indiana University and general editor of the University of Chicago series, *Folktales of the World,* wrote in the foreword of the eighteenth volume, *Folklore of Germany,* concerning the motivations of the Grimms. In selecting and refining their household stories, Dorson said, the Grimms placed stress on some attitudes as particularly Germanic. In this way they conveyed the impression that their tales reflected praiseworthy national traits of the German people. These included authoritarianism, militarism, violence toward the outsider, and the strict enforcement of discipline. The social classes were set apart: the king, the count, the leader, the hero are glorified, while the lower class, the servants and peasants dependent upon them and obediently executing their commands, is praised. In contrast stand the avaricious, mendacious middle class of merchants and quack doctors and scheming Jews—outsiders who intruded through the dark forest into the orderly system of manor and village. Hence the loathing for outsiders.

Professor Dorson recognized the nexus:

> In the wake of the Grimms, late nineteenth century nationalists extolled the brothers and their *Märchen* for helping acquaint Germans with a sense of folk unity and add historical past. Under the Nazis the original edition of the tales with their bloodletting and violence was reintroduced.

> Apart from the distortions by the Nazis, modern German folktale scholarship has largely disavowed the promises and methods of the Grimms. The powerful interest they generated in *Märchensammlung* and *Märchenforschung* has maintained its momentum up to the present time, but with altered directions and revised emphases.*

Nationalism and the Grimm Brothers

"Not a narrow nationalism but the philosophic romanticism of Schelling, Görres, Cruezer and Kanne, the view that the mythos glimpsed more of truth than reason, impelled the brothers Grimm to make such great collections of folk poetry as the *Kinder- und Hausmärchen.*"[1] And again: "The brothers

---

*Folktales of Germany, ed., Kurt Ranke, tr. Lotte Baumann (Chicago, 1966), pp. xvii–xix. Kurt Ranke is generally regarded as the outstanding folklore scholar in contemporary Germany.
[1]R. Stadelmann, "Grimm, Jakob Karl and Wilhelm Karl," in *Encyclopedia of the Social Sciences* (New York, 1937), p. 173.

Grimm had no thought of breeding an overweening nationalism, but rather of paving the way for a profounder comprehension of German character, a national self-knowledge."[2] These two conclusions, reached in 1937 by Rudolf Stadelmann, then of the University of Freiburg i. Br., tend to relieve the famed German philologists, founders of scientific Germanistics, of the onus of "narrow" and "overweening" nationalism that has caused an enormous amount of trouble in recent years. Because nationalism, far from weakening, is growing even stronger as nations everywhere grow more national in thought and in deed, an examination of nationalistic aspects of the work of the two gifted brothers would seem to be in order.

Did nationalism, whether narrow or wide, play a vital rôle in the lives and works of the brothers Grimm? Did they venerate national, indigenous, anonymous folk poetry merely on esthetic grounds or in the belief that it contained primitive folk wisdom which became peculiarly German in character? Is there any evidence to show that the *Hausmärchen,* though beloved among many generations of children all over the world, were designed originally to stimulate German national sentiment and to glorify German national traditions?

Die Brüder Grimm, Jakob Ludwig Karl (1785–1863) and Wilhelm Karl (1786–1859), are inseparably linked in the history of German antiquarianism, philology, and folklore. The two were together all their lives. As children they slept in the same bed and worked at the same table, as students they had two beds and tables in the same room. Even after Wilhelm's marriage in 1825, Uncle Jakob shared the house, and they both lived "in such harmony and community that one might almost imagine the two children were common property."[3] The two scholars eventually became leaders of that band of distinguished men who in the nineteenth century devoted themselves to the scientific study of German language and literature and who, at the same time, fashioned the early framework of philology which was used later by some of the linguistic paleontologists in their search for the elusive Aryan by "race."[4] There is versatile genius here, for it is not usual for the same minds to evolve an authoritative grammar and a book of popular fairy tales.[5] Most of the major works of the Grimm brothers stressed national indigenous literature, such as their great collections of folk poetry, as well as their standard works on the history of the Germanic languages, law, folklore, and comparative mythol-

---

[2]*Ibid.,* p. 174.
[3]R. Cleasby, *An Icelandic-English Dictionary* (Oxford, 1875), p. lxix.
[4]See Louis L. Snyder, *Race: A History of Modern Ethnic Theories* (New York, 1939), pp. 65–66.
[5]C. Spender, "Grimms' Fairy Tales," *Contemporary Review,* 102 (1912), pp. 673–679.

ogy. The Grimms were certain that every language has its own peculiar spirit standing in mysterious relationship to the national character. They preferred knowledge of native literature to all foreign lore, because "we can grasp nothing else as surely as our innate powers" and because "Nature herself guides us towards the Fatherland."[6] From the beginning they were attracted by all national poetry, either epics, ballads, or popular tales, and they received full satisfaction in the study of the language, traditions, mythology, and laws of their countrymen.

When Jakob in 1805 visited the libraries of Paris, he quickly became homesick and wrote to his brother that he always dreamed of the Fatherland: "At night I am always home in Germany."[7] Four years later he informed Wilhelm that he would not go to a certain vacation resort "because there are too many Frenchmen there."[8] After watching a festival bonfire in 1814, he wrote to Wilhelm: "I wished that a colossal Bonaparte, a *Puppe aus Heu*, be thrown ceremoniously into the fire and burned."[9] When his friend Benecke received a call to Edinburgh in 1821 and asked for his advice, Jakob replied: "I cannot advise you but I can say that, if I were in your place, I would not emigrate. That would be a difficult thing."[10] In his inaugural lecture at Göttingen, Jakob wrote: "The love for the Fatherland is so godlike and so deeply impressed a feeling in every human breast that it is not weakened but rather strengthened by the sorrows and misfortunes that happen to us in the land of our birth."[11] When Bettina in 1838 sought to get the Grimms positions in France after they had been dismissed at Göttingen, Wilhelm Grimm wrote to Dahlmann: "What's the use of doing it? What can become of the matter? All our work would be paralyzed and extinguished in short order if we renounced our Fatherland."[12]

In 1817 the brothers went to Göttingen, where Jakob received an appointment as professor and librarian, Wilhelm as underlibrarian. In 1837 they were among the *"Göttinger Sieben"* who signed a protest against the king of Hanover's abrogation of the constitution. Both were dismissed from their positions and banished from the kingdom of Hanover.[13] On the surface the

---

[6]Stadelmann, *op. cit.*, p. 174.
[7]T. Matthias, *Der deutsche Gedanke bei Jakob Grimm* (Leipzig, 1915), p. 45.
[8]*Ibid.*, p. 52.
[9]*Ibid.*, p. 48.
[10]*Ibid.*, p. 45.
[11]Jakob Grimm, *De desiderio patriae*, in *Göttinger Gelehrte Anzeigen*, November 13, 1830.
[12]Matthias, *op. cit.*, p. 46.
[13]See Veit Valentin, *The German People* (New York, 1945), pp. 407–408; S. H. Steinberg, *A*

protest of the Grimms seems to have been motivated by liberal sentiment, but actually they had no extreme faith in parliamentary government. To them constitutions had a negative value—as dikes against a devastating flood, while positive fertility was given by the benevolent grace of a monarch.[14] Wilhelm IV had established a constitution and Ernst had by two successive decrees revoked it. In the sight of the Grimms, Ernst had perjured himself, and it was the duty of *Georgia Augusta,* the University of Göttingen, to protest.[15]

In 1840 Jakob wrote to Lachmann: *"Der Welt bin ich nicht feind und hänge heiss an allem Vaterländischen."*[16] In his dedication to his *Geschichte der deutschen Sprache,* Jakob Grimm confessed that his book was meant to be political, since the German people had been responsible for throwing off the Roman yoke, bringing "fresh freedom to the Romans in Gaul, Italy, Spain, and Britain," and with their own strength decided the victory of Christianity "by erecting an unbreakable wall against the constantly pressing Slavs in Europe's middle."[17] "All my works," Jakob wrote later in one of his last essays, "relate to the Fatherland, from whose soil they derive their strength."[18] The distinguished scholar of modern nationalism, Hans Kohn, concluded that "Jakob Grimm, one of the most violent Pan-Germans, expressed his confidence that the peace and salvation of the whole continent will rest upon Germany's strength and freedom."[19]

Romanticism and German Nationalism

From the outset the Grimm brothers took the Romantic position which was closely allied with the rising German nationalism. Following closely upon the lead of the early Romantics—the Schlegel brothers, Ludwig Tieck, Novalis, Herder, Fichte, Schelling, and Schleiermacher, the Grimms in their philological investigations sought to unlock the poetry and the experiences of the German people, which were encased in words and grammatical forms.[20]

Short History of Germany (New York, 1946), p. 195; and Matthias, pp. 25–34.

[14]W. P. Ker, *Jakob Grimm* (London, 1915), p. 10.

[15]*Ibid.*

[16]Matthias, *op. cit.,* p. 49.

[17]*Ibid.,* pp. 43–57.

[18]G. P. Gooch, *History and Historians of the Nineteenth Century* 4th ed. (London and New York, 1928), p. 61.

[19]Hans Kohn, *Prophets and Peoples, Studies in Nineteenth Century Nationalism* (New York, 1946), p. 194.

[20]S. Liptzin, *From Novalis to Nietzsche* (New York, 1929), p. 4.

Many of the German Romantics saw their organic-genetic conception of culture as the expression of the Germanic national soul,[21] which had its beginning in the heroic Middle Ages.[22] Like the Romantics the Grimms issued a plea for the claims of the imagination, of emotion and feeling, of individualism, and above all for a synthetic expression of the national genius in all its manifold aspects of literature, art, religion, and philosophy.[23] But where the Romantics enriched the imagination by presenting the many-colored life of other ages and countries, they remained mostly artists and poets, not scholars, philologists, and historians; the Grimms, on the other hand, functioned in the Romantic circle by giving to it the critical scholarship that hitherto had been lacking.[24] "I strove to penetrate into the wild forests of our ancestors," wrote Wilhelm Grimm, "listening to their whole language, and watching their pure customs."[25] As a group the Romantics profoundly venerated folk poetry and especially the fairy tale.[26] Novalis pronounced the folk tale the primary and highest creation of man.[27] Even the great Schiller had written in extravagant terms:

> *Tiefere Bedeutung*
> *Liegt in dem Märchen meiner Kinderjahre,*
> *Als in der Wahrheit, die das Leben lehrt.*[28]

It was this type of romanticism, stressing folk language, customs, personality, and the idea of *Volksgemeinschaft*, or community of the people, which was an important factor in the historical evolution of modern nationalism.

Planning and Publication of the Fairy Tales

The idea for a collection of children's stories may be traced directly to Herder, who in 1773 aroused immediate attention to folk literature with an essay

---

[21]Robert R. Ergang, *Herder and the Foundations of German Nationalism* (New York, 1931), p. 4.

[22]G. Salomon, *Das Mittelalter als Ideal in der Romantik* (Munich, 1922), pp. 46 ff.

[23]See F. Wertham, *The Show of Violence* (New York, 1929).

[24]Gooch, *op. cit.*, p. 54.

[25]J. and W. Grimm, *Fairy Tales* (New York, 1944), p. 943. Hereafter cited as *Fairy Tales*.

[26]H. Hamann, *Die literarischen Vorlagen der Kinder- und Hausmärchen und ihre Bearbeitung durch die Brüder Grimm* (Berlin, 1906), p. 8.

[27]J. Campbell, "The Work of the Grimm Brothers," in *Fairy Tales*, p. 834.

[28]Friedrich von Schiller, *Die Piccolomini*, in *Schillers Werke, herausgegeben von J. J. Fischer* (Stuttgart and Leipzig, n.d.) [The excerpt is from Act III, Scene 4, p. 317.]

entitled *Ossian und die Lieder alter Völker*.[29] Such a collection, Herder once remarked, would be a Christmas present for the young people of the future.[30] in 1805 Jakob Grimm was taken to Paris by his teacher, Savigny. "I have been thinking," Wilhelm wrote to Jakob, "that you might look for old German poems among the manuscripts. Perhaps you might find something unknown and important."[31] Soon after Jakob's return the brothers began their laborious collection of German sagas and fairy tales. The work proceeded under difficult conditions, for in 1806 the armies of Napoleon overran Kassel. "Those days," wrote Wilhelm, "of the collapse of all hitherto existing establishments will remain forever before my eyes. . . . The ardor with which the studies in Old German were pursued helped overcome the spiritual depression."[32] Working thus in difficult times but nevertheless hearing "the horns of elfland faintly blowing,"[33] the Grimms completed their first volume, which appeared at Christmas, 1812, the winter of Napoleon's retreat from Moscow. It was an immediate success, the masterpiece for which the whole Romantic movement had been waiting.[34]

The name of the Grimms quickly became a household word throughout the Germanies,[35] and eventually it was carried throughout the civilized world in a series of translations. Even the natives of Africa and the South Seas have borrowed tales from the Grimms.[36]

With the publication of the *Hausmärchen* the Grimms not only accomplished for the fairy tale what Arnim and Brentano had done for the *Volkslied*,[37] but they also established a universal standard for the telling of fairy tales.[38] The Grimms were ideal interpreters of this literary form. Fascinated by folk-poetry and themselves gifted with a persisting sense of childlike wonder, the dignified scholars at the same time had a rare ability to pass on their own enthusiasm to children. They saw to it that any child could follow

[29]E. Lichtenstein, *Die Idee der Naturpoesie bei den Brüdern Grimm und ihr Verhältnis zu Herder, Vierteljahrschrift für Literaturwissenschaft und Geistesgeschichte*, vol. VI (1928), pp. 513–547; E. Laas, *Herders Einwirkung auf die deutsche Lyrik von 1770 bis 1775, Grenzboten* vol. XXX (1871), pp. 581 ff.; W. A. Berendsohn, *Grundformen volkstümlicher Erzählerkunst in der Kinder- und Hausmärchen der Brüder Grimm* (Hamburg, 1921), p. 8; and Ergang, *op. cit.*, pp. 102, 106, 114, 139, 174, 208, 234, 236, 240.
[30]Gooch, *op. cit.*, p. 56.
[31]*Ibid.*, p. 55.
[32]Campbell, *op. cit.*, pp. 835–836.
[33]Spender, *op. cit.*, p. 673.
[34]Campbell, *op. cit.*, p. 838.
[35]Stadelmann, *op. cit.*, p. 173.
[36]Campbell, *op. cit.*, p. 839.
[37]Gooch, *op. cit.*, p. 56.
[38]G. M. Priest, *A Brief History of German Literature* (New York, 1909), p. 253.

the tales. The youngster loves a beginning, a plot, and an ending, together with a clean-cut moral, and the Grimms gave them all of these. The Grimms recognized that the child loves to know how old people are, what they wear, what they say, and why they say it, details which attract the attention of young minds. That the Grimms knew their way around in the child's world is attested by the simple and subtle humor of the tales. Children love houses built of bread, roofed with cake, and finished with sugar windows. They are delighted to learn that witches have red eyes and cannot see far, that a kettle can be scoured to resemble gold, and that a dwarf fishing can get his beard entangled in his line. They love the little bean who laughed so much that she burst and had to be sewn up with black cotton by a friendly tailor, thus explaining why every bean since that day has a black seam in it.[39]

 The Grimms obtained their folk tales from the lips of peasant women, shepherds, waggoners, vagrants, old grannies, and children in Hesse, Hanau, and other areas.[40] Their first concern in collecting the stories was "faithfulness to the truth," and they sought to keep the tales "as clean as possible," adding nothing and changing nothing.[41] Wilhelm Grimm stated explicitly that he and his brother were most careful to avoid embellishing the tales which in themselves were so rich and rewarding.[42] Jakob Grimm, too, was certain that "stories of this kind are sought for with full recognition of their scientific value and with a dread of altering any part of their contents, whereas formerly they were only regarded as worthless fancy-pieces which might be manipulated at will."[43] In their thorough commentary on the stories the Grimms gave painstaking and accurate references to the exact source from which each tale was taken. For example, nineteen of their finest tales were taken from Frau Katerina Viehmann (1755–1815), the wife of a tailor, who lived at Niederzwehrn, a village near Kassel. "Anyone believing that traditional materials are easily falsified and carelessly preserved, and hence cannot survive over a long period, should hear how close she always keeps to her story and how zealous she is for its accuracy."[44]

---

[39]Spender, *op. cit.*, pp. 673 ff.
[40]W. Schoof, *Zur Entstehungsgeschichte der Grimm'schen Märchen, Sonderabdruck aus den Hessischen Blättern für Volkskunde*, XIX (Frankfurt am Main, 1931), *passim*. See also R. Steig, *Zur Entstehungsgeschichte der Märchen und Sagen der Brüder Grimm, Archiv für das Studium der neueren Sprachen*, vol. 107 (1901).
[41]Liptzin, *op. cit.*, p. 99.
[42]*Ibid.*
[43]H. B. Paull, *The Grimms' Fairy Tales and Household Stories.* Reviewed in *The Athenaeum*, 3148 (1888), pp. 237–239.
[44]J. Bolte and G. Polivka, *Anmerkungen zu den Kinder- und Hausmärchen der Brüder Grimm* (Leipzig, 1912–1932), vol. IV, pp. 43–44.

The fact that the brothers Grimm took down the tales with almost fanatical accuracy does not at all invalidate the thesis that the *Märchen* have played a role in the historical evolution of German nationalism. Quite the contrary— the many sentiments typical of German nationalism which are found in the tales, as will be demonstrated, existed among the old peasants, nurses, and workers from whom the Grimms obtained their material. What the anthologists did was to catch the varied strands of German national tradition and weave them into a pattern glorifying German folk stories. Themselves superb patriots who always believed in sanctifying the ancient German tongue,[45] the Grimms, consciously or unconsciously, stressed those peculiar traits which have since come to be known as important elements of the German national character. Moreover, in the very cooperative action by which the tales were written a quality of national validity and individual unity appears.[46]

Analysis of the Tales

The environment of the Grimms' tales was one which reflected similarities of family life in the same culture. The milieu consisted of farmland, villages, towns, and the forest, but the sea was alien. In the village lived the peasant, the tradesman, and the artisan, near the castle of the king and his court. The forest, a dark jewel containing evil spirits and lovely treasures, was a fascinating but frightening unknown, where witches lived in huts and princesses in enchanting castles. The family was a cohesive unit, with the good and able father, respected and obeyed, at its head; its cohesiveness was challenged by such unattractive elements as poverty, the stepmother, and inheritance trouble. There was no primogeniture, hence the Salic law with its cycle of unification, disruption, and unification prevailed.

Society consisted of royalty, the aristocracy, the military, the professionals, merchants, artisans, and peasants. Class distinctions were definite. The upper and lower classes are depicted favorably in the tales, but the middle class, consisting of merchants, innkeepers, doctors, clerics, and Jews, is condemned for its greed and quackery. Virtue is always rewarded and sin punished, though virtue was complicated somewhat by heroes lying, cheating, stealing, and slaying to gain an end.

There is plenty of evidence in the fairy tales to show the existence of what

---

[45]J. and W. Grimm, *Deutsches Wörterbuch* (Leipzig, 1854), vol. I, preface.
[46]Campbell, *op. cit.*, p. 848.

may be called universal factors of personality, qualities which are typical of many peoples from all parts of the world. But at the same time there is also evidence of the existence of such relatively uniform and striking attitudes as respect for order, obedience, discipline, authoritarianism, militarism, glorification of violence, and fear of and contempt for the stranger.

A strong respect for the desirability of order is indicated in the opening paragraph of *The Sole*:

> The fishes had for a long time been discontented because no order prevailed in their kingdom. None of them turned aside for the others, but all swam to the right or left as they fancied, or darted between those who wanted to stay together, or got into their way; and a strong one gave a weak one a blow with its tail, and drove it away, or else swallowed it up without more ado. "How delightful it would be," said they, "if we had a king who enforced law and justice among us!" and they met together to choose for their ruler the one who would cleave through the water most quickly, and give help to the weak ones.[47]

The concept of obedience is emphasized again and again. A little hare tells a musician: "I will obey you as a scholar obeys his master."[48] When the Devil orders a father to cut off the hands of his own child, the father asks his daughter to understand his predicament. She replies: "Dear father, do with me what you will, I am your child." Whereupon she lays down both her hands, and allows them to be cut off.[49] A king's son, seized with a desire to travel around the world "took no one with him but a faithful servant."[50] When Hans serves his master for seven years, the master gives him as reward "a piece of gold as big as his head."[51] A diligent servant is the first out of bed every monring, the last to go to bed at night, and whenever there was a difficult job to be done, which nobody cared to undertake, he was always the first to set himself to it. Moreover, he never complained, but was contented with everything, and was always merry.[52]

This concept of obedience, together with its corollary—discipline, amounted to something more than mere obedience of the child to its parents. It was closely akin to that type of authoritarianism manifested in attitudes toward the family, society, and the state. The father is head of the home and the ruler of the family; it is wrong and dangerous to challenge his authority. Society itself is static, with definite gradations from top to bottom. The state is

---

[47]*Fairy Tales*, no. 172.
[48]*Ibid.*, no. 8.
[49]*Ibid.*, no. 1.

[50]*Ibid.*, no. 22.
[51]*Ibid.*, no. 83.
[52]*Ibid.*, no. 110.

supreme and the end of all striving. In the state the king is supreme. His word is law and his orders must be strictly obeyed, even if forfeiture of life be the result. He may on occasion order death or grant wealth at a mere whim.

The nature and personality of the king become dominant themes in the *Märchen*. The land of the tales is made up of many small kingdoms, in each of which the king emerges as the strong, all-powerful personality. When a king made a great feast and invited thereto, from far and near, all the young men likely to marry, he marshalled all of them in a row according to their rank and standing: first came the kings, then the grand-dukes, then the princes, the earls, the barons, and the gentry.[53] When Adam and Eve enter Heaven, the Lord saw their pretty children, blessed them, laid his hands on the first, and said, "Thou shalt be a powerful king."[54] When a bird sings well, it is identified as "the king of the birds."[55] It was decided among the birds that he who flew highest should be king.[56] The king is mighty: "such a person arrives in the carriage in full splendor like a mighty king, not like a beggar."[57] The king is wise: "a long time ago there lived a king who was famed for his wisdom through all the land."[58] The verdict always comes before the king.[59] The king is generous: when he hears of a poor peasant's poverty, he presents him with a bit of land.[60] He is handsome: when peasants dress up in splendid garments, and wash, "no king could have looked so handsome."[61] The king is kindly; he always looked kindly at frightened people,[62] and, feeling compassion, raised a poor soldier from poverty.[63] He is a lover of all the better things, including all kinds of fine trees.[64] He is sentimental: "tears rose to the king's eyes."[65] He is omnipresent and omniscient: when a shepherd boy's fame spreads far and wide because of his wise answers, the king naturally hears of it and summons him;[66] when a horn sings by itself "the king understood it all, and caused the ground below the bridge to be dug up, and then the whole skeleton of the murdered man to come to life."[67] Similarly, the various members of the king's family take top rank in the social hierarchy.[68]

The love and reverence for the king, emphasized so strongly in the fairy tales, are a part of a major theme of the stories: the life of the hero. How the hero makes his way through thick, weird forests, how he outwits ferocious

---

[53]*Ibid.*, no. 52.
[54]*Ibid.*, no. 180.
[55]*Ibid.*, no. 102.
[56]*Ibid.*, no. 171.
[57]*Ibid.*, no. 54.
[58]*Ibid.*, no. 17.
[59]*Ibid.*, no. 94.
[60]*Ibid.*

[61]*Ibid.*, no. 106.
[62]*Ibid.*, no. 11.
[63]*Ibid.*, no. 146.
[64]*Ibid.*, no. 91.
[65]*Ibid.*, no. 94.
[66]*Ibid.*, no. 152.
[67]*Ibid.*, no. 28.
[68]*Ibid.*, nos. 19, 65, 94, 126, 128, 129, 166.

animals, and how he wins a propitious marriage, these exert a tremendous appeal to the child's mind. The hero, be he prince, soldier, peasant's son, servant, or tradesman, falls into two categories: he is a cunning, clever fellow, destined from the very beginning to conquer fate by his strength, courage, and brains, or he is slightly stupid and guided in his victorious course by good fairies.[69] In both cases obviousness is the chief characteristic. The clever hero appears less often than the dullard, but his is a glorious life overshadowed by the wings of death. A simpleton son, by a trick of fate, gains his father's inheritance away from his two intelligent, older brothers.[70] In *The Golden Goose,* the youngest son, Dummling, attains success and happiness despite his stupidity.[71]

The greatest virtue of either the clever or dullard boy is courage. When Strong Hans beats some robbers, "his mother stood in a corner admiring his bravery and strength."[72] When a young soldier is asked if he is fearless, he replies: "A soldier and fear—how can the two go together"?[73] The cunning little tailor was not frightened by a bear that had never left anyone alive who had fallen into its embraces, but was on the contrary, quite delighted, saying: "Boldly ventured is half-won."[74] When the seven Swabians make up their minds to travel about the world and seek adventures and perform great deeds, they reserve the place of honor at the front for Master Schultz, "the boldest and the bravest."[75] One of the longest of the tales is concerned with a youth who went forth to learn what fear was.[76] Little Thumbling the tiny son of a diminutive tailor, was no bigger than a thumb, "but he had some courage in him."[77]

The virtue of courage is closely associated with another dominant theme of modern nationalism: the veneration of the military spirit. Again and again the tales show that war is good, that fighting gives great moral vigor, that bearing arms is the highest of all possible honors, and that the military instinct is a blessing. There are many great deeds of valor, reminiscent of the *chansons de geste* of the Middle Ages. In *Iron John,* a country was overrun by war, whereupon the king gathered together all his people, and did not know

---

[69] V. Brun, "The German Fairy Tale," *Menorah Journal*, XXVII, pp. 147–155.
[70] *Fairy Tales*, no. 63.
[71] *Ibid.*, no. 64.
[72] *Ibid.*, no. 166.
[73] *Ibid.*, no. 101.
[74] *Ibid.*, no. 114.
[75] *Ibid.*, no. 119.
[76] *Ibid.*, no. 4.
[77] *Ibid.*, no. 45.

whether or not he could offer resistance to the enemy, who was superior in strength. But the gardener's son came to the rescue. "When he got near the battlefield a great part of the king's men had already fallen, and little was wanting to make the rest give way. Then the youth galloped thither with his iron soldiers, broke like a hurricane over the enemy, and beat down all who opposed him. They began to fly, but the youth pursued, and never stopped, until there was not a single man left."[78] A young fellow, who enlists as a soldier, conducts himself bravely, "and was always the foremost when it rained bullets."[79] When three soldiers desert the army, they receive due punishment for it, not by the authorities but by a dragon, who turns out to be the Devil.[80]

The moral is clear: it is not wise nor desirable to desert the army. When the valiant little tailor announces that he is ready to enter the king's service as a soldier, "he was therefore honorably received and a special dwelling assigned to him."[81] "When there is order to be maintained in the kingdom, the king angrily, as is expected, orders a captain to march out with his troops."[82] Even the animals are infected with the war spirit: "when the time came for the war to begin, the willow-wren sent out spies to discover who was the enemy's commander-in-chief"[83] [the spies were gnats, who were the most crafty, and who flew into the forest where the enemy was assembled].[84] Force is accepted as normal and desirable: when a cat jumps upon her friend, the mouse, and swallows her, the story ends: "Verily, that is the way of the world."[85]

Cruelty and violence and atrocity of every kind are characteristic of the fairy tales and myths of all peoples. On a certain level of civilization punishment is meted out without any seeming relation to guilt. Thus Achilles pitilessly drags the corpse of gallant Hector ten times around the walls of Troy, and Ulysses kills his wife's suitors for no greater sin than revelling. These things are common enough. "But typical of the German fairy tale is the juxtaposition of the commonplace and the intimate with the horrors of death and all the tortures of a calculated cruelty."[86] While the king's son is busy putting on his clothes, a giant surprises him, and puts both his eyes out.[87] A king orders a witch cast into the fire and miserably burnt, while her daughter is to be taken to the forest to be torn to death by wild beasts.[88] A wicked

[78]*Ibid.*, no. 136.
[79]*Ibid.*, no. 101.
[80]*Ibid.*, no. 125.
[81]*Ibid.*, no. 20.
[82]*Ibid.*, no. 54.
[83]*Ibid.*, no. 102.

[84]*Ibid.*
[85]*Ibid.*, no. 2.
[86]Brun, *op. cit.*, pp. 153–154.
[87]*Fairy Tales*, no. 121.
[88]*Ibid.*, no. 11.

stepmother is placed in a barrel filled with boiling oil and venomous snakes.[89]
An equally wicked mother-in-law is bound to the stake and burnt to ashes.[90]
The two false sisters of Cinderella have their eyes pecked out by pigeons;[91] the
cook of a hunter decides to throw Fundevogel into boiling water and eat him;[92]
an old woman cuts off the head of her beautiful step-daughter, whereupon
drops of blood from the girl's head carry on a conversation.[93]

And so it goes, with Hansel and Gretel shoving the wicked witch into the
oven for a merited cremation, bad step-mothers torn to death by wild beasts,
others forced to dance in red-hot slippers, and tailors having their eyes gouged
out one by one. To find a comparable obsession with vengeance and death it
would be necessary to turn to ancient Egypt. But where the Egyptians linked
death with elaborate ritual and a traditional piety, the characters in the *Märchen* challenge it in a mood of hysterical fear and revenge. Throughout the tales
there is a bias toward elementary justice very much like the early Hebrew-
Babylonian concept of an eye for an eye.

Much of this, of course, is typical of the primitive instincts of children,
which are not very different, in the final analysis, from those of the savage.
Dr. Frederic Wertham points out that the lack of respect for human life can
begin in childhood in the comparative indifference to torture, mutilation, and
death.[94] One of my students, Miss Bertha Pinsky, demonstrated the existence
of this callousness to violence in a series of experiments with her own class of
six-year-olds. Finding it difficult to maintain order among this group of
pupils, she hit upon the expedient of reading the Grimms' fairy tales to them.
"I was amazed to discover that I could obtain perfect silence by reading any
one of the more violent tales. The children were simply fascinated. The entire
class howled with delight when I read to them *The Jew Among Thorns,* in
which an old Jew is forced to dance among thorns to the tune of a fiddle."

When these primitive sadistic and masochistic social attitudes carry over
into the adult years, trouble can be expected. It is to the eternal discredit of the
Nazi leaders of Germany that they elevated obscene glorifications of violence
and crime into a place of authority. All the cruel pieces of the fairy tales,
which had been eliminated under the Weimar Republic, were restored in
Hitler's Germany, and the study of folklore was raised to a special place of
honor.[95]

Still another obvious theme of the *Märchen* was fear of and hatred for the

---

[89]*Ibid.,* no. 9.
[90]*Ibid.,* no. 49.
[91]*Ibid.,* no. 21.
[92]*Ibid.,* no. 51.

[93]*Ibid.,* no. 56.
[94]Wertham, *op. cit., passim.*
[95]Brun, *op. cit.,* pp. 154–155.

outsider, characteristic of primitive tribalism and modern nationalism. The stepmother is invariably a disgusting old woman who performs evil deeds with inhuman zest and cruelty. She is diabolically cunning in seeking to do away with her stepchildren. If she has any children from her first marriage, she will seek to displace her stepchildren so that her own flesh and blood will acquire the family fortune. In *Hansel and Gretel,* the stepmother purposely loses her stepchildren in the forest so that they will no longer be in the family.[96] A king, fearing that the stepmother of his children might not treat them well, and even do them injury, takes them to a lonely castle in the midst of a forest.[97] A little boy takes his younger sister by the hand and proclaims: "Since our mother died we have had no happiness. Our stepmother beats us every day, and if we come near her she kicks us with her foot. God pity us, if our mother only knew."[98] But when a wicked stepmother is taken before a judge, she is placed in a barrel filled with boiling oil and venomous snakes, and dies an evil death.[99] The stepmother's real crime is disruption of the family, the alienation of the children and even the father. She is an alien in the home, an outsider, a foreigner in the state. She must be hated and eliminated because she will throw the accepted order into chaos with her new ideas and foreign attitudes and methods.

The virulent type of anti-Semitism which is a concomitant of German nationalism,[100] appears often in the *Märchen.* It was taken as a matter of course that poverty and discontent were directly attributable to the Jew, who was "the unproductive exploiter and employer of other people's labor." The peasant suffers most from the machinations of the Jew.[101] Though the merchant is always a villain, the Jewish merchant is something more—a foreigner, the product of a strange and ancient civilization, who is universally disliked. He is a greedy moneylender who cheats his fellow man, and moreover he is a sycophant and a serio-comic villain. He is always dressed shabbily, has a yellow or gray beard, and it is plainly his fault when some honest person gets into trouble and goes to the gallows.

In *The Bright Sun Brings it to Life* a Jew appears as a prophet of death to a hapless tailor.[102] *The Good Bargain* is concerned with the struggle between a

---

[96]*Fairy Tales,* no. 15.

[97]*Ibid.,* no. 49.

[98]*Ibid.,* no. 11.

[99]*Ibid.,* no. 9.

[100]See I. Cohen, *Anti-Semitism in Germany* (London, 1918), and F. von Hellwald, *"Zur Charakteristik der jüdischen Volk,"* *Das Ausland,* XLV (1872), pp. 951–955.

[101]S. Maccoby, "Modern Anti-Semitism," *Contemporary Review,* CXLVIII (1935), pp. 342–348.

[102]*Fairy Tales,* no. 115.

shrewd peasant and a deceitful Jew, in which the peasant says: "Ah, what a Jew says is always false—no true word ever comes out of his mouth."[103] In *The Jew Among Thorns* an honest and clever servant, who played a fiddle, one day meets a Jew with a long goat's beard. When the Jew, who is watching a bird in the thorn bushes, crawls into the bushes to fetch the bird, the good servant's humor leads him to take up his fiddle and play.

> In a moment the Jew's legs began to move, and to jump into the air, and the more the servant fiddled the better went the dance. But the thorns tore his shabby coat from him, combed his beard, and pricked and plucked him all over the body. "Oh, dear," cried the Jew, "what do I want with your fiddling? Leave the fiddle alone master; I do not want to dance."

> But the servant did not listen to him, and thought: "You have fleeced people often enough, now the thorn-bushes shall do the same to you"; and he began to play over again, so that the Jew had to jump higher than ever, and scraps of his coat were left hanging on the thorns.

The story concludes with a courtroom scene, in which the judge "had the Jew taken to the gallows and hanged as a thief."[104]

The effects of such tales upon generations of German youth may well be imagined. In Nazi Germany the unexpurgated fairy tales were read by children and a large part of Nazi literature designed for children was merely a modernized version of the Grimms' tales, with emphasis upon the idealization of fighting, glorification of power, reckless courage, theft, brigandage, and militarism reinforced with mysticism.[105]

It is reasonable to conclude, then, that, with their fairy tales, as well as their dictionary and grammar, the brothers Grimm contributed as much to the German revival and to German nationalism as generals, diplomats, and political figures. The place of the Grimms in the development of German nationalism was recognized a half century ago by Carl Franke:

> To the spirit of German schoolchildren the tales have become what mother's milk is for their bodies—the first nourishment for the spirit and the imagination. How German is Snow White, Little Briar Rose, Little Red Cap, the seven dwarfs! Through such genuine German diet must the language and spirit of the child gradually become more and more German. . . .

---

[103]*Ibid.*, no. 7.

[104]*Ibid.*, no. 110.

[105]V. Petrova and A. Vibakh, "Nazi Literature for Children," *The Living Age,* CCCXLVII (1934), pp. 365–366.

Indeed the brothers Grimm have earned our innermost love and highest admiration as citizens and as men. For they belong doubtlessly in the broadest sense among the founders of the new German Reich. . . . They exhibited all the German virtues: the inner love of family, true friendship, the kindly love for the Hessian homeland, the inspiring love for the Fatherland. . . . With full right they earn therefore a place among Germany's greatest men.[106]

Summary and Conclusions

1. Nationalism played a vital role in the lives and works of the Grimm brothers, who were convinced that all their writings, including the fairy tales, derived their strength "from the soil of the German Fatherland."

2. From the beginning of their work the Grimm brothers took the Romantic position, closely allied with the rising German nationalism, in which they stressed the claims of the imagination, emotions, and feelings.

3. In planning and collecting the fairy tales the Grimms, consciously or unconsciously, were motivated by a desire to glorify German traditions and to stimulate German national sentiment.

4. An analysis of the *Märchen* gives ample evidence to show an emphasis upon such social characteristics as respect for order, belief in the desirability of obedience, subservience to authority, respect for the leader and the hero, veneration of courage and the military spirit, acceptance without protest of cruelty, violence, and atrocity, fear of and hatred for the outsider, and virulent anti-Semitism.

5. The fairy tales thus played a significant role, hitherto little recognized outside of Germany, in the development of modern integral German nationalism. "They have enabled us to understand that we, the German people, bear the power and conditions in ourselves to take up and carry on the civilization of old times, that we are a folk with a high historical mission."[107]

A Question of Authenticity

The *Hausmärchen* continue to attract the attention of children everywhere as well as fascinated scholars. Some German folklore specialists are now reluc-

---

[106]Carl Franke, *Die Brüder Grimm, Ihr Leben und Wirken* (Dresden and Leipzig, 1899), pp. 40, 52, 150–151, 153.
[107]*Ibid.*

tant to accept the judgment of Hermann Grimm, son of Wilhelm Grimm, that
the collection of tales "spring from the soil of Germany." The most recent
attempt to purge the tales of what is called romantic politicizing was made in
1976 by Heinz Rölleke, a Wüppertal Professor of German, who for many
years was a lecturer at the University of Cologne. Rölleke discovered a
manuscript copy of sixty-three of the original tales and compared them with
the first edition of 1812.[108] His research led him to question the German origin
of some of the tales as well as their very authenticity.

According to Rölleke, the *Fairy Tales* are not as German in spirit as has
been generally accepted. The Grimm brothers had quoted "elderly peasant
women from Hesse" as the main verbal source of their stories. Nineteen of
the tales, they noted, came from Frau Katerina Viehmann, the wife of a tailor.
"It was one of those pieces of good fortune," Wilhelm Grimm wrote in 1819,
"that we got to know an old peasant woman who lived in a small village
called Niederzwehrn, near Kassel, and who told us the greatest and best parts
of the second volume. She was still hale and hearty, and not much over 50
years old. Her face was firm, pleasant and somehow knowledgeable, and her
eyes clear and sharp. She retained the old stories in her head."[109] Further, in
1895 Hermann Grimm told of how an aged woman called "Old Marie" had
told his father and uncle most of the remaining stories of the first volume,
such as *Little Red Riding Hood* and *The Sleeping Beauty*.

Rölleke's research revealed that Frau Viehmann[110] came from a French
Huguenot family, grew up speaking French, and took some of her stories
straight from Charles Perrault, a 17th-century French writer. "Old Marie"
was a woman named Marie Hassenpflug, also from a Huguenot family; she
was brought up in the French tradition and—far from being a peasant woman
steeped in German folklore—was the wife of a president of the government.
Thus, Rölleke dismisses the traditional explanation that these were genuine
"Hesse folk tales" as Wilhelm Grimm had contended but rather the product
of comparatively well-educated people from good families in Switzerland or
other French-speaking areas. As an example he quotes the story of *The Sleep-*

---

[108]This manuscript was originally owned by Clemens Brentano, who acquired it in 1810 because
of his active assistance in preparing it. On his death it passed eventually to a Trappist monastery
in Alsace, and from there to an auction in New York in 1953, at which time it was acquired by
Martin Bodmer, a Swiss national. The Bodmer family passed it on to Rölleke, who used it for his
systematic analysis of the tales.
[109]Quoted by Mathias Schreiber in *Kölner Stadt-Anzeiger*, April 17, 1976. Schreiber's article, on
which this section is based, gives an excellent résumé of the Rölleke thesis.
[110]Rölleke calls her *Dorothea* instead of *Katerina* Viehmann.

ing Beauty, which hitherto had been held to be particularly German. The story, concerning a princess who was put to sleep for a century by an evil fairy until she was awakened by a kiss from a prince, was told to the Grimms by "Old Marie." Rölleke insists that it is a word-for-word repetition of Perrault's *Histoires ou contes du temps passé,* a collection of French fairy tales which appeared in 1697. He cites other tales as also not reflecting the German folklore language of old peasant women.

Rölleke does not assert that the Grimms were literary swindlers who were aware of the questionable authenticity of the tales. He agrees that they listened to the two old women and that the brothers simply acted within the spirit of the times. Nevertheless, he does conclude that it is an exaggeration to say that the tales were irreproachably German and genuine.

Rölleke deserves much credit for his discovery that Frau Viehmann and "Old Marie" were of French Huguenot background and that several of the tales were French in origin. Yet this does not invalidate the theory of the importance of the tales in the development of German nationalism. Far from it. The methods of the Grimms may well have been faulty, but they endowed their tales with nationalistic bias.

The fact that Frau Viehmann and "Old Marie" were of Huguenot origin does not lessen their role in German cultural life. Historically, many Huguenots or French Protestants who fled from France after the revocation of the Edict of Nantes by Louis XIV in 1685, settled in England, America (the Carolinas, Pennsylvania, and New York), and Germany (especially in Brandenburg and the Rhineland). Of Calvinist persuasion, the Huguenots were skilled as artisans and traders, and wherever they went they constituted one of the most advanced and industrious elements in society. Invariably, they became assimilated in their new homelands, while at the same time retaining many of their old cultural forms. Undoubtedly, they brought with them folklore tales of French origin. But this does not mean that the German folk tales therefore became exclusively French.

Secondly, the Huguenots were but one element among the many ethnic and cultural groups which formed the German nationality. Neither Germans nor any other people are born with a sense of national consciousness: the need for security may be biological but national consciousness is engrained environmentally through family, school, and public life. Because the old women interviewed were of Huguenot origin does not mean that the authenticity of the tales is thereby demolished.

Finally, it is not as much the tales themselves as the *usage* made of them by the Grimms that makes them vital in the development of German romantic-nationalism. As linguistic paleontologists, the Grimms believed that their tales "sprang from the soil of Germany." That was the way they were presented. Perhaps, indeed, some of the tales came not from peasant women but from bourgeois Huguenot families. It may also be true that, despite their denials, the Grimms idealized and stylized the stories. But the two brothers always emphasized the Germanness of their tales. They gave romantic pictures of German medieval life, with its special conglomeration of kings, princes, princesses, peasants, frogs, and pumpkins. Even if Sleeping Beauty were originally French, the Grimms converted her into a fair German maiden. The motivation may well have been unconscious, but it was certainly inspired by the sentiment of nationalism.

The brothers Grimm had no idea that one day their folk tales would become the best-known German book in existence with translations into many languages throughout the world. For them the stories were particularly German and a reflection of true German folkish culture. The elements of loyalty, greed, and cunning may have common international implications, but regarded *in toto,* a special combination of German characteristics, both stereotypes and national, remain in the German versions of the tales.

3

Political Consolidation: German Nationalism as a Force for Unification

Let us put Germany in the saddle. She will know how to ride.

Otto von Bismarck

The Nature of German Nationalism

It is the nature of nationalism to act in different ways by adjusting itself to the milieu in which it operates. Thus, nationalism can be at one time a force for unification and at another a mechanism for disruption. It was a prime stimulus for the unification of Germany under Prussian auspices, but it was also a disintegrative factor in the conglomerate Austro-Hungarian Empire and eventually helped to break up that central European state.

By the early part of the 19th century other European states, notably England and France, had long since achieved their national consolidation. But this sense of national identity had escaped the Germans. It is more correct to refer to the 19th century "Germanies" rather than Germany. Far from a unified national state it was a geographical expression with residues of feudalism and manorialism. Nationalism was to be the cement which bound the structure of German society.

What had been a fragmentized social order was transformed by nationalism into a centralized state under Prussian domination. The German people became united by strong bonds of community interests. As in other countries, the German flag was to symbolize glory and prestige. The German people came to regard their special culture and way of life as equal to or superior to

55

those of other peoples. Where once the individual German had given his paramount loyalty to the Church, lord, guild, or university, he now regarded his primary allegiance to be to the national state. This was the essence of modern nationalism.

In the process the component parts of German society outgrew their feudal divisions while hostile factions combined in a process of unification. The Germanies at the end of the 18th century consisted of a combination of independent sovereignties varying in size from the kingdom of Prussia with its Hohenzollern dynasty and *Junker* nobility, to tiny principalities most of which boasted of a special army, flag, and system of tariffs. True to the feudal tradition, larger and lesser lords quarreled among themselves in defense of their territories and rights. As a matter of prestige each lord was anxious to impress his neighbors by displaying ostentatious wealth or an efficient army. Some of the larger states were brought to the edge of bankruptcy by efforts to imitate the splendors of Louis XIV's Versailles. The construction of a viable national state out of these diverse elements seemed to be an impossibility at the end of the 18th century.

The French Revolution of 1789 was decisive not only for the course of French history but also for that of the remainder of Europe. Rulers of German states and principalities were appalled by the events in Paris. They denounced the revolution as insurrection gone wild. All were fearful that similar troubles might break out at home. German intellectual advocates of the Enlightenment were inclined to greet the social changes in France as harbingers of a new European order, but they were few in number and they had little influence. News of the Reign of Terror was received with dismay. German rulers, both large and small, wanted no part of the new liberalism, constitutionalism, and cosmopolitanism.

The Napoleonic Impetus

The original stimulus for German nationalism came from outside German territory. Napoleon set the boundaries of the German states much as they would exist in the 20th century. This was by no means altruism on Napoleon's part. Utilizing the principle of *divide et impera,* he was anxious to bolster the smaller states at the expense of the larger purely for his own convenience. In the process German princes, impressed by the successes of the French conqueror, made it a point to work with him. The rulers of Bavaria, Baden,

Saxony, and Württemberg, among others, deemed it to their advantage to ally themselves with the devil instead of trying to fight him.

Napoleon was always the practical activist. As early as 1803 he set up a kind of glorified real estate office in Paris with the purpose of redistributing the German ecclesiastical states and free cities among the secular princes. In this process he was able to reduce the conglomerate German states and principalities to about thirty. The next step on July 21, 1806, was to unite the German states he had created or enlarged into what he believed to be a permanent Confederation of the Rhine. This union, he decreed, was to be "forever separated from the territory of the German Empire." Several days later he sent a message to the Imperial Diet announcing the end of the Holy Roman Empire. Thus was ended the largely Germanic and North Italian territory originally organized under Otto I, who had been crowned emperor by papal authority in 962 A.D. The Holy Roman Empire was abolished not by the Germans in the name of their own nationalism but from the outside by the French conqueror who wanted to establish a French-dominated Europe. Francis II, the last emperor, thereafter ruled as Austrian Emperor. Napoleon had induced him to abdicate as Holy Roman Emperor but retain the title of Francis I, Emperor of Austria.

The old Holy Roman Empire, which had lasted for almost a thousand years, was no more. The independence of its component parts was now legally recognized. The end of theocracy in the Germanies was decreed from Paris, not in Potsdam or Aachen. This consolidation survived the downfall of Napoleon and eventually led to German national unification.

At this time Prussia, which had been careful to avoid the Corsican adventurer, began to take steps to throw off the Napoleonic yoke. Frederick William III, most cautious in his attitude toward France, now allowed himself to be carried away by the war party in Berlin. The once timid Teutonic poodle suddenly decided to attack the giant French mastiff. It was a dangerous mistake and a good opportunity for the delighted French conqueror. He would have a final reckoning with the Prussians. The confrontation was brief and decisive. Napoleon arrived in Franconia at the head of 200,000 troops and inflicted severe defeats on the Prussians at Jena and Auerstädt in October 1806. The Prussians panicked as French troops surged into Berlin to seize monuments for transportation to Paris. The Prussian monarch fled. Prussia lost half her territory and was forced to pay an enormous indemnity.

Napoleon had inflicted on Prussia the most humiliating defeat in her history. The disaster was not complete, however, for out of it emerged the impulse for revenge, which was to prove a powerful stimulant for German nationalism. It was not a unique phenomenon. When Napoleon decided to spread his ideas of the French Revolution as he interpreted them into other countries by military force, he invariably ignited the fires of nationalism.

Spurred on by hatred of the conqueror, the Prussians decided that the best way to defeat the French was to imitate them. The extraordinary reforms of the French Revolution had brought fresh vigor to the French people. Perhaps the German people, under Prussian leadership, could seek a similar set of reforms for their own good. But they would not attempt to accomplish this task by means of violent revolution in German streets but by the considerably more civilized method of "entrusting the future to those in authority." Prussia would revise her social structure by decree, by a revolution turned upside down in which the impulse came from those who traditionally held the reins of power. Then she could proceed to the problem of the larger German nationalism.

Accordingly, the wheels of reform were set in motion. Karl Freiherr vom Stein was called to head the reform movement. His attitude was forthright. "I hate the French," he said, "as much as it is allowed a Christian to hate." Vom Stein presided over the complete overhaul of the Prussian bureaucracy. Frederick William III found his reformer intractable, obstinate, and disobedient, as well as "somewhat eccentric," and on one occasion dismissed him only to call him back to office. The two worked together to bring the landed nobility under royal control, a necessary step to avoid particularistic and feudal vestiges. They called in Karl August von Hardenberg to eliminate medieval economic restrictions, set up a new system of municipal government, and create a more efficient bureaucracy. At about the same time, Wilhelm von Humboldt introduced educational reforms designed to increase the authority of the state. Perhaps most important of all for Prussia's future goals was August Wilhelm von Gneisenau's reorganization of the army and the introduction of military conscription.

What was the goal of these reforms? All were designed with one purpose in mind—to make Prussia the most powerful of all German states, to give her a leading role in the overthrow of the French conqueror, and to help prepare the way for German unification. The reforms gave a very special character to the Prussian system. Education was geared to service to the state. Militarism was solidified. Individual freedom was sacrificed to the concept of service to the state, obedience, and respect for authority. All the reforms were couched in the language of liberalism, but in practice they meant exactly the opposite.

The Prussian way of life which emerged from these reforms was later to be welded on to the unified national state.

Such was the heritage of Napoleonic conquest. The flame of German nationalism was lit from Paris.

The Role of Romanticism

Meanwhile, added to Prussian political and military leadership, was a marked changed in the intellectual atmosphere. Here a generating intellectual movement took on political overtones and helped contribute to the formation of 19th century German nationalism. Romanticism was a European-wide movement, but in the Germanies it took on a special complexion and, perhaps more than elsewhere, contributed to the shaping of German nationalism. As in other countries, nationalism in Germany had behind it a combination of intellectual, economic, political, and psychological factors.

The motivating intellectual factor was the special form of German romanticism. In order to forget their humiliation and despair, Germans turned in relief to their past, to those days when the glorious German Empire had been the fulcrum of European power. They were attracted by their own idea of an organic folk community wrapped in the cloak of tradition. A humiliated people could mobilize their heroic past as a bulwark against the principles of 1789 and the machinations of Napoleon. They would return to the glory of the Middle Ages with its traditional folk songs, fairy tales, sagas, and poetry with accent on imagination instead of reason. In the medieval mind they would find that "freedom" which had little in common with French and English egalitarianism. They would think with the blood and give free rein to all that was uniquely German.

The movement began as early as the 1770s in the *Sturm und Drang* (Storm and Stress) period, ably depicted by Goethe in *The Sorrows of Young Werther*. Young Germans turned to the world of mysticism and intuition, to nature, to love for the vague and the mysterious. They denounced the effete "pygmy French" as proponents of a sterile rationalsim (*Vernuftelei*). During the early 19th century this Storm and Stress movement merged imperceptibly into the new romanticism sweeping Europe. Eventually, the German form moved over the boundary from literary into political romanticism. In essence it was a reaction against the democratic rationalism expressed in the French concept of liberty, equality, and fraternity. The French Revolution, it was said, was an explosion of immoderate forces, a tragic watershed which would not be repeated on the German scene. Germans would stress law, order, security, and legitimacy.

Politically, German romanticism was linked with the rising spirit of nationalism. It would look to the past to find justification for the future German state. The idea was to find deep roots in history for all things German. Scholars turned to the study of German antiquity, the German landscape, German art forms, German institutions and traditions, the German language. They denounced the *philosophes* of the French Enlightenment as shallow intellectuals barren in sensitiveness and imagination. They would turn to the mysticism of the past glorious days when to be a German meant something special. They rejected the concept of universalism and world citizenship as an unattainable ideal and called for a New Germany.

All these motivations harmonized well with the rising sense of national consciousness and the formation of German nationalism. The special form of German nationalism, however, was destined to run a tragic course. What started out as cultural nationalism, epitomized in the work of Johann Gottfried von Herder, who, unlike Bolingbroke and Rousseau, saw nationalism as a cultural rather than a political phenomenon, eventually ended up as aggressive integral nationalism.

Leading the way for German romanticism was the trio of Arndt, Fichte, and Jahn. Ernst Moritz Arndt, poet of the War of Liberation, had only contempt and hatred for Napoleon. He did whatever he could to arouse a crusading spirit against the French conqueror. He excoriated those German princes who had sold their souls into French bondage and urged continued resistance to French armies. The defeats at Jena and Auerstädt, he said, were tragic, but they were not the last word in Germany's destiny. "It is possible," he said, "to defeat Napoleon with his own weapons. His soldiers are only ordinary mortals. . . . German generals, trust and believe in your men. They are firm, stout-hearted, loyal and courageous. They must be inspired by the Fatherland when the final moment comes."

To Arndt the word "Fatherland" had almost magical connotations. Again and again he sang its praise:

> Where is the German's Fatherland?
> Name me at length that mighty land!
> "Wher'er resounds the German tongue,
> Where'er its hymns to God are sung."

Be this the land,
Brave German, this thy Fatherland.

Added to Arndt's soaring spirit of nationalism was the work of Johann Gottlieb Fichte. Taking the chair of philosophy at Jena in 1794, he began to attract attention by a series of brilliant lectures. Later he was appointed *Rektor* of the new University of Berlin, where he spent the rest of his life. When German morale was at a low point in the winter of 1807–1808, Fichte delivered his famous fourteen lectures, "Addresses to the German Nation." In impassioned tones, he urged resistance to the death against the invader Napoleon. The forefathers of the German people, he charged, had never submitted to Rome, hence they must act in the same spirit and refuse to give in to the Corsican. The German people, alone of all the peoples in the world, were capable of the highest perfection. They deserved to be the cultural leaders of the entire world. Other European peoples had damaged their heritage by using an adopted or derived language—only the Germans spoke an original ancient dialect, pure and perfect.

Fichte insisted that the German concept of freedom was rooted in the highest moral traditions. Indeed, the Germans had a world mission and they must prepare for it by achieving their own national regeneration:

Our most urgent present problem is to preserve the existence and continuity of all that is German. All other differences vanish before the higher point of view. Love for the Fatherland must reign supreme in every German state.

The third of this trio of German romantics was Friedrich Ludwig Jahn, an eccentric demagogue who praised Germany's great heroic past. The best way to rebuild the shattered morale of his countrymen, he said, was to turn to physical well-being. Too many Germans, he charged, had been infected with Gallic cosmopolitanism and had become soft and effeminate. It was important that they begin to use traditional Swedish exercises to build their bodies and to become strong and self-assertive. In this way they could become loyal citizens of a powerful national state:

All people have their own peculiar thoughts and feelings, loves and hates, joys and sorrows, hopes and yearnings, ancestors and beliefs. German means national. Our feeling of nationalism, or Germanness, has been disappearing more and more because of our sins. We must return to the past and re-create Nation, Germanness, Fatherland.

There were many others who contributed to this glorification of the past as a basis for future greatness. Friedrich von Schlegel described the Rhine as "the all too-faithful image of our Fatherland, our history, and our character." Jakob Karl and Wilhelm Karl Grimm, the famous Grimm brothers, called attention to indigenous national literature and collected the fairy tales as a special contribution to German culture. (See chapter 2.) Karl Theodor Körner composed stirring war songs; Ludwig von Arnim collected old popular legends and songs; Adam Müller described the state as of infinitely greater importance than the existence of the individual—a concept directly opposite to that of Rousseau and the *philosophes;* Friedrich Ernst Daniel Schleiermacher expressed pietism in patriotic terms.

In all the work of the German romantics there was the common theme of an organic folk community. Again and again came the call for national cohesiveness. Behind it was a kind of vague mysticism, an irrationalism which came to affect the special tenor of German nationalism.

Nationalism in the Prussian Image

Invigorated by reform, Prussia took the lead in breaking the Napoleonic yoke in the War of Liberation, 1813–1815. Prussian troops under Marshal Blücher were among the victors at Waterloo. The Napoleonic grip was ended, but there was still the Austrian Metternich, the reactionary genius of Europe. German students, organized into *Burschenschaften* (fraternities), pledged themselves to oppose tyrants at home and abroad and demanded an end to Metternich's meddling from Vienna. On October 18, 1817, during the jubilee year of the Protestant Revolt, students held a much publicized celebration at the Wartburg at which they consigned to the flames varied symbols of tyranny. On March 23, 1819, a fanatical student murdered a reactionary journalist who was suspected of being in the pay of the Russian royal court. In response to these "insurrections," symptomatic of a rising nationalism, Metternich drew up the Carlsbad Decrees, which established a rigid censorship, provided for the supervision of suspect students, and paved the way for the arrest of vociferous patriots. The Austrian made it clear that he had enough of revolutionary Young Germany.

This political activity was matched in the economic sphere by a new drive for unity. Something had to be done to remedy the chaotic tariff system with its bewildering variety of water, inland, and provincial tolls. We have seen that between 1818 and 1834 the *Zollverein,* or customs union, was fashioned to achieve economic reform. Proposed originally by Friedrich List, the Württemberger political economist, the *Zollverein* was taken over by Prussian administrators. (See chapter 1.) For Prussia the customs union meant economic power—a prelude to political dominance in German affairs.

The Bankruptcy of Liberal Nationalism

The attempt to unify the Germanies on the basis of liberalism failed. When the Metternichian system of reaction began to disintegrate, the Germans at long last had the opportunity to express their sense of nationalism along liberal lines. But the course of German history was destined to take another turn. A different kind of nationalism emerged.

Metternich's system began to weaken as early as 1830 when there were revolutions in France, Belgium, and Poland and reverberations in the Germanies. Minor German princes were forced to grant constitutions. The new sense of German nationalism was revealed at a meeting in Hambach in the Palatinate when some 25,000 people gathered to call for national unity based on the sovereignty of the people and for a European confederation of free republics. Metternich, watching from Vienna, was appalled by this evidence of liberalism and democracy.

When in 1848 another revolution exploded in France, it spread quickly to the Germanies. Beginning in Baden and Württemberg, it diffused through the German states until soon the whole country was aflame. Metternich's system collapsed and its author fled to England.

The course of the revolution of 1848 revealed the powerful sense of national consciousness which had appeared in the Germanies. German liberals issued a call for a preliminary parliament, a *Vorparlament,* which met and called for general elections for a National Assembly designed to create a constitution for the German people. The National Assembly convened on May 18, 1848, in St. Paul's Cathedral in Frankfurt am Main. A provisional representative government was established. Archduke John of Austria was chosen as *Reichsverweser* (Imperial Regent). Several months later the Assembly adopted a declaration of rights modeled on the French Declaration of the Rights of Man and Citizen and the American Bill of Rights. The territorial problem seemed unsolvable. The Assembly had to contend with the goals of the multinational Austrian monarchy and the Prussian desire for leadership in

German affairs. Would there be a "Big German" (*Grossdeutsch*) solution including all the Germans in Austria, or would there be a "Little German" (*Kleindeutsch*) settlement which would favor Prussian hegemony in the race for guidance of German affairs?

Conservative trends still militated against the formation of a national state under liberal auspices. When the Prussian King Frederick William IV was offered the crown of a united Germany by the Assembly, he refused it arrogantly with the comment that he could not accept an offer "from the gutter." He was not going to accept, he complained, "a dog-collar chaining me to the revolution." The Assembly had additional cause for worry: there were bitter internal dissensions, complicated rivalries, and eternal political bickering. Finally, disgruntled members withdrew from the Assembly. A last-ditch rump parliament, which met at Stuttgart, was dispersed by force.

Gradually, the tide of revolt began to turn against the revolutionaries. The princes, once humiliated and at one time fearing for their lives, suddenly came to life when it became evident that the revolutionaries were not going to win the battle of the streets. The liberals felt the wrath of the victors. Hundreds fled from the Germanies. Carl Schurz, Franz Sigel, and others emigrated to the United States, there to play an important role in the American Civil War. Heinrich Heine and Karl Marx chose exile. The composer Richard Wagner and the historian Theodor Mommsen returned to an authoritarian Germany. The poet Ernst Moritz Arndt penned a remarkable prophecy:

> Away! Our heroes' arms grow tired,
>   And stricken sore the strongest fall.
> A truce of life no more desired!
>   Away! The death-knell tolls for all.

The momentum of the revolution was lost. On February 4, 1850, the king of Prussia took an oath to a conservative constitution, providing for a three-class system of voting which insured the domination of the propertied classes and at the same time gave the monarch an absolute veto on all legislation.

There were attempts to appease Austria. Frederick William IV and his chief minister, Joseph von Radowitz, proposed a friendly arrangement between Protestant Prussia and Catholic Austria, by which the two nations would agree to a common policy for all Germany. Radowitz organized the Erfurt Union (sometimes called the Prussian Union), an association of princes under Prussia's protection, and urged that this new organization be placed on an equal basis with the old *Bund* centered at Frankfurt am Main. Prince Felix Schwarzenberg, Metternich's successor, opposed the Prussian plan and insisted that only Austria could effectively rule Germany. On September 1, 1850, Schwarzenberg officially announced the renewal of the old German *Bund*.

There were now two German *Bund*s. The dispute soon turned into open conflict. The Elector of Hesse–Kassel, a member of the Erfurt Union, finding himself in constitutional difficulties with his parliament, called on the Frankfurt Diet for assistance. Both confederations prepared to send troops to the rescue. War seemed inevitable. Schwarzenberg undoubtedly preferred a decision by arms, but Francis Joseph I, the Austrian monarch, was reluctant to make war on his royal friend Frederick William IV. The Prussian king, faced with insubordination by the rival princes of his Union and uncertain of support by the *Junker* nobility, decided that it was best to retreat. When the Russian Tsar Nicholas I, who was opposed to German unity of any kind, indicated that he would intervene in favor of Austria, the Prussian monarch gave up altogether. He dismissed Radowitz and sent the more yielding Theodor von Manteufel as successor to deal with the Austrians. The result was the Agreement of Olmütz, signed on November 29, 1850, by which Prussia renounced the Erfurt Union and recognized the revival of the German Confederation. Once again Austria had surged to power in German affairs. For Prussian patriots this was the "humiliation of Olmütz" for which there must one day be revenge against Austria. They were agreed that German nationalism must be fixed in a Prussian—not Austrian—image.

Historians have ascribed varied reasons for the failure of the Revolution of 1848 in the Germanies. It was unsuccessful, Lewis Namier said, because most members of the Frankfurt Assembly were not true liberals but rather nationalists and imperialists. "The professional lambs at Frankfurt, bitten by the Pan-German dog, caught rabies." At that time, Namier continued, the Germans managed to make other nations believe that there was something especially noble and liberal-minded about the collectivity of Germans—"one of the legends of history." Peter Viereck pronounced the Revolution as "a pathetic muddle": "The liberal university professors, Metternich's fiercest foes and now so prominent in 1848, were often far from the cloudy idealists pictured in our textbooks. The majority were more Bismarckian than Bismarck ever realized."

Erich Brandenburg laid the blame for the failure not on the Frankfurt Assembly but on "the power and self-assertation of the larger individual states, above all the two great powers" [Austria and Prussia]. Koppel Pinson attributed the failure to "the enormous disparity between the political aspirations of the German liberals and the mass support and actual power and influence they commanded." Edmond Vermeil saw the cause not so much in external factors as in the mentality of the German people, molded and developed by peculiarly German romanticism. German liberalism, he said, was extraordinarily weak, bowing before the work and will of pure politics. A. J. P. Taylor deemed it barren speculation to discuss the causes for failure: "There was no successful revolution in Germany, and therefore nothing to fail. There was merely a vacuum in which the liberals postured until the vacuum was filled." According to Taylor, it was a missed opportunity: "For the first time since 1521, the German people stepped to the center of the German stage only to miss their cue once more. German history reached its turning point and failed to turn. That was the fateful essence of 1848."

Others seek a clue in economic and social conditions. Franz Schnable wrote about the close nexus between the constitutional movement and industrial development at this time. Oscar J. Hammen observed that "economic and social factors helped to precipitate and to determine the course of the Revolution of 1848." Hans Rosenberg described the events of 1848 as lending a powerful stimulus to the creation of economic conditions essential to an industrial state.

These scholars disagree on causation but all agree that the Revolution of 1848 did not satisfy the rising nationalism of the German people. The demand for unity, for a united German Fatherland, had to be met one way or another. The revolution revealed that the goal was not to be achieved by liberal nationalism. The year 1848 turned out to be a dangerous one in German history. On the surface it seemed that at long last the streams of rationalism—social contract, egalitarianism, constitutionalism—were converging. For the first time in their history the Germans had the opportunity to determine their own destiny. For once, critical decisions were out of the hands of autocratic princes and in the hands of men who understood the currents of Western liberalism. At a critical moment German intellectuals found themselves to be spokesmen for their compatriots. They would seek unity through persuasion, progress through moderation, and a united Germany through rational behavior. They failed.

When the wave of revolution receded, liberalism was submerged in a stronger movemement of forceful nationalism. The German people were bypassed by currents of liberty, equality, and fraternity and were left instead with Prussian discipline, authority, and efficiency. The professed aim of the

Revolution had been "through unity to freedom," but events showed that unity was to be achieved through power. German unification would depend upon cohesion through force. For the rest of the 19th century, the ethical concept of liberty as a postulate of the human spirit fought a losing battle in Germany. It was a dangerous residue.

Bismarck as Blood-and-Iron Chancellor

The failure of the Revolution of 1848 left the German people frustrated in their aspirations for national unity along liberal lines. The role of Prussia was vital in future developments. The coronation of William I on October 16, 1861, gave hope to depressed nationalists who had been dissatisfied with the leadership of Frederick William IV. Meanwhile, the Prussian general staff, appalled by the humiliation at Olmütz in 1850, began to reorganize the army for another confrontation with Austria. More than ever Prussia was determined to make a moral conquest of all Germany and to lead the way in national regeneration.

There were many apostles of German nationalism at mid-century, but one was ready to combine theory with action. Otto von Bismarck had some very positive views. "I am a *Junker,*" he said, "and I mean to profit from it." In 1870 French Foreign Minister Jules Favre gave Bismarck grudging admiration as "a statesman surpassing everything I can imagine." British historian A. J. P. Taylor described Bismarck as "the greatest of all political Germans, [who] assembled in his own person all the contradictions of German dualism." Erich Eyck went so far as to attribute not only the unification of Germany to Bismarck but also all the great landmarks of European history from 1860 to World War I. According to Eyck, Bismarck was responsible for the transformation of the spirit and mentality of the German people.

These estimates of Bismarck are by no means exaggerated. Here, indeed, was one of the most extraordinary individuals of modern times. Conservative, aristocratic, monarchist, Lutheran, Otto von Bismarck had no use for "phrase-making and constitutions." He made it plain that he intended to achieve by force what he believed could not be achieved by the honeyed words of liberals. The reactionary genius of 19th-century Europe, he defended all that was traditional in German life, especially the existence of the Hohenzollern monarchy and the way of life preferred by *Junker* landlords. A *Realpolitiker,* he was convinced that only through guidance and domination from above and not by revolution from below could Germany achieve her rightful place in the family of nations.

Bismarck's sense of nationalism was of a very special kind. Originally a Pomeranian patriot, he came to the conclusion that Prussia was destined for leadership of a united Germany. His sentiment of local patriotism changed eventually into a broader Prussian loyalty. Bismarck was to be transformed from a Prussian to a German nationalist, but he never for a moment forgot his Prussian ties. Nationalism to him meant that all Germany was to be dominated by Prussia. "Never," he said, "did I doubt that the key to German politics was to be found in princes and dynasties, not in publicists, whether in parliament and the press or on the barricades." The opinion of the cultivated public as uttered in parliament and the press might promote and sustain the determination of the dynasties, but provoked their resistance more frequently than it urged them forward in the direction of national unity.

Bismarck was convinced that nothing must stand in the way of Prussia's drive for hegemony in German affairs. "If I have an enemy in my power, I must destroy him." His goal always was to win a united Germany, but this was to be attained along two corollary lines: (1) the preservation of his own social class—the *Junkers,* and (2) the destruction of the political philosophy of liberalism. "I am no democrat," he once told Carl Schurz, "and cannot be one. I was born and raised an aristocrat."

Bismarck was forty-seven when he was named Minister-President of Prussia. His appointment was made during a critical constitutional conflict. William I, the new Prussian king, wanted to reorganize the military by increasing the strength of the standing army at the expense of the traditional militia. The Prussian *Landtag* refused to grant him the necessary funds and accused him of wanting the change in order to stifle democratic sentiment. Meanwhile, the Progressive party, opposed to the monarch, increased its representation in the elections of May 6, 1862. The depressed king seriously considered abdication.

In this crisis Minister of War Albrecht von Roon prevailed upon William I to call Bismarck to Berlin. The Pomeranian *Junker* began his ministry by withdrawing the budget for the next year. His words were sensational: it was essential, he said, that Germany should look not to liberalism but to her own power:

> Bavaria, Württemberg, and Baden may indulge in liberalism, but no person will because of that reason assign Prussia's role to them. Prussia must gather up her

strength and maintain it in readiness for the opportune moment, which already has passed by several times. Since the Treaty of Vienna, Prussia's borders have not been favorable for a really healthy state. Not by parliamentary speeches and majority votes are the great questions of the day determined—that was the great mistake of 1848 and 1849—but by iron and blood.

The last sentence of Bismarck's historic speech was to be vital not only for the course of German history but also for European history in the 19th century. With the rhythm of the phrase changed from ''iron and blood'' to ''blood and iron,'' it gave direction to the quality of Germany's search for nationhood. German national unification, it meant, was to be achieved not through discussion and arbitration and agreement but through force.

Bismarck's solution for the conflict between king and parliament was simple—he dissolved parliament. From 1862 to 1866 he ruled arbitrarily without legislative consent, collecting funds and invigorating the military without sanction of the *Landtag* or the voters.

The Road to National Unification

The stages by which the Pomeranian *Junker* achieved the national unification of Germany are so well known that they need only the briefest recapitulation here. The first step was to settle a quarrel with tiny Denmark, which at one and the same time would test the Prussian army and mold German public opinion in Prussia's favor. The problem of Schleswig-Holstein had won the attention of European diplomats for some time. It was exceedingly complicated. Lord Palmerston described it somewhat facetiously: ''Only three men have ever understood it. One was Prince Albert, who is dead. The second was a German professor, who became mad. I am the third, and I have forgotten about it.'' On the downfall of Napoleon, the Treaty of Vienna in 1815 combined the duchies of Schleswig and Holstein, both of which had large German populations, and united them with Denmark. Holstein was a part of the German Confederation. The king of Denmark, as duke of Holstein, was a member of the Confederation and was represented at the Diet in Frankfurt.

As soon as he became Minister-President of Prussia, Bismarck decided that he would annex the provinces to Prussia. ''I have not the smallest doubt,'' he said, ''that the Danish business can be settled in a way desirable to us by war.'' All he needed was a favorable opportunity. It came on November 13,

1863, when the Danish *Rigsraad* passed a new constitution which Bismarck claimed would incorporate Schleswig into Denmark. This, he said, was a violation of the promise that King Frederick VII of Denmark had given to Austria and Prussia in the Protocol of London in 1852. The matter was brought to a head two days later when the Danish king died.

Bismarck was careful to win Austrian support for his plans. On February 1, 1864, Prussian and Austrian troops crossed the frontiers of Schleswig. The Danes, hoping desperately for British help, elected to fight. But London, fearful of becoming involved, asked only that the integrity of the Danish monarchy not be violated. It was a short war—two giant powers against a small state. By April 18 the whole of Schleswig was in the hands of the invaders.

The result of the Danish war turned out to be a tremendous stimulus to the sense of German nationalism. The German public received news of the military victory with an outburst of jubilation. In the face of hostility everywhere Bismarck had brought about, with almost reckless speed, the most important acquisition of territory since the days of Frederick the Great.

The next stage in the unification of Germany was a terminal struggle between two conflicting nationalisms, both artificially constructed but both seeking a dominant position in Central European affairs. Prusso-German nationalism was consolidating in nature and geared to the problem of unifying all the German states under Prussian leadership. The conglomerate Austrian empire, composed of a wide variety of ethnic and political groups, hoped to extend its sway over all German-speaking peoples while at the same time frustrating any particularistic tendencies inside the empire.

Bismarck's own goal was clear. He would stimulate a sense of German national consciousness by eliminating Austrian influence in German affairs. He had never forgotten the humiliation of Olmütz. First he carefully isolated Austria from possible foreign assistance. In early April 1866 he concluded an agreement with Italy which promised Venetia to the Italians as a reward if they maintained a benevolent neutrality in case of an Austro-Prussian conflict. This alliance was made in defiance of the German Confederation, which prohibited any member from making any pact with a foreign power against any other member of the *Bund*. At this time Bismarck knew that Napoleon III, despite his pretensions for French glory, was in no position to thwart Prussian designs. Bismarck would have to goad Austria into an act of aggression and then strike back.

The made-to-order issue was there. Bismarck had been careful to include

Austria in his war with Denmark over Schleswig-Holstein. Now he would trigger a quarrel over the spoils. On June 1, 1866, Vienna challenged Bismarck by submitting the "problem" of Schleswig-Holstein to the Federal Diet at Frankfurt. On June 12 the Austrian ambassador at Berlin and the Prussian envoy at Vienna asked for their passports. Two days later the Diet passed an Austrian motion calling for mobilization of all non-Prussian armies. This "hostile" act gave Bismarck the opportunity for which he was waiting. He announced that the German Confederation was finished. He urged all German states to join a successor union under Prussian leadership. In his mind this was a necessary step to the fashioning of a proper German nationalism. The canny Bismarck now had his war with Austria. "If we are beaten," he said, "I shall not return. I can die only once. and it befits the vanquished to die."

Once again the war was short, so short in fact that it has been called the Seven Weeks' War. The Prussian army, superbly organized, quickly demonstrated its superiority over the Austrians. On July 3, 1866, Prussian arms won a decisive victory at Königgrätz (Sadowa). Again Bismarck revealed his diplomatic genius. The Prussian king and his triumphant *Junker* military leaders wanted to cap the Prussian victory with a march through the streets of Vienna. But Bismarck, always the chess-playing diplomat, was thinking of the future: he insisted upon moderate peace terms. After clashing arguments, in which Bismarck wept false tears, the king gave in to his insistent minister. The Treaty of Prague called for Austrian recognition of the end of the *Bund,* the incorporation of Schleswig-Holstein into Prussia, and the annexation of Venetia to Italy. The indemnity of 20,000,000 thalers was small and Austria lost no territory. Bismarck's policy was shrewd: he wanted Austrian neutrality in the event of a major conflict with France. "We shall need Austria's strength in the future for ourselves."

The Austro-Prussian War of 1866 furnishes historians with a fascinating dilemma. Was it Bismarck's intention from the very beginning to make war on Austria as a necessary step to German unification under Prussian auspices? There have been arguments on both sides. Erich Eyck concluded that Bismarck never had any scruples about a war of this kind, which he regarded as a kind of "fraternal" conflict. But it is another question as to whether he *wanted* the war. According to Eyck, Bismarck would have been willing to do without war if he had been able to achieve his aim by normal diplomatic means. While Bismarck was not from the beginning intent upon war with Austria, he was engaged in a policy which made the war unavoidable. Simiarly, Otto Pflanze described the twists and turns of Bismarckian diplomacy in the conquest of Schleswig-Holstein, "a performance of incredible dexterity." Most historians accept the view that, consciously or unconsciously, Bismarck carefully prepared the ground for the war against Austria.

Victory against Austria brought with it a unique pardon for Bismarck's brusque unconstitutional tactics. On September 9, 1866, the Prussian *Landtag,* its members delighted by the triumph over Austria, passed a bill retroactively approving Bismarck's budgets of 1862 and 1864. The vote was 230 to 75. It was a decision which brought an end to the idea of meaningful parliamentarianism in Germany. Moreover, the Prussian victory meant that Prussian Hohenzollerns replaced the Austrian Hapsburgs as the dominant dynasty in German life. In 1867 Bismarck created the North German Confederation, a union of twenty-three states and smaller principalities in North and Central Germany. He wrote most of its constitution, which was similar to that adopted later by the Second German Reich in 1871. Bismarck himself, the Federal Chancellor, became the responsible minister of the North German Confederation. "Let us put Germany in the saddle," he said. "She will know how to ride."

The final step in the creation of the Second German Reich was the Franco-Prussian War of 1870–1871. Bismarck's successful wars of 1864 and 1866 had aroused the fear and envy of Napoleon III. Sensing that a unified Germany would react to the disadvantage of France on the Continent and at the same time anxious to revive the glory of Napoleonic legend, Louis Napoleon was determined to hinder German unification. Publicly, he stated that he would not interfere with changes "that have been evoked by the German nation," but in his private circle he confided that if Bismarck attempted to absorb the South German states into the North German Confederation, "our guns will go off by themselves." Napoleon III's confused diplomatic meddling gave Bismarck the chance to strike the final blow for German unity.

It was an unequal battle between the German statesman and the French monarch. With great diplomatic cunning, Bismarck isolated Napoleon III from foreign help. He brought the Prussian army to a high state of efficiency and awaited his opportunity. It came in the conflict over the proposed Hohenzollern candidacy for the throne of Spain. The specter of a revived empire of Charles V was a nightmare for the French ruler. When King William was approached by the French ambassador at Bad Ems and requested to abandon once and for all time any claims to the throne of Spain, the king telegraphed an account of the meeting to Bismarck in Berlin. Bismarck unscrupulously edited the dispatch and released it the next day, July 14, 1870, Bastille Day in France. In its abbreviated form the telegram gave the impression of an ultimatum to the French and an insult to the Germans. France declared war at once.

Within two months the French armies were soundly defeated and Napoleon was taken prisoner at Sedan. After the siege and capitulation of Paris, the war was ended by the Treaty of Frankfurt, May 10, 1871. There was no generosity in the German terms.

German unification was now completed on the basis of Bismarck's policy of iron and blood. The historian Heinrich von Sybel wrote as a passionate patriot: "Tears run down my cheeks. By what have we deserved the grace of God, that we are allowed to live to see such great and mighty deeds? What for twenty years was the substance of all our wishes and efforts, is now fulfilled in such an immeasurably magnificent way." On January 18, 1871, King William of Prussia was proclaimed William I, German Emperor, at the Hall of Mirrors in Versailles. It was the triumphant culmination of the process by which German nationalism was finally molded in the Prussian image.

Appraisals of Bismarck as German Nationalist

Prussian professor-patriots, awed by Bismarck's career and his accomplishments, lauded him in sugary panegyrics. But after Germany's defeat in World War I revealed the impermanency of his Second Reich, there was a reappraisal of Bismarck's *Realpolitik*. According to Erich Eyck, Bismarck was responsible for initiating the three wars of national unification and bears partial blame for his unwillingness to educate the German people in the way of democracy and liberalism. Another school, represented by Franz Schnabel and Werner Richter, reject what they call the "legend" of Bismarck's day-by-day building of the unified Reich and instead say that he never at any time had more than a general idea of what he sought ultimately to achieve. He did not manipulate history, they say, but rather simply took advantage of situations as they arose. Bismarck used nationalism for his own end, took it into custody, and subordinated it to the needs of the people.

For the historian of nationalism, one key factor remains amidst the plethora of conflicting views: the transformation of Bismarck from narrow Prussian to broader German nationalism was one of the more important factors in the history of 19th-century Europe. A politically narrow-minded Prussian *Junker,* a traditional nationalist, was to elongate his vision and give direction to German nationalism. In setting its tone of reliance upon *Macht,* the master of Friedrichsruh—perhaps unconsciously if one wants to be charitable— prepared the way for that aggressive nationalism which was to lead William II to exile and Hitler to self-destruction while bringing humiliation and tragedy to the German people.

C H A P T E R

4

Nationalism and Colonial Expansion: German Penetration into South West Africa, 1880 to 1885

A people needs land for its activities, land for its nourishment. No people needs it as much as the German people which is increasing so rapidly and whose old boundaries have become dangerously narrow. If we do not soon acquire new territories, we are moving to a frightful catastrophe. . . .

Once more, as 2,000 years ago, when the Cimbri and the Teutons were hammering at the gates of Rome, sounds the cry, now full of anguish and unappeased desires, now arrogant and full of confidence—sounds more and more strongly the cry "We must have lands, new lands!"

From a Pan-German pamphlet on *Lebensraum*

Until the decade of the 1880s neither the German government nor the public showed much interest in the acquisition of a colonial empire. In 1868 Bismarck said: "All the advantages claimed for the mother country are for the most part illusory. England is abandoning her colonial policy. She finds it too costly." But after 1880, imperialist sentiment became highly fashionable among Germans once the first steps toward a colonial policy were taken in Africa. The German Colonial Society, organized in 1882, had more than ten thousand members within three years. The rapidly burgeoning German imperialism clashed head-on with the older established British form.

Adapted from Louis L. Snyder, "The Role of Herbert Bismarck in the Angra Pequena Negotiations between Germany and Britain, 1880–1885," *The Journal of Negro History*, XXXV, no. 4 (October, 1950), pp. 435–453.

This article, originally published in *The Journal of Negro History,* traces the first faltering steps of German colonialism, with accent on Herbert von Bismarck's role in the Angra Pequena negotiations between Germany and Britain in the years from 1880 to 1885. Behind the facade of normal diplomatic relations may be sensed the gradual hardening of sentiment between two Great Powers, one dedicated to the task of maintaining its vast empire, and the other seeking to break into the circle of colonial powers.

The negotiations between Germany and England on this African problem took place in an atmosphere of conflicting nationalisms. The hard-line nature of German nationalism may be noted in the behavior of Herbert Bismarck, who revealed a stiff-necked pride in Germany's status on the international scene. After the ascent of William II to the throne in 1888 and his subsequent dismissal of the elder Bismarck in 1890, the German Emperor embarked on a New Course dedicated to a Big Navy and more colonialism. The increasing economic competition between the two countries plus a cascading armaments race and a psychological clash of differing ways of life eventually led to the outbreak of World War I. Here once again nationalism was to play a major role in the determination of diplomatic relations.

Bismarck's Conversion to Imperialism

The dispute between Germany and Britain over Angra Pequena during the years 1880 to 1885 is of special significance. The acquisition of South West Africa as the first German colony took place in the face of strong British resistance and contributed to the severe strain which culminated in World War I. Moreover, the incident brings into relief such important political trends of the late 19th century as the rising German nationalism, the growth of imperialism in Germany and England, the difficult diplomatic task of conducting negotiations between a democratic and an autocratic state, the conflict inside England between different systems of colonial thought, and, above all, the diplomatic techniques of Bismarck.[1] How Bismarck successfully embarked Germany on a colonial policy has been admirably handled in several books,[2]

---

[1]W. O. Aydelotte, *Bismarck and British Colonial Policy* (Philadelphia, 1937), p. vi.
[2]Notably M. v. Hagen, *Bismarcks Kolonialpolitik* (Stuttgart, 1923); P. T. Moon, *Imperialism and World Politics* (New York, 1936); M. v. Koschitzky, *Deutsche Kolonialgeschichte,* 2 vols. (Leipzig, 1887–88); W. Stuhlmacher, *Bismarcks Kolonialpolitik nach den Aktenveröffentlichungen des Auswärtigen Amtes* (Halle, 1927); M. E. Townsend, *The Origins of Modern German Colonialism, 1871–1885,* (New York, 1921), and *The Rise and Fall of Germany's*

but relatively little attention has been paid to his utilization of the talents of his son, Herbert, in the involved negotiations of the undercover battle by which Germany obtained a foothold in Africa.

Before 1871 Bismarck had neither thoughts nor the possibility of acquiring colonies for Germany; from 1871 to 1881 he adopted a course of watchful waiting for the desired opportunity; after 1881 he inaugurated a cautious but definite colonial policy.[3] His attitude in 1871 was expressed in the typical Bismarckian aphorism: "A colonial policy for us would be just like the silken sables of Polish noble families who have no shirts."[4] In conformity with the anti-imperialist *Zeitgeist* he looked upon colonies only as a means of providing sinecures for officials and he concluded that they were too costly a luxury for Germany.[5] In the middle 1870s he regarded as obstacles to a German colonial policy the *Kulturkampf,* the jealousy of France, the acute irritableness of England, and Germany's own insecure position in international affairs.[6] But in the early 1880s the *Kulturkampf* was at an end, the *revanche* policy of France had been softened, and Germany's position in Europe had been strengthened in 1882 by the Triple Alliance. Bismarck, who as early as 1863 had been called "the crazy Minister at Berlin" by Palmerston,[7] was now in a position to defy England's sensitiveness. Impatient at British delays and knowing that he held trump cards, he assumed a bullying attitude. With brutal frankness he let it be understood that his support for British claims in Egypt could be had only at a price—colonies for Germany.[8] He got what he

---

Colonial Empire, 1884–1918, (New York, 1930). See also P. Darmstaedter, *Geschichte der Aufteilung und Kolonisation Afrikas,* 2 vols. (Berlin, 1913 and 1920); W. H. Dawson, *The German Empire, 1867–1914,* 2 vols. (London, 1919); and A. Zimmerman, *Geschichte der Deutschen Kolonialpolitik* (Berlin, 1914).

[3]A. L. Hodge, *Angra Pequena* (Munich, 1936), p. 11.

[4]See M. Busch, *Tagebuchblätter,* 3 vols. (London, 1898), vol. II, 157; *cf.* also R v. Poschinger, *Fürst Bismarck als Volkswirt,* 2 vols. (Berlin, 1889), vol. 1, pt. 4, p. 63, footnote 9: *"Ich will auch gar keine Kolonien. Die sind blos zu Versorgungsposten gut ... diese Kolonialgeschichte wäre für uns genau so, wie der seidene Zobelpelz in polnischen Adelsfamilien, die keine Hemden haben."*

[5]P. T. Moon, *Imperialism and World Politics* (New York, 1936), pp. 23–24.

[6]M. E. Townsend, *The Rise and Fall of Germany's Colonial Empire, 1884–1918* (New York, 1930), pp. 84–85. [Hereafter cited as Townsend (B). Townsend (A) refers to *The Origin of Modern German Colonialism, 1871–1885* (New York, 1921).]

[7]H. Temperley and L. M. Penson, *Foundations of British Foreign Policy* (Cambridge, 1938), p. 251.

[8]P. Knaplund, ed., *Letters from the Berlin Embassy, Selections from the Private Correspondence of British Representatives at Berlin and Foreign Secretary Lord Granville, 1871–1874, 1880–1885* (Washington, 1942), p. 17. Volume II of the 1942 annual report of the American Historical Association. This valuable collection has thrown new light on the estrangement of Britain and Germany which ultimately led to the tragedies of World Wars I and II. [Hereafter referred to as *L.B.E.*]

wanted—Angra Pequena, South West Africa, the creation of a colonial empire, and the beginning of a new epoch in modern history.

The Clash in Africa

The Bay of Angra Pequena, located along the South West African coast at 26.38 degrees south by 15 degrees east, was discovered by Bartholomew Diaz in 1487.[9] In 1796 a Captain Alexander landed in the name of Great Britain. In 1805 a group of German missionaries, in the service of the London Missionary Society, landed at a small village on the coast, and in 1814 a settlement was founded at Bethany, a village 125 miles east of Angra Pequena Bay.[10] In 1842 a German missionary, Knudsen, representing the Rhine Missionary Society, settled at Bethany,[11] and other Germans established homes in the Walfisch Bay area on the coastline to the north.[12] In 1877 the Governor of the Cape Colony, Sir Henry Bartle Edward Frere, uncomfortable because of the settlement of so many Germans in the Angra Pequena and Walfisch Bay areas and annoyed by the numerous disputes between the German missionaries and the natives, vainly urged his home government to place both Damaraland and Namaqualand, virtually all of South West Africa, under the British Empire. In March 1878 the British Government placed under its protection Walfisch Bay and the surrounding territory for fifteen miles.[13] With no

---

[9]Hodge, *op. cit.*, p. 7. Encouraged by the discovery of the mouth of the Congo by Diego Cam, King John II appointed Bartholomew Diaz in 1486 as commander of an expedition under orders to commence his investigations at the Congo and proceed southward. Before rounding the "Cape of Storms" (later re-named the "Cape of Good Hope" by the king), Diaz discovered numerous capes, bays, and islands, including the Bay of Angra Pequena. In accordance with King John's instructions, Diaz erected in every conspicuous place stone columns (*padrões*) bearing the Cross and the Royal Arms, as a symbol of subjugation to Christianity and Portugal. In the middle of the sixteenth century, as Portugal revived its colonization in West Africa, Paulo Dias set up a Portuguese colony in Angola, to the north of what is now South West Africa. Although Portugal naturally claimed sovereign rights over all the lands discovered by her explorers, the English and the Germans in the late nineteenth century acted on the new principle of "effective occupation," which recognized the sovereignty only of an occupying power. The "Great African Hunt" of the early 1880s riveted the attention of would-be colonizers on "unclaimed land" that had long been under presumptive Portuguese control. England, the recognized ally and patron of Portugal, had no compunctions about disposing of the property of an allied nation behind the latter's back, and Bismarck, of course, showed no concern for either the rights or sensibilities of the natives or the Portuguese. Always the *Realpolitiker*, acting exclusively in terms of blood-and-iron, the German Chancellor regarded the first great colonizing country of modern times as fair game now for more powerful European nations.

[10]M. v. Koschitzky, *op. cit.*, vol. II, sec. 3, 41.

[11]*Ibid.*, p. 41.

[12]*Ibid.*, p. 42.

[13]*Cf.* v. Hagen, *op. cit.*, vol. IV, pp. 1, 295.

help coming from Britain the German missionaries protested to Berlin, which sent a German warship to Walfisch Bay in August, 1881.[14]

As a result of the Rhine Missionary Society's requests for protection, Count Münster, the German Ambassador in London, communicated a note to the British Government asking for the extent of British sovereignty in South West Africa.[15] On November 29, 1880, Lord Granville, the British foreign secretary, replied that:

> Her Majesty's Government cannot be responsible for what may take place outside British territory, which only includes Walfisch Bay and a very small portion of the country immediately surrounding it.[16]

A month later, on December 30, 1880, in a note from the Colonial Office, London, to the Cape Government, Britain defined the extent of her claims.

> Her Majesty's Government are of the opinion that the Orange River should be maintained as the northwestern limit of the Cape Colony, and they will give no countenance to schemes for the extension of British jurisdiction over Great Namaqualand and Damaraland.[17]

The British had cause to regret these two declarations of 1880, for soon it became obvious that Bismarck had embarked seriously on a policy of colonization.

By this time the missionary issue had been complicated by more important economic matters. Trading possibilities in Africa had interested the German Hansa merchants, especially F. A. E. Lüderitz, the head of a large mercantile house in Bremen. In 1876, Lüderitz, as spokesman for a merchant group, unfolded to Bismarck a complete scheme for founding a colony in South Africa, but his plan was for the moment rejected as impractical.[18] Lüderitz was not discouraged. In 1881 he founded a factory at Lagos on the African Guinean coast, and with trade increasing rapidly, gradually developed the idea of setting up more factories as the nucleus for a German colony.[19] On November 16, 1882, Lüderitz asked his own Foreign Office whether he would receive imperial protection for his factory and for his contracts with native

---

[14]See *Das Deutsche Weissbuch, Reichstag Aktenstück Nr. 61, Angra Pequena. A. Korrespondenz betreffend die Niederlassungen der Rheinischen Missionsgesellschaft im Hererolande, I*, and *Anlage zu IV*. [Hereafter cited as *D.W.*]

[15]*D.W., Angra Pequena, A. Anlage zu IV*.

[16]*D.W., Angra Pequena, A. Anlage zu II*.

[17]*D.W., Angra Pequena, A. III*.

[18]Townsend (*B*), p. 128.

[19]Hodge, *op. cit.*, p. 15.

chieftains.[20] With a secret agreement from Bismarck that he would be given imperial protection if he could acquire a harbor in which no other nation could assert a claim, Lüderitz decided to go ahead with his plans.

Course of Negotiations

On February 4, 1883, Bismarck opened the negotiations by addressing a note to Britain through his son, Count Herbert von Bismarck, then chargé d'affaires in London, asking if Britain exercised any authority over the Angra Pequena region.[21] Britain replied on February 23, 1883, that:

> The Cape Colony Government has certain establishments along the coast, but without more precise information as to the exact location of Lüderitz's factory, it is impossible for the British Government to say whether it could afford this protection in case it were required.[22]

This was an evasive and even procrastinating reply, inasmuch as Britain had already declared that this part of the coast was outside her jurisdiction. Lüderitz, with his secret promise of protection from Bismarck, now acted. He sent his agent, Heinrich Vogelsang, in April 1883 to Angra Pequena, where a landing was effected, a treaty signed with the natives, and the German flag hoisted on May 2, 1883.[23]

This news was greeted in German colonial circles with undisguised joy, in England with ridicule.[24] In the Cape Colony it was received with indignation and incredulity. The Cape Colony, which hitherto had shown no desire to occupy Angra Pequena, even now did not choose to show the slightest intention of seizing the unoccupied remainder of the coast.[25] Apparently, neither Britain nor the Cape Colony realized that this was the founding of the first German colony in Africa.

On August 18, 1883, the German Government notified the German Consul

---

[20]*D.W.*, *Angra Pequena*, *B. Nr. 1*. Cf. Townsend (*A*), p. 157.

[21]*D.W.*, *Angra Pequena*, *Nr. 2*. An important portion of this document was left out in the version published in the German White Book. Herbert Bismarck was also asked to say that "now as formerly, we have no thought of any overseas project." The full version of Bismarck's instructions to his son will be found in *Reichsarchiv, Vermischtes Südwestafrika* 1. Cf. Aydelotte, *op. cit.*, pp. 28–29.

[22]*D.W.*, *Angra Pequena*, *B. Anlage zu Nr. 4*.

[23]Townsend (B), p. 128.

[24]Hodge, *op. cit.*, p. 17.

[25]E. Fitzmaurice, *The Life of Granville*, 2 vols. (London and Bombay, 1905), vol. II, p. 348.

at the Cape that if the rights of other nations were not interfered with thereby, they would be prepared to give protection to Lüderitz's settlement. A German gunboat took up a permanent station in the Bay of Angra Pequena. A German corvette, the *Carola,* appeared in the Bay and gave notice to the commander of the British gunboat, the *Boadicea,* which had arrived from the Cape, that he was in German territorial waters.[26]

Britain's reply to Bismarck's inquiry, which finally came after nearly nine months,[27] stated that, although British sovereignty had been proclaimed at Walfisch Bay and the islands off Angra Pequena, any claim to sovereignty or jurisdiction by a foreign power between Angola and Cape Colony would infringe on Britain's legitimate rights.[28] Bismarck's note of December 31, 1883, was hard in tone and demanded by what rights or title could Britain claim sovereignty over a territory formerly considered independent.[29] Britain did not reply to this note.

From December 1883 to April 1884 the thermometers of public indignation and national chauvinism rose rapidly in Germany, to Bismarck's not altogether disinterested delight. On April 24, 1884, the German Chancellor sent a telegram to the German consul at Capetown declaring officially that Lüderitz's settlement was under Imperial protection, thus officially inaugurating the German colonial empire.[30] The old Kaiser Wilhelm I could say happily: "Now I can look the Great Elector in the face when I cross the long bridge in Berlin."[31]

So far, so good—from the Bismarckian viewpoint. The Chancellor had proceeded cautiously and cleverly and had been successful in quieting any British suspicions of German colonial aspirations. Although the correspondence of 1880 had definitely delimited British claims, it did not prevent Bismarck from continuing his inquiries at London as a means of maintaining Germany scrupulously in the right. Thus far British indifference, pusillanimity, and procrastination had played into Bismarck's hands. But now the issue

---

[26]*Ibid.,* p. 349.
[27]Townsend believes that Britain's delay in the affair is largely explained by the necessity felt by the British Colonial Office (Lord Derby) of consulting the Cape Government, and also by the failure of the British ministers to recognize Bismarck's colonial designs. Lord Granville and others misinterpreted Bismarck's colonial policy as mere "election maneuvres." (Townsend [B], p. 94, footnote 67.)
[28]Townsend (B), p. 90.
[29]*D.W., Angra Pequena, B. Nr. 9.*
[30]Townsend (B), p. 91; *cf.* Townsend (A), p. 169. See also *D.W., Angra Pequena, B. Nr. 12.* This telegram was kept secret from Britain, which did not learn of its contents until May 26, 1884.
[31]Townsend (B), p. 91.

was getting serious. There were embarrassing inquiries in the House of Lords about rumors that "Germany intended to steal Angra Pequena from Great Britain,"[32] and the British press spoke of "insults to the Home Country."[33] The Chancellor's diplomacy was put to a hard test. How to complete the negotiations on Angra Pequena without losing the main objective and without goading the British too far became for Bismarck a matter of prime importance.

From Bismarck's viewpoint the proper presentation of his own views to the British was complicated by his belief that the German ambassador in London, George Herbert Münster,[34] was "more English than German" and had been content to allow the question of Angra Pequena to hang fire.[35] Eccentric both physically and mentally, with a disproportionately large head that reminded Bülow of "a pumpkin on a long stalk,"[36] Münster was by nature courteous and considerate, qualities which Bismarck considered of doubtful value in negotiations at a high level with British diplomats on a critical issue. Münster's personal connections with England, both by birth and marriage, made him anxious to interpret the unpleasant communications, of which he was at this time frequently the bearer, in the most conciliatory manner possible.[37] Often he took it upon himself to soften down the asperities of Bismarck's notes in the interest of maintaining cordial relations, thereby increasing the number of his enemies at the German Foreign Office, who clamored for his recall so that Herbert Bismarck might replace him.[38] Münster on his side had only contempt for the German Foreign Office under Bismarck, to whom he referred as the "Central Ox."[39] Although an Anglophile, Münster believed that Germany had nothing to fear from British statesmen, who impressed him as "wealthy amateurs who live from hand to mouth, without really understanding the situation."[40]

From April 27, 1884, when he returned to his London post, to the first

---

[32]*The Times*, London, May 12, 1884.
[33]Hodge, *op. cit.*, pp. 37–38.
[34]George Herbert Münster (1820–1902) had been born in England and was married to the sister of the Earl of Rosslyn. He had been a member of the *Reichstag* under the Confederation and the Empire from 1867–1873, and was German ambassador to France.
[35]Busch, *op. cit.*, vol. II, p. 370.
[36]Prince v. Bülow, *Memoirs*, 4 vols. (Boston, 1931–32), vol. IV, p. 550.
[37]Fitzmaurice, *op. cit.*, vol. II, p. 370.
[38]*Ibid.*
[39]Bülow, *op. cit.*, vol. IV, p. 550. "When he (Münster) received a written censure from 'the great Otto,' he said indifferently in the very presence of Herbert Bismarck: 'How annoyed he must have been when he wrote this!'"
[40]Lord Vansittart, *Lessons of my Life* (New York, 1943), p. 10.

week of June, Münster made a number of serious mistakes which made him *persona non grata* with the "Central Ox." In the first place, he did not make it clear on the Angra Pequena question that Germany would deal only with the British Government and not with the Colonial Office or the Cape Colony. Secondly, he failed to realize Bismarck's intention of founding a colony at Angra Pequena.[41] And finally, Münster had not pointed out with the emphasis that Bismarck desired the possibility of a reversal of British policy in Egypt if Germany were not satisfied on the Angra Pequena question, until he had been severely reprimanded in writing,[42] and even then he had not done it effectively. Clearly, then, Bismarck was not satisfied with Münster as an intermediary in the delicate negotiations.

Enter Herbert Bismarck

In this emergency Bismarck turned quite willingly to his son. The eldest son of the Chancellor, Herbert Count von Bismarck-Schönhausen, was born in 1849, served with distinction in the Franco-Prussian war, and entered the foreign service in 1874 at the age of twenty-five. Until 1881, with some interruptions, he served as his father's private secretary. From the end of 1881 Bismarck sent Herbert to the various foci (*Brennpunkten*) of European politics, namely London, Paris, St. Petersburg, and Vienna, sometimes as an attaché to the German embassy, at other times on special missions. The son kept in close touch with his father through letters and reports.[43] What he did with enormous successs was "to act as an instrument of his father, almost as an extension of his father's personality."[44] Like his father, Herbert could be charming, witty, and ingratiating, but also, when occasion demanded, rough, arrogant, and overbearing. These were qualities which Bismarck considered to be desirable and essential at the time of the Angra Pequena negotiations. It was something more than fatherly pride which animated Bismarck—certainly the most colossal among 19th-century diplomats; he fairly worshipped this

---

[41]See Aydelotte, *op. cit.*, pp. 59–89, especially pp. 79–82.
[42]Bismarck to Münster, June 1, 1884, in *Die Grosse Politik der Europäischen Kabinette, 1871–1914, Sammlung der Diplomatischen Akten des Auswärtigen Amtes* (Berlin, 1922), vol. IV, no. 743. Bismarck regarded his support of British claims in Egypt as a *quid pro quo* for British support of German claims in Angra Pequena. He was certain that the complexities of Egyptian finance could not be unraveled without his help. Münster apparently either did not understand Bismarck's attitude or was unwilling to make the Chancellor's feelings known to the British.
[43]W. Windelband, *Herbert Bismarck als Mitarbeiter seines Vaters* (Stuttgart, 1921), pp. 6–8.
[44] Aydelotte, *op. cit.*, p. 162.

son, whom he hoped to build up as his own successor. When the fledgling
German emperor, William II, rebelled against Bismarck, forcing his resignation in 1890, he was motivated in part by fear of the formation of a "Bismarck
dynasty."

Bismarck had already tested his son by sending him on a mission to London
in 1881–1882 and had been satisfied by the results. On November 20, 1881,
the Chancellor sent a personal message through Gerson von Bleichröder, his
own banker, to Lord Ampthill, the British representative at Berlin, saying that
he had decided to send his eldest son as second Secretary to London and that
he personally hoped and flattered himself that it might be regarded as a
compliment and as an earnest desire to wipe out the painful impression made
by a scandal which had taken place the previous summer at the German
Embassy in London.[45] Several days later Bismarck wrote to Ampthill, asking
him as a personal favor to recommend his son, Herbert, "to Lord Granville's
benevolence."[46] The British ambassador promptly reported to London:

> Bismarck adores this son, who is a remarkably clever youth, and hopes to make a
> great stateman of him. He has often told me in confidence that Herbert, young as
> he is, would already make an abler ambassador than all the members of the
> German diplomatic body taken together.[47]

Knowing full well he and his family were not "in ordeur [*sic*] of sanctity" in
high quarters, Bismarck kept Herbert's visit to England a secret at the Palace
from all except the Emperor, until the newspapers revealed his arrival.[48]

Lord Granville, the British foreign secretary, received the young Bismarck
cordially, giving him a magnificent reception despite a "Berlin letter" sent
him by the Queen painting Herbert Bismarck in black colors.[49] He found
Herbert "clever, well-informed, bright, and easy to please,"[50] and was certain that the visit would do much to dispel "the want of knowledge of each
other which some politicians display."[51] Granville was almost pathetically
eager to lionize the young cub as a means of softening the heart of the

---

[45]Lord Ampthill to Lord Granville, November 26, 1881, *L.B.E.*, p. 235. Unfortunately, there is
no further information available on this scandal.
[46]*Ibid.*
[47]*Ibid.*
[48]Lord Ampthill to Lord Granville, December 17, 1881, *L.B.E.*, p. 238. The German Crown
Princess, Queen Victoria's daughter, was bitterly anti-Bismarck.
[49]Lord Granville to Lord Ampthill, December 14, 1881, *L.B.E.*, p. 238.
[50]*Ibid.*
[51]Lord Granville to Lord Ampthill, March 29, 1882, *L.B.E.*, p. 258.

growling father. Similarly, members of English society vied with one another to give Bismarck's son a hearty welcome. Regarding the visitor as the political as well as personal heir of the dynasty,[52] the British hosts effusively flattered the paternal vanity of the great man whose power was then at its zenith.

Herbert Bismarck himself was not a little astonished by the cordiality of his reception, both by the official world and by society, and he allowed that he had never been made so much of before.[53] He quickly assumed a position which made it clear that he was the representative, though not officially accredited, of his father.[54] Without consulting his nominal chief, Münster, he sent his father, Holstein, or Rantzau private reports of the gossip he picked up in London clubs, which were then forwarded to the Emperor and occasionally made use of in the press.[55] Bismarck and his wife were delighted. They thanked Granville and Lady Granville through Ampthill for the cordiality of the reception to their beloved boy, whereupon Ampthill reported to London that "He (Bismarck) said he could never be sufficiently grateful for the reception his son had met with in England."[56] And again: "Princess Bismarck never ceases to talk in grateful and eloquent language" about Granville's kindnesses to her son.[57]

It was a happy state of affairs: the British had invested their kindness politically, Bismarck seemed to have a growing preference for England, and relations between Britain and Germany seemed to be improving.

This love feast was rudely disturbed in 1884 by the shadows of Angra Pequena. Feeling that the time was now ripe for a showdown with Britain, Bismarck decided to use his trump card—the threat of withdrawing his support for Britain's policy in Egypt. On June 14, 1884, just before a debate in the *Reichstag,* he informed Ampthill that he "deplored the delay in answering his questions, which had been respectfully and loyally put," and feared that "public opinion in Germany would resent the fact that after six months delay the Cape Government had been wedged in between German aspirations and interests and Angra Pequena."[58]

In the meantime Herbert Bismarck had arrived in London on a special

---

[52]Fitzmaurice, *op. cit.,* vol. II, pp. 256–257.
[53]Lord Ampthill to Lord Granville, February 25, 1882, *L.B.E.,* p. 254.
[54]Fitzmaurice, *op. cit.,* vol. II, p. 256.
[55]Busch, *op. cit.,* vol. III, p. 60.
[56]Lord Ampthill to Lord Granville, March 25, 1882, *L.B.E.,* p. 257.
[57]Lord Ampthill to Lord Granville, April 1, 1882, *L.B.E.,* p. 258.
[58]Lord Ampthill to Lord Granville, June 14, 1884, *L.B.E.,* pp. 333–334.

mission for his father to deal with the Angra Pequena question. Bismarck planned his attack well: on the same day that he was interviewing the British ambassador at Berlin, June 14, 1884, his son Herbert was having his first long conversation with Granville in London.[59] Herbert first complained of the long delay in answering his father's inquiries, to which replies might have been given in a few days. He then insisted that the German Government would negotiate only with the Foreign Office and not with the Colonial Office, and then accused Lord Derby, the colonial secretary, of duplicity by taking advantage of the delay to press the Government of the Cape Colony to take action anticipating that of the German government. Granville meekly laid the blame for delay on Britain's "peculiar" form of governmental machinery and defended Derby:

> I answered that there was no doubt that the delay was regrettable, that I had said as much in the House of Lords, and had added that, although it had been unavoidable, whatever blame there might appear to be, rested with Her Majesty's Government. I fully admitted, I said, that in matters of this sort, the German Government had only the Foreign Office to look to as organ of Her Majesty's Government, but practically, I could not act except on acquaintance with the views of the Colonial Office, and with our peculiar organization, the latter department could frequently give no opinion without first communicating with our colonies, especially when the latter had representative institutions.

> It was a complete misunderstanding of Lord Derby's action to suppose that his action in consulting the Government of the Cape Colony was intended in any sense to be hostile to the German Government. On the contrary, he had acted in the belief derived from some of the questions which had been asked by the German Government that it was their desire that the German settlers should receive British protection.[60]

Herbert Bismarck then made clear the importance that his father attached to Angra Pequena and stated that his father intended to set up an arrangement at Angra Pequena that would preclude the possibility of the annexation of that place by any other power.

With the groundwork prepared, Herbert Bismarck now produced his father's sharpest weapon. While Prince Bismarck still entertained the same friendly feelings towards Her Majesty's Government and was desirous of supporting its policy in Egypt, he thought it right that Granville should be

---

[59]Lord Granville to Lord Ampthill, June 14, 1884, *Foreign Office Papers,* Public Record Office, London, 64/1102.
[60]*Ibid.*

warned that the feeling in Germany as regards these colonial questions was so strong that, with the best of wishes he felt he would be unable to afford Britain the same friendly assistance as hitherto, unless he could give some satisfaction to public opinion on the subject. To this Granville replied that he "objected to anything in the nature of a bargain between us. Each question ought to be discussed on its own merits." Herbert Bismarck then insisted that he did not raise any question of a bargain, but that "the German Government expected their rights to be respected." "We have the painful impression," he informed Granville, "that you will evade the question and are awaiting reports, whether you can want the thing." Granville denied this strenuously and said: "If it is your *right* you will see England at your feet at once."[61]

On June 17, 1884, Herbert Bismarck and Granville met for the second time. This interview proceeded along the same lines as the previous one, although there were differing accounts by the participants. Herbert Bismarck reported that Granville had said that in England it was the opinion that the national possessions were already too great and that England had not the slightest reason to oppose German colonization.[62] Granville wrote to Ampthill that he had asked Herbert Bismarck to let him know definitely what Germany claimed: "Did they wish, I said, to protect the German settlers only, or were they desirous of undertaking the protection of both the German and the British settlers, or thirdly—did they claim to extend protection to all settlers of whatever nationality who might obtain concessions?"[63]

During these two vital interviews Herbert Bismarck adopted a policy of calculated rudeness which appears to have been planned well in advance. Thus, in the first conference of June 14, 1884, Granville said that since the problem of Angra Pequena affected his colleagues more than it did him, he would be pleased if Herbert Bismarck would confer, in his presence, with Lord Derby and Lord Kimberley. Herbert curtly refused the invitation.[64] In the second interview of June 17, 1884, Granville brought up the question of sovereignty at Angra Pequena. Herbert Bismarck, who had been prepared for this very question by his father in an exchange of telegrams, retorted not over-politely that he thought it "a question of mere curiosity if you ask about sovereignty: it can be all the same to you, what another power does in a

---

[61]Count Herbert Bismarck to Prince Bismarck, June 14, 1884, *Reichsarchiv, Vermischtes Süd-westafrika* III.

[62]Count Herbert Bismarck to Prince Bismarck, June 17, 1884, *Die Grosse Politik*, IV, no. 746.

[63]Lord Granville to Lord Ampthill, June 18, 1884, *Foreign Office Papers*, 64/1102.

[64]Aydelotte, *op. cit.*, p. 94. Herbert Bismarck wanted to make it clear that neither he nor his father would deal with the Colonial Office.

country not belonging to you." Moreover, he was sure that "my Government would decline to give an answer in a matter that is of no concern to you."[65]

This was an extraordinary way for a thirty-five-year-old diplomat to address the seventy-year-old minister of a great power, but the elder Bismarck was delighted with his son's toughness.[66] Herbert Bismarck seemed to be carried away with his role of tough negotiator; he sent home scornful reports on almost all the British ministers.[67] The British, on their part, were not unaware of the policy of rudeness adopted by the two Bismarcks. Thus, Sir Charles Dilke reported that he attended a cabinet meeting at Lord Granville's house at a time when Herbert Bismarck was there also. "He (Herbert Bismarck) had been very rude to Lord Granville about Angra Pequena, which was mentioned to the Cabinet, which could do nothing."[68]

Victory for the Bismarcks, Father and Son

Here is an excellent illustration of Bismarckian diplomacy. From the beginning Bismarck was sure of his ground. The British were taken in a trap and he was well aware of it. Eighty-eight years previously British troops had been landed on the South West African coast, yet Britain had never claimed it or set up a government. British diplomats handled the Angra Pequena matter with varying amounts of indifference, delay, expressions of ignorance, and the earnest hope that somehow in some way South West Africa could be saved either for Britain or the Cape Colony, and the embarkation of German colonialism in Africa discouraged or prevented. Bismarck met these tactics with brusqueness and rudeness, carefully planned for its effect and executed by his son, whom he regarded as his amanuensis. The idea was to convince the British Foreign Office that he meant business. Thoroughly disgusted with the

---

[65]Count Herbert Bismarck to Prince Bismarck, June 17, 1884, *Die Grosse Politik*, IV, no. 746.

[66]As witness this report by journalist Busch of the Bismarck inner circle: "Lord Granville asked Herbert Bismarck in the course of negotiations respecting Angra Pequena whether he were not contemplating an ultimate expansion of territory towards the interior (query, towards the east, in the direction of Bechuanaland and the Boer Republic); he retorted, not over-politely, that that was 'a question of mere curiosity' and indeed 'finally a matter that does not concern you.' The Chief [Bismarck] showed him [Bucher] the letter in which that was reported, and was pleased with his son's sturdiness." (Busch, *op. cit.*, II, 373.)

[67]E. Eyck, *Gladstone* (Leipzig, 1935), p. 436.

[68]S. Gwynn and G. M. Tuckwell, *The Life of the Rt. Hon. Sir Charles W. Dilke, Bart.*, 2 vols. (London, 1917), vol. II, p. 81. On another occasion Dilke wrote: "Count Herbert Bismarck came over again. If at his former visit he had only tried to get us to dismiss Lord Derby, on this occasion he wanted to dismiss Lord Granville and Lord Derby." (Quoted in C. G. Robertson, *Bismarck* [London, 1918], p. 427; *cf.* also Eyck, *op. cit.*, p. 436, and Fitzmaurice, *op. cit.*, vol. II, p. 430.

temporizing methods of British ministers and convinced that Münster had not represented German interests with sufficient energy, Bismarck sent his son to London with explicit orders to carry on diplomacy-by-irritation.

On June 22, 1884, another confidential conference was held between Herbert Bismarck and Granville, during the course of which the British foreign minister said that the Cabinet, having thoroughly examined the Angra Pequena question, had come to the conclusion that Britain was not in a position to question the right of the German Government to afford protection to its own subjects who had settled there.[69] Thus, in three interviews Herbert Bismarck had achieved a preliminary settlement of the South West Africa issue, with the British Government giving Bismarck all that he had wanted. Britain had been forced to admit that the German protection over the mainland acquired by Lüderitz was justified, and she had been compelled to withdraw her claims to this area of Africa, with the exception of Walfisch Bay.

The British had sustained a bitter diplomatic defeat, but the fact that they gave in eventually to Bismarck's demands was another indication that realism and not sentiment ruled the Foreign Office. It would seem that the only satisfactory answer to Herbert Bismarck's rough diplomacy-by-irritation should have been equally harsh and stiff-necked treatment, but the British were by now well aware of the weakness of their own position and the corresponding strength of Bismarck's. It was felt that the Chancellor's support in Egypt was well worth the loss of Angra Pequena. In London there was much criticism in the press about "this ignominious chapter in the colonial history of England"[70]; in Berlin the press happily applauded "the clever manipulating and use of great patience" by the Bismarcks, father and son, who joyfully toasted each other in mutual admiration.

There were some further repercussions,[71] although the matter was basically settled. In July 1884 the Cape Colony suddenly declared that with Lord Derby's sanction, she had annexed South West Africa. Bismarck promptly dispatched three warships to the spot, and on August 7, 1884, the German flag was hoisted. Britain had no desire to go to war about Angra Pequena, hence she explained that the annexation order referred only to such lands as were not actually occupied by the Germans.[72] Germany's great colonial adventure was under way and German nationalism had been given further powerful stimulus.

---

[69]Count Herbert Bismarck to Prince Bismarck, June 22, 1884, *Die Grosse Politik*, IV, no. 747.
[70]See *The Times*, London, December 13, 1884.
[71]*Cf.* Aydelotte, *op. cit.*, pp. 113–135.
[72]E. F. Henderson, *A Short History of Germany* (New York, 1917), p. 470.

German Nationalism and Imperialism

German penetration into Africa was a logical concomitant of the German nationalism which had been developing since the early 19th century. After the failure of liberal nationalism in the Revolution of 1848, German nationalism took on special characteristics of its own, including the Bismarckian concept of *Macht* as opposed to parliamentary majorities. Berlin thought in terms of prestige. If Britain, France, Portugal, Belgium, and Holland could be colonial powers, then nothing on earth could stop the Germans from establishing their own empire. If others could absorb huge territories in Africa, then why not the Germans with their advanced economic, social, and cultural life? It was only reasonable to have African colonials parade through the streets of Berlin. It was a matter of prestige—of national pride, of national power.

The acquisition of South West Africa was merely an initial step in colonial expansion. There was widespread public support. In 1882, in the midst of the Angra Pequena negotiations, the *Deutsche Kolonial Verein* (German Colonial Society) was founded in Frankfurt am Main by Freiherr Hermann von Maltzen. Business leaders rallied to the support of the new organization. Two hundred members appeared at the first meeting; by the end of 1884 the membership list had reached more than 9,000. The society published a journal dealing with colonial subjects, established a bureau of information for prospective emigrants, offered prizes to colonial planters, and awarded scholarships to students.

Even more vigorous was the *Alldeutscher Verband* (Pan-German League). In 1886 Dr. Karl Peters, one of the most successful of German colonialists, called a German General Congress in Berlin for the promotion of German interests overseas. In the 1890s this became the Pan-German League. Its propaganda complained that the wave of enthusiasm which had swept the German people to great heights in 1870–1871 had been displaced by a certain apathy. National sentiment was being obliterated by economic interests and social questions. Other peoples had taken advantage of "the holy possession of their race," but Germans had spent their energies in internal party struggles, and had wallowed in deceptive self-content. "National tasks should not be placed behind our social and economic goals. We must strengthen our national feeling, and bring home to the mass of our people the fact that Germany's development did not end with the year 1871."

To counter this disintegration of national sentiment, the Pan-German League presented four basic aims in section 1 of its constitution:

1. Preservation of the German *Volkstum* in Europe and overseas and its support wherever threatened;

2. Settlement of all cultural, educational, and school problems in ways that shall aid the German *Volkstum*;

3. The combatting of all forces which would hinder German national development;

4. An active policy of furthering German interests in the entire world, in particular continuance of the German colonial movement to practical results.

This type of propaganda indicated that the commitment was made. German nationalism, from the first steps of the Angra Pequena negotiations, had merged with aggressive imperialism. The combination of nationalism and imperialism led straight into the abyss of World War I.

CHAPTER

5

Clashing Economic Nationalisms: The Battle between German and American Pork, 1879 to 1891

[Ambassador] Sargent's appointment and continued service are inconsistent with Germany's national dignity.

Otto von Bismarck

After unification in 1871 the Second German Empire aroused the attention of the entire world by her phenomenal economic progress. Prussia-Germany emerged from parochialism and traditional disunity to become an industrial giant. Once the stepchild of Western Europe, she now competed with the nations of the world for industrial leadership. What Friedrich List had envisioned early in the 19th century now became hard fact.

An intensified economic nationalism preceded that aggressive political nationalism which aggravated the international scene in the decades before the outbreak of World War I. The United States and Germany succeeded to the place once held by Britain, which had given direction to the First Industrial Revolution in the middle of the 18th century. The economic rivalry between Germany and Britain was more and more accentuated as the slogan "Made in Germany" began to challenge "Made in Britain."

On another level there was an increasing competition between German and American production, although it never reached the bitter stage which marked Anglo-German rivalry. Bismarck's new protective tariff policy, instituted in

Adapted from Louis L. Snyder, "The American-German Pork Dispute, 1879–1891," *The Journal of Modern History*, XVII, no. 1 (March, 1945), pp. 16–28.

the late 1870s, eventually led to friction between Germany and the United States. Conservatives, anxious to protect German industry and agriculture against foreign competition, were angered by the competition from American imports, including pork and pork products.

The story of the battle between German and American pork, which had its serious as well as amusing sides, was one facet of the tariff confrontation between the two countries. At the same time it presents a fascinating microcosm of conflicting economic nationalisms.

Bismarck's Conversion to Tariff Protection

During the decade following German national unification in 1871 Bismarck was converted to the cause of a protective tariff policy. He became convinced that the acute sufferings of German industries and the depression of prices had been due in large part to the government's moderate free-trade practices. In reaching this decision the Chancellor undoubtedly was influenced by the views of his confidential assistant, Lothar Bucher, who warned him that Germany was being swamped by the surplus production of foreign nations.[1] The battle between proponents of laissez faire (parliamentarians, liberals, bankers, and merchants) and protectionists (agrarians and manufacturers) was eventually won by the champions of protection.[2] Finding himself unable to convert the National Liberals to protection, Bismarck negotiated with the Center, which agreed to support him if he dropped the *Kulturkampf*. Accordingly, he introduced his new tariff policy with the explanation: "I had the impression that under free trade we were gradually bleeding to death."[3] The new tariff schedule was adopted on June 12, 1879.[4]

---

[1]Bucher was contemptuous of British free traders. He considered the Manchester free-trade movement the most colossal and the most audacious campaign of political and economic deception which the world had ever seen. See Moritz Busch, *Bismarck, Some Secret Pages of his History* (New York, 1898), vol. 1, p. 437.

[2]Since the death by suicide in 1846 of Friedrich List, founder of a system of national protection, many scholars had proclaimed that the salvation of Germany lay in protection. The jurist Ihering, the economist Roscher, the historians Treitschke and Mommsen, the political economist Schmoller, and others condemned free trade as impracticable and unattainable for Germany (J. Ellis Barker, *Modern Germany* [6th ed.; New York, 1919], pp. 169–83 [an earlier edition of this book (1905) appeared under the name of "O. Eltzbacher"]).

[3]Speech of May 2, 1879. See J. W. Headlam, *Bismarck and the Foundations of the German Empire* (New York and London, 1899), p. 420.

[4]In 1881 Hamburg and Bremen were brought within the customs frontiers of Germany, with the exclusion of their free harbors for goods in transit.

Bismarck's shift from laissez faire liberalism to economic nationalism was a natural outcome of the steadily strengthening nationalism of the 1860s and 1870s. It reflected the relative decline of the National Liberal and Progressive parties (strongly free trade) and the enhanced position of the Conservative and Center parties (strongly paternalistic). In the 1880s Germany became a world power instead of purely European power, and its prosperity increased greatly. The change in basic economic policy coincided with the beginning of Germany's great industrial development which led to the international economic and political friction that culminated in the world wars of the 20th century.

Effect on German-American Relations

The new course had a vital effect upon German-American relations. The metamorphosis of Germany from a food-exporting to a food-importing country, a result of German industrialization, profoundly affected the attitude of German agrarians to imports from America. The growth of American agriculture and the improvement of ocean transportation had brought American agricultural products into European markets in great quantities. Bismarck's tariff of 1879 embodied an agrarian, as well as an industrial, protective policy. Two conflicting interests had to be served: it was necessary to protect German farmers against the large imports of American grain, livestock, and foodstuffs, and yet at the same time German industrialists had to receive raw materials, including foodstuffs, at a price low enough to enable them to compete with foreign manufacturers in the final selling of their products.[5] Significantly, the high protective policy that developed in the United States after the Civil War had been dictated by the manufacturing interests, while the German protective system had been sponsored by both the manufacturers and the agrarian party.[6]

There was no formal comprehensive commercial treaty between the United States and the German Empire. The two nations used the old treaty between Prussia and the United States, which placed both on the "most-favored-nation" basis in commerce and navigation. Controversies on interpretation had been frequent. By 1878 the issue of commercial relations had become serious. The beginning of recovery from the world depression had been marked by the increased purchasing power of the masses in Germany (as

---

[5]Jeanette Keim, *Forty Years of German-American Political Relations* (Philadelphia, 1919), p. 65.
[6]*Ibid.*, p. 66.

elsewhere in Europe); moreover, a series of crop failures helped prepare the way for a demand for the huge supplies of American wheat.

A Matter of Pork

While the problem of the importation of American wheat was a thorny one, wheat was not the only product of American agriculture whose importation caused concern among the German agrarians. American exportation of live-stock (mainly pork) and meat products had attained such proportions that neither German production in particular nor European production in general could keep abreast of it. Before 1879 Russia and Austria-Hungary had supplied Germany with meat products, but by that year America was sending a large supply to Germany and other European countries. A regular ship line to England was used by American packers for the purpose of supplying Europe with meats. The superabundance of pork in the United States was indicated by the fact that, while Europe, as a whole, produced more swine than the United States, still the relative amount available in the United States was four times as great as in Europe, as shown in the accompanying table.[7] American packers exported at least 60 percent of their pork and pork products (meat, ham, lard).[8] In 1879 there were 1,081,892,318 pounds, estimated to have had a value of $77,157,330; and in 1880 these figures were exceeded by the exportation of 1,326,157,330 pounds, valued at $100,799,414.[9]

PRODUCTION OF SWINE (IN MILLIONS)

Europe (1875) 43.5
United States (1878) 32.2

NUMBER PER 1,000 INHABITANTS

Europe (1880) 156
United States (1878) 690

The American packing industry was exceptionally extensive in its organiza-tion and production. American stockyards, particularly at Chicago, were known throughout the world. The shipment of hogs to Chicago exceeded

---

[7]Sargent to Frelinghuysen, Berlin, November 18, 1882, U.S., *Foreign Relations, 1883,* Part I (Washington, 1884), p. 307.
[8]Alexander von Peez, *Die amerikanische Konkurrenz* (Vienna, 1881), p. 36.
[9]Sargent to Frelinghuysen, Berlin, November 18, 1882, *Foreign Relations, 1883,* Part I (Washington, 1884), p. 308.

50,000 per day; from 10,000 to 15,000 hogs were slaughtered and packed daily.[10] The Anglo-American Packing and Provision Company in two seasons—from March 1, 1880, to March 1, 1881—packed more than a million hogs; Armour and Company in the same period, approximately the same number; in all, more than five and a half million hogs.[11]

The importation of large quantities of pork and pork products into Europe tended to lower the price and bring it within the range of the poorer classes. Lard became an important and extensively used article of food in Germany only through its import from America; German lard, on the other hand, because of its higher price, remained a luxury.[12] In 1881 and the first half of 1882 Westphalian and Oldenburg hams cost 1.05 to 1.10 marks per pound, and American hams from 60 to 64 pfennigs.[13] The attitude of German agrarians toward this state of affairs may well be imagined.

In 1880 Bismarck precipitated a quarrel with the United States by banning the importation of American pork and pork products. For a decade thereafter the bitter controversy threatened to develop into a customs war. The ban upon American pork and pork products was not, however, exclusively a German phenomenon but occurred simultaneously in several European countries.[14] On February 20, 1879, the sanitary department of Italy, alleging the frequent discovery of trichinae in hog's meat coming from Cincinnati, prohibited all pork imports of whatever character from the United States.[15] In September 1879 the Hungarian council general of public health likewise prohibited the importation of American pork into Hungary. In the same month the prevalence of trichinae in American pork was reported to the International Medical Congress at Amsterdam by Dr. Ludwig von Grosse, who announced that the Austro-Hungarian Empire intended to prohibit the American product.[16] In the early part of 1880 the publication of reports by several British consular offi-

---

[10]Memorial of the Merchants of Hamburg to the Bundesrat, Nov. 21, 1882, translation in Sargent to Frelinghuysen, Berlin, Dec. 11, 1882, *Foreign Relations, 1883*, Part I (Washington, 1884), p. 321.

[11]"Scanlan report," *Foreign Relations, 1883*, Part I (Washington, 1884), p. 310. On the other hand, the largest German packing-house, J. D. Koopman, packed only from 130,000 to 140,000 German hogs yearly—exclusively for London.

[12]*Berliner Tribune*, November 10, 1882.

[13]*Ibid.*

[14]For the actions of European governments on American pork and pork products see August Sartorius von Waltershausen, *Das deutsche Einfuhrverbot amerikanischen Schweinfleisches* (Jena, 1884), Cf. Keim, pp. 67–70.

[15]Soon afterward, on May 6, 1879, the Italian restriction was made general against all foreign pork.

[16]American pork was prohibited in the Austro-Hungarian empire more than a year later (March 19, 1881).

cers in the United States, alleging the prevalence of hog cholera in the West to an alarming extent, aroused popular excitement in England. The import of live swine and swine products was checked in England for a time, but no prohibitory legislation ensued. Apparently cholera was mistaken for trichinosis. The reports of the British consuls appeared to provide a strong basis for prohibitions in other European countries. The first German ordinance came only on June 25, 1880. It was followed by a decree of the French chamber on February 8, 1881, upon the advice of the Consultative Committee of Public Health. Turkey, Greece, and Austria-Hungary followed the German and French example for professed sanitary reasons, but efforts to enact similar prohibitions in Belgium and Switzerland failed. Although confined at first to scientific and hygienic considerations, the movement soon took on a commercial aspect. Protectionists loudly condemned American pork on sanitary grounds, while men of science and practical economists attacked the prohibitory edicts as unnecessary.

Beginning of the Controversy

The pork dispute between Germany and the United States began with the above-mentioned imperial decree of June 25, 1880, prohibiting the importation from the United States of all sorts of pork except hams and sides of bacon.[17] The reason given for the decree was that a recent epidemic of trichinosis had been due to the eating of diseased pork. Hams and sides of bacon were exempted from the decree because these could be inspected properly for trichinosis.[18] The full effect of the prohibition was not felt until 1882: in 1880 the value of German imports of butchered animals from America amounted to 7,743,000 marks, increasing to 12,497,000 marks in 1881 and sinking to 861,000 marks in 1882.[19] In 1882 the request of the United States

---

[17]Everett to Frelinghuysen, Berlin, Feb. 23, 1882, *Foreign Relations, 1882*, Part I (Washington, 1883), p. 158.

[18]The *New York Herald* (December 4, 1882) found this exemption extraordinarily inconsistent and accused Germany of bravely trying not to appear ridiculous in her protective measures: "If the dreadful parasites are to be made an excuse for enabling German hog raisers to maintain the high prices of the native pork, it is just as well for Germany to be consistent and exclude the hindquarters of the American pig as well as those portions of the animal's carcass that are less costly and in more active demand. The Germans are to be pitied, for the American ham is a good thing to have in the house; still, so is consistency."

[19]Otto Graf zu Stolberg-Wernigerode, *Germany and the United States during the Era of Bismarck* (Reading, Pa., 1937), p. 151.

for a modification of the decree for the benefit of the meat products of two large American packing companies was refused.[20]

Sensing victory in the campaign against American pork, German agrarian interests began to apply pressure on the government for total exclusion. On March 27, 1882, a circular was addressed to agricultural societies in Germany by a committee appointed by the Congress of German Agrarians, asking that petitions be prepared and sent to the Chancellor and the *Bundesrat* demanding prohibition of all American cattle, meat, and meat preparations. Through the spring and summer of 1882 Bismarck's office was deluged with petitions.[21] It soon became apparent that the chancellor intended to go ahead with the prohibition edict. The *Berliner Tageblatt*,[22] alarmed by the probability of the decree, warned against the step: "Should this prohibition go into effect we should have cause to regret it, for the reason that it would result in making meat dearer to the mass of people, or even restrict them in its consumption. American meat undoubtedly is, and always was, cheaper than the domestic article, and the claim that it is unwholesome is not sufficiently proved to justify its exclusion from our market." Nevertheless, on November 21, 1882, Bismarck transmitted a memorandum, together with the exclusion bill, to the *Bundesrat*, characterizing meat inspection in America as unsatisfactory.

From December 1882 to March 1883 there was an acrimonious debate in the German press and in the *Reichstag* over the question of total exclusion of American pork and pork products. The chambers of commerce of all the German seaports, which expected to be hard hit, protested against the contemplated legislation.[23] Westphalian farmers, who imported a large quantity of American bacon and hams, which appeared on the market as Westphalian *Schinken*, sent a deputation to protest to Bismarck against the measure.[24] The *Berliner Tageblatt* again warned that the prohibition would be "disastrous"; the *Weser Zeitung* expressed fear of retaliation; and other opposition newspapers termed the measure "injurious" and "ill-advised"[25] On January 9, 1883, a vigorous debate on the pork question took place in the *Reichstag* following an interpellation addressed to the chancellor by the opposition par-

[20]Everett to Frelinghuysen, Berlin, Mar. 27, 1882, *Foreign Relations, 1882*, Part I (Washington, 1883), p. 158.
[21]*New York Herald*, December 19, 1882.
[22]Nov. 3, 1882.
[23]*New York Herald*, December 9, 1882.
[24]*Ibid.*, December 17, 1882.
[25]Quoted in *ibid.*, January 15, 1883.

ties. According to Ambassador Aaron A. Sargent's account, the arguments of deputies Eugen Richter, Dr. Friedrich Kapp, Dr. Wilhelm Theodor Barth, and Gerhard Ahlhorn, in summary, were: (1) the previous prohibition of American pork had been injurious; (2) the chancellor had made no efforts to collect or present any evidence of the unsoundness of American pork; (3) cases of trichinosis arose from the use of German chopped meat, fresh from the butchers; (4) the poorer classes were deprived of a source of cheap food on flimsy and sensational evidence; (5) the *Bundesrat* had no right to make the prohibition under the tariff law of 1839, its only pretense of authority, for that law gave only the right of temporary suspension in cases of emergency; and (6) it was undesirable to disturb the good relations with the United States, which was then engaged in reducing tariffs. Representatives of the government (Ministerial Director Marcard, Secretary Buchard, and Federal Commissioner Köhler) replied to the effect that (1) the *Bundesrat* had as yet come to no conclusion and no one had the right to announce its intentions in advance; (2) the German poor were not dependent upon pork, which was only 3 per cent of their food; and (3) American pork was definitely infected with trichinae, "as proved by scientific opinion." Bismarck arrived in the midst of the debate. Excusing himself, on the plea of ill-health, from speaking at length, he indicated that he was not moved by the pleas of the opposition and dismissed the matter sarcastically by terming pork "the poor man's trichinae."[26]

It was clear that Bismarck was determined to prohibit American pork despite all opposition. Therefore, President Chester A. Arthur, on February 15, 1883, directed that the Imperial Government be informed of his intention appoint an impartial and competent commission to examine the raising of hogs and the curing and packing of hog products in the United States. The proposal also invited Germany to send her own commission of experts to co-operate with the American experts, who were "scientists of known probity."[27] The invitation was declined on July 11, 1883, (more than four months after the *Reichstag* had accepted the bill), on the ground that in a matter concerning domestic sanitary legislation, the German government could not enter into any arrangement which might imply an obligation on its

---

[26]Sargent to Frelinghuysen, Berlin, January 13, 1883, *Foreign Relations, 1883,* Part I, 328–29. Sargent's report of the debate was accurate. See Germany, *Stenographische Berichte über die Verhandlungen des Reichstages* (29th sess., [1882–83]) (Berlin, 1883), vol. II, pp. 810–26.
[27]Frelinghuysen to Sargent, telegram, Washington, February 15, 1883, and letter, Washington, February 16, 1883, *Foreign Relations, 1883,* Part I (Washington, 1884), pp. 335–36.

part to accept or to be bound by a state of facts existing outside its jurisdiction. "Germany by its strict and rigorously enforced legislation afforded the same protection to its people at home against all danger from German cattle and hogs; it could therefore not treat the foreign products better than its own. An investigation of the American methods of raising hogs and preparing hog products by a commission of German experts in the United States could not effect a material change in this respect."[28] This type of reasoning was faulty: the suggested investigation by German experts might well have shown that American methods were as careful and American pork as healthful, as the German.[29]

The Role of Ambassador Sargent

A complicating factor in the dispute was Bismarck's strong personal animosity toward Aaron A. Sargent, who had been American minister in Berlin since March 2, 1882. Formerly, the Chancellor had always enjoyed cordial relations with American ministers.[30] With the historian George Bancroft, the poet Bayard Taylor (translator of *Faust*), and the educator Andrew D. White, Bismarck had maintained close personal relations, reminiscent of his intimate friendship during his student days at Göttingen with John Lothrop Motley.[31] But the Chancellor heartily disliked Sargent, and it is not at all unlikely that Bismarck's somewhat bad-tempered handling of the pork issue was influenced, to some extent, by his attitude toward the American minister. Sargent, like Bismarck, was a man of strong and forceful personality, aggressive in political contests, untiring and persevering in pursuit of his ends, a good German scholar, and an able debater.[32] Unlike his predecessors at Berlin,

---

[28]Von Eisendecher to Frelinghuysen, Washington, May 2, 1883, U.S., *Senate Reports* (48th cong., 1st sess.), III (doc. No. 354: "Swine Products of the United States"), 145.

[29]Cf. Keim, p. 68.

[30]Throughout the period from 1862, when Bismarck became minister-president and minister of foreign affairs of Prussia, to 1890, when he resigned as German chancellor, there were ten American ministers in Berlin: Norman B. Judd (Illinois, appointed in 1861), Joseph A. Wright (Indiana, 1865), George Bancroft (New York, 1867), J. C. Bancroft Davis (New York, 1874), Bayard Taylor (Pennsylvania, 1878), Andrew D. White (New York, 1879), Aaron A. Sargent (California, 1882), John A. Kesson (Iowa, 1884), George H. Pendleton (Ohio, 1885), and William Walter Phelps (New Jersey, 1889).

[31]L. L. Snyder, *Die persoenlichen und politischen Beziehungen Bismarcks zu Amerikanern* (Darmstadt, 1932), pp. 39–65.

[32]Cf. *Dictionary of American Biography*, XVI, pp. 353–354.

Sargent was a masterful machine politician; and undoubtedly in some of his actions he stepped beyond the bounds of effective diplomacy.[33]

Soon after arriving in Berlin, Sargent worked energetically to forestall any further action by the German government against American pork and pork products. In a long series of dispatches to Washington he heatedly criticized the German position. A typical passage from these messages follows:

> I have sought by every means to oppose the measure, and have lost no opportunity to show that the health of American swine is unimpaired and American products are entirely wholesome. I do not think these latter propositions are now seriously disputed by people of intelligence. The movement is merely selfish, and in disregard of the interests of the United States. The only argument that would be effective against the measure would be the fear of reprisals. We could not insist upon any people receiving from us articles deleterious to health, but we can as little submit to the exclusion of our products upon false pretenses— pretenses so obviously false in this instance.[34]

During the winter of 1882–83, when the debate on the impending decree of prohibition was at its height, Sargent advised Washington to increase import duties against Germany. On February 23, 1883, he presented a note to the German government in which he expressed the warning that the American Congress would be forced to undertake measures of retaliation if the decree were put into effect. Bismarck, regarding the note as a case of interference in the internal affairs of Germany, inquired in Washington as to whether the American minister was acting on instructions from his government: "The tenor of [the note's] argumentation suggests that he [Sargent] did not take this step without assistance from the opposition in the *Reichstag*. If such be the case, it will, much to my regret, be very difficult for Mr. Sargent to acquire that position of confidence with us which his predecessor enjoyed and which corresponds to the continued friendly relations between the two Gov-

---

[33]Stolberg-Wernigerode (pp. 152–65) gives a decidedly unfavorable picture of Sargent. He accuses the American minister of conducting his office more or less in the spirit of American party politics, maintains that Sargent received his political information from Bismarck's political opponents, and dismisses his earlier experiences as only those of a journalist and a representative in congress. Stolberg-Wernigerode's treatment of the pork dispute is colored by a strong sympathy for Bismarck's point of view. He accuses the Americans of "stubborn self-righteousness" in the conflict (p. 166) and concludes that "they were not nearly so firmly convinced of the unfairness of the criticism raised as they pretended to be" (p. 150).
[34]Sargent to Frelinghuysen, Berlin, January 1, 1883, *Foreign Relations, 1883*, Part I (Washington, 1884), p. 326.

ernments.''[35] The German minister in Washington replied that the content of the note presented by Sargent was not based on instructions from Washington.[36] Although Secretary of State Frelinghuysen regarded the threatened prohibition as unwarranted and injurious, he disapproved of the headstrong action of the American minister and sent him what amounted to a mild reprimand: "So far as your intimation touches the operation of the laws of international trade, it is unexceptionable. . . . But when you go further and indicate the possibility that this Government may resort to retaliation if its views be not assented to by Germany, you introduce an element which it was not intended to present."[37]

Sargent's zealous efforts had no effect. The draft of the ordinance originally presented to the *Bundesrat* in late 1882 was accepted by that body in late February 1883 and by the *Reichstag* on March 6, 1883. It reads as follows:

1. The importation from America [the United States] of pigs, pork, bacon, and sausages of all kinds is prohibited until further notice.
2. The Imperial Chancellor is empowered to permit exceptions to this prohibitive rule, subject to the necessary measures of control.
3. The restrictive ordinance of the 25th June, 1880 with respect to the importation of pork and sausages from America is abolished.
4. The present ordinance comes into force thirty days after its promulgation.[38]

A few days later Bismarck wrote to the *Bundesrat* recommending that, in order to prevent evasion of the law, pork products be admitted into Germany only on attested proof that they were not from America.[39] Several months later the German admiralty ordered the commanders of men-of-war to limit their supplies of American pickled pork to what was necessary for the sustenance of the crews during the passage home of the vessels from foreign stations.[40]

In the *Reichstag* and in the opposition press, sporadic criticism of Bismarck's policy continued, but to little avail. Particularly strong objections were made to Bismarck's procedure in banning American pork. It was pointed out that the *Bundesrat* claimed power under an article in the tariff laws of July 1, 1869, article 2 of which read: "Exceptional measures may be adopted

[35]Bismarck to Eisendecher, Berlin, March 3, 1883; quoted by Stolberg-Wernigerode, p. 153.
[36]*Ibid.*
[37]Keim, p. 39, n. 17.
[38]Sargent to Frelinghuysen, Berlin, December 11, 1882, *Foreign Relations, 1883,* Part I (Washington, 1884), p. 319. The text of the ordinance appeared in the *New York Herald,* December 2, 1882.
[39]*New York Herald,* March 15, 1883.
[40]*Ibid.,* August 7, 1883.

temporarily under extraordinary circumstances for the prevention of dangerous contagious conditions, or for other sanitary or precautionary reasons, for a part or the whole of a district [of the customs union].'' The power granted was apparently for temporary use, but it was obvious that Bismarck intended to keep the ordinance in effect. Moreover, the Chancellor blandly ignored the fact that no decrease in the number of cases of trichinosis in Germany was noted to match the precipitous decline in the importation of American pork.

During the year following the total exclusion of American pork, Sargent continued his outspoken criticism of Germany's ''unfriendly discrimination.'' On March 10, 1883, the *New Yorker Handels-Zeitung* published an article, supposedly by Sargent, dated January 1, 1883, in which it was intimated that the prohibition was dictated not by reasons of public health but for the benefit of the German agrarians. In Germany newspapers favorable to the government pounced upon this ''indiscretion'' and bitterly attacked the American minister on the ground that he was acting outside his official capacity. The *Norddeutsche Allgemeine Zeitung*[41] warned: ''If the report suggests reprisals in order to force American trichinae upon German consumers, it uses an argument similar to that which formed the basis of the Chinese Opium War.'' Sargent explained to Washington that his views had been distorted,[42] and in an interview with the *Boersen-Kurier* he denied vehemently that he had written any article for the *New Yorker Handels-Zeitung*.[43] As a matter of fact, Sargent had sent a report to the State Department on January 1, 1883, in which he had repeated the arguments of opposition newspapers;[44] how this report got to the German-American newspapers in New York and how it appeared under Sargent's signature remains a mystery.

By this time it was obvious that Sargent's position in Berlin was considerably shaken. The American minister became *persona non grata* to Bismarck when he was required to transmit the unfortunate Lasker Resolution to the German government. The Lasker incident was only a minor irritant, but it aroused considerable ill-will in both countries. (See chapter 7.) Edward Lasker, leader of the left wing of the National Liberal party, had made a lecture trip to the United States in the winter of 1883–84. In his addresses before American audiences he criticized Bismarck's domestic policies, par-

---

[41]April 24, 1883.
[42]April 28, 1883, *Foreign Relations, 1883,* Part I (Washington, 1884), pp. 377–78 and 381–82.
[43]*New York Herald,* May 2, 1883.
[44]*Foreign Relations, 1883,* Part I (Washington, 1884), p. 324.

ticularly the Chancellor's new policy of protection. Lasker died suddenly while on his tour (January 5, 1884). A few days later, the American House of Representatives passed a resolution addressed to the family of the deceased and to the German *Reichstag* expressing the sympathy of the House upon the death of the German statesman. Sargent, as was customary, delivered the resolution on February 9, 1883, but Bismarck refused to accept it because it contained a eulogy of a detested political opponent.[45] The great Chancellor was capable of acting in a petulant and childish manner on occasion, and his reaction to the Lasker Resolution was a manifestation of a peculiar sensitiveness. In addition, Bismarck probably desired to seize the occasion to rid himself of the American minister. Bismarck now made it clear that Sargent's appointment and continued service were inconsistent with Germany's "national dignity" and that his "journalistic agitation" and his relations with the German opposition parties made it imperative that he be recalled. Sargent resigned in April 1884. President Arthur immediately offered him the ministry to Russia, which he declined.

Reaction of the American Press

The German prohibition of American pork apparently gave more offense in the United States than the earlier prohibitions of other European countries. If the objections in the American press following the earlier prohibition were lively, they were now even more vehement. German-Americans who had settled in the pork centers of the Middle West made no secret of their anger because of lost business.[46] Especially rankling was the fact that, while in ordinary tariff procedure exclusion was effected by a general law covering the same products from all countries, the German government had insisted upon banning only American pork—"and that on a pretext which, being officially set up by a responsible government, tends to injure the reputation of American hog products in all other countries."[47]

---

[45]Stolberg-Wernigerode's judgment that "on such occasions the Chancellor's self-control seems particularly admirable" (p. 158) is a surprising one, considering the fact that there were obviously no ulterior motives in the action of the American Congress.

[46]Stolberg-Wernigerode hints that at the same time they were glad to use occasions like the pork dispute to demonstrate their sympathy for the opposition parties in Germany. "Indeed, there existed a certain community of interests between those groups and German free traders, and they joined hands in fighting Bismarck's new economic policy" (pp. 151–52).

[47]*New York Herald*, March 17, 1883.

Typical of the attitude of the American press was the headline of an article on the pork dispute reading: "Avenging the American hog."[48] For American cartoonists the pork dispute was a welcome subject. On March 1, 1884, there appeared a cartoon in *Frank Leslie's Illustrated Newspaper* which criticized Bismarck both for his rejection of the Lasker Resoulution and his policy on American pork. The Chancellor, bearing a huge porcelain pipe in one hand and a foaming jug of beer in the other, with a pretzel hanging from his cap, is shown walking along the street. From his pocket hangs a slip of paper labeled "Lasker Resolution." Passing in the opposite direction is a huge hog, whose belly is wrapped in an American flag and from whose tail the Stars and Stripes wave proudly. The caption reads: "We do not greet each other when we meet on the street!" In the April 5, 1884, issue of the same magazine appeared another cartoon entitled: "President Arthur apologizes." Bismarck is shown seated on a throne, the legs of which are beer mugs. The hands and feet of a hog are substituted for the Chancellor's own extremities. Covering the pedestal of the throne is an American flag. President Arthur is depicted bowing before Bismarck in a most humble and apologetic manner. On the wall is a sign: "We have enough hogs—Bismarck." Sargent, the American minister, is shown leaving through the door headed for a new post at St. Petersburg.[49] Yet, however humorous the conflict might appear to some, to the meat packers of Chicago and Cincinnati, the mid-western farmers, the representatives of the farm states in Congress, and the state department the issue was a distressingly serious one.

The Trichinosis Issue

Throughout the controversy Bismarck had contended that American pork was infected with trichinae, that the prohibition concerned problems of public health, and that the "Federal Council could not take the trichinae of the poor under their special protection." From the Chancellor's viewpoint the prohibition was a measure of internal legislation found necessary "after careful investigation on sanitary grounds." Let us examine these accusations. There is abundant evidence to show that here, as in other diplomatic maneuvers,

---

[48]*Ibid.*, January 18, 1884.
[49]L. L. Snyder, "Bismarck in American Caricature," *American-German Review*, V, no. 1 (1938), pp. 42–45.

Bismarck deliberately utilized a smoke screen to hide his real intentions. The interdiction of American pork was much less a sanitary than a protectionist measure.[50]

There were, indeed, cases of trichinosis in Germany which could be traced to the eating of pork; but most of these cases of death or disease had resulted from the use of freshly slaughtered German, Russian, or Hungarian pork. The German (and also European) practice of eating pork uncooked[51] was a dangerous one and undoubtedly was responsible for the sporadic outbreaks of trichinosis which the German government attributed to American swine.[52] The *Berliner Tribune* quoted official German reports showing that from 1877 to 1879 there was an average of 33 deaths annually from trichinosis; yet "there has not been proved to be one case of death, or even disease, from eating American pork."[53] In an interview with an American newspaperman, Professor Rudolf Virchow, the eminent German pathologist, condemned the prohibition against American pork as "utterly illogical, unnecessary, and unjustifiable on the ground of sanitary reasons."[54] Asked by the French Chamber of Deputies to give his opinion on the necessity of the prohibition,

---

[50]Of the relatively few specialists in German-American relations, two outstanding scholars, Alfred Vagts and Count Otto zu Stolberg-Wernigerode, agree that the prohibition was influenced basically by Bismarck's desire to restrict menacing imports in the interests of home consumption. Stolberg-Wernigerode, however, shows much sympathy for the German case: "There can also be no doubt that inadequate meat inspection in America had given cause for complaint for some time. Only microscopic inspection was considered by European experts as a sufficient guarantee against trichinosis, and such inspection was not compulsory in the United States.... Stubborn denial of American mistakes resulted in a controversy with Germany which was by no means negligible" (p. 150). Vagts, on the other hand, considers the prohibition understandable as a measure of protection, but he describes the sanitary excuse as "unworthy of belief and inconsequential" (*Deutschland und die Vereinigten Staaten in der Weltpolitik* [New York, 1935], vol. I, p. 1).

[51]Yet, Americans—the greatest pork-consuming people in the world—usually cooked their meat, thereby eliminating the danger of trichinae. American farmers often ate pork two or three times daily. Of 40,000 deaths in Chicago, only two were traced to trichinosis. See Michael Scanlan, *American Pork: Result of an Investigation made under Authority of the Department of State of the United States* (Washington, 1881). The reference above is to the résumé in *Foreign Relations, 1883,* Part I (Washington, 1884), p. 310.

[52]Even today Germany is plagued by recurrent outbreaks of trichinosis, probably due to the practice of eating raw pork. In October 1941, the Reich medical authorities had to issue a general warning to the public against trichinosis (Howard K. Smith, *Last Train from Berlin* [New York, 1942], p. 320).

[53]*Berliner Tribune,* Dec. 30, 1882. The newspaper furthermore maintained that the methods of preparing export meat in the United States were absolute death for trichinae. Throughout the pork dispute the *Berliner Tribune,* powerful organ of the Progressive party, strongly opposed Bismarck.

[54]*New York Herald,* January 15, 1884. See also Vagts, vol. 1, p. 2. The anti-Bismarck and pro-American German Liberal party sought to lift the prohibition by appealing to science, utilizing Virchow's microscope and pen to prove that there was no danger from American pork.

he answered that no case of trichinae in American hog meat had been found in Germany during the last ten years.[55]

That the sanitary reasons were a thin pretense was indicated by a painstaking report made by the United States department of agriculture. In February 1881 the New York Produce Exchange, foreseeing the danger to the export trade, made representations to the United States government, which immediately ordered an investigation. Mr. James G. Blaine, the secretary of state, through Michael Scanlan, chief of the statistical bureau, made a searching investigation at Chicago and Cincinnati, centers of the packing industry. Scanlan received strict instructions to investigate every phase of the pork industry—from the raising of pigs to the manufacture of pork products. Accompanied by experts and stenographers, he visited the principal breeders, traders, exporters, packing houses, abattoirs, and shippers. His thoroughly competent report[56] concluded that the breeding and fattening of American swine was so superior to the standards prevailing everywhere else in the world that the percentage of infected hogs was much smaller in the United States than elsewhere. The *Berliner Tribune* was impressed by the Scanlan report: "To assume that an industry which is carried on with such painstaking cleanliness and such order and regularity would expose its interest to the danger of ruining the entire product, by introducing diseased swine, would indicate a total ignorance of the principles underlying its prosperity. The American speculates, but he does not adulterate, for he well knows that it would ruin his trade forever. 'To mix and to fix' is better understood in Europe than in America."[57]

Bismarck's Real Motive

An indication of Bismarck's real motive in banning American pork may be found in his remark to an American journalist in July 1884: "It is absolutely necessary for us people of Europe to protect ourselves in time against your competition, for whenever the point arrives that the United States is not checked in its inroads on our agriculture, complete ruin will overtake our landholding classes."[58] Bismarck considered the large landowners as pillars

---

[55]The references above are to the résumé of the "Scanlan Report," *loc. cit.*, pp. 309–10.
[56]Published on April 26, 1881. See note 51. The references above are to the résumé, *ibid.*
[57]November 11, 1882.
[58]Wolf von Schierbrand, *Germany, Welding of a World Power* (New York, 1902), p. 354.

of the monarchy, as men of noble lineage, whose sons formed the flower of the German army. He was anxious to shield them from foreign competition, especially if their status as a class was endangered.[59] The key to the problem, according to the German Liberals, was that the German proprietors resented that a pound of American pork could be bought in Germany at less cost than the home product. "If the price of pork rises 5-pfennigs per pound, a hog of 300 pounds gains 15 marks in value on present prices; the result is that large farmers who slaughter yearly from 500 to 1000 head have a gain of 7500 to 15,000 marks."[60] To the contention of the Liberals that his prohibition of the importation of "sick hogs" would lead to a higher cost of food, Bismarck answered: "*Agitationslüge.*"[61] He brusquely dismissed the American arguments that he had banned the American product "not on hygienic grounds but simply as a matter of protection for the German farmer at the expense of the German poor."[62]

There was considerable resentment in the United States when it became clear that Bismarck did not intend the prohibition to be a temporary measure. During 1884, members of Congress received numerous letters from their constituents urging retaliatory action against Germany. The prevalence of anger over a wide section of the country was indicated by a series of bills and resolutions introduced into both the House and the Senate bearing on the problem of retaliation. Both President Arthur and Secretary of State Frelinghuysen believed, however, that a customs war with Germany was undesirable and that it was wiser to move slowly. In his message to Congress (December 1883) Arthur suggested "equitable retaliation," but he alluded in general to invidious distinctions against American products by foreign governments and not specifically to the prohibition of American pork by Germany. Frelinghuysen felt that the mere introduction of legislative bills would have a sufficient effect and advised against any retaliatory legislation.[63]

By 1885 Germany had imposed additional duties on wheat and rye and had contemplated measures hostile to American petroleum. A House resolution called for instructions to the Committee on Foreign Affairs to "inquire into and report whether the interests of the United States do not demand the adoption of like discriminatory measures against such principal articles im-

---

[59]Vagts, vol. I, pp. 6–7.
[60]Sargent to Frelinghuysen, Berlin, January 1, 1883, *Foreign Relations, 1883*, Part I (Washington, 1884), p. 325.
[61]Otto von Bismarck, *Gedanken und Erinnerungen* (Stuttgart and Berlin, 1928), p. 498.
[62]*New York Herald*, December 27, 1882.
[63] Frelinghuysen to Arthur, January 30, 1884, *ibid.*, January 31, 1884.

ported from the German Empire as are grown or manufactured in the United States."[64] The Committee on Foreign Affairs later reported on the resolution and resolved that the President be requested to take immediate steps to obtain from the German Empire the benefits of the most-favored-nation clause in the treaty of 1828 with Prussia, still in force. Nothing, however, developed from this request for "immediate action."

End of the Dispute

Two closely related developments finally led to the end of the pork dispute. The first one, initiated by the American Congress, was designed to meet the German government halfway by agreeing to inspect American meats before exportation. In 1886 a bill was introduced in the Senate (S. 1644) providing for an inspection of meats for exportation. In the discussion of the bill on the floor, Senator George F. Edmunds of Vermont made reference to Germany's claim of disease "when it is obvious as a matter of fact that it is merely a method of excluding American productions."[65] There was no action, however, for four years. Then, on August 30, 1890, came an act of Congress in the form of a law providing for meat inspection. In a debate before the *Reichstag* in late January 1891 Dr. Barth introduced a resolution requesting the government to withdraw the order of March 6, 1883. Karl Heinrich von Boetticher, the Vice-Chancellor, objected on the grounds that the American inspection law did not make examination compulsory and that it was made on the product already boxed. The resolution was defeated by a vote of 133 to 106.[66] On March 3, 1891, Congress passed an act making microscopic inspection of meat compulsory.[67] Thus, one of the critical objections of the Germans to American pork was removed, and the German government was given an opportunity to lift the ban without losing face.

Of considerably greater importance was the second development, the prospect of possible American retaliatory action. Although the American government until this time had rigidly avoided the promulgation of retaliatory legisla-

---

[64]U.S., *Congressional Record* (48th Cong., 2d sess. [1884–85]), XVI, Part III (Washington, 1885), p. 2028.

[65]U.S., *Congressional Record* (49th Cong., 1st sess. [1885–86]), XVII, Part II (Washington, 1886), p. 1760.

[66]Phelps to Blaine, January 24, 1891, *Foreign Relations, 1891*, Part I (Washington, 1892), pp. 501–2.

[67]Wharton to Count von Arco Valley, Washington, June 15, 1891, *ibid.*, pp. 527–28.

tion (despite the fact that members of Congress continually introduced such measures), it became evident that retaliation was now imminent. The victory of Benjamin Harrison over Grover Cleveland in the presidential elections of 1888 resulted in the dominance of the protective tariff party. According to the McKinley Tariff of October 1, 1890, the president, under section 3, had the power to reimpose a duty on German sugar and sugar products imported into the United States after January 1, 1892. Germany at this time exported large quantities of beet sugar to the United States. During the illness of Count von Arco Valley, the German minister to the United States, the German chargé d'affaires, Mumm von Schwartzenstein, sought to forestall his prospective action by intimating the intention of his government to accept the inspection law as satisfactory and revoke the prohibition of American pork. The American President replied, with a touch of sarcasm, that the two questions were unrelated, as American pork had been shut out because it allegedly exposed German consumers to disease.[68] Nevertheless, an agreement was reached in the form of an exchange of declarations, since called "The Saratoga Agreement."[69] Germany agreed to import American pork and pork products but only with an official certificate stating that the meat had been examined and found free from qualities injurious to health. In return, the American government agreed not to take advantage of the clause in the McKinley Tariff regarding German sugar. With this *quid pro quo* the pork dispute was terminated.

Significantly, the Saratoga Agreement was not negotiated until after Bismarck's resignation in 1890. Bismarck rarely changed his course. In retirement at Friedrichsruh he bitterly criticized the new government through the columns of the *Hamburger Nachrichten*. He expressed dissatisfaction with the Saratoga Agreement, holding that "it attached officially the same trustworthiness to a foreign certificate as to that heretofore only enjoyed by a domestic certificate."[70] To the retired Chancellor the American hog remained unacceptable.

American Pork and German Nationalism

At first glance the pork dispute seems to be merely a miniscule difference of opinion between the iron-willed German Chancellor and the tough meat bar-

---

[68]Wharton to Phelps, Washington, June 15, 1891, *ibid.*, p. 511.
[69]Keim, p. 74; also Stolberg-Wernigerode, pp. 167–68.
[70]Stolberg-Wernigerode, p. 168.

ons of Chicago. But behind the sour outbursts and the pens of satirical cartoonists on both sides was an accelerating economic rivalry which was to bring both countries on the path leading to World War I. The Second Reich and the United States were leaders in the New Industrial Revolution, the former contributing chemical miracles and the latter presenting the key of mass production. For a neo-mercantilist power such as united Germany, protection against foreign products, especially American goods and materials, was considered to be a *sine qua non* for national expansion and international prestige. American pigs may have been unpopular in Berlin, but American economic competition was a critical matter which had to be faced squarely by a country seeking not only a place in the business sun but also a role as a national power.

CHAPTER

6

National Character:
Bismarckian Authoritarianism

> I have your own fortune and the prevention of the marriage more at heart than the whole empire.
>
> Otto von Bismarck

Among German national traits—beyond the periphery of mere stereotypes—during the Bismarckian era was obedience to the proper authority, to *die Obrigkeit*. Where other peoples stimulated by the Enlightenment developed a tradition of dissent, the Germans were environmentally influenced to maintain respect for those in authority. This tendency to subservience and obedience took firm hold in family life, in the schools, and in the individual's relationship with his government. Historically, it has more than minor significance.

From 1862 to 1890 Otto von Bismarck, apostle of Prussian Junkerdom, was at the fulcrum of political power in Germany. In many ways Bismarck set the pattern for that type of authoritarianism which was to have dangerous consequences for his people. From his viewpoint the matter of control from above was simplistic: in the family situation all power emanated from the father, while the mother was delegated to the pleasures of *Kirche, Küche, Kinder* (Kirk, Kitchen, Kids). Similarly, on the national scale all power in the *Vaterland* (Fatherland), came from the proper authorities. Bismarck was convinced of the necessity for this kind of authoritarian rule: "I was never a democrat."

Adapted from Louis L. Snyder, "Political Implications of Herbert von Bismarck's Marital Affairs, 1881, 1892," *The Journal of Modern History*, vol. XXXVI, no. 2 (June, 1964), pp. 155–169.

This tradition of subservience to authority carried over into the 20th century and became one of the contributory causes for the rise of Hitlerism. To millions of Germans the *Fuehrer* represented state power obtained legally, and the authority of that power was not to be challenged. Vestiges of this weakness for authoritarian rule may be seen even in the post-1945 Federal Republic of West Germany, where for a time Konrad Adenauer, *"der Alte"* ("The Old Man") remained the father-figure in a new Germany which had already chosen the path of Western democracy. The trait seems to be disappearing in contemporary Germany.

How the elder Bismarck reacted in a family situation concerning the marital affairs of his son Herbert is described in this chapter. Even as an adult the son dared not challenge the authoritarian father. In microcosm this incident reflected that national characteristic in which the German citizen was trained to show deep respect for authority.

Bismarck's Pride and Prejudice

The aura of politics permeated the private life of Otto von Bismarck, founder and Chancellor of the Second German Reich. In 1881 he prevented the marriage of his elder son because the intended bride had too close a family relationship with his detested political enemies. In 1892, when his son was married finally in Vienna, he saw the nuptials marred by an imbroglio between William II and himself.

Herbert Count von Bismarck-Schönhausen[1] (1849–1904) entered the foreign service in 1874 at the age of twenty-five and remained with it until 1881. For the next several years he represented his father on diplomatic or special missions in London, Paris, St. Petersburg, The Hague, and Vienna. In London, as the unofficial link between his father and English political circles, he played an important role in the involved negotiations of the undercover struggle by which Germany obtained her first foothold in Africa.[2] In 1885 Herbert von Bismarck became undersecretary in the foreign office. From 1886 to 1890

---

[1]There is no full-length biography of Herbert von Bismarck. Wolfgang Windelband, who published a twenty-eight-page pamphlet, *Herbert Bismarck als Mitarbeiter seines Vaters* (Stuttgart, 1921), intended to write such a biography, but he never completed the work. Herbert von Bismarck's political speeches were collected and edited by Johannes Penzler, *Fürst Herbert von Bismarcks politische Reden* (Berlin and Stuttgart, 1905).
[2]See chapter 4.

he was foreign secretary, resigning along with his father in 1890. Later he served several terms in the *Reichstag*.

There was a deep mutual affection between father and son. What Herbert did with success was to act as an instrument of his father, almost an extension of the older man's personality. "This brings the character of his services almost down to the level of a private secretary, but he did work which no one else could have done and which was of the greatest importance to Bismarck."[3]

Ironically, the son's private happiness was ruined by a father who loved him deeply. After his unfortunate love affair in 1881, Herbert was left embittered, rough, and overbearing. The marriage fiasco was also responsible in all probability for his increasing addiction to alcohol, which helped bring about his death just short of his fifty-fifth birthday. Both the tragic affair of 1881 and Herbert's nuptials in 1892 brought down on the Bismarck family the wrath and ill will of its enemies. On each occasion the Chancellor, a man who knew how to hate, set himself violently against those he accused of attacking his honor and pride.

The Princess Elizabeth Carolath

For the details of the marriage tragedy of 1881 we are indebted to Prince Philipp zu Eulenburg-Hertefeld (1847–1921), for years an intimate of the Bismarck household and a close friend of Herbert von Bismarck. Wit and poet, musician and architect, Eulenburg had a distinguished military and diplomatic career, which came to an abrupt end in 1902 owing to continued ill-health. Later, he lived in retirement, broken only by his trial in 1908 on a morals charge.[4] Herbert looked upon Eulenburg as the only one who could understand his predicament; the elder Bismarck saw in Eulenburg the clever mediator who could persuade Herbert to abandon the woman he wanted to marry; and the deserted Princess Carolath bore Eulenburg no grudge because he wrote her such kind and touching letters.[5] Eulenburg's account of the affair

---

[3]William Osgood Aydelotte, *Bismarck and German Colonial Policy* (Philadelphia, 1937), p. 162.
[4]See Eulenburg's biography by his friend and literary executor, Johannes Haller, *Aus dem Leben des Fürsten Philipp zu Eulenburg-Hertefeld* (Berlin, 1924).
[5]*Memoirs of Prince von Bülow*, trans. Geoffrey Dunlop and F. A. Voigt (4 vols.; Boston, 1932), vol. IV, p. 483.

was published in a German periodical in 1923.[6] In the same year this posthumous article was incorporated into a volume of reminiscences.[7]

A painting by Gustav Richter shows Princess Elizabeth Carolath as a beautiful, radiant young lady with dark brown hair and blue eyes. According to his own account, Philipp Eulenburg fell in love with her when she was the eighteen-year-old Countess Elizabeth Hatzfeldt, daughter of Prince Hatzfeldt-Trachenberg and a member of what many regarded as an eccentric family. Her marriage to Prince Carolath-Beuthen had been an unhappy one. Herbert von Bismarck had met her in the seventies and had been promptly smitten. Courting her with typically Bismarckian fire, he urged her to divorce her husband and become his wife. The ambitious young lady was quite anxious to marry into the Bismarck family. She was immensely attracted by the idea of becoming the Chancellor's daughter-in-law.

Empress Augusta's Anti-Bismarck Fronde

Unfortunately for her future, Elizabeth Carolath was connected too closely with the anti-Bismarck fronde. One of her sisters was married to Baron Walther von Loë,[8] and the other to Count Alexander von Schleinitz,[9] treasurer of the court household. Both her brothers-in-law were leaders of the anti-Bismarck faction. The Chancellor regarded them as among his most bitter political enemies and calumniators. The Hatzfeldt-Loë-Schleinitz crowd, according to the Bismarcks, was a part of the Augusta party, the real front against the Bismarcks. To understand the Chancellor's violent reaction against his son's contemplated marriage, we must pause and take note of his feud with Augusta, in 1881 the German empress and queen of Prussia.[10]

---

[6]Prince Philipp zu Eulenburg-Hertefeld, "Herbert Bismarcks Tragödie," in *Deutsche Rundschau*, XLIX (1923), pp. 225–248. The article consisted mostly of letters exchanged between Herbert von Bismarck and Eulenburg. Before his death Herbert asked Eulenburg to destroy the correspondence. Eulenburg, however, anxious to reveal the role he had taken in the matter and interested in showing the extent of his relationship with the Bismarcks, arranged for publication of the correspondence after his own death.

[7]Prince Philipp zu Eulenburg-Hertefeld, *Aus 50 Jahren* (Berlin, 1923), pp. 81–107. This book was concerned primarily with Eulenburg's early life.

[8]See Walther von Loë, *Erinnerungen aus meinem Berufsleben* (Stuttgart and Leipzig, 1906).

[9]See *Aus den Papieren der Familie von Schleinitz* (Berlin, 1905).

[10]On Augusta see Heinz Bosbach, *Fürst Bismarck und die Kaiserin Augusta* (Cologne, 1936); *Kaiserin Augusta, aus ihrem literarischen Nachlass* (Berlin, 1912); F. Nippold, *Das Kaiser-Augusta Problem* (Leipzig, 1914); and H v. Petersdorff, *Kaiserin Augusta* (Leipzig, 1900).

Born the Princess of Saxe-Weimar, Augusta was a woman of great beauty, but dictatorial in manner. Until her death in 1890, the Chancellor had to bear what he called Augusta's "intolerable accessory and opposition government." His conflicts with Augusta he spoke of as "the hardest fought battles of my life."

The Bismarck-Augusta feud began as early as the revolution of 1848 at a time when Augusta had been married for nearly twenty years to Prince William of Prussia, brother of the king, Frederick William IV (1795–1861). As the king's madness became more evident, Augusta hoped that she and her husband would ultimately ascend the throne. In March 1848, after an unfortunate affair in which troops he once commanded fired on the people, Prince William fled to London. In the meantime, Bismarck, the young squire of Schönhausen, strongly royalist, came to Berlin to offer his services as well as his ill-armed peasants to the king "against the revolutionaries." Giving up the king as hopeless, he moved to obtain active orders from Prince William. He was referred to the princess. Bismarck then went to Potsdam, where he collided head-on with a conspiracy already under way.[11] Augusta, fearing that both the king and her husband had lost any possibility for power, decided to obtain the succession for her son. She negotiated for help from Georg von Vincke, leader of the moderate Liberal party in the Prussian chamber.[12]

In his memoirs, published fifty years later, Bismarck gave his own version of the encounter. Augusta, he wrote, refused to inform him of the whereabouts of her husband. She declared excitedly that it was her duty to defend her son's rights. Bismarck continued: "In the name of his party, and apparently

---

[11]On the Augusta-Bismarck meeting at Potsdam, see *Aus den Papieren der Familie von Schleinitz*, pp. 311, 314; Friedrich III, *Tagebücher von 1848–1866* (Leipzig, 1929), pp. 28, 30, 32; Leopold von Gerlach, *Denkwürdigkeiten aus seinem Leben* (Berlin, 1891–92), vol. I, pp. 146 ff.; G. Grundman, *Der gegenwärtige Stand der historischen Kritik an Fürst Bismarcks Gedanken und Erinnerungen* (Berlin, 1925), vol. I, pp. 11–12; R. Pahncke, *Die Parallelerzählungen Bismarcks zu seinen Gedanken und Erinnerungen* (Halle, 1914), pp. 22–24; and H. von Petersdorff, *Deutsche Männer und Frauen, Biographische Skizze* (Berlin, 1913), p. 271; and E. Marcks, *Bismarck und die deutsche Revolution, 1848–1851*, ed. W. Andreas (Stuttgart and Berlin, 1939), p. 23.

[12]Some years later Bismarck had a duel with Vincke, ostensibly over a parliamentary difference, but in reality, as Bismarck admitted later, because of the acrimonious difficulties in March 1848 concerning Augusta's plans. According to Erich Eyck, Bismarck detested Vincke because the latter was aware of his moral defeat in the meeting with Augusta at Potsdam. *"Legt man hingegen Augustas Darstellung zugrunde, so musste ihm die Erinnerung an seine Niederlage im Potsdamer Stadtschloss peinlich sein, und es versteht sich leicht, dass ihn tiefe Abneigung gegen den Mann erfullte, der vielleicht ihr einziger Mitwisser war"* (Erich Eyck, *Bismarck* [3 vols.; Erlenbach-Zürich, 1941], vol. 1, p. 190).

under instructions from higher quarters, Vincke was anxious to obtain my support for a move to induce the *Landtag* to ask the king to abdicate. The prince of Prussia was to be passed over, presumably with his own consent. The princess of Prussia was to be regent for her son during his minority. I . . . declared that I would counter any such proposal with one to take proceedings against its authors for high treason.''[13] Bismarck concluded: ''I never told Emperor William anything about this affair, not even at a time . . . when I could not help but look upon Queen Augusta as my opponent, although to remain silent was the hardest test to which my sense of duty and my nerves were put at that time in my life.''[14] Bismarck was not altogether innocent. It is probable that he came to see Augusta on behalf of Prince Charles, a younger brother of the king, a reactionary whom Bismarck would support to take over leadership in the counterrevolution. Augusta indignantly declined. She never forgave Bismarck for what she believed to be his support for an intrigue on behalf of Charles.[15]

From this point on the ambitious *Junker* and the strong-willed queen were bitter enemies. In Bismarck's letters and conversations there were many embittered attacks upon the woman he regarded as an obstacle both to himself and to the progress of Prussia-Germany. He was certain that his unwanted transfer from Frankfurt to St. Petersburg in 1858 was due to her machinations.[16] According to Max Lenz, Augusta opposed Bismarck's appointment as minister-president in 1862 because of ''his attitude in the March days of 1848, his reactionary views as diplomat and politician, and his frivolous and arrogant personality.''[17] In 1866 Augusta and her clique worked feverishly against the war with Austria. In Bismarck's view, Augusta's tactics in those days were definitely antinational.[18] According to Lothar Bucher, Bismarck's assistant, Augusta, in an outburst of pique following the end of the Franco-Prussian war, held up the victory celebration in Berlin for several weeks while

---

[13]Otto von Bismarck, *Die gesammelten Werke*, critical edition of *Gedanken und Erinnerungen* titled *Erinnerung und Gedanke*, ed., G. Ritter and R. Stadelmann (Berlin, 1932), vol. XV, p. 29.
[14]*Ibid.*, pp. 29–30.
[15]Eyck, vol. I, p. 89.
[16]See M. Duncker, *Politischer Briefwechsel* (Stuttgart and Berlin, 1923), p. 83; and H. Robolsky, *Die Damenpolitik am Berliner Hof. 1850–1890* (Berlin, 1897), p. 45.
[17]Max Lenz, *Geschichte Bismarcks* (Leipzig, 1902), p. 270; see also E. Zechlin, *Bismarck und die Grundlegung der deutschen Grossmacht* (Stuttgart and Berlin, 1930), pp. 252–256.
[18]See Loë, pp. 53 ff.; E. Marcks, *Kaiser Willhelm I* (Leipzig, 1897), p. 231; Alfred, Graf von Waldersee, *Denkwürdigkeiten* (2 vols.; Stuttgart and Berlin, 1922), vol. 1, p. 23; and J. Ziekursch, *Politische Geschichte des neuen deutschen Kaiserreiches* (3 vols.; Frankfurt am Main, 1925–30), vol. II, p. 413.

she took the cure at Baden-Baden.[19] On May 14, 1875, Bismarck, in a letter to Count Georg zu Münster, the German ambassador in London, complained about Augusta's private correspondence with Queen Victoria. He accused her of playing politics and of hampering the work of responsible ministers.[20] Bismarck suspected Augusta of passing state secrets to Princess Victoria, wife of Crown Prince Frederick, heir to the German throne. He was sure that Princess Victoria was giving these secrets to her mother, Queen Victoria. To the Chancellor this was treason.

The feud between Augusta and Bismarck became more intense when she and her adviser, Alexander von Schleinitz, joined hands to support the anti-Bismarck fronde. Schleinitz worked with Ludwig Windhorst[21] and Count Harry von Arnim[22] in opposing Bismarck and Bismarckian policies. All three were favorites of Augusta, who, through them, sought to embarrass the Chancellor.

Little wonder then that Bismarck regarded a marriage linking his adored son with the Augusta clique as a catastrophe to be avoided at all costs. His reaction was violent. Not only was the Princess Carolath a divorced woman, but she was also a Catholic. The father was unimpressed with the son's plea that his intended bride was willing to become a Protestant. In the Chancellor's view this intention was not sufficient to excuse the facts that the Augusta-Loë-Schleinitz cabal had conspired secretly against the Bismarckian political program, and that it had slandered and libeled the Bismarck family by circulating false rumors about it to the press. It was just too much. The angered

---

[19]It is probable that Bucher heard the story from Bismarck. Bucher recounted it: "In the spring of 1871 our troops were supposed to return early. The queen wanted to be present at the victory parade but would not end her cure at Baden-Baden. Therefore, a pause of four to five weeks, which cost our treasury nine millions" (M. Busch, *Tagebuchblätter* [Leipzig, 1899], vol. II, p. 417). See also Lucius von Ballhausen, *Bismarck: Erinnerungen* (Stuttgart and Berlin, 1920), p. 31; and Waldersee, vol. 1, p. 134.

[20]*Die Grosse Politik der Europäischen Kabinette, 1871–1914*, ed. J. Lepsius, A. Mendelssohn-Bartholdy, and F. Thimme (40 vols.; Berlin, 1922–27), vol. 1, p. 281.

[21]Ludwig Windhorst (1812–1891), a little man with a huge head and colossal mouth, was the parliamentary leader of the Catholic Centrist faction in the *Reichstag* and the Prussian Diet. A fierce political opponent, Windhorst aroused the savage enmity of Bismarck, who once said: "Hate is just as great an incentive to life as love. My life is preserved and made pleasant by two things—my wife and Windhorst. One exists for love, the other for hate" (Ziekursch, vol. II, p. 229).

[22]Count Harry von Arnim (1824–1881), a pro-French and pro-Catholic diplomat, had been a companion of Bismarck's youth. Arnim believed that he himself would become Chancellor one day. Arrested in 1874 for embezzling state papers, he avoided prison by leaving the country, but then published pamphlets attacking Bismarck for "personal jealousy." Condemned to prison for five years for treason and libel, he was allowed to return to Germany to be tried anew but died on May 19, 1881.

elder Bismarck would not allow this camarilla to invade the sanctity of his home. His wife, Princess Bismarck, added her agreement: "I'll fight tooth and nail to see that the society of Loë, Schleinitz and Hatzfeldt do not come to our table!"[23] The clash of wills left all three principals sick and miserable. When the Bismarck family physician, Dr. Eduard Cohen, visited the Chancellor on April 3, 1881, he found him to be suffering from a strong catarrh and in a high state of nervousness which the doctor attributed to Bismarck's "misunderstanding with his son."[24]

Herbert Bismarck's Dilemma

In early April 1881, when she heard the shocking news of Bismarck's frim opposition to her marriage, Princess Carolath fled to Venice, where she collapsed. "I was so sick," she wrote to Eulenburg on April 14, "that it was believed I wouldn't live, and even now I am so weak that I can scarcely take a few steps. . . . I shall try to regain my strength and seek to begin a new life."[25] The rejected lady maintained an embarrassed and inconclusive correspondence with Herbert. On April 20 Herbert urged Eulenburg to write to the Princess "because the poor woman has no one to whom she can talk from the heart."[26] He added that he intended to go to Venice in May. "When I come back, I shall make a final attempt with my father. My present feeling is that it is a matter of life and death, and what will happen God knows! I seem to be faced by the absolute impossibility of devoting to the Princess what remains to me of life."[27]

Father and son now had several painful interviews which left both shattered. At the first meeting, on April 28, 1881, the elder Bismarck, with tears in his eyes, informed his son that he was determined absolutely not to go on living if the marriage took place. At the second interview, two days later, Bismarck warned his son that it was incompatible with his honor that his name be connected with those of Hatzfeldt, Loë, and the others. He beseeched Herbert to remember that he did not bear the Bismarck name for himself alone, that anything which affected his father's name affected him and his

---

[23]Joachim von Kürenberg, *Johanna von Bismarck* (Berlin, 1935), p. 262.
[24]See Otto von Bismarck, *Die gesammelten Werke, Gespräche,* ed. W. Andreas (Berlin, 1926), vol. VIII, p. 404.
[25]Eulenburg, "Herbert Bismarcks Tragödie," p. 232.
[26]*Ibid.*
[27]*Ibid.,* pp. 232–33.

brother, William, as well. He would, therefore, oppose Herbert's marriage *"mit Zähnen und Nageln"* ("with teeth and nails").[28]

The Chancellor now placed additional pressure on his son. He was Herbert's superior in governmental service, and as such his permission was necessary for the marriage. He hinted at the possibility that Herbert might be disinherited if he went through with his plans. Herbert described this development in a plaintive letter to Eulenburg dated April 31, 1881:

> In the meantime, I am forbidden to leave the service. Therefore, I cannot marry without permission (there is no legal possibility until after the lapse of ten months). In addition, I must remember that I have nothing to offer the princess, since, according to the terms of the law of primogeniture, as recently changed with the emperor's approval, any son who marries a divorced woman is automatically disinherited. Since my father has nothing except the two great entailed estates, I should have no inheritance whatever. This would be all the same to me, since I would not live very long after the marriage anyhow; the split with my parents and their ruin would be the death of me.[29]

In the same letter Herbert wrote that his father had said again that "if the princess were to bear his name, it would drive him to suicide."[30]

A week later, on May 6, Princess Carolath wrote to Herbert that she expected him in Venice by the middle of May. She did not wish to live any longer. Herbert's father had no heart. She quoted the Bible: "For this cause shall a man leave his father and mother, and shall cleave unto his wife."[31] When apprised of the contents of this letter, the infuriated Chancellor demanded that his son pledge upon his honor that he would not go to Venice. If he made the pilgrimage, he would have to accept the company of his father. "I have your own fortune and the prevention of the marriage more at heart than the whole empire."[32]

The hapless Herbert was caught in a dilemma. He knew that it was impossible to keep the proposed journey to Venice a secret. The anti-Bismarck cabal would exaggerate the marriage hegira out of all proportion. The Bismarcks

---

[28]*Ibid.*, p. 235. The Chancellor was more satisfied with the marriage of his son, William, to Sibylle von Arnim of the house of Kröchlendroff on July 6, 1885. Bismarck and Sibylle's mother were brother and sister (see Kürenberg, p. 261).
[29]Eulenburg, "Herbert Bismarcks Tragödie," p. 236.
[30]*Ibid.*
[31]*Ibid.*, p. 237.
[32]*Ibid.*

would be ridiculed mercilessly, probably with cartoons showing the Chancellor in a gondola speeding to rescue his son from the arms of a designing woman.

Herbert bared his heart in his letters to Eulenburg. A selection of his thoughts reveals his terrible inner conflict. "I wonder whether or not I have lost my reason." "I feel that I am one of those unfortunates being torn apart by four horses." "I regard it as a point of honor that I should marry her, even though my love for her were gone." "I blame myself for all that has happened, and am loathsome to myself." "The rest of my life stretches out before me in prospect like an interminable avenue of trees leading to a flat, sandy waste."[33] As tactfully as possible, Eulenburg advised Herbert not to separate himself from his parents. Eulenburg equated filial loyalty with patriotism. "In all seriousness," he wrote, "I feared for the life of Prince Bismarck, whose health was degenerating. If the marriage took place, it would have meant the withdrawal of the Chancellor from all affairs of state and his retirement to Friedrichsruh to await death. . . . I did my duty with a bleeding heart."[34]

Embarrassing Aftermath

Princess Carolath herself ended the marriage plans. She wrote Herbert crisply that she despised him, and let him know through others that she would have nothing further to do with the house of Bismarck. Never again did she send a word, a letter, or a greeting to the man who had deserted her. "Suffering the fate of Ariadne," wrote von Bülow, "she was left to languish on Naxos."[35] Apparently, she retained her beauty for some time. She turned to a brilliant social circle in Venice, where natives and visitors alike were apt to point out her private gondola with the black-gold livery as belonging "to the woman scorned by the Bismarcks." She survived for thirty-three years in the Palazzo Modena, where she died in January 1914.

The outcome of the affair gave a tremendous amount of fuel to the anti-Bismarck camarilla. Herbert Bismarck was denounced as a shameful lout who

---

[33]*Ibid.*, pp. 237–45.
[34]*Ibid.*, p. 245.
[35]Bülow, vol. II, p. 114.

had arranged Princess Carolath's divorce and had then betrayed her. Said General von Loë, reacting with what he believed to be proper military spirit: "If Herbert were not the son of the Almighty Chancellor, he would be brought before a court of honor and it would be a farewell appearance."[36]

The Chancellor emerged shaken and scarred from the ordeal. A classic hater, he was caught between two conflicting emotions—his love for his son and his overwhelming hatred for his enemies, "that mob of vile conspirators." If there were a matter of honor concerned, then the honor of the Bismarcks was by far the weightier. Having won his victory, the elder Bismarck tried to dismiss it from his mind. In a letter dated December 27, 1881, to A. W. Hildebrandt, a former servant, he avoided details: "My sons are, unfortunately, not yet married. Herbert is at the embassy in London, and the youngest works here under me; both, thank God, are in good health, which, unfortunately, I cannot say about my wife."[37]

Herbert Bismarck was the real loser. The marriage tragedy left permanent scars. From a clever, confident, rising diplomat, aged thirty-two, he became a hard misanthrope who hated people and earned their contempt in return. He was never able to rid himself of feelings of guilt.[38] He was now open to accusations of cowardice. He was denounced as a weakling who was overpowered by fear of his father, as a selfish rascal who had no taste for being disinherited, and as a man completely lacking in a sense of independence.

New Marriage Plans

In the first week of April 1885 Herbert was at dinner with a rising figure in the German diplomatic service, Bernard von Bülow, when the latter told him of his desire to marry Countess Marie Dönhoff. "When he realized I meant what I said, [Herbert] seemed surprised, embarrassed, and at first, dumbfounded. Two conflicting emotions possessed him. On the one hand was his desire to show me he was my friend; on the other a very understandable envy that I was to know a happiness denied him.... He had loved Princess Elizabeth

---

[36]Kürenberg, p. 262.
[37]Otto von Bismarck, *Die gesammelten Werke, Briefe*, ed. W. Windelband and W. Frauendienst (Berlin, 1933), vol. XIV-2, p. 934.
[38]Bülow, vol. II, p. 14. "I am still convinced," Bülow wrote, "that the struggle through which he fought his way in those days left permanent traces upon Herbert, that the wound in his heart was never entirely healed."

Carolath passionately. He loved her still, and, I believe, never ceased to love her. He could never rid himself of a feeling that he had failed in the first great love of his life, that his behavior in this crisis had neither been wise nor quite correct."[39] Herbert tried to change Bülow's mind. While admitting that Countess Dönhoff was "gifted, truly good, and uncommonly charming," he pointed out that she was a foreigner, and German diplomats should not wed foreigners. "Besides she is a Catholic. . . . She is a friend of the Crown Princess, of Mimi Schleinitz, of Cosima Wagner, Frau von Helmholtz, and other women who hate my father. I do not think my father will give his consent to such a match. I cannot even advise him to. I shall even advise with all my energy against it."[40]

Bülow, understandably resentful, refused to tolerate this interference in his private life. He spoke plainly: "If consent to my marriage is withheld—a marriage from which I hope not only my own life's happiness but that of the woman I love—I shall resign." Shortly after this meeting Bülow was informed by Herbert: "My father will ask His Majesty's consent in person. As soon as this is granted the Empress will receive your wife in special audience."[41]

If the marriage fiasco of 1881 had political implications, Herbert Bismarck's actual marriage in 1892 produced an even greater political explosion. It seemed that both Bismarcks, father and son, were to have little relaxation or private peace in their lives. Now past the age of forty-two, Herbert decided that it was time to settle down. He realized that his father, now seventy-seven, wanted heirs for the male side of the family as well as a successor to Herbert in the princely Bismarckian line.

At the instigation of his father, Herbert became engaged to a Hungarian heiress, the Countess Marguerite Hoyos, whose mother was English and whose father was half-Austrian, half-Hungarian.[42] The elder Bismarck was delighted by the match. He had encouraged the courtship on the ground that a union of his eldest son with a representative of a people who owed him so much was desirable, thus repeating in the domestic life of the Bismarck family the alliance between Prussia and Hungary.[43]

---

[39]*Ibid.*, vol. IV, p. 586.
[40]*Ibid.*, pp. 586–87.
[41]*Ibid.*, p. 592.
[42]*Ibid.*, p. 587.
[43]F. P. Stearns, *The Life of Prince Otto von Bismarck* (Philadelphia, 1899), p. 405.

Bismarck and William II: A New Clash

On May 5, 1892, when the engagement was announced, William II sent this telegram of good wishes to Herbert:

> Best thanks for your friendly announcement and heartiest wishes for your happiness on the occasion of your engagement to Countess Marguerite Hoyos.
>
> WILHELM, *Imperator Rex*[44]

There was little spontaneity or warmth in this communication. Since Chancellor Bismarck's resignation on March 17, 1890,[45] the elder statesman and the blustering young emperor had engaged in a long-range personal vendetta. Smarting under his defeat, the ex-Chancellor not only resented the way in which he had been dismissed, but also was bitterly grieved in having his hopes for a "Bismarck dynasty" dashed to pieces. He had hoped that Herbert would be his successor in the chancellery.[46] Despite his battle with the Bismarcks, William II considered it to be good manners as well as good politics to pretend that he was delighted by the news of the forthcoming wedding.

The young emperor might not have been so quick to send congratulations had he known that the elder Bismarck himself intended to go to Vienna for the ceremony. The news brought excitement to Berlin. Word spread through the anti-Bismarckian court circle and among Wilhelmstrasse officials that the fallen Chancellor had sinister political designs in making the journey to the Austrian capital. One rumor had it that Bismarck on one occasion had remarked that he would "open the eyes" of Francis Joseph to the young Kaiser.[47] There would be a triumphant procession of the Bismarcks through German cities. Once in Vienna, the dangerous lion and his cub would be counted on to mend their political fences and prepare the way for a return to power. To the uncomfortable monarch and his advisers this was but an exten-

---

[44]Quoted in Siegfried von Kardorff, *Wilhelm von Kardorff: Ein nationaler Parliamentarier im Zeitalter Bismarcks und Wilhelm II, 1828–1907* (Berlin, 1936), p. 267.

[45]On Bismarck's dismissal see Hans Delbrück, "Bismarcks Entlassung," in *Vor und nach dem Weltkriege* (Berlin, 1926); E. Gagliardi, *Bismarcks Entlassung* (Tübingen, 1927); W. Mommsen, *Bismarcks Sturz und die Parteien* (Stuttgart, 1924); and K. F. Nowak, *Kaiser and Chancellor* (London, 1930). "Not a finger has been lifted, not a pen taken up, so far as individuals and journals in an independent position are concerned, to advocate Bismarck's continuance in office. The Iron Chancellor has lost his sureness of touch, he had begun to vacillate, while the will of the youthful and energetic ruler was coming more and more strongly into play" (*Vossische Zeitung,* March 18, 1890).

[46]Koppel S. Pinson, *Modern Germany* (New York, 1954), p. 284.

[47]O. Gradenwitz, *Bismarcks letzter Kampf, 1888–1898* (Berlin, 1924), p. 243.

sion of the concerted effort to arouse popular enthusiasm for the Bismarck dynasty, thus embarass the emperor, force him to oust General Leo von Caprivi, Bismarck's successor as Chancellor, and then recall Bismarck.[48]

Bismarck's own advisers, especially his confidential agent, Gerson von Bleichröder,[49] urged him not to make the trip and argued that it would be interpreted as a new venture into the political arena.[50] But the old man would not listen. Had not Herbert already ascertained that the Austrian emperor would receive him? Was he not assured of an audience and a welcome in Vienna? Further, as was the privilege of any father, he was determined to go to Vienna "to please the family of the daughter-in-law."[51]

When it became obvious that nothing could deter Prince Bismarck from making the trip to Vienna, it was decided at the highest level to stigmatize him officially as a person not to be received and also to arrange a social boycott of the family. On June 9, 1892, a letter signed by Chancellor Caprivi was dispatched to Prince Heinrich VII von Reuss, the German ambassador in Vienna:[52]

> After an audience with His Majesty, I inform Your Excellency of the following concerning the forthcoming marriage of Count Herbert Bismarck. The rumors of a reconciliation of Prince Bismarck and His Majesty do not take into account the

---

[48]Pinson, p. 284.

[49]Gerson von Bleichröder (1822–93) was a Jewish banker to whom Bismarck gave a general power of attorney to manage his property. Army generals, especially Count von Moltke, and the entire anti-Bismarck clique distrusted Bleichröder and sought to separate Bismarck from him. Herbert Bismarck shared this view on Bleichröder, whom he regarded as "an evil in himself" and as "that stinking brute." In a letter to Friedrich von Holstein sent from St. Petersburg on March 3, 1884, Herbert wrote: "My father on the whole knows that Bleichröder is a filthy swine, but it is absolutely necessary to remind him of the fact from time to time by obvious proofs, so that the impression is never temporarily erased. Bl., like most of his kind, is sometimes useful, but only if one treats them badly and keeps them in constant fear. I am afraid this does not happen often enough" (*The Holstein Papers,* ed. Norman Rich and M. H. Fisher [3 vols.; Cambridge, England, 1955–61], vol. III, p. 107). For a definitive treatment of the relations between Bismarck and Bleichröder, see Fritz Stern, *Gold and Iron: Bismarck, Bleichröder, and the Building of the German Empire* (New York, 1977).

[50]Gradenwitz, pp. 242–43, claims, on rather dubious evidence, that Bleichröder was the source for the rumor that Bismarck intended to visit Vienna on a political mission. According to Gradenwitz, Bleichröder was present in Friedrichsruh at the time; hence he obviously was the guilty one.

[51]*Memoirs of Prince Chlodwig of Hohenlohe-Schillingfürst,* ed. Friedrich Curtius (2 vols.; New York, 1906), vol. II, p. 446. According to A. O. Meyer, the original idea was to have the wedding at Fiume, the residence of the bride's parents, but it was changed to Vienna for the greater convenience of Bismarck (*Bismarck: Der Mensch und der Staatsmann* [Stuttgart, 1949], p. 691).

[52]See Horst Kohl, *Denkwürdige Tage aus dem Leben des Fürsten Bismarcks* (Leipzig, 1898), p. 93; and Karl Wippermann, *Deutsche Geschichtskalender* (Leipzig, 1885 ff.), 1892, vol. II, p. 26.

indispensable presumption of a first step upon the part of the Prince. But even if this did take place, the reconciliation could never go so far that public opinion would take it that the Prince had won any kind of influence in the leadership of national affairs. His Majesty requests Your Excellency that, should the Prince or his family make any approach to Your Excellency's house, you limit yourself to the conventional forms, and avoid accepting any invitation to the wedding. His Majesty will not accept any notice of the wedding. You are instructed to inform Count Kálnoky [foreign minister of Austria-Hungary] of this fact in whatever manner may seem best to you. These indications as to behavior apply to the staff of the embassy as well as to yourself.[53]

It is probable that Friedrich von Holstein,[54] from 1878 to 1906 counsellor (*Vortragender Rat*) in the political department of the German Foreign Office, had a hand in drafting this communication. Eulenburg's biographer, Johannes Haller, states categorically: "This unfortunate step was wholly Holstein's work."[55] Otto Gradenwitz wrote that Holstein had a double purpose in mind: to boycott Bismarck and at the same time to prepare the way for Eulenburg's appointment as ambassador in Vienna.[56]

On June 12, 1892, three days after the official dispatch had been sent to Vienna, William II sent a handwritten communication to Francis Joseph:

---

[53]*Reichsanzeiger*, July 7, 1892.

[54]Friedrich von Holstein (1837–1909) was, after Bismarck and William II, the most important personality in the political history of the Second Reich. Until he resigned he played a commanding role in the determination of German foreign policy. The traditional view holds that Holstein, when in 1874 a young diplomat attached to the German embassy in Paris, had been employed by Bismarck to report on the activities of Count Harry von Arnim (see n. 22). Holstein was obliged to testify against the accused in the Arnim trial. Therefore, it was further believed, Holstein, feeling himself disgraced, had withdrawn from society and had become a hermit-like recluse possessed with an undying hatred for Bismarck, who had ruined his life. Later Holstein worked against Bismarck so venomously that the ex-Chancellor turned against him as "that man with the hyena eyes." According to the journalist Maximilian Harden, Bismarck, when attacking the leaders of the New Course in 1890, stated: "I owe the Arnim scandal to Holstein; if he had not poisoned the well from the beginning, I would have gotten along with that talented comedian without an open conflict" (*Die Zukunft*, LV [1906] p. 458).

With the publication of *The Holstein Papers*, this traditional view has been revealed as somewhat unfair to Holstein. The new materials give a different version of Holstein's part in the Arnim affair: "Holstein's responsibility for the ruin of Arnim can be established only on a single point: he wrote letters to friends in the foreign ministry in which he pointed out Arnim's opposition to Bismarck's policy, and he recommended Arnim's transfer from Paris" (Norman Rich, "Holstein and the Arnim Affair," *Journal of Modern History*, XXVII [1956], p. 53).

[55]Haller, p. 110.

[56]O. Gradenwitz, *Akten über Bismarcks grossdeutsche Rundfahrt, Sitzungsberichte der Heidelberger Akademie der Wissenschaft, Philosophisch-historische Klasse*, (Heidelberg, 1921), vol. XII, p. 23. (Hereafter cited as Gradenwitz, *Akten*.) On Holstein's role in sending the Vienna dispatch about Bismarck see also Hans Delbrück, "Von der Bismarck-Legend," *Historische Zeitschrift*, CXXXIII (1926), p. 80; H. O. Meisner, *Der Reichskanzler Caprivi. Eine biographische Skizze* (Tübingen, 1955), pp. 713–17; and Helmuth Rogge, *Holstein und Hohenlohe* (*Stuttgart*, 1957), p. 387.

At the end of the month Bismarck goes to Vienna, ... in order to receive planned ovations from his admirers. ... You are aware that one of his masterpieces was the secret treaty *à double fonds* with Russia, which, negotiated behind your back, was annulled by me. Since his retirement, the Prince has carried on a most perfidious war against me and Caprivi, my minister. ... He seeks, with all the art and shrewdness he possesses, to twist matters so that the world shall believe that I am making advances to him. The main feature of his plan is that he has asked you for an audience. ... Therefore, I venture to beg you not to complicate my situation in my own country by receiving this unruly subject of mine before he has approached me and said *peccavi*.[57]

It was impossible to keep communications of this kind secret in the Berlin atmosphere, suffused as it was with gossip and intrigue.[58] The "unruly subject" soon learned about the contents of these two insulting letters. At first he reacted as if he were still a student at Göttingen: he would challenge Caprivi to a duel. The seventy-seven-year-old Bismarck would defend his name, rank, and honor. "But when I turned the matter over in my mind I remembered that I am an officer, and that the affair would be submitted to a court of honor composed of elderly generals. I should never have got him to face my pistol."[59] Still, it took great effort by the family to calm down the furious old man. Privately, Bismarck denounced the emperor's communication, which he called a *"Uriasbrief"* ("Uriah letter")[60] as "a contemptible piece of effrontery."

The Wedding in Vienna

The Bismarcks left for Vienna on June 18.[61] The *Norddeutsche Allgemeine Zeitung* announced erroneously that the former Chancellor and his party

[57]For the full text see Gradenwitz, *Bismarcks letzter Kampf, 1888–1898,* pp. 240–242.

[58]William II's letter to Francis Joseph was not published until 1919, after World War I, when it appeared in the *Österreichische Rundschau,* LVIII (1919), 109–10, and then only in fragmentary form. Bismarck, however, as he revealed quickly in the *Hamburger Nachrichten,* learned about the Kaiser's letter shortly after it was sent. See Gradenwitz, *Bismarcks letzter Kampf, 1888–1898,* pp. 244–245.

[59]Bismarck later told a guest at Friedrichsruh: "I still have a sharp eye up to 100 meters" (Meyer, p. 693).

[60]"Letter of Uriah" (II Sam. 11:15), a treacherous letter, importing friendship but in reality a death warrant. It refers to the biblical story of Uriah the Hittite, a captain in David's army, who was sent to the most dangerous area of the battle line, where he was killed. David then took as his wife Bathsheba, who had been Uriah's spouse.

[61]On Bismarck's journey to Vienna, see Hans Blum, *Fürst Bismarck und seine Zeit* (6 vols.; Munich, 1894–95), vol. VI, pp. 445–64; Kohl, pp. 93 ff.; Meyer, pp. 691–93; and Adolf von Westarp, *Fürst Bismarck und das deutsche Volk* (Munich, 1892).

would arrive in Berlin at the Lehrter station, whereas they actually came in at the Anhalter station. Nevertheless, a huge mob was there clamoring for a speech. "My duty is to be silent," said Bismarck. An onlooker countered: "When you keep silent, then will the stones speak!"[62] City officials met the Bismarck party at the station in Dresden. The city was in banners, the Bismarcks' private car covered with flowers. "Our unity is unbreakable," said the prince in a speech. That night, from his rooms at the Hotel Bellevue, he reviewed 13,000 torchbearers and 1,600 singers.[63] At 10:30 P.M. on the evening of June 19 the party arrived at Vienna, where the reception was so stormy that Bismarck and Herbert were nearly trampled by the crowds.[64] By the next day, however, it became obvious that there was an official and social boycott.[65] Unimportant mayors and representatives of prominent citizens did wait upon the Bismarck family, but there were no invitations from kings and princes.[66] The nobility, "the true aristocracy," remained aloof.[67]

Emperor Francis Joseph, unwilling to disturb political relations with Berlin, did not receive the Bismarcks at court.[68] Reuss found himself in an embarrassing position. He had been instructed not to receive the family. He was not even to allow the German *Gesangverein* in Vienna to take part in any demonstrations for the visitors.[69] Because he could not very well disobey his emperor, Reuss took to his bed and became diplomatically ill. However, his wife, daughter of Grand Duke Alexander of Saxony, proclaimed loudly that *she* was not in the diplomatic service; she would receive the ex-Chancellor and his family with great deference in her home.[70] On the afternoon of June 20 Bismarck left his card with Kálnoky at the Foreign Office.[71] That evening there was a gala party at the home of Count Palffy, a relative of the bride's family, with whom the Bismarcks were staying. The guests included Kálnoky, the ambassadors of Russia, England, and Italy, and the military attaché of the German embassy in Rome.[72]

The intended humiliation of the Bismarcks went to almost ludicrous propor-

---

[62]Blum, vol. VI, p. 445.
[63]*Ibid.*, vol. II, p. 446; Kohl, p. 94.
[64]Blum, vol. VI, p. 446.
[65]Ziekursch, vol. III, p. 71.
[66]Stearns, p. 405.
[67]Hohenlohe, *Memoirs,* vol. II, p. 446. See also Blum, vol. VI, p. 448.
[68]Arthur von Brauer, *Im Dienste Bismarcks* (Berlin, 1935), p. 354.
[69]Otto von Bismarck, *Die gesammelten Werke, Briefe,* ed. W. Windelband and W. Frauendienst (Berlin, 1933), vol. XIV-2, p. 1005.
[70]Brauer, p. 354.
[71]Kohl, p. 94.
[72]*Ibid.*

tions. Neither the resigned Chancellor nor his son was supposed to wear a military uniform because such attire could be worn in foreign countries "only with permission."[73] The old man was infuriated by this ban. "I don't know about rules on uniforms," he wrote to his son, William, "and I do not believe they are in effect. Think of it, at my age, to have to ask what I should wear!"[74] However, when Bismarck was driven to the church on the morning of June 21, he was dressed in the uniform of a cuirassier.[75]

Despite the plethora of premediated insults, the ceremony went off happily at noon on June 21 at the Helvetian Reform Church.[76] There was no official representation at the wedding. The ex-Chancellor gave a toast at the wedding dinner: "To the political unity of the two great powers."[77] At 5:00 P.M. that afternoon the couple, orange blossoms in hand, went off on their honeymoon.[78]

From Marriage Ceremony to Political Sparks

The elder Bismarck remained in Vienna for two more days. Despite his age, he visited the Prater, the Rathaus, and mounted the 158 steps of the Festsaal.[79] On June 23, aching for battle, he carried out his carefully made plan for revenge. In a long interview with M. Benedikt, editor of the *Neue Freie Presse*, he openly attacked the German government and accused it of stupidity:

> Austria, in the commercial treaty, has, of course, turned to account the weakness and ineptitude of our negotiators. This result must be ascribed to the fact that in our country men have come to the front whom I had formerly kept in the background—the reason being that everything had to be changed. . . . For my part, I am no longer under any obligations towards the personalities now in office, or towards my successor. All the bridges have been broken down. . . . The

---

[73]Bismarck, *Die gesammelten Werke, Briefe*, vol. XIV-2, p. 1006.
[74]*Ibid.*, Bismarck was so angered that he wrote only about uniforms in his letter to William. A postscript added: "If the ban exists, then it must be for street wear only, not for indoors, otherwise gentlemen from many lands would have to make more daily changes than they possibly could" (see *Bismarck's Briefe an seinen Sohn Wilhelm*, ed. W. Windelband [Berlin, 1922], p. 24).
[75]Blum, vol. VI, p. 447.
[76]Kohl, p. 94; Blum, vol. VI, p. 447.
[77]Blum, *loc. cit.*
[78]*Ibid.*
[79]Meyer, p. 693.

tie which used to connect us with Russia has been severed. Personal authority and confidence are lacking in Berlin.[80]

This tough talk resulted in an uneasy sensation in Berlin. Something had to be done to discredit the "garrulous old man." Eugen Richter,[81] leader of the Progressives, referred to legal paragraphs which could be used against Bismarck for this interview, and even reckoned how many years the ex-Chancellor would have to serve in jail.[82]

The return journey of the Bismarcks was made by way of Munich (June 24), Augsburg (June 26), Kissingen (June 27), Jena (July 30), Berlin (August 6), and Varzin (August 8).[83] The German public, aware of the shabby treatment accorded Bismarck in Vienna, greeted him with an outburst of enthusiasm.[84] Never in his active political life had the Junker of Friedrichsruh enjoyed such popularity. He was astonished: "My six weeks' journey was a triumphal tour—such as I had never dreamed. . . . Everywhere the people greeted me joyfully."[85] Crowds of many thousands met him at the railway stations. There were torchlight parades and choirs. Hans Blum, with commendable *Gründlichkeit,* reported that during his five weeks in Kissingen, Bismarck received 320 dispatches totaling 10,000 words.[86] At Jena, where the Bismarcks had breakfast, a golden tablet was placed on the wall: "Here lived Prince Bismarck on 30 and 31 July 1892."[87]

Bismarck exploited the situation with a series of political speeches.[88] He called the German people to war against their government. In the past, he admitted, the "inner building" of the Reich demanded a certain dictatorial activity: "Now, however, one need not look upon dictatorship as a lasting institution of a great empire."[89] According to Johannes Ziekursch, "the man who had done everything to lessen the influence of the *Reichstag* in the

---

[80]For the full text see Hermann Robolsky, *Bismarck, 1888–1898* (Berlin, 1899), pp. 278–86.

[81] Richter (1838–1906), one of Bismarck's most obstinate opponents, opposed the Chancellor on virtually every political matter. Bismarck despised him so much that he usually left the *Reichstag* chamber whenever Richter rose to speak (see H. Röttger, *Bismarck und Eugen Richter im Reichstage, 1879–90* [Bochum, 1932]).

[82]Robolsky, *Bismarck, 1888–1898,* pp. 286–87.

[83]Blum, vol. VI, pp. 449.

[84]Hans Blum, *Persönliche Erinnerungen an den Fürsten Bismarck* (Munich, 1900), p. 198. See also Ziekursch, vol. III, p. 171.

[85]Gradenwitz, *Akten,* p. 51.

[86]Blum, *Fürst Bismarck und seine Zeit,* vol. VI, p. 459.

[87]*Ibid.,* p. 463.

[88]See Raymond J. Sontag, *Germany and England, Background of Conflict, 1838–1894* (New York, 1938), p. 276.

[89]Ziekursch, vol. III, p. 71.

1880's, the man who had broken political parties, now spoke in terms of a majority in the *Reichstag.*"[90]

All Europe was amused by the press battle which followed. While the Bismarcks were in Kissingen, the *Norddeutsche Allgemeine Zeitung* sharply attacked the ex-Chancellor for his interviews and speeches. It recognized "with horror that his memory is failing him." It accused him of "wounding the monarchical sentiment and of undermining respect for the Kaiser."[91] Bismarck replied vigorously in the *Hamburger Nachrichten* that the attacks on him were "tasteless absurdities."[92] On July 7, 1892, Caprivi published the text of his June 9 communication to Reuss.[93] Undoubtedly, this "vassal-like act of loyalty" was an effort to turn the scorn of an angered public from the Kaiser to himself.[94] Every German now had the opportunity of reading how the new Chancellor had humiliated his predecessor.

Not all governmental figures were convinced that it was necessary to discredit Bismarck publicly. Count Paul von Hatzfeldt,[95] the German ambassador in London, counseled moderation. In a letter to Holstein from Ems on July 1, 1892, Hatzfeldt gave his opinion on the best way to handle the situation and added comments on the attitude of the public at this stage of the conflict:

Since you have not yet written to me, I assume that the storms of war have died away for the present and that His Highness has not started another offensive. This will still come, about that we must not deceive ourselves. In my humble opinion it will then be advisable *for the time being* to observe *great composure in the manner* of our replies and also to preserve the appearance that we are only acting in self-defense, and that only *with bleeding hearts* did we criticize the demigod of the past. Everything I see in the Press about public opinion strengthens me in this opinion. The situation obviously is that the great majority condemn H.H.'s action, and even his friends have little to say in his defense, but that everyone, including the vast number of impartial and honourable people, is painfully disturbed by the thought that a conflict could arise which would result in hurling from his pedestal the sole remaining representative of the great past. Therefore it

[90]*Ibid.*
[91]*Norddeutsche Allgemeine Zeitung,* June 27 and 28, 1892.
[92]*Hamburger Nachrichten,* July 4, 1892. The *Hamburger Nachrichten,* alone among the German newspapers, opened its columns to the fallen Chancellor.
[93] The July 7, 1892, edition of the *Reichsanzeiger* contained not only the Caprivi communication to Reuss but also the text of an article from the *Norddeutsche Allgemeine Zeitung* attacking Bismarck (see Paul Liman, *Fürst Bismarck nach seiner Entlassung* [Berlin, 1904], p. 112).
[94]See Fritz Hellwig, *Carl Ferdinand Fhr. v. Stumm-Halberg, 1836–1901* (Heidelberg-Saarbrücken, 1936), p. 442.
[95]Paul, Count von Hatzfeldt-Wildenburg (1831–1901) was state secretary in the Foreign Ministry, 1881–85, and ambassador in London, 1885–1901.

seems to me that moderation is called for; this will be all the easier to exercise because it will hardly be preserved by the other side. For should H.H. take up the cudgels he will hardly show moderation (which he has never known) and he himself will then probably supply the means for a severe counter-attack, which would then have the approval of the great majority of the nation.[96]

William II lost face in the struggle. Many Germans had regarded his virtual dismissal of Bismarck in 1890 as a hard but necessary action, indicative of the emperor's tact and genius. Now they were certain that William possessed neither tact nor genius. Paul Liman attributed the beginning of the estrangement of the German people and their emperor to the Uriah letter and its aftermath.[97]

Bismarck the Ultimate Politician

Both affairs revealed Otto von Bismarck as the complete political animal who seemed unable to draw any firm lines between his private and public lives. He regarded his victory over Princess Carolath in 1881 as a triumph over his political enemies. He had not permitted his son to become allied with the detested families in whose homes scandal was directed against the house of Bismarck. At the marriage of Herbert with Countess Hoyos the seventy-seven-year-old Bismarck, officially stigmatized by William II and his court circle, fought back vigorously to defend his name, rank, and honor. The effect on German public opinion was so strong that for a time there was real concern in the Wilhelmstrasse.

Mirror on German Nationalism

Herbert Bismarck's marital affairs, sad and tragic as they were for him, had additional significance. They reflected in miniscule an outcome of that form of authoritarianism which became a part of German nationalism. Fear of and

---

[96]*The Holstein Papers,* vol. III, p. 413. In a subsequent letter, dated July 10, 1892, also sent from Ems, Hatzfeld wrote: "I am afraid that in regard to His Highness things are developing as I expected and that he will not give up the struggle. Caprivi's position is now a good one, however, because even [Caprivi's] opponents will not follow the Prince through thick and thin" (*ibid.,* p. 415).

[97]Paul Liman, *"Herbert Bismarck: Ein Gedenkwort," Westermanns Monatshefte,* DLX, XVII (October, 1904), p. 431.

respect for authority existed in the German way of life at that time. All levels of German society, from the lowly office clerk to the successful son of the mighty Chancellor, were affected by this kind of subservience. It must be taken in account in any investigation of national character during the Bismarckian era.

The strength of the paternal bond was so great that the son had to desert the woman he loved and accept the appellation of ''cad,'' surely a humiliating epithet for a proud *Junker*. Little wonder that he turned to alcohol as a way out of his misery.

It would be wrong to assume that this kind of authoritarianism was solely and specifically German. Similar incidents have occurred in other countries, and others have shown this kind of paternal behavior. But subservience, discipline, and respect for authority, when added to other characteristics, gave the German national character of the late 19th century a special quality of its own.

CHAPTER

7

National Pride and Individual Eccentricity: Bismarck and the Lasker Resolution, 1884

My Lords, I am a Christian, but not as Reich Chancellor. When I get my ears boxed should I ask for a second blow?

Otto von Bismarck

When Edward Lasker, one of Bismarck's most persistent political opponents, died while on a visit to the United States, the American Congress, in a spirit of innocent good will, sent a resolution of sympathy to the German people. As was the diplomatic custom, the resolution was forwarded to the German *Reichstag* through the German Chancellor. Bismarck, in a classic display of arrogance, refused to accept the expression of condolence.

The action of the German Chancellor was due to a combination of national pride, bitter political sensitiveness, and sheer cussedness. Bismarck had little use for the English mode of political sportsmanship acquired on the playing fields of Eton or in the debating rooms of Oxford and Cambridge. He felt a deep aversion for his political opponents. He had only contempt for Ludwig Windhorst, leader of the Catholic Center Party and his opponent in the *Kulturkampf*. His aversion for Lasker was even greater.

Adapted from Louis L. Snyder, "Bismarck and the Lasker Resolution, 1884," *The Review of Politics*, vol. I, no. 1. (January, 1967), pp. 41–64.

Added to this political hatred was a somewhat perverted sense of national pride. In his early days Bismarck had been a Prussian rather than a German nationalist, but with the unification of Germany under Prussian auspices and with Prussian power dominant in the German state, the Chancellor was able to change his parochial nationalism into a broader form. Bismarck's resentment against the United States, a powerful rival in the Second Industrial Revolution, was being augmented at this time, especially in the matters of the pork dispute (see chapter 5) and compounding differences on naturalization and citizenship of German-Americans. He was in no mood for pleasantries from the American Congress. By interpreting a well-meant gesture from the American people as an unwarranted interference in German domestic affairs, Bismarck was giving way to his well-known sense of pique as well as to a clumsy interpretation of national pride.

The following study traces the story of how the German Chancellor handled the Lasker resolution.

Career of an Intellectual Politician

Edward Lasker, German parliamentarian, was born on August 14, 1829, in Jaroczin, a small village in the province of Posen, the Polish area of Prussia. The offspring of an orthodox Jewish family, the young man studied the *Talmud* and translated Schiller into Hebrew verse.[1] At first he showed a preference for philosophy and mathematics but turned later to history, political science, and law. Influenced by contemporary pre-Marxian socialism, he, together with his fellow students, fought on the barricades during the revolution of 1848. It became clear to him after passing his law examinations that he could not expect an adequate appointment in the civil service of reactionary Prussia.[2]

In 1853 Lasker went to England, where he studied English law and institutions and became an adherent of John Stuart Mill. There he also became the fiancé of the beautiful but ailing Maria Kinkel, daughter of the German refugee professor and poet, Gottfried Kinkel.[3] Young Maria died of consump-

---

[1]For Lasker's early years see Paul Wentzcke, *"Glaubensbekenntnisse einer politischer Jugend,"* in Paul Wentzcke, ed., *Deutscher Staat und deutsche Parteien, Festschrift für Meinecke* (Munich and Berlin, 1922), pp. 87–96.

[2]*Ibid.,* p. 194.

[3]Veit Valentin, "Bismarck and Lasker," in *Journal of Central European Affairs,* vol. III, no. 4 (January, 1944) pp. 4–5. Valentin intended his article to be a chapter of a biography, which would be published after the war under the title, *Edward Lasker or the Tragedy of German Liberalism,* but he died before he could complete the task.

tion before the marriage could take place. Deeply distressed, Lasker remained a bachelor for the rest of his life. He returned to his homeland in May 1865, happy "that I no longer need to be a foreigner and now can hear the German language."[4] A new era was opening as the Prince of Prussia became regent in 1858. Lasker now began a career as radical publicist, lawyer, political leader, and author[5] which made him one of the most important, popular, and distinguished political figures in Germany.

In 1858 Lasker became an assessor at the city court in Berlin. In 1865 and 1866 he was elected to the Prussian *Landtag,* where he represented Magdeburg (1868-1873) and Frankfurt am Main (1875-1879). From 1867 until his death he represented the district of Sonneberg-Saalfeld in the North German *Reichstag* and its successor, the German *Reichstag.* Until 1866 he belonged to the Progressive Party, and then became cofounder of the National Liberal Party.

A highly controversial politician throughout his career, Lasker was defended and attacked by colleagues and contemporaries. "Without doubt he was the best known and most popular member of the *Reichstag* when I entered that body," said Robert von Mohl in 1874.[6] Another *Reichstag* colleague, Dr. Carl Braun, reported in 1878: "Lasker was an attorney and could have had a rich practice but he scorned it. He loved neither wine, women, nor song. He had no hobbies. Parliament absorbed him completely. At night he studied the publications of the house, mornings he sat on committees, afternoons he attended meetings, evenings he spent with his party fraction."[7]

Historians echoed these favorable estimates. Johannes Ziekursch praised Lasker as "a sharp, juristic head filled with ice cold logic," a man with an unlimited drive for work, and a devastating debater.[8] William Harbutt Dawson judged him to be "a distinguished German statesman whose firm and consistent exposition of free and liberal ideas . . . have greatly promoted the social, political, and economic conditions of his nation."[9] Veit Valentin wrote that Lasker "had the character of an Aristides," that he was "a man of

---

[4]Wentzcke, *op. cit.,* p. 96.

[5]Among Lasker's major works were: *Zur Verfassungsgeschichte Preussens* (Leipzig, 1874); *Die Zukunft des deutschen Reiches* (Vortrag, 1877) (Leipzig, 1884); *Wege und Ziele der Kulturentwicklung* (Leipzig, 1881); *Biographie und letzte öffentliche Reden, mit Nekrolog von Karl Baumbach* (Stuttgart, 1884).

[6]Robert von Mohl. *Lebenserinnerungen* (2 vols., Stuttgart, 1902), vol. II, p. 176.

[7]Robert W. Dill, *Der Parlamentarier Eduard Lasker und die parlamentarische Stilentwicklung der Jahre 1867-1884* (Erlangen, 1956), p. 189.

[8]Johannes Ziekursch, *Politische Geschichte des neuen deutschen Kaiserreiches* (3 vols., Frankfurt-am-Main, 1925-1930), vol. II, p. 287.

[9]William Harbutt Dawson, *The German Empire, 1867-1914, and the Unity Movement* (2 vols.. New York, 1919), vol. II, p. 33.

great personal integrity, notable for his penetrating mind and his gifts as a writer."[10] Otto Becker referred to Lasker's "sarcastic dialectic and his masterly intellectualism."[11]

Other historians saw Lasker in a more unfavorable light. Charles Lowe, who published a biography of Bismarck three years before the Chancellor's death, described Lasker as "the learned and laborious little Jew."[12] Frank P. Stearns, in a biography published a year after Bismarck's death, denounced the mud-throwing against Bismarck in the days of the May Laws and the *Kulturkampf* (1875) and made this charge: "The socialistic Lasker made himself particularly conspicuous in this dirty work."[13]

Confrontation with Bismarck

To Otto von Bismarck, founder of the Second German Reich and German Chancellor, hate was just as great an incentive in life as love.[14] He developed a deep hatred for Lasker, whom he dubbed "the sickness of Germany."[15] The battle of words between the two men was carried on "with unsurpassed personal bitterness, irritability, and grim vindictiveness."[16] Bismarck resented Lasker as the chief-of-staff of the National Liberals, and as a political *enfant terrible*.[17] "Lasker and his followers annoy me," said Bismarck, "and then at the decisive moment act quite differently from what I ought to expect of them."[18] Bismarck complained in later years that he could never pass a bill without a "Lasker amendment," that gave his bill a more liberal flavor than he liked.[19]

---

[10]Veit Valentin, *The German People*, tr. Olga Marx (New York, 1946), p. 489.

[11]Otto Becker, *Bismarcks Ringen um Deutschland* (Heidelberg, 1958), p. 375.

[12]Charles Lowe, *Prince Bismarck, An Historical Biography* (2 vols., London, 1885), p. 375.

[13]Frank P. Stearns, *The Life of Prince Otto von Bismarck* (Philadelphia, 1899), p. 294.

[14]Ziekursch, *op. cit.*, vol. II, p. 229.

[15]On January 25, 1875, in conversation in Berlin with *Reichstag* delegate Christoph von Tiedemann and the historian Heinrich von Sybel, Bismarck said: "Lasker is really a state sickness; he is more of a plant louse than Windhorst" (Otto von Bismarck, *Die gesammelten Werke* [Berlin, 1923 ff.], vol. VIII, p. 139).

[16]Ziekursch, *op. cit.*, vol. II, p. 360.

[17]On May 15, 1894, in conversation at Friedrichsruh with Regierungsrat Heinrich von Poschinger and the historian Heinrich von Sybel, Bismarck said: "In the long run there could be no lasting alliance with the National Liberals. The main cause of our break was the *enfant terrible* Lasker" (Bismarck, *Die gesammelten Werke*, vol. IX, p. 387).

[18]Heinrich von Poschinger, *Conversations with Bismarck*, ed. Sidney Whitman (New York, 1900), p. 113.

[19]Erich Eyck, *Bismarck* (3 vols., Zürich, 1941–44), vol. III, p. 44.

In his memoirs, *Gedanken und Erinnerungen,* Bismarck had little to say about the man he detested. He reprinted a letter dated August 4, 1879, to the Bavarian king in which he denounced both Lasker and Eugen Richter as revolutionaries "whose inflammatory harangues to the propertyless classes were so clear and naked that advocates of monarchy could have nothing in common politically with them."[20]

It would be incorrect to attribute Bismarck's hatred for Lasker to anti-Semitism. The adult Bismarck discarded anti-Semitism as a reactionary prejudice of his youth. He regarded Ferdinand Lassalle as one of the most brilliant of men; he employed Gerson von Bleichröder as his confidential financial agent and gave him power of administration for the Bismarck properties; and Dr. Eduard Cohen remained his physician and friend. Bismarck entrusted both his health and his property to Jews. The traditional prejudices of his class persisted to some extent. To his Boswell, Moritz Busch, Bismarck on occasion referred to "the little Jew Lasker,"[21] and once wrote to Busch about "Bambergé, Laskère, and Rickèrt," the accents indicating something foreign about these Jews.[22] But Bismarck added that "these Jews are not dangerous: they don't go to the barricades and they pay their taxes conscientiously."[23]

Underneath the cold exterior the Chancellor may have had a small sense of admiration for Lasker. One day he said jokingly to him: "I'll wager that we shall one day become colleagues." Lasker replied earnestly with a witticism that Bismarck could appreciate: "Does Your Highness really have the intention of becoming an attorney?"[24] When at a tea party one of the guests became sarcastic about Lasker and accused him of uttering a total of 927,745,328 words in parliamentary debate—"154 times as many words as the whole of the Old Testament," Bismarck was not amused. He astonished the company by remarking that "a good lawyer easily makes a good Minister of Public Worship, either Falk or Lasker."[25]

Bismarck's enmity for Lasker was due primarily to the Chancellor's opposition to every attempt to strengthen parliamentary power in Prussia and Germany. He told Moritz Busch that Lasker, like the National Liberals, and especially the left wing, was not national but liberal and particularistic. To

---

[20]Otto von Bismarck, *Gedanken und Erinnerungen* (3 vols. in 1, Stuttgart and Berlin, 1928), p. 326.
[21]Moritz Busch, *Tagebuchblätter* (3 vols., Leipzig, 1899 ff.), vol. II, p. 565 ff.
[22]*Ibid.*, vol. III, p. 9 ff.
[23]*Ibid.*
[24]Carl Braun, *Randglossen zu den politischen Wandlungen der letzten Jahre* (Bromberg, 1878), p. 161.
[25]Poschinger, *op. cit.*, pp. 263–264.

that he was opposed.[26] And Bismarck complained to Dr. Cohen: "I cannot rule with such men as Lasker and Forckenbeck."[27]

There could be no lasting conciliation between these men of opposing sentiments. Bismarck and Lasker had dissimilar socio-economic backgrounds. On the one side was the legal-minded constitutionalist Lasker, representative of the capitalist world, purveyor of the ideas and ideals of the Enlightenment. On the other was the *Junker* opportunist, the Prussian statist, who resented any attempt to check or break his power. The early mutual respect of these two men finally degenerated into hatred. Veit Valentin described the competiton in a somewhat oversimplified passage:

> They had nothing in common, the little Jew of Jaroczin and the reactionary *Junker* of old Prussia who became a revolutionary, a destroyer, a master of international intrigue, the builder of the new German Reich, the creative genius of the period, the man of destiny, the pioneer of the German future.... The development of his feud is an amazing chapter of German political psychology.[28]

During the early part of his political career, Lasker headed a majority which supported Bismarck for the best in German constitutional and legal life. He entered into a kind of *entente cordiale* with Bismarck in October 1866, on the occasion of the "indemnity" debate. This concerned the government's infringement of the constitution since 1862 by spending funds without legal sanction. The German Progressive Party split into two on the issue: twenty-four members of the moderate right wing of its parliamentary section, headed by Lasker, Forckenbeck, and Bennigsen, announced their complete accordance with the aims of Bismarck's foreign policy. This marked the birth of the National Liberal Party, which, as chief spokesman of the middle class, was to take a leading part in building the new Reich in the next generation.[29]

Thus the political relationship of the two men began on a plane of mutual admiration. This was true despite the fact that in supporting the constitution of the North German Confederation, Lasker made it clear that he desired for the Chancellor a position equivalent to that of the English Prime Minister.[30] A clue to the later clash came on April 1, 1870, Bismarck's birthday, when

[26]Busch, *op. cit.*, vol. II, p. 587 ff.

[27]Bismarck, *Die gesammelten Werke*, vol. VIII, p. 497.

[28]Valentin, "Bismarck and Lasker," *op. cit.*, pp. 401–402.

[29]On the party split see Otto Pflanze, *Bismarck and the Development of Germany: The Period of Unification, 1815–1871* (Princeton, N.J., 1963), pp. 330–31; Fritz Löwenthal, *Der preussische Verfassungsstreit, 1862–1866* (Munich, 1914), pp. 302 ff.; Martin Spahn, *"Zur Entstehung der nationalliberalen Partei,"* *Zeitschrift für Politik*, I (1907–1908), 302 ff.; and Gordon A. Craig, *The Politics of the Prussian Army, 1640–1945* (Oxford, 1955), p. 177.

[30]Erich Eyck, *Bismarck and the German Empire* (London, 1950), p. 148.

Lasker sharply criticized what he called a miscalculation (*Verrechnung*) of 30,840 *talers* in war costs. Bismarck angrily replied that Lasker in his speech had made a number of needle pricks against his person (*"eine Anzahl von Nadelstichen für meine Person mit aufgenommen"*), and he denounced such "oratorical arabesques."[31] Busch reported that a few days later, on April 4, 1870, Bismarck for the first time expressed a wish to render the "Lasker fraction" innocuous and thus split the National Liberals.[32] Bismarck was further angered when, on January 7, 1871, Lasker, while discussing the new constitution in the Prussian Diet, criticized Bismarck's knowledge of jurisprudence.[33]

From 1873 to 1878 the personal relations between the two men remained on a level of courtesy, though there was touchiness in the background. In early 1873 Lasker made several sensational speeches of great eloquence in the Prussian Diet in which he demanded an investigation of grave malpractices by well-known aristocrats and high officials in the matter of railway concessions. Lasker's arraignment resulted in the resignation of Count von Itzenplitz, Minister of Commerce, a rare instance in the parliamentary history of Prussia in which public opinion forced the king to dismiss one of his ministers. It also led to the pensioning of Privy Councillor Hermann Wagener, founder of the conservative *Kreuzzeitung* and one of Bismarck's intimate friends.[34] Lasker was beginning to earn Bismarck's total enmity.[35]

In June 1873 Lasker further annoyed Bismarck by complaining of the government's method of submitting bills to the *Reichstag* without adequate speed and preparation. In an angry speech Bismarck accused Lasker of being extremely skilled in sharpening his arrows and then dipping them, not exactly in poison, but in some acid liquor. "I must protest any distinction between the government and the people. We are all the people. I protest when anyone monopolizes the name of the people and tries to exclude me from it."[36]

---

[31]Bismarck, *Die gesammelten Werke,* vol. II, p. 115. The debate took place at a session of the *Reichstag* of the North German Confederation on April 1, 1870.

[32]Busch, *op. cit.,* vol. I, p. 25.

[33]*Stenographische Berichte über die Verhandlungen des Hauses der Abgeordneten* (Berlin, 1871), pp. 150–51.

[34]Cf. Lowe, *op. cit.,* II, 392–93. Lowe added: "Of these malpractices Herr Lasker, a Jew, undertook the exposure all the more readily, as the delinquents were not members of his own speculating and gambling race, but blood-proud Junkers and titled Christians" (p. 392). Thus the historian Lowe, like many Germans of the day, tended to make Lasker responsible for the financial crash of 1873. See also Valentin, *The German People,* p. 488.

[35]Lasker's speeches on the railway scandals made an enormous impression throughout Germany and raised his popularity to a pinnacle. See Eyck, *Bismarck,* vol. III, pp. 63–64.

[36]*Stenographische Berichte über die Verhandlungen des Reichstages* (Berlin, 1873), June 16, 1873, p. 1178.

In the autumn of 1874 Lasker began work with a *Reichstag* committee on a series of Judicature Acts for establishing uniform legal tribunals and procedures throughout the Empire. Bismarck could not very well object to Lasker's brilliant work in this capacity. but there were increasing areas of friction. When in 1876 Bismarck laid before the *Reichstag* a bill directed against the Socialists, his measure was denounced by Lasker for its elastic clauses (*Kautschuk,* or India-rubber paragraphs) and it was defeated.[37] When on April 3, 1877, the Grand Duke Friedrich von Baden, in an interview with Lasker, discussed Bismarck's work unfavorably and even hinted at the possibility of the Chancellor's resignation,[38] Bismarck began to concentrate his hatred of the National Liberals on Lasker's person.[39]

The uneasy period of neutrality ended and the two men broke into open enmity in 1879 when Bismarck inaugurated his new protective tariff policy. Lasker opposed him sharply at every stage as bitter scenes occurred in the *Reichstag* with Lasker directing shafts of ridicule at Bismarck and the latter striking back with acid criticism at his tormenter.[40] Matters were not helped when Bismarck's son, Herbert, was defeated by Lasker for a *Reichstag* mandate for Meiningen.[41]

Bismarck was a chivalrous political fighter in other cases,[42] but he could not bring himself to tolerate Lasker. There was no other politician as effective

---

[37]Lowe, *op. cit.,* II, 406. In 1878, following an attack on the life of the emperor, Bismarck obtained legislation directed against workers' associations, publications, and rights of meeting. Lasker called these anti-Socialist laws "a political and juridical monstrosity." See Ralph Flenley, *Modern German History* (London, 1959), p. 278.

[38]Ludwig Bamberger, *Bismarcks grosses Spiel, Die geheimen Tagenbücher Ludwig Bambergers,* ed. Ernst Feder (Frankfurt-am-Main, 1932), p. 321.

[39]Valentin, "Bismarck and Lasker," *op. cit.,* p. 408.

[40]*Ibid.,* pp. 409–410. See also Dill, *op. cit.,* pp. 172–175; and Eyck, *Bismarck,* vol. III, pp. 286–287.

[41]Valentin, "Bismarck and Lasker," *op. cit.,* 410; Eyck, *Bismarck,* vol. III, pp. 357–58. In the elections of 1879 Herbert Bismarck, with the blessings of his father, had deliberately stood for a Reichstag seat from Meiningen in order to silence Lasker inside "Lasker voting territory" with the ring of the Bismarck name. Herbert was soundly trounced.

Herbert Bismarck had used these tactics once before. He was a Conservative candidate for Lauenberg in the *Reichstag* elections of July 17, 1878. His campaign was singularly inept, characterized by overconfidence and a somewhat tactless treatment of the voting public. Herbert identified his candidacy with his father's views. "As to my other views, you know all about them, my position relative to my father, the Reich Chancellor, and you will understand that I identify my political position with his. This is well-known to you. I won't bore you with clarifying my program and I won't ruin your lovely afternoon." The overconfident Herbert was defeated in a close contest, polling 3,894 votes against the National Liberal candidate, Dr. Hammacher, who received 4,276 votes. See Johannes Penzler, ed., *Fürst Herbert von Bismarcks politische Reden* (Berlin und Stuttgart, 1905), p. 8.

[42]For example, Bismarck never broke off his personal relations, not even during the most emotional stages of the *Kulturkampf,* with his fierce political enemy, leader of the Catholic Center Party, Ludwig Windhorst (1812–1891).

as Lasker in attacking Bismarckian domestic policies. Lasker thoroughly understood the constitution, Reich legislation, military law, and every phase of German political life. He was effective in pinpointing before the public Bismarck's antiparliamentarianism, anticonstitutionalism, and opportunism. For Bismarck, Lasker meant permanent political danger.

Lasker's Death in New York

In the summer of 1883, the frail Lasker, worn out by his labors, journeyed to the United States in search of rest and health. He visited New York, Chicago, and Washington, where, at the opening of Congress, German-Americans gave him a warm ovation. In Galveston he lived as a guest of his brother, Moritz Lasker, who had emigrated from Germany to Texas and had become a successful business pioneer. He was present as a German guest of honor in September 1883, when the Northern Pacific Railway was completed to join east and west.[43]

During the evening of January 4–5, 1884, Lasker had dinner with the banker Jesse W. Seligmann in his New York residence. While on the street on his way home, Lasker complained of illness and within a few minutes was dead of a heart attack.[44]

The news of Lasker's death was received with sorrow in Germany. The *Reichstag* Vice President and later Minister, Lucius von Ballhausen, commented: "With him ends one of the most important and for a time the most popular parliamentarian of the new Reich. He was next to Bismarck and Bennigsen after 1870 the most frequently mentioned name in the *Reichstag.*"[45] The *Berliner Boersen Courier,* Progressive, lauded Lasker for his "personal disinterestedness," his "pure character," and his "devotion and unselfishness."[46] Even Conservative newspapers joined in tribute. The *Berlinische Zeitung* spoke of Lasker as "in the true sense of the word a

---

[43]Dill, *op. cit.,* p. 200.

[44]There were extensive reports of the death in *The New York Times,* January 6, 1884; the *New York Tribune,* January 6, 1884; and the *New Yorker Staats-Zeitung,* January 6, 1884. Lucius von Ballhausen believed the death to have been caused by typhus (Freiherr Lucius von Ballhausen, *Bismarck-Erinnerungen* [Stuttgart, 1921], p. 278), while Dr. Zinn, a psychiatrist and early political friend of Lasker, attributed the collapse to nerve fever (Bamberger, *op. cit.,* pp. 272–273). However, after an autopsy performed by four physicians in New York, it was revealed that Lasker's death was due to a combination of four diseases: (1) degeneration of the blood vessels; (2) two spots of softening of the brain; (3) dilation and fatty degeneration of the heart; and (4) edema of the lungs. (*The New York Times,* January 7, 1884.)

[45]Lucius von Ballhausen, *op. cit.,* 278.

[46]January 7, 1884.

self-made man."[47] The *Berlin Post* (Conservative) praised Lasker's "very extraordinary oratorical talents and remarkably steady industry" as well as his "growing flood of popularity."[48] The *Neue Preussische Zeitung* (Conservative and Protestant) described Lasker as "a man of uncommon genius, who was also imbued with an idealism that ever aims at the best."[49]

The American press was unanimous in praise of the dead parliamentarian. The *New York Tribune* called him "preeminently the greatest lawyer" and concluded that "German liberalism loses one of its most distinguished leaders."[50] An editorial in *The Nation* stated that the German people had lost one of their truest and purest as well as most useful servants. "Lasker will be remembered in Germany not only as a brilliant orator and wise legislator, but as a man of unspotted purity of life, of the warmest patriotism, and of that unquestioned disinterestedness of motive which makes a public character especially dear to the popular heart."[51]

Despite the widespread paeans of commendation, when the funeral services, burial ceremony, and public meetings were held in Berlin at the end of January and beginning February, attended by some 5,000 persons, not a single representative of the federal or state governments or of the *Bundesrat* put in an appearance. No one doubted that Bismarck had forbidden such persons to take part in the services.[52]

"The U.S. House of Representatives Resolves. . . ."

On January 9, 1884, Thomas P. Ochiltree, member of the House of Representatives from Texas, introduced the following resolution:

> *Resolved,* That this House has heard with deep regret of the death of the eminent German statesman, Eduard Lasker.

---

[47] January 7, 1884.
[48] January 8, 1884.
[49] *Ibid.*
[50] January 6, 1884.
[51] *The Nation,* XXXVIII, No. 967 (January 10, 1884), pp. 28–29. The editorial was unsigned but *Poole's Index to Periodical Literature, Jan. 1, 1882–Jan. 1, 1887* (New York, 1938), p. 250, attributed it to Carl Schurz.
[52] Eyck, *Bismarck,* vol. III, p. 378. Correspondent F. Rapp reported to *The Nation* from Berlin on "Official Indignities to Lasker" and noted that the American government was not officially represented. A leader of the Prussian *Landtag,* a Mr. von Koeller, gave as a reason for his absence the "arrogant and anonymous German-American Turners and radicals of Cincinnati, Louisville, and other cities who had, in rather unbecoming terms, entreated him to have sufficient courage to take part in the proceedings." Lasker had been a member of the Prussian *Landtag* for fifteen years. *The Nation,* XXXVIII, no. 974 (February 28, 1844), pp. 184–185.

That his loss is not alone to be mourned by the people of his native land, where his firm and constant exposition of and devotion to free and liberal ideas have materially advanced the social, political, and economic condition of those peoples, but by the lovers of liberty throughout the world.

That a copy of these resolutions be forwarded to the family of the deceased as well as to the minister of the United States resident at the capital of the German Empire, to be by him communicated through the legitimate channel to the presiding officer of the legislative body of which he was a member.[53]

Bismarck Declines

The resolution was considered and adopted without objection. It was expected that the address of sympathy would be handed over to the German *Reichstag* through the usual diplomatic channels. The American ambassador in Berlin, Aaron A. Sargent, in routine manner sent it on to Bismarck, the German Chancellor and responsible Foreign Minister. Bismarck declined to transmit the resolution to the *Reichstag* and sent it back to the United States through the German ambassador in Washington to Secretary of State Frelinghuysen with an expression of regret. He was not in a position to agree with the expressed judgment in the resolution, hence he could not present it to the Emperor.[54]

The American press reacted angrily. An editorial in the *New York Tribune* reflected the widespread indignation about Bismarck's "fantastic performance, malicious, resentful, and ill-mannered [which] dishonors himself and his government."[55] A few weeks later the same newspaper stated that Bismarck's action "serves to remind national legislators of the futility of making any incursions into the realm of foreign politics even when they are influenced by generous motives."[56]

Meanwhile, on January 27, the Executive Committee of the Liberal Union of the *Reichstag* sent a letter to the House of Representatives expressing its "warmest thanks" for the Lasker resolution:

> *Berlin, January 27, 1884*
> The undersigned executive committee of the Liberal Union has the honor to express, at the request of all its members who are today present from the various parts of the German Empire, to the House of Representatives at Washington its

---

[53]*Congressional Record*, 48 Cong., 1st sess. (January 9, 1884), p. 329.
[54]Bismarck's action became known almost at once, although the formal return of the resolution to the House of Representatives was not made until March 7, 1884 by the German ambassador in Washington. (*The New York Times*, March 8, 1884.)
[55]*New York Tribune*, February 17, 1884.
[56]*New York Tribune*, March 3, 1884.

warmest thanks for the resolution which they have passed in honor of Eduard [*sic!*] Lasker, its late leader and friend.

The Liberal Union combines with this acknowledgment of its thanks the most heartfelt wishes for the welfare and prosperity of the powerful and progressive United States of America, and for the strengthening and further development of the mutual friendship between both nations.

The executive committee of the Liberal Union:

L. BAMBERGER
RUECKERT
V. FORCKENBECK
K. SCHRADER
G. V. BUNSEN
FRIEDRICH KAPP[57]

This letter touched off a lively debate in the House, in which Mr. Deuster of Wisconsin lauded the communication as "a condemnation of the discourteous, if not contemptuous attitude which Prince Bismarck has seen fit to assume toward the principal legislative body of a friendly nation."[58]

A few days later there was a dramatic sequel. At the 2nd sitting on March 7 of the 4th session of the 5th legislative period of the *Reichstag,* President Albert von Levetzow called for memorials for deceased delegates. Immediately Heinrich Rickert, Independent Liberal, "in the name of the numerous friends of the deceased delegate Lasker" expressed his gratification to the House of Representatives of the United States for its resolution. This was greeted with calls of "Oho!" from the Right and lively "Bravos!" from the Left. The chairman declared Rickert out of order. Wilhelm Freiherr von Hammerstein, Conservative and chief editor of the *Kreuzzeitung,* rose to protest against "the misuse of the tribune for a political demonstration." Eugen Richter, leader of the Progressives, angrily denounced the "unauthorized meddling" ("*die unbefugte Einmischung*") of the Reich Chancellor. In the midst of shouts and bell ringing by the chairman, the Imperial Secretary of the Interior, Heinrich von Boetticher, passionately defended his chief on the ground that Bismarck was not subject to criticism by members of the *Reichstag.* Richter replied that the Chancellor most assuredly was open to such criticism. After further bitter exchanges the president closed the session.[59]

---

[57]*The New York Times,* February 29, 1884.
[58]*Congressional Record,* 48 Cong., 1st sess. (February 28, 1884), 1464.
[59]*Deutscher Reichstag, Stenographische Berichte,* March 7, 1884, 9–12. See also Eyck, *Bismarck,* vol. III, pp. 378–379; Dill, *op. cit.,* p. 202; and *The New York Times,* March 8, 1884.

On March 10, Secretary of State Frederick T. Frelinghuysen "replied to the insult" (in the words of *The New York Times*) by declining courteously to take back the Lasker resolution.[60] That same day an angered Congressman, a Mr. Hiscock, offered another resolution calling for a reiteration of regret at the death of Lasker:

> Whereas it has come to the knowledge of this House that a communication from it to the Parliament of the German Empire, entirely friendly in its intent, respectful in its character, and sent through the regular channels of international communication, has been arbitrarily intercepted and returned to the Department of State of the United States by the person now holding the position of Chancellor of the German Empire: Therefore, [be it]
> *Resolved,* That this House cannot but express its surprise and regret that it should be even temporarily within the power of a single too-powerful subject to interfere with such a simple, natural, and spontaneous expression of kindly feeling between two great nations, and thus to detract from the position and prestige of the crown on the one hand, and from the rights of the mandataries of the people on the other.
> *Resolved,* That this House does thereby reiterate the expression of its sincere regret at the death of the late Edward [*sic!*] Lasker and of its sympathy with the Parliament of the German Empire, of which for so many years he was a distinguished member.[61]

This resolution was referred to the Committee on Foreign Affairs, where it was buried.

Now thoroughly annoyed, Bismarck on March 12 journeyed from Friedrichsruh to Berlin, and the next day, at the 4th sitting of the spring session, delivered an angry speech defending his action. In scathing words he attacked Lasker amidst cries of "Shame!"

Bismarck commenced by recognizing the good intentions of the American House of Representatives.[62]

> I should have refrained from mentioning this matter, except for the manner in which the *Reichstag* has discussed it, and for the charge of interference made by Herr Richter. The relations of Germany and America have always been good. The Government has constantly tried to cultivate them. Ever since I have been

[60]*The New York Times,* March 11, 1884.
[61]*Congressional Record,* 48 Cong., 1st sess. (March 10, 1884), 1766.
[62]Condensed from Bismarck, *Parlamentarischen Reden,* ed. Wilhelm Böhm and A. Dove (Stuttgart, Berlin, Leipzig, n.d.), vol. XIII, pp. 143–165. Bismarck's speech ran for 22 pages in text form. See also Heinrich von Poschinger, *Fürst Bismarck und die Parlamentarier* (3 vols. Breslau, 1894 ff.), vol. III, p. 127, and Adolf Wermuth, *Ein Beamtenleben* (Berlin, 1922), p. 54.

Minister the relations between the two countries have been satisfactory. After the war with Austria in 1866 and after the Franco-Prussian War, America gave numerous proofs of sympathy, not only with the prosperity of the Empire, but also with the person of the Chancellor. Nothing has occurred to disturb these good relations. From the outset I regarded the resolution regarding Herr Lasker as an expression of the good feeling of the American Congress toward Germany, the good feeling which has been promoted and cultivated by myself.[63]

With the groundwork thus laid, Bismarck began to explain his action.

I would have presented the resolution to the *Reichstag* had I not been prevented by its form. It was not confined to a general expression of sympathy, but it expressed the conviction that Herr Lasker's labors had been very useful to Germany. This clause was directed against the policy, which, in the Emperor's name, I have been pursuing for years. Now, the question arises whether Herr Lasker was right. If he was, then the Emperor's policy, my policy, was wrong. Herr Lasker belonged to an opposition group, who made immense capital out of Herr Lasker's merits.[64]

At this point Bismarck was interrupted by loud cries of "Pfui!" and "Shame!" from the Left. He turned indignantly toward the quarter from which the cries came, and advancing, shouted:

The cry of "Shame!" is an insult to me, and demands from me the protection of the president. I hope the anonymous slanderer will give his name. He should have cried "Shame" on those who carried on political intrigues at Herr Lasker's grave. As Chancellor, I can do nothing, of course, without the Emperor's approval, and I could not be expected to ask his permission to present such a resolution to the *Reichstag*. Herr Lasker introduced himself in America as the champion of German freedom against a Government of despotic tendencies impersonated in the Chancellor.

Am I to make myself my enemy's postman? Even on the assumption that Americans are not intimately acquainted with our circumstances, the American minister at Berlin, or some other official who possessed sufficient knowledge might have sent a confidential warning against conferring on me the part of postman. This was not done. There I instructed Herr Eisendecher, the German minister at Washington, that I could not possibly forward the resolution.

The resolution, moreover, did not emanate from Congress, but only from the House of Representatives. I never intended to annoy America or disturb our relations. I am simply unable to make the opinion of Herr Lasker, adopted by the

---

[63]Bismarck, *Parlamentarischen Reden*, vol. XIII, p. 145.
[64]*Ibid.*, p. 147.

American House of Representatives, my own. My desire is that the good relations that have subsisted between the two countries for a century may still
continue. My action was forced upon me by the abuse to which I was subjected
here at home as a consequence of the vote of the House of Representatives.
Prussia has withdrawn all temptations from other powers to interfere in the affairs
of America and to recognize the Southern states. Indeed, Prussia might still claim
the merit of having prevented a recognition by the benevolent attitudes she
maintained.[65]

Bismarck then went on to say that from his knowledge of the political past
and the industrial development of the German people, he could not accept the
judgment that Lasker's "firm and constant exposition of and devotion to free
and liberal ideas have materially advanced the social, political, and economic
condition of those peoples." ("That means us," Bismarck said amidst laughter.)

"I cannot submit this resolution because I must take on a judgment which I
cannot regard as true."[66] Bismarck recalled the making of the German constitution and he charged that in everything Lasker did he made it worse. He
accused Lasker of sabotaging the work of Rudolf von Bennigsen, leader of the
moderate faction in the National Liberal Party, "my political and personal
friend." He accused Lasker of turning the whole Liberal fraction to the Left.
"Shall I be thankful to the gentleman for that? Or shall I become the organ of
praise for him? I cannot forgive all this."[67]

Delegate Haenel of the University of Kiel, leader of the Progressives, arose
to say that it was a matter of record that Lasker had spoken well of Bismarck
while in America. It was also a matter of profound regret that Prince Bismarck
should have uttered no single word in praise of Lasker. People are accustomed
to reserve proof for the living. Why had not Bismarck spared the dead?[68]

Bismarck retorted that he had not sat in judgment on the dead, but those
who had tried to glorify the dead had done so. He denied the alleged friendli-
ness of the Lasker party toward him. Herr Lasker had consistently and persis-
tently opposed him. "My Lords, I am a Christian, but not as Reich Chancellor. When I get my ears boxed should I ask for a second blow? . . . In principle
Lasker was my friend, in fact he was my enemy; one does not cancel the other
out. He did praise me, but he fought me."[69]

[65]*Ibid.*, p. 149 ff.
[66]*Ibid.*, pp. 154–155.
[67]*Ibid.*, p. 157.
[68]*Ibid.*, p. 160.
[69]*Ibid.*, p. 161.

Angered, sarcastic, Bismarck ended his speech repeating what he had already said, accusing his political enemies of trying to injure him through the mouth of a dead man. If his enemies, he thundered, thought he would take all this without reacting, they were making a mistake.

Reaction in the United States

When news of Bismarck's speech reached the United States, there was an explosion of indignation. The American press reacted angrily, with the exception of the *New York Herald,* which found the speech "an unusually full and comprehensive explanation." "The Prince is somewhat illogical in comparing himself to a postman, . . . but aside from such small defects it is a good and vigorous and courteous presentation of his opinion, and ought to mollify the American Eagle."[70]

But most Congressmen were not appeased. They reacted with bitterness: "nonsensical" (S. S. Cox); "simply absurd" (Hewitt); "Bismarck is the foremost representative of the principle of absolutism, to which this government is opposed" (Rice); "A great big statesman made a great big mistake" (Gov. Curtin, chairman of the Foreign Affairs Committee and ex-minister to Russia). Congressman Ochiltree, who had introduced the original Lasker resolution, was thoroughly incensed: "It is a complete hodge. . . . There never was an intention to do more than compliment the people of Germany by paying our tribute of respect to one of Germany's greatest men."

A few Congressmen defended Bismarck, notably a Mr. Deuster, a German-American member of the Foreign Affairs Committee. Mr. Kasson, ex-minister to Austria, believed that "Prince Bismarck evidently regarded his refusal as a purely internal question."[71]

On March 19 the Committee on Foreign Affairs reported to the House on the Lasker matter. It stated that the original resolution of January 9 should have been received and transmitted by Bismarck in the same spirit of cordiality and goodwill by which it was prompted, but the Committee refrained from "expressing an opinion as to whether the course pursued by the authorities of the German Empire in regard to them was not in accordance with the proprieties governing the internal relations of said empire, as a matter not within its province of consideration." The Committee then complimented the State

---

[70]*New York Herald,* March 14, 1884.
[71]*The New York Times,* March 14, 1884.

Department for its "dignified position" in the Lasker matter. The Hiscock resolution of March 4, it stated, contained language that "under present circumstances was superfluous and irrelevant and not necessary to vindicate the character or dignity of this House."[72]

The Committee on Foreign Affairs then presented a final resolution which read:

> *Resolved.* That the resolution referring to the death of Dr. Edward Lasker, adopted by the House on January 9 last, was intended as a tribute of respect to the memory of an eminent foreign statesman who had died within the United States, and an expression of sympathy with the German people, of whom he had been an honored representative.
>
> *Resolved.* That the House, having no official concern with the relations between the executive and legislative branches of the German Government, does not deem it requisite to its dignity to criticize the manner of the reception of the resolutions or the circumstances which prevented them reaching their destination after they had been communicated through proper channels to the German Government.[73]

This set off a full-scale debate in the House. Mr. Cox of New York said that Bismarck "has insulted this Republic," and suggested that the right way to dispose of the matter was "to lay the whole business on the table and get rid of it." On the motion there were 83 ayes and 125 noes.

Exasperated beyond endurance, Mr. Ochiltree of Texas asked for and obtained the floor. "This," he said, "is an American House of Representatives, and not a *Reichstag.*"[74] He deeply deplored the report of the Committee on Foreign Affairs: "It is not becoming, sir, to the dignity of this body to enter into any explanations whatever as to the meaning of the original resolution: it speaks for itself. The semi-apologetic tone is unworthy of the Representatives of this great nation."

Ochiltree then went far beyond the fifteen minutes allotted him by the Speaker. He lauded Lasker, "a man of proscribed and persecuted race," who had elevated himself to a high position in his country. "I do not believe there was another German so profoundly versed in the great principles of Anglican and American liberty as was Dr. Lasker." "Suppose Matthew Arnold, Lord Coleridge, or Herbert Spencer, none of whom ever wrote anything surpassing

---

[72]*Congressional Record,* 48 Cong., 1st sess. (March 19, 1884), 2073.

[73]*The New York Times,* March 20, 1884. In reporting the news story *The New York Times* editorialized in its news columns by accusing the Foreign Affairs Committee of attempting to "rectify the blunder" committed by the House with its original resolution. The newspaper reported a "general interest in getting out of this scrape."

[74]*Congressional Record,* 48 Cong., 1st sess. (March 19, 1884), p. 2073.

Lasker's lectures to the working classes or his powerful essays on constitutional or budget questions, were to die in the same way. Would a resolution of condolence have been regarded with disfavor?" "To compliment Lasker was to rebuke the Prince Chancellor, a courtier, cold, haughty, . . . ever a subtle flatterer and sycophant to royalty, . . . a man possessed of intense selfishness—the alcohol of egoism."

Ochiltree insisted that he had introduced the original resolution with the approval of a member of the Foreign Affairs Committee. "Little one reckons when throwing a garland into the open grave of one who had done only good to his fellow-men whether the act would be repelled with the thrust of a bayonet."[75] He quoted Andrew White, president of Cornell University, on Lasker: "As a statesman, few equaled him in the work of adjusting society to a new time."[76] And had not Carl Schurz said: "Where is the nation that would not be proud to name him among their own?"[77]

Ochiltree then went on to dissect the government of Germany with emphasis upon its despotic character and its claim of constitutional government. In repetitious phrases he denounced Bismarck for attempting to ascribe ulterior motives to this mere act of courtesy, this simple display of goodwill, and for charging that the passing of the resolution was aimed at interference with the political affairs of Germany. He closed with praise for "Eduard Lasker, the friend of constitutional liberty."[78]

Other speakers took the floor. Mr. Deuster of Wisconsin and Mr. Phelps of New Jersey, both members of the Committee on Foreign Affairs, expressed their resentment of Bismarck's action.[79] Throughout the debate members referred again and again to "dignity becoming the House of Representatives." The resolution was finally adopted. After the vote Congressmen congratulated each other on what they regarded as a satisfactory and final disposition of the provoking Lasker affair.[80]

A Compendium of Motives

The incident thus ended with a residue of ill-temper and sullenness on both sides. What were the causes of Bismarck's unexpected and ungracious action?

---

[75]*Ibid.*, p. 2074.
[76]*Ibid.*, p. 2075.
[77]*Allgemeine Zeitung*, Munich, January 26, 1884.
[78]*Congressional Record*, 48 Cong., 1st sess. (March 19, 1884), p. 2079.
[79]*Ibid.*, p. 2080.
[80]*The New York Times*, March 20, 1884.

As in most matters concerning the German Chancellor, there is no simple explanation but rather a compendium of motives, each of which contributed to Bismarck's decision not to accept the resolution.

1. Bismarck had only contempt for Lasker as a political enemy. Lasker was much too intelligent, much too able, much too dangerous. The Chancellor despised the dead Lasker as much as he resented the live Lasker. He had no use for the principle of *De mortuis nil nisi bonum:* let others wallow in the usual obituaries and sudden praise for the dear departed. "This most loyal servant of the Emperor did not respect the Higher Majesty of death and history."[81]

2. Rightly or wrongly, Bismarck believed that he would have to get the Emperor's permission before he could transmit the resolution to the *Reichstag,* and to get this permission he would have to accept and recommend the contents of the resolution. This was the explanation he gave to Freifrau von Spitzemberg, a visitor at Friedrichsruh, on February 15, 1884, shortly after he had returned the resolution. He added: "After thirty years' experience I can say that Lasker is not a great man and benefactor of the German people."[82]

3. From the very beginning Bismarck was convinced that the Lasker resolution had been the result of a scheme originated inside Germany by his political foes. When, on March 22, 1884, he received an address from the workingmen of Marggabowa thanking him for his action in the Lasker affair, Bismarck replied that the recognition of Herr Lasker's merits included a condemnation of the policies of the German Government and that this was known to the *German originators* of the resolution.[83] Bismarck was certain that his political opponents were using even Lasker's death to continue the struggle against his own policies. The resolution was therefore a political document and he would treat it as such.[84] The German press supported his accusation that Lasker's death was being used for political purposes.[85] He

---

[81]Valentin, "Bismarck and Lasker," *op. cit.,* p. 415.

[82]From Frau von Spitzemberg's unpublished diary, in Bismarck, *Die gesammelten Werke, VIII,* 501.

[83]*The New York Times,* March 22, 1884.

[84]This was the view of Moritz Lasker, the brother who accompanied the remains of Edward Lasker to Berlin for the funeral. In an interview he said: "Bismarck, having discovered the grave mistake in excluding all official recognition at the funeral services of Dr. Lasker, seized upon this resolution which, in contrast with his own action, had met with the warm sentiment of the German people, to give it the importance of a political document, and by returning it to weaken the influence of the friendly sympathy which existed between the two nations, in behalf of the ideas which Dr. Lasker lived to advocate and support." (*New York Tribune,* February 26, 1884.)

[85]F. Rapp, correspondent for *The Nation,* reported that for some weeks the Lasker affair was a sensation throughout Germany. "All the hounds of the Reptile Fund have been let loose to

would therefore strike back at those who were attacking him through a dead man.

4. Bismarck had never forgiven Lasker, the out-and-out free trader, who found it impossible to remain in the National Liberal Party after Bismarck began his protectionist policy in 1879 by instituting a corn duty.[86] When in 1880 Lasker announced his decision to leave the party and enter a parliamentary group called the Secessionists, he was denounced in diatribes by an angry Bismarck.[87] In Bismarck's eyes this was desertion and he would never honor a deserter.

5. Bismarck could not bring himself to forgive or forget the fact that Lasker had defeated his adored son Herbert in the elections at Meiningen in 1879. This was a grievous blow to Bismarck's clan instincts. After Lasker's victory Bismarck lodged complaints with the government of Saxe-Meiningen and with the Duke of Saxe-Meiningen concerning *Landrat* (district governor) Baumbach who, Bismarck charged, had used his influence to insure Herbert's defeat.[88]

6. A clue to another possible motive may be found in the *Norddeutsche Allgemeine Zeitung,* Bismarck's newspaper, which, on March 10, 1884, three days before Bismarck delivered his speech before the *Reichstag,* associated the Lasker resolution with the pork dispute between Germany and the United

manifest their meanness coupled with ignorance.'' (The press bureau of the Prussian Ministry of the Interior and a similar organization of the Imperial Home Office furnished numerous journals with complete articles gratis. Such communications appeared simultaneously throughout the country. Radical and Socialist opponents labeled this the "Reptile Press," which, they said, was inspired in wholesale manner by Bismarck.)

Rapp went on to report that the *Norddeutsche Allgemeine Zeitung* denounced the Lasker resolution as interference in German home matters and described the incident as an American electioneering trick, a means by which the House of Representatives was seeking "to maintain its power at the next presidential elections." Further, the paper stated flatly that the resolution was composed by members of the *Reichstag* "who write and speak English" and that it was sent to Washington with directions to have it adopted at once and sent back to the Chancellor. *The Nation,* XXXVIII, no. 797 (March 20, 1884), p. 251.

[86]Stimulated by the agrarian crisis of the 1870's, Bismarck switched from *laissez-faire* protagonist to advocate for protection to assure a new source of revenue for the Reich and to use tariffs as a weapon of foreign policy. The first tariff law was passed by the *Reichstag* on March 12, 1879 by a vote of 217 to 117. On the changes in Bismarck's economic policies see Oswald Schneider, *Bismarck's Finanz- und Wirtschaftspolitik* (Munich, 1912); Joseph B. Esslen, *Die Politik des auswärtigen Handels* (Stuttgart, 1925); and Wilhelm Röpke, *German Commercial Policy* (New York, 1934). In Alfred Vagts's view the agrarian encounter between the United States and Germany "received its diplomatic-ideological clarification or darkening through Bismarck's (agrarian-unchivalrous) bearing at the death of Lasker in 1884." Alfred Vagts, *Deutschland und die Vereinigten Staaten in der Weltpolitik* (2 vols., New York, 1935), vol. I, p. 1.

[87]Eyck, *Bismarck,* vol. III, p. 379.

[88]Valentin, "Bismarck and Lasker," *op. cit.,* p. 409. Baumbach sued his local adversaries for slander, and von Swain, chairman of the Bismarck election committee, was found guilty and sentenced.

States. "American newspapers," it reported, "forget that a short time previously an unmistakably retaliatory bill in regard to pig-meat was presented to
Congress."[89] In 1880 Bismarck had precipitated a quarrel with the United
States by banning the importation of American pork and pork products on the
ground that American meat was infected with trichinosis.[90] German interests
applied pressure for total exclusion of American pork, while American meat
packers protested that their own methods were as careful as German procedures and that American pork was healthful.[91] Bismarck himself regarded the
prohibition of American pork as necessary for the success of his protectionist
tariff policy.[92] The notoriously thin-skinned Chancellor resented such sarcasm
as expressed in cartoons in American publications.[93]

7. A complicating factor in the dispute was Bismarck's animosity toward
Aaron A. Sargent, who had been American ambassador in Berlin since March
2, 1882, and who had collided with Bismarck on the pork issue. Bismarck had
had cordial relations with previous American ministers,[94] but he disliked
Sargent, whom he believed guilty of conducting his office in the spirit of
American party politics.[95] Sargent aroused the Chancellor's anger by his
outspoken criticism of Germany's "unfriendly discrimination" against
American pork.[96] Already *persona non grata,* Sargent added fuel to the re-

[89]*Norddeutsche Allgemeine Zeitung,* March 10, 1884.

[90]See chapter 5.

[91]See Jeanette Keim, *Forty Years of German-American Political Relations* (Philadelphia, 1919),
p. 68.

[92]In July 1894, Bismarck told an American journalist: "It is absolutely necessary for us people of
Europe to protect ourselves in time against your competition, for whenever the point arrives that
the United States is not checked in its inroads on our agriculture, complete ruin will overtake our
land-holding classes. It was the knowledge of American competition, with which, without protective lines, we are unable to cope in our smaller and older and poorer lands, which dictated my
agricultural policy." Wolf von Schierbrand, *Germany: The Welding of a World Power* (New
York, 1902), p. 354.

[93]See *Frank Leslie's Illustrated Newspaper,* March 1, 1884.

[94]From 1862, when Bismarck became Minister-President and Minister of Foreign Affairs of
Prussia, to 1890, when he resigned as German Chancellor, there were ten American ambassadors
in Berlin: Norman B. Judd (Illinois, appointed in 1861), Joseph A. Wright (Indiana, 1865),
George Bancroft (New York, 1867), J. C. Bancroft (New York, 1874), Bayard Taylor (Pennsyl-
vania, 1878), Andrew D. White (New York, 1879), Aaron A. Sargent (California, 1882), John
A. Kesson (Iowa, 1884), George H. Pendleton (Ohio, 1885), and William Walter Phelps (New
Jersey, 1889).

[95]This view was supported by Otto Graf zu Stolberg-Wernigerode in his *Germany and the United
States in the Era of Bismarck* (Reading, Pa., 1937), pp. 152–165. Stolberg-Wernigerode accused
the American ambassador of receiving his political information from Bismarck's political opponents, and deprecated Sargent's earlier experience as journalist and as politician in the House of
Representatives.

[96]On March 10, 1883, the *New Yorker Handels-Zeitung* published an article, supposedly by
Sargent, dated January 1, 1883, in which it was intimated that the prohibition of American pork
had been dictated by German agrarians. Sargent explained to Washington that his views had been

sentment against him when he was required by the duties of his office to deliver the Lasker resolution to Bismarck.[97]

The Reptile Press, reflecting Bismarck's attitude, broke into bitter denunciations of Sargent. The *Deutsche Tageblatt* attacked him for his relations with the Progressives,[98] and accused him of being "a corrupt speculator and railroad swindler, laden with curses of numberless victims."[99] The *Norddeutsche Allgemeine Zeitung* accused Sargent of "going for information to the Free Trade, Liberal, and radical parties."[100] Other German newspapers accused Sargent of intimacy with Georg von Bunsen, *Reichstag* delegate from 1871–1887[101] and Bismarck's political enemy.[102]

The American press vigorously defended Sargent. The *New York Tribune* in an editorial complained of Bismarck's treatment of the United States Minister at Berlin and denounced "the gross and deliberate disrespect to the government which appointed him, and whose honored and trusted agent he is."[103] In another editorial the same newspaper insisted that "Mr. Sargent was not in the remotest degree responsible for the Lasker resolution, which he had transmitted merely as a clerical function."[104] *The New York Times* reported from Berlin that members of the diplomatic corps were highly indignant at the brutal attack on Sargent.[105]

8. Finally, for Bismarck the entire affair was an affront to the "national dignity" of the German people. These were the exact words he used when he was informed that members of the diplomatic corps in Berlin were highly indignant about the attacks on Ambassador Sargent. At this time he made it clear that Sargent's appointment and continued service were inconsistent with Germany's "national dignity" and that Sargent's "journalistic agitation" and his relation with German opposition parties made it imperative that he be recalled.[106] To the German Chancellor, German nationalism was a euphemism for his own political power.

---

distorted (*Foreign Relations, 1883*, Part I (Washington, 1884), 377–78 and 381–82), and in an interview with the *Boersen-Kurier* denied that he had written any such article for the *New Yorker Handels-Zeitung* (*New York Herald*, May 2, 1883).

[97]Stolberg-Wernigerode stated that "on such occasions the Chancellor's self-control seems particularly admirable." Stolberg-Wernigerode, *op. cit.*, p. 158.

[98]*Deutsche Tageblatt*, February 20, 1884.

[99]*The Nation*, XXXVIII, no. 977 (March 20, 1884), p. 251.

[100]*Ibid.*, p. 252.

[101]Erich Eyck, *Bismarck*, vol. 1, p. 424.

[102]*The New York Times*, March 14, 1884.

[103]*New York Tribune*, February 21, 1884.

[104]*Ibid.*, March 9, 1884.

[105]*The New York Times*, March 14, 1884.

[106]*Ibid.*

Any or all of these motives may have played a role in Bismarck's behavior in the Lasker affair. Lasker, in Bismarck's eyes, had committed the unpardonable political crime of opposing Bismarckian policies. Not even death could salve the Chancellor's personal hatred for a man he suspected of seeking his overthrow.

In England death made a difference. It was customary for the leaders of all political parties to give a respectful memorial talk on a deceased opponent, as for example Gladstone's stirring speech on Disraeli, or Salisbury's moving address on Gladstone. Perhaps this represented in miniature the wide gulf in political *Kultur* between Gladstone's England and Bismarck's Germany.

Relation to German Nationalism

One of the distinguishing characteristics of nationalism in general and German nationalism in particular is the disposition of those in political power to spring automatically to the defense of what is called "national honor." Bismarck, the supreme egotist and the classic hater, identified himself with a sense of national honor. He would have no one interfere with matters of strictly national concern. Lasker, in his view, was a dangerous domestic political foe and one who stood in the way of the Chancellor's plans for heightened national prestige. No one, not even the estimable American House of Representatives, had the right to tell him—the German Chancellor—how to run German affairs.

Bismarck's motivations in the Lasker resolution case were, indeed, pluralistic and complex, and among them was an extreme sensitivity to national sovereignty and outside interference. The graciousness and goodwill expressed by the American Congress had little effect on the German Chancellor, who regarded his domestic political opponents as disloyal to the national state of which he, Bismarck, was custodian, guide, and leader. In his mind it was absolutely necessary to take every step possible to defend the national honor of that great state—even if it meant blowing up a really picayune event into the winds of a political tornado. To the mighty Bismarck, German nationalism had to be defended even from a thoroughly dead and despised political opponent.

8

Nationalistic Myths in the Weimar Republic

Glow Holy Flame! Glow! Glow! Never Die Out for the Fatherland!
                                                            Karl Götz

The Nightmare of Defeat

The German people hoped for a miracle in the closing months of World War I. Living in a dream world, they endured hunger, privation, and misery in the hope that everything would straighten itself out. They were certain that eventually there would be cries of joy and the ringing of bells. Official communiqués still announced victories on the battlefields. No German territory had fallen to the enemy.

Then, seemingly overnight, came the news of defeat. William II was thrust aside and his Hohenzollern dynasty consigned to the dustbin of history. A new Republic was proclaimed. The triumphant Allies occupied German territory; war prisoners were not sent home; the naval blockade was maintained. All this was fiercely resented and all of it was associated in the German mind with the Weimar Republic, the illegitimate child of defeat.

The new government was tarnished from the very beginning by the odium of defeat. The Weimar Republic was born without adequate planning, almost as an afterthought. The architects of Weimar worked in a hurry to produce a government which they believed would be regarded with favor by the Allies and which would assure them of easier terms of peace. They had but little

This chapter is based on the article, "Nationalistic Myths in the Weimar Republic: An Iconographic Study," by Howard L. Adelson and Louis L. Snyder, in *Museum Notes VIII*, The American Numismatic Society (New York, 1955), pp. 190–216. I am indebted to Professor Adelson, who did the major research, for permission to reprint this study.

mass support. If it be true that a democracy can be successful only if it is wanted by the people, then the German democracy was doomed from the very start. To Germans the Weimar Republic was an artificial creation, a stopgap government pending restoration of the Hohenzollerns.

Constructed on this weak frame, unsupported by public opinion, lacking help from the outside, the Weimar Republic was betrayed by friends and foes alike. It was unable to weather attack from both Right and Left. It was not strong enough to withstand political chaos, economic trials, social distress, and psychological anxiety. What had started out as a bold experiment in democracy ended in the nightmare of Hitlerism.

To such a pass had an errant nationalism brought the German people. But by no means had the persistent ism disappeared from the German scene. Nationalism was still alive despite the humiliating defeat. Not the least important factor in stimulating the revival of German nationalism was the Treaty of Versailles, which was designed to punish Germany and her allies for causing all the loss and damage of the war. The treaty set up the Polish Corridor which divided Germany into two parts, a violation of nationalism which was certain to result in repercussions.

There were many aspects of nationalism, both old and new, in the Weimar Republic. One facet—cultural nationalism—is of special interest. It is an indication of the all-encompassing nature of nationalism that all elements of a people's culture—from anthems to textbooks, from novels to stagecraft, from folk dancing to festivals—can be affected by a sense of national consciousness. The Weimar Republic was no exception to this historical truism.

In the Weimar Republic vestiges of the older form of nationalism was combined with a new mythology expressed in iconographic terms. This was a highly specialized cultural form which contributed in its own way to the persistence of nationalism among a defeated and humiliated people. The emphasis here is on the production of satirical medals, which contributed to the mythology of nationalism in the postwar Republic. More popular inside Germany than elsewhere, these medals reflected the status of the society in which they were produced.

Karl Götz, Satirical Medalist

The satirical medal has been in almost constant use as a most effective means of expression by some government, body of men, or individual since it was inaugurated on a large scale with the issue of a series of anti-Papal pieces during the Reformation. Whenever events have stirred the deepest emotions in men there has been a concomitant peak reached in the number of satirical medals which have appeared. The Reformation called forth the anti-Papal specimens of the 16th century in all their special vulgarity; the French defeat at Sedan in the Franco–Prussian War occasioned not only a series of struck and cast pieces but even some hand-tooled specimens made by altering coins.

Never, however, was the satirical medal more popular than during the grim days of World War I and the postwar period. All the combatants made use of this vehicle for propaganda at home and abroad, but the satirical medal achieved particular significance in Germany where many of the best known sculptors, medallists, and die-sinkers created specimens to satisfy the ever-increasing demand.[1]

The most active of the German medallists engaged in answering the public clamor for such satirical pieces was Karl Götz. Born on June 28, 1875, in Augsburg, Götz studied in Augsburg, Berlin, and Utrecht in the Netherlands. He then spent five years in Paris. He began his active career as a medallist in Munich in 1905 with a piece in bronze and silver in honor of the Emperor Louis of Bavaria. This was followed by a prolific series, which, before his death on September 8, 1950, numbered some 650 pieces. Götz was awarded the Silver State Medal at the International Medallic Exposition at Geneva, and posthumously a similar medal at the World Exposition held in Madrid in 1951.

The striking nature of Götz's art was first exhibited by his medal commemorating his marriage on April 27, 1912, to Margarete Stangl of Augsburg. A bronze oval, 47 × 60 mm., showing Götz facing front and a profile of his wife in the obverse was joined with a reverse depicting a centaur, obviously representing Götz, with a nude woman representing his wife perched on his back. In the field to the left was the coat of arms of Augsburg

---

[1]On these commemorative satirical medals see J. Menadier, *"Der Geist der deutschen Schaumünze zur Zeit des Weltkrieges,"* *Blätter für Münzfreunde,* LII (1917), pp. 201–216, 225–238, 245–249; Max Bernhart, *Kriegsmedaillen bayerischer Künstler* (München, 1915); and George F. Hill, *The Commemorative Medal in the Service of Germany* (London, 1917). The most extensive catalogue of the satirical pieces of the various powers engaged in the First World War is to be found in M. Frankenhuis, *Collection M. Frankenhuis. Catalogue of Medals, Medalets and Plaques Relative to the World War 1914–1918* (Enschede, Holland, n.d.). The older Dutch edition, *Collectie M. Frankenhuis, Medailles, Medaillons, Penningen en Plaquettes met betrekking tot den Wereldkrijg 1914–1918. Catalogus der Verzameling M. Frankenhuis* (Enschede, Holland, n.d.), is not as complete as the English edition. All references are, therefore, given to the English edition with those to the Dutch edition, wherever possible, placed in parentheses immediately following.

while in the right field there was a representation of the Munich child in swaddling clothes symbolizing the union of the two cities in this marriage.[2]

The Lusitania *Medal*

Götz achieved real prominence during World War I when he began his successful series of satirical medals lampooning the Allies and commemorating various events. By far the most successful and effective of these little propaganda pieces was devoted to the sinking of the *Lusitania*. From an artistic standpoint it is not comparable with many other designs even of a satirical character which came from Götz's studio, but it certainly caused the greatest furor of any piece. It may be briefly described:

> *Obv.* Death is represented as a booking clerk at a window in the office of the Cunard Line selling tickets to a throng of passengers one of whom holds a newspaper with the words *"U Boot Gefahr"* (Submarine Danger). Above the window are the words *"Cunard Linie"* (Cunard Line), below the window *"Fahrkarten Ausgabe"* (Booking Office), and along the side of the window in a vertical band is the name "CUNARD." A bearded man in a top hat in the crowd with his index finger raised in warning apparently represents a German official who is being ignored by the crowd. Across the top is the semicircular legend *"Geschäft Über Alles"* (Business Above All). In the exergue K. G.

> *Rev.* The *Lusitania*, loaded with munitions and aircraft, is shown sinking stern first into the Atlantic. Above are the words *"Keine Bannware"* (No Contraband). Below is the inscription *"Der Grossdampfer / — Lusitania — / durch ein deutsches / Tauchboot versenkt / 5 Mai 1915"* (The liner *Lusitania* sunk by a German submarine, 5 May 1915).[3]

---

[2]A virtually complete manuscript list of medals by Karl Götz can be found in the Library of the American Numismatic Society. This manuscript list will hereafter be referred to as "Götz". A medal showing a profile of Margarete Götz by her husband is illustrated in Max Bernhart, *Die Münchener Medaillenkunst der Gegenwart* (München and Berlin, 1917), Plate 20, no. 137. In addition, Karl Götz issued a self-portrait at the age of sixty in 1935. Götz was mentioned very briefly in the first edition of L. Forrer, *Biographical Dictionary of Medallists* (London, 1904), vol. II, p. 286, as a "contemporary Die-sinker whose signature I have seen in conjunction with that of Schwener on a medal commemorating the Sixth Centenary of the University of Heidelberg, and on a portrait-medal of Prof. Dr. Virchow." Specimens of Götz's work may be found in the Münzkabinet in Munich, the Kaiser Friedrich Museum in Berlin, the German Museum at Nuremberg, the Vienna Museum, the American Numismatic Society, and other museums.

[3]Hill, *op. cit.*, p. 24, fig. 11. The medal described by Frankenhuis, *op. cit.*, no. 1428 (696), is a later imitation with a corrected date.

Actually the *Lusitania* was sunk on May 7, 1915, and the British were quick to seize upon this discrepancy to draw sinister deductions. It is to the credit of George F. Hill, that even during the war he wrote, "But it must be doubted whether the German naval authorities would have confided their intentions to Herr Götz in Munich, although it is quite possible that he may have begun his design at the time when the impudent German warning to intending passengers was published in the American Press."[4] Nevertheless, the British use of this medal in the form of reproductions for anti-German propaganda and Lord Balfour's mention of it in a speech gave it even greater notoriety than other pieces commemorating the same event.[5] In German eyes this piece "castigated the levity of mind of the Cunard Line" and was a celebration of a naval victory to be contemplated with joyful pride.[6] For German children it was a prized possession, and it was traded zealously for more valuable objects.

Götz, of course, tried to undo some of the damage done by the incorrect date by lampooning the English propaganda and the speech of Lord Balfour in a second satirical piece.[7] Needless to say, this did not put an end to the propaganda barrage by the British, and even after the war the *Lusitania* medal was still being distributed in England and the United States at cut-rate prices with inflammatory literature to show the barbarous nature of the Germans.[8]

---

[4]Hill, *op. cit.*, p. 23.

[5]Cf. Frankenhuis, *op. cit.*, no. 641. This is a medal by L. Gies issued to commemorate the same event but bearing the correct date. Another medal by W. Eberbach, one of his "Dance of Death" series, deals with the same event. See Frankenhuis, *op. cit.*, no. 1477 (748).

[6]"*Gemeint ist eine der gegossenen Spottmünzen von Karl Götz in München, die den Leichtsinn der Cunard-Linie geiselt* [sic]." This is quoted by Hill, *op. cit.*, p. 22, from the *Blätter für Münzfreunde,* LI (1916), p. 136, which was the organ of the Dresden Numismatic Club and the Bavarian Numismatic Society. A circular of anti-German character issued after the Armistice in 1918 by Sandstrom and Mahood of Warren, Pennsylvania, offering copies of this medal for sale at a cost of fifty cents each or three for a dollar as well as three dollars for a dozen, quotes the *Kölnische Volkszeitung* of May 10, 1915, as saying "With joyful pride we contemplate this latest victory of our Navy." J. Menadier, *"Der Geist der deutschen Schaumünze zur Zeit des Weltkrieges,"* *Blätter für Münzfreunde,* LII (1917), pp. 245–246, speaks very highly of the *Lusitania* medal, but it must be remembered that during the war Menadier is supposed to have greeted visitors to the Berlin museum with the phrase *"Gott strafe England"* which is found on so many smaller pieces and even some larger medals.

[7]Frankenhuis, *op. cit.*, no. 1451 (720).

[8]See note 6. One of the authors purchased a copy as late as 1939 in the Caledonia Market in London. The legend on the box reads: "The *Lusitania* (German) Medal: An exact replica of the medal which was designed in Germany and distributed to commemorate the sinking of the *Lusitania.* This indicates the true feeling the War Lords endeavour to stimulate, and is proof positive that such crimes are not merely regarded favourably, but are given every encouragement in the land of Kultur."

Götz's reputation as a medallist, however, was firmly established by this unique piece and its predecessors. Critics of medallic art discussed his work which was really the best of the entire school of satirists which was then flourishing. These cast pieces of fifty-eight or sixty millimeters, which had to be produced very quickly to retain their topical interest, show that he was a first-rate designer with an excellent sense for the use of a round or oval field to the best advantage. His satirical pieces were compared with his earlier work of a more serious nature. Max Bernhart felt that his earlier work, like that of his contemporaries, was under French influence because it was produced during a period when it was believed that only French medals were worthy of recognition and all who undertook medallic art earnestly studied in France. His later work, principally satirical, according to Bernhart, took on a more Germanic character and was less susceptible to foreign influences. Bernhart thought it worthy of high praise.[9]

Hill, on the other hand, also discerned two styles in Götz's work. The first of these he felt was intended to appeal to those familiar with Renaissance art, particularly German art of the 16th century. The second style he exemplified by the *Lusitania* medal and dismissed briefly by saying, " . . . it corresponds to the satirical print, and makes no attempt at composition, but simply crowds into the space available all the details that it is thought will amuse the public."[10] This is probably somewhat harsh and does not do full justice to a medallist who merited seven pages in Forrer's *Dictionary of Medallists* in 1923.[11]

Mythology of Nationalism in Iconographic Terms

The importance of Götz's work for the historian, however, rests not so much on the satirical medals issued during the war, for which a great many parallels among all the combatant nations can be found, but on the series of post-war pieces of like nature commenting upon contemporary events and lampooning prominent figures. A large and representative collection of these pieces exists in the cabinet of the American Numismatic Society in New York; some purchased in 1922 and others presented by the late Wayte Raymond in 1934. After World War I very few medallists continued to issue satirical pieces, and

---

[9]Max Bernhart, *Kriegsmedaillen bayerischer Künstler*, pp. 9–10.
[10] Hill, *op. cit.*, p. 26.
[11]L. Forrer, *Biographical Dictionary of Medallists*, vol. VII, pp. 379–386.

the field was largely monopolized by Götz. From his hand a continuous stream of medals poured forth in the form of reasonably priced castings in base metals which were purchased by innumerable Germans and carried in their pockets to display to one another. The overwhelming importance of these medals of the Weimar period as a historical source lies in the fact that they provide a deeper insight into the German view of the course of history. Within this series of medals the elements of the older nationalistic and a new mythology are combined in iconographic terms. It was this new mythology which was to dominate German history in the thirties and forties.

Götz's personal role loomed in heroic proportions as he continued to comment on the current scene and historic events. There were advantages which he enjoyed that no other German political satirist could claim; the medallic productions were apparently uncensored at a time when other means of expression were controlled. The necessity for issuing these cast pieces as quickly as possible so that they would retain their topical interest meant that they were primarily expressions of emotion rather than of well-planned intellectual effort. The popularity of the medals indicated that Götz read, or better still shared, the sentiments of most Germans, but since he was a creative artist, he was able to give these emotions the most complete expression. In another sense he was also a molder of public opinion and one of the creators of the new mythology which was to be treated as historical reality during the Nazi regime. His medals followed hard upon the events themselves, and even if the sympathies of the German people had already been stirred, it was Götz, and others like him, who helped shape these emotions.

Imperial Germany, with Prussia at its head, had a political mythology of its own which, to be sure, had undergone changes during the history of the Empire, but which had maintained its absolute values and supported the imperial throne and its incumbent. History and reality were bent to accord with this imperial mythology. The defeat of 1918, however, had made the concepts of the empire and the emperor no longer tenable. A series of medals by Götz in the last year of World War I shows the glorification of Bismarck, his prophetic vision, and the decline of royal prestige. Nevertheless, before any new mythology could be created the older one had to be cast aside and the ground levelled in preparation for the changed edifice. The core of German nationalism had to be saved without its great symbol, the emperor. William II was the perfect subject for the destruction of the older concept. Unlike the brave hero, William had not chosen to die sword in hand on the steps to his throne as German nationalists such as von Bülow would have desired.[12] He had instead written a terse note to his son, abdicated, and fled the country.

The Kaiser Image

The flight of the Kaiser at the end of the war and the question of war guilt affected most Germans very deeply, but their comments on this question in the current literature had to be somewhat guarded. Götz, however, took a leading role in the destruction of the Kaiser image. In a piece issued in 1918, Götz showed *Germania* casting out the Kaiser for ineptness while the reverse depicted William II on the wall at Amerongen and Bismarck standing in a garden below the wall with a whip hidden behind his back. Bismarck addresses William II in the Berlin dialect asking him to come down from his perch with the obvious intention of punishing him.[13] The incapacity of the Kaiser as a ruler was obvious to all Germany, and Götz issued a full series of medals castigating William II as a deserter and a poor emperor in virtually the same terms utilized by von Bülow. On a medal dated November 9, 1918, commemorating the flight of the Kaiser to Amerongen, Frederick the Great is seen pinching William's ear while the unruly monarch calls out *"Mais Monsieur."* On the reverse of this piece William's uniform hangs with a sign draped across the chest reading "William the Deserter." In the background the gallows with which the former monarch had been threatened can be seen with the hangman's noose.[14]

Still another medal commemorative of the same event compares the greatness of Germany in 1871 with the disappearance of the ruler. The scene in the Hall of Mirrors at Versailles in 1871 is shown and above it the inscription "O Ancient Imperial Grandeur." The reverse shows the head of a pig which has been designed to resemble the face of the Kaiser with the inscription "Where

---

[12]Cf. Prince Bernhard von Bülow, *Memoirs of Prince von Bülow,* trans. by Geoffrey Dunlop (Boston, 1932), vol. III, p. 322. William II afterwards insisted that he had abdicated and fled to Holland upon the advice of Field Marshal von Hindenburg that this was "the last possible way out." On the afternoon of November 9, 1918, von Hindenburg handed the Kaiser a note signed by himself which said: "I cannot take the responsibility for Your Majesty's being carried away to Berlin by mutinous troops, there to be handed over as a prisoner to the revolutionary Government. On that account I must advise Your Majesty to go to Holland." Quoted in Joachim von Kürenberg, *The Kaiser: A Life of Wilhelm II, Last Emperor of Germany,* trans. by H. T. Russell and Herta Hagen (New York, 1955), p. 372.
[13]Götz, p. 258. *"Wilhelm soll'st mal runter kommen."*
[14]Götz, p. 233.

have you disappeared?''[15] On still another piece the Kaiser is represented riding a hobby horse in a warlike attitude with upraised sword calling out, "I will lead you." On the reverse the results of his leadership are shown in the form of a one-legged soldier grinding an organ as a beggar while his wife and children follow him in the streets. The inscription on this side of the medal, "Towards Glorious Times" is merely the continuation of that on the obverse.[16]

Certainly one of the most interesting of those medals referring to William II is the piece which shows the Bavarian viewpoint of the artist. The obverse depicts William II writing one of his famous "Dear Nicky" letters to Czar Nicholas II while the reverse shows Dr. Eisenbart, the prototype of the medical quack in German literature, diagnosing the cause of the imperial foolishness in the words, "He is not mad, but a Berliner."[17] William II as the symbol of Prussia and Berlin as well as an incompetent ruler brought forth the scorn of many Germans from all parts of the country.

Germany, however, was not doomed, for even though the naval mutineers are shown on one medal rudely expelling the Kaiser, the obverse of that same piece symbolized Germany as a sturdy oak standing in a storm and the date is November 9, 1918.[18] Even more striking is the medal showing the Allied powers binding the fallen German hand and foot while in the exergue is the inscription "Foch's turn to speak." The reverse pictures a number of raised fists, and it bears the inscription "A nation of 70 millions suffers—but does not die."[19]

The contrast between the figure of William II as the incompetent destroyer of the Empire and Bismarck, the hero, was patent. It was utilized to the fullest advantage as the starting point for the new mythology. The timing was perfect because it was just twenty years since the death of the Iron Chancellor. On the obverse of one medal the head of the Chancellor was shown issuing from the clouds with the quotation, "Twenty years after my death I will arise from my tomb to see whether or not Germany stands in honor before the world." The answer, of course, is given on the reverse where a horse symbolic of government, is being mounted by a male figure which represents revolution, while in the foreground Germania turns from the scene and covers her eyes to shut out

---

[15]Götz, p. 239. *"O Kaiserherrlichkeit / wohin bist du entschwunden."*
[16]Götz, p. 238. *"Ich führe euch / herrlichen Zeiten entgegen."* William II actually used this expression in a speech. Cf. Joachim von Kürenberg, *op. cit.,* p. 155.
[17]Götz, p. 257. *"Nicht geisteskrank aber Berliner."*
[18]Götz, p. 232; Frankenhuis, *op. cit.,* no. 1484.
[19]Götz, p. 215; Frankenhuis, *op. cit.,* no. 1439. This piece refers specifically to the Armistice.

this grim view. On the ground can be seen the imperial crown and sword, and the date 1918 runs across the top of the piece.[20]

Barbed lampoons continued to be launched against the Kaiser even in his privileged exile. In 1921 William II was represented approaching the Netherlands Tax Office, hat in hand, announcing that he was only a poor man with one and a half millions. This side of the medal is labelled "Appearance." The reverse is labelled "And Reality," and shows the royal figure in the form of a king in a deck of playing cards encompassing a treasure labelled as "160 millions in gold."[21] In the same year the third volume of Bismarck's *Reflections and Reminiscences,* a part of which was particularly critical of the former Kaiser, was published. All Germany was entranced by the section which heaped ridicule and scorn on the former Kaiser. The contrast between the great Chancellor and the inept monarch was once again utilized. Bismarck had shown his disapproval of William II by choosing as his epitaph the words, "A True German Servant Of The Emperor William I;" the third volume of his *Gedanken und Erinnerungen* was more specific as to the reasons for this dislike. The natural result was that earlier the Imperial Court had forbidden its publication. When it did finally appear, Götz showed the book bound in chains beside the imperial crown with the inscription, "Bismarck's legacy to the German people." The reverse shows the German Michel, the representation of the good simple German, pushed back from the volume by a figure clad in the judicial robes of the Empire with the legend, "Not for you Germans."[22]

When, however, the Kaiser was identified with Germany on the question of war guilt, as the newly created myth required that he be, he was exonerated of

---

[20]Götz, p. 216; Frankenhuis, *op. cit.,* no. 1491. "*20 Jahre nach meinem Tode will ich aufstehen aus meinem Sarge um zu sehen ob Deutschland in Ehren vor der Welt bestanden hat oder nicht.*"

[21]Götz, p. 277. "*Schein / und Sein.*"

[22]Götz, p. 278. The name "Michel" is the popular form for the personification of the ordinary German, corresponding to John Bull in England and Uncle Sam in the United States. He is generally depicted as a good-natured simpleton, who allows anyone to take advantage of him. The figure betrays a deep trend of self-pity in German popular consciousness; the feeling that the Germans are constantly being stepped upon by other peoples. Grimm's *Wörterbuch* defines it as the "Designation of an honest, well-meaning, but awkward and intellectually limited person," and yields references to the use of the special term in that sense as early as the middle of the 16th century. The substance of the concept of the Michel is, of course, to be found even earlier in Luther's *Address to the Christian Nobility of the German Nation*. One of the earliest and most effective representations of the figure is to be found in the character of Simplicius Simplicissimus in a novel of the Thirty Years' War, *Die abentheurliche Simplicissimus,* by Grimmelshausen. Götz made constant use of the Michel in his postwar medals, always showing him with a sleeping cap.

the principal blame even though he remained an object of derision. Thus Russia, John Bull, and France are pictured on a medal standing around a powder keg with the inscription, "The Designedly Guilty for the War," while on the reverse William II seated on a bag of sixty million gold marks is proclaimed "The Unintentionally Guilty."[23]

Nationalistic Response to War Guilt

The entire question of war guilt was a very live issue in post-war Germany and stirred German emotions to the deepest degree. In two pieces Götz makes specific reference to it. On a medal of 1919 Clemenceau is shown in the guise of a schoolmaster questioning the Kaiser's sons about the origins of the war; all spring forward to confess their guilt (figure 1). On the reverse, which bears the inscription "The Loafer Called Before the Court," Bethmann-Hollweg is shown with his hand raised as though to testify before Clemenceau, Lloyd George, and Wilson, and he says in Berlin dialect, "Mr. Criminal Judges, I am reporting" (*Herr Kriminell, ick melde mir*). There is, however, a double nuance in this form of expression which would be improper in a German criminal court. The first words of the expression would seem to be addressed to the court, much after the use of "Your Honor" in American practice. Thus Götz seems to indicate, as had been done on the earlier medal, that the true criminals are seated in judgment.[24]

Figure 1

---

[23]Götz, p. 235. "*Die absichtlich Schuldigen des Weltkriegs / Der unabsichtlich Schuldige.*"
[24]Götz, p. 237.

Figure 2

The last of the medals dealing with war guilt is somewhat poignant in its approach, but it is still obvious as another step in the creation of the myth of a world which placed its hatred of Germany above truth. It is oval in shape, and the obverse is devoted to a triumphal procession showing the bound Kaiser following a chariot driven by Clemenceau beating a drum (figure 2). Following the former ruler is a Negroid soldier. Above this is found the word CIRCENSES, an obvious reference to the Roman motto *Panem et circenses.* In the exergue there is the Latin inscription *Mundus vult decipi ergo decipiatur* (The world wishes to be deceived, therefore let it be fooled).[25] The reverse shows the German generals and admirals led off into captivity by the French and English with the inscription above reading "Oh! Germany, High In Honor." At the rear of the procession we see the stricken German eagle standing on a perch labelled "Articles 227 and 230," the so-called Honor Clauses, which arraigned the Kaiser and other German leaders as war criminals. Below the entire scene is the inscription "The revenge of the enemy is filled with hate."[26]

Denunciation of Communism and the Weimar Republic

The events surrounding the end of the war itself and the separatist communist republic in Bavaria inspired still another genre of Götz medals which illustrated his loyalty to the local royal family and hatred of the communists who would rend Germany apart in the service of foreigners. The Bavarian Revolution is portrayed in the form of Death in a Bavarian costume crashing through

---

[25]This expression is attributed to Cardinal Caraffa in the 16th century but it occurs in many languages in various forms perhaps at even earlier dates.
[26]Götz, p. 231. *"Der Gegner hasserfüllte Rache."*

the gates while holding the scales of justice in its hand. One of the gates is labelled 1180, the date on which the Wittelsbach family acquired possession of Bavaria, and the other is inscribed *"Verfassung 1818,"* obviously referring to the establishment of the liberal constitution in that year. On the reverse Curt Eisner is shown mounted on a lion trying to put a sleeping cap on the lion's head. Eisner himself is labelled in royal fashion "Curt Eisner I" and a circular inscription, purportedly from Eisner, reads, "And I am Prime Minister."[27] The cowardice of the king's bodyguard and the actual departure of the royal family formed the subject for another medal which expressed the deep sympathy of the artist.[28] A concomitant of this feeling of affection for the Wittelsbachs, however, was a hatred for the red republic which was expressed in a third medal on the subject. Levin, Teller, and Mühsam were shown in caricature on one side while Eisner danced with the barbarous Russian Lenin to the tune of the "Internationale" on the other. The cry "Out of the Reich" which Götz placed upon this latter scene was sufficient to mark the foreign character of the new political entity.[29] Another facet, the hatred of leftwing political groups, was thus added to the new mythology.

More important than the transient Bavarian Republic, however, was the establishment of the Weimar Republic itself. This was the milieu within which the new mythology was to be created. It was the successor state; democratic in structure, it was supposed to fulfill Wilson's dream of a Germany freed from absolutism. It was impossible for any German to be completely indifferent to the new state, but who was to mold the sentiments of the people? Götz's response to this new entity which had been born in the disgrace of national defeat displays a cynicism which can only be suspected as evoking a similar attitude among the German people from the very moment of the creation of the Republic. The censored literature does not, and indeed it cannot, show the depth of the contempt which the Germans felt for the democratic Republic from the very beginning. Its popularity, if any, was limited to the few intellectuals while the masses had their emotional response mirrored in these medals. The Weimar Republic was doomed from the moment on November 9, 1918, when it was proclaimed in the New Market at Cologne. The Götz medal commemorating the event has a classic obverse

---

[27]Götz, p. 214. *"Und Ministerpräsident bin ich."* Kurt Eisener (1867–1919) was an Independent Socialist who proclaimed a Bavarian Republic on November 7, 1918. He was assassinated in a counterrevolution in February 1919, the first of many prominent radicals to meet this fate.
[28]Götz, p. 222.
[29]Götz, p. 234. *"Los vom Reich."*

Figure 3

showing Father Rhine below and the scene in the New Market above (figure 3). The reverse, however, portrays the young mediaeval soldier of Cologne standing with shield and lance while on either side there is a bit of doggerel in the Cologne dialect:

> Hold fast Amril
> Thou Cologne youth
> Whether it turns out
> Sweet or sour.[30]

A more vitriolic comment on the establishment of the Republic was forthcoming in 1919 (figure 4). On the obverse *Gallia* was pictured snuffing out

Figure 4

---

[30]Götz, p. 275. *"Halt fass Amril*
           Do Kölsche Boor
           Mag et falle
           Söss ov soor."

the broken imperial eagle which was fitted with a face resembling that of the former monarch. In the exergue the motto of the French Republic was rendered in German, *Freiheit, Gleichheit, Brüderlichkeit.* On the reverse two washwomen were shown laboring over a laundry tub while at the top there was a representation of the National Assembly at Weimar. A bit of alliterative doggerel, such as was popular in German poetry of a much earlier period, separates these two parts of the design and expresses the tone of the medal.

> We washwomen of Weimar,
> Besotted with folly,
> Are washing week-in and week-out
> The revolting dirty laundry of vile adversaries,
> As if the savage raging of World War
> were of little importance.[31]

The German of the postwar period could hardly refrain from comparing the old Empire with the new Republic always to the disparagement of the younger state. From the moment of the creation of the Weimar Republic, the scorn which attached to William II for his incompetence was fastened upon his successors in power as upstarts. This, too, was to be part of the new mythology. On one piece commemorating the assumption of power by Ebert the obverse is devoted to a lampoon of William II wearing a fool's cap and reading the Golden Book of Munich in which it is written, "The highest law is the will of the king" (*Summa lex regis voluntas*) (figure 5). Across the upper portion of the medal is a paraphrase of the Old Testament: "Obey my

Figure 5

---

[31]Götz, 218. *"Wir Weimarer Waschweiber waschen wochenlang wahnbetört wüster Widersacher widerliche Wäsche, wohlgemut weiter wurstelnd wie wenn Weltkriegs wildes Wüten wenig wichtig wäre."*

commandments so that I shall be your God and you will be my people." The reverse depicts Ebert, who is shown in a business suit on a throne, about to be crowned with the cap of the German Michel and labelled in regal fashion "Ebert I." The reverse legend is the natural continuation of that on the obverse: "But they did not want to heed nor to give ear but rather followed their own counsel."[32] The scorn implicit in this piece speaks volumes for the German attitude immediately following the collapse of the Empire in 1918. The Republic, in the new mythology, was the punishment that the Germans must endure for the ineptness of the Kaiser.

In 1919 Götz commemorated the first anniversary of the Republic with a piece which pointed to the contrast between the Republic and Empire in a sardonic vein. On the obverse the Kaiser is shown toasting his officials on October 15, 1890, with the words, "Your are the noblest of the nation." On the reverse the mourning survivors are pictured placing a capstone labelled "German Republic" on the tomb of the Empire which bears the inscription "Amerongen R.I.P."[33]

Foreign Affairs and the Occupation of German Territory

The greater part of German emotional response to the collapse following World War I, however, was directed towards the problems of foreign affairs and the occupation of German soil. Götz's comments in this field are particularly illuminating and important as expressions of the new political doctrine. The arrival of President Wilson in Europe aboard the *George Washington,* which is mistakenly dated as March 16, 1919, was greeted with a medal showing Europa on a kneeling bull waving greetings to the President.[34] In the exergue was an inscription declaring Wilson to be the "Savior of Mankind" while around the upper part of the piece was the word "Welcome." Nevertheless, the reverse showed some of the scepticism with which the Germans

---

[32]Götz, p. 234. *"Gehorchet meinem Worte so will ich euer Gott sein und ihr sollt mein Volk sein / Aber sie wollten nicht hoeren noch ihre Ohren zuneigen sondern wandelten nach eigenem Rate."* J. Ellis Barker, *Modern Germany: Its Rise, Growth, Downfall and Future* (New York, 1919), pp. 33–34, says that William II wrote the phrase *Suprema* [sic] *lex regis voluntas* in the Golden Book at Munich as a demonstration of his attitude towards parliamentary and popular opposition.

[33]Götz, p. 236. *"Ihr seid die Edelsten der Nation / die trauernden Hinterbliebenen."*

[34]Götz, p. 226. Wilson actually returned to Paris on March 14, 1919. The word *"Weltlauschen"* which has been translated as "The World Is Listening" has the connotation of "eavesdropping" as well.

viewed the coming peace conference. A gigantic ear attached to the globe of the world was depicted with the phrase "The World is Listening."

This scepticism gave way to complete disillusionment and hatred by the time of Wilson's departure for the United States. On a medal dated June 28, 1919, the laureate American President is shown sailing for home in a seat which bears the words "World Imperialism Is Our Aim", while in the exergue the inscription reads, "With a calm spirit he sailed for home" (figure 6). The reverse design is a gigantic mousetrap clearly indicative of what the Germans in their reinterpretation of history felt had been a monstrous hoax perpetrated upon them. The mousetrap itself is specifically called "Wilson's Mousetrap," and in a further inscription in the exergue American action is referred to as "systematic roguery." What is it that the Germans remembered a year later as the great betrayal or "systematic roguery?" On October 3, 1918, Prince Max of Baden had requested an armistice on the basis of the Fourteen Points. Wilson responded on October 8th setting forth the demand that the Germans evacuate Belgium and northern France and give guarantees that they would not renew hostilities. It was also pointed out that Prince Max had yet to prove that he spoke in the name of the German people. In a conciliatory note of October 12th Prince Max gave the necessary assurances and requested the formation of a joint commission to supervise the evacuation of the occupied territories. Wilson's response of October 14th, however, rejected this proposal for a joint commission and indicated clearly that the only acceptable armistice would be one which guaranteed the supremacy of the American and Allied armies. This was the great betrayal in German eyes. It had severe repercussions inside Germany. Instead of an arrangement between

Figure 6

equals, Germany was asked to accept the fact, for fact it was, of defeat. The pain of that recognition was not to be lost, and when the Götz medal was cast in the next year under the mousetrap was placed the inscription "Telegram 14. 10. 18."[35] Thus was added to the myth the concept of a planned Wilsonian betrayal.

With England, the United States was now placed among the heartless and deceitful nations which had taken crude advantage of German suffering. When the blockade was finally lifted on July 12, 1919, Götz commemorated the fact with a new medal showing starving Germans on the ground behind the iron wall of the blockade (figure 7). Above this scene were the words, "England's Deed of Shame." On the reverse, America, in the shape of Uncle Sam, was represented as the Good Samaritan selling foodstuffs to the starving, wounded German Michel at outrageous prices.[36] The theme was persistent and repetitive—always the cruel exploitation of a patient, suffering Germany.

In the new myth of history Versailles was the "hour of reckoning" between Germany and her foes, the Carthaginian Peace *par excellence,* and Clemenceau was the villain of the scene. By contrast the German hero of the moment was Philip Scheidemann. At the "hour of reckoning" on May 7, 1919, Clemenceau was satirized in gruesome form presenting the treaty to Scheidemann with his actual words, "You asked for peace. We are ready to give it to you." On the reverse, Scheidemann was depicted in heroic style casting aside the text of the Allied proposal from which the snakes of hatred issued with open jaws. For Scheidemann, as the inscription says, it was to be

Figure 7

---

[35]Götz, p. 227.
[36]Götz, p. 229.

Figure 8

a peace of right and not of might.[37] By this act of resigning rather than becoming a party to the new treaty, Scheidemann became the proclaimer of German virtue before the world at the end of the first act in the drama to show that unreasoning power and not ethical concepts had dictated the contents of the treaty. For this brief interval of time, only a few weeks, Scheidemann enjoyed his heroic role as the man who had proclaimed the desire that his arm might wither before he agreed to the terms of the treaty. Later, when as a governmental leader he was actively engaged in a policy of fulfillment of the treaty, he bore the hatred of the German people and the popular denomination of "Scheidemann of the withered arm."

The facts of world history as viewed by Götz, and we must believe that many Germans followed his lead, pointed to the signing of the treaty in 1919 as "Germany's Day of Crucifixion" for her "guilt" in the war (figure 8). But on the reverse of a medal portraying this crucifixion of a nation, the "true villains" Wilson, Sonnino, Lloyd George, and Clemenceau, were depicted as casting dice in a game for the cloak while the *manus Dei* issued from the heavens and inscribed the word "Bolshevism."[38] The old Germany was suffering on the cross while the terrible punishment of Bolshevism hovered over the world as the Divine vengeance for the victors.[39] Here was an added

---

[37]Götz, p. 225.

[38]Götz, p. 224.

[39]Götz and the German middle class as well as the aristocracy represented by men like von Bülow had a deep aversion to the new danger of Communism. Shrovetide 1919 was represented by a medal showing the German eagle with tears starting from its eyes and a padlock on its beak while a liberty pole on its back served to stimulate some few dancers to perform and orators harangued a crowd in the background. On the other face the evil visage of the "New Danger from the East" was shown in all its horror with snakes and bombs. The carnival with which the Lenten season was begun witnessed a helpless Germany in which the danger of Communism had a free hand. Cf. Götz, p. 223.

feature to the myth—the initial suggestion that the Allies never understood that Germany was the vital bulwark against Bolshevik expansion.

The Treaty of Versailles and German Nationalism

The Treaty of Versailles was in the German mind to be compared with the immediate cause of the outbreak of the war in its capacity to cause further difficulty. Götz certainly viewed it in that light in a piece which celebrated the signing of the peace and bore the inscription "A Day of Commemoration of Two World Crimes." A hand, labelled Sarajevo, can be seen rising with a burning torch from which the earth has been ignited while another arm, denominated as Versailles, comes down to seize fodder for the raging flames. In such proceedings the Germans refused to take an active part, and Götz cleverly pointed to this fact on a strange reverse. It should be remembered that the German government had refused to send anyone to "receive" the treaty from the Allies, and only when the word "negotiate" was used did they consent to send Count Ulrich von Brockdorff-Rantzau. Brockdorff-Rantzau repudiated the treaty when it was delivered to him, and, indeed, he delivered a scathing denunciation of it while maintaining his seat as the symbol of German equality before the world. At a later date the explanation was to be given that he was too weak from hunger to stand. He refused to be placed in the criminal's dock and took specific exception to the articles regarding the war guilt of the Germans. Opposition, however, to the Allied demands was hopeless in the light of Germany's weakness and the strength of her opponents. Germany was forced to sign, but only Hermann Müller, who later became a Chancellor of the Republic, and Dr. Bell, a Centre Deputy, would agree to affix their signature to the document. No German statesman of standing, not even Erzberger, whom von Bülow and the rest of the Germans castigated during the Weimar period as the real traitor, consented to perform this odious deed. Götz emphasized this fact with a reverse showing the pen and the treaty with a legend reading, "The Historic Golden Pen Not Used By the Germans."[40] Even so, in 1921, Erzberger was to be assassinated by disgruntled nationalists.

It seems obvious that Götz intimated that the treaty had been signed by individuals under pressure and that the state was not committed to observe its

---

[40]Götz, p. 228. *"Gedenktag zweier Weltverbrechen / die historische goldene Feder von den Deutschen nicht benützt."*

terms. The fact that the names of Hermann Müller and Dr. Bell can be distinguished on the document represented on the medal makes it certain that this piece was issued after the actual signing and not in the interval when the German government was wavering about its course of action. Even though the Weimar Assembly had voted to sign the document by a clear majority, Götz continued to maintain his position, and it seems apparent that a great many Germans shared his views. A policy of fulfillment was not popular from the beginning. Müller himself was stoned by the Paris mob as he left the scene of his disgrace that night because he had prevented the occupation of the Rhine which the French wished so avidly. On the following day a Berlin newspaper expressed the emotions of Germany in less symbolic form. "Lest we forget! The German people will strive to attain that place among the nations of the world to which we are entitled. Then, vengeance for 1919."[41]

Revenge was added to the myth in a medal portraying Bismarck's mausoleum in the Saxon Forest with the inscription: "Germany's Honor, Greatness and Good-Fortune Lie Buried in the Saxon Forest—1 April 1899 (figure 9). On the reverse under the date 1919 can be seen the head of Bismarck and his two clenched fists rising through a mist below which is the terrible inscription: "What I created with the help of the German people over a long time—that has been destroyed by the delusion of a single individual. The German people have struck themselves from the list of great powers by

Figure 9

[41]Quoted by Victor L. Albjerg and Marguerite Hall Albjerg, *Europe from 1919 to the Present* (New York, Toronto, London, 1951), p. 82.

subscribing to the Peace of Versailles. It (Germany) was formerly hated, it is now justifiably despised. It must, therefore, despise itself so much until this disgrace will be cleansed with the blood of our enemies."[42]

Two aspects of the final settlement weighed most heavily on the German mind and provided the subject matter for other medals. The first of these was the reparations payments. German feeling was exacerbated when, at the end of January 1921, the Allies set the total reparations at 55¼ billion dollars to be paid in 42 annual installments each of which was supposedly equal to 12 percent of the value of Germany's exports. The Germans responded with an offer of 7½ billions which was rejected and resulted in the occupation of Düsseldorf by the Allies, but before that point had been reached inflamed German public opinion was voiced in a nationalistic medal which recalled the glories of the War of Liberation against Napoleon. At the same moment the medal castigated the hatred and vindictiveness of the Allies as well as the blindness and simplicity of the Germans who permitted this robbery. The nude figure of a German bound by his arms to a cross as the symbol of martyrdom with the legend "42 Years," for the 42 annual installments, above the head, set the tone of the medal. The inscription which surrounded the figure made its meaning even clearer.

> Enslaved
> From hate and vindictiveness
> From blindness
> Denuded of human rights

The reverse contained the famous lines of the poet of the War of Liberation, Ernst Moritz Arndt (1769–1860), who in the early part of the 19th century had proclaimed the superiority of German as opposed to Latin and Slavic languages and demanded the union of all German-speaking peoples. Familiarly called "Father Arndt" by the German people, Arndt was a chauvinist who detested everything French. These lines had been enshrined in the songs of German youth, but now they were interpolated between the large word "No" and the source of the evil *Pariser Diktat*. Below the words *Pariser Diktat* was placed the date "28 Jan. 1921" which made the immediate cause of the

---

[42]Götz, p. 230. *"Deutschlands Ehre, Grösse und Glück begraben im Sachsenwalde—1 April 1899 / Was ich mit Hülfe des deutschen Volkes schuf in grosser Zeit—das hat der Wahn eines einzelnen zerstört. Das deutsche Volk hat sich durch Unterzeichnung des Friedens von Versailles selbst aus der Reihe der Grossmächte gestrichen. War es früher gehasst, so wird es jetzt mit Recht verachtet. Es muss sich sogar selbst verachten bis diese Schmach mit dem Blute unserer Feinde abgewaschen wird!"*

protest evident. The words of Arndt in such a setting had the force of a new call on the Deity for liberation.

> The God who made Earth's iron hoard
> Scorned to create a slave.
>
> *Der Gott der Eisen wachsen liess*
> *Der wollte keine Knechte.*[43]

By 1923 the hatred and vituperativeness of Götz had risen to the point where savagery entered into the symbolism for the reparations payments. In that year a new medal showed a baby with an immense bloodsucker attacking it and the inscription "Bloodsucker on the Rhine" (figure 10). To give even greater concreteness to the imagery, the Michel was shown in a press with a bursting abdomen from which coins were pouring while the heads of French soldiers were represented on the mechanism for turning the press to apply still greater pressure. The legend "The Boches are completely squeezed dry," left nothing to the imagination.[44]

Hatred of the Allies because of the annexations of German territory was even more vivid. This was the second "evil" aspect of the settlement. It was

Figure 10

[43]Götz, p. 279. *"Frohnen*
    Aus Hass und Rachgier
    Aus Verblendung
    Entbloesst sein aller Menschen Rechte."

   The translation of the poetry of Ernst Moritz Arndt is taken from Alfred Baskerville, *The Poetry of Germany* (Baden-Baden and Hamburg, 1876), p. 155. It attempts to preserve the poetic quality rather than simply the actual literal meaning of the words. On an earlier medal commemorating the conference at Spa, July 5–16, 1920, about reparations, the obverse shows the German Michel carrying the heavy burden which had been placed upon him. Götz, p. 270.

[44]Götz, p. 294. *"Boches' fest ausgepresst."*

the inspiration for more medals of a sadistic nature. From the German point of view the telegram of October 14, 1918, had been a monstrous betrayal, Versailles was the crucifixion of a nation, the reparations nothing more than robbery, and the annexations were the boldest denial of the rights of self-determination which the peaceful German Michel had accepted. On one medal inscribed "After the Peace," Götz depicted the bottle of heady liquor labelled "Peace Food" resting by a document inscribed "The People's Right of Self-Determination." Flying above the scene was a monstrous three-headed bird grasping a sword in its talons. One head was that of Lloyd George, another that of the French cock, while the third was President Wilson. On the reverse the hairy hand of a savage beast with long claws was represented snatching at the tombstones of Eupen and Malmédy. This scene was encircled with the inscription "Belgium's Robber March."[45] The territories of Eupen and Malmédy with the little enclave of Moresnet were transferred to the Belgians on September 20, 1920, without a plebiscite. The treaty, however, provided a means for the expression of popular opinion. Registers were placed at various locations, and the residents who objected to the annexations could sign their names in these. This was certainly a mockery of the very concept of self-determination. In view of this and the fact that these lands had never been Belgian, the German reaction was extremely sharp.

Even deeper wounds were inflicted by the Polish occupation of the eastern regions of the former German Empire. The seizure of Upper Silesia after a plebiscite in which a clear majority of the Silesians had chosen to remain German appeared to be a simple act of vengeance. Götz expressed German reaction to this with a medal showing the German eagle standing on a jar labelled "German Majority" while *Gallia* was depicted as whipping the eagle and savage little Poland resorted to pulling at its tail feathers. The reverse of this piece was even more ominous in that the border between Germany and Poland was shown in the form of an angry face with the inscription "The Border Itself Presents A Front Against Poland."[46]

Pan-Germanism was also added to the nationalistic reinterpretation of history. By the terms of the treaty the union between Germany and Austria (*Anschluss*) was specifically forbidden, but the medals clearly demonstrate that the character of German nationalism was such that even the losses suffered by Austria under the Treaty of St. Germain were viewed as attacks on the German people. To the Germans the Tyrol was an integral part of their country

[45]Götz, p. 283. *"Belgiens Räuberzug."*
[46]Götz, p. 284. *"Die Grenze selbst macht Front gegen Polen."*

because it was inhabited by German-speaking people even though it had formerly been Austrian. After a plebiscite which resulted in favor of Germany, the Tyrol was, nevertheless, given to Italy. Götz's medal portrays an arm raised with an Alpine cap in hand while two Italian soldiers are seen tugging at the sleeve and arm. The inscription left no doubt as to the meaning: "Decision to join the Reich." On the reverse the German eagle was depicted lying helplessly on its back and plucking with its beak at the band which bound its feet. It was this feeling of helplessness which apparently affected the Germans most deeply because the inscription on the piece reads, "All of Germany lay in disgrace and pain—and with her her land, the Tyrol."[47]

It was widely believed that the author of Germany's woes was Clemenceau. He was the villain of the story in the eyes of the Germans. A medal of 1921 depicted the former French Premier in the shape of a hunchbacked elf tearing pages from the book of German folk tunes while on the ground there lay several songs about the Rhine and one specifically about Strassburg.[48] Strassburg was, of course, the *wunderschöne Stadt,* and von Bülow in his *Memoirs* makes specific mention of its loss, along with that of Metz, as particularly painful.

The New Nationalist Mythology

Under these circumstances pacifism was a luxury which the German mind rejected. The simple character of the German, according to the new myth, was a source of advantage to his enemies which they were not slow to utilize. To represent this no better form of symbolism existed than the Michel which embodied all of those traits and which had appeared on the medals in the dark days of the defeat. The new mythology presented the Germans as earnestly desiring peace, but because of their simplicity they were being forced to pay the heaviest price for it. A medal with the inscription "Peace at any price" depicts the Michel being tormented from one side by a French soldier standing on the Rhine while a Polish trooper adds his abuse from Upper Silesia (figure

---

[47]Götz, p. 285. *"Abstimmung an's Reich! / Ganz Deutschland lag in Schmach und Schmerz—mit ihm sein Land Tirol."* The medal bears the date April 20, 1921, but the plebiscite actually took place on April 24, 1921. Perhaps this little error of fact may be seen as the result of the deep emotion felt by Götz. The reverse inscription is taken from the poem *Andreas Hofer* by Julius Mosen (1803–1867). Hofer was the Tyrolian hero against the French in 1810. This poem became a German folk song.

[48]Götz, p. 286.

11). Germany was the lamb on the reverse crying "Never again war" while the savage wolf reared above him to pounce upon him and to devour him.[49] There could be no doubt of the significance of the piece which bore the legend "Pacifism."

Götz was clearly of that school of nationalist Germans who viewed success as the measure of truth. This, too, was accepted in the myth as ideal. The international affairs of Germany pained him as shown by the many medals in which he commented on the inflation and the differences between rural and urban life during the Republic as well as the various shortages. His comments on politics, however, tended to be innocuous or simply anti-Communist unless they were directed at failure. The Kapp Putsch of 1920 was one such event which called for a comment poking fun at the "Five Day Chancellor" as well as at the government which had fled from the capital.[50] The Hitler Putsch of November 8, 1923, was another such event, but in this latter instance the medallist was distressed by the fact that both antagonists, von Kahr and Hitler, were nationalists. The obverse shows Hitler mounting the rostrum, pistol in hand, to arrest von Kahr while a Munich citizen sits below with beer steins in hand, wide-eyed with amazement. The inscription in Bavarian dialect reads, "Nationalist Against Nationalist" (*National [ge]gen National*). On the reverse the Feldherrnhalle was represented as a stage setting across the top of which is the inscription *Münchner Theater*. This inscription seems to have been intended to have a double entendre. Not only was it the scene of the events, but the word "Theater" may also be used to designate a

Figure 11

---

[49]Götz, p. 291. *"Nie wieder Krieg."*
[50]Götz, p. 260.

Figure 12

foolishly dramatic occurrence. This is implied in its use on this piece, for from the left the Nazis are represented as half-grown boys rushing out on to the stage with the swastika and a gallows while just behind the curtain in the opposite wing von Kahr is shown with a cannon. Between the two parties a Communist is caricatured as dancing with glee while pointing at both participants. In the foreground there is the inscription "Last Performance—On to Berlin."[51]

Intense preoccupation with foreign affairs, however, was the rule, as shown in a satirical piece leveled at Poincaré and Chancellor Wirth who had boldly proclaimed with deep insight that the real enemy of Germany was the right-wing political group (figure 12). The obverse pictures Wirth as Bismarck's successor proclaiming this political doctrine while the reverse shows an armadillo-like creature wearing a French helmet labelled Poincaré and the legend "Not right—not left, on the Rhine Herr Chancellor."[52]

France was the *bête noire* of history in the new interpretation. Clemenceau, the real villain, received his just deserts as "The Father of the Victory" when

---

[51]It is interesting to note that on this very early Hitler medal the name of the principal actor is misspelled. Götz, however, continued to issue medals throughout the Nazi period, though none of those of this later period are marked by the use of satire or lampooning. Apparently the artist, who was a nationalist, if we may judge from his work, accepted the New Order as inevitable and desirable. He sought to glorify it in his work. One piece shows Hitler shaking hands with the elderly von Hindenburg who has just appointed him Chancellor. Still another shows the young German soldier behind a shield marked with a swastika and bearing the words "National Front" (*National-front*) slaying a dragon. The encircling inscription reads: *"Mit Hindenburg für Deutschland."* Lest the impression be given that it was because of Hindenburg that this piece was issued there is still another showing a storm-trooper waving flags with the encircling legend, *"Deutschland Erwache."*

[52]Götz, p. 293. This piece is dated June 25, 1922.

he was defeated for the Presidency. Götz celebrated this with an exceptionally vulgar piece which ignored the reason for the defeat, the leniency of the Treaty of Versailles.[53] This medal, however, was only the forerunner of an entire series of even more tasteless and pornographic pieces on the subject of French occupation troops. In German eyes Foch and the French army were lascivious villains who preyed upon German women and introduced Negro troops to exercise their lust on the defenseless females of the Reich. The "Black Disgrace" formed a recurrent theme which lent itself to pornography in a truly fantastic fashion reminiscent of the Ku Klux Klan. Götz utilized it fully as a means of incitement.[54] Even white French troops shared in the opprobrium while France itself was referred to as the "Bordello Nation."[55] Not only were the French purportedly guilty of assaulting women and forcing them into brothels, but in the spirit of revenge, they even stooped to the desecrtion of the graves of the German heroes[56] (figure 13).

Under these circumstances the occupation of the Ruhr in 1923 by the French, because the Germans had defaulted in their reparations payments, resulted in a spate of newer anti-French medals, but this time the attitude was not entirely negative. New German heroes appeared in the persons of those who opposed the French and Belgian occupying authorities. Massive resistance, which was not always as completely passive as the textbooks would have us believe, provided the new heroes who were necessary for a new history. The fourteen people slain in Essen on Easter in 1923 were visualized

Figure 13

---

[53]Götz, p. 259.
[54]Götz, pp. 262, .265, 274.
[55]Götz, p. 295.
[56]Götz, p. 273.

as dead heroes.[57] Albert Leo Schlageter, who had been executed before a French firing squad for sabotage, returned in the new mythology not as a former German officer who had indulged in sabotage against the French and was punished, but as a hero who had been murdered by the oppressors. To him Götz dedicated a medal with the burning words, "Glow Holy Flame! Glow! Glow! Never Die Out For The Fatherland!"[58]

With the creation of new heroes in a new mythology there arose a new hope from the well of mediaeval imperial legends. The *Kyffhäusersage,* which was taught to every German schoolboy, provided the basic foundation. Frederick Barbarossa (1123–1190), Holy Roman Emperor and first of the Hohenstaufen dynasty, according to this legend, had not really died, he was merely asleep in the Thuringian hills, and at the proper moment he would awaken to seize his sword and shield and lead the united peoples of Germany to victory against her enemies. This legend has origins in the tales of the earliest Germans, but in Westphalia it was connected with still another tale of Byzantine origin. According to the Byzantine version, the last emperor of the Byzantine Empire would at some future time establish his kingdom in Jerusalem; then hang his shield on a withered tree, in some cases a birch (*Birke*); deposit his sword on the Mount of Olives; and surrender the kingdom to God. When the Antichrist appears the emperor will resume his armor, fight the holy war to subdue the demon, and in the final victory he will establish the true kingdom of God. In Westphalia the connection with the shield hung on a birch tree caused this final battle to be called "*die Schlacht am Birkenbaum.*" Götz pictured such a tree with broken fetters attached and a head and two arms rising from the ground while above this figure was the inscription, "The Day Will Come." On the reverse a shepherd is represented with his flock near a gravestone with the date 1923 viewing the distant sky in which appear the words: "Between the Lippe and the Ruhr—The Last Battle at Birkenbaum."[59]

The sequel was a foregone conclusion. There were medals with storm troopers and the words "Germany Awake," pieces commemorating the victories of the new Germany at Munich, and, finally, a serious glorification of the German victory over the French and the armistice of June 21, 1940. As

---

[57]Götz, p. 297.

[58]Götz, p. 300. "*Glüh' heil'ge Flamme glüh! Glüh' u. erlösche nie für's Vaterland.*" Schlageter was later elevated to the hierarchy of Nazi saints.

[59]Götz, p. 298. "*Es kommt der Tag / Zwischen Lipp' u. Ruhr—Die letzte Schlacht am Birkenbaum.*" Some German historians, notably G. Vogt, insist that the real hero of the legend is Frederick II, not Frederick I. There were many other legends of a slumbering future deliverer—Siegfried in the hill of Geroldseck; the Saxon Widukind in a hill in Westphalia; and Charlemagne in a hill near Paderborn.

surely as the new mythology had been created, it reached its fulfillment in the horrors of World War II and its pinnacle in the representation of the meeting of French and German officers in an old railroad car. This medal bears the tragic words which are the culmination of the tragedy, "In the historic 'car' in the forest of Compiègne ended the tragedy of 'German Shame' which had its origin at that spot on November 11, 1918."[60]

Mirrored in these medals is the creation of a new legend and an explanation of German mass psychology in the years between the wars. The defeat was declared to be a great betrayal even before the armistice had been signed. Wilson's telegram of October 14, 1918, which stipulated recognition of German defeat as one of the essentials of an armistice, was the starting point. The treaty itself was not to be accepted in good faith. It was imposed on Germany because of the admirable simplicity and credulity of the German people. The Michel figure was ideally suited iconographically for this purpose. The savage French and Poles were the true enemies of Germany and not the rightists or leftists within the Republic. The Republic itself was merely a plaything without reality which indulged, like laundry women, in washing the evil filth of Germany's opponents. The war guilt lay not with the incompetent Kaiser but with the evil plotters among the Allies.[61] Seizures of German territory were unjust. Reparations were unjust and placed impossible burdens on the simple German Michel. Opposition to the Allied powers was heroic. Nationalists must not fight one another. The day of final victory, the golden age of the future, would surely come. This new mythology, which distorted the historic facts, was full blown within five years of the surrender, long before the Nazis achieved prominence. It was carefully cultivated within Germany, and it was recited by the well-meaning abroad. For the Nazi ideology it was highly useful material.

German satirical medallic propaganda thus contributed heavily to the perpetuation of old and the creation of new nationalist myths. Similar myths have emerged in all modern countries, but in Germany they took on a special character of philosophical mysticism and barren abstraction. This was due in part to a resurgence of romanticism in its most confused form, what Frederic

---

[60]Götz, p. 260. "*Im historischen "Wagen" im Walde von Compiègne endete die Tragödie 'deutscher Schmach' welche am 11 Nov. 1918 von dort ihren Ausgang nahm.*"

[61]The campaign against the "war guilt lie" was carefully organized under the direction of Alfred von Wegerer (1880–1945). A General Staff Officer in World War I, von Wegerer was to write the history of a triumphant Germany or to justify Germany's position in the event of defeat. From 1921–1936 he headed the Central Office for Research on Causes of the War (Berlin), which issued the publication *Die Kriegsschuldfrage* (since 1929 the *Berliner Monatshefte*). German satirical medals generally reflected accurately von Wegerer's stand on war guilt.

Lilge has called "a demoralization of the mind by intellectuals afraid of the intellect." In its older form, the tradition of irrationalism, mysticism, and intuition, inaugurated by Julius Langbehn (1851–1907), was further stimulated by a Frenchman, Arthur de Gobineau (1816–1882) and a Germanized Englishman, Houston Stewart Chamberlain (1855–1925); and later by Oswald Spengler (1880–1936) and Alfred Rosenberg (1893–1946). The peculiar content of German extremist nationalism, so obvious in the satirical medals, stressed the traditions of State-worship, unconditional loyalty to the ruler (no matter what his character and the spirit inspiring him), and the replacement of responsibility by blind obedience. To these were added the new facets commemorated in bronze by Götz. All this culminated in the ideology of Hitlerism, with its fanatical nationalism, its infantile mysticism, and its uncompromising hostility to liberalism, democracy, and humanitarism.

The evidence is as solid as the bronze of these very popular medals. The only features lacking are "the stab-in-the-back"[62] of the glorious German army, anti-Semitism, and a *Führer Prinzip*. These, however, were native elements in Germany and did not require a new creation. Beyond them was the newly created essential myth.

---

[62]Götz did not use the "stab-in-the-back" (*Dolchstoss*) theory in his medals although its content was closely associated with the myths he helped to perpetuate. According to this legend, German arms had never been conquered on the battlefield, but German collapse had been due to treachery on the home front by Social Democrats and Jews in Berlin. The courageous German army, which had not expected attack from that quarter, had been "stabbed in the back." The theory was attributed to General Maurice, head of the British Armistice Commission, but he denied this. (Cf. Frederick Maurice, *The Armistice of 1918* [London, 1943].) After the war a *Reichstag* Inquiry Commission examined the legend with painstaking care, and found no basis for it whatsoever. "Whatever its origins, it fitted neatly into the introspective, romanticist, soul-searching character of a great deal of the conservative German tradition, which sought explanation for German weakness in the *Zerrissenheit* of the German national body." (Koppel S. Pinson, *Modern Germany, Its History and Civilizations* [New York, 1954], p. 344.) See also F. C. Endres, *Die Tragödie Deutschlands* (Munich, 1922), pp. 436–437, and Harry R. Rudin, *Armistice 1918* (New Haven, 1944).

9

Detritus I:
The Nationalism of Adolf Hitler

He who is not attacked by the Jews is not a true nationalist.

Adolf Hitler

What I tell you three times is true.

Alice in Wonderland

Infantilism and Monomania

Carlton J. H. Hayes once said that nationalism could be either a blessing or a curse. Certainly nationalism in the mind of Adolf Hitler degenerated to its most obnoxious form—bare and vicious, integral and extreme, romanticized to the point of irrationalism. Hitler's sense of nationalism was harsh and aggressive, infantile and monomaniacal, distinguished by overtones of paranoia. Barbara Ward expressed it succinctly: [Hitler emerged on the scene] "to work out in extreme institutional form and with the total logic of the lunatic the unlimited pretensions of Western nationalism."[1]

Any attempt to understand the nature of Hitler's nationalism must take into consideration the character and personality of the man. Whether or not he was mentally ill in a clinical sense has become a matter of dispute. How to explain his mind has become a major task among psychohistorians, psychiatrists, psychologists, and psychoanalysts. It began as early as 1943 when the psychiatrist Walter C. Langer undertook a psychological analysis of Hitler for the U.S. Office of Strategic Services.[2] The efforts have continued to the present day.

[1] Barbara Ward, *Faith and Freedom* (London, 1934), p. 190.
[2] Walter C. Langer, *A Psychological Analysis of Adolph Hitler: His Life and Legend,* with the collaboration of Henry A. Murray, Ernst Kris, and Bertram D. Lewin, With *Source Book.* Typescript prepared in 1943 for M.O. Branch of the U.S. Office of Strategic Services, National

Virtually all observers have come to the conclusion that Hitler's emotional makeup was abnormal, but they disagree on whether or not he was insane. Some psychiatrists hold that Hitler was not psychotic but highly neurotic. Others suggest that he was the victim of several kinds of insanity, including paranoia (systematic delusions), schizophrenia (disintegration of personality), and dementia praecox (incoherence in thought and action). Some call attention to Hitler's psychotic suspicions: "I never met an Englishman who did not say that Churchill was off his brain." "There is no doubt about it—Roosevelt is a sick brain." Others emphasize the *Fuehrer's* delusions of grandeur. Still others point to his monomania: "Jews are destroyers of civilization (*Kultur-zerstörer*) . . . parasites in the bodies of other peoples."[3]

It has remained for a historian to write the most extraordinary one-sentence analysis of the mind of Hitler. Hugh R. Trevor-Roper, Regius Professor of Modern History at Oxford University, put it bluntly: "A terrible phenomenon, imposing indeed in its granite harshness and yet infinitely squalid in its miscellaneous cumber—like some huge barbarian monolith, the expression of giant strength and savage genius, surrounded by a festering heap of refuse— old tins and dead vermin, ashes and eggshells and ordure—the intellectual *detritus* of centuries."[4]

The dominant trait in Hitler's personality, the characteristic which most profoundly affected his sense of national consciousness, was infantilism. He had little capacity for mature intellectual or emotional development. Ernst Nolte pointed out that Hitler never emerged from his boyhood and completely lacked the experience of time and its broadening, reconciling powers. "If at the age of fifty he built the Danube bridge in Linz down to the last exact detail as he had designed it at the age of fifteen before the eyes of his astonished boyhood friend, this was not a mark of consistency in a mature man but the stubbornness of the child who is aware of nothing except himself and the mental image and to whom time means nothing because childishness has not been broken and forced into the sober give–and–take of the adult world."[5] Hitler's favorite film was *King Kong*, which he never tired of viewing. This continuing adolescence lasted to the day of his death in the *Götterdämmerung* of his Berlin bunker.

Archives, Washington, D.C. This was the basis for Langer's *The Mind of Adolf Hitler*, which appeared in 1972 in book form. The *Source Book* was not used and there were additions, modifications, and omissions of the original report.

[3]For these and similar quotations, see *Hitler's Secret Conversations*, with an introduction by Hugh R. Trevor-Roper (New York, 1953), *passim*.

[4]Hugh R. Trevor-Roper, in the introduction to *ibid.*, pp. xxix–xxx.

[5]Ernst Nolte, *Three Faces of Fascism, Action Française, Italian Fascism, National Socialism,* tr. by Leila Vennewitz (New York, 1966), p. 289.

Hitler's sense of nationalism remained fixed in a teenage image despite his rejection of what he called "the old nationalism." He equated his love for Germany with the crash of military music, waving banners, tramping feet, and national anthem. His national consciousness was consistent with that form of German nationalism which arose in the early 19th century as a protest against the Western Enlightenment. He was a product of a persistent emotionalism, though on a primitive and immature level. Unfortunately, the scatterbrained prejudices of the boy were to become the political program of the man. The tragic outcome was the death of millions.

The Making of a Nationalist

Clues to Hitler's special type of nationalism may be found in the experiences of his youth and early political career. He was born on April 2, 1889, in the Austrian border town of Braunau. How he was transformed from an Austrian subject into a German nationalist became a major theme of his book *Mein Kampf.* "When I look back now after so many years, I see two things of importance in my childhood. First I became a nationalist. Second, I learned to understand and grasp the real meaning of history."[6] He boasted that even at the age of fifteen he understood the difference between dynastic "patriotism" and racial "nationalism." Even though he was an Austrian, he would sing *"Deutschland über Alles!"* with fervor at his school. He preferred it to the *Kaiserlied* in spite of the warnings of his teachers. "In a short time I developed into a fanatical German nationalist."[7]

For the young Hitler it was a heady experience. "We sat at the feet of our old professor enthusiastic to the bursting point, sometimes even breaking into tears. Our little version of national fanaticism was a means by which he could educate us, for he only had to appeal to our national honor once to bring us around to his viewpoint more quickly than he could in any other way."[8] The old history teacher at the *Realschule* at Linz was Dr. Leopold Pötsch, whose eloquence made a deep impression on the young student.

At the same time the youthful Hitler had only contempt for those teachers who attempted to instill in him a sense of loyalty to the Hapsburg dynasty. In his *Table Talk,* Hitler later told of his dislike for such a teacher:

[6]Adolf Hitler, *Mein Kampf* (Munich, 1931), vol. 1, p. 8. Tr. by the editor.
[7]*Ibid.,* pp. 12–13.
[8]*Ibid.*

When Father Schwartz entered the classroom, the atmosphere was at once trans-fixed. He brought revolution in with him. Every pupil took to some new occupa-tion. For my part, I used to excite him by waving pencils in the colors of Greater Germany. 'Put away those abominable colors at once!' he'd say. The whole class would answer with a long howl of disapproval. Then I would get up and explain to him that it was a symbol of our national ideal. 'You should have no other ideal in your heart but that of our beloved country and our beloved house of Hapsburg. Whoever does not love the Imperial family, does not love the Church, and whoever does not love the Church, does not love God. Sit down, Hitler!'[9]

Actually, the youthful Hitler's dissatisfaction with Austria reflected a simi-lar spirit among the lower middle class in his area. Like others, he distrusted the Hapsburgs because of their repeated concessions to non-Germans. The Danube monarchy was a hodgepodge of a dozen nationalities, on which the German-Austrians had attempted unsuccessfully to stamp their culture and way of life. The minorities—Czechs, Slovaks, Serbs, Croats—called for na-tional and social equality. To these demands, young Hitler was bitterly op-posed. He regarded the Hapsburg dynasty as a "foul carcass" and joined the Germans in Austria who insisted on "Home to the Reich," which meant away from the Hapsburgs toward the Prussian German Reich. He went to the extreme of a radical Pan-Germanism and carried the black, red, and gold banner, the old German colors of the Napoleonic period. He was proud of the fact that he was often beaten for this kind of behavior.

The young Hitler's enthusiasm for all things German increased as the years went by. His musical taste for Wagnerian operas remained with him for the rest of his life. He was fascinated by German mythology. As a youngster he spent a good part of his time roaming through nearby forests and communing with the spirits of Teutonic heroes about whom he had learned from Wagner-ian operas. He devoted much of his reading time to the exciting adventure stories of the German novelist Karl May, who without ever having seen North America wrote scores of tales about American Indians and cowboys.

Hitler's contempt for everything Austrian increased even more when, in October 1907, at the age of eighteen, he went to Vienna, where he was twice refused entry to the Academy of Fine Arts to pursue a career as painter of architect. It was a crushing blow from which he never recovered. With charac-teristic lack of logic he blamed it all on Austria, the Austrians, and the Hapsburgs. He was appalled by the lack of national pride (*Nationalstolz*) in

[9]Adolf Hitler, *Hitler's Table Talk,* tr. by Norman Cameron and R. H. Stearns (London, 1953), p. 187.

the Austrian capital. Here he learned something that he had never dreamed of before, that "only he through education learns to know the cultural, industrial and, above all, the political greatness of his Fatherland, only he is able to win that inner pride which ought to go with the honor of belonging to a nation. And I can fight only for something I love. I can only love that which I esteem. I can esteem only that which I at least know."[10]

In 1912 Hitler, now in his early twenties, went to Munich, the capital of Bavaria. Drawn by his zeal for Germany and the Germans, he was additionally motivated by his desire to escape arrest as a deserter from the Austrian army. On several occasions he had received orders to report for military service in Austria, but he had paid no attention to the correspondence. In Munich he immediately felt at home. "A German city!" he wrote with enthusiasm. "What a difference from Vienna!"[11] Here German nationalism became the fulcrum of his political ideology. He found Social Democracy "nationally unreliable."[12] He rejected "the Jewish teachings of Marxism" because they "denied the value of the individual in mankind and disputed the importance of nationalism and race."[13] He studied the parliamentary system and found it wanting. "A feeling of national self-preservation convinced me even then that I ought to care little for national representation."[14] He concluded that there was only one thing of importance for a nation—"the general national necessity of existing" (*allgemeine nationale Lebensnotwendigkeit*).[15]

On the outbreak of the Great War in August 1914, Hitler volunteered for service not in the Austrian army but in the Bavarian List Regiment. He sent a note to the Bavarian king asking that he be allowed to serve in the Bavarian forces. He was delighted when his application was accepted immediately. He was sent to the front to fight for his adopted Fatherland. An obedient and efficient soldier, he won the Iron Cross, First Class. Later he stated that the six years he spent as a German soldier provided the foundation for his hardness, resolution, and perseverance. He was certain that everything he had won of virtue and of worth had been given to him by his service in "this unique, unconquerable, old German army." He was shattered by news of the formation of the Weimar Republic. "My brow burned with shame. My hatred of the men who had committed this crime grew and grew. I, however, decided to become a politician."[16]

---

[10]*Ibid.*, p. 34.
[11]*Ibid.*, p. 38.
[12]*Ibid.*, p. 56.
[13]*Ibid.*

[14]*Ibid.*, p. 82.
[15]*Ibid.*, p. 121.
[16]*Ibid.*, p. 225.

Before and after the war, in the cafes of Vienna and Munich, Hitler gradually crystallized his ideology and sense of nationalism. Among his spiritual godfathers were Machiavelli, Napoleon, Treitschke, Nietzsche, Wagner, Stoecker, Mussolini, and Feder. His own ideology was a mixture of dissent against and contempt for the existing order. Outstanding was a sense of nationalism combined with overriding hatred for Jews. The Prussian historian Heinrich von Treitschke was a hero to Hitler because of his deep sense of national consciousness and especially for his dictum: "The Jews are our misfortune!" In the same way Hitler turned to Richard Wagner because the composer had immortalized the spirit of the Teutonic gods in crashing martial music and because Wagner had once said: "The Jew is the plastic demon of the fall of mankind!" Hitler never ceased to praise Wagner: "My youthful enthusiasm for the Bayreuther master knew no bounds. Again and again this enthusiasm drew me to his works."[17]

Citizenship: Hitler's Transferred Nationalism

We have seen that, ironically, the man who represented German nationalism in its most extreme form was not even a German. Living in Munich in the mid-twenties, Hitler was fearful of being deported by the Bavarian government. He was still on parole because of the Munich Beer Hall *Putsch* and did not possess German citizenship. Banned from public speaking, he knew that he could easily be sent over the border to his native Austria. To lessen the threat of deportation, he formally renounced Austrian citizenship on April 7, 1925, a step which the Austrian authorities promptly accepted. He now became *staatenlos,* literally a man without a country. It was a considerable handicap for a budding politician. In defiant speeches he declared that he would never lower himself to beg officials of the Weimar Republic to make him a German national, a designation he felt he deserved because of his war service. Nevertheless, he secretly attempted to have the Bavarian government grant him citizenship but without success.

The issue came to a head in January 1932 when Hitler decided to run for the presidency against the incumbent, war hero Paul von Hindenburg. His candidacy without German citizenship was impossible. On February 25, 1932, the Minister of the Interior of the Nazi-controlled state of Brunswick announced

---

[17]*Ibid.,* p. 15.

that he had appointed Hitler an attaché of the legation which Brunswick by tradition maintained in Berlin. By becoming an official Hitler automatically became a subject of Brunswick and hence a citizen of the German Reich. He could now pursue his campaign for the presidency.

By no means was this a rare example of transferred nationality. There are countless cases in the Age of Nationalism of individuals born in one country, emigrating to another, and then becoming zealous patriots in their adopted homeland. The German-born Carl Schurz left his country during the revolution of 1848 and later emerged as a highly respected American politican, journalist, orator, and reformer. He served as a general of volunteers during the American Civil War. His career was distinguished not only for personal integrity, for honesty in public office, but also for his devotion to his adopted country.

On occasion, the outsider becomes more Roman than the Romans themselves. This was the case in the career of the English-born Houston Stewart Chamberlain, who went to Germany at the age of fifteen, later married as his second wife Eva, the daughter of Richard Wagner, and thereafter devoted himself to the cause of German nationalism. Violently pro-German and anti-British, Chamberlain proposed theories of Teutonic racial supremacy. He became a German citizen in 1916 in the midst of World War I, and died in his adopted country in 1927. In the land of his birth he was denounced as "a renegade Englishman" and "a vicious turncoat."

By far the outstanding example of transferred nationality is to be found in the life of Napoleon Bonaparte, Emperor of the French. A Corsican by birth, heredity, and training, Napoleon never quite assimilated the traditions of his adopted country, although he regarded himself as the ultimate Frenchman. Educated in France from the age of nine, he nevertheless remained Corsican in temperament, likes, and dislikes. Whenever he lost his temper, he like other members of his family invariably lapsed into the Corsican dialect. The transplanted Corsican was to become the greatest champion of French nationalism and the one single figure most responsible for the spread of nationalism throughout Europe. His last words, uttered on May, 5, 1821, at St. Helena, were: "My God! . . . The French nation! . . . My son! . . . Head of that army!" On his tomb at the Invalides in Paris were inscribed at his behest these words:

> I wish my ashes to rest on the banks of the Seine, in the midst of the French people whom I have loved so much.

Perhaps there should be added to any discussion of transplanted nationalism the prescient words of the German poet Goethe: "May God help the German people if ever a Napoleon appears among them!"

Opposition to Bourgeois Nationalism

The character, personality, and intellect of Hitler embraced a world of contradictions and paradoxes. The orator who could hypnotize huge audiences was in private conversation an insufferable bore. The man who displayed love for children and dogs was unmoved by the slaughter of thousands of human beings. The man who considered himself to be a born genius, the greatest German of all time, could not abide the company of intellectuals, academicians, or scholars.

There were similar contradictions in Hitler's political ideology. There was, indeed, consistency in one overwhelming monomania—his lifelong aversion to Jews and Judaism, a hatred he maintained to the instant of his death. But there was inconsistency in his conception of nationalism. His basic definition was traditional: "The highest form of nationalism finds its expression only in an unconditional devotion of the individual to the people."[18] It was typical, however, of his thinking that his sense of national consciousness had very special qualities.

Throughout his political career Hitler made it plain that he had only contempt for what he called "bourgeois nationalism," conveniently forgetting that he himself advocated many elements of the very type of nationalism which drew his sarcastic comments. His opposition to bourgeois nationalism reflected hatred for the Weimar democracy. He accused democratic statesmen of practising a barren and decadent nationalism. Middle-class political leadership, he charged, promoted a dull, listless nationalism by which the ignorant masses were trained to give useless lip-service to country, flag, and anthem. He, too, wanted glorification of these symbols of nationalism, but on a vastly different basis. The men of Weimar, he said, just did not work adequately for the fulfillment of Germany's destiny.

Hitler made it clear that good nationalists, such as himself, would never be guilty, as were "bourgeois patriots," of working hand-in-hand with Marxist

---

[18]Adolf Hitler, *My New Order* (London, 1942), p. 223.

traitors. Truly national-minded leaders would never ally themselves with international bandits:

> The attacks of the general enemies of our people and Fatherland are joined inside the country by the proverbial stupidity and ineptitude of the bourgeois national parties, the indolence of the broad masses, and by cowardice. . . . These patriotic, national and in part folkish champions, however, find it considerably easier to launch their war cry . . . in union with Marxist betrayers of their people and country, rather than fight an earnest war against these very elements.[19]

How he arrived at this combination of nationalism and socialism was a favorite theme for Hitler in many speeches. In a speech delivered at Hamburg on August 17, 1934, he told how after the end of World War I two views struggled for mastery among the German people:

> [Millions lived] in a world of Socialist conceptions which they might not be able to define in detail but which as a whole appeared to them as fixed and necessary. Over against this world of Socialist conceptions there stood the national idea. Here, too, definitions might vary greatly, but here, too, the word "National" embraced a sum of ideas which led up to a general conception for which millions were ready to give their all. Now the decisive factor was that the qualified representatives of these two views—or those who regarded themselves as such—maintained on principle that between these two worlds not only was any connecting link lacking but that they must of necessity stand opposed to each other in deadly enmity.

> The Socialist world was mainly inhabited by those who worked with the hand, the national world by those who worked with the brain. If these divided worlds were not to lead to the annihilation of Germany, one of the two, within a not too distant future, must emerge as victor, for in the long run a nation cannot survive when its brain workers see in the organized workers with the hand their deadly enemy and vice versa. The worst therefore which threatened us was thus not a victory of Marxism over *bourgeois* nationalism, but the worst fear was that this state of things should harden into permanency—that the German people should slowly but finally split into two self-sufficing bodies with different outlooks upon the world. The religious division within our people can teach us that such a development is possible.

> This, my fellow-countrymen, was the situation which met me and millions of others at the end of the War. That was the picture that the homeland offered to the returning soldiers and which was but more clearly marked in the following months and years. In such circumstances it was not difficult to foresee the future of the German nation.

---

[19]*Hitler's Secret Book,* tr. by Salvator Attanasio (New York, 1961), p. 3.

If the Nationalism of our *bourgeois* world and the Socialism of our Marxists could never unite; if, in consequence, the mass of the intelligentsia finally lost all relation to the mass of the people; and if lastly the nation, i.e. the German people, fell in consequence into complete disintegration and weakness, and therefore into economic annihilation, then both these theories could have no value for this people. For theories do not exist to annihilate peoples, but to make them happier. . . .

Thus, my fellow-countrymen, when I entered political life it was with the burning vow in my heart that I would root out from Germany this world of the political parties—that I would set in its place a community of the German people.

And from the first day I saw clearly that this goal could not be reached in weeks or months or even in a few years. I realized the immense work which such a decision entails. Just as surely as an examination of the terms Socialism and Nationalism leads to a single definition, so certain is it that the realization of such a definition means unending work in educating the people. One can easily state, so far as the mere understanding of the statement goes, that the highest form of Nationalism finds its expression only in an unconditional devotion of the individual to the people. It will never be denied that the purest form of Socialism means the conscious elevation of the claims of the people, its life and its interests above the interests and the life of the individual. But it is a task of immeasurable difficulty to find immeasurable new sources of strength in the inexhaustible well-spring of our own people (*Volkstums*).[20]

Again and again Hitler came back to this theme. Both Marxism and the bourgeois parties were international–minded. The bourgeois parties, he charged, never grew out of a narrow point of view based on class; they never succeeded in extending the term "national" to include the whole nation. The Marxists were not alone responsible for the German collapse; the bourgeois nationalists were just as guilty.

For this watered-down bourgeois nationalism, Hitler offered to substitute his own brand of "people's nationalism," which would reflect the overwhelming strength of the Nazi Third Reich.

Hitler's "People's Nationalism"

In his speeches and writing Hitler made it plain that he would substitute for an outmoded bourgeois nationalism a new vigorous national consciousness. Only in this way, he warned, could Germany right the wrongs of Versailles, once

[20]*The Speeches of Adolf Hitler*, ed. by Norman H. Baynes (London, 1942), vol 1., pp. 94–97.

again take her place as a leading Great Power, and eventually obtain the *Lebensraum,* the living space so vital for her existence. Any other approach was merely wishful thinking. Hitler regarded it as his own task as *Fuehrer* of the German people to build a new version of German nationalism, which would assure their rightful status in the world, through the complete and vigorous use of propaganda.

It was absolutely necessary, Hitler insisted, that Germans base their sense of nationalism on the will to self-preservation. It was not enough to rely on the listless nationalism of the German middle class. All Germans, from workers to aristocrats, would have to be retrained for a new national discipline and a new national will. They must not wait for an accidental national emergency to create the right kind of nationalism. The new nationalism must be fashioned in advance in peacetime. What is ultimately decisive in the life of a people, he asserted, is the will to self-preservation and the living forces that are at its disposal for this purpose. Weapons can rust, forms can be outdated; but the will can always renew both and move a people into the form required by the need of the moment. The warning was implicit: the only hope of the German people lay in their willingness to join him in the creation of the right kind of nationalism.

The new German nationalism, Hitler said, would cast off restraints from both right and left. It would be free of bourgeois jingoism. It would never accept the middle-class idea of national assimilation of un-German ethnic stocks nor the bourgeois belief in a possible "Germanization."[21] Nor would it allow itself to be influenced by the traitorous tendencies of Marxist internationalism.

The new German nationalism, in Hitler's views, must be based on the all-important values of race. The old decrepit bourgeois nationalism had been infected by "pacifistic-democratic poisoning." "The source of a people's whole power does not lie in its possession of weapons or in the organization of its army, but in its inner value which is represented through its racial significance, that is the racial value of a people as such, through the existence of the highest individual personality values, as well as through its healthy attitude toward the idea of self-preservation."[22]

Hitler defended two vital adjuncts—terror and war—as necessary for the

---

[21]From a speech delivered to the *Reichstag* on May 21, 1935. See *My New Order, op. cit.,* p. 246.

[22]*Hitler's Secret Book, op. cit.,* p. 27. See later sub-section of this chapter titled "The Innovator of Racial Nationalism," for a more detailed discussion of Hitler's racial nationalism.

existence of the new people's nationalism. Terror was necessary on the domestic scene; war was the only logical instrument of foreign policy. "Terror," he said, "is the most effective political instrument. I shall not permit myself to be robbed of it because a lot of stupid bourgeois mollycoddles choose to be offended by it."[23] He would destroy any domestic political, social, or ideological principles which opposed his New Order "in conformity with Germany's history, character, and destiny."

[margin note: openly violent in order to preserve Nationalit]

In foreign policy Hitler maintained consistently that only through war could Germany's mission be achieved. It was just like the cowardly bourgeoisie, he said, to pacify their consciousness with legal proceedings. "There is only one legal right, the nation's right to live."[24]

In fashioning his new people's nationalism Hitler in effect accepted the more extreme forms of German integral nationalism and added to it a radical tinge. To the older Pan-Germanism he presented a new argument for the living space necessary for the survival of the German people. Nationalism, in his view, was sterile and useless unless it stimulated a people to fight not only for their existence but for the goal of achieving a master's status in world society. In Hitler's vocabulary, nationalism was merely another synonym for power.

Revolutionary Dualism: Nationalism and Socialism

Hitler regarded as his major political achievement a new combination of isms—the marriage of nationalism and socialism. Although not the originator of the idea, he was responsible more than any other individual for its consummation in Germany. After winning his way to leadership of the German Workers' Party in 1920, he decided to form his political base on a combination of his sense of nationalism plus his own interpretation of socialism. He contemptuously rejected the ideology of international socialism and proclaimed that socialism at the national level was the only true path for Germany's future greatness. He revised the name of the party and called it the *National Socialist German Workers*' Party (NSDAP). He furthermore saw to it that the propagandistic acronym "Nazi" (combining the first syllable of *Na*tional plus the second syllable of *Sozi*alist) would feature the union of nationalism and socialism.

---

[23]Hermann Rauschning, *Hitler Speaks* (London, 1939), p. 87.
[24]*Ibid.*, p. 87.

Almost immediately there began a struggle between the right (nationalist) and left (socialist) wings of the political movement. Hitler, well aware that money and power were more likely to come from the right, chose the nationalist side and eliminated the leftist advocates of a Second Revolution by the Blood Purge of June 30, 1934. For the rest of his career, however, he never abandoned his original idea of combining nationalism and socialism as the core ideology of his Third Reich.

The dualism of nationalism and socialism and the reasons for it remained one of Hitler's favorite subjects in his speeches and conversations. It became a kind of *idée fixe* in his mind. He referred to it again and again. In one of his earliest speeches on April 12, 1922, he expressed the "fundamental principles" of his movement:

> 'National' and 'social' are two identical conceptions. It was only the Jew who succeeded through falsifying the social idea and turned it into Marxism, not only in divorcing the social idea from the national, but in actually representing them as utterly contradictory. . . .

> 'National' means above everything to act with a boundless and all-embracing love for the people and, if necessary, even to die for it. And similarly to be 'social' means to build up the State and the community of the people, that every individual act in the interest of the community of the people, and must be to an extent convinced of the goodness, of the honorable straightforwardness of the community of the people as to be ready to die for it.[25]

A little over two weeks later, on July 28, 1922, Hitler came back again to his favorite subject. Speaking on "Free State or Slavery," he said that he saw a vast battle going on between the ideals of the nationalists (*Ideale der national-völkisch Gesinnten*) and those of the supra-State internationalists. He set the beginning of the battle at one hundred twenty years ago, at the beginning of the 19th century, "when the Jew was granted citizenship in the European States." Again he identified nationalism with socialism:

> Every truly national idea is in the last resort social, *i.e.* he who is prepared so completely to adopt the cause of the people that he really knows no higher ideal than the prosperity of this—his own—people, he who has so taken to heart the meaning of our great song *'Deutschland, Deutschland über Alles,'* that nothing in this world stands for him higher than this Germany, people and land, land and people, he is a Socialist!

---

[25]*The Speeches of Adolf Hitler, op. cit.,* vol. 1, p. 15.

And he who in this people sympathizes with the poorest of its citizens, who in this people sees in every individual a valuable member of the whole community, and who recognizes that this community can flourish only when it was formed not of rulers and oppressed but when all according to their capacities fulfill their duty to their Fatherland and the community of the people and are valued accordingly, he who seeks to preserve the native vigor, the strength, and the youthful energy of the millions of working men, and who above all is concerned that our precious possession, our youth, should not before its time be used up in unhealthy, harmful work—he is not merely a Socialist, but he is also National in the highest sense of the word.[26]

Interviewed by a reporter for the London *Sunday Express* in September, 1932, Hitler was careful to give him a definition of his movement. He defined a nationalist as "one to whom duty to country or community comes before self-interest; in other words, 'one for all,' but with justice for the one where interests clash." He defined a Socialist: "Socialist comes from the word 'social,' meaning in the main 'social equity.' A Socialist is one who serves the common good without giving up his individuality or personality or the product of his personal efficiency." He then went on to assure his English interviewer that the Nazi term "Socialist" had nothing to do with Marxian Socialism. "Marxism is anti-property; true Socialism is not. Marxism places no value on the individual, or individual effort, or efficiency; true Socialism values the individual and encourages him in individual efficiency, at the same time holding that his interests as an individual must be in consonance with those of the community."[27]

After achieving political power with the chancellorship on January 30, 1933, Hitler became even more convinced of the validity of his concept concerning the nationalism-socialism dualism. In a wireless message to the city of Danzig, whose return to Germany he advocated, he told how in 1918 and 1919 the two ideals of nationalism and socialism stood opposed to one another, how they declared themselves to be mutually incompatible and, therefore, enemies for all time. He, however, was certain that one must define afresh the two apparent extremes and thereby awake an unparalleled strength on behalf of the nation of the whole people. It was necessary, he said, to approach the two ideals without preconceptions, scrutinize them from a higher standpoint, and then come to the conclusion that fundamentally both conceptions were one and the same. "Then a new idea for the people (*Volksgedanke*)

---

[26]*Ibid.*, vol. 1, pp. 35–36.
[27]*The Sunday Express*, London, September 28, 1930.

was born! Through the intimate marriage of Nationalism and Socialism there was developed a force at which formerly the old parties stopped, but before which today they have surrendered. Thus was created forces which have led to the formation in our people of a new political will."[28]

Hitler was inordinately proud of being the best man at this "marriage" of nationalism and socialism. Again and again he boasted that he had outwitted "the old parties." In a speech to the Nazi Old Guard on February 24, 1934, on the anniversary of the founding of the NSDAP, he reverted to his favorite theme: "In uniting Nationalism and Socialism we have scared away from us both the bourgeois Nationalists and the international Marxists to find immeasurable new sources of strength in the inexhaustible well-being of our own people (*Volkstum*)."[29]

Hitler took great delight in reiterating his theme. In an election speech to the Sudeten Germans on December 2, 1938, he told how he had discovered the two ideals "which could unquestionably inspire men to bring them under their spell—the Socialist and the Nationalist ideals." "I was then resolved to take these two ideals into a single whole. If I succeeded in that, then the nation might be saved. If not, the nation would more and more tear itself to pieces, and would finally go down in impotence and ruin. Naturally my opponents said at once: 'Such a union is impossible: Nationalism and Socialism are ideas that can never be fused!'"[30] Hitler complained that party leaders at the time were really unqualified to consider whether such a union was possible. "If anyone was qualified," he added in somewhat questionable logic, "it was the German front-line soldier."[31]

The Innovator of Racial Nationalism

The second outstanding characteristic of Hitler's nationalism was his monomania on the subject of race. He never retreated from his extreme racial nationalism. As a youth in the back-street cafes of Vienna, he had had his first exposure to the theories of the Frenchman Count Arthur de Gobineau and the Germanized Englishman Houston Stewart Chamberlain, as well as the racial anti-Semitism or Paul Anton de Lagarde and Jörg Lanz von Liebenfels. While in prison at Landsberg in 1924, Hitler dictated his own simplified version of

[28]*The Speeches of Adolf Hitler, op. cit.*, vol. 1, p. 101.
[29]*Ibid.*, vol. 1, pp. 93–94.
[30]*Ibid.*, vol. 1, p. 91.
[31]*Ibid.*

Aryan-Nordic racial supremacy. As political party leader in the late 1920s, he hammered away incessantly at his fixed idea. As dictator of the Third Reich, he came to the conclusion that it was time for the task of cleansing the Teutonic-Aryan-Nordic race. Racialism was the ultimate illiteracy of this fanatical mind.

Between 1833 and 1855 Joseph Arthur, Comte de Gobineau (1816–1882) published his four-volume work, *Essai sur l'inégalité des races humaines,* which became the bible of racialist literature. The thesis held that all human races are anatomically, psychically, and psychologically unequal. Civilizations degenerate and fall not through fanaticism, luxury, corruption of morals, irreligion, or bad governments—these were all unmeaning accidents—but when the primordial race-unit was so broken up and swamped by the influx of foreign elements that its effective qualities were destroyed. As long as the blood and institutions of a nation kept to a sufficient degree the impress of the original nation, that nation would continue to exist.

Gobineau contended that as soon as isolated groups grew great and civilized, when the majority of the people had mixed blood flowing in their veins, only then was it asserted that all men are equal. Our present civilization, he wrote, was created by the intermingling of Germanic tribes with the races of the ancient world. "The richness, variety, and fertility of invention of which we honor our modern societies, are the natural, and more or less, successful result of the maimed and disparate elements which our Germanic ancestors instinctively knew how to use, temper, and disguise."[32]

The white race, said Gobineau, was the one superior race. All modern civilizations derive from the white race, and none can exist without its help. "A society is great and brilliant only so far as it preserves the blood of the noble group that created it." And again: "There is no true civilization among the European peoples, where the Aryan branch is not prominent." And finally: "European peoples degenerate only in consequence of the various admixtures of blood which they undergo; their degeneration corresponds exactly to the quantity and quality of the new blood."[33]

Gobineau's racial ideas made little impression on Frenchmen, who respected him as scholar, savant, and diplomat, but who rejected the implications of racial superiority. In Germany, however, the idea of the inequality of races received wholehearted acceptance. Here was pleasant, if unscientific,

---

[32]All quotations from Arthur de Gobineau, *Essay on the Inequality of Human Races* (New York, 1915), *passim.*
[33]*Ibid.,* ch. 16.

verification of the superiority of the German way of life. Gobineau's exaggerated praise for the conquering early Germanic tribes was taken to mean a similar high level for current German society. The composer Richard Wagner, an ardent German nationalist, introduced Gobineau to the German public. Historic Nordicism, he believed, was a perfect expression of the superiority of the German Spirit. Ludwig Schemann translated Gobineau's work while praising "the conquering strength of this man." All good Germans, said Schemann, should regard Gobineau as one of the most extraordinary men of the 19th century, as "one of the greatest God-inspired saviors and liberators sent by Him across the ages." In 1904, after Wagner's death, Schemann founded the Gobineau *Vereinigung* at Freiburg. The new society quickly won a large membership.

The cult of Gobinism spread throughout the Germanies. Had he lived, Gobineau himself would probably have objected to the appropriation of his theories by German racialists. Although he believed that where the Germanic element never penetrated, "our special kind of civilization does not exist," still he saw no identity between those heroic Germans (*les Germains*) and modern Germans (*les Allemands*). Actually, he found no Teutons who really belonged to the race that had created modern European civilization. Gobineau stated that if any nation might lay claim to present descent from the pure Aryan race, it was England. But German Gobinists conveniently took those portions of the *Essay* which fortified their conviction that they were the finest representatives on earth of a superior race.

Gobineau gave the racial myth form and content, but it remained for an Englishman, the son of a British admiral, to take over Ayran doctrine and fashion it into a battle hymn for Aryan-Nordic-Teutonic racial supremacy. Houston Stewart Chamberlain (1855–1927), born at Southsea, moved to Germany, married Wagner's daughter, and eventually became more German than the Germans themselves. In 1898 he published the first edition of his *Foundations of the Nineteenth Century,* which was immediately hailed in Germany as a historical masterpiece. More than 60,000 copies were sold when Emperor William II proclaimed it to be "a work of the highest importance." Three editions were exhausted within three years.

Chamberlain sought to reveal the basis on which the 19th century, "an inexhaustible theme," rested. During the era from 1200 to 1800, he wrote, the Teutons emerged as the creators of a new culture. They entered the history of the world as a positive force opposed to the diminutive but influential race of Jews. To this day, he said, these two powers, Jews and Teutons, stood, "wherever the recent spread of the Chaos had not blurred their features," now as friendly, now as hostile, but always as alien forces face to face.

The work of Teutonism, Chamberlain said, was "beyond question the greatest that has hitherto been achieved by man." "What is not Teutonic consists either of alien elements not yet exorcized, which were formerly forcibly introduced and still, like baneful germs, circulate in the blood, or of alien wares sailing, to the disadvantage of our work and further development, under the Teutonic protection and privilege, and they will continue to sail thus, until we send these pirate ships to the bottom."[34] All achievements in science, industry, political economy, and art were stimulated by the creative Aryan race. The 19th century, in this vew, rested upon a secure Teutonic foundation.

In Germany, Chamberlain's book was praised for its learning, its splendid critical acumen, and the method in which the facts were marshaled in support of its main thesis. One critic hailed it as "one of the most significant historical works of the 19th century," while another praised it for its "vast and powerful edifices of argument." In England, however, Chamberlain's book was denounced as "the crapulous eructations of a drunken cobbler," and as "a clever synthesis of Schopenhauerism and Gobinism reflecting the more audacious and brutal affirmations of the mystical alliances between Teutonism and the divinity of progress."

Judged by present-day standards, Chamberlain's *Foundations* is one of the worst historical works ever published. It is a case study in dogmatism and rationalization. The logic is cunningly forceful but imperfect: the author became strangled in his own mystic and romantic intuition; his arguments are coated with sophistry; his conclusions suspect. Chamberlain boasted that he was "incapable of lying." Yet, he was so overcome by the necessity of proving the superiority of the Aryan race that he again and again lapsed into what he called "prophetic visions" and "historical intuition." As pointed out by reviewer Theodore Roosevelt: "He likes David, so he promptly makes him an Aryan Amorite. He likes Michelangelo and Dante, and Leonardo da Vinci, and he instantly says that they are Teutonic; but he does not like Napoleon, and so he says that Napoleon is the true representative of the raceless chaos. . . . He greatly admires the teachings of the apostle Paul, and so he endeavors to persuade himself that the apostle Paul was not really a Jew, but

---

[34]Houston Stewart Chamberlain, *Foundations of the Nineteenth Century,* tr. by John Lees, 2 vols. (London, 1911), p. 228.

he does not like the teachings of the epistle of James . . . and accordingly he says that James was a pure Jew.''[35]

The course of German nationalism was influenced by the type of racialism advocated by Gobineau and Chamberlain. It was a process of osmosis by which racial ideas were imprinted indelibly on the mind of a young Hitler searching for an ideology. Konrad Heiden classifies Hitler as an apostle of the apostles of Gobineau and Chamberlain—of Hans F. K. Günther and Alfred Rosenberg. These two "scientists" added variations of their own.

Hans F. K. Günther, luminary of Nazi *Rassenforschung* (racial research), held that the original Nordics were a Neolithic people who eventually settled in Central and Southern Germany, wandered to the Balkans, into Italy, and then into France and Spain. But, said Günther, the "original Nordic blood" of these people disappeared, while it still flowed freely in its purest form in the veins of the Germans. The Nordic man, according to Günther, was distinguished by a highly developed sense of reality, which, in combination with an energy that might arise to boldness, urged him on to ever higher undertakings. To prevent denordicization, or disappearance of Nordic blood, became the great historical mission of the present German descendants of the Nordic *Urmensch,* or early Nordic man.

The second important and outstanding apostle of Gobineau and Chamberlain was Alfred Rosenberg, who was the philosophical *Fuehrer* of Nazi intellectualism during the Third Reich and who was hanged at Nuremberg in 1946. In 1930 Rosenberg wrote *The Myth of the Twentieth* Century, which became a kind of second bible for the Nazi movement. For Rosenberg the key idea of the 20th century was "the myth of Blood, which under the sign of the swastika unchained the social world-revolution." "It is the awakening of the race soul, which after long sleep victoriously ends the race-chaos."[36] By 1938 the book had run into 142 editions and had sold 713,000 copies.

In the early 1920s, long before the publication of his book, Rosenberg had already played a role in shaping the quality of Nazi racialism. How much he influenced Hitler is problematical, but he certainly expressed the exact ideas which Hitler accepted for the rest of his life. In the *Fuehrer*'s mind, connection between nationalism and racialism was a close one—each merged into the other. German nationalism to Hitler meant the necessity for purging those disintegrative elements which stood in the way of Aryan-Nordic greatness. George Bernard Shaw dismissed Nazi racialism as "pernicious nonsense,"

---

[35]Theodore Roosevelt, in *Outlook,* vol. 98 (July 29, 1911).
[36]Alfred Rosenberg, *Der Mythos des 20. Jahrhunderts* (Munich, 1934), pp. 21–23, 116–118.

but to Hitler the purity of race was the one great ideological need of the German people. Circumstances were to thrust him into a position of power from which he could decree the kind of nationalism he wanted for the German people.

Hitler presented his own combination of nationalism and racialism in the pages of *Mein Kampf* with a kind of breathless air of discovery—as if he had found the secret key to the mystery of the universe. That his ideas were historically and scientifically fallacious made absolutely no difference to him. This was truth because he willed it to be truth.

For Hitler the one superior race was the Aryan. "History shows us in terrifying clarity that every mixture of blood between the Aryan race with lower races has resulted in the downfall of the bearer of *Kultur*. North America, whose greater proportion of population consists of German elements, which have mixed but little with lower colored races, shows a civilization and a *Kultur* different from that of Central or South America, where the Romanic immigrants became assimilated to a great extent with the original inhabitants."[37] This was the effect, Hitler insisted, of race mixture. Germanic America, on the other hand, had remained "racially clean and unmixed."[38]

The ideologist of racial nationalism warned his countrymen that he who failed to understand the laws of race brings misfortune upon himself. He urged them to "join the parade of victory" (*Siegeszug*) of the best races.[39] Cut the Aryan race from the face of the earth and deep blackness, comparable to the Dark Ages, would descend upon mankind.[40]

Hitler divided all humanity into three classes: (1) founders of civilization (*Kulturbegründer*); (2) bearers of civilization (*Kulturträger*); and (3) destroyers of civilization (*Kulturzerstörer*).[41] In the first category, founders of civilization, Hitler placed the Aryan "race," especially the Germanic and North American civilizations. The second category came about, he said, because of the gradual worldwide spread of Aryan civilization. These "bearers of civilization" included such peoples as the Japanese and "other morally subjugated races." Only in their outer form would Japan and other "bearers of civilization" remain Asiatic; inwardly they would become Aryanized.

In his third classification, "destroyers of civilization," Hitler placed,

---

[37]*Mein Kampf., op. cit.,* p. 313.
[38]*Ibid.*
[39]*Mein Kampf, op. cit.,* p. 317.
[40]*Ibid.*
[41]The German word *Kultur* cannot be translated accurately as either "culture" or "civilization." It is a generic term which includes the whole range of a people's philosophy and way of life.

above all, the Jews. "In strong contrast to the Aryan is the Jew. Scarcely any people on earth has its instinct of self-preservation so well developed as the 'chosen people.' "[42] The Jew never had a *Kultur* of his own: he always borrowed from others and developed his intellect in contact with the minds of other peoples. Unlike the Aryan, the Jew's desire for self-preservation was a selfish characteristic which never went beyond the good of the individual himself. The Jewish "sense of belonging together" (*Zusammengehörig-keitsgefühl*) was based on "a very primitive herd instinct."[43] The Jewish race was "nakedly egoistic" and it possessed only an imaginative *Kultur*. "There is no idealism to be found in it.[44] The Jews were not even a race of nomads, because the nomads had at least some idea of what it meant to work. "They are parasites in the bodies of other peoples, making states within the state and refusing to leave."[45]

Hitler refused to recognize Judaism as a religion. "Judaism," he wrote, "is composed of a people without positive racial characteristics."[46] The Talmud was not a religious book dedicated to preparing the individual for immortality, but on the contrary was devoted to the materialist life of the present world. The religious teaching of Judaism was concerned primarily with keeping the Jewish blood pure, not with religion itself.

These destroyers of civilization, Hitler warned, were working for the ruin of Germany. "The black-haired Jewish youth waits for hours with satanic joy in his eyes for the unsuspecting [Aryan] girl, whom he shames with his blood and thereby robs the nation. . . . He tries to destroy the racial characteristics of the German with every means at his command. . . . It was the Jews who brought the Negro to the Rhine,"[47] always with the same thought and clear aims in the back of their heads—to destroy the hated white races through bastardizing, to tumble them from their cultural and political heights and raise themselves to the vacant place.

Worst of all, Hitler charged, Jewish sentiment ran counter to the healthy spirit of German nationalism. The Jews were responsible for organized Marx-

---

[42]*Mein Kampf, op. cit.*, p. 329.
[43]*Ibid.*, p. 330.
[44]*Ibid.*, p. 331.
[45]*Ibid.*, p. 334.
[46]*Ibid.*, p. 335.
[47]Hitler here referred to Allied occupation in the Rhineland after the World War of 1914–1918. Actually, the troops sent in for occupation duties were French colonials from Africa, but this made no difference in Hitler's rationalization. To him black troops were racially indecent, and all indecency could be attributed to the Jews.

ism and the ideology of the dictatorship of the proletariat. Jewish Marxism, he wrote, was the cause of the current corruption of national blood and national ideals in Germany. Marxism, with its international flavor, had overcome good German nationalism, until he himself had appeared to act in the role of savior of Germany's national honor. The Jews had always wanted "to root out the national bearers of intelligence and make slaves of a country." He pointed to the "terrible example of Russia, where 30,000,000 were allowed to die of hunger in a truly savage manner, undergoing inhuman torments, while literary Jews and stock-exchange bandits obtained the rule over a great people."[48] He, Hitler, would never allow that to happen to the good German people.

It was vitally necessary, Hitler said, to continue the battle against the Jews. "A racially clean people could never be subjugated by the Jews." Everything on this earth can be made better. Every defeat can become the triumph of a later epoch. There could be "a renaissance of the German soul" as long as the blood of the German people could be kept pure. Race was the key. The defeat of the Germans in 1918 could be explained on a racial basis. The World War was simply "the last attempt of the forces working for national preservation against the steadily advancing pacifist Marxian crippling of the national body." What Germany needs today, Hitler warned "is a Teutonic State of the German nation."[49]

In thus identifying race with nationalism in such simplistic terms, Hitler succeeded in adding mist to the fog already surrounding both nationalism and racialism. His attempt to extract a "pure German race" out of complex and intermingled strains which formed the German nation was so demonstrably fallacious that it did not deserve the attention of normally intelligent human beings. Yet the emotional appeal of Hitler and Nazism was so great and so effective that millions of Germans who should have known better were willing to accept even this bizarre teaching as long as it helped to right the wrong of Versailles. No nation in modern times is racially pure, nor can that state be achieved. But this made absolutely no difference to Hitler. Nationalism to him meant a pure race and a clean race and every nonnational element must be purged mercilessly. It was his own duty to awaken patriotism and national pride among the German citizens by reminding them of their racial heritage.

---

[48]*Mein Kampf*, p. 358.
[49]*Ibid.*, p. 367.

The Politics of Aggressive Nationalism

In Hitler's view the form of nationalism he advocated reflected the "true" course of history. He believed that man, throughout his existence on earth, had become great only through struggle. This was a law of life. The whole world of nature is locked in a mighty clash between strength and weakness, with eternal victory going always to the strong over the weak. Therefore, there could never be a solution to the German problem until the German people return to the fundamental principles which control the existence of every nation—struggle, purity of blood, ingenuity of the individual. This was the Hitler credo.

Hitler had no understanding of nor use for the complexities of nationalism. His approach was simplistic—there were superior nations and there were inferior nations and the advantage was always with those peoples who practiced an aggressive nationalism and were willing to use their strength to rectify past wrongs and set the stage for future greatness. Young Germans must be prepared for future conflict. They must become "as swift as the greyhound, tough as leather, and hard as Krupp steel." Germany must have a "violently active, dominating, brutal youth, indifferent to pain." The young must always be prepared for inevitable conflict—the law of life.

The *Fuehrer* urged his fellow Germans to pay no attention to what he called "outworn principles of humanity." They must reject that liberal nationalism which emphasized rational give-and-take negotiations and compromise between equals. In his estimation this was merely deplorable weakness. The German people could preserve themselves and rise above the animal world only by "brutal struggle." They must deny out of hand the egalitarianism of a Rousseau or the pacifism of a Bertrand Russell. They must despise "humanitarian stupidity." They must never forget that they were a higher form of life, and it was far better to be numbered among the tigers and wolves than among the sheep.

Thus spoke the "thriving earthworm" to his entranced people. Had Bishop Berkely known Adolf Hitler he would undoubtedly have included him in his category of "a sorry patriot and a sorry statesman."

Like Heinrich von Treitschke, Hitler regarded war as "a biological necessity" and as the logical outcome of an aggressive nationalism. War was desirable for the German people: "For the good of the German people we must work for a war every fifteen or twenty years. An army whose sole purpose is to preserve peace leads only to playing at soldiers—consider Sweden or Switzerland. Or else it constitutes a revolutionary danger for its own country.''[50] The Leader would prepare his people for conflict: ''It is my duty to make use of every means of training the German people to severity, and to prepare them for war.''[51]

Hitler was certain that if war came he would know how to handle it. ''We must shake off all sentimentality and be hard. Some day, when I order war, I shall not be in a position to hesitate because of the ten million young men I shall be sending to their death.''[52] He would have no second thoughts about it. ''In this business [of war] I shall go straight ahead, cold-bloodedly. What they may think about me, at this juncture, is to me a matter of complete indifference. I don't see why a German who eats a piece of bread should torment himself with the idea that the soil that produces this bread has been won by the sword.''[53] People forget wars: ''In time wars are forgotten. Only the works of human genius are left.''[54]

From the beginning of his political career Hitler insisted again and again that the iniquitous Treaty of Versailles had robbed Germany of her precious territory. He went one step farther than other politicians by making it clear that he would seek change not by petitioning or begging for redress, but that he would use force in the holy task of acquiring the territory that had wrongfully been taken. The idea of the territorial imperative and the winning of territory by war remained with him for the remainder of his life.[55] The mania was there even in the closing seconds before his suicide. The valedictory words, which he addressed to the German Armed Forces while he was preparing for suicide in his Berlin Bunker as the Russians were hammering at the gates of the city, were an exhortation to win territory for the German people in the East.[56]

Meanwhile, it was necessary to prove to the world that the man of war was actually a man of peace. While secretly advocating war as the only means of attaining his goal, Hitler informed the world in major speeches that ''Germany needs peace.''[57] This was merely a reflection of his belief that that the bigger the lie the more people would believe it. Hitler would break into

---

[50]*Table Talk*, *op. cit.*, p. 28.
[51]Rauschning, *Hitler Speaks*, *op. cit.*, p. 90.
[52]*Ibid.*, p. 87.
[53]*Table Talk*, *op. cit.*, p. 69.
[54]*Ibid.*, p. 210.
[55]See chapter 12.
[56]See Hugh R. Trevor-Roper, in the introduction of *Table Talk*, *op. cit.*, p. xxxii.
[57]*My New Order*, *op. cit.*, p. 247.

paroxysms of fury when anything or anybody stood in the way of the war he wanted.

This perverted sense of nationalism was an important contributory factor to the outbreak of World War II. The fundamental causes of both World Wars in the 20th century were much the same. They were beyond the control of individual actors in history. These basic causes included economic rivalries, unresolved political disputes, social ideologies, international anarchy, and the armaments race. For the immediate cause, affected by individuals, the blame for starting World War II can be placed squarely on Hitler and Nazi Germany. The German people, at the time of the Third Reich, in choosing to follow Hitler and his close circle of followers, share a measure of responsibility, but the immediate origins of the conflict are clearly to be found in their *Fuehrer's* will to war.

This is the orthodox view held by most historians despite the revisionist theory of A. J. P. Taylor.[58] The surest proof of Hitler's intentions may be seen in the evidence of the Hossbach Memorandum. On November 5, 1937,

---

[58]In his *Origins of the Second World War* (New York, 1962), A. J. P. Taylor, the Oxford University historian, published the first important revisionist study on the origins of the conflict. Taylor implied that Hitler was not guilty of having been the prime instigator of the war. In a brilliant study he sought to counter the verdict of the Nuremberg Trial that Hitler bore the main responsibility for the outbreak of war. According to Taylor, the fault lay chiefly with others, notably Prime Minister Neville Chamberlain, who by their own combination of mistakes actually pushed Hitler into aggression. British errors, Taylor charged, helped bring on a war that Hitler never wanted. There were no Nazi plans, he said, for world conquest. Hitler, in Taylor's view, was a blunderer who was pressed into aggression by outsiders under circumstances beyond his control. Hitler was no better or no worse than any other contemporary statesman. He never wanted the annexation of either Austria or Czechoslovakia. He was maneuvered into the Czech crisis by Chamberlain. He never had any intentions of seeking to implement the blueprint of *Mein Kampf*.

Taylor's book was greeted by a chorus of disapproval. The most significant denunciation came from his colleague, Hugh R. Trevor-Roper, Regius Professor of Modern History at Oxford. Trevor-Roper accused Taylor of willfully misusing documents and perverting the evidence, and of being an apologist for Hitler, Stalin, and the general policy of appeasement. The thesis, Trevor-Roper said, was "illustrated with all [Taylor's] old resources of learning, paradox, and *gaminierie.*" The Taylor concept, he charged, was demonstrably false and the book "utterly erroneous." Nazi Germany, Trevor-Roper said, was not really a totalitarian state, but a vast personal despotism in which the power of the arch-villain Hitler was absolute, and in which his followers vied with one another for his favor in the manner of an oriental court.

Other scholars joined Trevor-Roper in denouncing Taylor's thesis. G. F. Hudson considered Taylor's revisionism as too painful to be accepted by any person of academic standing. Some refused to accept Taylor's thesis that Hitler only wanted a free hand to change conditions in the east which Westerners regarded as intolerable and that he had no ambitions directed against Britain and France. Had Hitler had his way, said one critic, Taylor himself would long ago have perished in Buchenwald or Dachau.

Central to the controversy was the Hossbach Memorandum, discussed in the text above. On the Taylor/Trevor-Roper confrontation, see Roman Rome, "The Origins of the Second World War and the A. J. P. Taylor/Hugh Trevor-Roper Controversy," *Intellect,* vol. 104, no. 2368 (September/October, 1975), pp. 126–129.

Hitler called a secret meeting of his closest advisers and informed them that he planned to go to war. He carefully outlined the steps he intended to take in order to achieve *Lebensraum* for Germany in the east, and the means he would use to provide for Germanization there. With him at the conference were Colonel Friedrich Hossbach, his military aide who took the notes later used for the memorandum; Field Marshal Werner von Blomberg, Minister of War; Gen. Werner Freiherr von Fritsch, Commander-in-Chief of the Armed Forces; Adm. Erich Raeder, Commander-in-Chief of the Navy; Colonel General Hermann Goering, Commander-in-Chief of the *Luftwaffe;* and Constantin Freiherr von Neurath, Foreign Minister. After pledging his colleagues to secrecy, Hitler informed them of his decision and urged them to regard his words as a political testament in the event of his death.

Five days later Colonel Hossbach used his notes to write out a memorandum, which was later (November 24, 1945) introduced in evidence at the Nuremberg Trial. The document revealed that at the conference Hitler began by asserting that the "solid racial core" of the German nation gave it the right to greater living space. The future of Germany, he said, depended on satisfaction of its need for space. Expansion could not take place without destroying resistance. The problem was how to gain the most at the lowest cost. Once it was decided to use force, timing and execution were to be determined. The latest would be between 1943 and 1945. Any later date would be to Germany's disadvantage. "Nobody knows today what the situation would be in the years 1943–45. One thing only was certain, that we could not wait any longer."

The Hossbach Memorandum revealed Hitler's intentions. Added to the pages of *Mein Kampf* and to the entries in Hitler's *Table Talk,* it provides proof of a premediated plan for war. There is further damaging evidence. On August 22, 1939, one day before the signing of the Non-Aggression Pact with Soviet Russia and one week before the invasion of Poland, Hitler made these confidential remarks to his generals:

> No one will ever have the confidence of the German people as I have. There will probably never again in the future be a man with more authority. My existence is, therefore, a factor of great value. . . .
>
> Our enemies have men who are below average, no personalities, no masters, no men of action. . . .
>
> For us it is easy to make decisions. We have nothing to lose, everything to gain. . . .
>
> All these favorable circumstances will no longer prevail in two or three years. . . .

/herefore, conflict is better now. I am afraid that at the last minute some *Schweinehund* [pig dog or filthy fellow] will make a proposal for mediation....

I shall give a propagandistic reason for starting the war, no matter whether it is plausible or not. The victor will not be asked, later on, whether he told the truth or not. In starting and waging a war, it is not the Right that matters, but Victory.[59]

"*I am afraid that at the last minute some* Schweinehund *will seek a proposal for mediation.*" In this special language of the streets, Hitler made doubly clear his desire for war. No sophistry, no extenuating circumstances can argue away Hitler's words in this passage. He wanted war and he worked zealously to bring it about. To such a pass had his sense of "new nationalism" brought him and the whole German nation along with him.

Beyond Nationalism

Boiled down to its essentials, Hitler's sense of nationalism was a combination of emotional naiveté, political shrewdness, and weak historiography. The Nazi leader never really abandoned the older form of 19th and early 20th-century nationalism. At the same time, with a sure belief in his own intellectual infallibility, he sought to present himself as the champion of a revolutionary world order beyond nationalism. Like Napoleon, who saw himself as the future arbiter of a United States of Europe, the German dictator defined himself as the creator and leader of a New Order.

The old nationalism, Hitler said, was no longer acceptable. In contemptuous terms he dismissed "the clichés of nationalism." The traditional conception of the state, he said, had become meaningless, and, indeed, had only a transient reality. The nation as it existed in his contemporary world was only a political expedient of democracy and liberalism. Hitler deemed it necessary for Germans to get rid of this false conception and in its place set up the critically important ideology of race.

The New Order, in Hitler's estimation, could not be conceived of in terms of national boundaries of peoples with a historic past, but on the ground that race transcends all borders. It was nonproductive to bring about adjustments and corrections of frontiers and regions of colonization. This could be com-

---

[59]See Louis L. Snyder, *The War: A Concise History, 1939–1945* (New York, 1960), pp. 48–53, for a discussion of Hitler's war guilt.

pared to the ploughing of sand. One must now think in terms of race. The concept of the nation was a revolutionary change from the purely dynastic feudal states. Just as this idea introduced a revolutionary concept, that of the people, so did the National Socialist revolution take the final step by rejecting the old historic order and recognizing the purely biological values in world society.

At this point Hitler modestly threw a bone to his critics. "I know perfectly well, just as well as those tremendously clever intellectuals, that in the scientific sense there is no such things as race."[60] The tactician, having thus protected his rear, then went ahead to defend his cause.

The *Fuehrer* placed himself in the hurricane eye of this new revolution. It was his own duty "to arouse the forces that slumber in our people's blood."[61] "I shall bring into operation throughout all Europe and the whole world this process of selection which has been carried through by National Socialism in Germany."[62] He would see to it that the process of dissolution would run its course in every nation, no matter how old and firmly knit its social system. The active section of the nation, the militant Nordics, would rise again and become the ruling element over shopkeepers and pacifists, "those puritans, speculators, and busybodies." "I have to fuse those nations into a higher order if I want to get rid of the chaos of an historic past that has become an absurdity. And for this purpose the conception of race serves me well."[63]

Then the thunderous warning: "No Jewish God can save the democracies. There is a stern time coming. I shall see to that. Only the tough and manly elements will endure. And the world will assume a new aspect."[64]

Hitler admitted that his task was a major one, much more difficult than that which faced Bismarck or any other German. "I must first create the nation before even beginning to tackle the national tasks before us."[65]

Such was Hitler's blueprint for a New Order beyond the old nationalism. It was presented to captive audiences with all the self-assurance of a half-educated zealot with delusions of grandeur. ("When one enters the Reich Chancellery, one should have the feeling that he is visiting the master of the world."[66]) Hitler's arguments were grotesque and riddled with flippant irrelevancies. Often he was illogical in mixing heterogeneous ideas and on

---

[60]Rauschning, *Hitler Speaks, op. cit.,* p. 230.
[61]Adolf Hitler, *Hitler's Secret Conversations, 1914–1944* (New York, 1953), p. 29.
[62]Rauschning, *Hitler Speaks, op. cit.,* p. 230.
[63]*Ibid.,* pp. 229–230.
[64]*Ibid.,* p. 230.
[65]*Ibid.,* p. 26.
[66]*Hitler's Secret Conversations, op. cit.,* p. 67.

occasion he was simply unintelligible. One is reminded of the grand historical allusions of Houston Stewart Chamberlain who insisted that Christ as well as all Renaissance culture giants from Michelangelo to da Vinci were blue-eyed, fair-haired Nordics.

In the final analysis, the Hitler intellect was a product of private study rather than formal school work. He was a voracious reader of second-rate literature. He absorbed much from conversations with acquaintances, especially in the backwaters of Vienna cafes. Here he was briefed on elementary history, nationalism, and anti-Semitism. Here he learned such basic historical facts that the French Revolution was the watershed which produced modern nations and modern nationalism. To such ideas he added his own interpretation that his National Socialist revolution was the exact recent counterpart of the French Revolution. Instead of the old nation and nationalism, National Socialism, he argued, introduced the new vital racial nationalism. Such was history as seen by the master of Berchtesgaden, who distrusted intellectuals and had an exaggerated opinion of his own intelligence and knowledge of history.

10

Detritus II:
Nationalism in the Third Reich

Hitler knew how to penetrate through to the instincts of his audience. To compensate for misery, insecurity, unemployment, and hopelessness, this anonymous assemblage wallowed for hours at a time in obsession, savagery, license. This was no ardent nationalism. Rather, for a few short hours the personal unhappiness caused by the breakdown of the economy was replaced by a frenzy that demanded victims.

Albert Speer

The Structure of Nationalism in the Third Reich

German nationalism took on a new complexion at the point at which Hitler's special sense of national consciousness converged with the national aspirations of the German people. Among the products of this dangerous alliance was a sentiment which contributed much to the outbreak of World War II.

The process of this convergence presents a classic case in historical causation. Behind the union was a multiplicity of causes, a complex blend of economic, political, social, and psychological trends. Not one element is exclusive of the others and no one in itself is sufficient to explain the character of Nazi nationalism.

The economic aims of nationalism in the Third Reich were the outcome of an expansionist tendency already revealed in the years preceding World War I. The earlier economic dynamism was associated closely with imperialism, the urge toward territorial expansion on the European continent and the desire to succeed the British as the world's leading imperialist nation. As a result of World War I, the national economy plunged to a low point. Before 1914 Germany had held a position of economic strength. There was considerable change for the worse during the postwar era, culminating in the disastrous inflation of 1923. There was some improvement in the middle 1920s, but the depression of 1929 hit Germany with the impact of a sledge hammer.

Added to economic woes was public dissatisfaction with the political situation. During the Second Reich, the authority of the Hohenzollern monarchy was undisputed by almost all Germans. The citizen identified himself with the monarchy, the legal custodian of law and order. This was a stable system in which every individual had his safe and secure place. It was a well-ordered society satisfactory to both the authoritarian government and the submissive citizen.

Most Germans regarded the Weimar Republic as a poor substitute for the safe monarchy. They were uncomfortable with this child of defeat. Bewildered by the onrushing political chaos, they lost that sense of pride which they had in the old regime. Any political party which could offer them a renewed sense of security and national pride would attract their enthusiastic support. For the politically ambitious Hitler it was a situation made to order.

Added to the political chaos were cracks in the social structure. The Weimar government was unpopular with all social classes. The industrialists and *Junkers,* who maintained a tight hold on the nation's purse strings, were in deadly fear of communism; they had no confidence in the government's attempt to steer a middle course between right and left. They would turn to any political movement which guaranteed relief from this overwhelming dread of communism.

For an ambitious politican there was political support to be found at the bottom of the social scale among the working class—farmers and urban proletariat. Socialist-minded, the German proletariat at first was opposed to the proliferating Nazi movement, but its will to resist collapsed quickly because of Hitler's early successes. It was won over by Nazi propaganda, especially by the early "socialist" appeal of National Socialism. For German workers the choice between nationalism and foreign Bolshevism was an easy one.

Even more important was the attitude of the middle class, the German bourgeoisie. Nazi ideology was greeted enthusiastically by the small independent businessmen, clerks, artisans, shopkeepers, white-collar workers, and civil servants. All had been hit hard by the 1923 inflation, which had wiped out their savings, pensions, and insurance policies in one devastating blow. A class which had believed in the virtue of thrift had been almost destroyed. A desperate government printed more and more paper money in a frantic attempt to save the mark and the bourgeoisie.

How to keep afloat in very dangerous waters became a problem for every middle-class citizen. The bourgeoisie lost its favored position in society. It could no longer look down on the proletariat. Dealt one blow after another, it turned in desperation to anyone or anything—man or movement—which could give it some hope for the future. To this disgruntled class Hitler offered the life belt of a popular ideology. His promise to relieve economic misery won him the support of millions. By exalting the Nordic race he gave Germans of all social strata a new sense of pride. By preaching aggressive nationalism he attracted the attention of those who had already been convinced of the necessity for Germany's place in the sun. He knew how to awaken the response of a miserable people.

There were also deep psychological motivations for the new nationalism. The apotheosis of the little man, Hitler utilized national symbols to justify his own loyalty to Germany. He, the Austrian, the outsider who had been excluded from German life, became a dedicated convert to German nationalism. Like many other Austro-Germans, he wanted to be welcomed back to the Great German Reich as one of its national sons. He would teach his compatriots to avoid the pitfalls of an outmoded bourgeois nationalism and have them join him in a crusade for a new, racially pure, and dominant German nationalism.

When the character structures of both Hitler and the German people converged, traditional German nationalism turned to Nazism. For those Germans burdened by seemingly insurmountable troubles, the National Socialist government became identical with Germany. Hitler's brand of nationalism was accepted automatically as the new German nationalism precisely because he, the guardian of law and order, represented authority from above. To a people psychologically motivated to authoritarianism, the two—Hitler and Germany—came to be regarded as interchangeable. To oppose the *Fuehrer* meant to oppose Germany. Any attack on National Socialism came to be looked upon as an attack on Germany.

This type of psychological response affected even those Germans who had little use for Nazi ideology as well as those who were indifferent to it. The Nazi party was able to win the loyalty of a large majority of the German people because it was successful in "legally" capturing the apparatus of power. For the average German, trained for generations in submission to the legal authority, it was a perfectly normal response. The German sense of morality and decency almost vanished in the glare of Hitler's new nationalism.

This was the great dilemma which faced the German people during the

Third Reich. Should they obstruct the "legally" constituted government even if that government performed criminal acts? Civilians did not realize that even a legal government could be opposed. This was their ultimate tragedy—the false identification of State and Nation, of Government and Fatherland, of Germany and Hitler.

Coordination of Private and National Mentalities

Let us examine in more detail this coordination of Hitler's personal sense of nationalism with that of the German people.[1] Most observers who have worked on the history of the Third Reich have recognized the significance of this convergence. In his *Hitler Among the Germans,* Rudolph Binion similarly stated that Hitler's uncanny personal power over Germans came from his having coordinated his private fury with the national traumatic need. Binion believes that this was "a stupendous stunt," which took "the devil's own psychological genius."[2] The *Fuehrer* had a "castration complex" as well as a deep-rooted fear that he might himself have been "defiled" by Jewish blood. John Toland, too, suggests that the depth and passion of Hitler's hatred of the Jews had psychological roots and may have been his fear that his own father, born illegitimate, might have had a Jewish father who had seduced a servant-girl.[3]

Hitler's new nationalism, with its accent upon the primacy of race, became the ideological base of the Third Reich. Millions of Germans, who until then had never been concerned with thoughts of Aryanism or Nordicism, accepted without question the ideology of pure, superior, and inferior races. Intoxicated by the exuberance of Hitler's verbosity, they adopted his brand of racialism with little or no attention to its scientific absurdity. The *Fuehrer,* as Carl Jung remarked, told every German what he had been thinking and feeling all along in his unconsciousness about the destiny of Germany, especially since the defeat in World War I. He struck a responsive chord when he appealed to the German inferiority complex. The broad masses were convinced that it was supremely right to attack the vicious Treaty of Versailles. Heads of families who listened transfixed to the *Fuehrer*'s fulminations on race came home unable to remember a single line of what they had heard but

[1] See Louis L. Snyder, *Encyclopedia of the Third Reich* (New York, 1976), entry on Adolf Hitler, pp. 150–160.
[2] Rudolph Binion, *Hitler Among the Germans* (New York, 1976), *passim.*
[3] See John Toland, *Adolf Hitler* (New York, 1976), pp. 4–5.

certain nevertheless that they had been made aware of the ultimate truth. Academicians who prided themselves on their scientific objectivity indifferently recognized racial theories which before 1933 they would have rejected as ludicrously spurious.

In the Third Reich, Hitler's special form of nationalism attracted the allegiance of a wide variety of individuals—from the beer-drinking taxi driver to Martin Heidegger, one of the most influential philosophers of modern times. Scornful of the *Massenmensch* (mass-man), Heidegger, philosopher of pessimism, astonished his peers throughout the world by his cooperation with the Nazis. This can be attributed, perhaps, to his powerful sense of German nationalism: he believed German was the only language, apart from Greek, that lent itself to good philosophy. This kind of nationalism, instigated by morbid romanticism, might well explain his attitude: "The *Fuehrer* himself and alone is the present and future German reality and its law." Coming from a giant intellect such as that of Heidegger, this was puzzling eyewitness news for the rest of humanity.

Once he was able to combine his own sense of nationalism with the kind of national will he wanted, Hitler set into motion the gigantic armaments program which he needed to destroy the residue of Versailles. The German people, like a nation of sleepwalkers, were entranced by their leader's bold and imaginative decisions, by his seemingly extraordinary grasp of military strategy, and by his understanding of their psychological needs. He was able, perhaps a bit too soon for his plans, to get his war in 1939.

This was the end result of Hitler's nationalism. His brand of nationalism turned out to be one of the most destructive forces in history. Under the impact of war fever, he went about the task of cleansing the race. Many millions of Germans, unaware that their patriotism was being perverted, became unwitting accomplices to a gigantic crime.

Hitler's Usage of Nationalism

German nationalism turned ugly during the hectic years of the Third Reich. It reflected the aggressiveness of the half-educated Hitler and his immediate entourage. The *Fuehrer* instinctively knew how to penetrate to the psychological needs of his people. Millions responded happily to his baton. An unhappy people, made miserable by the breakdown in their economy, were given new hope. They were entranced by the sight of Nazi discipline in a time of chaos, by the display of energy in an atmosphere of hopelessness.

Hitler would use nationalism to build a new society. In 1937 he informed his architectural adviser Albert Speer. "We will create a great empire. All the Germanic peoples will be included in it. It will begin in Norway and extend to northern Italy. I myself will carry this out. If only I keep my health."[4] As late as May 8, 1943, Goebbels noted in his diary: "The *Fuehrer* expresses his unshakable conviction that the Reich will one day rule all of Europe. We will have to survive a great many conflicts, but they will undoubtedly lead to the most glorious triumphs. And from then on the road to world domination is practically spread out before us. For whoever rules Europe will be able to seize the leadership of the world."[5]

Highly successful in his campaign to mold German nationalism in the special image he wanted for it, Hitler went ahead to use it in his own way to implement the blueprint of *Mein Kampf.* In utilizing German nationalism for his own purposes, Hitler claimed to represent the true interests of the German people. In part this was a legitimate claim, for he did in fact appeal to special elements in the character of the German people. Untrained in the ways of democracy and doubtful of its efficiency, they sought a strong hand at the helm. The *Fuehrer* was prepared to give them the iron leadership they craved. They wanted law and order. He won the battle of the streets against the communists. Sentimental and romantic, they loved a parade. He gave them such bread-and-circuses that had not been seen on earth since the time of the Romans. They loved the sound of music. He gave them the catchy *Horst Wessel Lied* and a thousand marching bands. They were angered and humiliated by the Treaty of Versailles, "that Carthaginian Peace." He went beyond wordy denunciation to activism and sent his troops into the Rhineland. They were distressed and humiliated by the lack of jobs. He promised to rectify this blight and in fact within a year conquered unemployment by putting the jobless into the army. In these and many other ways Hitler paid attention to the aspirations of a disgruntled people. The Germans were quite willing to accept the nationalism of this wonder-man.

The German people were not unique in their national hopes. Other peoples also held such sentiments, but they were not ready to reject liberal-humanitarian motivation in favor of a risky new nationalism. Others, too, were stirred by the traditions of their past, but among the Germans this romantic search for the great past took on a special intensity. Hitler understood this longing and took full advantage of it. He sensed that the most

---

[4]Albert Speer, *Inside the Third Reich* (New York, 1970), pp. 110–111.
[5]Quoted by Speer, *op. cit.,* p. 222.

successful way to lead Germans was to present them with a metaphysical system that would give their national aspirations the consecration of history as well as divine guidance. He returned again and again to this theme. At the annual Nuremberg rallies he ostentatiously reconsecrated the bloody banners as a tribute to those of his followers who had lost their lives in the 1923 Beer-Hall *Putsch* at Munich. The *Fuehrer* knew his people well. He satisfied their idealism by exercises in bloated nationalism.

The new nationalism gave the Germans a Leader who epitomized their national will. He would lead a crusade to implement the historic German mission. A giant step had been taken by the great Otto von Bismarck, who virtually singlehandedly had brought about the unification of Germany and had established the Second Reich under firm Prussian *Junker* leadership. There had been a temporary, humiliating setback in 1918, but that had been due to traitorous Jews and Social Democrats in Berlin who had stabbed the Germans in the back (*Dolchstoss*). Now a new Leader had emerged from the streets of Vienna and Munich to become the heir and successor of German romanticism. This savior was ready to take up the torch for its corollary German nationalism. He would lead the people away from weak and listless German Christianity with its philosophy of turning the other cheek and make of them a nation of proud people. He would purge alien liberalism. He would extend the proud heritage of Prussian military efficiency and entrust German nationalism to Nazi patriots.

Intrigued by the early political successes of the onrushing Hitler, most of the German people were unwilling to face the fact that their fanatical leader was vulgarizing their past by his irrational behavior. They saw only the fireworks of victory. In January 1935 a plebiscite was held in the Saar by the League of Nations as stipulated under the Treaty of Versailles. The vote was an honest one. The inhabitants of the Saar, choosing between nationalism and liberty, chose German nationalism by an overwhelming vote. In the confrontation of ideologies in the Saarland, both socialism and Roman Catholicism gave way to nationalism.

On the German National Character

What explanation can there be for the descent of so advanced a people as the Germans, a people who gave the world the three B's—Bach, Beethoven, and Brahms, and then succumbed to the three H's—Hitler, Himmler, and Hess? It is a difficult question to answer. Causation in history is never simplistic. After World War II the otherwise distinguished German historian Friedrich Meinecke presented the thesis that the rise of Nazism was a "catastrophe" which hit the unsuspecting German people like a bolt of lightning from the heavens.[6] The interpretation is weak and inaccurate. Never in the history of historiography has so great a historian been as utterly wrong as Meinecke with his theory of catastrophe. On the contrary, the roots of Hitlerism lay deep in Germany history.

Perhaps a clue can be found in the national character of the German people. There is a difference of opinion on the existence of a German national character or for the national character of any people.[7] One point of view rejects it entirely as a metaphysical dream burdened with fallacious generalization and prejudice. It is charged that collectivity in this sense is an abstract idea and that it amounts to a mystical delusion. That each nation has a character of its own is rejected as mere superstition. On the other hand, there is a contrary view holding that national character is a demonstrable historical reality produced by variable social influences. A third point of view, equidistant between the two extremes, recognizes the existence of national character but without minimizing the difficulties which determine its meaning and nature. This position holds that there is a relative uniformity of national character as shown by the power of survival of national traits and by its existence well beyond the boundaries of mere stereotypes. Above all, it is never permanent. Transformations can and do take place in the personality of nations. This appears to be a reasonable and demonstrable position.

The key to the immediate pre-Hitler national character of the German people may be found in the fashioning of the German mentality in the late 18th century. The Western Enlightenment, the Age of Reason, which the French called the *Illuminé* and the Germans termed the *Aufklärung,* was centered in France, England, and the United States. It by-passed Germany. German intellectuals were well aware of its character, but they were not successful as catalytic agents in transmitting the ideas of the Enlightenment to the masses of their compatriots. The ideas are familiar—constitutionalism; parliamentarianism; liberty, equality, and fraternity (France) and life, liberty, and the pursuit of happiness (United States); freedom of speech, press, and assembly; and above all, toleration of dissent. At its base was the key factor—*exaltation of the individual*. These were the ideals toward which

[6]Friedrich Meinecke, *The German Catastrophe* (New York, 1950).
[7]For a more detailed discussion of national character see Louis L. Snyder, *The Meaning of Nationalism* (New Brunswick, N.J., 1954).

Western society looked as a goal, ideas which have not been completely realized.

The course of German history since Frederick the Great took an opposite turn. The ideas which attracted the French *philosophes* Rousseau, Montesquieu, and Voltaire, and such English rationalists as John Locke, Thomas Hobbes, and Jeremy Bentham, did not conquer the German mind. Instead, German intellectuals rejected the central importance of the individual and accepted the *exaltation of the state.*

The German mind of the 19th and early 20th centuries was molded in this tradition. The villain in the process was the philosopher Hegel, who saw civilization as a process of upward movement from P.M. to P.M.—from Primitive Man to the Prussian Monarchy. In this evolution Hegel deemed it absolutely necessary that the individual be subordinated to the state. Belief in this idea became a facet of the German personality. At the same time it was a dominant theme of German home life and public attitude. Virtually every teacher at the grammar school level and in the *Gymnasium* was trained in Hegelian dialectics.

Clamped in this rigid formula, the German mind, dominated by the consistent expansion of Prussia, acquired traits decidedly hostile to the Enlightenment. The characteristics—and they were more than just stereotypes—included discipline, obedience, worship of authority (*die Obrigkeit*), an inordinate respect for the military, a passion for law and order, and respect for legality. Outstanding was the idea of obedience to the proper authority. Where other peoples, stimulated by the Enlightenment, developed a strong tradition of dissent, the Germans tended to regard it as irrational to oppose the legal authority. This attitude persisted through the Bismarckian Second Reich, the era of William II, and even into the Weimar Republic. What was legal was right and acceptable. Let other peoples have their revolutions.

Most observers of the German scene accept the explanation that the Germans of the pre-Hitler period were shaped by a special way of life and that, despite deep differences among them, resembled one another in the basic patterns of behavior and beliefs more than they were like the peoples of other nations. The British historian A. J. P. Taylor recognized the term "national character" as the shorthand which the historian must use to express the effect on a community of geographical, political, and social surroundings.[8] Alex Inkeles expressed it this way:

---

[8] A. J. P. Taylor, *The Course of German History* (New York, 1946), p. 14.

The burden of the available work in the scholarly disciplines concerned with social relations indicates that there are distinctive patterns of reaction to given situations which may be used to distinguish the population of particular national states. These patterned responses, along with the symbols and value systems . . . are not independent of political and economic institutions; indeed they are intimately interwoven with them. But they may exercise an independent influence in the selective apprehension of experience, and have a profound effect on the opportunities for success of *new* institutional forms in the political and economic realm.[9]

Role of Authoritarianism

German authoritarianism at the governmental level existed precisely because over a long period of their history the Germans learned meekness and humiliation in the presence of the overbearing bureaucrat and the barking sergeant. Added to a rigidly formalistic and hierarchical occupational system was a strong authoritarian element implicit in the father-son relationship and the sharply subordinated role of women. To sociologist Talcott Parsons, this meant a special national character. "These elements were either peculiar to Germany or relatively far more important than for instance in this country. . . . Such conditions were much more favorable to the development of a strongly militaristic variety of nationalism."[10]

The British historian, L. B. Namier, agreed:

Most types of social groups can be found, in one form or another, in all nations, but attaining various degrees of development and importance; and some nations develop into one or two forms into dominant patterns which express national character and their communal life. Thus the pattern forms of England are Parliament and the team, of Germany the State and the army, or perhaps rather the army and the State. Characteristic of the English social groups is the degree of freedom which they leave to the individual and the basic equality of their members, the voluntary submission to the rules of 'the game' and the curious mixtures of elasticity and rigidity in these rules; most of all the moral standards which these groups enforce, or to which they aspire.

Characteristic of the German social group is the utter, conscious subordination of the individual, the iron discipline which they enforce, the high degree of organi-

---

[9]Alex Inkeles, quoted in Morroe Berger, "Understanding National Character—and War," *Commentary,* vol. II (1951), p. 159.
[10]Talcott Parsons, "Sources and Patterns of Aggression," in *A Study of Interpersonal Relations,* ed. by Patrick Mullahy (New York, 1949), p. 295.

zation and efficiency which they attain, and their resultant inhumanity. The State is an aim in itself, while that of the army is essentially amoral—*a-moral*—to smash the enemy. Whatever characteristics of the individual members of the two nations have gone to form these patterns, and whatever share circumstances had in their development, once crystallized these patterns powerfully react on the individual and mould him in turn. Removed from this setting the individual may develop, or at least seem to develop, in a different manner; still, it is the pattern which expresses the national character.[11]

In this framework, individual Germans did not ask about the morality or indecency of governmental officials. The ruler or leader was simply the personification of authority. He was the one to exercise control, to maintain law and order, and to be followed. This subservience to authority showed an extraordinary endurance in 19th- and 20th-century Germany. Not even the catastrophe of 1918 was powerful enough to break the bonds of this kind of spiritual serfdom. The bureaucracy emerged unscathed after defeat, the German army still retained its special stamp, and even the Weimar Republic was weakened by the traditional urge for strong authoritarian leadership.[12]

There are objections to this analysis.[13] How is it possible, it is asked, to endow a nation numbering millions with a single character or will? Is it not true that precisely opposite characteristics can exist in one people? Is it not obvious that Germany's political divisions in the past have been accompanied by cultural differences? Exactly what national character does one select? On the one side there may be the transcendental idealism of Kant, the classic humanitarianism of Goethe, or the decent tolerance of Lessing. On the other side is displayed the warmongering of Treitschke, the anti-Semitism of a long line of individuals from Adolf Stoecker to Alfred Rosenberg, and the irrationalism of Nazi racialists such as Hans F. K. Günther. Which is the real character? To those who ask such questions any reference to German national character is considered unhistorical and unworthy of attention.

Eugene Anderson attacked the idea of authoritarianism in Germany as a "kind of inverted racialism." "The German people," he wrote, "are often branded as irretrievably authoritarian in government and politics and in the manifestations of social life. The father of the family and the labor leader, the social worker and the school teacher, all are accused of conforming to a

---

[11]L. B. Namier, *Conflicts: Studies in Contemporary History* (New York, 1943), p. 79.
[12]See Talcott Parsons, "The Problem of Controlled Institutional Change," *Journal of the Biology and Pathology of International Relations,* VIII (1946), pp. 79–101.
[13]For a condemnation of the idea of national character, see especially Hamilton Fyfe, *The Illusion of National Character* (New York, 1940).

pattern of authoritarianism set by the long domination of monarchism and militarism and of their servant, bureaucracy.''[14]

A fair evaluation of this point of view hinges on Anderson's word ''irretrievably,'' which few historians of German nationalism would venture to use. Anderson found it ''irrelevant and unnecessary'' to explain any period in German history prior to that which exerted an immediate influence on the contemporary scene. He designated the years between the unification of Germany in 1871 and the overthrow of Hitler in 1945 as a historical period with a life of its own. ''Bismarck's work of national unification fixed the political, social, and institutional framework within which or against which German events have since moved.''[15]

Yet it was precisely in this period that the national character, which had been in formation for some generations before 1871, was solidified. Anderson himself recognizes this pattern: ''The qualities which German tradition regarded as the highest virtues became means of totalitarian domination. The Germans made a fetish of order, cleanliness, performance of duty, efficiency in craft or profession, concentration on the business at hand without interference in affairs about which they knew little, being obedient to officers and officials and to the last irrespective of the validity or morality of the order, ardent love of the nation and supreme loyalty to it. All peoples of our civilization have these traits in varying degrees, but in the Western democracies they are balanced by a strong sense of civic responsibility and of individual worth as a citizen. In no other country than Germany did such a combination of qualities obtain on such a broad scale, qualities which in favorable circumstances could be exploited to the ruin of a people.''[16] Here the analysis, including its accent on authoritarianism, is fair and reasonable and it is by no means ''inverted racialism.''

Inside Germany there are historians who reject the concept of authoritarianism in their history and furthermore claim that National Socialism had no deep roots in the ideological traditions of the older Germany. Instead, they assert, Hitlerism actually was imported into Germany from the West and had its roots in general Western historical development. It was the result, they say, of industrialization and mass democracy, which had their origins in England and France in the 18th and 19th century.

In this convenient fashion the responsibility for Hitler and Nazism is shifted

---

[14]See Eugene N. Anderson, ''Freedom and Authoritarianism in German History,'' in *The Struggle for Democracy in Germany,* ed. by Gabriel L. Almond (Chapel Hill, N.C., 1945), pp. 3–32.
[15]*Ibid.,* p. 5.
[16]*Ibid.,* p. 29.

beyond the borders of Germany. There is little evidence for this attempt to place the onus for National Socialism on the Western democracies. The very fact that this type of Fascism did not emerge in the advanced industrial nations to the point where it took over complete control is indication enough that it had no mass following in those countries. Dissent instead of conformity was the critical factor in the Western democracies. There were, indeed, waves of unemployment in the democracies, there were severe economic crises, but the industrial masses there did not seek a solution through totalitarian dictatorship. National Socialism appeared in Germany because the people were conditioned over a long period of time to the authoritarian values it represented. The Germans readily and even enthusiastically accepted the Hegelian exaltation of the state. They fell into the abyss of Hitlerism precisely because they lacked the Western urge to dissent.

Two important facts remain to be considered. First, by no means is German national character a *permanent* manifestation. The Germans of the Holy Roman Empire or the German Confederation were unlike those of the 19th and 20th centuries, as indicated by Hans Kohn:

> In the eighteenth century German intellectuals and the German people underrated the importance of power and overrated purity of spirit. They seemed to the western world an idyllic apolitical people of poets and thinkers. The attitude changed in the nineteenth century. From one extreme the Germans moved to another. They remained fundamentally apolitical, animated by haughty contempt for politics, but they became a dynamic nation whose will centered upon power and the power-state. From the life of the spirit, which characterized the period from 1870 to 1914, they turned to the pursuit of power. Having lived so long outside of active participation in political history, educated Germans tended to overstress the concepts of state and power. They rejected the rational and critical control of *Macht* by *Geist;* instead under the pretext of a synthesis of spirit and power, they idealized the power-state and transformed it from an instrument of spirit into its embodiment. Their leading thinkers of the early nineteenth century—Fichte, Hegel, and Marx—raised the nation, the state, and the economy to supreme concepts, regarded history with its conflicts as the unfolding of an ultimate and self-justifying reality, and distorted political processes to fit a semireligious utopianism. Under the influence of these and similar thinkers German thought after 1812 consciously deviated from the main lines of western development.[17]

The second point to be emphasized is that German national character must not be confused with the Hitlerian concept of racial character. The contention

---

[17]Hans Kohn, *The Mind of Germany* (New York, 1960), pp. 9–10.

that the German character is *congenitally* authoritarian, that is, Germans are born goose-stepping and they are biologically aggressive, is, of course, invalid. This was a popular propaganda device used by the Allies—and most successfully—during both World Wars. The traditions of authoritarianism, discipline, and servility were environmentally produced, not inborn characteristics.

The Lure of Racial Nationalism

Until Hitler appeared on the scene, German nationalism had little or nothing to do with racialism. The call for German expansion was geared to economic, political, and cultural considerations, not to ethnic theories. Indeed, scattered throughout Germany were many Gobineau societies dedicated to Aryan racial supremacy, but these were regarded, especially in the German scientific community, as unworthy of serious attention. When Hitler came to political prominence, he was driven by his monomaniacal obsession to impose his racial views on the masses. His direct appeal to fierce primal passions was largely successful.

Had this type of racial nationalism been confined to buzzing cafe gossip, it would have merited only a small footnote in the history of the 20th century. But the deadly serious *Fuehrer* intended to go ahead on what he regarded as the biological cleansing of the Aryan-Nordic race. It is difficult for the normal mind to grasp such irrationalism but Hitler intended to achieve his goal.

Once his followers realized how deeply Hitler felt about his racial nationalism, they entered into a lively competition with one another to spread his ideology. It made no difference that most of Hitler's racialism was nonsense and that it was rejected by scientists all over the world. This was the truth as the *Fuehrer* saw it—the intellectual wave of the future, the creative gift of the emancipated German mind to a better world. *Rassenreinheit* (racial purity) was to be the ideal of the Third Reich. The "blood" substance of the Germanic race" was hailed as "a preeminent and unique asset of the entire world."

Professor Ernst Hauer revealed the extent of the official thinking about the blood:

Blood is sacred. It contains from ancient times, the generating mystery of families, tribes, and peoples. . . . The origin of the spirit is in the blood. There is a divine power in the blood which forms human beings in conformity with their predestined patterns. . . . It thus comes about that we so ardently love blood and soil and Fatherland and the history of our people with all its struggles, that we profoundly worship all this because God himself meets us here, materialized and immediate.[18]

Hauer was not alone in linking "blood and soil and Fatherland," in combining racialism with nationalism, It became a central theme in Nazi thinking. Felix Fischer-Dodeleben insisted that it was not possible to build up a German-Nordic religion if one omitted or rejected the sacred preservation of the blood. "Our religions must correspond to the inheritance of our people."[19] He warned that it was a sacred duty to see to it that "in our family no member of it by marriage of alien race weakens or spoils our German blood."[20] "Nor can sacred German blood be allowed to become diseased by marriage with the mentally inferior."[21]

Others became lyrical in their estimate of the rhythm of the blood. "In blood," wrote Dr. E. Krieck, "lurks our ancestral inheritance; in blood is embodied the race; from blood arise the character and destiny of man. Blood is to man the hidden undercurrent, the symbol of the current of life from which men can arise and ascend to the regions of light, of spirit and of knowledge."[22] Dr. Wilhelm Kusserow stated that only the Nordic race could be expected successfully to control Jewish influence on culture and industrial life; it was—as the Christian religion was not—race–conscious. "The union of all Nordic persons and peoples is the final moral duty of the Nordic racial community. Only when this is achieved will the danger of the downfall of the creative Nordic Man be banished."[23]

Walter Darré, agricultural expert in the Third Reich, attacked the Jews because they rejected everything that pertained to the pig. "The Nordic peoples, on the contrary, accord the pig the highest possible honor. In the ancient cult of the Germans the pig occupies the first place and is regarded as the first among the domestic animals. The Semites do not understand the pig, whereas the animal occupies first place in the cult of the Nordic peoples."[24]

Nazi racial thinking ventured closer and closer to the grotesque. *Rassenkunde* (study of race) and *Rassenforschung* (racial research) were elevated to

---

[18]Quoted in N. Gangulee, ed., *The Mind and Face of Nazi Germany* (London, 1942), pp. 56 ff.
[19]*Ibid.*
[20]*Ibid.*
[21]*Ibid.*
[22]*Ibid.*
[23]*Ibid.*
[24]*Ibid.*

the plane of respectable sciences in the Third Reich. The quality may be judged from this passage in which Professor Hermann Gauch reclassified the animal world into Nordic men and lower animals (Jews):

> Generally speaking, the Nordic races alone can emit sounds of untroubled clearness, whereas among non-Nordics the pronunciation is impure, the individual sounds are more confused and like the noises made by animals, such as barking, sniffing, snorting, squeaking.... That birds can talk better than other animals is explained by the fact that their mouths are Nordic in structure—that is to say, high, narrow, and short-tongued. The shape of the Nordic gum allows a superior movement of the tongue, which is the reason why Nordic talking and singing are fuller....
>
> If non-Nordics are more closely allied to monkeys and apes than to Nordics, why is it possible for them to mate with Nordics and not with apes? The answer is this: It has not been proved that non-Nordics cannot mate with apes.[25]

Detailed comment or refutation of such nonsense is unnecessary. Perverted racialism is fit only for the theater of the absurd.

Derivative Bestiality—the Holocaust

The theme has been presented here that it was in large part the combination of two factors—Hitler's monomania on the subject of racial nationalism and the German disposition to accept a perverted "legal" dictatorship—which was responsible for the descent into barbarism now generally termed the Holocaust. So unique was this phenomenon that it became necessary to coin a new word to describe it—genocide, from *genos* (a people) and *cide* (slaughter of). There has been little to compare it with in the course of civilization, not the depredations of Attila the Hun in the fourth century nor the massacre of

---

[25]Hermann Gauch, *Neue Grundlagen der Rassenforschung* (Berlin, n.d.), p. 165. This passage can be compared with an earlier contribution by the composer Richard Wagner on "Jewish sounds": "The Jew speaks the language of the nation in whose midst he dwells from generation to generation, but he always speaks it as an alien. Our whole European art and civilization have remained to the Jew a foreign tongue. In this speech, this art, the Jew can only after-speak and after-patch—not truly make a poem of his words, an artwork of his doings. In the peculiarities of Semitic pronunciation the first thing that strikes our ear as quite outlandish and unpleasant, in the Jew's production of the voice sounds, is a creaking, squeaking, buzzing sniffle [*ein zischender, schrillender, summsender und murksender Lautausdruck*]. This mode of speaking acquires at once the character of an intolerably jumbled blabber [*unerträglich verwirrten Geplappers*). The cold indifference of his peculiar blubber [*Gelabber*] never by chance rises to the ardor of a higher heartfelt passion." From *Richard Wagner's Prose Works*, tr. by William Ashton Ellis, 8 vols. (London, 1897), vol. I, pp. 84–85.

Huguenots by Philip II in 1575. There was some similarity in the Turkish atrocities of 1894, when slaughter of the most brutal character aroused great indignation in Europe, only to be followed by the attempt in 1915 by Turkish authorities to exterminate the entire Armenian population. More than 800,000 Christian Armenians died in the massacre. During Stalin's collectivization of argiculture, his "revolution-from-above," 5,000,000 *kulaks* died of starvation, were deported, or sent to labor camps. In the Maoist revolution many Chinese lost their lives from the crime of belonging to the despised bourgeoisie. Throughout history, and especially in time of war, there have been outbreaks of man's inhumanity to his fellow man. Yet not one of these atrocities can match in sheer horror Hitler's plan to purge unwanted elements from German life.

The term Holocaust refers specifically to the physical destruction of at least six million Jews, added to Poles, Russians, Gypsies, and others during the existence of the Third Reich. Hitler's hatred was directed especially against Jews. The Jews had been subjected to waves of persecution throughout their history, but never to a state-inspired movement of this magnitude carried through systematically and with such terrible consequences. There were warnings. As early as 1922 Hitler announced his plan to execute Jews on the gallows, though at that time he was not aware of the facilities of modern technology. He came to the conclusion that nothing would stand in the way of eliminating Judaism. Again and again he stated his goal, but too many Germans chose to ignore him. In the pages of *Mein Kampf* and in most of his speeches, he reverted to this compulsion. Once he had the opportunity, he was determined to wipe out all vestiges of Jewish influence in German life simply by destroying the existence of those tainted by Jewish blood. If, he said, at the start of World War I, someone had only submitted 12 to 15,000 of these Hebrew enemies of the people to poison gas, then the sacrifice of millions at the front would not have been in vain.

Soon after he became Chancellor on January 30, 1933, Hitler ordered a boycott of Jews as his response to what he called "the atrocity campaign against Germans" sponsored by Jews abroad, especially in the United States. The Nazi bureaucratic machine swung quickly into action. Jews were dropped from local governments, law courts, and universities. Nazi zealots threw bricks through the windows of Jewish-owned shops. Synagogues were wrecked by Nazi ruffians. Jewish doctors were denied the use of hospitals. Jews were forbidden to take part in cultural activities on the pretext that there were too many of them in the art world. Jewish men, women, and children were attacked on the streets and the police did not help.

From September to November 1935 Hitler ordered legal steps to define the status of Jews in Germany. The Nuremberg Laws on Citizenship and Race, the so-called Ghetto Laws, gave official sanction to the union of German nationalism and German racialism. Citizenship was withdrawn from persons of non-German blood. Abroad there was much criticism of the Nuremberg Laws but Hitler paid no attention. By mid-1938 every Jew was required to apply to the police for an identity card to be shown on demand. Male Jews were also ordered to add the name "Israel" and females the name "Sarah" to any non-Jewish first name. All passports held by Jews were to be marked for identification with a special J.

On November 7, 1938, Enrst vom Rath, a third secretary of the German embassy in Paris, was assassinated by Herschel Grynszpan, a young Jew. This act set into motion two days later the *Kristallnacht,* the Night of the Broken Glass, in which thousands of Jewish-owned stores were attacked and synagogues burned down. Hermann Goering now began to speak about "our final reckoning" with the Jews. On January 30, 1939, in a speech before the *Reichstag* celebrating the sixth anniversary of the beginning of the Nazi regime, Hitler publicly threatened the extermination of Jews (*Vernichtung*). Few Germans or Jews took the warning seriously.

No one knows the precise moment when Hitler finally decided upon the physical destruction of all Jews.[26] The concentration camp at Auschwitz was built in May 1940. In the summer of 1941, Rudolf Hoess, who had been commandant at Auschwitz for a year, was ordered to report to Heinrich Himmler. Himmler informed Hoess that Hitler had given the orders for a solution of the Jewish question, and that he, Himmler, had chosen Auschwitz for an important death camp because of its easy access by rail and because "it offered space for measures ensuring isolation."[27] On July 31, 1941, six weeks after the invasion of Soviet Russia, Hermann Goering gave Reinhard Heydrich absolute power to organize what he called "a complete solution":

Complementing the task that was assigned to you on January 24, 1939, which dealt with carrying out emigration and evacuation, a solution of the Jewish problem as advantageous as possible, I herewith charge you with making all necessary preparations with regard to organizational and financial matters for bringing about a complete solution of the Jewish question in the German sphere

[26]On the course of the Holocaust, see Eugen Kogen, *The Theory and Practice of Hell,* tr. by Heinz Norden (New York, 1950); Gerald Reitlinger, *The Final Solution* (New York 1961); Raul Hilberg, *The Destruction of the European Jews* (Chicago, 1961); and Nora Levin, *The Holocaust* (New York, 1968).
[27]Levin, *The Holocaust, op. cit.,* p. 292.

of influence in Europe. Wherever other governmental agencies are involved they are to cooperate with you. I request, furthermore, that you send me an overall plan . . . for the implementation of the desired final solution of the Jewish question.[28]

The most critical decision was made at the Wannsee Conference held on January 26, 1942, when the details were worked out for the Final Solution (*Endlösung*). Adolf Eichmann, who was Heydrich's specialist at ss headquarters, was designated for the task of liquidation. Heydrich informed the Nazi authorities at Wannsee that undoubtedly a great number of Jews would disappear through natural diminution (*naturliche Verminderung*), but that the remainder who survived "must be treated accordingly," because these people, representing a natural selection, had to be regarded as the germ cell of a new Jewish existence.

The actual process was now under way by which Jews were to be purged physically from German life. Preparations were made for the removal of Jews from concentration camps for dispatch to extermination centers. In the midst of World War II the *Gestapo,* the ss, and Nazi administrators followed Hitler's wishes in the ghastly task of eliminating non-Aryans from German life. The extermination camps at Maidanek, Treblinka, Chelmno, Belzec, and Sobibór went into action around-the-clock. At Auschwitz, most notorious of the death camps, 12,000 victims were gassed in one day. Hoess testified at Nuremberg how he had used Zyklon B, a crystallized prussic acid, which was dropped into the death chamber from a small opening. "It took from three to fifteen minutes to kill the people, depending on climatic conditions. We knew when the people were dead because the screaming stopped."

In late 1944 the extermination camps in Poland were threatened by onrushing Russian troops. By this time Himmler and some of his ss followers were doubting the efficacy of the slaughter program. It was becoming increasingly difficult to dispose of the bodies. Auschwitz was captured by the Russians in January 1945. A few months later Himmler made the gesture of releasing some Jewish prisoners for evacuation to Switzerland, hoping by this display of humanity to salvage his reputation. It was, however, far too late to undo the damage. British and American troops now overran the concentrations camps in Germany proper.

The entire civilized world reacted with horror when the extent of the

---

[28]Letter from Goering to Heydrich, July 31, 1941/Ps-710, from the English translation of the American edition, on *The Trial of the Major War Criminals, Nazi Conspiracy and Aggression* (Washington, D.C., 10 vols., 1946–1948).

Holocaust was revealed. Some captured Nazi leaders on trial at Nuremberg maintained that the atrocities were in reality the invention of Allied propaganda. At the same time millions of Germans finally came to the realization that the name of their country had been stained by an inexcusable lapse into barbarism.

Such was the result of the wrong kind of nationalism preached by the wrong kind of leader. It was also the wrong kind of nationalism for the Germans themselves. They had shown a willingness to sacrifice their rights and liberties to Nazi authoritarianism while gaining a questionable equality and prosperity. The outcome was suicide for Hitler, the death of millions of Germans, cities in ruins and ashes, and a sense of humiliation and shame which would torture the minds of surviving Germans.

C H A P T E R

11

Hans Kohn on German Nationalism

Nationalism in the West was based on the concept of a society which was
the product of political factors; German nationalism substituted for the
legal and rational concept of 'citizenship' which the Germans call
Staatsbürgerschaft—the infinitely vaguer concept of 'folk'—in German
Volk—which lent itself more easily to the embroideries of imagination and
the excitation of emotion.

Hans Kohn

Two American names stand out in the historiography of nationalism: the late
Carlton J. H. Hayes of Columbia University, from whose seminar on
nationalism emerged a stream of dedicated specialists; and the late Hans
Kohn, a scholar of worldwide renown. In the winter 1967 issue of *Orbis,* the
quarterly journal of world affairs published by the Foreign Policy Research
Institute of the University of Pennsylvania, the entire issue was dedicated to
Hans Kohn. Among the twenty-four articles was this tribute, which traced
Kohn's special interest in German history and German nationalism.

Discovery of a Creative Scholar

My first contact with the admirable and stimulating scholar, Hans Kohn, came
in the summer of 1937 when, as a neophyte historian groping for solid
ground, I was sent a book for review by the editor of the now defunct *Journal
of Social Philosophy.* It was a small volume of 176 pages titled *Force or*

Adapted from Louis L. Snyder, "Hans Kohn on Germany," *Orbis,* X (Winter, 1967), pp.
1327–1340. The present tense is retained in the discussion of Kohn's works. Kohn died in
Philadelphia, Pennsylvania, on March 15, 1971.

Reason: Issues of the Twentieth Century, published by Harvard University Press.

The book was a revelation. My reaction was one of complete enthusiasm, as indicated in the opening paragraph of the review:

> In this small but strikingly brilliant volume, Professor Kohn analyzes some of the aspects of the post-war world and traces their historical background. Without attempting to cover all the ramifications and implications of the various factors of present-day civilization, he coordinates these factors in masterly fashion and draws sound conclusions. To a perplexed world he offers a rekindled faith in the dignity of human nature and in the democracy which is being challenged by the current vogue of Force and *Machtpolitik.*

The review went on to examine the book in detail and pronounced it "a rare work which stands out among the hundreds of books being written these days." It praised Kohn's "fine historical intuition and his ability to describe the complex strains of historical development." It ended: "For the historian and layman it is a work of genuine intellectual art."

Each succeeding work by Kohn accented this early impression. Because our interests ran parallel—nationalism and German history—each paragraph from Kohn's pen became for me the object of close attention as well as increasing appreciation. It became clear to me that here was one of the great analytical minds of the 20th century, a master of creative scholarship, one of those rare historians whose flowing style matched a scintillating intellect.

Kohn's Early Awareness of Nationalism

Kohn's lifelong concern for the German problem was conditioned by the fact that he was born in the midst of it and in his early years became aware of its manifold facets and paradoxes. His early education was German in language and cultural form, though not necessarily *Germanic* in content. His ancestors had lived for generations in the Czech countryside and his immediate forebears settled in Prague. He spent his early years in the twilight of the Austro-Hungarian Empire which was to fall victim to the rising tide of nationalism, a development the young Kohn witnessed at first hand.

Prague at the end of the 18th century was culturally and socially a predominantly German city. German and Czech students collaborated in the heady days of the Revolution of 1848, but soon turned into bitter enemies. Germans began to speak of a Pan-Slavic danger; the Czechs saw Germans as enemies of their own national aspirations. From then on the two groups were locked in implacable struggle.

By 1900 Prague was preponderantly a Czech city. German was spoken by only about 5 percent of the population. But this relatively small group was a cultural and economic factor far greater than its size would indicate. Kohn grew up among this German-speaking minority with its separate cultural and social life. His first language was German. He attended the elementary school in the Herrengasse and obtained a thorough and vigorous classical training under Father Anton Hesky. He then entered the Altstädter Gymnasium in 1902, where he remained for eight years, from his eleventh through his nineteenth year, from the lowest *Prima* to the highest *Octava*.

In his autobiography, *Living in a World Revolution,* Kohn described the milieu in his inimitable fashion:

> The German minority did not feel the lack of "roots" in Prague. Our roots were there. We even accepted without much reflection the strange fact that in Prague the two national groups lived strictly separated lives. There was little, if any, social or cultural contact between them. Each had its own schools and universities, theaters and concert halls, sport clubs, and cabarets, restaurants and cafés— in all fields of life and activity there reigned a voluntary segregation, a kind of tacitly acknowledged "iron curtain" which separated two worlds living side by side, each one self-contained, scarcely communicating. In few other cities was nationalism as living and all-pervasive a force as in Prague at the beginning of the twentieth century.

It was this experience of his youth which, Kohn believes, predestined him to develop an awareness of the importance of nationalism. It also gave him insight not only into the German minority of Prague but into the Germans and Germany—the powerful neighbor to the north that was to become the keystone of Central European as well as European politics. In a series of superb studies on Germany and the Germans, Kohn became one of the world's foremost scholars on the history of the country and its people.

On German Romanticism and Nationalism

Kohn was one of the first historians to reveal how German history took a course almost diametrically opposed to the Western Enlightenment. Within the context of the intellectual traditions and social structure of the modern West, the Age of Reason represented a movement for a more open society—a society distinguished by the pursuit of individual happiness, the security of individual liberties, constitutionalism, tolerance, cosmopolitanism, the unfettering of thought, and a community of free citizens based on law. Western rationalism represented the intellectual side of a politico-economic pattern, in which the secularized bourgeoisie abandoned in fact and in theory the universal, imperial concept of the medieval world and supported such vital changes in the political and social order as democracy and liberalism. This "open society" placed reliance on the autonomy of the individual, on voluntary association, on a rational and humanitarian regard for one's fellow man.

Kohn sees this development as running counter to the course of German history. The German socio-political order was not changed essentially by the intellectual trends of the Age of Reason. The Germans persisted in retaining a politically vague universalism, as well as a tendency toward an authoritarian uniformity of state and faith. Where Western rationalism exalted the individual, the German idea stressed collective power and the state. Where the West was impressed by social contract and the universal similarity of nations, Germany turned to the irrational folk-concept—the myth of the blood and the idea of inferior and superior nations. Where the West appealed to individual rights, Germany turned to collective rights. The West was optimistic; Germany lacked self-assurance and relegated common citizens to the position of lackeys of the state. Rejecting the ideals of the Enlightenment, Germany developed an authoritarian or what Kohn calls a "closed society."

In this connection Kohn points to the nature of German romanticism, which gave nationalism and tradition their strongest expression. He sees German romanticism, poor in creative genius, mobilizing the totality of the past to fight against the principles of 1789. German romantics started as extreme individualists, and developed a longing for an organic folk-community that would immerse the individual in an unbroken chain of tradition. To them the nation-state or folk-state was not a societal organization based on human law with the purpose of assuring man's liberty, security and happiness, but an organic personality, God's creation like the individual himself, only greater and more powerful.

Kohn's studies reveal Georg Wilhelm Friedrich Hegel as a rationalist whose conception of the state resembled that of the romantics. Other Prussian professor-prophets, above all Heinrich von Treitschke, helped to mobilize national enthusiasm and to popularize Hegel's theory of the nation-state as the source of all law and ethics, as a superpersonality, whose essence was power (*Macht*). Hegel's dictum: "All the worth which the human being possesses—all spiritual reality, he possesses only through the state" led to dire consequences for the German people.

As an analytical historian of remarkable insight, Kohn sees the course of German history as suffused with tragedy. He presents the idea of polarity in German history: that dichotomy of ideas and procedures that has never been resolved. The history of Germany is described as a struggle for a working compromise between uniformity and disruption. Uniformity was contrary to the political and cultural divergencies among the Germans. At no time in German history was there a central power strong enough to crush the centrifugal tendencies of the component parts. At no time were the individual parts weak enough to allow themselves to be submerged into a highly centralized body, with the exception of the short-lived Hitler Reich. Where England and France emerged in early modern times as unified states, in the Germanies there persisted a fruitless struggle in pursuit of an idealistic world-empire—the recreation of the defunct, vague and shadowy Holy Roman Empire.

Kohn calls attention to the fact that the Germans themselves recognized their pessimistic attitude which divided them from the English-speaking peoples and made difficult mutual understanding in the realm of political thought. Germans easily succumbed to the fascination of such terms as *Schicksal* (fate) or *Verhängnis* (doom), words used as a matter of course in German writing and conveying an untranslatable overtone of unreality. Many German intellectuals were certain that they understood the course of history in a deeper way than the "superficial" peoples of the West. In a kind of higher spirituality these Germans found a compensation for their country's allegedly undeserved national misfortunes.

Kohn sees another tragic element in German history in the misconception of *Geist* (spiritual depth) and *Macht* (authoritarian power). In the 18th century the Germans, both intellectuals and others, underrated the importance of power and overrated purity of spirit. This attitude changed in the 19th century from one extreme to the other. Germans remained fundamentally apolitical, animated by a haughty contempt for politics, but still they emerged as a dynamic nation whose will centered on power and the power-state. From a life of the spirit, they turned to the pursuit of power. Having lived so long outside active participation in political history, the Germans tended to overstress the ideas of state and power. Their leading thinkers raised the nation, state and economy to supreme concepts, regarded history as the unfolding of ultimate and self-justifying reality, and distorted political processes to fit a semi-religious utopianism. Though other Western peoples distrusted power and feared its abuse, modern Germans felt an almost religious reverence for power (Ranke regarded it as a manifestation of a spiritual essence) and for its embodiment in the state. Thus power and state found popular symbols in army and uniform. Even the humblest Germans had a feeling of belonging.

These views on the general nature of the course of German history show Kohn at his analytical best. Many historians are so disgusted by the developments of German history that they either turn away from its study or denounce German nationalism, leadership and propensity for arousing hatred and contempt. Others become ardent defenders. Kohn is refreshingly free from either ingrained prejudice or bias. He sets himself the task of understanding. He is not interested in pointing at guilt but in explaining causation, motivation, roots. He rejects hostility and seeks clarity. His is that highly desirable approach based on just what happened: *was ist geschehen?* His work on German history remains an imposing contribution to historiography.

Analysis of German History

Let us turn to two works by Kohn specifically concerned with German history. In 1960 he published his *The Mind of Germany: The Education of a Nation*. Every page of this major work sparkles with the craftsmanship of a master historian. This is intellectual history at its very best. It remains today a dispassionate and objective classic on German intellectual history in modern times.

In this book Kohn projects "a tentative reply" to a question upon which much of the fascination of German history rests: How was it possible for a people such as the Germans, who had won enormous prestige in scholarship, music, literature and philosophy, deliberately to attempt national suicide? Kohn answers that responsibility for the disaster must be borne by those Germans who had rejected the humanitarian traditions of the West. The sentiment of nationalism had led the Germans on an errant path. "Perhaps the Germans have presented the most outstanding example in our times of the moral catastrophe, into which the malady of a self-centered nationalism and the accompanying *trahison des clercs* can lead."

In a series of penetrating chapters Kohn uses his favorite procedure of examining the foundations of German historical development by concentrating on key individuals in intellectual history. He absolves the magnificient Goethe from contributing to those deleterious pre-modern social and intellectual foundations which were retained by modern German society: Goethe, in Kohn's view, was a cosmopolitan who spurned the cult of the Middle Ages fostered by the romantics. Kohn shows how such romantics as Novalis and the Schlegel brothers placed abnormal stress on *German-ness,* with deplorable results later. He describes the integral nationalism of Turnvater Jahn and his intellectual war against the West. He quotes Heinrich Heine as issuing a warning against a unified Germany that would terrorize all Europe. His chapter on Richard Wagner is filled with psychological insight: "What separated Nietzsche from Wagner was not only the master's Germanophilism and racialism but also Wagner's character, his lusting for honors, women, and gold."

With this inductive approach, Kohn goes on to show how German liberalism began to wither in 1848, how in 1866 liberalism surrendered to nationalism, and how the liberal intellectuals finally surrendered to the might of Bismarck's *Eisen-und-Blut* empire.

In 1951 and 1952 Kohn made several visits to Germany, primarily to observe the progress of German historiography. The outcome of these visits was another outstanding volume published in 1954: *German History: Some New German Views.* In this book Kohn collected and edited essays written since 1945 by German historians. The scholars represented range from the deceased Friedrich Meinecke to his biographer, the thirty-four-year-old Walter Hofer, then *Dozent* at the University of Berlin.

The essays are uniformly excellent. Karl Buchheim discusses the *via dolorosa* of the civilian spirit in Germany. Franz Schnabel, the leading spokesman of the non-Prussian school of German historiography, re-evaluates the Bismarck problem, concluding that the Iron Chancellor, despite his achievements, never realized that in history only those forces are preserved which devote themselves to world and historic goals. In another essay on Bismarck, Alfred von Martin informs his countrymen that they had trod the path of error "because they are always impressed by the cavalryman's boot and a fist banged on the table."

Of equal merit are Hans Hertzfeld's treatment of militarism, Ludwig Dehio's review of Germany and the epoch of World Wars, Johann Albrecht von Rantzau on the glorification of the state in German historical writing, and Walter Hofer on revisionism in German history. Meinecke gives a penetrating picture of his predecessors Ranke and Burckhardt, but fails to emphasize their misunderstanding of the moral and historical resources of modern Western democracy. In a concluding essay Hajo Holborn, the Yale historian, calls for the formulation of a new concept of German history.

The importance of Kohn's *German History* lies in the encouraging fact that German scholars are beginning to face squarely the trends and ideas of their past, and to understand the meaning and consequences of state-worship and the power-complex implicit in Bismarck's rigid policies. They are now asking themselves whether the road followed by professional historians since Ranke had not been a wrong one, especially in the matter of value judgments. "There are some hopeful signs at present," Kohn writes, "that several German historians are seeking ways which will help to integrate the Germans into the West and thus provide a new opportunity for their creative contribution to a common civilization based on a common heritage."

Kohn's Analysis of German Nationalism

Although these two books give us a general pattern of Kohn's conception of the course of German history, by no means do they represent all his interest in and knowledge of that subject. In a series of studies published in scholarly journals, he examines every conceivable phase of modern German history. For convenience in discussing this work we shall divide it into four major subjects: (1) German nationalism; (2) Germany between East and West; (3) Germany and Russia; and (4) the nature of contemporary Germany. Each of these subjects is handled in Kohn's graceful style (few writers outside of Conrad, Koestler and Kohn have mastered so well the intricacies of writing in another language).

First, the concept of German nationalism combines two of Kohn's major interests as a historian: the course of German history, and the sentiment of nationalism. Nationalism has been Kohn's lifelong interest; it is fair to say that he is today our leading authority on the subject.

Kohn sees nationalism, reflecting the course of German history, characterized by two interwoven strains: an emphasis upon liberal constitutional rights after the Western pattern, and a struggle for national power strengthened by authoritarianism. In his view it was unfortunate that the second strain became predominant in three decisive moments of German history: the War of Liberation—1813, the Revolution of 1848, and national unification in 1871. "It was Germany's misfortune that she had a Bismarck and not a Gladstone, not even a Cavour."

German nationalism arose in the early 19th century as a newly awakened response against Napoleon and French missionary nationalism. The struggle against the French conqueror was led inside Germany by writers and intellectuals, who saw German nationalism not only as a rejection of Napoleon's rule but also of all the principles upon which the American Revolution and the French Revolution had been based. In essence this was a repudiation of liberal and humanitarian nationalism.

In the Revolution of 1848 the professors at the Frankfurt Assembly strove mightily to achieve German unification on a liberal basis, but they collapsed along with the revolution. The result was a nationalism based eventually on Bismarck's policy of *Blood and Iron.* And in fact German unification in 1871, following three wars, was achieved in a milieu of authoritarianism and militarism.

Kohn is at his best in describing the subsequent course of German nationalism in the 19th century. He shows in broad strokes how nationalism began to emphasize instinct against reason, how it stressed the power of historical tradition against national attempts at progress and a more just order. He describes how German nationalists tended to regard liberalism and equality as brief aberrations, "against which the eternal foundations of societal order would prevail." A temporary rebirth of liberal nationalism was reversed in Germany by Bismarck, who achieved national unification on a conservative basis and defeated German liberalism. Bismarck's annexation of Alsace-Lorraine, for example, was against the will of its inhabitants, and certainly contrary to the principle of nationalism grounded on the free will of man. Only a small number of Germans dismissed the Bismarck ethos or doubted his wisdom.

Kohn sees the tragedy of German history in this unfortunate course of German nationalism. Bismarck's Second German Reich, a product of victorious war, a state suffused with authoritarianism and militarism, collapsed just two decades after his death in 1898. The Prussian monarchy disappeared in 1918 after the severe defeat of World War I. The Weimar Republic, "a republic with few republicans, a democracy with few democrats," was unwanted, unloved, misunderstood. Nationalism underwent a frenzied rebirth in Hitler's Third Reich, "which revived, expanded, popularized, and vulgarized the glories of the Second Reich.'' As in 1813, 1848, and 1870–1871, a sense of national power and greatness was reborn, only to collapse ignominiously in the debacles of 1918 and 1945.

Germany between East and West

The second major Kohn interest concerns Germany as fulcrum between East and West. Here Kohn recognizes the major influence of geography on history without succumbing to the blandishments of geopolitics. Germany likes to call herself the heartland of Europe: Kohn points out that geographically this is true. But spiritually and culturally Germany, throughout most of European historical development since Roman times, has been a frontier land of Western civilization. In the Middle Ages and in the 18th century, the Germanies were actually an integral and important part of the West. This centrally located area was the catalyst through which the course of civilization flowed westward.

But as a competent historian Kohn never limits himself to simplistic interpretations and is well aware of the paradoxes of history. Despite its role as the mediator between West and East, there were times from Arminius to Hitler when Germany spearheaded war against the West. From the days of German romanticism in the early 19th century onward, Germany often influenced anti-Western ideas among the peoples farther to the east. Added to romanticism was German historicism, partly a reaction against the abstract principles of the Enlightenment. Originating with Möser, Hegel and Marx, German historicism was revived and altered by Dilthey and Troeltsch, and it was given a subtle interpretation by Meinecke. Primarily a philosophical approach to history, historicism was used to explain the differences between German and West European intellectual life. Where the rationalists believed in reason, intellect and pragmatism as the keys of history, the historicists placed greater emphasis upon soul, intuition and ''wisdom without reflection.'' Stripped of its imposing façade, its ponderous verbiage, and its nuanced intellectualism, historicism was a highly rationalized anti-Western argument in support of Prussianism and German nationalism.

In Kohn's estimation, Germany's troubles stemmed from the tragic consequences of departing from the Western tradition. Everything the Germans considered of value in their own history was developed in contrast to Western ideas and experience. The war of 1914–1918 was widely regarded inside

Germany as a war against the West. Behind it was a long historical process extending back to the 18th century. In Kohn's view, the fact that Germany was attracted by the East and could think of preparing for the Second German War was partly the fault of the West. World War II, an extension of a new conflict between East and West, was, in Kohn's interpretation, directly Hitler's work. "Hitler's attack on Russia forced the democracies and the Soviet Union into an unwilling cooperation which, given the nature of Russian communism, could not last despite some widespread disillusions in the West."

In clarifying this Janus-like attitude of Germany between East and West, Kohn pinpoints the meaning and substance of German history. Torn between the open society of the West and the closed society of the East, the Germans until 1945 became the spearhead of the struggle against the West. Their role as spoiler of the Western tradition makes understandable the deep distrust of Germany still prevailing in many European countries.

German and Russian Confrontation

The third major Kohn interest, closely tied to his second, is concerned with the old streams and new realities of the relationship between Germany and Russia. Kohn's knowledge of Russia is not limited to that of the armchair historian. Serving as a young man in the Austro-Hungarian Army in World War I, he was taken prisoner during the Carpathian campaign in the early hours of March 21, 1915. From then on, until January 21, 1920—for almost five years—he was to remain a prisoner in Russia, chiefly in Siberia. These years, which in many ways he has always regarded as the decisive years of his life, gave him a continuing personal encounter with war, revolution and colonialism, as well as a remarkable front-line seat at the drama of Russian history. Few historians can match Kohn's keen understanding of the impact of Germany and Russia on each other.

Kohn sees the confrontation of Germany and Russia in both world wars as the extension of old historical aspirations and trends. Fundamentally, this was a rivalry between Germans and Slavs for control of central eastern Europe, and the Germans eventually lost the competition. The forces of history showed tremendous staying power: the rivalry continued and it was even accelerated in the era between Bismarck and Hitler. In *Mein Kampf*, Hitler made it clear that he would never be trapped in a two-front war, and that in spect he would never repeat the experience of the Wilhelminian Reich. despite the bitter scorn he poured on his predecessors in both Wilhelmi-n and Weimar periods, he had the same sort of decisive dreams and made .ie same errors of the past, exaggerating them in every instance.

Russia emerged from World War II the strongest military land power in Europe and Asia. Following her own path, so different from that of Western liberalism, she assumed the defense of all the former Russian Pan-Slavic and Pan-Asiatic aspirations in most advanced form. A new situation was created in Europe: Russian power and German folly were at the bottom of it. Since the time of Bismarck, Germany had been the strongest power in Europe in numbers, industrial equipment and efficiency. Now she found herself dwarfed in all three fields by Russia.

In both cases—in Russia and Germany—the key to the future, in Kohn's estimation, is to be found in contact with the West. Kohn believes that the hope for a better world lies in the full integration of Russia with the West, a process which began in the 18th century and ended abruptly in November 1917 with the Bolshevik Revolution. He feels that growing contact with the freedom of the West, if not artifically suppressed by the Soviet government, might start again that fermentation and that revolutionary cycle which began when Russia's victorious troops under Alexander I came into contact with and learned about Europe.

The New German National Character

Kohn adds to that "hope for the future" the reintegration of Germany into Western civilization. This leads us to Kohn's fourth major theme: the nature of contemporary German development. Here he sees extraordinary progress. A new opportunity has arisen for the creative contribution of contemporary Germans to a common civilization based on a common heritage. Kohn believes that the new German Federal Republic is safely anchored to the West and that the new German generation is finding inspiration and social solidarity in a return to the principles of human freedom. Germany's two hegemonial wars of the 20th century brought the peoples and civilization of Europe to the brink of catastrophe. But out of this cataclysm has come one great gain: a democratic Germany that is finally taking its rightful place in modern Western society.

Kohn sees 1945 as a critical date of German history. At the close of World War II there existed no German state, no German administration, no German government. German cities had been reduced to rubble and ruin by Allied bombing; the country was overcome by ghastly poverty and hopelessness.

Then came the miracle: political, economic, intellectual. Partly due to the efficiency and discipline of the German people, but also because of American assistance, Germany rose from the ashes in the form of the German Federal Republic, the most modern state the Germans ever conceived. Politically, the old centralization and uniformity fostered by the cult of power was replaced by a federal structure. Prussia ceased to exist; the mystique of the old German Reich lost its hold over the German mind. The new Germany was protected against the dangerous trend of centralization.

A decade after 1945 the West German economy attained a recovery almost without parallel in history. Unemployment was reduced, the currency reserve rose, public figures showed surpluses despite tax reduction, and production rose rapidly. It was an extraordinary spectacle. The recovery of West Germany was a classic case of the free-market economy operating successfully with a limited number of strategically selected controls, and helped greatly by politico-economic developments outside Germany's borders.

Some observers attribute the beaverlike activity of contemporary Germans to a desperate search to forget the past and sublimate their guilt feelings by a highly neurotic concern for work and more work. Whatever the reason, the Germans rapidly rose to the top of the European economic structure, with German goods again flowing to the markets of the world and the German mark widely recognized as one of the most stable of currencies.

Kohn, with his deep interest in intellectual history, is more attracted by changes in the German mentality than in Germany's economic success. He sees the Germans of today as far less addicted to metaphysics, to *Weltanschauung,* than in earlier times. As an advocate of the idea that national character is always in process of change, Kohn believes that the Germans have taken on a sober and practical quality different from the past. They now think within the framework of political and social realities instead of ephemeral nationalist ideas. The traditional German love for the uniform and the paraphernalia of militarism has gone.

Most important of all, Kohn sees the German mind as finally attuned spiritually with the West and the Free World. This is the culmination of a long period in which the German mind oscillated between West and East, apparently unable to choose between the two, again and again selecting Eastern ideas at precisely the wrong moment. Kohn sees this unsatisfactory state of affairs as changed—at long last. In his view this is one of the most promising developments of the 20th century. The alienation from the West has come to an end in a process that has been going on for a long time. The war in 1914 inflamed the anti-Western, folk-centered and militarist passions in Germany precisely at a time when a *rapprochement* with Western liberal democracy seemed to be on the way. The situation changed after World War II, when the defeat of Germany preserved liberty and civilization not only in the greater part of Western and Central Europe but also in Germany itself.

Fundamentally, Kohn's view is an optimistic one. It has been challenged by historians who point to the isolated outbursts of pro-Nazi sentiment, as yet small but nevertheless existing. There are continuing reports of Nazi reunions and the conviction that "We really didn't lose the war!" Some observers point to the tragedy of the Weimar Republic, which was unsuccessful in forestalling Hitler, and ask how confidence can be placed in a people who react irrationally at critical moments in their history.

Kohn is not impressed by these arguments. He sees the new German trend toward the West as considerably more decisive than the past tendency to fall to totalitarian tyranny. The German Federal Republic, he feels, is the first real attempt to create a Western-oriented, liberal and democratic Germany. The West, he says, can be satisfied. The chances of a free Germany in the Western sense are far greater today than at any time in the past hundred years, despite the recrudescence or occasional manifestation of the older form of German nationalism.

Beyond the Fragmentation of Nationalism

Kohn's attitude toward contemporary Germany reflects his general sense of optimism. He sees global conditions in the second half of the 20th century, with the rapid advances in communication and transportation, as leading to a world society beyond the fragmentation of nationalism. He calls again and again for international cooperation on a worldwide basis, corresponding to the new reality of the common destiny of mankind.

The tortuous course of German history, with its many tragedies, has attracted the attention of scholars. Certainly the task of clarification is a difficult one. With his extraordinary insight, his analytical mind, and his masterly prose style, Kohn takes a place on a high plateau among those great historians who have contributed something of value in the interpretation of the history and intellectual development of the Germans.

CHAPTER

12

On German Aggression: Territorial Imperative?

Man is a territorial species and . . . we defend our homes or our homelands
for biological reasons, not because we choose to but because we must.

Robert Ardrey

The Problem of German Aggression

The matter of German aggression has engaged the attention of several generations of historians. On the one hand are those who from the evidence in the
archives assert that German integral nationalism was aggressive at its roots
and that it was one of the main contributors to the outbreak of both World
Wars in the 20th century. Add this driving impulse for territory, say these
historians, to such motivations as economic rivalries, social chaos,
militarism, and international anarchy, and one finds the Germans responsible
for both wars.

On the other side are the revisionist historians who refuse to acknowledge
this drive for expansion and insist that the causes for both conflicts are to be
found in the nature of European society. The Germans, say the revisionists,
were no more responsible than other peoples. Revisionist schools emerged in
1918 and 1945 to distribute the onus in several directions.

Some historians prefer to make a distinction between the two wars. One
group, including Bernadotte Schmitt, attributed World War I to German aggression. From the viewpoint of these historians the German General Staff
wanted war and prepared for it for some forty years. Admittedly, non-German

Adapted from Louis L. Snyder, "Nationalism and the Territorial Imperative." *Canadian Review
of Studies in Nationalism,* I, no. 1, pp. 1–21.

as well as German statesmen had made serious errors in the everyday diplomatic moves, but these errors were ultimately irrelevant when compared with the German drive for war.

Revisionists such as Harry Elmer Barnes disagreed. They presented the explanation that although German statesmen did make moves that contributed to a war situation, they should not be accused of deliberately plotting war. It was false, said the revisionists, to paint Germany's prewar record as uniquely aggressive. In fact, Germany's statesmen worked energetically to prevent the conflict, because they knew that the great gains made in times of peace might be jeopardized. This point of view was most acceptable to German historians then in the midst of an organized campaign to combat what they called the *Kriegsschuldlüge* (war-guilt lie).

A third approach held that responsibility for World War I was equally distributed and that the war was the result of unresolved economic clashes, diplomatic intrigues, national rivalries, sword rattling, and a psychologically unsound conception of security. Those who took this attitude had in mind not only the crisis of June and July 1914 but also the general cultural and institutional situation behind the assassination at Sarajevo. Serious mistakes of judgment were made on all sides during the critical weeks. Most historians accept this view that while individuals may have been responsible for diplomatic errors, it was the milieu which was the danger not personal mistakes. Lloyd George explained the catastrophe in these words: "The more one reads of the memoirs and books written in the various countries of what happened before August 1, 1914, the more one realizes that no one at the head of affairs quite meant war. It was something into which they glided, or rather staggered and stumbled."

In a sense this view relieved Germany of sole responsibility for the outbreak of war in 1914. Then in 1961 more fuel was added to the controversy by the publication in Germany of *Griff nach der Weltmacht* by Fritz Fischer, a historian at the University of Hamburg. Translated into English in 1967 under the title *Germany's Aims in the First World War,* the book shocked Fischer's colleagues by presenting the thesis that Germany deliberately aimed at world domination in 1914–1918. This was by no means a popular, undocumented account: it was a minutely detailed and carefully researched study based on both Western and German archives. Fischer linked the development of German war aims with the general climate among Germany's rulers in the prewar years. He showed how hopes of annexing territory on both western and eastern frontiers were the logical result of ideas which had gained wide currency for some years before 1914. Moreover, he revealed the tenacity with which German leaders had clung to their original aims.

Fischer's book made much of the earlier war literature obsolete. The German historian described a nightmare world in which Germany's war aims were placed above any other consideration. He had brought home an unpleasant fact—Germany's drive for territorial expansion was just as strong before 1914 as it was in 1939.

The intellectual battle on aggression before World War I rages on. There is more general agreement that the blame for *starting* World War II rests solely and squarely on Adolf Hitler. Admittedly, the general economic, political and psychological climate in the late 1930s was such that war could be expected. But it is clear that continued aggressions by Nazi Germany provided the immediate sparks for the conflagration. The very existence of the Third Reich, with its goals already blueprinted in Hitler's *Mein Kampf,* was a threat to peace. It is clear from Hitler's writings, conversations, and especially from secret reports captured during the war, that Hitler wanted his war. "For the good of the German people," he said privately in his *Secret Conversations,* "we must wish for a war every fifteen or twenty years. An army whose sole purpose is to preserve peace leads only to playing at soldiers—compare Sweden and Switzerland." At the same time this master of the lie informed the world: "I am not crazy enough to want a war. The German people have but one wish—to be happy in their own way and to be left in peace."

Highly competent scholars agree on this interpretation—among them the British historians John W. Wheeler-Bennett and Lewis Namier, and the Americans William Langer, Norman Rich, and Gerhard Weinberg. All see a continuity in Hitler's thinking, what amounted to an ideology of aggression. Hitler was convinced that German security was absolutely dependent upon territorial expansion in Eastern Europe. He was certain that France would attack Germany once German armies were committed against the Soviet Union. His war policy was neither a mistake nor was it forced on him.

The inevitable revisionism came with the work of A. J. P. Taylor, to which we have already referred. (See chapter 9, footnote 58.) Taylor came to the conclusion that equal if not more blame should be placed on the British and French statesmen than on the German *Fuehrer.* There is one piece of evidence which Taylor was unable to explain adequately. At a secret meeting held on November 5, 1937, Hitler outlined to his military leaders the practical steps

for undertaking aggression against other countries. The minutes were recorded by Colonel-General Friedrich Hossbach, Hitler's adjutant for the
Wehrmacht, the armed forces. No revisionist, including Taylor, has been able
to explain away these words:

> The *Fuehrer* then stated: The aim of German policy is the security and preserva-
> tion of the *Volk* and its propagation. This is consequently a problem of space. . . .
> The question for Germany is where the greatest possible conquest can be made at
> lowest cost. . . .
>
> If the *Fuehrer* is still living, then it will be his irrevocable decision to solve the
> German space problem no later than 1943–1945. . . . For the improvement of our
> military political position it must be our first aim, in every case of entanglement
> by war, to conquer Czechoslovakia and Austria simultaneously, in order to
> remove any threat from the flanks in case of a possible advance westward. . . .
> Once Czechoslovakia is conquered—and a mutual frontier of Germany-Hungary
> is obtained—then a neutral attack by Poland in a German-French conflict could
> be more easily relied upon. Our agreements with Poland remain valid only as
> long as Germany's strength remains unshakeable. . . .
>
> The *Fuehrer* believes personally that, in all probability England and perhaps also
> France, have already silently written off Czechoslovakia. . . . Without England's
> support it would also not be necessary to take into consideration a march by
> France through Holland and Belgium. . . . Naturally, we should in every case
> have to secure our frontier during the operation of our attacks against Czecho-
> slovakia and Austria. . . .
>
> Military preparation by Russia must be countered by the speed of our operations;
> it is a question whether this needs to be taken into consideration at all, in view of
> Japan's attitude.

This is it—the ultimate evidence. Seldom in the annals of historiography
have historians been presented with a more clear-cut revelation of aggressive
thinking than the Hossbach Memorandum. It is not a falsified document—
this is plainly what the man said.

There have been many attempts to explain the nature of German aggression. Recently there has emerged a new treatment of the concept of the
territorial imperative and its corollaries of expansionism, aggression,
nationalism, and crusading imperialism. The idea is highly controversial and
provocative and some observers believe that it should be ignored. It would
seem to be the better part of wisdom to look into it. While not referring
specifically to the German scene, certainly the concept may be applied to
Germany as well as to other nations of the 20th-century world.

The Multidisciplinary Approach to the Study of Nationalism

The most recent attempt to elucidate the nature of nationalism comes from disciplines adjacent to that of the historian. This view holds that nationalism, stripped to its essentials, is merely the behavior of the human animal in defending the territory he has staked out for himself. It is claimed that this is an extension of the behavior of lower species. Just as many species of lower animals are governed by the territorial imperative, so have human beings turned to nationalism as their version of the same instinct.

The projection of this thesis has led to a bitter confrontation among scientists. This quarrel is of special interest to those social scientists who have concerned themselves with the problem of clarifying this most complex historical ism.

The difficulty is that nationalism is so suffused with inconsistencies, contradictions, and paradoxes that there is little agreement as to exactly what it is. There are difficulties in arriving at a satisfactory meaning for a historical phenomenon which some scholars believe to be the most important thing in the world. In the search for clarification such historians as Carlton J. H. Hayes, Hans Kohn, and Boyd C. Shafer did pioneer work in setting up a traditional approach to the study of nationalism.[1] But because nationalism is first and foremost a state of mind, what Hans Kohn called "an act of consciousness," it is obvious that the study of nationalism cannot remain exclusively the sphere of the historian, but by logical necessity must be treated from an interdisciplinary or multidisciplinary viewpoint.

For this reason historians have waited patiently for assistance from other disciplines. The contributions range from bad to good to excellent. On the questionable side was the attempt made by the psychiatrist Richard M. Brickner to show that German nationalism was paranoid in nature and that virtually the entire German people were mentally ill.[2]

---

[1] See Carlton J. H. Hayes, *Essays on Nationalism* (New York, 1926); *France: A Nation of Patriots* (New York, 1930); *A Generation of Materialism, 1871–1890* (New York, 1941); *Historical Evolution of Modern Nationalism* (New York, 1931); and *Nationalism: A Religion* (New York, 1960); Hans Kohn, *The Age of Nationalism* (New York, 1962); *American Nationalism* (New York, 1967); *Nationalism and Imperialism in the Hither East* (London, 1932); *Nationalism and Liberty: The Swiss Example* (London, 1956); *Nationalism in the Soviet Union* (London, 1933); *Nationalism: Its Meaning and History* (Princeton, 1955); *Prelude to Nation-State* (Princeton, 1967); and *Prophets and Peoples: Studies in Nineteenth Century Nationalism* (New York, 1963); *Nationalism: Myth and Reality* (New York, 1955) and *Faces of Nationalism* (New York, 1972).

[2] Richard M. Brickner, *Is Germany Incurable?* (Philadelphia, 1943).

This extreme view is balanced by contributions from other disciplines. Thus, the sociologist Konstantin Symmons-Symonolewicz has done first-rate work in analyzing nationalism as a social movement with accent on the nation as a we-group, while the political scientist Hans J. Morgenthau has recounted well the incongruities of nationalism in his A-B-C paradox (the existence of every nation-state is paradoxically a denial of the very right of nationalism to others).[3]

To the traditional classifications of nationalism by Hayes, Kohn, Shafer, and their disciples has been added the quantitative approach of the political scientist Karl W. Deutsch and the psychologist Leonard Doob, both of whom seek a more inductive treatment of nationalism.[4]

Such work, however, comes under the category of exceptions to the general rule. On the whole, the work on nationalism in neighboring disciplines has seldom been in depth and has added little to the overall knowledge of this important historical phenomenon.

The Lorenz-Ardrey-Morris Combination

In recent years, naturalists, biologists, and anthropologists have entered the arena. One group consists of the naturalist Konrad Lorenz, the biologist Robert Ardrey, and the anthropologist Desmond Morris. Let us arbitrarily name it the LAM group, although there is no unity in their work. And let us look into their thesis in detail, despite the attitude of some scientists and historians that their work is so fallacious that it is wrong to dignify it by any attention. The present observer begs to dissent—our knowledge of nationalism is so incomplete that we cannot afford to ignore any line of investigation.

Briefly stated, the LAM thesis asserts that man, like the lower animals, has been moved instinctively and unconsciously to defend his own living space in what is called the "territorial imperative." This term is defined as an instinct by which animals regulate the distances among their members and stand aloof from other species. According to this theory, the ownership of land is not a

---

[3]Konstatin Symmons-Symonolewicz, *Nationalist Movements: A Comparative View* (Meadville, Pa., 1970); Hans J. Morgenthau, "The Paradoxes of Nationalism," *Yale Review*, XLVI (June, 1957), pp. 481 ff.
[4]Karl W. Deutsch, *Nationalism and Social Communication: An Inquiry into the Foundations of Nationality* (Cambridge, Mass., 1966); *An Interdisciplinary Bibliography on Nationalism, 1933-1955* (Cambridge, Mass., 1956); and *Nationalism and Its Alternatives* (New York, 1969); and Leonard Doob, *Patriotism and Nationalism: Their Psychological Foundations* (New Haven, 1964).

human invention but rather one that has existed and now exists widely among such animals as lions, wolves, eagles, ring-tailed lemurs, seals, gorillas, and many other species who set aside a specific amount of territory as their private domain and aggressively attack invaders who would seek to take it from them.

This territorial propensity, according to the LAM school, is revealed in remarkable uniformity when, by means of revolutionary trial and error, species incorporate a zealous regard for territory into their general behavior complex. The instinct is said to be innate and to be even stronger most of the time than the sex drive. What it does is to give the species security from predators as well as access to a vital food supply.

The LAM thesis does not halt at this point. It goes on to apply the idea of territorial imperative to the human species on the assumption that man is a higher form of animal and, despite his greater brain capacity, lives and acts according to the same motives that influence the lower animals. It is claimed that when human beings form social grouping to defend their title to the land or the sovereignty of their country, they are acting for reasons no different from and no less innate than similar motivations in the lower animal world. Thus, man's territorial expression is a human response as an imperative affecting both men and lower animals.

It follows, according to LAM reasoning, that the nation-state is merely an invention of man to indicate the territory of his in-group. With this hypothesis, nationalism reflects a sense of consciousness that leads man to protect his own territory from those who would take it from him. From this point of view nationalism becomes, not a historical phenomenon whose emergence was as artificial as the building of the Panamal Canal, but rather the natural expression of an innate drive for security, a drive existing in all animals from the barnyard rooster to *Homo sapiens*.

The Work of Konrad Lorenz

The origins of the LAM school may be found in the work of the Austrian naturalist Konrad Lorenz, who is generally considered to be one of the most important founders of ethology, the science of animal behavior under natural conditions of life.[5] Lorenz was born in Vienna on November 7, 1903, the son of an orthopedic surgeon. After attendance at the Schotten *Gymnasium,* he

---

[5]The modern science of ethology is concerned with depicting character, customs, and moral motives, or the study of manners, customs, and mores. Lorenz is especially interested in the branch of ethology concerned with the behavior of lower animals.

took doctorates at the University of Vienna in medicine, philosophy, and political science.

In 1940 Lorenz wrote an article in the *Journal of Applied Psychology and Personality Science,* in which he supported "race-preserving" measures to avoid the "degeneracy" in man that is typical of domesticated animals. The latter, he wrote, unlike their relatives in the wild, are not bred along strictly racial lines and hence are ugly and degenerate. The danger, he warned, was that socially inferior human material is enabled to penetrate and finally annihilate the healthy nation. He suggested that the racial idea, as the basis of the Third Reich, had already accomplished much in this respect. Later, in 1943, Lorenz re-stated and elaborated these ideas in a 174-page article in the *Journal of Animal Psychology.* This attitude, seemingly in support of racial doctrine, strongly appealed to Nazi authorities, who were anxious to obtain "scientific" evidence for Hitler's monomania on the subject of race.

Such views were later to prove embarrassing to Lorenz. In 1973 he was awarded the Nobel Prize in physiology and medicine along with Niko Tinbergen and Karl von Fritsch, both specialists in animal behavior. On announcement of the award, Simon Wiesenthal, head of the Documentation Center at Vienna, who had made a career of running down Nazi war criminals, wrote to Lorenz and asked him to decline the prize as a gesture of contrition for his writings on racial purity during the era of the Third Reich. At a news conference held in Stockholm in October 1973, Lorenz said: "I deeply regret [these writings]. I have very different notions now concerning the Nazis."

Meanwhile, after the war Lorenz headed the Max Planck Institute for Behavioral Psychology at Seewiesen in Bavaria. Here his experiments with geese attracted worldwide attention. His book, *King Solomon's Ring,*[6] published in 1952, was followed in 1963 by a study, *Das sogennante Böse: Zur Naturgeschichte der Aggression,*[7] specifically concerned with the problem of aggression. The theme of this book may be reduced to a single formula: one particular instinct which is common to animals and man is aggression. Lorenz stated the analogy:

> An impressive example of behavior analogous to human morality can be seen in the ritualized fighting of many vertebrates. Its whole organization aims at fulfilling the most important function of the rival fight, namely to ascertain which

---

[6]Konrad Z. Lorenz, *King Solomon's Ring* (New York, 1952).
[7]Konrad Z. Lorenz, *Das sogennante Böse: Zur Naturgeschichte der Aggression* (Vienna, 1963). The English edition was translated by Marjorie Kerr Wilson under the title *On Aggression* (New York, 1966).

partner is stronger, without hurting the weaker. Since all human sport has a similar aim, ritualized fights give the impression of "chivalry" or "sporting firmness."[8]

Lorenz's basic assumption was that human behavior, and particularly human social behavior, far from being determined by reason and cultural tradition alone, is still subject to all the laws prevailing in phylogenetically adapted instinctive behavior.[9] We have a fair amount of knowledge of such laws, Lorenz wrote, from studying the instincts of animals. He drew the conclusion that "man's social organization is very similar to that of rats, which, like humans, are social and peaceful beings within their class, but veritable devils toward all fellow-members of their species not belonging to the community."[10]

Lorenz began his account by recording his observations of strikingly colored coral-reef fish in tanks and in the sea. He noted how each territory holder, excited by invaders of its own species, attacked and drove off the trespasser. He then went on to reveal how territorial defense fighting in lower vertebrates, birds, and mammals became crucial in natural selection. Such defense, he is convinced, is a basis for food-getting, mating, rearing of the young, and in general for promoting survival.

At the root of the Lorenz instinct conception among lower animals is what he calls the "spontaneity" of behavior. All instincts, he suggested, are characterized by spontaneity. It is this character of spontaneity that makes the aggressive drive so dangerous. Aggression follows a set formula: a specific energy accumulates in that part of the central nervous system responsible for the coordination of behavior, builds up spontaneously, and is discharged when the response is performed.

From this background Lorenz attempted to prove the evolution of human behavior. It runs parallel, he believes, to the biological forms among all the lower animals. The mechanism of territorial defense fighting is similar in man and the lower animals. Intra-specific aggression is deeply rooted in man's biology. "It is more than probable that the destructive intensity of the aggression drive, still a hereditary evil of mankind, is the consequence of a process of intra-specific selection which worked on our forefathers for roughly forty thousand years, that is, through the Early Stone Age."[11]

---

[8]Lorenz, *On Aggression,* pp. 110–111.
[9]*Ibid.,* p. 237.
[10]*Ibid.,*
[11]*Ibid.,* p. 42.

Lorenz pointed out that both man and the lower animals are addicted to ritualistic displays in which aggression is warded off with little or no contact. In man there are inhibitory controls on aggression both through natural selection and through cultural processes. These controls may fail in split-second emergencies. Man can dedicate himself to a point where he will kill his brother while convinced that what he is doing is in defense of the highest moral values. Lorenz shared this concept with Freud, who also spoke about inevitable violent expressions of irresponsible human conflict.

Lorenz saw in sport one of the many instances in which phylogenetic and cultural ritualization has hit on a similar solution of the same problem. Both man and the lower animals have achieved the difficult task of avoiding killing without destroying the important functions performed by fighting in the interest of the species. "All the culturally evolved forms of 'fair fighting' from primitive chivalry to the Geneva Convention, are functionally analogous to phylogenetically ritualized combat in animals."[12] The Olympic Games, for example, "are virtually the only occasion when the anthem of one nation can be played without arousing hostility against another. This is so because the sportsman's dedication to the international social norms of his sport and the ideals of chivalry and fair play is equal to any national enthusiasm."[13] Thus, sporting contests between nations are beneficial not only because they provide an outlet for the collective militant enthusiasm of nations, but because they promote acquaintance between different nations.

With this argument Lorenz headed straight into the territory of the historian of nationalism. While he does not mention the specific term "nationalism," it is nevertheless clear that, in combining his theory about instincts in general and intra-specific aggression in particular, he is actually referring to nationalism as a pattern of human behavior. He sees a compounding danger of human society becoming increasingly disintegrated by "the malfunction of the social behavior pattern."[14] He warns about the danger of isolating art forms in national patterns: "Art is called upon to create supranational, suprapolitical values that cannot be denied by any narrow national or political group. It turns traitor to its great mission when it allows itself to be harnessed to any political aim whatever."[15]

What can be done about the aggression that has become so powerful a characteristic of integral nationalism? Lorenz suggests that man must find some

---

[12]*Ibid.*, p. 280.
[13]*Ibid.*, p. 281.
[14]*Ibid.*, p. 276.
[15]*Ibid.*, p. 287.

method for ritualizing and channeling aggressive instincts, by encouraging people of different ideologies and races to become acquainted, by directing the militant enthusiasm of youth toward "genuine causes," and by improving the understanding of the underlying mechanisms fundamental to aggression. "Enthusiastic definition with any value that is ethical in the sense that its content will stand the test of Kant's [categorical] question, will act as an antidote for national or political aggression."[16]

Robert Ardrey and the Territorial Imperative

The LAM thesis began to take on its special character with the work of Robert Ardrey, a dramatist turned anthropologist and biologist. Born in Chicago on October 16, 1908, Ardrey graduated from the University of Chicago in 1930. As an undergraduate he began his study of the sciences of man under Professor William Fielding Ogburn. He started his career in the midst of the depression, for a time earning his living as a lecturer in anthropology at the Chicago World's Fair and as a statistician. During World War II he served with the Office of War Information.

After the war Ardrey turned to journalism. The editors of *The Reporter* sent him to Africa to write about the Mau Mau. His African journey was to prove a turning point in his interests and in his career. An accidental experience in South Africa resulted in a return to his early concern with human behavior. In February 1955 he was introduced to Professor Raymond A. Dart, the South African paleoanthropologist, who took Ardrey to the basement of the medical school and showed him his collection of fossilized jawbones. Ardrey was fascinated, especially by the jawbone of the *Australopithecus,* whom Dart identified as a creature between ape and man who had haunted African savannahs more than a million years ago. From this moment on Ardrey assumed the task of "rescuing Dart from neglect and contumely." A by-product of this determination was Ardrey's decision to study the genesis of man in Africa.

For the next six years Ardrey worked energetically on his first biological study, *African Genesis,*[17] which appeared in 1961. The basic idea of Ardrey's book was derived from an article by Dart titled "The Predatory Transition from Man to Ape," in which the South African paleoanthropologist argued that man's ancestry was carnivorous, predatory, and cannibalistic in nature.

---

[16]*Ibid.*, p. 291.
[17]Robert Ardrey, *African Genesis* (New York, 1961).

According to Dart, "Wars and atrocities accord with early universal cannibalism, with animal and human sacrificial practice of their substitutes in formal religions and with worldwide scalping, head-hunting, body-mutilating and necrophilic practices of mankind in proclaiming this common bloodlust differential."[18] Ardrey attempted to demonstrate the validity of Dart's description of what he called an osteodontokeratic culture among the *Australopithecines*. These early men, Ardrey concluded, were killers, hence it followed that human beings, too, are killers.

African Genesis quickly stirred up a storm. Written in a fast-paced, interesting style, as were all Ardrey's later works, this book attracted the attention of both scholars and the general public. Reviewers of professional background immediately attacked the book with biting criticism; the general public, including armchair biologists and anthropologists, heaped encomiums on a "fascinating" book and called for more. This pattern was to be repeated with all of Ardrey's work on evolutionary behavior.

Five years later Ardrey published his major work, *The Territorial Imperative,*[19] which propelled him to the forefront of the LAM school. In this book Ardrey attempted to show that man's aggressiveness is based on his "innate territorial nature." According to Ardrey, man has an inborn compulsion to defend his exclusive territory, preserve, or property. This territorial nature is genetic and ineradicable.

In Ardrey's view, man's territorial expressions are but human responses to an imperative acting with similar and equal force on both the lower animals and man. The territorial imperative is no less vital for the existence of contemporary man than it was to the small-brained proto-man millions of years ago. It is, Ardrey contends, an expression of the continuity of human evolution from the environment of the early animals to that of man. Any human group in possession of a social territory will behave in accordance with the universal laws of the territorial principle. The territorial concept, no matter whether we like it or not, is as much an ally of our enemies as it is of ourselves and our friends. This territorial imperative, in Ardrey's view, is one of the basic evolutionary principles operating in our lives. Furthermore, it amounts to a biological law on which we have founded our human edifice of morality. "Our capacities for sacrifice, for altruism, for sympathy, for trust, for respon-

---

[18]Raymond A. Dart, "The Predatory Transition from Ape to Man," *International Anthropological and Linguistic Review,* I (1953), pp. 201–208.

[19]Robert Ardrey, *The Territorial Imperative: A Personal Inquiry into the Animal Origins of Property and Nations* (New York, 1966).

sibilities to other than self-interest, for honesty, for charity, for friendship and love, for social amity and mutual interdependence have evolved just as surely as the flatness of our feet, the muscularity of our buttocks, and the enlargement of our brains, out of encounter on ancient African savannahs between the primate potential and the hominal circumstance. Whether morality without territory is possible in man must remain as our final, unanswerable question.''[20]

This estimate of morality plays an important role in Ardrey's thinking. He believes that morality, the personal sacrifice for interests larger than ourselves, had its origins in dim evolutionary beginnings. It is as essential, he says, to the life of animals as in the lives of men. It could probably not exist in the human species without property privately or jointly defended. It is closely connected with the concept of the territorial imperative.

In a later book Ardrey summarized his efforts made in the earlier volume:

> In *The Territorial Imperative* I inspected the history and nature of a biological force called territory, first diagnosed in bird life by the British amateur ornithologist Eliot Howard. Today we can predict that in many other species than birds the male will defend the territory—his exclusive bit of the world's space—against all intrusion with a high probability of success even though the intruder be the stronger. A corollary to the proposition I called the amity-enmity complex, the likelihood that a group of defenders of a territory will be drawn together, united, and their efforts commanded by the intruding enemy. I suggested that man is a territorial species and that we defend our homes or our homelands for biological reasons, not because we choose to but because we must.[21]

With this last sentence, suggesting that we defend our homelands for biological reasons, Ardrey, for better or for worse, invades the scholarly territory of the social scientist and especially that of the specialist on nationalism. He sees the biological nation as a social group holding exclusive possession of a continuous area of space, which isolates itself from others of its kind through outward antagonism, and which through joint defense of its social territory achieves leadership, cooperation, and a capacity for concerted action. ''It does not matter too much whether such a nation be composed of twenty-five individuals or two hundred and fifty million. It does not matter too much whether we are considering the true lemur, the howling monkey, the

[20]*Ibid.*, p. 351.
[21]Robert Ardrey, *The Social Contract: A Personal Inquiry into the Evolutionary Sources of Order and Disorder* (New York, 1970), p. 23.

smooth-billed ani, the Bushman band, the Greek city-state, or the United States of America. The social principle remains the same.''[22]

Ardrey finds it difficult to understand why in the past students of man ''have failed to gain from students of the animal any notion concerning the biological origins of the nation.''[23] He repeats again and again that nations as well as animals ''obey the laws of the territorial imperative.''[24] This territorial imperative, he insists, ''is as blind as a cave fish, as consuming as a furnace, and it commands beyond logic, opposes all reasons, suborns all moralities, strives for no goal more sublime than survival.''[25] The continuity of evolution from the world of the animal to the world of man ''ensures that a human group in possession of a social territory will behave according to the universal laws of the territorial principle.''[26]

Ardrey is specific on two terms closely associated with the phenomenon of nationalism—patriotism and xenophobia. What we call patriotism, he says, is a calculable force, which, ''released by a predictable situation, will animate man in a manner no different from other territorial aspects.''[27] Patriotism, he says, is a biologically innate instinct and not an environmentally produced historical phenomenon. As a clinching argument he uses Pearl Harbor, the news of which made his response ''instinctive, instant, voluntary, universal.''[28] Like other Americans, he says, he was subjected to a command ''of genetic origin,'' an inheritance from the experience and natural selection of tens of thousands of generations of human and hominid ancestors. If this remarkable uniformity were not innate, he asks, by what processes of social conditioning had Americans been instilled with such love of country as to guarantee that when challenge arose they acted as one?

At this point Ardrey plaintively admitted that no school of thought anywhere would accept his proposition as correct.[29] This is typical of the defensive attitude he has taken to the bitter criticism accorded his views.

On xenophobia, the fear and hatred of strangers or foreigners, and a main component of several forms of nationalism, Ardrey sees a close connection. Animal xenophobia, he says, is universal. ''The stranger is driven out of the group's social space and is physically attacked if his attentions persist. The howling monkey roars, alerting his fellows in the clan; the spider monkey barks; the lion, without ceremony, attacks. However the animosity for strang-

---

[22] Ardrey, *The Territorial Imperative*, p. 191.
[23] *Ibid.*, p. 204.
[24] *Ibid.*, p. 219.
[25] *Ibid.*, p. 236.
[26] *Ibid.*, p. 232.
[27] *Ibid.*
[28] *Ibid.*
[29] *Ibid.*

ers is expressed, either through attack or avoidance, xenophobia is there, and it is as if throughout the animal world invisible curtains hang between the familiar and the strange."[30]

Ardrey sees this xenophobia in human as well as in animal life. He believes that general evidence supports the conclusion that xenophobia is a factor in the life of all societies. "If an animal society is based on a territory, then joint defense of the territory against an intruding stranger not only enhances energy but must enjoin mutual trust and sacrifice, just as a human being defending its homeland must seldom have problems with the social contract."[31]

This xenophobia, Ardrey says, leads to war. "Can we wonder that warfare, satisfying such natural demands, has flourished throughout human history? Can we wonder that man, like other social animals, carries with him a dual code of behavior?"[32] In support of his contention Ardrey quotes Geoffrey Gorer, one of his critics, as saying that there must be few human groups that do not distinguish between the killing of an insider and the killing of an outsider. The one is murder, the other carries a variety of distinctions. Ardrey calls S. L. Washburn as a witness: "Almost every human society has regarded the killing of members of certain other human societies as desirable."[33]

The Contribution of Desmond Morris

The third of the LAM trio is Desmond Morris, a British anthropologist who also has written prolifically on biology and zoology. Born at Purton, Wiltshire, in 1928, he studied at Oxford. In 1956 he became head of the Granada TV and Film Unit at the London Zoo, and in 1959 he was appointed Curator of Mammals at the Zoological Society of London. He has published widely in scholarly as well as popular journals.

In the 1960s he published a wide variety of books, including *Biology of Art* (1962), *The Mammals: A Guide to Living Species* (1965); *Men and Snakes* (1965); *Men and Apes* (1966); *Men and Pandas* (1966); *The Naked Ape* (1968); and *The Human Zoo* (1969). The last two books won him worldwide attention.

In general Morris supported the thesis that man is merely a higher form of

---

[30]Ardrey, *The Social Contract,* p. 269.
[31]*Ibid.,* p. 276.
[32]*Ibid.*
[33]*Ibid.*

animal and is motivated by similar drives that influence the lower animals. In his *The Naked Ape*[34] he makes an analogy between man and ape and contends that *Homo sapiens* has in reality remained little more than a naked ape. In acquiring new motives, he says, man has lost none of the early old ones. We can understand the nature of human aggression only if we consider the background of our animal origins.

Unlike Lorenz and Ardrey, Morris denies the existence of an innate, aggressive drive. He emphasizes instead the existence of genetically determined signals which both apes and men send to their fellows. Where Lorenz and Ardrey regard a spontaneously engendered drive as impelling human beings to aggression, Morris on the other hand views many of our aggressive acts as genetically governed responses to certain environmental conditions and to signals sent to us by other people.

While the three leaders of the LAM school differ on certain incidentals, in general they agree that both lower and higher animals live and act according to similar motivations. They see the territorial imperative working in both lower and higher animal worlds and they conclude that man's social behavior expressed in such drives as nationalism is precisely the same as the motives impelling lower animals. Nationalism thus becomes man's way of protecting his territory against those who would take it away from him.

Whirlwind of Denunciation

For a time the LAM thesis aroused hopes among scholars of nationalism that—at long last—the scientific world had something of value to contribute to the study of nationalism. The feeling arose that possibly scientists could now provide in-depth information that would help clarify the meaning of nationalism and explain its persistent paradoxes. The theory of man's instinctive behavior, like that so common in the animal world, might well provide the groundwork for a new approach to the study of nationalism. If this view were to be accepted generally by anthropologists, biologists, naturalists, sociologists, and psychologists, then there was hope for new evaluations by historians.

But then came a collective shock. The views of the LAM school far from attaining acceptance among scientists of various disciplines, fell into the

---

[34]Desmond Morris, *The Naked Ape* (New York, 1968).

whirlpool of the old hereditary-environment clash. Few arguments among scholars have caused such bitter difference of opinion as that seeking to explain man's behavior either on inherited instincts or environmental learning. The idea of a territorial imperative, especially, considered to be a variation of the old "instinct of property" or "philoprogenitiveness" began to be denounced as "a curiosity repudiated by scientists half a century ago" and as "a crude Hobbesan war of all against all."

The main charge against the LAM school was oversimplification. They were accused of presenting a grossly simplified conception of the causes and possible remedies of aggression.[35] It soon became clear that scientists as a group were unwilling to go along with the concept of the territorial imperative and its implications.

Most of the criticism was leveled at Ardrey. He was denounced as "a popularizer of data he does not understand," as "a fallible guide," as "a simple-minded adolescent." His "layman's version of science" was described as "distorted, shallow, even downright erroneous." His work was "shot through with ambiguity." It was erroneous, it was charged, to permit Ardrey "to propagate false doctrine on the ground that it is provocative and controversial." He was accused of being master of the kind of statement that has so many possible interpretations that "literally any position may be said to have been asserted."

The psychologist J. P. Scott found Ardrey's evidence to be "presented naively." "*The Territorial Imperative* is good theater and third-rate reporting, full of entertainment and wild analogies. . . . To him a band of lemurs in Madagascar is just like that of a modern nation. . . . He has written down [ideas] as they have come to him and the result is a sort of intellectual pizza pie, with tasty bits of information embedded in a mass of partially baked ideas."[36]

The anthropologist Geoffrey Gorer spoke highly of Ardrey's ability but cast doubt on his conclusions:

Unfortunately, Ardrey's diligence and research have so stopped short at *Homo sapiens*. His views on human behavior are almost entirely impressionistic, imbued with the sophistication of a cosmopolitan writer who reads news magazines. . . . He is a reliable man when he discusses *proconsul* or *au-*

---

[35]See Leonard Berkowitz, "Simple Views of Aggression," *American Scientist*, LVII (1969), pp. 372–383.
[36]J. P. Scott, in *The Nation*, (January 9, 1967), pp. 53–54.

stralopithecus, the birds and the bees, mice and monkeys, for he relies on expert authorities; when he discusses man he relies on himself.[37]

Gorer saw Ardrey's three final chapters of *The Territorial Imperative* as filled with oversimplifications, questionable statements, omissions, and plain inaccuracies. In a disappointed tone he accused Ardrey of dramatizing the employment of ambiguous metaphors and symbols and of bringing to these some rather ambiguous conclusions.[38]

Others joined the chorus of rebuke. Edmond Leach denounced Ardrey for "explicitly comparing man's killing propensity to a wolf."[39] The most severe critic of all, the anthropologist Ashley Montagu, attacked the entire LAM school in a book he edited, *Man and Aggression.*[40] Montagu holds a low opinion of Ardrey's *The Territorial Imperative:* "Mr. Ardrey's book constitutes, perhaps, the most illuminating example of the manner in which a man's prejudices may get in the way of his reason and distort his view of the evidence."[41] Montagu was certain that "the evidence does not support Mr. Ardrey's theories."[42] The critic reserved special scorn for Ardrey's theory of innate depravity. "[This theory] is an unsound thesis, and it is a dangerous one, because it perpetuates unsound views which justify, and even intend to sanction, the violence which man is capable of learning, but which Mr. Ardrey erroneously believes to be inherited from man's australopithecine ancestors."[43]

What we are witnessing in Ardrey's "territorial imperative," Montagu says, is a revival in modern dress of the good old "instinct of property, which scientists have long since rejected. Mr. Ardrey is more enamored of his theories than of his facts."[44]

The psychoanalyst and social philosopher Erich Fromm pointed out that analogies are easily made, especially the implication that man is dominated by an instinct for defense of his territory, inherited from his animal ancestors.

---

[37]Geoffrey Gorer, "Ardrey on Human Nature: Animals, Nations, Imperatives," in *Encounter,* XXVII, no. 6 (June, 1967), p. 67.

[38]*Ibid.*

[39]Edmond Leach, in *The New York Review of Books* (December 15, 1966), p. 8. Leach, professor of anthropology at the University of Cambridge, titled his review of books by Lorenz and Ardrey, "Don't Say Boo to a Goose."

[40]Ashley Montagu, *Man and Aggression* (New York, 1973). The first edition appeared in 1968. Montagu's book, which presents the case of the environmentalists against the instinctivists, is a model of scholarly criticism.

[41]*Ibid.,* p. 4.

[42]*Ibid.,* p. 6.

[43]*Ibid.*

[44]*Ibid.,* p. 9.

The popular picture of animal aggressiveness, he says, has largely been influenced by Ardrey's concept of territorialism. Fromm judges the idea as "quite erroneous" for several reasons:

1. There are many animal species for whom the concept of territoriality does not apply. Fromm quotes the psychologist J. P. Scott as saying that territoriality occurs in higher animals such as the vertebrates and anthropoids and even here in a very spotty fashion.

2. A distinction must be made between the territorialism of the species and that of the individual. Territories are generally selected primarily on the basis of properties to which the animals react innately. All animals of the same species seem to select the same general type of habitat. But the personal binding of a male to its own territory is the result of a learning process.

3. Observation of apes reveals that the various groups of primates are quite tolerant and flexible on the matter of their territory. This simply does not justify the analogy to a society guarding its frontiers and forcibly preventing the entry of any "foreigner."

4. Defense of territory has the function of *avoiding* the serious fighting that would become necessary if the territory were to be invaded to such an extent as to generate crowding. "Actually the threat behavior in which territorial aggression manifests itself is the instinctively patterned way of upholding spatial equilibrium and peace. *The instinctive equipment of the animal has the function that legal arrangements have in man. Hence the instinct becomes obsolete when other symbolic ways are available to mark a territory and to warn: no trespassing.* [Author's italics.] It is also worth keeping in mind that . . . most wars start for the purpose of gaining advantages of various kinds and not in defense against a threat to one's own territory—except in the ideology of the war makers."[45]

The most effective criticism of the LAM school centered on its extrapolations from animals to people. Critics admitted that it was one thing to state that heredity plays an important role in human behavior, a fact that could not be denied, but it was another matter to identify human instincts by comparing our behavior with that of distant cousins among the lower vertebrates. It is a fundamental fallacy, they say, to describe animal behavior in human terms, and it is false to present the rigid notion of instinct as innate and inflexible.

Stephen Jay Gould, the Harvard biologist, sees a confusion of analogies in the work of Lorenz:

---

[45]Erich Fromm, *The Anatomy of Human Destructiveness* (New York, 1973), pp. 114–115.

Similarities in nature fall into two different categories—homologies that reflect common descent (the arm bones of man and bat, to choose the standard example), and analogies that record separate evolutionary development (wings of bat and butterfly). Homologous similarity arises from a common genetic source: analogous similarity does not. Analogies may be fruitful if separately-evolved behaviors perform the same function in two species; more often, they are treacherous and misleading, especially when the subjects are so different as humans and stickelback fishes. Virtually all of Lorenz's speculations about human behavior are based on analogous similarity.[46]

Defense of the LAM School School

Ardrey was unimpressed by the plethora of complaints. He replied that he did not seek the confession box. "I recognize, of course, that no school of thought prevailing on any continent will inform you that my proposition is correct."[47] Again and again he reiterated his theory of a dominantly innate instinct leading men as well as animals to defend their territory. In a later book, *The Social Contract,*[48] he admitted that the territorial imperative was, perhaps, somewhat less than imperative because, in addition to physical space, it could well include social and psychological space and status seeking. Furthermore, he was quite willing to accept the revision that the territorial imperative could be expressed in retreat and accomodation as well as aggression. However, Ardrey was by no means willing to abandon his original proposition. He continued to insist that the gap between animals and men should be ignored and that man was not unique in his status as an animal.

Others came to the defense of Ardrey and the LAM school. Defenders insisted that the territorial imperative was in reality in accord with a rapdily growing body of experimental socio-psychological research. Perhaps there was a tendency to oversimplify. So what? This was to be expected when painting on so broad a canvas.

Among the defenders of Ardrey and the LAM school were those who looked with suspicion at the closed academic world and accused it of protecting its own boundary lines against a presumptuous playwright turned biologist. The criticism of Ardrey was dismissed as "the usual academic bellyache." Typi-

---

[46]Stephen Jay Gould, in a review of Alec Nisbet, *Konrad Lorenz* (New York, 1977), in *The New York Times Book Review,* February 27, 1977, p. 3.

[47]Ardrey, *The Territorial Imperative,* p. 232.

[48]Ardrey, *The Social Contract, op. cit.*

cal of this reaction was the following letter-to-the-editor by an individual who evidently represented the cause of amateur scholars: "So many of our pompous pedants, reared upon an unvaried diet of predigested pap, dribbling from 'accepted' sources, clinging to the shelter of 'recognized' authority so their togas will not be sullied by association with unapproved surmises, forget that to-day's dogma was yesterday's conjecture. The Gospel according to Scott, Foresman is not Holy Writ to the eager, inquiring mind. Through the ages, the Tree of Knowledge unfolds one leaf at a time; thus each generation of pedagogues has a new blanket of Ultimate Truth with which to smother the minds of their helpless charges."[49]

A Plea for Suspense of Judgment

The intellectual battle goes on. On the one side there remain the instinctivists like Lorenz, who argue that man's destructiveness has been inherited as an inner trait from his ancestors. On the other side are the environmentalists or neobehaviorists such as B. F. Skinner,[50] who insist that there are no inborn human traits for man's actions are always the result of social conditioning. Both sides present their arguments with fervid and sometimes passionate arguments, and neither side seems quite willing to tolerate the views of the other.

In watching the battle from the sidelines it would be well to consider past experience with such controversies. There are many examples of how ideas which we accept today were once regarded as the work of charlatans. Though their parallel is not an exact one, defenders of Ardrey point to Galileo's difficulties with the "authorities," and present the truism that Aristotelian "truth" was succeeded by Copernican truth. One can sympathize with the letter-to-the-editor writer who suggested that "today's dogma was yesterday's conjecture."

There is support for this point of tolerance in the scientific world. Zing Yang Kuo, the student of behavior, is not overly impressed with the LAM school and its so-called territorial defense, which he calls merely a fancy name for the reaction pattern to strangers, "flavored with anthropomorphism and nineteenth-century Darwinism." But at the same time he urges caution

---

[49]Marshall L. Levin of Fort Lauderdale, Florida, in *Saturday Review,* November 7, 1970, p. 35.
[50]See B. F. Skinner, *Biology and Man* (New York, 1964); *The Meaning of Evolution* (New Haven, 1949); and *Science and Human Behavior* (New York, 1953).

and suggests that "further and more systematic experimental explorations are necessary to decide the issue."[51] This gentle reminder from the scientific world is precisely the view that should be taken by the student of nationalism. Let both instinctivists and environmentalists continue their experimentation and observation to build up a body of scientific knowledge which will demonstrate more adequately than is possible now the truth or falsity of the territorial imperative.

Historians of nationalism, too, are beginning to show more and more interest in the territorial imperative. So discriminating a historian as Boyd C. Shafer suggests that it is *possible* that men have some instinctive desire for land of their own, an inherent feeling about what is exclusively their own. "This could be the 'territorial imperative' that... Ardrey has so vehemently put forward as an explanation of nations."[52] At the same time, with care typical of his studies on nationalism, Shafer quite rightly states that vehemence is really scant foundation for proving the existence of the territorial imperative. He asks: "Why the nation rather than some other territorial grouping?... Why national loyalty than loyalty to city, empire, or just the place of birth and maturation?"[53]

In his presidential address to Phi Alpha Theta on December 28, 1973,[54] Shafer again referred to the territorial imperative while discussing the puzzle as to why men, despite their articulate leaders and major communicators, remain dominantly nationalist when nationalism, with its accompanying international anarchy, so often leads to war. Men resort to war, it is argued, either through ignorance, or apathy, or their aggressive nature. Yet all three reasons are so general that they throw little light upon peace and war. Here Shafer spoke about the work on aggression by Lorenz, Ardrey, and Morris. The puzzle has not yet been solved: "That men are ignorant or apathetic seems a truism; that men by nature are aggressive depends on time, place, and circumstance."[55] Shafer neither attacks or defends the LAM school; he reserves judgment and maintains an open mind pending further observation and experimentation. This is, indeed, the proper attitude for historians of nationalism. Keeping in mind Shafer's recommendation, what position should be taken by the historian of nationalism in this continuing controversy?

---

[51]*Cf.* Zing Yang Kuo, "Studies on the Basic Factors in Animal Fighting," VII, Inter-species Co-existence in Mammals, *Journal of General Psychology,* 97 (1960), pp. 211–223.
[52]Boyd C. Shafer, *Faces of Nationalism* (New York, 1972), p. 323.
[53]*Ibid.,* pp. 322–323.
[54]Boyd C. Shafer, "Webs of Common interests: Nationalism, Internationalism, and Peace," *The Historian,* XXXVI, no. 3 (May, 1974), pp. 404–405.
[55]*Ibid.,* p. 404.

First, it is useless for the social scientist to take sides in the long and continuing struggle between the instinctivists and environmentalists. The historian of nationalism must wait patiently for more evidence as the scientists battle with hypotheses, theories, propositions, and laws. He must preserve a benevolent neutrality and do what he can to discourage either side from presenting such criticisms as "simple-minded," "adolescent," "uncritical," and "plainly erroneous." Considering the extent of our present knowledge, it is impossible for either side to ridicule the other out of the academic market.

Second, the historian of nationalism should make it clear that he does not intend to reject out of hand the LAM school and its territorial imperative. On the contrary, he should give every encouragement to Lorenz, Ardrey, Morris, Lionel Tiger, Anthony Storr, and all the other instinctivists. It is to the credit of the LAM school that it has brought an awareness of a major research problem to the attention of many scholars who would not have considered it seriously in the past. Furthermore, our knowledge of the science of man is currently not so overwhelmingly exact that we can dismiss the work of those who seek parallel modes of behavior between lower and higher animals.

Third, the historian of nationalism, without becoming mired in the quicksands of the heredity-versus-environment clash, should place increasing emphasis upon special phases of the study of nationalism brought out in the controversy. For example, he might well consider transferring his interest from such components of nationalism as language, institutions, traditions, customs, and the will for social homogeneity to a closer examination of the territorial drive. Is the urge to protect or to defend territory the exclusive or dominant motive in the conflict between nations? Is it a major factor governing the human animal in his group actions? What are the historical parallels in human aggression? And what special combinations of time, place, and circumstance lead to territorial aggression?

Fourth, historians of nationalism should do what they can to test the theses of the LAM group in specific cases to see if they can provide any mechanism for historical explanation. Is there any evidence among the current mini-nationalisms (Welsh, Scots, Croats, Flemings, Ukrainians) or the macro-nationalisms (Pan-Arabism, Pan-Slavism, Pan-Americanism) to support the general contention of the territorial imperative? Do historians from their view see any parallels between human and animal behavior?

Answers to such and similar questions would be more productive for the study of nationalism than the process of ridiculing the LAM thesis out of existence. Perhaps the quantitative approach, including computerization, might be of some value in this effort.

What the scholar of nationalism should recall is the possibility that the work of the LAM school may well one day add a new dimension to his subject. By this reasoning nationalism could become a calculable force which, released by a predictable situation, animates man as well as other territorial species. But further examination is needed before one accepts or rejects the LAM hypothesis of human behavior.

Specificity—On Hitler's Aggression

Attacks on the theory of the territorial imperative continue.[56] Yet, should the concept be bolstered by more convincing evidence, it will in all probability be considered in its human phase as closer to patroitism than to nationalism. The two terms—patriotism and nationalism—and often used interchangeably, but there are differences. Patriotism is derived from *patria,* signifying land, fatherland, or country. Nationalism comes from *natio,* literally a person born, or a *people* having common historical traditions. Patriotism is concerned with love for a *country;* nationalism refers to the historical sentiment of a *people.*

Even more important in the distinction between patriotism and nationalism is the association with defense and aggression. Patriotism is distinguished by its defensive quality. The great patriot is the man who sings praises to his country and defends it courageously in time of war. The typical 19th-century patriot was Giuseppi Mazzini, who was overwhelmed by his love for Italy. Nationalism, on the other hand, has developed to a point where it is inseparable from the notion of power and aggression. A malleable force, it may be used either to justify the use of power to forge the union of a nation or it may be applied to condone a mission for expansion. In either case nationalism, as compared with defensive patriotism, takes on a coating of aggression that makes it a prime cause for war.

This leads us back to our theme of German nationalism and specifically to the nature of Hitler's aggressive nationalism. Champion of the superiority of the Indo-European-Aryan-Nordic-Teutonic "race," Hitler believed it his mission to preside over the territorial expansion of his own chosen people. There was nothing defensive about this charismatic activist. His compulsion

---

[56]See Ashley Montagu, *The Nature of Human Aggression* (New York, 1976). In this fascinating book, Montagu takes issue with the LAM school and its popularization of the view that humans are inescapably killers. Instead, according to Montagu, human behavior is determined not by genes alone, because in specific circumstances, people are capable of all kinds of behavior, but by the interaction of the individual's experience and his genetic constitution.

was always to attack and to attack again. As a military leader in World War II he contemptuously dismissed any tactics of defense-in-depth or retreat-for-recuperation. He ordered his generals to attack, win, or die. In late 1942 he reacted hysterically to the bad news from Stalingrad: "The Sixth Army will stay where it is. I am not leaving the Volga." He was furious with General Friedrich von Paulus, who had surrendered. "I have no respect for a man who is afraid of suicide and instead accepts captivity." To the attack-minded *Fuehrer*, von Paulus was a traitor.

The kind of nationalism advocated by Hitler went far beyond the territorial imperative and its defensive connotation. In fighting off invaders of their territory, the lower animals react defensively without impinging on the turf of other animals. With Hitler the opposite was true. He rejected traditional bourgeois nationalism and set up his own form of aggressive racial nationalism. With it was an element of destructiveness which went far beyond the bounds of defense.

What was the nature of Hitler's aggressive nationalism? The anatomy of his malignant aggression was analyzed convincingly by the psychoanalyst Erich Fromm in a clinically professional psychobiographical study.[57] In tracing the development of Hitler's necrophilia (love for the dead), Fromm first describes early roots from infancy to age six (1889 to 1895); childhood from ages six to eleven (1895 to 1900); preadolescence and adolescence from ages eleven to seventeen (1900 to 1906); Vienna (1907 to 1913); and then Munich. The characterological analysis reveals Hitler as a withdrawn, extremely narcissistic, unrelated, undisciplined, sadomasochistic, and necrophilic individual, but one who had considerable gifts and talents.

This background contributed much to Hitler's special form of nationalism. To him the outbreak of World War I was a godsend: he thanked heaven for the event which at one stroke solved the problem of what to do with his life. The war came at that point when he had failed as an artist: it replaced his sense of humiliation with a feeling of pride. "He was no longer an outcast: he was a hero fighting for Germany, for its existence and glory, and the values of nationalism."[58]

The war ended with defeat and revolution. The defeat might have been bearable for Hitler but the revolution was not. The revolutionaries attacked everything that was sacred to his reactionary nationalism and they had won.

---

[57]Erich Fromm, *The Anatomy of Human Destructiveness, op. cit.* See chapter 13: "Malignant Aggression: A Clinical Case of Necrophilia," pp. 369–433.
[58]*Ibid.*, p. 394.

His humiliation was all the greater because some of the revolutionaries were Jews. "[The Jews] made him the hapless spectator of the destruction of his nationalist, petit-bourgeois ideals."[59] He transformed his personal defeat and humiliation into a national and social defeat and humiliation. "This time not *he* had failed and been humiliated, but Germany; by avenging and saving Germany he would avenge himself, and by wiping out Germany's shame he would wipe out his own."[60]

Although Fromm traces what he calls Hitler's "nationalist, petit-bourgeois ideals," he does not take into account, however, the critical change by which Hitler's sense of nationalism went beyond nationalist bourgeois ideals. Influenced by the anti-Semitism he found in the cafes of Vienna and Munich, Hitler became contemptuous of "bourgeois nationalism" and began calling for a new racial nationalism. Casting aside traditional bourgeois nationalism, he regarded himself as the innovator and champion of a new form of racial nationalism that would change world history.

Fromm shows convincingly how Hitler's sense of nationalism was colored by a malignant destructiveness which was to have tragic consequences. Hitler's main objects of destruction were cities and people. The enthusiastic planner of a new Vienna and Berlin was the same man who wanted to destroy Paris, level Leningrad, and eventually demolish all Germany. At the same time he called for the physical destruction of Jews, Poles, Gypsies, and Russians, all of whom he held responsible for the political and moral contamination of the German people. The more victory became doubtful, the more depressed he became. On January 27, 1942, a year before Stalingrad, he said: "If the German people are not ready to fight for their survival (*Selbstbehauptung*) . . . then they have to disappear (*denn soll es verschwinden*)."

Despite such necrophilic manifestations, millions of Germans, as well as people all over the world, regarded Hitler as a great patriot motivated by love of country. To Germans he was the savior who would liberate them from the chains of Versailles, the administrative genius who would straighten out the economic chaos, and the master builder who would construct a new, prosperous Germany. Seldom in history have so intelligent a people been so utterly wrong in judging their leader.

From the psychoanalytical point of view Hitler unconsciously repressed his own sense of destructiveness. He sought to rationalize any destruction he

---

[59]*Ibid.*, p. 394–395.
[60]*Ibid.*, p. 395.

ordered as being only for the survival, growth, and splendor of the German nation. Always the aggressor, he nevertheless constantly spoke in terms of *defense* against real or imagined enemies. A convinced Social Darwinist, he claimed to be acting only "to preserve the species." He spoke of his "duty" and "noble intentions," but repressed the awareness of his craving for destruction. Clinically, Fromm says, Hitler dealt with his repressed strivings by denying their existence and developing exactly opposite traits: this reaction formation explains his vegetarianism, his refusal to witness murders or executions, and his reluctance to visit the war fronts because he could not tolerate viewing dead and wounded soldiers.[61]

Fromm concludes that, although in conventional terms Hitler was not psychotic, in dynamic, interpersonal terms he was a very sick man:

> In analyzing Hitler we have found a number of severely pathological traits: we hypothesized the presence of a semi-autistic streak in the child; we found extreme narcissism, lack of contact with others, flaws in his perception of reality, intense necrophilia. One can legitimately assume the presence of a psychotic, perhaps schizophrenic streak in him. But does this mean that Hitler was a "madman," that he suffered from a psychosis or from paranoia, as it has been sometimes said? The answer, I believe, is in the negative. In spite of the mad streak in Hitler he was sane enough to pursue his aims purposefully and—for a while—successfully. With all the errors in judgment he made due to his narcissism and his destructiveness, it cannot be denied that he was a demagogue and a politician of outstanding skill who at no point showed frankly psychotic reactions.[62]

To the German people this narcissistic, sadomasochistic, and necrophilic *Fuehrer* presented himself as a "good" nationalist who always worked for the welfare of his people. But to his special type of nationalism Hitler added a malignant sense of aggression and destructiveness which turned out to be more curse than blessing. With unbending will, covered with a veneer of amiability and control, this apotheosis of the little man promoted his brand of German nationalism to the point where it became a grave danger not only for the Germans but for all Europeans and other peoples throughout the world. Millions of youth, German and non-German, had to be sacrificed in the task of bringing this apostle of destruction to the point of self-destruction.

---

[61]Fromm's clinical analysis here does not take into account Hitler's actions following the unsuccessful bomb plot on his life at his Eastern Headquarters in Rastenburg on July 20, 1944. The enraged *Fuehrer* had the conspirators hanged by the neck with piano wires and allowed to strangle slowly. All this was photographed by Nazi camermen. Hitler stayed up most of one night and ordered a projectionist to roll the films again and again so that he could relish every moment.
[62]Fromm, *op. cit.*, p. 432.

13

German Nationalism after 1945

I was 15 years old when the war ended. No part of our fatherland suffered as much from the war as this area, where the Ardennes offensive was launched. We don't want nationalism, but we're entitled to a normal feeling of national pride—it's the most natural thing in the world.

Helmut Koht, head of the
Christian Democratic Party,
in the national election
campaign, October 1976.

The Bitter Fruits of Aggressive Nationalism

Aggressive nationalism was not profitable for the German people. In two 20th-century wars they were defeated and each time she had emerged humiliated and prostrate. In World War I Germany mobilized 11,000,000 men and incurred a casualty list of 7,148,558, or 64.9 percent (1,779,700 killed, 4,216,058 wounded; 1,152,800 prisoners or missing). These were enormous human losses. In addition, by the Treaty of Versailles, Germany lost all her colonies, 15.5 percent of her arable land, 12 percent of her livestock, nearly 10 percent of her manufacturing plants, two-thirds of her coal reserves, two-thirds of her iron ore, and more than half of her lead.

The situation in 1945 was even more devastating. Hitler's Third Reich was supposed to live for a thousand years but it succumbed in just over twelve years. It was necessary to mobilize a large part of the world's population for the task of putting an end to a nationalism gone berserk. The price was great. Including Austrians, Germany had a peak strength of 10,200,000 men and lost 3,500,000 of these in battle, killed, wounded, missing in action, or captured. Again property damage was tremendous. At the close of World War I, no important part of German territory was in possession of the Allies, but in 1945 it seemed that the entire country had been laid waste by a gigantic scythe. About 90 percent of all major German cities with over 100,000 population were wholly or partly destroyed. Berlin was a heap of ruins; Dresden was devastated by fire bombs; the heart of Hamburg was wiped out. Transportation was in chaos. The bridges across the Rhine were smashed and lying on the river bed. Most of the railway system was battered and seemingly beyond repair. More than 7,000,000 Germans were homeless.

Such was the heritage of that "national regeneration" promised by the master of Berchtesgaden. Stunned and bewildered, the Germans seemed unable to comprehend the extent of the disaster. When reason returned, they began the process of abandoning the kind of perverse nationalism that had brought them to catastrophe.

Transformation I: The Political Miracle

The three decades which followed 1945 saw a remarkable political, economic, and psychological change in German life. What happened in the New Germany reveals once again that history remains an open book on whose pages new and startling developments are written.

At long last the Germans turned away from the tyranny of their past. For more than a century they had been fascinated by the ideas of *Geist* (spiritual depth) and *Macht* (authoritarian power). Within this framework they accepted the concept of strict obedience to the legal power of the state. They would follow the leader—no matter what the extent of his sanity. They dismissed the very idea of dissent as foreign to their being. Politically, West Germany emerged as a viable democracy, with a smoothly functioning government oriented to the Western free world.[1]

To be sure, there was assistance from the outside. The Potsdam Agreement of the Allies divided Germany into four control zones—American, British, Russian, and French—cutting across the former state and provincial boundaries. Greater Berlin was split into four sectors thus forming a fifth zone. The occupying authorities purged Germany of Nazis and Nazism and put an end to the National Socialist political structure.

In September 1949 Dr. Theodor Heuss was elected first President of the

---

[1]On the political character of the Bonn Republic, see Richard Hiscocks, *Democracy in West Germany* (New York, 1957); Gordon A. Craig, *From Bismarck to Adenauer: Aspects of German Statecraft* (Baltimore, 1958); Elmer Plischke, *Contemporary Government of Germany* (Boston, 1961); and Arnold J. Heidenheimer, *The Government of Germany* (New York, 1961).

Federal Republic of Germany. West Germany now embraced slightly more than half the area of prewar Germany, but had at least three-quarters of its population. The new constitution provided for a federal parliament. The capital was established at Bonn, the old university city. The center of gravity of German political life was thereby shifted from Potsdam and its military milieu to the Rhineland, home of the liberal tradition in the 1840s. All this was symbolic of a new spirit and a shift in policy. The Germany liberated by the Allies was not rebuilt as a Reich but as a working democratic republic.

The Bonn Republic was different from the Weimar Republic created after 1918. Germany's new democracy was ideologically and structurally far stronger than its predecessor. Few Germans understood the Weimar democracy, burdened as it was by violence, assassinations, resistance to occupation, and a flawed cultural and artistic life. Righting the wrongs of Versailles took first priority. This was fertile ground for the machinations of ambitious politicians. Weimar was not Bonn.

The conversion was late, but Germans had finally turned to the ideals of the Western Enlightenment. Some historians expressed doubt about the sincerity of the change. Others were impressed. Hans Kohn saw the German Federal Republic as the first real attempt to create a Westernized and liberal Germany. "The West, and with it the German liberals, can on the whole be satisfied with the progress achieved by the Germans in the last ten years. Naturally the old trends are still there, and are still strong, and it could not be otherwise. These last five years [1958–1963] Germany has been extremely successful, and in modern times Germans were rarely able to bear success without becoming overbearing."[2]

Transformation II: The Economic Miracle

The political transformation of Germany after 1945 was more than matched by what is generally termed "the German economic miracle."[3] West Germany emerged as Europe's most dynamic industrial state. Within a decade the German economy achieved a recovery almost without parallel in history. It was an astonishing performance. Production rose, the currency reserve was

---

[2]Hans Kohn, *Reflections on Modern History* (Princeton, N.J., 1963), p. 239. See also chapter 10.
[3]On the German economic miracle, see Henry C. Wallich, *Mainsprings of German Revival* (New Haven, 1955); Ludwig Erhard, *Prosperity Through Competition* (New York, 1958); and Wolfgang F. Stolper, *Germany between East and West* (Washington, D.C., 1960).

enhanced, unemployment was almost wiped out, and the national treasury showed a large surplus.

In the beginning the Federal Republic was heavily subsidized by Western sponsors, especially the United States. Under the conservative Chancellor Konrad Adenauer, German consumer goods began flowing in such quantities to the world markets that some countries, notably Britain, began to fear an unfair economic competition. The German automotive industry, starting with gutted factories and scattered labor forces, began to sell not just automobiles but complete assembly lines to foreign countries. By 1951 West Germany boasted of an industrial output 58 percent higher than in 1936. She became the most important creditor in the European Payment Plan with an accumulated credit of nearly a half-a-billion dollars. From 1951 to 1956 German exports tripled in value and began to close in on second-place Britain and first-place United States. In 1955 West Germany had a trade surplus of $286 million while Britain had a deficit of $985 million. Within another few years West Germany had sufficient surplus resources to give economic and technical aid to many underdeveloped nations. This record continued into the 1970s.

It was truly an economic miracle. Much of it was achieved by the brilliant leadership of Ludwig Erhard, Economics Minister who became chancellor in 1963. Germany's incredible prosperity, he said, had been due to "the purposeful use of economic means and strict adherence to the market economy." Whatever the explanation it was a unique phenomenon in contemporary history.

Away From the Old Nationalism

The extraordinary political and economic changes took place in a psychological climate which rejected the old nationalism. For two centuries German nationalism had wavered between two forms: one grounded on authoritarianism and militarism and the other on liberal constitutionalism. We have seen that the first form was triumphant at decisive moments in recent German history. In the War of Liberation against the foreigner Napoleon, heir of the French Revolution, Germans were freed from the French dictator only to lose their liberties to their own home-grown tyrants. The revolutionaries of 1848, both liberals and radicals, proved themselves to be far too weak to assure a meaningful transformation of the German social order. The national unification of 1871 was achieved not by liberal means but by Bismarck's iron-and-blood policy. The

Weimar Republic of 1919 to 1933 had a beautifully written constitution but its squabbling multiplicity of parties was a poor imitation of a working democracy.

There are few signs in the current Federal Republic of West Germany of the kind of extreme nationalism which caused so much trouble in the course of German history. True, there has been a revival of national consciousness after the debacle of 1945, but the new German nationalism exists inside the mainstream of established democratic procedures.[4] The ugly marks of the Third Reich have almost vanished. German politicians speak increasingly of national values, but the old spirit of aggression is gone. Instead, they mention "national substance," "national pride," "national identity," and "national achievement." Some express a sense of uncertainty. "Our reason tells us," said Hans Christ, "that we are Europeans, but our feelings waver, for we cannot be both a nation and European."[5]

The old mystical and irrational cloak of German nationalism has been discarded, at least for the time being. The new Germany has been structured in such a way that there is no trend to over-centralization. Prussia, the traditional defender of its own brand of German nationalism, has disappeared while the center of gravity shifts to the west and southeast in areas more agreeable to Western constitutionalism. A new sense of national consciousness works within the liberal-democratic framework of the West.

Contemporary German political leaders and scholars accept the new trend. The historian Ludwig Dehio, editor in 1952 of the *Historische Zeitschrift,* said it clearly: "The prerequisite for any really creative response after the period of the two World Wars is the unconditional recognition of the terrible role we have played in this period." Dehio called for a radical transformation in the sort of nationalism that had dominated Germany: "Today liberty—that is the liberty of the individual, not of the state—can only be preserved as the common property of a consolidated group of nations, and any nation which draws aside to save its own unity will lose it. A hundred years ago the most pressing goal was national unity; for the preservation of freedom offered no problem in the sense that it does today, whereas unity was the natural demand within the system of nation-states which is lying in ruins today. Now, however, after the Third Reich has abused and thrown away our unity by denying freedom, unity must be subordinated by the superior and wider aim of freedom, for today a demand for unity surely has an anachronistic flavor about it.

[4]C. L. Sulzberger, in *The New York Times,* February 21, 1965.
[5]Hans Christ, *Die Rolle der Nationen in Europa, Gestern-Heute-Morgen* (Stuttgart, 1962), p. 65.

No political watchword can be transplanted into a new situation without carrying with it traces of the soil in which it grew previously.''[6]

This accent upon benevolent nationalism of a free people functioning in a free society is something novel in the course of German history. Rejecting worship of the all-embracing State in favor of sovereignty of the individual has had favorable repercussions. A great and gifted people have traveled and now abandoned the long and rocky road of the wrong kind of nationalism.

German Youth and German Nationalism—the **"Ohne Mich"** *Syndrome*

German youth played a major role in this critical transformation. In postwar Germany young people were appalled by the excesses of National Socialism and particularly by their parents' toleration of the worst features of Hitlerism. They reject nationalism because it was responsible in large part for Hitler's rise to power in 1933 and for the subsequent war of 1939. In its place they prefer a general European frame of reference. Young Germans who traveled abroad were shocked to find that their peers in other countries often held them responsible for the crimes of Nazism. They protested that they were not even born during that barbaric era and that it was unfair to blame them for the sins of their elders. It was a frustrating experience. At home they spoke bitterly to their distressed parents.

Trapped in an uncomfortable dilemma, most young Germans decided to "play it cool" (*Gelassenheit*). They discarded the old slogans. Hans Magnus Enzenberger, a young poet, denounced the worship of national sovereignty: "The beer hall is the only place where it is still taken seriously.''[7] As for German youth in general, most preferred an attitude of "ohne mich" (without me) if nationalism were to be revived.

The new attitude is important because German youth played a significant part in the emergence of German nationalism.[8] The Young Germany of the War of Liberation in 1813 set a standard for the rest of the century. Young Germans willingly supported the Fatherland in the fashioning of the old nationalism. Hitler used them in his thrust for power in the late 1920s and gave them top priority during the life of the Third Reich.

---

[6]Ludwig Dehio, quoted in Hans Kohn, *The Mind of Germany* (New York, 1960), pp. 350–351.
[7]Quoted in *Time*, June 4, 1965, p. 23.
[8]See Howard Becker, *German Youth: Bond or Free* (New York, 1940).

This is not to say that contemporary German youth is lacking in patriotism. Young Germans listen patiently as the rest of the world talks of self-determination. They feel themselves a part of the German past but they do not accept its exaggerated and militant nationalism. Eleanor Lansing Dulles recognized the trend: "Those [German students] who were born after World War II think they owe little to the past. In a sense they are people without parents. They are intense in their desire for freedom, and they take a position that is designed to prevent a new authoritarianism. There must be no second Hitler. The new type of nationalist feeling which they do not clearly recognize, can become a strong political force unless they are kept in tune with internationalism."[9]

It is a fair evaluation. Taking a position designed to prevent a new authoritarianism is something new in German history. In the past all confrontations between liberalism and the power-from-above concept ended in the triumph of authoritarianism in one form or another. Young Germans, the citizens of tomorrow, have chosen the moderation of liberal nationalism.

The Specter of Neo-Nazism

New German administrators take the same line as German youth. The pragmatic architects and their successors of the Federal Republic of West Germany, aware of the experiences of their Weimar predecessors, have succeeded in the critical task of giving stability to their new system of government. They have avoided the excesses of polemics and especially appeals to national consciousness. Advocates of a new restrained nationalism, they urge German participation in the European family.

This moderate approach left a vacuum and any movement dedicated to the revival of Nazism was attracted to it. Some observers of the German scene predicted a quick and sustained revival of National Socialism. They were wrong: while there has been some evidence of such a trend, it is small and insignificant.

There were, indeed, attempts to revive the Nazi past. There emerged in postwar Germany a political movement which called itself rightist and conservative but which critics denounced as a barely disguised new National Socialism. By 1950 there were at least a dozen small political parties which

---

[9]Eleanor Lansing Dulles, *The Wall is Not Forever* (New York, 1967), p. 172.

could be described as neo-Nazi in spirit. Each in its own way imitated the outer forms of Hitlerism.

The most vociferous of these neo-Nazi parties was the *Nationalde-mokratische Partei Deutschlands* (NPD), formed in the 1960s on the consolidation of several right-wing groups. At its core was a hard cadre of self-professed superpatriots. It was led by Adolf von Thadden, who sought to give the movement an air of respectability by disavowing any connection with the Nazi regime. A gifted speaker, von Thadden was more polished than the crude, ungrammatical Hitler. Preaching the message of a revived German nationalism, with accent on the national mission, he attacked the Nuremberg war crimes trials as "a national pollution." He advocated pensions for all, including former ss members who had fought for the Fatherland during the war. Germans, he said, must regain their discipline and pride.

The platform of the NPD appealed to the sense of German nationalism. It included these demands:

1. Recall all foreign troops, including Americans, from German soil.
2. Deport all 1.3 million foreign workers.
3. Put an end to the one-sided war crimes trials because "in other countries millions of war crimes against German men, women, and children go unpunished."
4. Protest against all lies about German responsibility for World War II.
5. Put an end to the practice of extorting money from Germany.
6. Demand the return of territories on which Germans had lived for centuries (lands beyond the Oder-Neisse line; Austria).
7. Decline any further American aid.

Critics charged that this platform was neo-Nazi. They pointed out that a dozen of the eighteen members of the executive board of the NPD were former card-holding Nazis and that half of them held high rank in the ss and were entitled to the Nazi golden badge. In response, NPD leaders denied that they were in any way anti-Semitic, even though some of them made veiled insults against Jews and Israel. NPD speakers at political rallies claimed to have "inside news" that the gas chambers found in Nazi extermination camps had been constructed by American troops after the war in order to throw guilt on innocent Germans.

In 1965 the NPD claimed a membership of 16,298. In the November 1966 state elections it had twenty-three candidates in Bavaria and Hesse, polling 225,000 votes (2.9 percent) in Hesse and 390,000 (7.4 percent) in Bavaria. In

Nuremberg, the former site of Nazi rallies, the NPD received 13.1 percent of the total vote; in Bayreuth, home of Wagnerian tradition, it won 13.9 percent. In April 1967 the NPD was supported by 6.9 percent of the voters in the Rhineland-Palatinate and 5.8 percent in Schleswig-Holstein.

These early successes touched off a lively debate on the possibility of a Nazi revival. On December 20, 1966, the American Council on Germany issued a statement casting doubt about the rebirth of Nazism and warned against "the danger of condemning an entire people for the views of a small minority."[10] The statement was signed by twenty-nine American authorities on Germany, including George N. Schuster, Hans J. Morgenthau, Henry A. Kissinger, Robert Strausz-Hupé, Hajo Holborn, and Harry D. Gideonse, all highly respected observers of the German scene. Critics objected on the ground that a similar view was expressed during the early days of the National Socialist movement, but others defended it. Lowell Dittmer concluded that NPD's potential was very limited.[11] Paula Sutter Fichtner observed that the rightist-radical parties in Germany and Austria had little attraction for the German public and that there was no basis for active cooperation between these neo-Nazi "forces of German nationalism."[12]

These conclusions appear to be correct. The NPD declined steadily in voting power. In the elections of November 1972 it received only 0.6 percent of the total vote. Other nationalist parties also lost strength. The neo-Nazi parties used all the old drum-and-bugle parades and rallies even in the same Nuremberg squares, but the former emotional response was lacking. Bonn authorities vigorously opposed this sort of revival, so much so that they were accused of stepping beyond the limits of democratic practice. In justification they pointed to the tragic effects of unrestrained nationalism in the past and described their own attitude as reasonable protection.

Dichotomy: Nationalism in the German Democratic Republic

After World War I the peacemakers of Versailles divided defeated Germany into two parts separated by the Polish Corridor. Germans were outraged by the isolation of East Prussia. This "punishment" promoted the spirit of German

---

[10]*The New York Times,* December 30, 1966.

[11]Lowell Dittmer, "The German NPD, A Psycho-Sociological Analysis of 'Neo-Nazism,'" *Comparative Politics,* II, no. 1 (October, 1969), pp. 79–110.

[12]Paula Sutter Fichtner, "NPD-NDP: Europe's New Nationalism in Germany and Austria," *Review of Politics,* XXX (July, 1968), pp. 308–315.

nationalism. Hitler carefully used Danzig and the Polish Corridor as tools to whip the German people into a frenzy of sustained nationalism.

Again in 1945 the victorious Allies divided defeated Germany into two parts, the Western-oriented Federal Republic of West Germany and the Soviet-dominated Democratic Republic of East Germany. In the ensuing years West Germany took her place as an affluent capitalist state, while East Germany became a satellite of the Soviet Union. Once again students of nationalism predicted that German nationalism would be promoted by this dichotomy.

That has not happened. Here is another example of the fact that nationalism can act in many differing ways. Instead of working for the union of the two Germanys, nationalism seems to be promoting the existence of two permanently separated states. The language and many aspects of culture remain the same, but this time the ideological differences are so strong that the two countries go their separate ways, each content with its own form of nationalism. In the immediate postwar period, nationalists in West Germany insisted that the agricultural areas of East Germany were essential to exploit the full potential of a united Germany. That view gradually disappeared in the elixir of West German prosperity. At the same time, the Democratic Republic of East Germany, like communist states elsewhere, opted for its own brand of nationalism superimposed on its loyalty to international communism.

Not the least important contribution to permanent division was the Berlin Wall. In August 1961 the German Democratic Republic announced the closure of the border between East and West Berlin ostensibly to keep out Western saboteurs. Within weeks a wall of solid cement blocks topped with broken glass and barbed wire was built. Eventually, the wall was extended to the boundaries between East and West Germany.

For a time the Berlin Wall stimulated a revival of national sentiment and increased public calls for reunification. This sentiment gathered some strength during the administration of Chancellor Konrad Adenauer from 1949 to 1963.[13] Adenauer was successful in integrating the Bonn Republic into Western Europe and NATO, but at the same time he hoped to bring about a reunion of the two Germanys. For a time he seemed to have public support. The most enthusiastic advocates of reunification were the thirteen million refugees from East Germany who had escaped to the West. These refugees were living reminders of a truncated nation.

---

[13]On divided Germany, see Rudolf Walter Leonhardt, *This Germany: The Story Behind the Third Reich* (New York, 1964).

Adenauer was unsuccessful in his goal. The old Chancellor believed that a powerful West would sooner or later impose terms on the Russians and that such terms would include the reunification of Germany. He was mistaken. It became clear eventually that this policy was wrong in exaggerating the possibilities of both Western strength and Russian weakness.[14] Adenauer did not understand that nationalism remains one of the most paradoxical and eccentric of the historical isms.

Estrangement between the two Germanys grew during the administrations of Willy Brandt and Helmut Schmidt. East Germany has gone far on the road of developing a nationalism of her own. Although wedded to Marxism-Leninism and closely associated with the Soviet Union, it has become a quasi-independent national state. It has assumed a coherent national image of its own. It has nationalized all basic industries and collectivized agriculture, projected a new conception of citizenship which stressed collective involvement rather than private profit. John Starrels expressed it well: "The regime was able to articulate its image of what is called 'the new socialist man.' Building on the experiences—real or imagined—of such people as Adolf Hennecke, the SED [Socialist United Party] began to generate a concept of nationalism which underlined the need of individuals to enlist their full strength in the cause of economic mobilization. A proliferation of adjectives touching on such virtues as 'industriousness,' 'readiness to help others,' 'cooperativeness,' 'responsibility toward the affairs of the nation,' and unrestrained 'loyalty' to East German society, catches the spirit of the effort."[15]

This new idea of nationalism emerged in East Germany during the early and middle 1960s, at roughly the same time as the building of the Berlin Wall. Politicians began to express a sense of pride in "socialist achievements." Walter Ulbricht spoke glowingly of the new nation: "All citizens of the German Democratic Republic can be proud of the fact that in their German state the socialist revolution has been carried out, the exploitation of man by man has been abolished, a powerful nationally-owned industry has been created, and in agriculture the union of farmers into agricultural production cooperatives has taken place."[16] In such convenient fashion was international socialism converted into nationalism.

By the mid-1960s the earlier all-German appeal was stilled in both East and

---

[14]See Klaus Epstein, *Germany After Adenauer*, Foreign Policy Association Headline Series, no. 164 (New York, April 1964), p. 7.
[15]John Starrels, "Nationalism in the German Democratic Republic," *Canadian Review of Studies in Nationalism*, vol. II, No. 1 (Fall, 1974), pp. 27–28.
[16]Walter Ulbricht, *Whither Germany?* (Dresden, n.d.), p. 334.

West Germany. Both areas placed emphasis on their unique national consciousness. The nationalism of the West harmonized with a planned capitalism; the nationalism of the East functioned within the spirit of collectivity. There were, of course, clusters of minorities in both areas which still called for unification.

It remains to be seen whether or not there will arise a strong movement for union inside the two German states. There is a split between generations: some older Germans prefer the traditional nationalism, while young people prefer the new form. East German youngsters are inclined to hold a vision of German politics which does not pass beyond the borders of their country. They prefer voluntary acceptance of the collective spirit and comradeship offered by social, economic, and political institutions. The German Democratic Republic, they believe, has established itself as a nation-state in its own right. Peter Christian Ludz presented this point of view: "The consciousness of a German history and the superiority of a democratic Germany will perhaps not be lost on those who are now twenty-five to thirty years old. But even assuming a continuation of a steady economic upswing in the GDR, this consciousness will probably not be stronger than the consciousness of the fact that two independent German states and social systems resulted from World War II and must be respected as such."[17]

Changing National Character?

One of the few certainties in the study of national character is the dictum that national character is by no means fixed and permanent. The character of a people accurately reflects the era in which they live and it may undergo change under the impact of historical development. We have seen how the passive Germans of the 18th century were transformed in the 19th into a highly disciplined people strongly affected by the ideology of power. Young Germans who fought against Napoleon in the War of Liberation were willing to sacrifice their lives for the Fatherland. No French bourgeois decadence for them, no British constitutional chaos. They had an abiding faith in the German soul and in the German mission to save the world. For the rest of the 19th century the German national character was molded in the Prussian image—discipline, thoroughness, obedience, pedantry, punctuality, love of decora-

---

[17]Peter Christian Ludz, *The German Democratic Republic: From the 60's to the 70's* (Cambridge, Mass., 1970), p. 30.

tion and titles, respect for the military. This kind of national character helped prepare the way for the two world conflagrations of the 20th century.

Those Germans who survived the slaughter became convinced that aggressive nationalism was not the answer to Germany's problems. A weary people had enough of unrestrained nationalism. They were now inclined to shove the tragic Nazi experience back into the recesses of their minds. The arch culprit, the misleader, was now dead. Let Germans get to work.

Germans now began to desert that romanticism of the past which had placed its accent upon unrestrained nationalism. There was less interest in interminable philosophical speculation and in the transcendental idealism of the past. Instead of flags, anthems, and the goose step, Germans turned to a skeptical, literal-minded, cautious materialism. Escape to prosperity became a kind of national occupational therapy. Young Germans turned from parades to jobs in the belief that careers were open to talent. The resultant *Wirtschaftwunder,* an economic miracle, impressed the whole world.

Psychologically, the new national character was geared to Western democracy. For the first time West Germans were playing a really meaningful role in their own government. This was new and challenging for them. They wanted no more of that gigantic hoax called National Socialism. They would accept a moderate, rational nationalism which had no room for excesses. They would accent national pride and national dignity instead of the national image of the mailed fist. The old curse of integral nationalism was gone and the national character was changed.

Defensive Re-nationalism in Contemporary Germany

The kind of defensive nationalism which has emerged in West Germany reflects the economic situation in Europe. Defeated Germany moved from the bottom of the European heap to its pinnacle. West Germany used her immense economic power to keep the sick nations of Europe alive and to maintain the viability of the NATO alliance. Bonn contributed a major share to the International Monetary Fund for use by economically endangered Britain, Italy, Portugal, and Turkey. This was very different from the national egotism of the past.

There were varied reactions to this new state of economic affairs. Other European nations, notably Britain and Italy, suffered a decline in national pride as they were forced to ask economic help from Bonn as a means of keeping afloat. Inside Germany, political leaders far from being pleased by the widening economic gap, reacted with dismay. They were worried lest increasing economic discontent throughout Western Europe lead to the intensification of what was now called Eurocommunism, or communism with a Western-oriented democratic tinge.

The trend climaxed in the national elections of October 1976. The opposition Christian Democratic Union (CDU) received the largest vote in the election, but lost the chancellorship. During the campaign the CDU made an issue out of the so-called generals' affair, in which two senior air force generals were dismissed for a political indiscretion involving a former Nazi *Luftwaffe* flying ace. Opposition orators denounced the Social Democratic (SPD) government of Helmut Schmidt for allowing the summary dismissal of the two generals.

This clash represented in miniscule the quarrel between two forms of nationalism—one closer to the old traditional aggressive form and the other a defensive re-nationalism played in a low key. To counter the possibility of a revival of nationalism in its dangerous form, Bonn took a political path designed to lessen the display of its own strength and to bolster its partners in the NATO alliance. It wanted no renascence of William II's loud protest that Germany must fight her way to a place in the sun because "all the nations of the world are directing the force of their bayonets against Germany." Nor did it want a revival of Hitler's vow to achieve *Lebensraum* on the ground that a superior German Aryan race was ready for territorial expansion.

The re-nationalism proposed by the current West German government, and enjoying widespread public support, is a hopeful development. If it sets a standard for Europe and for the rest of the world, it may well presage an era of peace and prosperity. Certainly it is far from that form of arrogant, aggressive nationalism which brought little but misery and despair to the German people in the past. One can only hope.

Bibliographical Note

There is a vast bibliography on the general subject of nationalism, but the number of studies on the specific field of German nationalism is meager. Relatively little attention has been paid to this speciality. Hans Kohn, who along with Carlton J. H. Hayes was a pioneer American scholar on nationalism, was interested in anything related to German nationalism. He was attracted by the lives and career of those German Romantics who were regarded as apostles of German nationalism, including Turnvater Jahn, Heine, Wagner, Nietzsche, Rilke, and others. Kohn's book, *The Mind of Germany: The Education of a Nation* (1960) is a classic analysis of the German mentality.

My own *German Nationalism: The Tragedy of a People* (1952, 1969) is one of the few studies directly concerned with the origin, nature, and development of German nationalism. All major works on nationalism have chapters or sections devoted to this special subject, including such studies as Boyd Shafer, *Nationalism: Myth and Reality* (1955) and *Faces of Nationalism* (1972), and Frederick Hertz, *Nationality in History and Politics* (1951).

A most important stimulus to the study of German nationalism was the famed seminar at Columbia University led by the late Carlton J. H. Hayes. Highly original, Hayes was an enthusiastic teacher who succeeded in transferring his own interests to those students he selected for his seminar. Under his sponsorship there appeared a stream of dissertations and post-doctoral studies on every form of nationalism, including several specifically concerned with German nationalism. Among such works were: Walter C. Langsam, *The Napoleonic War and German Nationalism in Austria* (1930); Robert R. Ergang, *Herder and the Foundations of German Nationalism* (1931); Koppel S. Pinson, *Pietism as a Factor in the Rise of German Natiomalism* (1934); Louis L. Snyder, *From Bismarck to Hitler: The Background of Modern German Nationalism* (1935); and Oscar I. Janowsky, *Nationalities and National Minorities* (1945).

A challenging and provocative recent study on German nationalism appeared in an article by Robert M. Berdahl, "New Thoughts on German Nationalism," in *The American Historical Review*, LXXVI, no. 1 (February,

1972), pp. 65–80. Berdahl finds much of the older literature to be inadequate. He is especially critical of Kohn and others who have suggested that 19th-century Germany spurned the values of the Enlightenment and developed a romantic, aggressive nationalism different from other European forms. He grants that these writers have given valuable insights into the ideas of individual German chauvinists such as Turnvater Jahn and the historian Heinrich von Treitschke, but he believes that Kohn and his school have overemphasized the exclusiveness of German nationalism. According to Berdahl, these observers did not explain why nationalism emerged in Germany at a certain time nor why German nationalists were more aggressive than others. He concludes that in Germany, as elsewhere, nationalism was generated primarily among a people "by the growing awareness of its economic backwardness and by the desire for a modern economy." He also suggests that once a country has become industrialized, nationalism is merely one of the ideologies employed to integrate a society in which traditional loyalties have been undermined.

It is an interesting thesis but it also comes under the category of historical faddism. Berdahl's views are in accord with the recent tendency to overemphasize economic motivations as the solution to all the problems of nationalism or any other ism. This is a typical example of the approach of scholars-in-search-of-a-thesis. Neither economic determinists nor quantitative historians have been able to throw as much light on the genesis and development of nationalism as has Kohn in his study of cultural and psychological motivations. At the same time Kohn understood well the economic aspects of nationalism.

Special studies on German nationalism have appeared in such journals as *The American Historical Review, The Journal of Modern History, Review of Politics, The Journal of Contemporary History, Historische Zeitschrift,* and *Revue historiques.* The new *Canadian Review of Studies in Nationalism,* edited by Thomas Spira, is now the only important scholarly journal in the world devoted exclusively to the study of nationalism. It has published several excellent articles on German nationalism.

In Europe the most important work on nationalism in general and on German nationalism in particular is being done currently at the Historisches Seminar of the University of Cologne in the German Federal Republic. Historian Theodor Schieder and his students have produced a number of specialized works which compare favorably with the work done in Hayes's seminar at Columbia. Recent studies include *Sozialstruktur und Organisation*

Europäischer Nationalbewegungen (1969), edited by Peter Burion under the sponsorship of Professor Schieder, and *Staatsgründungen und Nationali-tätsprinzip* (1975), edited by Peter Alter again under the sponsorship of Professor Schieder. Both volumes concern typical national movements in Germany, Italy, Croatia, Denmark, Finland, and elsewhere.

The Schieder group takes a different line from that of the Hayes seminar in that it places a premium upon the inductive approach. It tends to emphasize the characteristics of nationalism or national movements in one specific coun-try, large or small but preferably small, and then channels the results to a level of overall contemplation. This in general is in line with European historical scholarship, which is microscopic in motivation as compared to the American scholars' preference for macroscopic treatment. American historians prefer to analyze nationalism from a perch high above earthly conflicts, while their European counterparts choose a ringside view.

Select Bibliography

Books Concerned Wholly or in Part with German Nationalism

Anderson, E. N. *Nationalism and the Cultural Crisis in Prussia, 1805–1815*. New York: Rinehart, 1939.

Barker, E. *National Character and the Factors in Its Formation*. London: Metheun, 1927.

Barzun, J. *Race: A Study in Modern Superstition*. New York: Harcourt, Brace, 1937.

Bauer, O. *Die Nationalitätenfrage und die Sozialdemokratie*. Vienna: Volksbuchhandlung, 1924.

Binkley, R. C. *Realism and Nationalism, 1852–1871*. New York: Harper, 1935.

Bossenbroek, W. J., ed. *Mid-Twentieth-Century Nationalism*. Detroit: Wayne State University Press, 1965.

Braunthal, J. *The Paradox of Nationalism: An Epilogue to the Nuremberg Trials*. London: St. Bodolph, 1946.

Chadwick, H. M. *The Nationalities of Europe and the Growth of National Ideologies*. Cambridge, England: Cambridge University Press, 1945.

Chamberlain, H. S. *The Foundations of the Nineteenth Century*. Tr. J. Lees. 2 vols. London: John Lane, 1913.

Count, E. W., ed. *This is Race: An Anthology Selected from the International Literature of the Races of Man*. New York: Schuman, 1950.

Demiashkievich, M. *The National Mind: English, French, German*. New York: American Book Co., 1938.

Deutsch, K. W. *An Interdisciplinary Bibliography on Nationalism, 1933–1955*. Cambridge, Massachusetts: Technology Press, 1956.

Dominian, I. *The Frontiers of Language and Nationality in Europe*. New York: Holt, 1917.

Engelbrecht, H. C. *Johann Gottlieb Fichte: A Study of his Writings with Special Reference to Nationalism*. New York: Columbia University Press, 1931.

Ergang, R. R. *Herder and the Foundations of German Nationalism*. New York: Columbia University Press, 1931.

Feis, J. *Begriff und Wesen der Nation: eine soziologische Untersuchung und Kritik*. Münster: Aschendorffsche Verlagsbuchhandlung, 1927.

Fichte, J. G. *Addresses to the German Nation*. Tr. R. F. Jones and G. H. Turnbull. Chicago: Open Court Publishing Co., 1922.

Fyfe, H. *The Illusion of National Character*. London: C. A. Watts, 1940.

Gooch, G. P. *Nationalism*. New York: Harcourt, Brace and Howe, 1920.

Hayes, C. J. H. *Essays on Nationalism*. New York: Macmillan, 1926.

———. *A Generation of Materialism, 1871–1890*. New York: Harper, 1941.

———. *The Historical Evolution of Modern Nationalism*. New York: E. R. Smith, 1931.

———. *Nationalism: A Religion*. New York: Macmillan, 1960.

Hertz, F. O. *Nationality in History and Politics*. New York: Oxford University Press, 1951.

Janowsky, O. *Nationalities and National Minorities*. New York: Columbia University Press, 1945.

Jaszi, O. *The Dissolution of the Hapsburg Monarchy*. Chicago: University of Chicago Press, 1929.

Kann, R. A. *The Multinational Empire: Nationalism and National Reform in the Habsburg Monarchy, 1848–1918*. New York: Columbia University Press, 1950. 2 vols. Octagon reprint, 1964.

Kedourie, E. *Nationalism*. New York: Praeger, 1960.

Kohn, H. *The Mind of Germany: The Education of a Nation*. New York: Scribner, 1960.

———. *Nationalism: Its Meaning and History*. Princeton: Van Nostrand, 1960.

———. *The Age of Nationalism: The First Era of Global History*. New York: Harper, 1962.

———. *Prelude to Nation-States: The French and German Experience, 1789–1815*. Princeton: Van Nostrand, 1967.

Kuhn, J., et al. *Der Nationalismus im Leben der dritten Republik*. Berlin: Paetel, 1920.

Langer, W. L. *The Diplomacy of Imperialism, 1890–1902*. New York: Knopf, 1935.

Langsam, W. C. *The Napoleonic Wars and German Nationalism in Austria*. New York: Columbia University Press, 1930.

Lemberg, E. *Geschichte des Nationalismus in Europa*. Stuttgart: Schwab, 1950.

May, A. J. *The Hapsburg Monarchy, 1867–1914*. Cambridge, Massachusetts: Harvard University Press, 1951.

Meinecke, F. *Weltbürgertum und Nationalstaat*. Munich: Oldenbourg, 1928.

———. *The German Catastrophe*. Tr. S. B. Fay. Cambridge, Massachusetts: Harvard University Press, 1950.

Michels, R. *Der Patriotismus*. Munich: Duncker und Humboldt, 1929.

Mitscherlich, W. *Der Nationalismus Westeuropas*. Leipzig: Hirschfeld, 1920.

Morani, G. M. *The Races of Central Europe*. London: Allen & Unwin, 1939.

Mosse, G. L. *The Nationalization of the Masses: Political Symbolism and Mass Movements in Germany from the Napoleonic Wars Through the Third Reich*. New York: Fertig, 1976.

Muir, R. *Nationalism and Internationalism: The Culmination of Modern History*. London: Constable, 1917.

Namier, L. B. "Pathological Nationalisms," in *The Margin of History*. London: Macmillan, 1939.

———. *Vanished Supremacies: Essays on European History*. London: Hamish Hamilton, 1958.

Oakesmith, J. *Race and Nationalism: An Inquiry into the Origins and Growth of Patriotism*. New York: Stokes, 1919.

Pinson, K. S. *A Bibliographical Introduction to Nationalism*. New York: Columbia University Press, 1935.

———. *Pietism as a Factor in the Rise of German Nationalism*. New York: Columbia University Press, 1934, 1957.

Platt, W. *National Character in Action*. New Brunswick, New Jersey: Rutgers University Press, 1961.

Pundt, A. G. *Arndt and the National Awakening in Germany*. New York: Columbia University Press, 1935.

Rose, J. H. *Nationality in Modern History*. New York: Macmillan, 1916.

Roucek, J. S. *Twentieth Century Political Thought*. New York: Philosophical Library, 1946.

Roussakis, E. N. *Friedrich List, the Zollverein, and the Unity of Europe*. Bruges, 1968.

Royal Institute of International Affairs. *Nationalism*. London: Oxford University Press, 1939.

Schaffner, B. *Fatherland: A Study of Authoritarianism in the German Family*. New York: Columbia University Press, 1948.

Schalk, A. *The Germans*. Englewood Cliffs, New Jersey: Prentice, Hall, 1971.

Schnee, H. *Nationalismus und Imperialismus*. Berlin: Hobbing, 1928.

Schneider, G. *Absonderung von allgemeiner Ursprung und Wesen d. Staatsideologie d. hist. Nationalismus*. Düsseldorf: Henn, 1973.

Schneider, H. W. and S. B. Clough. *Making Fascists*. Chicago: University of Chicago Press, 1929.

Shafer, B. C. *Nationalism: Myth and Reality*. New York: Harcourt, Brace, 1955.

———. Nationalism: *Interpreters and Interpretation*. New York: Macmillan, 1963.

———. *Faces of Nationalism*. New York: Harcourt Brace Jovanovich, 1972.

Snyder, L. L. *From Bismarck to Hitler: The Background of Modern German Nationalism*. Williamsport, Pennsylvania: Bayard, 1935.

———. *Race: A History of Modern Ethnic Theories*. New York and London: Longmans, Green, 1939.

———. *German Nationalism: The Tragedy of a People*. Harrisburg, Pennsylvania: Stackpole, 1952. Reprint Port Washington, New York: Kennikat Press, 1969.

———. *The Idea of Racialism*. Princeton: Van Nostrand, 1962.

———. *The Dynamics of Nationalism*. Princeton: Van Nostrand, 1964.

———. Varieties of Nationalism, New York: Holt, Rinehart and Winston, 1976.

Symmons-Symonolewicz, K. *Modern Nationalism: Towards a Consensus in Theory*. New York: Polish Institute of Arts and Sciences, 1968.

———. *Nationalist Movements: A Comparative View*. Meadville, Pennsylvania: Maplewood Press, 1970.

Tauber, K. P. *Beyond Eagle and Swastika*. 2 vols. Middletown, Connecticut: 1967.

Taylor, A. J. P. *The Course of German History*. New York: Coward-McCann, 1946.

Tims, R. W. *Germanizing the Prussian Poles: The H. K. T. Society of the Eastern Marches*. New York: Columbia University Press, 1941.

Vossler, O. *Der Nationalgedanke von Rousseau bis Ranke*. Munich: Oldenbourg, 1937.

Walzel, O. *German Romanticism*. New York: Capricorn Books, 1966.

Weber, E. *Varieties of Fascism*. Princeton: Van Nostrand, 1964.

Wertheimer, M. S. *The Pan-German League, 1890–1914*. New York: Columbia University Press, 1924.

Wiskemann, E. *Czechs and Germans*. London: Oxford University Press, 1938.

Periodicals

Berdahl, R. M. "New Thoughts on German Nationalism." *American Historical Review* LXXVI, no. 1 (February 1972), pp. 65–80.

Berlin, I. "The Bent Twig: A Note on Nationalism." *Foreign Affairs* LI, no. 1 (October 1972), pp. 11–30.

Blanke, R. "Bismarck and the Prussian Polish Policies of 1886." *Journal of Modern History* XLV, no. 2 (June 1973), pp. 211–239.

———. "Upper Silesia, 1921: The Case for Subjective Nationality." *Canadian Review of Studies in Nationalism* II, no. 2 (Spring 1975), pp. 241–260.

Braatz, W. E. "Two Neo-Conservative Myths in Germany, 1919–1932: The 'Third Reich' and the 'New State.'" *Journal of the History of Ideas* XXXII (October-December 1971), pp. 569–584.

Buchner, R. "Die deutsche patriotische Dichtung vom Kriegsbeginn 1870 über Frankreich und die elsässische Frage." *Historische Zeitschrift* CCVIII (April 1968), pp. 327–336.

Burkhardt, J. "Das nationale Interesse am deutschen Bauernkreig in der Geschichtsschreibung des neunzehnten Jahrhunderts." *Canadian Review of Studies in Nationalism* II, no. 1 (Autumn 1974), pp. 38–57.

Carsten, F. "'Volk ohne Raum': A Note on Hans Grimm." *Journal of Contemporary History* II, no. 2 (April 1967), pp. 221–227.

Chodorowsky, J. "J. G. Fichte: Precursor of the German Doctrine of 'Large-Area-Economy.'" *Polish Western Affairs,* no. 1 (1970), pp. 126–153.

Craig, G. "German Intellectuals and Politics, 1789–1815: The Case of Heinrich von Kleist." *Central European History* II, no. 1 (March 1969), pp. 3–21.

Deuerlein, E. "Die Bekehrung des Zentrum zum nationalen Idee." *Hochland* (September–October 1970), pp. 432–449.

Dittmer, L. "The German NPD. A Psycho-Sociological Analysis of 'Neo-Nazism.'" *Comparative Politics* II, no. 1 (October 1969), pp. 79–110.

Dorpalen, A. "Heinrich von Treitschke." *Journal of Contemporary History* VII, nos. 3–4 (July–October 1972), pp. 21–36.

Faber, K. -G. "Student und Politik in der ersten deutschen Burschenschaft." *Geschichte in Wissenschaft und Unterricht* (November-December 1969), pp. 68–80.

Fichtner, P. S. "Protest on the Right: The NPD in Recent German Politics," *Orbis* XII (Spring 1968), pp. 185–199.

———. "NPD-NDP: Europe's New Nationalism in Germany and Austria." *Review of Politics* XXX (July 1968), pp. 308–315.

————. "The Enduring Conflict: Hans Grimm and Twentieth-Century Germany." *South Atlantic Quarterly,* no. 2 (1972), pp. 177–188.

Grathwohl, R. "Gustav Stresemann: Reflections on His Foreign Policy." *Journal of Modern History* XLV, no. 1 (March 1973), pp. 52–70.

Grosser, A. "Specificités du nationalisme allemande." *Revue d'Allemagne* I (October-December 1969), pp. 421–435.

Haag, J. " 'Knights of the Spirit'; The Kameradschaftsbund." *Journal of Contemporary History* VIII, no. 3 (July 1973), pp. 133–153.

Hartwig, E. "Der alldeutscher Verband und Polen." *Wissenschaftliche Zeitschrift der Universität Jena,* no. 2 (1970), pp. 251–275.

Hayes, C. J. H. "Contributions of Herder to the Doctrine of Nationalism." *American Historical Review* XXXII (1972), pp. 719–736.

Jeimann, K. -E. "Nationalerziehung: Bermerkungen zum Verhältnis von Politik und Pedagogik in der Zeit der preussischen Reform, 1806–1815." *Geschichte in Wissenschaft und Unterricht* (April 1968), pp. 201–218.

Kennedy, P. M. "The Decline of Nationalistic History in the West, 1900–1970." *Journal of Contemporary History* VIII, no. 1 (January 1971), pp. 77–100.

Kimmich, C. M. "The Weimar Republic and the German-Polish Borders." *Polish Review* XIV, no. 4 (Autumn 1969), pp. 37–45.

Kohn, H. "Arndt and the Character of German Nationalism." *American Historical Review* LIV (1949), pp. 787–803.

————. "Father Jahn's Nationalism." *Review of Politics* XI (1949), pp. 419–432.

————. "The Paradox of Fichte's Nationalism." *Journal of the History of Ideas* X (1949), pp. 319–343.

————. "Romanticism and the Rise of Nationalism." *Review of Politics* XII (1950), pp. 443–472.

————. "The Eve of German Nationalism." *Journal of the History of Ideas* XII (1951), pp. 256–284.

————. "Begriffswandel des nationalismus." *Der Merkur* (August 1964), pp. 701–714.

Lader, H. "Die SED und die Nation." *Deutsche Studien* X (March 1972), pp. 32–45.

Lutz, R. R. "The German Revolutionary Student Movement, 1819–1933." *Central European History* IV, no. 3 (September 1971), pp. 215–241.

Maehl, W. "The Triumph of Nationalism in the German Socialist Party on the Eve of the First World War." *Journal of Modern History* XXIV (1952), pp. 15–41.

Marx, E. "Le nationalisme dans les manuels d'histoire de la R.D.A." *Revue d'Allemagne* (October–December 1969), pp. 502–518.

Messerschmid, F. "Deutsche Nation-historisch und politisch." *Geschichte in Wissenschaft und Unterricht* (May 1972), pp. 291–295.

Moses, J. A. "Pan-Germanism and the German Professors, 1914–1918." *Australian Journal of Politics and History,* no. 3 (1969), pp. 45–60.

Moslenhoff, F. "The Price of Individuality: Speculations about German National Characteristics." *American Imago* IV (1947), pp. 33–60.

Mosse, W. E. "The Conflict of Liberalism and Nationalism and Its Effect on German Jewry." *Leo Baeck Institute Yearbook* XV (1970), pp. 125–139.

Mueller, G. H. "Germany's Emergent Nationalism: Trends since the Berlin Wall." *South Atlantic Quarterly* (Autumn 1968), pp. 659–671.

Nipperley, T. "Nationalidee und Nationaldenkmal in Deutschland im 19. Jahrhundert." *Historische Zeitschrift* CCVI (June 1968), pp. 529–595.

Olson, J. M. "Nationalistic Values in Prussian Schoolbooks Prior to World War I." *Canadian Review of Studies in Nationalism* I (Fall 1973), pp. 47–59.

Oncken, H. "Deutsche geistige Einflüsse in der europäischen Nationalbewegung des neunzehnten Jahrhunderts." *Deutsche Vierteljahrsschrift für Literaturwissenschaft und Geistesgeschichte* VII (1929), pp. 607–627.

Passon, H. "Der Nationalismus in der deutschen jugendbildenden Literatur des 19. Jahrhunderts." *Internationales Jahrbuch für Geschichtsunterricht* XII (1968–69), pp. 54–95.

Peters, H. "Patriotische Offiziere in der antifeudalen Vormärzbewegung in Deutschland." *Zeitschrift für Militärgeschichte* no. 2 (1970), pp. 192–202.

Petzold, J. "Zur Funktion des Nationalismus, Moeller van der Brucks Beitrag zur faschistischen Ideologie." *Zeitschrift für Geschichtswissenschaft* XXI, no. 11 (1973), pp. 1285–1300.

Pflanze, O. "Nationalism in Europe, 1848–1871." *Review of Politics* XVIII (1966), pp. 129–143.

Pois, R. A. "Elements of Continuity in the Political Writings of J. G. Fichte." *Rocky Mountain Social Science Journal* (April 1971), pp. 11–21.

Renouvin, P. "Nationalisme et Imperialisme en Allemagne de 1911 à 1914." *Revue historique,* no. 497 (January–March 1971), pp. 63–72.

Schertzinger, M. "Le SPD et le nationalisme." *Revue d'Allemagne* I (October–December 1969), pp. 467–483.

Schieder, T. "The German Kaiserreich from 1871 as a Nation-State." *Historical Studies* (Dublin), VIII (1971), pp. 31–46.

Schmidt, R. J. "Cultural Nationalism in Herder." *Journal of the History of Ideas* XVII (1956), pp. 407–417.

Schroter, K. "Chauvinism and Its Tradition: German Writers at the Outbreak of the First World War." *German Review* XLIII (March 1968), pp. 120–135.

Stachura, P. D. "The Ideology of the Hitler Youth in the Kampfzeit." *Journal of Contemporary History* VIII, no. 3 (July 1973), pp. 155–167.

Starrels, J. "Nationalism and the German Democratic Republic." *Canadian Review of Studies in Nationalism* II (Autumn 1974), pp. 22–37.

Stein, L. "Religion and Patriotism in German Peace Drama during the Thirty Years' War." *Central European History* IV, no. 2 (June 1971), pp. 131–148.

Virtanen, R. "Nietzsche and the Action Française." *Journal of Modern History* XI (1950), pp. 191–214.

Wagner, J. F. "Transferred Crisis: German Volkish Thought among Russian Mennonite Immigrants to Western Canada." *Canadian Review of Studies in Nationalism* I (1974), pp. 202–220.

Index

An
Unlikely Story
of
Finding
Freedom

FLYING
FALLING
CATCHING

FLYING

FALLING

CATCHING

Henri J. M. Nouwen

and

Carolyn Whitney-Brown

HarperOne
An Imprint of HarperCollinsPublishers

FIRST EDITION

Designed by Joy O'Meara @ Creative Joy Designs

Illustrations: © Shutterstock (modified by The Book Designers)

Library of Congress Cataloging-in-Publication Data is available upon request.

ISBN 978-0-06-311352-7

22 23 24 25 26 LSC 10 9 8 7 6 5 4 3 2 1

to Geoffrey Whitney–Brown
because no one flies alone

When I saw the Flying Rodleighs for the very first time, it looked like everything that's important in life. I saw it together in one act.

—HENRI NOUWEN

The ten minutes that followed somehow gave me a glimpse of a world that had eluded me so far, a world of discipline and freedom, diversity and harmony, risk and safety, individuality and community, and most of all flying and catching.

—HENRI NOUWEN

CONTENTS

PROLOGUE

September 1996

When they received the phone call telling them of Henri's death, the five members of the Flying Rodleighs trapeze troupe were stunned. Before removing their flashy silver capes during their next performance, Rodleigh Stevens took a deep breath and offered a short speech dedicating the performance to the memory of their friend Henri Nouwen.

On the day of Henri's funeral, Rodleigh with his wife and colleague Jennie Stevens drove 170 miles to St. Catherine's Cathedral in Utrecht. They looked up into the stone Gothic arches and around the enormous space, amazed that it was so full.

"We should have expected this," Rodleigh whispered to Jennie. They knew that Henri was famous, with millions of books in print, translated into dozens of languages. They knew that Henri was a Roman Catholic priest from the Netherlands who had been a professor at Yale and Harvard, then over the past decade had given up his academic career to live with people with intellectual disabilities in Canada.

They had known Henri well for more than five years, but they were shocked when one speaker described Henri as "anguished" and "wounded." Rodleigh shifted uneasily and clutched the edge of the hard wooden pew to hold himself back from rushing to the front of the church to offer a corrective. His mind was full of images and memories of the very different Henri that he knew through visits, letters, and traveling together in Germany and the Netherlands with the Circus Barum.

Perhaps many of Henri's friends, aware of his yearning and inner pain, and many who for years read his personally revealing books on the spiritual life, would have been equally surprised to discover that Henri believed his most important book was going to be a work of creative nonfiction about his experiences with the Flying Rodleighs, a book that his sudden death in September 1996 left unfinished.

. • • •

The story you will read here is true. Every event actually happened, including Henri's rescue out a hotel window. Texts in italics are Henri's own words from his published or unpublished writings, talks or interviews.

Though Henri found acclaim and success writing books of spiritual wisdom, the Flying Rodleighs inspired him to imagine writing a different kind of book. When he died suddenly in 1996, he left hints of this new project: a transcript from his dictation immediately after meeting these trapeze artists for the first time in 1991, two chapters composed later, a journal written while traveling with the Flying Rodleighs, and other comments, reflections, notes, and journal entries.

In 2017, the publishing committee of the Henri Nouwen Legacy Trust approached me to "do something creative" with Henri's unpublished trapeze writings. I was a writer who knew Henri well. After completing my PhD in English literature at Brown University and training as a spiritual director in the United Kingdom and Canada, I lived at L'Arche Daybreak with my husband and children from 1990 to 1997, where Henri was also a community member. Shortly after Henri's death, I wrote an introduction to a new edition of his book *The Road to Daybreak*, as well as several other published pieces about him. Still, I was unsure about taking up Henri's unfinished project. I remembered many conversations with Henri about writing and about the Flying Rodleighs, but the trapeze imagery had never grabbed my imagination. I don't like heights.

When I read Henri's material, however, two questions intrigued me. First, why did the Flying Rodleighs' performance and lives strike Henri so powerfully at that moment in his life? Second, why didn't he write more than some fragments of a trapeze book? He wrote a lot of books between 1991 and 1996, and he talked continually about his desire to write this one. What happened?

I realized that my project was not to write the book that Henri would have written, but to tell the story of Henri and the Flying Rodleighs.

Combing through Henri's trapeze notes and drafts as well as Henri's other published and unpublished writing, I began to sense an overarching shape in his life's last few years. Four kinds of experiences stood out: Henri's reflections on artistry and beauty; times when his physical response helped him to articulate how *the body tells a spiritual story*; transformative points of immersion in specific communities; and moments of lightness, humor, relaxation, and delight.

Ideas for how I might bring Henri's experiences to the page began to form, but it took reading Rodleigh Stevens's memoir of his friendship with Henri, titled "What a Friend We Had in Henri," to give me details for a book that would read as engagingly as fiction while using true events. Rodleigh's memoir also helped clarify something that had been niggling at me: while Henri was often anguished and demanding, he was also delightful. Reading Rodleigh's account, at points I laughed out loud remembering our eager, awkward, insightful friend. There is a reason his friends still miss him all these years later.

Henri had envisioned writing this story as a work of "creative nonfiction." All of Henri's writing is creative, of course. His artistry is apparent even in his published journals, as Henri crafted himself into a character in his own narrative, selecting the details that he wished to share.

Even allowing for Henri's desire to tell a "creative" story, I needed to understand what actually happened the day of Henri's first heart attack. How is a patient in the midst of a medical emergency taken out a window? Dennie Wulterkens, a specialist who trained nurses to do this kind of rescue in the 1990s, responded to my email and explained the process in detail. Because we have been unable to identify the historic person who responded to the call, I have named the character of the nurse "Dennie" in thanks. Even in a medical crisis, Henri would have tried to learn the name of the person caring for him.

Except for "Dennie," all characters are real people, with their own names. My main artistic license is to imagine that during his heart attack in the Netherlands on September 16, 1996, Henri reflects back over parts of his life. This is not a biography. Many important people and experiences in Henri's life are not included.

Because I want you to hear Henri's voice as directly as possible, his writings are italicized and never rewritten. Occasionally I abbreviated or factually corrected them. Sources are provided in detailed notes at the end of the book.

"I wasn't thinking of using the Rodleighs as illustrations for great spiritual truths, but was simply trying to write a good story," Henri once told his German editor. I believe this is, as Henri hoped, a very good story. Along the way, you may also catch some unexpected insights. I know I did.

But first, jump in and enjoy the story!

Carolyn Whitney-Brown
Cowichan Bay, BC, Canada
September 16, 2021

I

The Call

1

Two paramedics in crisp white uniforms burst into Henri's hotel room. They are speaking rapidly in Dutch, his mother tongue. Henri, lying on the hotel bed still in his travel clothes, is relieved to see them.

One introduces himself as Dennie, and reaches out to shake Henri's hand. Henri's eyes behind his glasses are bright, but Dennie observes that his handshake is unsteady and his skin is cool. Dennie explains to Henri that he is a registered nurse with the Broeder De Vries ambulance service.

The other introduces himself as the ambulance driver, also a trained paramedic. He looks around the pleasant room, quickly assessing what Henri has with him in case he needs to go to the hospital. Henri has not unpacked any of his luggage.

Dennie shines his flashlight into Henri's eyes to check his pupils. He takes Henri's pulse and slips his arm into a blood-pressure cuff, all the while asking Henri questions: "What is your name? Where are you from?"

Henri is tired and feels dizzy, but answers as clearly as he can: he is Father Henri J. M. Nouwen. He arrived in Amsterdam at Schiphol airport that morning on an overnight flight from Toronto, Canada, and came straight to the hotel to rest.

"Do you know the date today, and where you are right now?"

"Yes," says Henri. It is Monday, September 16, 1996. He is in Hilversum, at the Hotel Lapershoek. He knows that he is on an upper floor, though he cannot remember his room number.

"What is your main complaint? Do you have any other complaints?"

"My chest hurts a lot. My arm is sore. I am hot and cold."

"When did it start? Have you ever had something like this before?"

"No," says Henri. "I wasn't feeling well yesterday, but I figured it was not serious, and I could rest as soon as I arrived. But it has been getting worse since I checked into the hotel a little over an hour ago."

Dennie evaluates Henri's blood pressure. Henri is glad the questions have paused. His mind is whirling with words and images, but speaking is too much effort.

This is, Henri thinks to himself, an interruption. He has mixed feelings. There have been many interruptions in his life. Some of them have turned out well.

·····

FIVE YEARS EARLIER, HENRI was in Freiburg, Germany, working on a book when he first saw the Flying Rodleighs perform their trapeze act. It left him breathless, almost in tears as a sudden bodily rush of adolescent infatuation swept over him. He was already fifty-nine years old, so he had not expected to be so stirred when he went to the circus with his elderly father. At first, he had assumed that his sensations were anxiety, because the act looked dangerous. It was only later that he recognized his own physical excitement. His response had been so dramatic that he repeatedly struggled to put words around it. First he had tried dictating a tape to be transcribed by Connie, his secretary back in Canada. He knew he was babbling, but he couldn't help himself.

What really got to me, what really fascinated me was the trapeze artists, and that's why I became so involved in the circus and, when I saw them at the very beginning it was absolutely fascinating. This was a group of five trapeze artists, four of them people from South Africa and one an American. I was just so impressed by this group that I kept thinking about them. They did incredible things in the air and somehow, and that was important that I realized that, that has always been why I went to the circus. It was never for the animals and never really for the clowns, but what I was always waiting for and what really grabbed me was the trapeze artists.

And these guys were really amazing. Actually, they weren't all guys; there were three men and two women, and I was just fascinated by the way they were moving freely in the air and making these incredible jumps, and catching each other, and I was just fascinated by their physical prowess.

But I was as much fascinated by the group as a team, the way they worked together because I realized there must be enormous intimacy among these people when everything is so dependent on co-operation, when everything is so dependent on mutual trust and everything is dependent on exact timing.

I realized from the very beginning that this group has to be really well together, and I saw that they enjoyed it, they really had fun doing it, and there was a kind of excitement in them that became very con-tagious for me.

It was kind of a WOW! you know, and I must confess that when I saw them they seemed to be in a way like gods, so far that I wouldn't even dare to come close to them. I had this emotional response that these people are really so far above me in their talent or in their giftedness. They are such great artists, who am I, a little tiny guy wanting to get to know them. It seemed to be impossible for me to even imagine myself knowing these people personally. I realized how strong that feeling was. It was like awesome, awesome, and there was something in me more than just a feeling of a fan who admires a musician or artist. It was as if these guys are indeed living in heaven; they are living in the air and I am living on the ground, and so I am not allowed to talk to them, being so far from each other.

I was so fascinated by my own emotional response to them that I wasn't at all comfortable to go and talk to them. They kept sort of being in my fantasies long after the show was over.

So I went to the show and saw it again, and I began, you know, watching all the other acts, but as soon as these Flying Rodleighs came on, I got all excited again. The whole way they walked right in there and they climbed up to the top of the tent and made these enormous jumps, and the music and their whole style, their smiling at each other, and the fun they had, and their timing, and the whole thing. I couldn't believe they were doing it. The second time I was even more fascinated than the first. It was just unbelievable and I got very nervous inside because I thought I am going to talk to these guys when this is over. It is like talking to people from another planet.

Henri could not get this experience out of his mind. Perhaps this unlikely new encounter with a troupe of trapeze artists wasn't an interruption from his writing, but rather was the start of a significant new book. Surely he could find a way to describe this experience. Something this amazing should be shared. It was all very exhilarating.

.••••

BUT NOW IT IS 1996 and he is lying on a hotel bed near Amsterdam with two paramedics hovering around him. Somehow five years have gone by since that trip to the circus with his father. It has never been far from his mind, yet he has only fragments of chapters, a diary kept over several weeks, and many ideas. He has failed, at least so far, to write his book about the Flying Rodleighs.

What would it feel like to let go, he wonders now, watching Dennie get out his medical equipment.

I never did write that book, he tries whispering to himself. It feels strange to admit that, as though it is a finished fact, as though he could have but didn't. A casual comment, small talk. Unless, of course, an astute listener were to ask, "Why?"

To that, he realizes, he does not have an answer.

2

Dennie unbuttons Henri's shirt and moves his undershirt aside to listen to his heart. The room isn't especially cold but Henri isn't accustomed to being bare-chested, especially in front of an audience. He shivers.

·····•

A FEW MONTHS AFTER meeting the Flying Rodleighs, Henri reread the typed text of his dictated words about the trapeze troupe and smiled. He loved remembering those magical days. He ran his fingers through his thinning hair and thought about the text. It didn't catch quite what he wanted to say. Or perhaps more accurately, this wasn't how he wanted to say it. He didn't want merely to describe his excitement, he wanted the reader to feel the same way. He sighed with frustration. He wanted to tell a story, a story of infatuation, even of falling in love with the Flying Rodleighs. But although he was a prolific writer, he had never attempted a *story*.

Always eager to learn, he bought two books about writing. Passages in Theodore Cheney's *Writing Creative Nonfiction* seemed to catch what he longed to do. *Use concrete details,* he wrote in the margin. "Develop the story scene by scene," he underlined.

He tried again, setting a sophisticated European scene, depicting himself as a spiritual writer peacefully composing a gentle book about love and inner freedom.

Visiting the south German city of Freiburg has always been a great pleasure for me. The most peaceful and joyful memories of the last few decades are from that city so beautifully situated between the river Rhine and the edge of the Black Forest.

In April 1991, I was there again for another month of writing. The L'Arche Daybreak community in Toronto, where I have found my home since 1986, encourages me to take at least two months a year away from the intense and busy life with mentally handicapped people and to "indulge" myself guilt-free in collecting thoughts, ideas and stories to articulate new visions about the ways in which God's Spirit makes its healing presence known among us.

I love Daybreak: the people, the work, the festivities, but I also realize that they can so completely absorb all my time and energy, that it is practically impossible to keep asking the question: "What is it all about anyhow?"

I spent most of my day in the guest room on the third floor of a small house of Franciscans, writing about "the life of the Beloved." Over the past years at Daybreak, the residents of Daybreak have helped me to rediscover the simple but profound truth that all people, handicapped or not, are the beloved daughters and sons of God and that they can find true inner freedom by claiming that truth for themselves.

This spiritual insight touched me so deeply that I wanted to spend a whole month thinking and writing about it in the hope that I would be able to help myself and others to overcome the deep-seated temptation of self-rejection.

"Nonfiction writers limit themselves to showing us how things really look to them in the world, leaving the reader to interpret what it all means," Henri read, and he underlined it, this time telling the story without interpretation.

However, this time in Freiburg was going to become unique. It bore a gift I could never have imagined before: the gift of a completely new image of humanity's belovedness—an image that would occupy my soul for many years. It was so surprising, so refreshing and so revealing that it would take me on a new journey, one that I could never have foreseen, not even in my wildest dreams.

Let me tell you how it came about. It all began with my father, who lives in the Netherlands and who had expressed a great interest in visiting me in Freiburg.

During the week my father and I were together, I forgot about my writing; we spent all of our time "going places," even though my father's weak heart prevented him from taking long walks. Since museums and churches were too tiring to visit, I looked for concerts or movies to entertain us. As I was going through the newspaper and asking people about interesting events to attend, someone jokingly said: "Well, the circus is in town!" The circus, the circus! I had not been to a circus for many years—I had not even thought about it since I had seen the Ringling—Barnum and Bailey Circus in New Haven, Connecticut. I said to my father: "Would you like to go to the circus?" There was little hesitation. "I'd love to go," he said. "Let's do it!"

Franz Johna, his wife, Reny, their son, Robert, my father, and I went to the circus. It was Circus Simoneit Barum, and it had just come to town. I didn't know what to expect. My main hope was that my father would enjoy it and that we all would have a good evening: hearty laughs, great surprises, pleasant conversation, and a good meal afterward. I was not at all prepared for an experience that would deeply influence my future thinking, reading, and writing.

The program was quite traditional: horses, tigers, lions, zebra, elephants, and even a giraffe and a rhinoceros. It all was delightful entertainment, but I would have forgotten the evening within a few days and gone back to my writing on "The Life of the Beloved" without any thought about the circus if there hadn't been the "Flying Rodleighs."

As the last act before the intermission, five trapeze artists, two women and three men, entered the ring as if they were queens and kings. After having greeted the audience with a movement that made their wide silver capes swirl about them, they removed them, handed them to the attendants, pulled themselves up into the large net, and started to climb the rope ladders that brought them to their positions high up in the tent. From the very moment they appeared, my attention was completely riveted. The self-confident and joyful way they entered, smiled, greeted the audience, and then climbed to the trapeze rigging told me that I was going to see something—better, experience something—that was going to make this evening unlike any other.

"A scene reproduces the motion of life; life is motion, action." He liked that. What he needed to communicate about the trapeze was motion and action. His other books had been shaped by a message he wished to convey, but this book was different. He was not entirely sure what his experience meant, just that it was so powerful and physical that he wanted to share it.

> *The ten minutes that followed somehow gave me a glimpse of a world that had eluded me so far, a world of discipline and freedom, diversity and harmony, risk and safety, individuality and commu-nity, and most of all flying and catching.*
>
> *I sat transfixed in my chair and couldn't believe what I saw.*

Yes, that's it, Henri thought as he paused in his writing. Flying and catching. It's everything I have always desired.

> *I still do not know precisely what happened that evening. Was it the presence of my eighty-eight-year-old father that made me see something eternal in a trapeze act that, for many, is simply one of the entertaining events in a two-hour-long circus program? (He certainly had something to do with it, since his visit had about it that wonderful quality of mutual freedom and mutual bonding that can develop when both father and son have become elders.) Or was it my intense concentration on the call to claim my own belovedness as an eternal gift and the call to proclaim that belovedness to others without condition?*
>
> *There is little doubt that my heart and mind were very disposed to see new visions and hear new sounds. And why wouldn't the angels of God come to me in the incarnation of five trapeze artists? It also is possible that my being so far away from the ordinary duties and re-sponsibilities in my community and the unusual opportunity of using*

time and space in such an unprescribed way opened me to a new, inner knowledge.

Sitting in the circus, I knew that I was free to see what I wanted and needed to see and that no one could force me to limit my vision to seeing simply a well-performed but never-perfect piece of aerial acrobatics.

Henri reread his paragraph. *No one could force me to limit my vision.* Why had he written that? It seemed a rather juvenile thought, as though he had to resist some judgmental outside authority that wanted to limit his perceptions or experience. But perhaps, he realized, feeling juvenile was precisely the point, because watching the Flying Rodleighs pulled him back to a much earlier moment in his life.

One thing I was certain of from the moment I saw the five artists entering the ring. They took me back forty-three years when, as a sixteen-year-old teenager, I first saw trapeze artists in a Dutch circus. I do not remember much of that event, except for the trapeze. The trapeze act gave rise to a desire in me that no other art form could evoke: the desire to belong to a community of love that can break through the boundaries of ordinariness.

Although I hadn't an athletic bone in my body and never participated to any significant degree in competitive sports, the trapeze became a dream for me. To be a trapeze artist symbolized for me the realization of the human desire for self-transcendence—rising above oneself, glimpsing the heart of things.

Sitting with my father in the Freiburg circus this teenage desire returned to my mind in full force. I had not thought about it for more than forty years, but how vivid and real it was—as if all those years had slipped by in one second. So much and so little had happened between 1948 and 1991. Perhaps all that had happened were just variations on the same desire for self-transcendence. Becoming a priest, studying psychology and theology, travelling all over the world, writing and speaking for the most varied groups of readers and listeners, leaving my country, teaching at different universities, and finally joining a community with mentally handicapped people—weren't they all attempts to be a flyer and a catcher?

As I sat there at the circus in Freiburg in April 1991, I suddenly saw my pure desire acted out in front of me and realized that what those five artists did was all I ever wanted to do.

A community of love that can break through the boundaries of ordinariness. My pure desire, repeated Henri to himself.

The Flying Rodleighs were stunning, the women in outfits that reminded him of swimsuits, and the men bare-chested in sparkling spandex tights. Henri had always been attracted to men. He had known that about himself since an early age. Among his close friends, Henri identified himself as a gay man who took his vows of celibacy as a priest seriously. But he was moved by more than the physical beauty of the Rodleighs. There was also the freedom, teamwork, and graceful community and joy between them.

Henri reread his words. *Variations on the same desire for self-transcendence.* Or maybe for escape? Or belonging? Even writing about the experience left Henri shaken with emotions he could hardly name, welling into tears. But it hadn't ended there. He pushed himself to keep writing.

A few days after that enlightening evening, my father returned to the Netherlands, and I returned to my writing project. Although Franz and Reny Johna, their son Robert and especially my father had enjoyed the circus, we didn't speak much about it anymore. Other events and other people asked our attention, and the human inclination to return to the familiar reduced the circus experience to a pleasant distraction.

However, back with the Franciscans, I overheard the superior say to one of the students: "Let's go to the circus tonight!" While I do not remember having been drawn to see the same movie more than once, the thought of going to the circus again filled me with excitement, and it wasn't hard to be invited by the superior and his students to join them. Just before leaving, I went to my room, picked up the Circus Barum program that I had bought a few days earlier, and looked up the page about the trapeze artists. There I read:

Strength and Spirit—in this presentation we meet a medical technician, a trained nurse, a teacher in athletics, a ship builder and a clown. Rod, the leader of the group, his wife Jennie, his sister Karlene and the catcher Johan Jonas all come from South Africa. Jon, the second catcher, is an American and comes from the Ringling Circus. All these talented people find themselves together in one of the best flying trapeze acts.

As I read this description of the five artists, my heart started to beat faster. It seemed as if I had been given a look behind the curtain of one of the most moving acts I had ever seen. I suddenly experienced feelings that were quite new for me: curiosity, admiration, and an intense desire to be close, but also feelings of awe, distance, and a strange sense of shyness. I don't remember ever having been an ardent fan of anyone. My room was never decorated with posters of sports heroes or music stars. But now I felt that strange mixture of worship and fear that must make up the heart of an adolescent who has fallen in love with an idol on an unreachable stage.

3

Dennie reaches under the blanket and feels Henri's feet and ankles. Somewhat swollen, he says, but that could be because he got off an overnight flight just hours earlier. He asks the driver to hand him the LifePak 10 monitor-defibrillator, and secures three EKG leads to Henri's chest.

He attaches a finger clip to Henri's right hand, explaining that it can measure the amount of oxygen in his blood. Henri is grateful that Dennie is explaining what is happening. It makes him feel safer.

"I also need to insert an IV to check your glucose levels and perhaps to give you medication," Dennie says, "and I will do that now in case your blood pressure drops and it becomes more difficult to find a vein. Are you right-handed or left-handed?"

Right-handed, responds Henri, wincing as the nurse inserts the needle in the back of his left hand.

"Can you raise your head?" Dennie asks. Henri tries, and immediately feels faint and dizzy. Suddenly the room is full of motion. Dennie looks at the monitor-defibrillator and grabs his portable radio.

Henri hears his voice, speaking urgently now, asking his dispatcher to notify the fire department with a top-priority request to assist with the rescue of a patient from an upper floor of Hotel Lapershoek. They will go to Ziekenhuis Hilversum: Could the dispatcher ensure that there will be a team waiting in the ICU for a heart patient?

Henri waits for the dizzying movement to subside. He does not feel in imminent danger, but the call sounds like an emergency.

The ambulance driver is now on the phone calling down to the front desk. Two fire trucks will be arriving, he tells the hotel manager. Can someone from maintenance come now to open the largest moving window? Yes, immediately.

Dennie puts the portable radio into its holder and turns back to Henri. He sees that Henri is struggling to make sense of what he overheard. Henri would probably appreciate a direct answer to his unspoken questions.

"This situation is a bit unusual," Dennie gently explains. "We have the ambulance waiting in the parking lot, but the elevator is too small for a stretcher. You need to stay horizontal, so there is no way to go down in the elevator. We cannot take you down the stairs, either. They are too steep and your blood pressure is low."

Henri seems to be following the explanation. Dennie takes a breath and makes sure he has eye contact with Henri because this next bit of information is the most important.

"We have called the fire department. They will take you out through a window."

Henri's eyes widen. Is he in pain, or frightened? Dennie is not sure. He doesn't seem tense. Henri looks like he would like to say something, but remains silent.

Out a window. Even in his discomfort, Henri is intrigued. Just nine months ago in Prague he wrote in his journal, *I have learned a new word:*

defenestration. It happened, he learned, in 1419 and again in 1618 when people threw their opponents out the window, and probably in 1948 as well. Henri had added lightheartedly, *I had never heard of this strange 'custom' but I have decided to keep my windows closed!*

Fortunately, the paramedics now proposing to defenestrate him seem friendly.

.••••

ALL HIS LIFE, THE experience of people at the top, the high-flyers in any field, held a particular fascination for Henri. Even back in his university days, Henri's friends saw him as a social climber. But Henri did not cultivate relationships only with important people. He was interested in everyone, in every social strata. Like his father, he liked people who did things well, with artistry, with discipline, with conviction. Where did it come from, this wide-ranging curiosity, the insistent desire to experience the world from another perspective, to get inside other people's skin?

It went deeper than curiosity. Maybe it was a kind of self-rejection. All his life, Henri had wanted a different body. For as long as he could remember, his body had hungers that were never satisfied. His mother blamed the strict instructions she had been given when he was an infant, to feed him only every four hours no matter how hungry and desperate he was. She figured he was always hungry, and that was inscribed in his flesh as soon as he was born. Growing up in wartime Holland and then through the hungry winter of 1944–45 without enough food anywhere deepened that body hunger.

Henri knew also that he had always felt uneasy in his own body, that his body had yearnings and desires that he never dared to put into words. His body wanted more freedom. Even as a teenager, he wanted to be like trapeze artists, part of the freedom and transcendence of an artistic physical community.

·····

HENRI IS SEIZED WITH a desire to tell Dennie more about himself. Surely Dennie would be interested to know about the Flying Rodleighs. An interviewer in 1995 asked Henri, "How will you apply the principles of the Flying Rodleighs in your life in the years to come?" And Henri had responded with enthusiasm, *"One principle is that I'd like to be freer. Just take more risks, you know, and trust that. And actually that has happened. In a very deep way just doing this crazy thing, for me to rent a camper and to go travelling through Germany with the circus—that's a little crazy in the first place, certainly when you're over sixty years old. On a deeper level, I mean, it has given me a sense that my life is just beginning."*

But even though Dennie's attention is focused on Henri's body, Henri is feeling too tired to explain all this. And anyway, traveling with the Flying Rodleighs came later.

4

C. S. Lewis wrote in *A Grief Observed* that no one had ever told him that grief felt so much like fear, "the same fluttering in the stomach, the same restlessness . . . I keep on swallowing." Henri swallows. His feelings in the hotel room seem like fear, but they are also like something else, oddly like the excitement that gripped him five years earlier. No one ever told Henri that fear feels so much like adolescent desire, the same pounding of his heart, the queasy feeling in his gut, the uneasy restless twitching, the unsettling emotion overflowing into tears. His body's responses now in Hilversum are not so different from what he had felt in 1991 when he first encountered the Flying Rodleighs.

•••••

Looking at the pictures of the five artists in the circus program, I found myself wondering about the ways these lives had become connected and given shape to their ten minutes of air ballet. I said to myself: "Who is Rodleigh? Who is Jennie? Who is Karlene?

Who is Johan? Who is Jon? Who are these people flying and catching in a circus tent somewhere in Germany? I wish I could talk to them, look closely at them, touch them and maybe become their friend."

I was embarrassed by my own desires, but simply decided not to let my embarrassment bother me too much. After all, . . . nobody was looking, . . . far from home, . . . far from work, . . . far from duties and obligations, . . . far from the regular pattern of my life. Why not be a teenager, a fan, an all-out admirer? What did I have to lose?

It is clear from all these inner ruminations that I was having a difficult time dealing with my stirred-up emotions. A little later, as I walked with my Franciscan hosts to the circus, I kept thinking: "I wonder how I could get to meet these artists? Will they be open to see me, to talk to me, to give their time and attention, or will they just treat me as one of their many fans who ask curious but foolish questions and who have to be whisked away like bees from a jar of marmalade?" I realized that my Franciscan companions had none of these questions and certainly wouldn't understand them.

As we walked through the entranceway, decorated with hundreds of little lights, bright pictures of lions and tigers and the faces of clowns, I noticed the circus director, Gerd Simoneit, standing there. The moment I saw him I knew that this was my chance to find a way to the circus group. As my companions walked on into the circus tent to find their seats, I walked up to him and said in German: "Good evening, sir. I saw your show a few nights ago and really enjoyed it, especially the Flying Rodleighs. I wonder if there is any chance of meeting the artists?"

His response was very surprising. Pointing to a woman with a small girl passing in front of the popcorn and soft drinks stand, he said: "That's one of them; why don't you ask her?"

Karlene was uneasy when the circus owner, Mr. Simoneit, pointed at her. Circus rules meant that she should not be out front where patrons could see her wearing her makeup, but she had promised her daughter Kail an ice cream from the refreshment wagon. Instead of a reprimand, Simoneit sent a tall, slender, middle-aged Dutchman bounding over to her.

"Hello, do you speak English?" he asked.

"Oh yes," she said, "I am from South Africa."

He was beaming with such joy and she was so relieved, that he immediately felt like an old friend. Her small daughter Kail, busy with her ice cream, ignored them. Amused by Henri's nearly inarticulate admiration and his clear desire to meet the troupe, Karlene invited him backstage to meet all of them during the intermission after their performance. She figured such a starstruck, gray-haired fan would entertain her brother Rodleigh. Then she and Kail hurried out of sight to the privacy of the backstage area.

As I walked back to the circus tent trying to find where my Franciscan friends had gone, I felt as if I had just taken a huge jump. It seemed as if I had just done something I had thought myself incapable of doing,—as if I had broken some kind of dangerous taboo. After having found my companions, I focused my attention on the director, Gerd Simoneit, who walked, microphone in hand, into the middle of the ring and announced the first act: Sascha Houke and his Arabian stallions. But my mind was elsewhere. Impatiently, I sat through the stallion act and the different acts that followed. Finally, more than forty minutes later, a group of Moroccans carried in the large net and with amazing speed built it up above the whole ring with large aprons on both ends, reaching to the far ends of the tent.

A clown tried to keep us occupied while everything was made ready for the trapeze act. Then, with great aplomb, the director announced the "dangerous, spectacular and aesthetically pleasing performance of . . . (here he paused to heighten the tension) . . . the Flying Rodleighs." To great applause they entered the ring, swirled their silver capes, took them off, lifted themselves into the net, climbed the rope ladder, and started their performance.

Once again I was completely captivated by the dazzling acrobatics, but this time I felt a strange fear. Having spoken with Karlene and knowing that I would meet them all within a few minutes, I had the strange sensation of worrying about their well-being. "I hope all goes well. I hope they won't make any mistakes," I kept thinking. Then it happened. As Karlene flew down from the top of the tent to be caught by her catcher, I saw that something had gone wrong. My body tensed up as I saw Karlene missing the catcher's hands and plunging down into the net. The net threw her body back up until it fell again and came to rest. The audience gasped but quickly relaxed when it saw Karlene straighten up, jump from the net, walk to the rope ladder, and climb back up to continue the show.

Henri's whole body shivers, remembering the distress he felt imagining the emotions of such a dangerous physical performance, an act permeated with the ever-present possibility of failure. Karlene simply climbed back up the ladder and carried on, but Henri found his own emotional response almost unbearable. It wasn't just the physical fall, but rather the possibility of public humiliation, of being judged harshly by a disappointed audience.

After that I could hardly watch anymore. I knew that the woman I had met for a few seconds at the concession stand was all right, but I was suddenly confronted with the other side of this air-ballet, not simply the dangers of physical harm, but the experience of failure, shame, guilt, frustration, and anger.

5

Dennie, seeing Henri shiver, interrupts his reverie. "Okay, the fire department will bring a stretcher up to us. The window for moving is down the hall, and we can take you there when they arrive. That window is big enough for your stretcher, so we will slide you out the window onto a lift mounted on a fire truck. I will stay with you as the lift lowers you to the ground."

For a moment, Henri wonders if he is having a bizarre dream, the kind of strange dreams that come when he forgets to take his nightly anti-anxiety medication. He has used Ativan for more than seven years, though he has considered trying to wean himself off it.

Just six months earlier, while waiting for spring to arrive, he raised the question of his medication with the doctor in New Jersey whom he had been seeing during his sabbatical. He explained that he was troubled by his experience after a fine lunch and animated discussion with friends.

"When I came home I felt quite weary. Tired, dizzy and out of focus. I realized that this was caused by not taking the Ativan tablet before going to bed each night," Henri told his doctor. *"Since I wasn't sure whether or not I had*

taken the tablet, I did not dare take another.” His voice trailed off, until he gathered his thoughts again. *“I think I have become addicted to it since my surgery in January 1989. Without the tablet, I get wild dreams and sleep restlessly and anxiously. So the whole day I felt out of sorts and without motivation.”*

His doctor nodded in understanding, then responded. “If you want to go off Ativan, you will need to be willing to feel like that for at least two weeks.”

Henri pondered this. *“I am not yet willing to do it,”* he finally admitted. *“It seems such a waste of time and energy.”*

Later that day, he carefully wrote about that conversation with his doctor in the publishable journal he kept during his sabbatical. Maybe readers might find this confession of vulnerability helpful, he thought. Many people depend on all kinds of medication to be well in their lives, and perhaps they will feel less alone knowing that he shares this experience. Writing about shared human experiences is part of his ministry, a way of laying down his life for others.

Now he vaguely wonders if other people have dreams of athletic paramedics throwing them out windows when they forget to take their medication. But no, he realizes, this is not a dream. He really is at a hotel in Hilversum, waiting for the fire department to arrive.

Suddenly Henri feels afraid, queasy with anxiety. It is one thing to say, as he often had, that the movement of his life has been from his mind as a popular professor, to his heart living in community with people with intellectual disabilities, to more recently discovering his body in a new way. The elegant movement from head to heart to body sounded convincing when he was standing firmly on the ground. But now his mind is spinning, his heart is apparently failing, and his body is about to be pushed out a window. Defenestrated. Alone.

He forces himself to think instead about that breathless first day of meeting his new friends.

. •••●

As soon as the artists had concluded their performance, received the applause, and disappeared behind the curtains, I excused myself to my companions and found my way to the back of the tent.

In a dark corner of the backstage area, the five artists were putting on their sweatsuits. When Karlene saw me she signaled me to come closer and told the group that we had met before the show and that she had invited me to join them after the act. There were no formal introductions. They just said "hello" and let me be there while they discussed their performance.

Rodleigh sighed as he headed backstage, ready to review why Karlene had missed her catch. When there was a failure, it was especially important to figure out what had happened so they would not repeat the mistake.

Joining the rest of the troupe, Rodleigh was not entirely pleased to see that a stranger had joined them, especially on a day when the act was flawed. Now they would not be able to discuss it in private. Oh well, he thought, I will explain that he can stay if he listens quietly and respectfully. We have work to do.

Rodleigh's sister Karlene introduced them to her new friend Henri, and Rodleigh found his ill humor soothed by Henri's heartfelt admiration and compliments. Then the troupe stood in a circle to discuss the performance, and Henri leapt right into the middle of their circle and interrupted with a barrage of questions, his large hands flailing. Annoyed yet also amused, Rodleigh kept trying to quiet Henri's excitement, but he persisted in standing right in front of each person so that they could not see each other. Yet it was hard to hold irritation. The offense was so unintentional, and Henri's facial expressions so comical that before the end of the meeting all five trapeze artists were laughing. Henri did not seem to mind. In fact, their mirth made him feel at home. When Rodleigh asked Henri why he stood right in front of the person talking, Henri explained that he could not hear their unfamiliar words very well and wanted to focus on the person talking. Rodleigh accepted the explanation and decided that if he ever met Henri again, he would remember to talk loudly and more clearly.

Listening to their exchange of words, I realized that I had entered a completely new world. Although they spoke clear English, I could not fully understand a single sentence. I picked up words such as "hop up," "lay out," "passage," "cradle" and other expressions which I couldn't even pronounce, let alone comprehend. It was clear, however, that every part of the ten-minute act was analyzed and evaluated in detail. No great issue was made of Karlene's fall into the net, even though that was what preoccupied me the most. They talked about it, but only as one aspect of a long, complicated routine.

After this discussion the group left the tent and moved in the direction of their caravans. As I walked with them, one of the men turned to me and said, "I am Rodleigh . . . well, this is your chance to ask me your questions." As he said this, I felt a certain distance and even fear of being an unwelcome intruder, and I really didn't have any particular questions. So I said, "Well, I was so moved by your

act that I wanted to meet you and maybe understand a little bet-
ter what your art is all about. . . . I really do not have any special
questions. I know too little to have any questions."

Seeing that Henri seemed determined to find out everything about the circus and the Flying Rodleighs' act in just one meeting, Rodleigh tried the old trick of turning the tables and instead asked Henri what he did for a living.

"I am a priest and I work in Canada with handicapped people and I write books," responded Henri.

Rodleigh stared with astonishment. It wasn't an answer he had expected from the tall, balding man with his helpless look of chronic confusion. He warmed to Henri's sparkling eyes, enormous behind his thick glasses, and his wide, eager smile.

He realized, however, that the fastest way to send Henri back to his seat would be to invite him to their practice the next day.

Rodleigh smiled and said: "If you'd like to, come to our practice
here tomorrow morning at eleven, and you can see for yourself what
it's all about!" I looked at him not fully believing the invitation. Why
did he invite me? Why did he want me to come and see for myself? It
seemed that Rodleigh took my interest in their profession more seri-
ously than I had taken it myself. But with all my inner questioning
there was little doubt about the answer: "I'd love to come," I said
quickly. "Thank you for asking me. For sure I will be there tomorrow
at eleven."

Rodleigh hurried back to his caravan, entertained by the curious interlude. He didn't really expect Henri would show up the next day.

As the five went through the little gate that separated the tent area from the caravan park, I waved them good-bye. "See you tomorrow," and found my way back into the tent where my Franciscan friends stood wondering where I had gone during the intermission. I didn't tell them. I just sat there silently looking at the tigers, the lions, the clown, and the tumblers. My mind wasn't there. I just kept wondering what my little visit during the intermission had set in motion.

As the circus band played their tunes and one act followed the other, I realized that I had already made my decision: as long as the Flying Rodleighs were in town, I was going to see them every chance I had, whether they were practicing or performing. I knew I had found something that was going to take me a big step closer to the understanding of the mystery of being alive! Everyone else may call the circus a nice distraction or a welcome interruption, but I decided to call it a new vocation!

As I awoke from my daydreams, I noticed that the director Gerd Simoneit was calling all the artists into the ring for the "finale." There I saw them again; looking bright and shiny in their red and gold decorated costumes, they waved to the cheering public. And as the Flying Rodleighs stood there waving among the lion tamers, clowns, equilibrists, stallion trainers, and tumblers, I felt tears welling up in my eyes. I knew that this evening would be the beginning of a new spiritual adventure, the end of which was known only to God.

It was an unexpectedly emotional experience, and while an emotional response was central to the story he was writing, Henri was still groping to understand and articulate it. He knew that some readers thought that he revealed too much, that he poured out his inner life indiscriminately, but he also knew that was a mirage, a persona that was truthful but not complete. Henri was careful about what he put into writing. He decided to finish the story of that evening.

> *While returning to the Franciscan convent, the superior and his student had little to say about the evening. They said they had enjoyed it, but their conversation quickly shifted to other subjects. I didn't tell them about my "secret." How could I explain to them that I was planning to go to the circus at least twice a day! Well, I didn't have to! I enjoyed having a little secret just as much as when I was a little boy digging tunnels in the backyard of my parents' home and hiding my treasures there.*
>
> *That night I didn't sleep too well. In my mind I kept looking upwards and seeing two women and three men moving freely through the air and I thought: "Isn't that what life is all about—flying and catching!" I knew my father would agree.*

Would his readers understand the dramatic irony of his narrative, that he was describing his "little secret," sharing the treasure that he was claiming to have hidden? That he was in some ways still that little boy, with secrets but also wanting his father to approve? Henri liked secrets, and thinking was safe. He had not tried to write down everything.

II

Falling

6

Fear and excitement can feel the same, thinks Henri on his bed at Hotel Lapershoek, restlessly breathing through the pain around his heart. He wants his father. His father's weak heart has worried him, but perhaps his own is in worse shape. How strange. Even though his father is now ninety-three, Henri knows he would come quickly, and wonders if he himself will forever be a prodigal son who lives far from his father but longs for him.

WHEN HENRI HAD A serious accident in 1988, his father flew across the ocean to be with him. Henri almost died of internal bleeding after being hit by the side mirror of a van while foolishly rushing on foot along the slippery edge of a busy, icy road north of Toronto. *Everything has changed,* he thought at that time. *None of my plans matter anymore. It is awful, painful, but maybe very good.*

That accident happened because he was trying to do too much, to prove that he could outmaneuver the winter weather and keep his planned commitments regardless of physical limitations. But on that cold morning as he lay in semidarkness by the side of the road, he felt *as if some strong hand had stopped me and forced me into a kind of necessary surrender.* In the following hours, full of intravenous tubes and surrounded by monitors, he was surprised that his feeling of powerlessness did not frighten him. Faced with the possibility of dying, he felt quite safe in his hospital bed with its railings on both sides. *Notwithstanding the severe pain, I had a completely unexpected sense of security.*

As he recovered from that accident, he observed how the most profound shifts in his life were due to interruptions. *A long time of solitude in a Trappist monastery interrupting a busy life of teaching, a confrontation with poverty in Latin America interrupting a rather comfortable life in the North, a call to live with mentally handicapped people interrupting an academic career.* Those were intentional interruptions. After all, as he liked to say, he is Dutch, with an impatient disposition and a need to be in control. He meticulously planned those key "interruptions." Other interruptions he chose spontaneously, such as Martin Luther King Jr.'s 1965 march in Selma that interrupted his studies in psychology at the Menninger Clinic in Kansas.

More disorienting had been unexpected interruptions, like the sudden death of his mother, or the breakage of a deep friendship that so completely shattered his sense of emotional safety that Henri spent months recovering in therapeutic retreat settings.

Oddly, the physical accident in 1988 that almost killed him had been less traumatic. The greater trauma was recovering. Before the surgery, he had worked to make peace with his life and impending death. After believing that he had wrapped up his life in reconciliation and goodwill, his recovery felt anticlimactic, even depressing as he resumed the various complicated relationships of his life.

Now in 1996, waiting with Dennie in his hotel room, Henri doesn't feel near death. He feels somewhat relieved by this interruption of his journey. He is pausing in Holland on his way to Russia, where he is scheduled to be filmed discussing Rembrandt's painting *The Return of the Prodigal Son*. The actual painting is enormous, more than half again as tall as Henri and many times wider. It will make a dramatic backdrop as Henri tells the story of the first time he saw the painting more than a decade ago, remaining in front of it for so long that eventually an official at the Hermitage Museum in St. Petersburg gave him his own special chair.

For this film, he plans to explain the dynamics of the painting, vividly reiterating many of the same points he made in his book *The Return of the Prodigal Son*. Henri looks forward to seeing the actual painting again, but has dreaded the trip. He is tired. He has not rested since arriving back in his community two weeks earlier after a busy sabbatical year. That sabbatical year was designed as a time to rest and write, but instead became a year full of stimulating travel, new friendships, and emotional complications. He has not felt ready to travel again so soon. Perhaps this interruption will turn out well.

Right now his chest aches severely and he can't deny that the sensation in his gut feels like fear. He tries to reinterpret the queasy feeling as excitement or desire. But combined with the unnerving pain in his chest, he can't remember what he might desire in these circumstances. Just to reach the ground safely. He offers that thought up as a small prayer. Prayer is to be fully present where you are, even for a moment, he has often announced. So now he wills himself to put everything else out of his mind and be fully present, like a trapeze artist in flight.

He lets go of the trip to Russia that is now interrupted. He puts out of his mind . . .

But actually, he realizes, he has no desire to be fully present in this insecure moment. He really wants to be fully present in a different time entirely, remembering what happened next after he met the Flying Rodleighs. He lets his mind shift back again to 1991, back to the day he first went to see the Rodleighs practice.

·····

"I am here to write, not to go to the circus!" I kept saying to myself. "I came all the way from Canada to have the quiet time to read, reflect and write about the life of the Spirit. I want to be alone, free from distractions and interruptions, and here I am accepting an invitation to watch the practice of a group of trapeze artists!"

The next morning while sitting at my desk, I kept looking at my watch. I couldn't concentrate on my writing. I could think of nothing but meeting the Flying Rodleighs again at their practice session at eleven o'clock. "What would it be like meeting them again? Would they be kind to me?" I was acutely aware that I had made them into some kind of unapproachable stars. The admiring child in me was so impressed by their invitation to come to their practice that everything else seemed less important.

At ten thirty I took the streetcar and a little before eleven I walked into the big tent. What a difference from last night! No audience— only empty seats.

Rodleigh was eager to work on his new routine that morning. He knew this first practice would include a lot of falls, because he would fly and be caught three times before returning to the pedestal board. Each attempt would be recorded on video so that he and the other troupe members could analyze what went wrong, then problem-solve how to improve. The timing was complicated and required precision, but the innovative sequence was exciting, and Rodleigh liked challenges. He would not have been surprised if Henri had not shown up at their practice session, but at eleven Henri was already pacing about, impatiently waiting for something to happen.

I waited for the Flying Rodleighs to appear. At eleven Rodleigh walked into the tent. He saw me and came up to me. "Good morning," he said. Pointing to one of the benches around the ring he said: "Why don't you sit down there. Karlene will be with you in a minute, and she will explain to you what you want to know."

His friendly, matter-of-fact attitude put me at ease. He was dressed in black tights and a T-shirt. Soon after Sascha and his horses had left the ring, the two other men of the trapeze troupe appeared and started to help Rodleigh set up the net. Then I noticed Karlene and her daughter and the other woman; they all looked more like maintenance people than artists.

Karlene came to me. "How are you this morning?" she asked. "Great," I said, "happy to be here." Karlene was carrying a little video recorder. "Looks like you are going to make a film," I said, somewhat surprised by this technological side to the practice session.

Meanwhile, the net was in position, and everyone, except Kar-

lene, was in place, high up in the tent. "Can you tell me, who is who?" I asked. "Sure, I am glad to," she said. "Well, you know my brother Rodleigh; he started the group. That's him, standing there on the pedestal board. With him, standing there, is his wife Jennie. And there high up on the center catch bar is Jon. He is from Detroit. He joined us a few years ago. And at the right, up there sitting in his catch trap is Joe. He is from South Africa like Rodleigh, Jennie, and me."

The little girl Kail climbed out from underneath the bleachers and assessed the tall stranger who was talking with her mother. She had met many new adult friends in her four years. This one looked promising. His hands were busy moving and his eyes were big and kind. She had just finished creating a sawdust cake. Standing directly in front of him so that he could not ignore her, she announced loudly, "I am making a birthday cake, and you have to pretend that it tastes good. Come and look!" Henri looked surprised, but he obediently followed her to the sawdust pile, where she had arranged two sticks as candles in her cake. "Now you have to pretend you have a fork and eat it." "Okay," Henri said. After following her instructions, he announced, *"It really tastes very good. You know how to make a good cake."* Kail beamed. But he seemed a bit too sincere. Maybe he would get confused and actually eat the cake, so she clarified, "We are only pretending, you know."

When I looked up from my little game with Kail, I saw Jennie falling into the net. She was wearing a safety belt with long ropes that came through pulleys high up in the tent. Rodleigh was standing on the floor now, holding the ropes. She had missed a trick and Rodleigh had broken her fall by pulling the ropes. He walked up to Karlene and replayed the video to see what had gone wrong; then he asked Jennie to try again.

Karlene said to me: "We are trying some new tricks. It always takes a long time to learn something new. But Rodleigh wants to keep improving our act. Some artists never change their act once they master it, but Rodleigh keeps trying new things."

"How long have you been doing this?" I asked.

"Oh. I am completely new at it. I just joined Rodleigh a little over a year ago. I was living in Hawaii with Kail. One day he called me and said: 'Why don't you come over, and I will teach you the trapeze.' I had been teaching athletics to little kids for some years and was ready for a change. Well, I flew over to Germany and Rodleigh immediately started training me at winter quarters in Einbeck. As teenagers we had done a lot of things together, but nothing like this. At first I was very scared, but I learned quickly. After a few months, Rodleigh put me in the flying act, and when our other flyer left, I had to take over from him. Anyhow, it's all quite new for me."

"My goodness, you learned all these things you were doing last night, in such a short time," I said, not hiding my amazement.

"Yes," she replied. "I was already past my thirties when I started to do flying trapeze, but Rodleigh said I could do it, and he kept encouraging me. Well, I like it, although after a fall like last night, I feel like I'm ready to quit."

While Rodleigh, Jon, Joe, and Jennie practiced and Karlene recorded the different tricks, I got my first impressions of these artists' life outside the limelight. During a free moment, Rodleigh said, with a smile: "Ten minutes in the air requires a lot of work. I hope you are becoming aware of it." I believed him but was still too new to know exactly what he meant. I understood that a good trapeze act requires much practice, but Rodleigh suggested that there was a lot more going on outside showtime than I knew.

Suddenly, I started to sense a burning desire to know, not just a little bit, but everything. One question after another piled up in my mind: "Who really are these people? What got them interested in doing these tricks? What brought them together? How are they living together going from town to town in Germany?"

7

Henri's breathing quickens as he relives the excitement of getting to know the Flying Rodleighs—his eager restlessness, the sense of being on the verge of a new discovery, his amazed thrill over meeting these remarkable artists—his adolescent infatuation—oh yes, those days were all so stimulating!

Dennie studies Henri. His breathing is becoming more rapid. He is probably frightened as well as in pain. Dennie puts his hand gently on Henri's arm to calm him. "Don't worry. We are looking after you. Breathe with me and it will help you to feel better."

Henri tries to focus, to breathe slowly in rhythm with Dennie. In, two, three, and out, two, three. Slowly. In, two, three, and out, two, three.

After a few breaths, he feels more connected with Dennie. He appreciates Dennie's gentle kindness and wonders how and when he decided to become a nurse. It seems like too much effort to ask.

"That's better," Dennie encourages him. "Now I am going to start you on oxygen. I need to take your glasses off to put the mask on."

Henri closes his eyes and remembers the first days of getting to know the Flying Rodleighs, a time when opening a window seemed like an agreeable and uncomplicated metaphor.

·••••

IS THIS TRAPEZE ACT perhaps one of the windows in the house of life that opens up a view to a totally new enrapturing landscape? Henri wondered as he watched the practice that morning.

And then there were all those other questions about the choices these men and women had made.

"Wasn't Rodleigh a medical technician, Jennie a nurse, and Karlene a teacher? What made them decide to leave their jobs and their countries and become flyers in a circus? And what about Joe and Jon, the catchers?" I really knew nothing about them and felt an urge to know the hows and the whats, the wheres and the whys of their lives.

Was this mere curiosity? Was I just prying into the lives of a group of strangers? I didn't know how to answer these questions, but I realized that the more I saw, the more I wanted to see and the more I knew, the more I wanted to know. I trusted that there was much more going on in me than curiosity. Wasn't the ten-minute spectacle of these five people in midair like a living painting put together by great artists?

I had spent days, years, studying the lives of Rembrandt van Rijn and Vincent van Gogh. I was not content just seeing their drawings and paintings. I wanted to know who these men were that had created works gazed upon by thousands of people day after day. And aren't these ten minutes of air-ballet like a painting made by five *painters, a painting that keeps thousands of people, young and old, spellbound every afternoon and evening?*

Nobody seemed to find it strange when I showed interest in the personal lives of Rembrandt and Vincent. And I had to get it all from books. They can't be spoken with. And here are five people drawing in the air—colorful, gracious, and most harmonious lines—while lifting up the hearts of so many! Is it no more than curiosity to want to know what is behind this perfect picture? Might it not be the desire to know the secret of the beauty and truth of human life?

THE PRACTICE ENDED. RODLEIGH and the other men rolled up the net, then bid farewell to Henri and watched him leave the circus grounds. Henri charged off, obviously late for his lunch. Rodleigh guessed that Henri's mind was full of new thoughts, and he chuckled as Henri almost tripped over a cable but didn't seem to notice. Rodleigh shook his head, still smiling as he walked back to his caravan, relieved that he would not have to answer Henri's questions that day.

When I took the streetcar back to the Franciscan convent, I was no longer wondering about my motives. I was convinced that the encounter with these five artists had indeed opened a new window in my life and that it would be very sad if I didn't look through it as long and attentively as I could.

Right there, in the streetcar going home, I decided to go to all the practice sessions, all the shows, and all the evaluation meetings. As long as the Flying Rodleighs were in town, I was going to be there, trusting that the landscape I would see would be worth all the time and effort.

At lunch I didn't mention my decision. After all, the Flying Rodleighs weren't as acceptable as Rembrandt or van Gogh, and I had no desire to prove to anybody that they were worth so much of my time and energy. After lunch, I went to bed and fell into a deep sleep. I knew I had found a treasure in a field. Now I needed to hide the treasure, see what I had, and then buy the field! When I woke from my nap, I felt glad to know that tonight I was going to the circus again!

After the evening show, the catcher Jon Griggs said to me: "I guess you like our show!" "I sure do," I said. "Every time I see it again, I like it more." Jon seemed at ease with my interest and quite eager to talk. "People seldom come to us after the show," he observed. "Maybe they are too shy. During intermission, they want to see the animals,— not us! And by the time the whole program is over, they have seen so many acts that they have already forgotten about the trapeze. I guess that's normal. That's circus life."

As we walked to the trailers Jon said: "You want to see my place?" "Sure," I said. I entered the trailer and noticed how small it was. There was a large colored photograph showing Rodleigh, Jennie, Karlene, Joe, and Jon in their trapeze costumes. "Nice picture," I said. "Yes, that's us," he answered proudly.

I was impressed with how easy it was to talk with Jon. No distance, no pretensions, no hesitations. He was so easy and self-confident. "Can I invite you for lunch someday?" I asked. "Then we can talk more."

"Yes, that would be great. Let me see. What about Saturday at noon? We have no practice and I don't have to be here before the afternoon show."

"Saturday is fine for me," I said. "I will pick you up here at

11:30, okay?" Jon seemed happy with the invitation, and I was excited with the chance to ask him many questions about catching and how he learned it.

Over the next days, Jennie and Rodleigh invited Henri for lunch and as a gift Henri brought them some of the books he had written. They thanked him warmly, and placed them on a shelf. After the matinee act, Rodleigh found Henri beaming with joy backstage, as eager to celebrate the successful act as if he had been part of it. Flipping through the books later, Rodleigh was perplexed to discover that the funny, gangly man who always looked like he would walk home in the wrong direction had been a professor of theology and psychology at some of the most prestigious universities in the United States.

Rodleigh now began to ask the same question that Henri himself was trying to resolve: Why was Henri so interested in the trapeze?

8

Henri had always been mesmerized by artists. Beauty, discipline, skill—all kinds of artistic endeavor enthralled him. Even the dramatic way that Rodleigh ended each performance was thrilling:

At the very end, they let themselves fall into the net all the way from the top. Rod, the last one, when he dives into the net—the net is like a trampoline—it throws him back up so high that he can catch the swing again. People aren't expecting that. So he comes down in the net and he falls all the way down, but then the net throws him back up so high that he catches the swing. So you think he's down, and he's up again.

Physical artistry and that kind of connection with an audience especially gripped Henri. He recalled one night in Holland in the mid-1980s. Staying at his father's home, he had been captivated by the artistic energy of two quite different performances when he came upon them playing at the same time on different television channels.

On one channel a rock concert with Tina Turner and David Bowie in Birmingham, England, was shown. On the other St. Matthew's Passion was performed in the St. Peter's Church in Leiden. I kept changing channels since I felt a strange attraction to both.

Tina Turner and David Bowie sang a song in front of a huge crowd of young people waving arms: "It is only love," or something like that. They sang with their whole bodies in such an increasingly gutsy way that they brought their audience gradually into a state of collective ecstasy: a sea of moving bodies, hands raised, eyes closed, totally surrendering to the sensual rhythm of the drumbeat. On the stage Tina and David held each other in a complex embrace while screaming their passionate song into their handheld microphones. Tina Turner's dress and movements were unambiguously meant to evoke sexual feelings; her dramatic staring into David Bowie's child-like clean-shaven face drove the crowd to a climactic frenzy. As they built up the tension with their lips nearly kissing, while screaming, "It is only love," the crowd merged into one dazed, anonymous being in the grip of these powerful feelings.

As I switched the channel I heard the voice of the Evangelist singing the passion of Jesus. Jesus stood before Pilate, silently, and the people cried: "Let Barabbas go, crucify Jesus." The choir sang the beautiful Bach chorales which meditate upon the divine love of our Savior. I thought, "It is only love," and felt a deep sadness invading me. The members of the choir were all above 40 years of age, dressed in formal black dresses, suits, white shirts, and ties. They looked stiff and serious while singing the sacred words of Jesus, their bodies remaining completely motionless. Only the director let his body move with the waves of Bach's melodies. The TV cameras never showed an *audience. Once in a while they pointed to the splendid architecture of the church and dwelled for a moment upon the ornate candelabra's soft yellow light.*

I switched back to Tina and David. She was back on the stage for another song with David. She was dressed differently. She said to her applauding fans, "Hi folks, sorry for letting you wait. I had to make myself pretty for you again . . . are you all ready for the next one?" And thousands of voices screamed, "Yea . . ." As the half-nude muscular drummer started to beat his huge drums the crowd turned back into that strange no-man's-land of dreams and desire, arms raised up, eyes closed, feet stomping.

Now the Bach choir sang, "Rest softly, Lord. Rest quietly. Your passion has come to an end. Have a great rest, dear Savior." Slowly the cameras moved back and gave a last view in the church as the final notes were sung. Then all was still for a moment and the program closed.

Meanwhile thousands clapped, yelled, stamped, and screamed as Tina and David held hands and bowed, jumped, laughed, and threw kisses into the Birmingham music hall. Both performances ended at the same time.

Henri sat clutching his elbows, nearly speechless. As a priest and a European, he felt an affinity with the profoundly beautiful and spiritual Bach concert. But the overt sexual energy of the other performance really grabbed him.

I sat there in my father's living room unable to grasp what I had seen. I felt part of both and distant from both events. Henri concluded, *I was exhausted and wondered what it all meant to see this at home with my father.*

He found himself wishing he could be in the huge, anonymous

Birmingham audience. Or even be on that stage. The physical energy he brought to his university lectures made him a popular professor, he knew, but there was a joyful freedom in Tina Turner and David Bowie's performance that he could hardly fathom. What would it be like to perform with that kind of utter conviction and uninhibited physical engagement?

Five years later in Freiburg, Henri and his father again joined an audience, and Henri was again overwhelmed by the physical power of a performance. This time Henri fell in love with an entire trapeze troupe. Not only did he want to get to know them and understand every detail of their act, but the rush of creative energy awoke his own yearning to be an artist himself—as a writer.

9

For the next few days, I kept going to the circus as often as possible. I attended the practice session, saw the afternoon or evening shows, sometimes both.

Henri urgently wanted to understand everything about the trapeze act, but found the details confusing. Rodleigh sat beside Henri, sketching the rigging in Henri's notebook and patiently repeating himself, often explaining the same material as the day before.

I gradually began to feel a little bit like an insider, at least as far as the Rodleighs were concerned. One day Rodleigh said: "I hope you don't pay each time you come to a performance. Just tell the box office people that we invited you. They will let you in." I did what he said, and, indeed, they let me in without a ticket. Meanwhile, I had become a familiar face to the entrance attendants, so I hardly needed to explain.

Once after an evaluation get-together, I tried to strike up a conversation with Joe, the South African catcher. While Jon, the American, worked from the center catch bar, Joe's place was on the swinging catch bar, opposite the pedestal board. Joe's muscular appearance, rough facial features, and dark tan made him look more like an ironworker than a trapeze artist. He always seemed a little off by himself and maybe a little shy.

"How did you feel about the show this time?" I asked him.

"Oh, fine," he said. "Rodleigh was just a little early so I had to adjust my swing a bit to catch him but it was fine."

I realized that I didn't understand what being early or late meant, but it was clear that it was the real issue for the catcher. Joe's speech was very difficult. He stutters heavily and isn't very talkative. But once I approached him, he was quite eager to speak.

"Do you like your job?" I asked.

He smiled at me and said very emphatically: "I love it. I love being in the catch bar and catching them!"

It was clear he meant what he said. Having seen the act many times, I became aware of the unique role of the catcher.

"You are not as much in the limelight as the flyers, but without you nothing can happen," I said.

He was quick to respond. "I really like it that way. The flyer gets all the attention, but their lives depend on the catcher! I don't want all the applause. I like what I am doing, and I have to give it all I've got. It's an important job to catch, and I love it, but I am glad to be a little less visible than the rest of them."

Henri wanted to stay backstage to watch the troupe warm up for the afternoon show, but he could not restrain himself from coming too close to their swinging arms to ask questions and try to carry on conversations. Finally Rodleigh sent him back inside the tent for his own safety.

That day, Rodleigh's new act did not go well and he fell into the front net, called the apron. Henri was alarmed seeing the fall, relieved to see that Rodleigh was not injured, and dismayed later to see all Rodleigh's painful red scratches from the nylon net.

"Why do you risk serious injury?" Henri asked. He was not entirely placated when Rodleigh responded with a string of stories about many previous accidents, although Rodleigh assured him that they overcame these mishaps through perseverance and hard work. Henri left perplexed, thinking all the way home about the hard and unusual life of circus performers.

The next day, Henri's questions took on a new tone.

"Why are you choosing to do a high-risk routine rather than something more predictable and safe?" he asked.

Rodleigh felt a bit defensive, but he knew that what sounded like criticism of the performance was concern for their safety. "The circus business is very competitive, Henri," explained Rodleigh, "and if the circus director is not satisfied with the audience response, we will be replaced next season. My job is to find the balance between difficulty and control, and build the routine intelligently."

Henri was listening attentively, so Rodleigh continued. "Also we are artists. We are proud people. So as a personal challenge, I try to make the most difficult tricks and routine look easy—fluid and graceful. I want to make the audience focus not on the danger but on the beauty."

On Saturday morning I met Jon at his trailer. We took the street-car to downtown Freiburg. I had wondered where to take him for dinner. The only place which seemed quiet enough for a good conversation was the "Red Bears," where my father had stayed. So I had made a reservation for 12:30. Since we were a half hour early, I asked Jon if he had already seen the Munster, the splendid cathedral. He hadn't and I wondered if he had seen anything at all of this city since the circus arrived.

Of all the medieval churches, the Munster is probably the one that had most impressed me. Its fascinating history, its location in the center of the city square, its magnificent tower with filigreed stone spire, its intimate interior . . . I had fallen in love with the Munster as I had fallen in love with the city.

But as I crossed the square and walked into the cathedral with Jon, I suddenly felt completely paralyzed in trying to convey to him any of the emotions that filled my heart.

"What do you think?" I said.

"I like it," he answered, but it was clear he felt like a cat in cold water. I immediately realized that everything the church meant to me was strange to Jon. He walked through it with an odd sense of obligation. I had taken him there, so here he was, but nothing spoke to him. The pillars with the Twelve Apostles, the splendid triptych on the high altar, the richly carved choir stools, the sculpture of Our Lady with the sea of lit candles and people praying in front to of it . . . nothing spoke a word to him. I wanted to explain. But how do you explain medieval Christianity to a trapeze catcher from Detroit?

Soon we were in the Red Bears, still early, but more at ease. We ordered lunch. It was probably the most expensive lunch I had ordered since coming to Freiburg. As I looked around and saw the middle-aged and older people in their formal dress and as the waiter filled our glasses, lit the table candle, and offered us napkins to put on our laps, I wondered if this was the most comfortable place for circus people to talk about flying and catching.

However, as soon as we began to speak about the circus, the surroundings didn't seem to bother me anymore. They certainly didn't bother Jon.

"What is it that makes the circus so fascinating?" I asked.

"Well," said Jon, after a moment of silence, "I guess we like to see animals do what really only people can do and to see people do what really only animals can do. Lions sit up like people and people fly like birds."

The two of us laughed.

"The circus is a fun world. It offers clean entertainment, and it's for everybody, young and old."

"The circus certainly got me hooked," I said. "The last time I was in Freiburg I spent all my free time in churches and museums. This time it's the circus that caught my imagination."

"Yes," Jon observed, "you have become a real fan."

I felt a little awkward being called a fan, but I had to confess that the word suited me.

We spoke about many circus things, and Jon told me anything I wanted to know. He never asked about me. Maybe he simply doesn't know what to ask. Maybe I was just as strange to him as the Munster.

We were back at the circus around three o'clock. People were lining up in front of the box office for the afternoon performance, which was to begin in half an hour. I could see it was going to be a full house. At four twenty-five I stepped into the tent just in time to see the Flying Rodleighs walking into the ring and swirling their silver capes, accompanied by the orchestra. As I saw Jon climbing up the high rope ladder, bare chested, wearing white tights and a golden belt and then stepping on the catch bar high up in the dome of the tent, uttering a shout to excite his audience, I had a hard time believing that two hours earlier I sat with this demigod in the Red Bears eating lunch.

The act went flawlessly. When Rodleigh, Jennie, Karlene, Joe, and Jon paid their final compliments in the ring and disappeared behind the curtain to the accompaniment of the applause and foot stomping of the more than two thousand enthusiastic spectators, tears came to my eyes. I knew that I had become part of this group of strangers and that in some mysterious way, the huge applause also embraced me.

10

Henri's eyes are still closed. Dennie notes that his breathing is speeding up again. He looks like the kind of nervous person who could become agitated when the exit from the window begins.

"Henri?" he asks, "I could start some medication now. It will help you. There are two drugs in the drip. Droperidol will minimize your anxiety and tension, and fentanyl is a synthetic morphine to reduce your pain. The negative side effect is that it could lower your blood pressure even further, but I think you need it. What do you think?"

Henri seems far away. Dennie gently prods Henri for a response. Henri's eyes flicker open, large and bleary above the oxygen mask, and Dennie makes the decision to start the drip medication.

.....

Sunday was the last day of the Circus Barum in Freiburg. After the afternoon show, as I was standing with the Rodleighs listening to their cryptic talk about the act, little Kail ran up to me and said: "Are you coming to see our trailer?" Karlene overheard her and said to me, "She really wants you to see our place. Come to us for a while after the finale."

An hour later, I was sitting with Karlene and Kail in their living room when Rodleigh knocked on the trailer door and invited me for supper along with Karlene and Kail. It was at supper that I first came to know Jennie. She welcomed me warmly around her small table.

"The trapeze is okay," she said, "but my real love is for making costumes."

As she spoke I became aware that all the costumes I had seen that week: the silver capes, the trapeze costumes, and the finale costumes were all made by Jennie.

"When I wanted to marry Rodleigh, I soon realized that becoming a trapeze artist was going to be part of the deal," she said smiling. "But I really got involved when I began to learn how to make our costumes. In the future, when we have become too old for the trapeze and we are going back to South Africa, I hope to start a business in costume design."

Jennie had nothing to hide. Spontaneous, direct, and very pragmatic, she made me feel right at home in the family. Here it all looked so normal and prosaic. Rodleigh, his wife, Jennie, his sister, Karlene, and the little Kail. That's the Stevens family in Germany. I was their guest for supper. Nothing special. Only that they all liked the flying trapeze.

After supper, Rodleigh said: "If you want to see something special, come tonight for 'pull-down.' Pull-down will show you how we disassemble our rigging while the Moroccans are taking down the tent. Forty-five minutes after the finale, we will be pulling out of the fairgrounds to the next town. Stay a little tonight until we leave. You will be impressed."

I did stay. During the intermission of the evening performance, Rodleigh, Joe, and Jon started already to load the truck with the net and the smaller parts of the trapeze rigging. Meanwhile, some of the animal wagons were already leaving the fairgrounds. But as soon as the finale was over, the whole place became a beehive of activity. Everyone knew exactly what to do. While the bleachers were taken down, the trapeze men started to disassemble the rigging. It was like a choreographed dance, meticulously planned and very quickly and carefully executed.

At five minutes to ten, Rodleigh closed his truck and connected it to the trailer. At the same time Jon and Joe were warming up their own trucks, and before I knew it, everyone was ready to leave.

"We are driving in convoy," Karlene explained. "Rodleigh leads, I follow, then Joe and then Jon. Rodleigh and Jon both have shortwave radios on their trucks, so that they can talk to each other on the road and keep an eye on what goes on between them. Once in a while, we lose each other because of stoplights and unexpected turns, but with the radios we can help each other to find our way back."

As Karlene spoke, I felt a sadness that I couldn't be part of that convoy. During the week, the Rodleighs had so much become part of my life that their leaving created a real pain in me. I realized too how difficult it must be for them to keep moving from place to place, never staying anywhere long enough to make lasting friends.

Was this the end? Would I see them again?

Then they began moving. I stood there waving at them all as they went into line and slowly turned out of the fairgrounds.

I felt lonely. Looking up, I saw the tent slowly coming down. It would take two hours to clear the place completely, but I had no desire to wait. Somehow, without the Rodleighs, the circus was just another circus, not worth staying up late for.

Walking away to catch a streetcar and go home, I felt a little con-fused. I still wasn't fully sure if I wasn't fooling myself with the new "vocation."

11

Dennie notices that despite the medication, Henri's body is still restlessly readjusting. He can't blame Henri for feeling unsettled. Being removed through a window is not a common occurrence.

But Henri is not thinking about his present state. He is back in 1991, remembering his sense of loneliness as he watched the Flying Rodleighs drive away and his sadness that he couldn't be part of that convoy. His legs twitch.

And now another memory is niggling for attention, drawing him back even further to another time when his whole body longed to join a community of people on the move together. As he wrote after the event, *It all began with a feeling of restlessness, an inner compulsion, a fierce gnawing, a painful question: Why aren't you in Selma?*

•····•

IT WAS MARCH 1965, and Henri was studying psychology at the Menninger Clinic in Topeka, Kansas. Police in Alabama had used tear gas and violence to stop a peaceful civil rights march, and Martin Luther

King Jr. called for church leaders and people of faith from around the country to come to Selma, Alabama, for a new march. As a Dutch citizen on a visa, Henri had many reasons not to go. It was more than eight hundred miles away. His friends assured him that it was a local matter and he was a foreigner who should not get involved. They suggested that in going he would be serving just himself, looking for thrills and excitement. But Henri couldn't shake off his desire to respond.

The march started on Sunday, March 21. At eleven o'clock that night, Henri was tossing and turning in his bed when he suddenly realized that he had made a mistake. His choice became clear. By midnight he was in his Volkswagen Beetle heading toward the southern United States to join the marchers. *The restlessness disappeared, and there was a deep, palpable certainty and sense of determination.*

Seven hundred miles later in Vicksburg, Mississippi, Henri picked up a twenty-year-old hitchhiker named Charles. *As we drove through the night Charles told me about the dark days of Mississippi.* Charles was Black, and Henri assumed that Charles would now share his privilege as a White person, since Henri was the older of the two and the driver of the car. But he soon discovered that as a White man and a Black man traveling together, they could not safely stop anywhere. Not for gas, not for a coffee, not even to use a restroom. *Gradually I felt my innocence and unquestioned sense of freedom disappear,* Henri realized. The restlessness that had launched him onto this road trip returned full force, but this time embodied as fear. *The fear gave me new eyes, new ears, and a new mouth.* Eighteen hours after setting out, Henri and Charles arrived in Selma feeling grubby, unshaven, and tired. As they drove on to catch up with the march, the heavily armed National Guard lining the streets reminded Henri of growing up in occupied Holland during the war.

Arriving, they were greeted by two twelve-year-olds who were registering people for the march with three questions: What's your name? Where do you live? Who should we contact if anything happens to you? The third matter-of-fact question was unsettling, yet the overall feeling was not anxious. *No matter what the setting, people ate, laughed, talked, and prayed,* Henri wrote. Always hungry, he was especially impressed by the abundance of food. *It was one of the mysteries of Selma. Thousands were fed during those five days in Selma, in Montgomery, along the road, and in the tents; there was always enough. It seemed as if nothing had been organized and everything was always threatening to collapse in confusion, but somehow it always turned out all right. I realized what it's like to live with people who know the necessity of improvising and reacting with immediate spontaneity.*

Henri listened as on the steps of the Montgomery legislature, Martin Luther King Jr. spoke slowly and powerfully: "We are on the move." King's voice rose and gathered momentum as he named the struggle for human freedom in the history of his people, and the many martyrs whose deaths were not in vain because, he repeated, "We are on the move. We will go back and we will continue to suffer but now we know: we are on the move."

At exactly four o'clock, the jurisdiction of the troops to protect the marchers ended and fear again pervaded Henri's entire body. He offered a ride north to three Black men, who advised him all along the way to stick to the main roads, stay carefully within the speed limits, and not drive after dark. *I only remember that we were scared,* wrote Henri later, *scared to death, and that we shook all over whenever we rode through a city and were wary of every state trooper that we saw.*

The omnipresent danger, so familiar to his companions, shocked the thirty-three-year-old Dutch priest. But what stayed with him most powerfully was his experience of community. Hungry for that kind of friendly commitment that could challenge violence and injustice, Henri reflected a few years later, *Resistance that makes for peace is not so much the effort of brave and courageous individuals as the work of the community of faith.*

As a priest, Henri often heard people confide that they felt inadequate, that they were "not enough." He understood that feeling because he often felt the same way. But, he tried to explain, of course you aren't enough! None of us can ever be enough by ourselves. The truth is that we are each part of a larger body, a community. *Individual people, even the best and strongest, will soon be exhausted and discouraged, but a community of resistance can persevere even when its members have their moments of weakness and despair. Peacemaking can be a lasting work only when we live and work together.*

HENRI WAS IN CHICAGO on Thursday, April 4, 1968, when he heard that Martin Luther King Jr. was killed. The news filled Henri with a distress and horror that were amplified by the apparent detachment of his mainly White community. His anguish grew and flooded his body for days until again, he made a sudden decision:

> *There was an empty seat left on the night plane to Atlanta and I knew I had to go. During the last four days, the sorrow and sadness, the anger and madness, the pains and frustrations had crawled out of the many hidden corners of my body and spread all over like a growing disease of restlessness, tension, and bitterness. I had been fighting it all the way, but now it was clear that only his own people could cure me. Only in the anonymity of their crying, shouting, marching,*

*and singing would I be able to meet the man of Selma again and find
some rest.*

Henri was amazed when he arrived the morning of King's funeral.
*In Atlanta everything was different. A strange lightness contrasted with all my
heavy feelings and expectations. No dark suits, but white dresses and colorful
hats as if people were on the move to a great festival.*

He was again welcomed warmly with unexpected kindness. *Perhaps my doubt at being welcome at the funeral of a Black man had made me
apprehensive. But there were only friendly questions: "Do you need any help?
Transportation, breakfast, a place to stay?"*

The funeral procession was, Henri realized, Martin Luther
King Jr.'s last march and everybody knew it. *But there was something
strange about his last march, something new. There was no fear. There were no
angry people on the sidewalks ready to throw stones. . . . When I looked back
over the mile of people behind me, I had the feeling that there was no end to
this victory march, no end to the stream of people singing the same song again
and again. "We shall overcome, we are not afraid, Black and White together."*

The funeral procession flowed into the quiet gardens of Morehouse
Seminary, and Henri collapsed onto the grass, too exhausted to watch
the speeches or songs on the stage. It was too much to absorb.

*Sitting on the ground surrounded by the countless people standing
around me, I felt safe and protected. A Black man smiled at me when
I woke up from a deep sleep. I felt exhausted, hungry, and heavy.
But a strange satisfaction went through my body. This was where I
wanted to be: hidden, anonymous, surrounded by Black people. It
had been a long, restless trip since that Thursday night. Nervous,
frantic, yearning, filled with grief and frustration. It had led me to*

the green lawns of Morehouse College. And here I rested, carried by people who kept on singing and praying.

.....

NOW DECADES LATER, EXHAUSTED, immobilized, and waiting for the stretcher, Henri wonders why remembering his early days with the Rodleighs has connected in his imagination with those extraordinary long-ago days in Alabama and Georgia. Maybe his restless body holds memories. Maybe he is trying to figure out the paths in his life that brought him to be so profoundly affected by the Flying Rodleighs. Points when he discovered something about his own limitations, but even more profoundly, saw his deepest desires for community and beauty embodied, in a funeral procession in Atlanta, and flying above him in Freiburg.

You know in this world where there is so much division, where there is so much separation, and so much violence, the Rodleighs in a way are peacemakers. They create community. They create something that the world so badly needs. Who doesn't desire friendship? Who doesn't desire belonging? Who doesn't desire to laugh? Who doesn't desire to be free? Who doesn't need discipline? Who doesn't need a sense of togetherness?

You know, it's all there in one act—what life is all about, what the world is all about.

12

At the end of the week when Henri met the Flying Rodleighs, they packed swiftly and Henri waved sadly as their vehicles pulled one by one out of the Freiburg fairgrounds. He wanted to be part of their procession. He felt bereft. But just five years earlier, Henri himself had led a convoy of trucks and trailers. It was the autumn of 1986. He was not part of a traveling circus, though the event was a bit over-the-top. After a year living with people with intellectual disabilities at a L'Arche community in France, he was moving everything he owned from Boston to L'Arche Daybreak in Canada, accompanied by a troupe of friends driving a variety of vehicles.

His Harvard companions were curious and a bit skeptical. Their academic friend was choosing to live with people who didn't know who he was, would never read any of his books, who were not impressed with his credentials or history. It was hard to see how this ambitious and impatient former professor would fit. But they also knew him as someone with a remarkable ability to build and nurture community. They loved him and the vibrant community he had gathered around him during his years in Boston. Those years had left him adrift and depressed, however, and they hoped this brave new experiment might help their friend find a deeper sense of home.

As they drove up Yonge Street north of Toronto, past ugly strip malls, used car dealerships, and an astonishing number of very Canadian donut shops, his friends wondered how this was going to work out for Henri, who loved beauty, historic architecture, and culture.

One by one, Henri's convoy turned through the split-rail fencing onto the gravel laneway of the L'Arche Daybreak farm property, a big old redbrick former convent to their right and a green barn and farm fields ahead.

On the welcoming end, there was also some bewilderment. Long-time community member Sue Mosteller had welcomed many people to Daybreak, people with and without intellectual disabilities. Most assistants came wearing jeans, carrying a backpack. Henri arrived in a parade of vehicles. The last to pull into the driveway was an enormous moving van. Over the next weeks, Sue watched as the whirlwind of Henri's energy and fame shook the quiet community.

But as his friends unloaded his many boxes of books, Henri was confident that the move to L'Arche Daybreak made sense. His physical experiences of solidarity, from Selma to Latin America to L'Arche in France, had quickened in him a yearning and vision that he had carried for decades.

Ready to serve the Daybreak community's spiritual life as a priest, Henri was surprised when he arrived to be asked to live in a house with people with intellectual disabilities and their assistants. Even more jarring for Henri was that he was expected to work as a regular house assistant.

I was told that L'Arche's mission was to "live with" core members, so I embarked on my new life with all the people in the New House. Manual work, cooking, and housekeeping skills were alien to me. I had been teaching for twenty years at universities in Holland and the United States, and during this time I had never given much attention to creating a home nor had I been close to people with disabilities. In my family and among my friends, I had earned a reputation for being impractical.

A few months into this new life, early in 1987, Henri had a chance to describe his household to an audience back at Harvard:

I live in a house with six handicapped people and four assistants. None of the assistants is specially trained to work with people with a mental handicap, but we receive all the help we need from doc-tors, psychiatrists, behavioral management people, social workers, and psychotherapists in town. When there are no special crises, we live together as a family, gradually forgetting who is handicapped and who is not. We are simply John, Bill, Trevor, Raymond, Adam, Rose, Steve, Jane, Naomi, and Henri. We all have our gifts, our struggles, our strengths and weaknesses. We eat together, play together, pray to-gether, and go out together. We all have our own preferences in terms of work, food, and movies, and we all have our problems in getting along with someone in the house, whether handicapped or not. We laugh a lot. We cry a lot too. Sometimes both at the same time.

Every morning when I say, "Good morning, Raymond," he says, "I am not awake yet. Saying good morning to everyone each day is unreal." Christmas Eve Trevor wrapped marshmallows in silver paper as peace gifts for everyone and at Christmas dinner he climbed

on a chair, lifted his glass, and said, "Ladies and gentlemen, this is
not a celebration, this is Christmas." When one of the men speaking
on the phone was bothered by the cigarette smoke of an assistant, he
yelled angrily, "Stop smoking; I can't hear." And every guest who
comes for dinner is received by Bill with the question, "Hey, how do
you keep a turkey in suspense?" When the newcomer confesses igno-
rance, Bill, with a big grin on his face, says, "I'll tell you tomorrow."

Despite the moments of hilarity, adjusting to this new life was hard
for Henri and for everyone around him. He was beyond impractical.
His companions were amazed at his incompetence. Henri asked for
help making tea, constructing a sandwich, and doing laundry. No one
could understand how this engaging and caring man had survived
for so long with such pitiful life skills. He felt disoriented and edgy,
relaxed only when he could escape to his office to write and answer
letters. Gradually, very slowly, Henri began to find a sense of belonging through Bill Van Buren, who was a founding member of L'Arche
Daybreak in 1969.

During the past few months I have developed a friendship with
one of the handicapped men in my house. His name is Bill. At first
he seemed simply interested in the many little things I would do for
him. And he used me well. Intuitively he knew about my guilt-ridden
desire to help and he let me help him as much as possible. He let me
pay for his beer, wash his dishes, and clean his room, even though he
himself could do all those things pretty well. I certainly didn't feel at
home with him.

But as the months went by and we came to experience many joys
and pains together, something started to change. One morning he

gave me a generous hug. One afternoon he proudly took me out for a beer and paid for it himself, and on my birthday he bought me a lovely gift. During dinner he wanted to sit close to me and during Mass his joking interruptions of my homily were replaced by heartfelt words of love and concern. Thus we were becoming friends.

·•••

DENNIE CHECKS THE OXYGEN levels on Henri's finger monitor and hides his concern. He tries to encourage Henri. "Things are moving along well. The fire department trucks are on their way. They will be here in a few minutes. We just have to wait. The medication I am giving you should help soon and your body will be able to relax."

Henri is not listening. He is remembering Adam.

·•••

Adam is the weakest person of our family. He is a twenty-five-year-old man who cannot speak, cannot dress or undress himself, cannot walk alone or eat without much help. He does not cry, or laugh, and only occasionally makes eye contact. His back is distorted and his arm and leg movements are very twisted. He suffers from severe epilepsy and, not withstanding heavy medications, there are few days without grand mal seizures. Sometimes, as he grows suddenly rigid, he utters a howling groan, and on a few occasions I have seen a big tear coming down his cheek.

Although Henri had spent time in L'Arche in France, he had not worked directly with any of the people with disabilities. He was quite afraid to enter this unfamiliar world. This fear did not lessen when he was asked to work directly with Adam.

I was aghast! I simply didn't think I could do this. "What if he falls? How do I support him as he walks? What if I hurt him and he cannot even tell me? What if he has a seizure? What if I make his bath too hot or too cold? What if I cut him? I do not even know how to dress him! So many things can go wrong. Besides, I don't know the man. I'm not a nurse. I have no training in this kind of thing!" Some of these many objections I voiced; most of them I just thought. But the answer was clear, firm, and reassuring: "You can do it. First of all, we will help you and give you plenty of time until you feel comfortable. . . . You'll learn the routine, and you will get to know Adam and he will get to know you."

So I began with fear and trembling. I still remember those first days. Even with the support of other assistants, I was afraid walking into Adam's room and waking up this stranger. His heavy breathing and restless hand movements made me very self-conscious. I didn't know him. I didn't know what he expected of me. I didn't want to upset him. And in front of the others, I didn't want to make a fool of myself. I didn't want to be laughed at. I didn't want to be a source of embarrassment.

A few months later, Henri was describing the routine to his Harvard audience:

It takes me about an hour and a half to wake Adam up, give him his medication, undress him, carry him into his bath, wash him, shave him, clean his teeth, dress him, walk him to the kitchen, give him his breakfast, put him in his wheelchair, and bring him to the place where he spends most of the day with different therapeutic exercises. When a grand mal seizure occurs during this sequence of activities, much more time is needed, and often he has to return to sleep to regain some of the energy spent during such a seizure.

In those early days Henri saw Adam as someone who was very different. Adam did not talk, so Henri did not imagine that they could ever communicate. The relationship was very physical. When Henri walked with Adam,

I had to get behind him and support him with my body. I worried constantly that he would trip on my feet, fall and hurt himself. I also was conscious that he could have a grand mal seizure at any moment: sitting in the bathtub, on the toilet, eating his breakfast, resting, walking, or being shaved.

At first I had to keep asking myself and others, "Why have you asked me to do this? Why did I say yes? What am I doing here? Who is the stranger who is demanding a big chunk of my time each day? Why should I, the least capable of all the people in the house, be asked to take care of Adam and not of someone whose needs are a bit less?" The answer was always the same: "So you can get to know Adam." Now, that was a puzzle for me. Adam often looked at me and followed me with his eyes, but he did not speak or respond to anything I asked him.

Gradually, very gradually, things started to change. My whole life had been shaped by words, ideas, books, and encyclopedias. But now my priorities were shifting. What was becoming important for

me was Adam and our privileged time together when he offered me his body in total vulnerability, when he gave me himself, to be un-dressed, bathed, dressed, fed, and walked from place to place. Being close to Adam's body brought me closer to Adam. I was slowly getting to know him.

13

While Dennie has been attending to Henri, the ambulance driver has gathered Henri's suitcases and carry-on bag. He has found Henri's medication, but he hasn't yet found a toothbrush or other toiletries. Dennie leans close to Henri to get his attention. "We can take one bag with us to the hospital now. Is everything you need for a night or two in your carry-on bag?"

Henri's fuzzy brain tries to decide. He won't need his notes about Rembrandt in the hospital, nor his suit. The brightly colored stole from Latin America that he wears to say Mass is in his carry-on, as well as some wafers, a small chalice for wine, a Bible, and his daily book of morning and evening prayers. Yes, that is all I need, he nods.

•••••

HENRI'S MIND FLOATS, WANDERING from the trapeze and the Rodleighs to his Daybreak community. *When I think about Circus Barum and Day-break, I think of two international communities of people who want to bring joy and peace to the world. The handicapped people at Daybreak and the talented artists of Circus Barum have much more in common than it would seem at first glance.*

But then why, Henri wonders, when he had moved to Daybreak and built a friendship with Bill and Adam and his new household, did he have a complete emotional breakdown in 1987?

His commitment for peace and social change had not diminished, and his living situation and work had refocused in a way that he had hungered for since Selma, moving from an *issue-oriented life* to a *person-oriented life*. And yet it nearly destroyed him.

That really was the problem. He had oriented his life around others, what they thought of him, how they responded. As a trained psychologist as well as a priest, Henri was aware of his insecurities. Close friendships had collapsed under the weight of his hopes and expectations before.

Possibly what changed at Daybreak was that he felt supported enough to finally risk facing this side of himself in a way that was impossible before. Did his new community trigger all his anguish? No, like a trapeze act, Daybreak and his new friends gave him a place where he could finally fall. And unexpectedly, a key part of that safety net was Adam.

I began to realize that the gentle safety of the New House was weakening many of the defenses I had created around my inner handicaps. In this loving, caring milieu, without competition, one-upmanship, and great pressure to distinguish myself, I experienced what I had not been able to see or experience before. I was faced with a very insecure, needy and fragile person: myself. Looking out from this vantage point I saw Adam as the strong one. He was always there, quiet, peaceful, and inwardly steady. Adam, Rosie, Michael, John, and Roy—they all showed themselves to me as the solid core of our community.

Toward the end of 1987 I realized that I was headed for a crisis. I wasn't sleeping well and I was preoccupied by a friendship that had seemed life-giving but had gradually become suffocating for me. It was as if the planks that had covered my emotional abyss had been taken away and I was looking into a canyon full of wild animals waiting to devour me. I found myself overwhelmed by intense feelings of abandonment, rejection, neediness, dependence, despair. Here I was in the most peaceful house, with the most peaceful people but raging inside myself.

Henri's friend Sue and others were deeply worried. Henri was barely holding himself together during the day, and at night in the safety of the small chapel in Daybreak's retreat house where Sue lived, she could hear Henri's anguished cries. Sometimes she would go sit with him as he writhed in physical agony.

I spoke to a few members of my community, at first obliquely but then quite openly and directly. I soon found myself speaking to a psychiatrist. Everyone said the same thing: "It is time for you to face your demons. It is time to bind your own wounds, to let others care for you."

It was a very humbling proposal. I had to leave the New House and the community for a place where I could live through my anguish in the hope of finding new strength and new peace. What did it all mean? I didn't know. I had come to live in community and to care

*for Adam. Now I had to leave Adam to others and fully acknowledge
my own disabilities.*

For years, Henri had been moved by the Bible story of Jesus's baptism, when a voice from heaven was heard identifying God's pleasure in Jesus as God's beloved child. For Henri, it was a voice he longed to hear personally: unconditional divine love affirming him.

I was going through the deep human struggle to believe in my belovedness even when I had nothing to be proud of. Yes, I had left the university with its prestige, but this life gave me satisfaction and even brought me admiration. Yes, I was considered a good, even a noble person because I was helping the poor! But now that the last crutch had been taken away, I was challenged to believe that even when I had nothing to show for myself, I was still God's beloved son.

As I lived through this emotional ordeal I realized that I was becoming like Adam. He had nothing to be proud of. Neither had I. He was completely empty. So was I. He needed full-time attention. So did I.

I found myself resisting this "becoming like Adam." I did not want to be dependent and weak. I did not want to be so needy. Somewhere, though, I recognized that Adam's way, the way of radical vulnerability, was also the way of Jesus.

During the months that I spent away from L'Arche Daybreak I was able—with much guidance—to hear a soft and gentle inner voice saying, "You are my beloved child, on you my favor rests." For a long time I distrusted the voice. I kept saying to myself, "It is a lie. I know the truth. There is nothing in me worth loving." But my guides were there, encouraging me to listen to that voice and let it become stronger.

Henri committed himself to six months of intensive psychological and spiritual accompaniment far from L'Arche Daybreak. Sue covered his pastoral ministry at Daybreak, spoke on the phone with him daily, and visited him. Through therapy, Henri began to understand more of his compulsion to get right into the lives of others. He wrote, *When you find yourself curious about the lives of people you are with or filled with desires to possess them in one way or another, your body has not yet come fully home.*

He began fumbling toward a new way of thinking about what he wanted to articulate as a writer, priest, and speaker. *A new spirituality is being born in you. Not body denying or body indulging but truly incarnational.* But opening himself to something new implied changes. *You will discover that many other spiritualities you have admired and tried to practice no longer fit your unique call.*

By July 1988, Henri was still fragile but he returned to the Daybreak community, where he was welcomed home. He now lived in the community retreat house, a four-bedroom family home that had been built in the early years of Daybreak. The community's small chapel was in the converted basement. The Daybreak woodworking shop had already built tall wall-to-wall bookshelves in the living room to make Henri's library available to everyone.

Sue and he would share the house and together they would care for Daybreak's spiritual needs. Henri occupied one of the small bedrooms, but he had a private phone line installed. He shared a bathroom with whichever random retreatants were staying in the house. Henri's new home was modest and he would have very little privacy, but he could welcome friends and community members. He liked living simply.

14

As Rodleigh drove away from Freiburg in 1991 in the convoy of circus trailers, he kept thinking about the new friend who had become so dear in just a week. Henri's gentle and friendly way of getting to know each of them was unusual—bold, yet sincere and attentive.

"We have a letter from Henri!" Rodleigh announced to Jennie about five weeks later. They were especially touched to read that Henri had felt completely welcome with the troupe. Really, thought Rodleigh, it hadn't been a big deal. In fact, it took relatively little effort to make Henri feel at ease. Henri was eager to be pleased, and each member of the Flying Rodleigh troupe genuinely liked him.

When Rodleigh and Karlene's mother died suddenly a few months later, Henri's sensitive and supportive letters meant a great deal to the grieving troupe members. They later told Henri about their struggle to perform immediately after hearing of their mother's death. "The way we got around it—I found out later that my sister and I both had the same feeling—was that we were doing our performance for our mother," Rodleigh told Henri. "Wherever she was, the feeling that I had was that it was a special moment, a special time."

By the end of the summer, Henri asked if he could visit them again. Everyone was pleased. Jon offered to host him in his new trailer, and Jennie prepared to feed Henri's voracious appetite.

After Circus Barum had left Freiburg and I had returned to Toronto, where I live in the L'Arche Daybreak community, I kept in touch with the Flying Rodleighs through letters. In November 1991—at their invitation—I returned to Germany to spend a week with them on their travels from town to town.

Henri took a taxi from the train station to join them on November 11 in Korbach, Germany, physically tired but as bright-eyed and excited as a child in a toy shop.

"That was wonderful!" were Henri's delighted first words following the afternoon performance just hours after he arrived. He tried to nap, but was too excited to sleep and joined Rodleigh and Jennie for supper.

"I'd forgotten how much he can eat!" Jennie laughed to Rodleigh.

After supper, despite his recent transatlantic flight, Henri watched their evening show as well. He was especially glad that he stayed awake, because Jon and Joe got into an argument during the evening's after-show debriefing. The troupe was embarrassed to deal with it in Henri's presence, but he loved it. He was delighted to see that the Flying Rodleighs were human and made mistakes and had to work on their relationships just like everyone else.

Sharing those intimate moments of emotional struggle, problem-solving, and commitment to a common purpose made Henri feel more involved, Rodleigh realized. Henri was almost imperceptibly becoming part of their family.

Hosting Henri turned out to be risky. One day the whole troupe went to get work visas at the Italian consulate, sixty miles away. Henri stayed in Jon's new trailer watching circus videos. When the troupe arrived back, he was on his knees in front of the TV, so entranced that he had forgotten the kettle that he had begun heating on the gas stove. The enamel exterior was charred black. Jon was not impressed, but as they got to know Henri better, they were just relieved that he hadn't burned down the whole trailer. Jennie and Rodleigh soon discovered that even drying the dishes was too dangerous for their awkward and overly enthusiastic friend, and they tactfully declined his further assistance.

They loved his presence, however. He was not just immersed in his subject, Rodleigh observed, but wallowing in it. They were tickled to see him sprawled across Jon's couch, expressing his thoughts with flamboyant hand gestures and an air of total belonging and contentment. He was especially intrigued by their perfectionism, their complete concentration, as well as the self-confidence and teamwork required to perform their ten-minute act. He often asked how they focused so completely, how they were able to put aside all the other things going through their minds, and Rodleigh could only say discipline and practice.

In mid-November, Henri interviewed each member of the troupe. He ended with Rodleigh, delving into Rodleigh's childhood, his family and religious background, his relationships, and his development as a creative artist. The three-hour interview ended abruptly as Henri bolted away to catch his train, and Rodleigh and Jennie found their trailer felt quite empty that afternoon after the show. Henri was eccentric and peculiar, but very lovable. By that evening, they were already missing him. He brought a different level of awareness to their lives, a deeper sense of themselves as a community, perhaps because of his own rootedness in community life.

During that week the idea grew in me to write a book—maybe even a novel?—about this remarkable group. They gladly gave me the freedom to interview them and write about them in any way I chose. Living with them for a week opened my eyes and heart to a new world of art, community, and friendship.

Back in Canada soon afterward, Henri announced his latest book idea to his friends Bart and Patricia Gavigan. Writers, filmmakers, and directors of a Christian ecumenical community and center in England, they had faithfully helped him through the early and later stages of his breakdown in 1987. Now they were in Toronto showing their new film *Zabelka: The Reluctant Prophet*, and Henri joined their workshop on nonviolence. That evening, he gave a keynote talk to thousands of Catholic school teachers, but by the time they got to their car in the underground parking garage he was bursting to tell them about a totally different kind of project.

"I feel like I am now at a crucial crossroads as a writer," he explained. "I want to write for a secular audience this time."

Bart groaned and rolled his eyes. Henri had been saying this for years.

But this time Henri had a new kind of project in mind. "I want my next book to be about the flying trapeze! I think it is such a good story that it will be a kind of cross-over book for me."

He paused. Now he had Bart's and Patricia's full attention, so Henri ventured an even deeper intuition: "I have never before attempted a book like this, but I believe this could be the most important thing I ever write. What do you think?"

"Go for it!" said his friends. Then lightheartedly picking up his own imagery for his new vision, they added, "Try a triple somersault!"

III

Teamwork

15

Here's what will happen next," Dennie says to Henri. "The fire department is sending two trucks. The truck with the aerial lift is a supporting unit, so it will come with a standard pumper truck. The pumper will have a crew of six, including the captain. He will coordinate the whole team, both the two in the aerial truck and the six men in his pumper truck. Most of them will come upstairs with the stretcher, so your room will feel a bit full, but everyone has a role. You will see that it is good to have many hands available."

I hope all those people know how to work well together, thinks Henri. He wonders if they like each other. The anticipated large crew reminds him of his very first impressions of the Flying Rodleighs, which he dictated onto a tape the week he first met them.

.....

Karlene was making these tapes with her camera and I was standing beside her. They were trying to do something new, and it was absolutely fascinating to see because it was very difficult and they couldn't do it. Every time they made that move either Rod was too late in arriving or Joe was too early in coming or Jon Griggs was too late in letting Rod go, or similar various little mistakes, denying them success or consistency. They couldn't figure it out. Rod wasn't caught by Joe and came down in the net. And that's not a small thing coming down in the net, to fall all the way from the top to the bottom. Falling in the net is really dangerous. It looks rather easy, but you can really hurt yourself, and they all suffer from painful shoulders, stiff necks, and all that.

But one of the things I saw was that these people really work well together. Rod was clearly the one who was the leader. Everybody listened very carefully to him. They are willing to follow his instructions, and there was a kind of gentleness about it.

And then they did some new practices with Rod and Jennie together on the Russian swing. This is a sort of big double-decker swing and they can give it an enormous amount of momentum by building the swing together. They take off from that swing and get propelled all the way to the top to Jon Griggs and he then throws them all the way to Joe, or they go right up into the middle of the air and mount to stands high up with Jon. It is just incredible.

On Friday I went to the practice again. They did the same thing—it went wrong—then it went well, and they tried all over again. They didn't practice very long and one of the reasons was that it was terribly cold. I realized how sensitive they are about health things because as soon as one of them gets sick or one of them is not able to do it, they can't do the act, and there are no replacements. So here are five people and they all have to be there. They all have to be healthy and in good shape.

And it has to be a good atmosphere to be successful. They had a flyer who was cocky and didn't want to help out with simple things. It isn't easy when one of them is not really connected and doesn't fit. So that's another aspect of the whole thing—how they work together, practice together, and so on. They really are sensitive to each other's needs.

·····•

THE MEDICATION IN THE IV must be working, Henri observes with relief. Dennie had said that it was a combination of two drugs. It could lower your blood pressure even further, Dennie had warned, so do not try to get up. Henri is not even tempted. Not now. He is remembering being inside an egg.

·····•

IN THE MONTHS AFTER Henri returned from his week traveling with the Flying Rodleighs, two big events for him happened at L'Arche Daybreak.

The first was in December 1991. Some of Henri's friends came for a discernment process to help Henri and Daybreak to reflect back over his five years at Daybreak and consider his future. For days, the community reminisced about Henri. Uproarious and touching and appreciative and annoying stories were told around dinner tables. As the three visitors listened to community members reflect on Henri's half decade, it became clear that Henri needed help to balance his community life with time away from the community to write.

The discernment process culminated in an evening event with invited dignitaries from three Christian churches: Catholic, Anglican, and the United Church of Canada. Alongside a more serious evaluation of Henri's contributions and challenges through his first five years at Daybreak, community members presented ridiculous songs and skits about Henri, such as a version of "The Man on the Flying Trapeze" with the lyrics adjusted to acknowledge Henri's infatuation with the Flying Rodleighs and his frequent flights around the world. Even though some of the skits were rather pointed, Henri did not feel hurt. "I didn't know that you knew me so well," he marveled afterward.

In January, L'Arche Daybreak threw him a big circus-themed sixtieth birthday party in the community meeting hall. Hung from the ceiling and along the walls were enormous homemade banners with exuberant paintings depicting clowns and trapeze artists. The guests were treated to skits, stories, songs, speeches, and general absurdity.

The highlight was when Robert Morgan, a long-term friend of L'Arche and of Henri's, invited Henri to be reborn as a baby clown. By then Henri had been softened up with lots of hilarious and affectionate attention. He was in his element. Without hesitation, he leapt to his feet to join Robert in the middle of the community gathering.

An actor, playwright, and professional clown himself, Robert carefully dressed Henri as a clown, layering over his clothes a baggy, shiny top, then an extravagant ruffled collar. Henri pulled a pair of calf-length pantaloons over his dress pants and shoes, then Robert added a final touch: a snug red beanie cap that came down over his ears. To the delight of his assembled guests, the distinguished author and former professor now looked very silly. He handed his glasses to one of the viewers and entered wholeheartedly into the transformation, beaming with anticipation.

Robert next produced a large white cloth sack decorated with a few bright swatches of fabric, and announced that this was a clown egg. He explained to Henri what would happen next.

Now to begin your life as a clown you have to go right back to the very beginning. This is a clown egg. . . . A little baby clown will come out of this egg. So you are going to come inside this. You have to realize that when you're in there—you know that Bible passage about being knitted in your mother's womb—that's what's going to happen to you inside this egg. You're going to be knitted together into a baby clown and you'll feel at some point that your body begins to work a little bit in there.

You know babies, when they're ready to come out, they have to come out. When you're ready, when you feel knitted together, what you can do is come out. Come out of the egg. But remember, you've never breathed, you've never even taken a breath. So you have to take your first breath. You can feel your body for the first time. You've never felt the air on your face. You've never opened your eyes to the light. You don't know what your hand is. You don't know a thing about your body. In fact, you don't know anything about anything! Isn't it wonderful being sixty?

Henri climbed into the cloth egg, and Robert dragged the bundle to the middle of the room and left it. Everyone watched eagerly.

Nothing happened for a while. Then, slowly, the sack began to twitch. It rolled over a few times. It wriggled, expanding and contracting. Finally, out of the opening emerged—a bare foot! A hairy calf with the cuff of the pantaloon at the knee! The room rocked with laughter, and the shy leg retreated back into the egg.

Moments later, it reappeared, cautiously, followed by the other leg. The two bare legs waved in the air, stretching their toes, exploring.

The sack rolled over again, and Henri's face emerged, wide-eyed, curious. With just his feet and head showing, he rolled onto his back, then reached up to grab his toes, just like a baby. He tried to put his toes into his mouth.

The baby clown sat up and looked around, blinking in newborn confusion. Gradually, with the assistance of some of his friends, mainly those with intellectual disabilities and the many children led by Robert, he gingerly rose to his feet, and found out how his arms worked. Imitating Robert, he discovered his voice, practicing first simple vowels then syllables as everyone present howled with laughter. With his arm around Henri's shoulders, Robert moved his attention beyond the discovery of his own body and introduced him to the assembled company, "your family."

"They love you, Henri," he explained, "and you will find that you love them, too."

The rebirth ended with Robert singing Bob Dylan's "Forever Young." Everyone who knew the words joined in: "May you always do for others, and let others do for you. May you build a ladder to the stars, and climb on every rung. . . ."

16

Yes, remembers Henri, that was the year he became so much younger, the year he turned sixty. He rediscovered his body, letting it be reborn from the clown egg into his loving and supportive community. He gave himself fully to the moment, open to transformation. Meeting the Flying Rodleighs the previous spring, he had felt like an infatuated adolescent. They gave him a whole new way to imagine what it might be to "climb on every rung." It was an unexpected ladder up to a new platform, but it felt risky. After all, every time the Rodleighs climbed, they knew they might fall. He could not get his new friends out of his mind.

His response to the Rodleighs' performance had been very physical, but his previous books had been about inward, spiritual movements and choices. He did not know how to put his experience into words. In fact, he felt what he termed *a certain inner resistance.* He decided to go to England to participate in a writing workshop led by Bart and Patricia Gavigan.

"What is the risk?" was a key question in the Gavigans' film-writing workshop in February 1992, and the question gripped Henri's imagination. *What is the risk?* he wrote in his notebook, thinking about his book about the Flying Rodleighs, and began making a list beginning simply with *time.* He continued with *security,* but also noted an *enigma: totally confident but do not know why.* It was like *traveling without maps, where your own map doesn't take you.* Henri found himself groping for a route beyond his own comfort zone, wondering how to explain his experience of the Flying Rodleighs on a *psychological–emotional level.*

What is this about? he wrote, and suggested some possible answers to himself: *Is this just an adolescent memory, just living out your fantasy?* There was clearly *sexual energy, with its invitation to fantasy,* and *that is in everyone.*

But Henri did not want to limit the power of the trapeze image. To make the experience accessible to all his readers, Henri wanted to identify *another reality* that would *desexualize* his experience.

Either way he saw a risk. He could explore his physical response to the trapeze act, or shift his attention to the safer *spiritual dimension,* which he named as *no more or less important than anything else.*

The problem, he realized, was that he wanted to write *not a spiritual book, but a book about life, examining life on all levels and letting them fall in their own place.* That meant trying to integrate the physical experience into a story about all of life. He had never before attempted to write anything like it.

YOUR journey has to be as vital as the circus story, wrote Henri, recalling Bart's encouragement. *Create curiosity, surprise people occasionally. Can you create apprehension? Even a feeling of foreboding? What is the end of the story? What is the climax?*

These were central questions to any good story, Henri realized. He had imagined that the climax had something to do with bringing together the world of the circus and the world of community with handicapped people. One of the first things that struck him about the Flying Rodleighs was the fun they had, the way they smiled at each other as they performed, the way they radiated a joyful spirit of community.

So when those two worlds of L'Arche and the trapeze meet, he thought, they could bring the reader into a kind of *total absorption, total delight.*

Working with Bart, Henri's own ideas, fantasies, and connections between communities seemed like a dramatic story of delight, risk, and surprise. But as the workshop carried on, writing from even that set of notes fell flat. He was losing the intense physical experience of seeing the Rodleighs.

HE NEEDED TO BE with them again. That spring, he initiated a daring plan to join the Flying Rodleighs' convoy for several weeks.

17

Back in Toronto, when I spoke about my experience with the Flying Rodleighs in my community, my desire to return and deepen my connection with the circus grew. Yes, I wanted to write about them, but to do that well I needed more immersion than a week would allow.

In May 1992 I flew to Amsterdam, rented a camper to have as my own little home for reading and writing, and returned to the circus. Since Rodleigh had given me their itinerary, I knew where to catch up with them. This happened to be close to the Dutch border, only one hour's drive from my father's home.

On Monday, May 4th, I arrived with my little mobile home in Geysteren—a small village in the Dutch province of Limburg—and parked in the front yard of my father's house. My father was excited about my plans, and he and a friend from the village helped me find all I needed for my camper to be self-sufficient.

Rodleigh and the troupe were delighted when Henri wrote to ask if he could travel with them for two weeks. For Henri writing would be a key focus, so he eagerly packed his books about creative writing. *As I drove away from my father's home, I said to myself: "This time I will keep a diary."*

Wednesday, May 6—Emmerich
Around noon I arrived in Emmerich. It wasn't hard to find the circus since all along the road there were "Circus Barum" signs. Last night the Flying Rodleighs had arrived here from the small town of Gogh, and this morning was "build-up" time. Around noon Rodleigh, Jon, and Joe were busy setting up the riggings, while the Moroccans were finishing the work on the tents.

I am happy to be here again. Another world, so different from my Daybreak community in Toronto and yet so similar. Animal trainers, clowns, acrobats, magicians, tumblers, flyers, and catchers living in a small "village on wheels" together with musicians, stable hands, electricians, and many handymen. They come from all over the world: Germany, Russia, Hungary, Italy, Spain, France, Morocco, South Africa, and the U.S.

When he arrived in Emmerich, the three men in the troupe welcomed him warmly, and took a break from setting up the rigging to park his camper in front of Joe's truck. The circus grounds were too small for all the circus vehicles, so the trailers were parked in a row along the street.

Henri was eager to watch as they resumed their work finishing the rigging and setting up the net. Recent rains had left the ground soft, so it took several tries and extra stakes to firmly anchor the net. Henri perched on a bleacher seat and immediately started writing notes. Rodleigh cheerfully braced himself for his friend's newest round of questions. In a hurry to be ready for the afternoon show, he was surprised by the level of technical detail that Henri requested. After the evening show, when the questioning continued, Rodleigh resorted to drawing diagrams for Henri. They shared a long discussion of Henri's latest book ideas, then Rodleigh walked Henri to his camper van, knowing he was likely to become disoriented in the darkness.

Karlene's new trailer arrived the next day, and Henri sprawled contentedly on her couch, chatting companionably as she and Kail unpacked.

Thursday, May 7

I have now seen the flying trapeze act of the Flying Rodleighs four more times, and each time I am stunned by their magnificent performance in the air. Their act has not changed since November. It remains spectacular, elegant, and very artistic. It also remains dangerous! Every time they have their evaluation meeting after the act, it becomes clearer to me how much can go wrong. It is all split-second work.

After the evening show, Henri's friends checked that his camper van had enough water in its tanks and charged its batteries for the trip. Rodleigh considered how best to arrange the convoy, and decided that he would lead, followed by Jennie driving Karlene's trailer, then Henri followed by Joe, with Jon at the rear.

As they set out in the dark, Henri discovered with dismay that writing in a new way was not actually his biggest challenge: driving the large van terrified him.

Rodleigh didn't realize how anxious Henri was about driving his big vehicle at night until they stopped. Rodleigh walked over, and saw that Henri was still clutching the steering wheel with white knuckles. Rodleigh asked him if he was okay. "I have never driven anything so large before," Henri blurted out desperately, "and I have never liked driving at night, and I don't know what to do now—I can't park it." He nearly wept with relief when Rodleigh took over the wheel of the camper van and parked it for him.

Henri slept well, however, and the next morning, Rodleigh found him up early, sitting at his table enjoying the view. Rodleigh connected Henri's electricity, and was startled to find that Henri had already used up all his water. He showed Henri how to refill his tanks, and warned him to be less extravagant in his water use.

By the time Henri sat down to write his journal later that day, the terrifying drive felt like history, and his focus had returned to his connection with Rodleigh and the trapeze act itself.

Friday, May 8—Borken

Last night we drove to the next town: Borken. It was a good 90-minute ride. We arrived safely, and I was glad because driving my camper at night fills me with fear.

I asked Rodleigh if he would be willing to give me a moment-by-moment commentary on the videotape of their flying trapeze act. He invited me to his trailer and gave me a very detailed analysis of the first movement in which he does a full-twist double-layout. The whole movement lasts less than 10 seconds, but this commentary, once I had transcribed it from the tape, filled three folio pages!

Saturday, May 9

During the afternoon performance Rodleigh missed his "long jump." It was a dramatic moment to see him pass Joe's hands and drop into the net. Then he repeated the jump, and this time, to the loud applause of the audience, Joe caught him safely.

It is strange, but after having seen the flying trapeze act countless times, I am not any less nervous. To the contrary. Since I now know more about the intricacies of the act, I am more aware of how much can go wrong, and I feel more tension than last year when I first saw it. I even said to myself, "I don't want to see it again; it makes me too anxious." But I know that I will see it many more times.

After the backstage evaluation session, Joe invited me for coffee in his caravan. We talked about catching. "I knew I couldn't catch Rodleigh on the first long jump," he said. "When I saw him passing Jon, I realized he was not getting close enough for me to touch him. He was out of my reach." I asked what the problem was. "It is the coordination between Jennie and Rodleigh on the Russian swing. The way Rodleigh was boosted up by Jennie made him go too high and not far enough." I tried to get some ideas as to how much flexibility Joe had in catching Rodleigh. I was amazed to hear him describe the many adjustments he could make to get Rodleigh safely in his hands.

He explained how he could see Rodleigh coming to him. Although he didn't observe details, he could see the total form of his body and was able to reach out to him in such a way that he could make a definite miss into a possible catch. "Sometimes I have to cross my arms so that I can catch both of his wrists and turn him so that we can come straight as we swing above the apron." As he spoke, I realized how much was happening within less than a second.

Joe also explained what it means for him when Rodleigh comes late or early: "When he is late I have to slow down my swing. When he is early I have to speed it up. I usually know whether he is late or early when I see him flying past Jon. Then I know mostly what to do. But when he gets up too high and his body moves back in the direction of the pedestal, I know there is no chance of catching him. Then I just have to let him go into the net."

The more I hear about the details of this short trapeze act, the more I am aware of how long it is. I know how, in a critical moment, life can go into slow motion. People in car accidents often tell you how much they saw, thought about, and felt from the moment they lost control of the wheel until the moment they hit the tree or another car. Some people even say they saw their whole life pass by in a second.

Now I realize what Joe sees, feels, and decides within the few seconds Rodleigh flies toward him. It must be like watching a movie in slow motion. I also realize that what is true for Joe is also true for Rodleigh, Jennie, Jon, and Karlene. Their ten-minute act is a long and complicated series of maneuvers that takes many hours to describe. What the public sees is the highly compact result of many thoughts, movements, choices, adaptations, successes, and failures that only slowly become visible to a trained eye. Often, when I join them after the act and congratulate them on their success—success for me means that nobody fell into the net during the act—they end up listing all their mistakes. In the beginning I didn't notice any of these "mistakes" and even now I mostly miss them.

The flying trapeze is a microcosm, even though it looks like a broad and free movement of flying and catching. Being with the Rodleighs is like being invited by a biologist to look through a microscope and become aware that a lot more is happening on my thumb than my naked eye can see.

Jennie welcomed Henri warmly when he dropped by late that afternoon. "I want to ask Rodleigh to check my description of the full-twist double-layout routine," he explained.

Jennie persuaded Henri to settle in and discuss the act with her. She knew that Rodleigh would be in no mood for a discussion. He was out trying to fix the heating system of the secondhand Mercedes-Benz that he purchased the day before. Hopefully the new, more spacious trailer for Karlene would have no problems. Henri happily accepted a cup of tea and tucked into Jennie's plate of cookies.

I asked Jennie to tell me more about boosting Rodleigh for the long jump. She gladly explained: "It requires real coordination. I have to time Rodleigh's leaving. I say: 'Ready . . . go.' But many things can go wrong. I can say 'go' too early or too late. Rodleigh can leave too early or too late. Since I weigh less than Rodleigh, I really depend on the momentum of the Russian swing and can't put my body weight behind it if I'm out of time with him."

Speaking about her adjustments, Jennie said: "When Rodleigh leaves too early, he will travel too long and end up too close to Joe. When he leaves too late, he goes too high up and does not come close enough to Joe. I have to make the corrections. When I see him leaving too late, I have to push harder; when I notice him leaving too early, I have to hold back." Her explanation puzzled me greatly. "How can your 'pushing' harder make any difference when Rodleigh leaves too late?" I asked, thinking that leaving means being away from the swing. "Well," Jenny said, "when Rodleigh leaves too late I see his body moving toward the cut-off too late. I then realize that I have to give him an extra boost."

That afternoon, Rodleigh had started the act feeling frustrated that the car he had just purchased already needed repairs. When he missed his long jump, the most dramatic part of their act, he felt his mood sink. It was his own fault, an obvious failure of concentration. He really did not feel like discussing it with anyone, especially not with Henri, but neither did he want to take his ill humor out on Henri, so he pushed himself to answer Henri's questions.

To his surprise, he felt better after talking with Henri about it. Henri had that effect, Rodleigh realized, not just for him but on every member of the troupe. Since Henri was not expecting perfection from people, he accepted human failure more easily than did Rodleigh.

The evening show of the Flying Rodleighs was stunning. Everything went smoothly—what a joy to see, what beauty and what grace! It was electrifying. The public applauded and stamped their feet with wild enthusiasm.

18

Saturday, May 9 evening

After the intermission I returned to the tent to see the Russian trio, Kaminski. They work on the Russian bar, three pole-vaulting poles taped together. The trio consists of two men and a woman. The men hold the bar on their shoulders while the woman leaps from the bar or pole somersaulting and twisting. The whole breathtaking act is done in a ballet-like fashion with riveting music. They are true disciples of the famous Moscow school. Rodleigh told me that it had taken them many years to train for this athletic routine, and they would do nothing else but this act in its present form for the rest of their professional careers. This really brought home to me the complication of artistic specialization. What they did was perfect, but it would never be different—a little like a pianist who can play one Chopin waltz perfectly but will never play anything else!

Karlene celebrated her new trailer with a little housewarming party that evening and no one was surprised when Henri was the first to arrive for more tea and biscuits.

Henri busily observed everything he could about the Flying Rodleighs, and Rodleigh couldn't help watching Henri with equal attention. After three days, Henri looked like he had been with them for years. Rodleigh noticed with amusement that he walked around the circus grounds with what Rodleigh recognized as his air of confidence, but what would likely appear to others like a confused lost child.

At least once a day, Rodleigh would go through a video of the day's performance with Henri and recount in minute detail what each person was doing and how it felt. Henri was mesmerized watching it in slow motion, marveling at how the human body could perform such a dance in the air. Day by day, he learned the new language of the trapeze.

As well as the physical discipline, he was fascinated by the mental focus required. As Rodleigh explained: "Once you're on that pedestal and once you're on the catch bar, you cannot think about anything else that is happening in your life at that time."

Beyond the obvious physical and mental challenges of the trapeze act, the troupe also had to face emotional upheavals without letting those affect their performance. Often he asked the Rodleighs about their feelings and about their interaction with each other.

Rodleigh enjoyed what he called these "psychological conversations" with Henri. As leader, he had to initiate discussions of any mistakes after each act.

"I have to be able to let them each know their mistake is okay," Rodleigh said to Henri. "I can't hide my disappointment in the overall performance that we did. But I cannot come back and say, 'Why did you do this? It's your fault. Why didn't you concentrate?' That's not going to instill any confidence in them for the next performance. I have to provide leadership so that the next time they go up they can feel, 'All right, now I'm going to do it' because each one has their own pride."

"What you say is incredibly important for life, not just for the trapeze," responded Henri. *"Your willingness not to accuse first, not to point your finger and say, 'You did something wrong' but simply to take the reality and continue to say to people, 'I will be with you, and you will do it well the next time.' That's a wonderful kind of discipline."*

Henri began to list various facets of Rodleigh's position in the troupe. "Your role is very complicated!" Henri said. "Everyone relies on you for their emotional strength and willpower. As troupe leader, you have to create peace when there is discord, make important decisions for the other troupe members, and offer concern and support for each in their personal lives."

Rodleigh felt his body growing tense. He had not thought about his role in that way before, and the pressure of all these new responsibilities weighed heavily. But then he realized that nothing had changed. Henri had just helped him to name the many roles that he was already carrying. He shifted his shoulders and relaxed.

Their conversations gave Rodleigh insight into both the lives of his troupe and Henri himself. He appreciated the way that Henri thought of them not only as artists but also as people.

Henri was pleased with Rodleigh's explanations, repeating them over again, putting them into his own words, finding parallels and similarities to his own life.

Sunday, May 10

This morning I went to a Catholic church in town, a two-minute walk from the circus entrance. There were a lot of church bells ring-ing through the air—as if they were competing with one another—but when I entered the church all was harmony and peace. By the time Mass began, the church was practically full. The celebration was carefully structured. The priest presided with great devotion, gave a well-prepared homily, and said the eucharistic prayer with conviction and clarity.

As in most German churches, there was much order and little intimacy. People scarcely greeted each other, and the sign of peace was omitted. I realized how similar, yet how different, this celebration was compared to my Daybreak celebrations. I felt deeply grateful to hear God's Word and to receive God's gifts, but also somewhat lost in this big church and its formal liturgy. Everything was so familiar yet so distant and strange.

No one from the circus was there. The circus tent and the church, standing a few hundred feet apart, are two completely separate worlds. For me, however, they are very connected, but no one seems to see this. Aren't they both trying to lift up the human spirit and help people look beyond the boundaries of their daily lives? And aren't they both, at the same time, in constant peril of becoming places for lifeless routines that have lost their vitality and transcending power?

I tried to stay a little longer in the church after most of the people had left. But I couldn't pray. I felt lost in this vast space in which everything was so aesthetically correct, so well arranged—flowers, candles, statues, etc.—and so meticulously clean. Looking for a more intimate place, I walked to the small side chapel, but an older nun was busy blowing out all the candles in front of a large bronze pieta, and made it clear to me that it was time to leave.

It was oddly comforting to leave the well-organized church and return across the rain-drenched field to his temporary home. Not that the circus lacked discipline, but like the community at L'Arche, the circus accepted that life would be messy.

As I walked back to the muddy circus grounds, I wondered how it all fit together. There is no reason to idealize the circus. Much that goes on there is quite unspectacular, inside as well as outside the tent. Nor is there any reason to romanticize the church. Much that goes on there is quite unspiritual. And still, the human heart searches for something larger, something greater than its own pettiness, and everyone who enters the circus or the church is looking for something that reaches out to the stars, or beyond!

Shouldn't there be something of a trapeze artist in every priest and something of a priest in every trapeze artist? I am sure there is, but neither seems to know it!

19

Sunday, May 10 [continued]

The afternoon trapeze act was very poor. There was not much spirit—as if everybody was tired. Karlene missed her layout to Joe. Joe had to let her fall into the net. After that, they finished the routine without much enthusiasm. Afterward Karlene was very depressed. She said: "You want to apologize to everyone and give them their money back. I feel awful."

Tonight I am in a bad mood. Rodleigh became impatient with my questions about the act and started to treat me in a very condescending way, asking me the kind of questions a policeman often asks when he gives you a ticket, such as: "Can't you read the sign that says 50 miles per hour?" I had to remind myself that Rodleigh had had a bad afternoon and that I am a very slow learner.

Tonight is another pull-down night. Forty-five minutes after the show we will be driving into the night to Datteln, the next town, about 57 kilometers away. "Count on an hour and a half," Jennie said. I hate driving in the dark—especially in this camper. But the circus goes on!

Rodleigh and the troupe knew that their trip would be slower with Henri because he drove slowly and cautiously. They consoled themselves that there was an advantage in arriving last to the fair-grounds: if there were problems, the other vehicles would have already discovered them.

Monday, May 11—Datteln

The trip was frightening. Rodleigh led the convoy, using the shortwave radio in his truck to talk with Jon, who, with his big car-avan, drove at the rear. Between Rodleigh's truck and trailer and Jon's caravan were Karlene and Jennie in the Mercedes, which towed Karlene's newly bought house on wheels. Then came Joe with his truck and trailer. I moved in behind Joe and could see Jon behind me in my mirror.

As I said, the trip was scary for me, but not for the others. They are accustomed to driving their mobile homes through the night on the narrow German country roads. But for me it was pure fear! My camper has five gears, and it wasn't easy to figure out which gear to use at different speeds. We kept going slowly at railroad crossings and through sharp bends, and each time I wondered which gear to go back to. It took a long time to get used to it, but eventually I began to feel a little more at ease.

Meanwhile, the fast-driving German cars kept moving in and out of our convoy. They obviously felt we were going too slowly and tried to pass us quickly, but the busy traffic coming toward us made their attempts look like Russian Roulette. Sitting high above the road, I could see this cat-and-mouse game between approaching and pass-ing cars, and I am surprised, still, that nobody was killed.

During trips like this there is ample opportunity to wonder why people are constantly risking their lives. It seems that everyone is so urgently trying to get somewhere that staying alive is less important than getting there!

Rodleigh surveyed the Datteln fairgrounds. They were so water-logged that other artists' trucks were stuck in the mud and would require a tractor to tow them out. Seeing that, he waved the Flying Rodleighs vehicles toward firmer ground, and they parked without problems. Weary from the drive, Henri was almost inarticulate with gratitude when Rodleigh again offered to park his camper van.

Last night, after we had arrived in Datteln, Karlene invited me for a hot drink. I was glad she did. As we spoke it became clear that she was aware of Rodleigh's impatience with me and wanted to make me feel better. "When you have grown up with acrobatics your whole life, you are not always aware that you use a language that is hard for outsiders to understand," she said. Jennie must have talked to her in the car about my conversation with Rodleigh. I was grateful for her kindness and for giving me a renewed sense of belonging.

In his diary the next morning, he continued to muse on the meaning of their traveling show:

As we drove through the night over the curving two-lane roads, crossing one little town after another, I found myself musing about the life of my five trapeze friends. As they move from place to place, they scarcely have time to notice where they are. The circus is usually at the outskirts of town, and the Rodleighs are too busy setting up their rigging, keeping their vehicles in shape, cleaning their trailers, and doing their act to have much time for relaxation.

The many two-day stands are truly exhausting. They arrive in a new town at about midnight and have to spend all the next morning setting up the trapeze. That alone is a four-hour job. Then at 3:30 and 7:00 there are the performances. Although the trapeze act lasts only ten minutes, getting dressed, the preparatory stretching, the evaluation afterwards, the changing of costumes for the finale, and the finale itself keep them quite busy throughout most of the time when the circus is on. During the second morning there is a little time for shopping, making phone calls, and doing business, but the rest of the day is filled again with the trapeze act. Then at 9:00 there is the pull-down and at 10:00 the convoy moves out for the next town.

Last night, as I drove my camper, in a bend in the road I could see the whole convoy in one glance. I thought: "What is this all about? Five people, four huge mobile homes, moving from one little German town to the next, sometimes in rain, sometimes in very cold weather, with never an excuse to stop for a while, to not perform, to not feel up for it, and all that for a ten-minute act that most people forget after they have seen it!"

It's the entertainer's life! Making people say "Ooh" and "Aaaah" and "Wow" and "Nooo"; making them feel tension and release, making them look up to the dome of the tent and say, "How can they do it? I can't believe it," and sending them home with that strange, but quickly passing sensation of having been in another world.

Is my own life very different? I travel here and there giving talks, make people feel safe or excited, and help them come to terms with *their feelings of loss, failure, and anguish, as well as their feelings of growth, success, and joy.*

Am I like circus people—an entertainer? Do I try to hold people up in between the many fragmented moments of their lives and give them a glimpse of "the beyond"? It fascinates me that the word "entertainment" comes from the Latin words inter (between) and tenere (to hold).

What's wrong with being an entertainer? Isn't Jesus the greatest of all entertainers? Isn't He holding people up in a life that constantly wants to go flat? Didn't Jesus come from another world and travel from place to place to let people look up for a moment and realize that there is more to life than they might have thought? And weren't most of those who listened to Jesus like circus-goers, going home with some excitement, but forgetting about it when everyday life reasserted its demands? There were many, many crowds during the three years He went from town to town to announce the Good News, but there were very few for whom His "performance" made a significant difference.

.••••

"The fire trucks are here," Dennie announces. "The team will run up the stairs with the stretcher and be here in just a minute to help get you down to the ambulance."

Entertainment is to hold between, "inter-tenere," Henri reminds himself. He knows that he will be well held between the window and the ambulance, but it doesn't strike him as exactly entertaining. Will it be a frightening trip down? He is glad that at least he does not have to drive the truck.

·····

Monday, May 11 [continued]

This morning I celebrated the Eucharist by myself in the camper. This was the third time during my stay in the circus. I have thought about inviting someone to be with me, but realize that it is better to remain "hidden." The idea of being a priest for the people in this circus has intrigued me, but the longer I am here the more I become convinced that only after a long hidden life here could any type of ministry emerge. The most religious people in this circus seem to be the Muslims from Morocco. I hear them sing at times and it sounds as though they are praying.

Of any Christian form of prayer or worship, however, I see no sign. But Rodleigh's kindness, hospitality, support, and generosity are such a gift to me that it is obvious that I have much more to receive than to give at this time. Right now it appears that I should live here a long time, get to know everybody in a simple and undemanding way, and then it would gradually become clear what ministry would mean.

Wednesday, May 13—Kamen

The trip on the German roads from Datteln to Kamen last night was short but again very tricky for me. At one point I realized I had forgotten to push back my camper's doorstep. Since I was afraid that this piece of metal sticking out was a hazard, I had to stop, walk around the camper, and push it in. Jon, driving behind me, and seeing what was happening, talked by radio to Rodleigh at the front of the convoy, and brought the whole circus troupe to a standstill. At first I couldn't get my camper to start again, but finally I got back on the road, and everyone started to move again. I felt embarrassed by my clumsiness, but realized that I had to accept it with a smile.

IT WAS TIME FOR lunch. Jennie glanced at Rodleigh and rolled her eyes. He knew what she was thinking. Henri had again charged into their trailer without noticing the mud he tracked in. They had discussed this with Henri, but he could not remember circus etiquette of removing his shoes before entering a caravan. He rarely even remembered to wipe them on the mat. He didn't mean to be rude: he was just oblivious. So Rodleigh and Jennie had privately agreed to overlook it, and laid down a trail of small rugs at the door and newspapers inside.

Jennie turned away to hide her smile as Henri managed to miss the newspapers and stomp his muddy shoes onto their carpets again. His face shone with excitement, eager to discuss how the sodden grounds were affecting the rigging and stakes of the safety net.

Wednesday, May 13—Kamen [continued]

Mud, mud, mud. Mud was everywhere at the Kamen fairgrounds. I walked over to Karlene's place, and we had some coffee. She was very open with me and spoke about all the "mood swings" of the troupe. "Rodleigh can be so critical of me. Sometimes I get so fed up with all his remarks about the way I keep my trailer, the way I am with my daughter, the way I do my act. A few weeks ago I was about ready to quit . . . but I have to confess . . . what makes him so critical is also what makes him such a good artist. He is a real perfectionist. You have to be a perfectionist when you want to be a good aerial acrobat. You not only have to do good tricks, but you have to do them with perfect style. A difficult trick, sloppily executed, does not make a good show. Well, his perfectionism comes through in all things. I guess I have to learn not to take his criticisms too personally."

Karlene also spoke about Jennie, Joe, and Jon. She spoke of them with great love and respect, but also letting me know that living so closely together, day in day out, with no outside friends, is far from easy. "You really have to give each other space. I need my own space, and I can't deal with people just walking in and out of my trailer all the time."

．•••．

SEVERAL FIREFIGHTERS IN BULKY dark uniforms enter Henri's hotel room with a stretcher, a sheet, and a blanket. Dennie moves quickly to unfold the large blanket. He and the firefighters spread it over the stretcher, then cover it with the sheet.

Dennie is speaking to Henri again. "Now everything will come together. We're on our way."

Strong hands smoothly lift Henri, and he is reminded of the Flying Rodleighs lifting him into their arms for a photo. Now Rodleigh pulls up the sides of the blanket to wrap Henri, and brings straps around to buckle him securely in the safety belt—or is it Dennie? Henri's mind is feeling fuzzy: the present moment and the past keep sliding together.

IV

Trust the Catcher

20

Waiting to begin his journey down the narrow hotel hallway, Henri shifts his attention to his own body, noticing the ache in his chest, and that familiar flutter in his gut. Fear? Or maybe not entirely fear. Apprehension—with a hint of curiosity? Even anticipation, despite being in the midst of a medical emergency? His mind wanders again, back to the physical effort and excitement of traveling with the Flying Rodleighs in 1992.

. • • • •

EVERY DAY HE FELT more and more like a writer, compiling notes for a new kind of writing. His attention in his diary shifted to focus on what kind of book he wanted to write and how to write it.

Wednesday, May 13—Kamen [continued]
The longer I am here, the more I find to write about. The flying trapeze act alone could keep me writing for months. I have collected some good personal stories of the three flyers and the two catchers; I

have a rather good description from Rodleigh of the act itself, but the gaps in my knowledge seem wider than ever.

I know nothing about the rigging. It would take me weeks to figure out the names of its different parts and the way they are pieced together. I know nothing about costumes, the way they are chosen and used. I know nothing about earnings and expenses and the countless administrative aspects of the act.

The more I learn, the more I realize how very little I know. Still, the more details I grasp, the better. I might not use all these details in my final story, but without knowing them I don't think I can make good choices in my writing. This makes me think of Rodin's statue of Balzac in Paris. Although the statue shows Balzac in a wide mantle, the preliminary studies show many nude models. Rodin wanted to know every detail of Balzac's body in order to be able to sculpt him well with the large mantle over his shoulders. I guess this is also true when you want to write a story about the flying trapeze. Even though you don't want to distract your reader with all the technical details, you have to know them quite well if you really want to describe the artistic power of the show.

Thursday, May 14

Reading Jon Franklin's Writing for Story and Theodore A. Rees Cheney's Writing Creative Nonfiction convinces me more and more of the power of writing. I have never really studied the craft of writing, but these books show me how much I have missed.

As I read these books, surrounded by the circus, I ask myself: "Why are you here? To learn about the circus or to learn how to write?" I now see how they are connected. I love the circus, but I *love it so much because it gives me so much to write about. I love to write, but I love it so much because I have the circus to write about. As I read these books on writing, I see how much there is to write about. At first it seemed that the spectacular trapeze act was the main subject, but as I enter more deeply into the circus world while reading these books, I see little stories everywhere and can be away from my camper scarcely more than ten minutes without wanting to run back and report what I have just heard or seen.*

So my life here is a strange running to and from the little writing desk in my camper: a strange tension between action and contemplation, between observing and reporting, between listening and writing, between walking around and sitting down.

My main discipline seems to be to remain focused. There is so much to see and hear that I easily get swamped by the countless impressions that come at me from all sides. Constantly I have to remind myself that I cannot go everywhere, cannot speak to everyone, cannot be part of everything.

The Rodleighs give me a good focus. Whatever I can learn from them, I really want to take in. But the rest—the clowns, the magic boys, the animal trainers, the Moroccan workers, and the Polish musicians—must remain on the periphery of my vision. Otherwise everything starts spinning, and writing becomes impossible.

Henri turned back to his *Writing Creative Nonfiction* book and read, "Faced with the search for structure, sit back and sift, shuffle and stack. Do any patterns, or things that look like possible patterns, take shape? . . . If the ending is there, it'll act as a magnetic pole drawing everything toward it." He marked the paragraph to make it easier to find later. Returning to his diary he noted:

Thursday, May 14 [continued]

I am convinced that I have been sent to the Rodleighs to discover something new about life and death, love and fear, peace and conflict, Heaven and Hell, something I can't get to know and write about in any other way.

Often I think: "How could I have ever imagined, even a few years ago, that I would sit for a few weeks writing in a camper in the midst of a circus in Germany?" But here I am, and it feels like the only good place to be right now. What tomorrow will bring, I will find out tomorrow. I am happy that I don't have to know that today.

During the afternoon show, just after Karlene had explained to me about the socks filled with magnesium-carbonate powder to dry the hands of the flyers and catchers, Joe's sock came loose and fell from the catch bar into the net. Rodleigh pointed to it, but nothing could be done, since the act was in full swing. The Moroccan ring-man smiled at me when he noticed that I had seen it happen.

The act went on as usual, but during the evaluation Karlene told me that it had scared her. "Joe sweats a lot, and he needs it to keep his hands dry in order to hold on to us."

The evening show went badly for Rodleigh. He missed the full-twist somersault and on his return he hit his calves at the pedestal board. After the act he was limping badly, but Jennie didn't make a big drama of it. "It is a strange place to get hurt," she said. "That has never happened before."

Friday, May 15—Wuppertal

We made it all right to the fairgrounds in the center of Wuppertal, despite my missing the exit to the freeway and Jon's having to go after me and bring me back to the convoy, and even despite Rodleigh's

turning off the freeway too early and having the whole convoy wan-
dering back and forth at the wrong end of town. When, by midnight,
all our trailers were neatly lined up, we felt some real excitement
about our new location. "I saw a large supermarket just before we
entered the grounds," said Karlene. Joe exclaimed: "Finally, a place
we can stay a while." Jennie remarked: "Except for not having grass,
we call this an ideal place," and Rodleigh added: "Nice and close
to the tent so we can hear the music and know when our time in
the show is coming." Jon was in an especially good mood because
his parents were arriving the following day from Detroit for a week.

This morning I decided to take the afternoon train to Freiburg to
visit friends. I felt a certain sadness about leaving, but was glad to
know that I would be back within a week and still be able to spend a
few days with the circus in Wuppertal.

Rodleigh stayed to do the rigging while Jennie took Henri to the
railway station. But first they checked Henri's caravan to make sure
that his electrical and gas appliances were turned off. After ten days
of traveling together, they were getting the hang of living with Henri.

21

In Freiburg, Henri eagerly laid out his thoughts about the trapeze to his friend and editor Franz Johna. After all, Franz had been with him that first night at the circus with his father.

Sunday, May 17—Freiburg

I sense that Franz still has some problems with my enthusiasm for the circus. In his presence, I feel as though I should choose a more serious subject. He finds it hard to see how this could lead to a spiritual book. But as we spoke, and as I explained that I wasn't thinking of using the Rodleighs as illustrations for great spiritual truths, but was simply trying to write a good story about good people who are doing good things, Franz began to warm up and even got excited.

It is important for me to be away from the circus and to be invited to "defend" my project. The more I talk about it, the more I realize that, first of all, I want to write a good story and that I have to trust that the story, alone, will carry within itself Good News.

Henri meandered along the side streets of downtown Freiburg, thinking happily, *Freiburg has become for me like a second hometown.* He bought a few new Vincent van Gogh prints. He didn't miss teaching university, but he enjoyed observing the many students with their briefcases going to and coming from various handsome old university buildings. *Just being here!* he exulted to himself.

Monday, May 18

I spent a good hour with Franz. We spoke mostly about writing a book with meditations for every day. Franz had already published such a book with daily readings by Carlo Martini, Carlo Caretto, and Heinrich Spaemann—compilations of excerpts from their earlier writings.

I wasn't too excited about doing another anthology. Many of my books no longer express my spiritual vision and, although I am not dismissing my earlier writing as no longer valid, I feel that something radically different is being asked of me.

My many encounters with people who have no contact with any church, my contact with AIDS patients, my experience in the circus, and the many socio-political events of the past few years all ask for a new way to speak about God. This new way includes not only content but form. Not only what I say, but also how I say it should be different.

What mostly comes to mind is stories. I know I have to write stories. Not essays with arguments, quotes, and analyses, but stories which are short and simple and give us a glimpse of God in the midst of our multifaceted lives.

The next day Henri spent the whole day at his desk, writing. The apartment on the third floor of Franz and Reny Johna's house was familiar and comfortable, and had always been a good place for him to write.

But I feel a certain inner resistance to working on the circus book, as if the project is too big for me and I still do not have enough knowledge about the trapeze to write it easily. Perhaps, he thought, he still was too much an observer. *I am still not fully capable of writing from within.* He tried to encourage himself that there was no end to the process of becoming part of one's subject, so just start writing, trusting that something will emerge. As he gradually slowed down, writing became easier.

But his visit was soon over.

Thursday, May 21—Wuppertal

This morning Franz took me to the railroad station. At 1:30 I was back at the circus. I had been wondering on the train how the week had been going for the Flying Rodleighs. Was Rodleigh's leg healed? Had there been a good audience during this long stay in one place? Would I find everyone in good spirits, less tired and frazzled than when I had left?

I soon discovered that it hadn't been an easy week at all. Rodleigh's injury still looked bad. Karlene had some internal bleeding in her stomach area, spent hours at the doctor's office, and was finally told that it was impossible to do any trapeze work as long as there was pain. Jennie had an extended medical checkup because of her heart murmur. The German clown collapsed in the ring as a result of a dust allergy and was taken to the hospital. Mrs. Kaminski fell from the Russian bar when she came down from her final trick; she hurt her leg badly. Peter, the Englishman with his dog act, had a real setback:

the clown's dog got loose and went after Peter's little circus dog and bit him so badly that Peter had to keep him out of the ring for nearly a week. And all the Hassani tumbling boys seem to have pain in their wrists and ankles!

Somewhat apprehensive, I went to the afternoon show, wondering how the trapeze act would go with two wounded artists. At first, nothing seemed too different. But when Rodleigh worked with Jon and wanted to make a front somersault from Jon to Joe, he failed to reach Joe's hands and came down into the net. Since he had planned to return from Joe to Jon and do some more tricks from Jon's hands, his fall forced him to cut all of that out and let Jennie continue the act from the pedestal board.

But the evening performance was completely different. Was it the simple determination to work well together in hard circumstances? Was it the large and enthusiastic audience? I don't know, and the Rodleighs probably didn't know, either, but the show was superb. Rodleigh flew to and from Jon and Joe with great ease and was caught without any visible strain. He made his somersaults and twists with tremendous grace and moved through the air as if the air was his. Jennie too went from the board and returned to it with much elegance, and when Jennie and Rodleigh concluded the act with their spectacular passage over the flying bar from and into the hands of Joe, the audience exploded in a burst of applause and foot stomping that made Gerd Simoneit send the whole troupe back into the ring for another bow.

The whole group was excited; they had felt the electricity in the air. Even Joe, who is usually quite reserved, didn't hide his enthusiasm. "It went really well," he said.

The next day, Henri deliberately spent the intermission with Jon's sister, who was visiting. He had been struck by an instruction in Cheney's *Writing Creative Nonfiction*, because it was something that came easily to him: "Listen to everyone—unsolicited comments by 'unimportant people' may explain even more than those received from the 'notables.'"

Saturday, May 23—Geysteren

Last night, during the intermission, I didn't join the Rodleighs for their evaluation, but spoke instead with Jon's sister Kristen, who has been going to every show since she arrived here with her parents from Detroit. Kristen loves the circus and can't get enough of it.

For a woman with Down's syndrome, she is very independent and quite articulate. The clowns, with their "boxing act" full of heavy sounding blows, were her favorites. She told me all about her family, her work, and her role in the Special Olympics, where she won two medals and a ribbon.

As we spoke I realized that the circus speaks not only to the young as well as to the old, but also to mentally handicapped people as well as to the sophisticated. Indeed, the circus has found a universal language that bridges many differences among people.

On this, my last day in the circus, I saw many connections between my L'Arche community in Toronto and this circus community. From a distance they seem so different, but looking at them closely they are quite similar. They are both communities for special people.

Saying good-bye wasn't easy after so many good days with such good people. But I felt ready to move on. I know the Rodleighs will be my friends for life. They might not yet know this, but leaving them last night didn't seem to be a leaving for very long. Just a time to gather up all my new impressions and find the story that lies beneath them.

After affectionate farewells in the early morning, Henri climbed behind the wheel and drove his camper van away from the circus in his characteristic way. Rodleigh winced as he watched Henri come very close to a parked car as he drove over a curb.

At 6 o'clock this morning, I left the fairgrounds in Wuppertal. An hour and a half later I crossed the border into the Netherlands and at 8:30 I was home with my father in Geysteren. He was very happy to see me and wanted to know all about the circus.

22

At the hotel in Hilversum, the ambulance driver shoves a large red emergency bag into Dennie's hands. Dennie pulls out some extra medication.

"I will keep this with us in case we need it in the next few minutes," he tells Henri. One of the firefighters is already waiting by the door with Henri's carry-on bag. Dennie hands the emergency bag back to the driver, who runs out the door with the firefighter. "They are heading downstairs to meet us at the bottom," Dennie adds.

He pauses, concerned by Henri's lack of response. Is he distracted by pain, is he afraid, or is he losing consciousness? Dennie keeps talking to keep Henri alert and present: "Now we are ready to go down the hall to the window. The hotel has opened it for us, and we will load your stretcher onto the aerial lift. Don't worry. I will be with you all the way."

The blanket wrapped around Henri is warm. Henri opens his eyes and tries to smile at Dennie, but realizes Dennie cannot see his mouth twitch behind the oxygen mask. Dennie tucks the oxygen bottle securely between Henri's legs. The heart monitor is held by one of the firefighters, who stays close so that the three leads remain firmly attached to Henri's chest. Another is preparing to carry the IV bag. He is impressed by their care and coordination as they confidently reach for the equipment they need. Each seems to know immediately what is needed and take their role without confusion. They must practice this.

It's another version of reaching out, Henri thinks. *Reaching Out* was the title of his second book, and Henri finds himself pondering how that book's main points are like the trapeze. From the pedestal, the flyer has to reach out to the trapeze bar. The catcher reaches out for the flyer. Even the book's subtitle emphasized motion and momentum: *The Three Movements of the Spiritual Life.* When he wrote the book twenty-one years ago, he articulated an *inward movement* from loneliness to solitude, then an *outward journey* from hostility to hospitality, and finally an *upward movement* from illusion to prayer. Readers found it practical and helpful, a spiritual self-help book just as the genre was starting to take hold, and it became Henri's first "best-seller."

But now, blearily watching Dennie and the careful teamwork of his rescuers, Henri wonders if he was thinking too much of a spirituality for just the individual. How could anyone reach out in those ways alone? Without a sense of being part of a larger body, even a team or community? The question isn't new. Already in 1983 while he was living in Latin America, Henri's new friends revealed to him *how individualistic and elitist my own spirituality had been. It was hard to confess, but true, that in many respects my thinking about the spiritual life had been deeply influenced by my North American milieu with its emphasis upon the "interior life" and the methods and techniques for developing that life.*

In fact, Henri reflected, he had fallen into *a spirituality for intro-*

spective persons who have the luxury of the time and space needed to develop inner harmony and quietude. Very different from the attentive, urgent, disciplined focus of Dennie's colleagues. Or of the Flying Rodleighs.

What do I want to say about the teamwork of the trapeze act? Henri asks himself now. Is beauty in its essence a shared spiritual endeavor? These artists have a desire for continual self-improvement, but they create beauty for others, and their act is lived out in teamwork and community. *I've seen very clearly that all together form one body, as a whole. If one part of the body isn't functioning, the whole body isn't functioning.*

.••••

BY THE END OF his time traveling with the Rodleighs in 1992, Henri felt excited about his project and eager to continue to learn how to write differently. Less than two weeks after Henri lurched away in his camper van, Rodleigh received a letter, thanking them for their kindness and hospitality. Henri confided that he now had lots of material for his book, and was considering writing it as his first attempt at a book for a secular audience.

Who would understand the wide-ranging connections he was seeing? On June 2, he wrote to John Dear, an American friend committed to community building and peacemaking, *One day I hope to be able to tell you about a very interesting month I spent recently with a German circus. In some ways, life in a circus is not dissimilar to life in a community of nonviolence.*

At the end of November, Henri again wrote to Rodleigh, now announcing that his ideas had swung back to introducing a religious element into the book and staying in more familiar writing territory.

Rodleigh chuckled to himself, privately wondering how Henri would be able to find enough connections between the Flying Rodleighs trapeze act and any religious topic to fill a book.

After sending his letter to Rodleigh, Henri picked up his pen feeling inspired. He could easily imagine using three movements as a way to tell the story of the Rodleighs. That format was both familiar and had been enormously successful. Readers loved it. He was excited as he scribbled out a draft outline of three movements. Each connected the Flying Rodleighs to his L'Arche community and to the Church.

From career to vocation, he wrote. This first movement would include *the personal journeys of each member of the troupe. Many assistants at L'Arche Daybreak had made similar choices.*

The second movement was from *individualism to community.* Henri outlined this section with a rush of enthusiasm. *To realize their vocation, the Flying Rodleighs had to live together because everything in the act depended on their teamwork and their care for each other. There could be no competition among them, no heroes, no anger or jealousy, and they had to practice their act continually together.* In other words, it was like L'Arche: *a lifestyle lived out in community with compassion, forgiveness, and a shared rhythm of life. "Look how they love each other!" is how Jesus said Christians would be recognized, and the same was true of the circus community.* Henri reread his notes, thinking about all the ways this section could help many of the lonely people who wrote letters to him.

Finally, he envisioned a third movement *from entertainment to inspiration.* He had been thinking about this ever since he journaled about entertainment on his road trip with the circus. *The point of the trapeze act is not just to distract people but to give them a glimpse of the beauty of life. Not only artistic beauty, but a beautiful vision of humanity in harmony, where it is possible for people to feel safe with one another.* In fact, the Flying Rodleighs offered *a vision of amazement, joy, rapture, beauty, elegance*—Henri's words tumbled over each other as he wrote. He imagined members of the audience like himself thinking, *I am not simply forgetting my trouble but I see who I am, can be, and want to be.* In that way, *the trapeze act is for others,* he wrote, *because it reveals the life of vocation and community, as does L'Arche.*

Then something shifted. Henri felt his shoulders droop. He put down his pen and hugged his chest tight, looking out the window beside his desk. The book he was outlining looked competent and full of important insights. The sections about the trapeze engaged him, but his energy dwindled and his focus slipped as he tried to outline the accompanying sections about L'Arche. By the time he tried to apply each insight to the spiritual life, he completely lost interest in his own subject.

He sighed as he admitted to himself that he had no real enthusiasm for this way of framing his experience. Perhaps the problem was that *Reaching Out* was published many years earlier. If his book about the Rodleighs also explored three spiritual movements, would he be like those exquisite Russian performers? Having created and perfected one act, the Kaminskis would do only that act for the rest of their careers.

Henri didn't want to have one trick, performing the same feat of writing again and again, even if his audience applauded every time. Like Rodleigh, Henri wanted continually to change his act, take a risk, try something new, even if it might fail or be uncomfortable. He abandoned the outline.

"I don't want to write just another book," he said to an interviewer a year later.

A lot of people have said, "Why don't you write another book about prayer, another book about God, another book about meditation?"

No, no, I want to write a book about the trapeze.

And they say, "What have you got in your head? Are you crazy?"

No, I'm not crazy, I'm just in love with the trapeze and with God and the two have something to do with each other.

Every time Henri returned to his trapeze book, he felt a sense of being called. He had explained this in his earlier diary, while on the road with the circus:

Why should I write about a trapeze act? I have no answers. The trapeze act was "given" to me last year, just as the print of Rembrandt's "The Return of the Prodigal Son" was "given" to me in 1983.

There is a strange "must" to my writing about the trapeze act. I still do not know precisely why the Flying Rodleighs are so important for me. I still cannot articulate fully the meaning of their show. But I know with great inner certainty that they hold an important secret for me that will reveal itself little by little if I remain faithful to my intuition.

23

Yes, he thinks, the trapeze was "given" to him. He had felt an immediate mysterious, physical connection. His most similar experience had occurred years earlier.

.••••

IT WAS 1983. SITTING in his friend Simone's small room at the L'Arche community in Trosly, France, Henri lost track of their conversation, distracted by her poster of Rembrandt's painting. His attention was utterly sucked into the scene before him. A son in ragged clothing was on his knees, leaning his head against his aged father, who stood tenderly laying both his hands on his son's back. The painting illustrated a story Jesus had told, about a younger son who demanded his inheritance, left home, and wasted it in extravagant, prodigal living. When he ran out of money and friends, the son returned home to his father, ashamed. But instead of rebuking him, the openhearted father embraced him, then hosted a homecoming party. His older brother, who had obediently stayed home, resented that his father took him for granted while welcoming home his irresponsible brother with a big feast. The painting showed not only the tender reunion of the father and younger son, but also the brooding anger of the older son.

The moment Henri saw it, he was immersed, convinced that the Rembrandt image had been "given" to him, bursting into his life as something so profound that he felt it in his own body.

So he meditated on Rembrandt's painting for several years. He carried small copies of it to give away on his travels, used a large poster-sized version for retreats, showed it to everyone, and thought about it endlessly. Yet for several years, he could not find a way to write about that painting that had gripped him so dramatically. A book just wasn't taking shape for him.

When he fell apart in a complete emotional and psychological and spiritual breakdown in 1987, he carried his Rembrandt print with him. From Daybreak to England then to Winnipeg, the days turned into weeks, and he looked at the image each day and through his long nights. It hovered always at the edge of his consciousness, even when he lay curled up on the floor moaning.

Stripped of his sense of self and security, mysteriously Henri started to find himself on the inside of the painting he had contemplated for so long. Slowly insights came. Not all at once, and not in a simple way. His identification with the younger son deepened. Now he felt as helpless, lost, and needy as that son, full of self-rejection and disgust. He tried to love that son. In England, his friend Bart Gavigan urged Henri to see himself also in the older son. Henri was the oldest son in his family, obedient and faithful, yet he had to admit that he often seethed with resentment and self-righteousness. Yearning for freedom, and for love without conditions, he felt envious of the courage and adventures of the younger son, who dared to set out and take a risk, even if it turned out badly.

As he began to find some peace in his own body, in his body's truth, his friend Sue offered a new insight. "Henri, whether you are the younger son or the elder son, you have to realize that you are called to become the father," she said. And suddenly more than five years of immersion in Rembrandt's painting snapped into focus.

These deeper self-reflections offered a way into the painting that anyone could share, finding their own feelings mirrored in the sons and the father. As he recovered his confidence, Henri offered retreats and talks about Rembrandt's painting, trying to articulate his own life through Rembrandt's image so that others could discover their own parallel experiences. The response was tremendous, and Henri felt encouraged each time that he could write with the authority of his own vulnerability. But it took a long time. Even with that depth of insight, another four years went by before the book was published.

When the book was done, he tried a few titles, starting with *A Dreadful Mercy*. Nobody liked that. He tried *A Dreadful Love*, then revised it to *Canvas of Love*. He resisted titling the book after Rembrandt's painting or Jesus's parable, because the word "prodigal" seemed archaic, and he hoped to reach a wider audience. His editors, however, convinced him that his readers would respond well to a book titled after both the painting and the parable.

His book *The Return of the Prodigal Son* was published in 1992, subtitled *A Meditation on Fathers, Brothers and Sons*. He dedicated it to his father, who was turning ninety. But like his books *Letters to Marc*, which he wrote for his nephew and other young readers, and *Life of the Beloved*, composed for a secular Jewish friend and others like him,

Henri's intended audience didn't flock to his book. *The Return of the Prodigal Son* did not catch on with men involved in the 1990s men's movement. Instead, it became enormously popular among clergy and spiritual seekers of all denominations.

For the second printing of his Prodigal Son book, Henri changed the subtitle to *A Story of Homecoming.*

•••••

WELL, HENRI THINKS NOW, perhaps my trapeze book will reach an audience completely different from the one I imagine. But the real point is that from the time Rembrandt's painting exploded into his life until that book was complete, nine years passed.

Relax, he tells himself. You saw the Flying Rodleighs five years ago. Somewhere inside you, it's all in motion.

It's all about motion, he realizes. Unlike a painting, nothing in a traveling trapeze act stays still. In fact, when he first watched the Rodleighs practice five years earlier, it was the movement and dynamism of the act that captivated him.

They were trying to do something new, and it was absolutely fascinating to see because it was very very difficult and they couldn't do it. It was a jump from one platform, they swing, they swing back, and then they make a salto—Rod was doing that and he was caught at the other end by Joe, one of the catchers. And then Joe threw him up, up to the high top where Jon Griggs was hanging and he caught him there in the middle, right in the middle of the circus, and then he had to throw him back to Joe, and then Rod goes with Joe back to the platform again.

THEIR STRUGGLE TO GET it right struck something deep in Henri—not just the swing of the flyer, but flyer and catchers whirling together, their momentum and energy feeding off each other. The soaring flyer had faith that the catcher would grab them to renew their momentum, then launch them onward to the next catcher. Trust and risk in continued motion together.

24

Henri twitches involuntarily. Now his fragile body is actually participating in physical risk. The sense of risk that he tried to grasp back in 1992 at the workshop with Bart seems comically theoretical and disembodied now that his body will soon be suspended in the air, at the top of the Hilversum fire department's aerial lift.

His chest still hurts, but not alarmingly. Henri is not worried. It will be a warning. He is being cared for, and he is only sixty-four. He even feels oddly relieved that this interruption has happened here in his home country, so that his father and brothers and sister can come to be with him.

Henri feels a surge of excitement as six uniformed firefighters surround him, lifting the stretcher and carrying it down the hall together. This is amazing: I have a disciplined and skilled troupe of rescuers preparing me to fly, marvels Henri.

> *When I saw the Flying Rodleighs for the first time, I had a feeling that they expressed one of my deepest inner longings to be totally free, as well as totally safe.*

He feels very safe.

To me it's very fascinating that this art can only function when all the members give full concentration to each other. They constantly have to be aware of where everyone is. Then there is harmony. The beauty of human communion becomes visible in this act.

••••

HENRI'S FRIEND FRANK HAMILTON read Henri's 1992 journal about driving his caravan with the Flying Rodleighs and it scared him. He knew that Henri was not the most attentive driver. In fact, his driving was notorious. In his journal he wrote about driving through little towns and down dark roads at one o'clock in the morning.

So in 1993, when Frank heard that Henri was again planning a visit with the Flying Rodleighs, he said, "Henri, you're going to Germany next June. May I go with you?"

Henri pondered this. The Rodleighs had started to feel like family. Would it work to add a friend to his visit?

"Why?" asked Henri.

"Because I could maybe help you with the driving," offered Frank. Frank was a steady long-term friend, a chaplain in the US military.

It didn't take long for Henri to decide, "You know, I would like that! I could relax with you driving and it would be fun to go together. I feel secure with you."

Henri began to imagine a new version of his trapeze project: a novel, beautifully illustrated with photos. Photographer Ron P. van den Bosch had known Henri for more than twenty-five years and they had collaborated on several books, but he was still startled when Henri broached the possibility of a new project together at the reception after a family funeral in Holland. After taking off his priestly robes but even before he had a coffee or a sandwich, Henri urgently asked Ron if he had any plans at the beginning of June, a few weeks later. When Ron said he was free, Henri explained that he wanted Ron to join him in Germany to take pictures of trapeze artists in a traveling circus. Struck by how swiftly Henri's attention was moving on from the sorrow of the funeral, Ron sipped his coffee and took his time answering. He was reminded of films about gangsters who make agreements and close deals at their many funerals. But Henri's bright eyes and eager enthusiasm were irresistible.

I came to know the trapeze life from within. I came to know how Rodleigh, and his wife, and his sister, and his friends were relating to each other. I came to know the danger of what they were doing. I came to know how complicated everything is around this one act—setting up the rigging, preparing, the costumes, the sound, the music. This one little act was a whole life, and what happens in these ten minutes was really the result of a life of work, a life of thinking, a life of commitment, a life of enthusiasm, and this really absolutely fascinated me. I just wanted to grab it from the inside.

The Flying Rodleighs eagerly agreed when Henri proposed another visit. They also were not surprised that Henri chose a time when they had an extended booking in one place so that he could stay at a local hotel rather than drive a caravan on the road with them.

Henri arrived with Frank in June 1993. Rodleigh and the whole troupe greeted Henri as a member of the family, pleased to see Henri bursting with his usual enthusiasm. Rodleigh felt a bit at a disadvantage, however, when Frank knew much more about the Flying Rodleighs than they knew about him. Soon Ron arrived and also greeted the entire troupe as though they were old friends. Clearly Henri liked talking about them.

Henri presented his plan: Ron would take a collection of high-quality photos for Henri's book. As Ron snapped pictures of the troupe setting up the rigging, Rodleigh noted that Ron seemed blissfully unaware that the troupe might find it hard to behave naturally with a camera lens right in their faces. Even Henri's friends were charmingly oblivious to their impact on others.

Henri was buzzing with pride. To Rodleigh, he seemed even more moved watching their act again, now that he had someone to share it with. Henri brought Frank and Ron for the traditional tea and biscuits after the show, and Henri and the Rodleighs caught up on their last few months. Henri was glad that Karlene's torn stomach muscle had healed well and she was again performing. Rodleigh showed Henri a video taken in Rome that showed his triple somersault, something he was not able to do with Circus Barum because the tent was not large enough. Henri loved the beauty of the move and watched it several times in slow motion.

When Henri, Frank, and Ron left, it was late and quiet on the circus grounds and Rodleigh could hear them talking excitedly almost all the way back to their hotel.

"What do you think?" Henri asked his friends earnestly as they walked through the quiet fairgrounds. "I don't know why I can't get started on this book. What do you think is the secret of my attraction to the Flying Rodleighs?"

Frank and Ron burst out laughing. "Well maybe, just maybe, because they are stunningly beautiful people, Henri!" chortled Frank. Ron added, "Did you happen to notice that they all have wonderful physiques as well as beautiful form?"

Henri pondered this for a moment. "I guess like Cirque du Soleil, they offer a very sensual circus experience. But I love the Flying Rodleighs performance much more."

"Sure," said Frank. "That makes sense. You admire their human bodies and acrobatic act, but you also have become close enough to touch them in their minds and even perhaps their souls. It puts the flesh and blood on them, so for you they are real people, not just a fantasy."

"Their artistry is beautiful," Ron reflected, "especially how they interact."

"Yes! And it's even more than that!" Henri enthused. "It's the way they have invited me into their lives. You know, they aren't religious people, but I think they have a spiritual hunger that they don't know how to talk about. And when I see them fly, I am in touch with a hunger in me that I don't know how to talk about, either."

Jennie's lunch the next day received lavish praise from Frank and Ron, while Henri was so caught up in explaining the lives of the performers that he barely noticed what he was eating. In the days that followed, they attended all the shows, enjoyed visits with each member of the troupe, and took many rolls of film.

One afternoon, Henri urged Ron to take a photo of himself and Frank with the troupe. Without Henri noticing, Rodleigh motioned to the others to pick Henri up in their arms and support him horizontally.

"Look at him, content as a Roman emperor being fed grapes by his servants," Rodleigh joked. "If he were a cat, he would purr!"

Ironically, the photos did not turn out, and Henri eagerly requested a repeat posing the next day, as relaxed and delighted as on the first spontaneous lift.

25

The highlight of the 1993 visit was on June 6, when Henri accepted Rodleigh's invitation to swing on the trapeze. Henri noted with some trepidation that the rungs of the rope ladder to the platform seemed uneven, with different spaces at different heights, but he hesitated for only a moment, then boldly started to climb as a helper held the ladder to minimize its swing. His eyes wide with concentration, Henri carefully climbed in his stiff leather-soled shoes and dress trousers. At the top, Karlene helped him onto the pedestal, and from that high vantage point they watched Rodleigh practice a double layout from Jon to Joe, testing out the height. He has to be high enough for Joe to catch him, explained Karlene.

I hold on to the pedestal with more fear than necessary. It is a safe place but I still feel somewhat anxious when I look down into the net and see the Sunday morning visitors on the seats. After his practice with Jon, Rodleigh comes up to the pedestal with the safety belt. Karlene puts the safety belt around me and Rodleigh hooks me on to the ropes. He powders my hands and asks me to hold onto the bar. It feels like taking a risk because the bar is a good distance from the pedestal. Rodleigh says: "Don't be afraid. I will hold you and drop you off the pedestal when you have a good grip with both hands on the bar."

He gives the instruction: "Keep your legs straight as you swing. Don't bend your knees. When you are ready to fall in the net, wait until I say 'hop' and then let your hands go, lift up your legs, so you fall into the net in a sitting position."

I grab on to the bar with one hand. Rodleigh stands behind me and embraces me around my waist. Then I put my other hand on the bar: "Keep your arms straight," Rodleigh says. Then he lifts me off the pedestal.

It feels great to swing through the circus tent. It is not scary. Just swinging back and forth. Ron stands on the King pole balcony and takes some pictures. After a few swings Rodleigh calls: "Next swing— let go." Then he calls: "Hop." I let go of the bar, lift my front feet, and fall in the net. The net is not as far away as I thought. Joe, who holds the ropes connected with the safety belt, makes the fall even lighter. I lie on my back in the net. People in the "audience" clap, laughing.

Rodleigh enjoyed seeing Henri on the platform, looking ready to explode with delight. Rodleigh was also interested in Henri's confidence. Most beginners show fear, but Henri seemed to have no fear of the height. He just wanted to reach out and grab the trapeze bar and swing. Rodleigh explained carefully to Henri what he needed to do, especially how to listen to Rodleigh's commands to ensure his safe landing in the net. Henri nodded earnestly in confirmation, but looking back Rodleigh realized that the silly grin on Henri's face should have alerted him that Henri was not actually absorbing anything Rodleigh said. The safety belt turned out to be a good decision.

Henri's eyes grew a few sizes larger as he left the pedestal board. Rodleigh wondered if Henri's involuntary gasp expressed fear or a quick call to his guardian angel, whom Rodleigh figured must be kept busy constantly looking after Henri. Henri's reaction to Rodleigh's call to let go and land in the net was hopelessly late and instead of landing in a sitting position, he put his feet down first. Joe supported his weight by holding firmly to the rope that was attached to the safety belt, then gradually loosened the rope to allow gravity to complete Henri's far-from-graceful landing in the net. Henri had no idea that he had not performed his fall perfectly. Rodleigh said Henri was smiling so hard that if it weren't for his ears, his lips would have touched behind his head!

Henri stood up gingerly in the net and tried to walk. The net bounced. His feet moved faster than his body. When it looked like he might catapult right off the net, Joe pulled on the ropes holding his belt to slow him down. Henri tried to turn, but the belt ropes twisted so he had to turn the other way, and then as the ropes pulled him, Henri began to negotiate the almost forty-foot trip backward, increasing in speed involuntarily, much to the mirth of his audience. Their laughing reached a crescendo when Joe mischievously loosened his grip on the ropes that Henri was using to help balance, and he landed unceremoniously on his back with his skinny legs waving above him. Even he saw the comedy. The whole atmosphere was lighthearted, the kind of scene that remains imprinted in the memory. Rodleigh treasured it: the laughter and friendship, Henri right in the middle with that everlasting smile on his face as he lay in the net after his great swing on the trapeze.

Rodleigh invites me to give it a second try. Again I climb up to the pedestal, get lifted off by Rodleigh, swing and fall in the net. Only afterwards I realize that I didn't use the opportunity to push the swing higher up and make some larger strokes. I did feel tired quickly and realized that my nervousness combined with my untrained muscle made me unable to try it a third time.

When Henri, Ron, and Frank returned to their hotel, they began brainstorming about Henri's book. "I really like them, Henri," began Frank. "I think they are hungry to sit down with someone like you, and not because they are impressed by your credentials."

Henri agreed. "They are wonderful, searching, beautiful people. But it is so good for me, too. I feel grounded by knowing them, maybe a bit like I feel around Adam at Daybreak. And they affirm me in a new way. I can give something different to them."

He pulled out his simple black hardcover notebook and settled into an armchair to jot down notes. "What do you think? What should I say in my book?" he asked.

"The act is like a Russian icon, which by distorting the natural world invites a viewer into a spiritual world," offered Frank.

They began to frame the trapeze act in mythic terms. The men—Rodleigh, Jon, and Joe—were *handsome, graceful, well formed, photogenic and strong, catching fair damsels and one another as they flew through the air.* They also *rescued one another from danger, falls, and death.*

But members of the troupe were not only mythic but unique individuals. If Henri were to write in a more creative way, he would need to bring each character vividly to life using specific details. Henri continued to write notes, now with the new subheading *Real People.* He began with Jennie: *Makes their caravan a warm, clean, and comfort-*

able home. Never idle—designing and hand-sewing complex patterns for their sequined costumes.

Rodleigh, they decided, represented *Integrity and Wholeness.* His sister Karlene was identified as a *Survivor* of some bad experiences, now carrying multiple roles as parent and provider to Kail.

Frank commented on the *Hospitality, Kindness, Attentiveness* of the troupe. They continued with notes on *Physique: Rod, Jon + Joe— Handsome, well built—Strong beautiful + intense faces.*

They were having fun. Frank conjured up menu items to describe the American Jon: *crew cut hair, with a wholesome buttermilk + cornbread sense about himself. A bit of a ham—loves to be photographed.* Regarding Joe, Frank commented, *I want to say, "Joe—you are neat."* The three friends nodded. There was something about Joe that touched them. *Dark wavy hair, deep dimples, turquoise earring, stutters. Short, fat hands + arms—muscular + graceful,* wrote Henri.

"But how can I communicate the profoundly embodied spiritual quality of the experience?" Henri asked. They considered this together. Soon Henri, Frank, and Ron were getting quite elated finding ways to express the intensely physical performance.

Ron commented, *"It's like people making love! Think about it: Bodies in tandem with one another, Harmony, Precision. They interact in the Air as lovers who have a good time."*

"Yup," added Frank. *"It's lovemaking season in heaven!"*

"And then afterward, all the participants have a discussion of the flaws," chortled Henri.

They nearly fell off their chairs laughing. Henri, speedily writing all this down, couldn't quite imagine how to write a book that would catch that kind of shared mirth, but he wished he could.

26

Rodleigh did not see Henri again until a brief visit in November 1993 when Henri returned with Ron and his daughter Marieke. Securely anchored in a safety belt, Henri amused everyone with his unique moves on the trampoline. He speedily ate the hearty lunch provided by Jennie and worried that Rodleigh was taking too many risks in developing a new act. Even knowing that the life of traveling circus performers was one of constant changes requiring attention and flexibility, he was concerned about how the new troupe member Slava fit into the act and whether that had implications for his research and book. After spending the night on the sofa in Jon's trailer, he left the next morning—a short visit with another fond farewell, reflected Rodleigh.

When Henri sent him a copy of *Our Greatest Gift* the next spring, Rodleigh hoped Henri would never know that he had not read any of the other books Henri had given him. It was not that he had no religious background, actually the reverse. He and Karlene had been raised as Seventh-day Adventists, a church that disapproved of what it considered the decadent, countercultural circus life. Rodleigh's call to be a circus performer was so compelling, however, that he followed it even though it meant leaving his faith community. Ever since then he was wary of judgmental religious beliefs that could pull him into self-doubt and guilt.

But Henri was different. Rodleigh was curious to see what Henri would write about his perspective on the Flying Rodleighs themselves. He looked at the slim hardcover book with its attractive cream-colored cover, read the friendly inscription from Henri, then flipped to the pages Henri identified in the accompanying letter.

One day, I was sitting with Rodleigh, the leader of the troupe, in his caravan, talking about flying. He said, "As a flyer, I must have complete trust in my catcher. The public might think that I am the great star of the trapeze, but the real star is Joe, my catcher. He has to be there for me with split-second precision and grab me out of the air as I come to him in the long jump."

"How does it work?" I asked.

"The secret," Rodleigh said, "is that the flyer does nothing and the catcher does everything. When I fly to Joe, I have simply to stretch out my arms and hands and wait for him to catch me and pull me safely over the apron behind the catch bar."

"You do nothing!" I said, surprised.

"Nothing," Rodleigh repeated. "The worst thing the flyer can do is to try to catch the catcher. I am not supposed to catch Joe. It's Joe's task to catch me. If I grabbed Joe's wrists, I might break them, or he might break mine, and that would be the end for both of us. A flyer must fly, and a catcher must catch, and the flyer must trust, with outstretched arms, that his catcher will be there for him."

When Rodleigh said this with so much conviction, the words of

Jesus flashed through my mind: "Father into your hands I commend my Spirit." Dying is trusting in the catcher. To care for the dying is to say, "Don't be afraid. Remember that you are the beloved child of God. He will be there when you make your long jump. Don't try to grab him; he will grab you. Just stretch out your arms and hands and trust, trust, trust."

Rodleigh had never read anything like this before. He looked out the window over the fairgrounds, turning it over in his mind. Catching. Dying. After rereading the passage several times, he put the book on the shelf with their other Henri books, and went to tell Jennie about it.

"What Henri wrote about us in his book is not religious exactly, but about something much more free, about how the spirit can fly," he told her.

Jennie was intrigued. "So while we thought you were just teaching him a new vocabulary of circus and trapeze terms, it turns out you were also giving Henri a new vision of his faith?"

"And even more, just like we experiment with new routines in our trapeze act, Henri is experimenting with these new images in his books and sermons," reflected Rodleigh. "It's fun to think about. I wonder if it has been as exciting and daring for him as it is for us doing our work."

27

Rodleigh was right: Henri was experimenting, finding his voice in daring new ways as he tried to communicate the insights stimulated by their friendship.

Soon after Rodleigh received Henri's book, Henri was in Minneapolis, smiling as he fingered the new medal on a wide red ribbon around his neck. The medal recognized Henri's contributions to the international movement of spiritual and pastoral care and counseling. Through the lengthy standing ovation that followed the presentation of the medal, he looked thoughtfully over all those attending the meetings of COMISS (Coalition On Ministry In Specialized Settings), weighing what to say in response.

Speaking without notes, he began by describing his friendship with Adam. But he also wanted to say more about community, so he began to share his experience of the Flying Rodleighs.

"I love these trapeze artists a lot!" he exclaimed. *"There are three flyers and two catchers. Three flyers who make these incredible triples, you know."* In his eagerness to communicate the momentum of the act, Henri rotated his arms vigorously to demonstrate, setting his COMISS medal

swinging and nearly dislodging his microphone. *"Better be careful here,"* he admonished himself, and his audience laughed.

I wonder if they realize that the catcher doesn't just wait for the flyer? Henri thought. Before getting to know the Flying Rodleighs, he had no idea of the complex dynamics of the act, the constant split-second decisions and adjustments made by each artist. How can I help them to imagine the attentive teamwork required when everyone is already in motion? He tried to embody the momentum, swinging his right arm to illustrate. *"The catcher is on a catch bar that moves. Meanwhile the flyer comes from the pedestal and does all these triples."* Henri swiveled his left hand high above him, and swung it down to meet his right hand flying in from his right side. When his right hand caught his left wrist, both in motion, Henri looked triumphant and the audience laughed and applauded Henri's successful act.

"And Rodleigh says, 'Henri, you know the greatest temptation for me as a flyer is to try to catch the catcher. Because the catcher will be there. I have to trust that. When I come down from my triple I have to stretch out my hands, and whether I'm here"—Henri paused to turn, stretching his arms out—*"or whether I'm there"*—Henri pivoted slightly—*"or whether I'm here"*—he shifted his body's direction yet again—*"I have to trust that he will be there."* Henri demonstrated, again locking one hand over his other arm in trapeze catching action. *"And will pull me right up into the cupola."* Henri jubilantly swung his right arm in a high arc.

"That's what I have to trust. And if I start"—Henri opted to use gestures rather than words, reaching his arms in front of him while stumbling and turning confusedly—*"then we break our wrists and we are in trouble."*

Henri's audience of ministers and caregivers again leapt to their feet to applaud his performance of trust and teamwork in motion.

A FEW MONTHS EARLIER, Henri had received an invitation to address the National Catholic HIV/AIDS Ministry conference in Chicago. By 1994, AIDS had become the leading cause of death among all people aged twenty-five to forty-four in the United States.

When the invitation from the conference organizers arrived, Henri could not decide. He said yes, then changed his mind and declined. He felt confused by whether he was the right person to address such a gathering. He worried about how much of a toll it would take on him personally. But his connection with the Flying Rodleighs was giving him not only new ideas but courage to leap into something new and risky. Henri agreed to go to the conference and give the closing address.

As Henri prepared to give his talk at the end of the conference, he was nervous. It had been a good week, but he took a deep breath and wiped his sweaty hands on his corduroy trousers as he looked out over hundreds of people and announced:

> *I am really very grateful for being here this whole week. As a beginning of my sharing with you I would just tell you in a way how it all came about. In 1981 the founder of the community of L'Arche—it is a community for and with people with mental handicaps—I had never met him before, but he looked at me when we met and he realized that I was not terribly happy, and sort of anxious, and looking for something new. But I didn't know what it was and he said, "Maybe our people have a home for you. Maybe our people have something for you that you really need." It took me quite a while to listen to that, and it was in 1986 that I finally left the academic world and joined the community of L'Arche. And my life has been*

very, very different, radically different since I got there, frighteningly different.

In 1991 or '2, I met another man called Rodney DiMartini [the executive director of the National Catholic AIDS Network] and he looked at me and thought I wasn't looking very happy.

This got a laugh from Henri's audience, and so he bravely continued:

And he thought I might be a little anxious about certain things, certainly about some of the things that he was interested in.

Henri's audience applauded, and Henri grinned back at them.

He said, "Henri, maybe our people have something that you really need." It's quite humbling to always walk into people who tell you that they think that you need something.

So it took me a few years and finally I said well maybe. But first I said no, and then I said yes, and then I said no, and he said you better say yes finally, and so I'm here.

Being in this conference has been a little bit like a new jump into something unknown—a little bit frighteningly unknown and not knowing what it will do to me.

Encouraged by the responsive audience, Henri tried to explain the growth that he was experiencing:

Maybe my whole life has been a life in which boundaries were pushed out and broken down, and it has been frightening for me every time a new boundary came tumbling down. So I've realized okay I might have started in community or in the Church or in the seminary or in my family as a safe clear place, and then bang, bang, bang, bang, bang all these boundaries keep falling, all these little hedges and fences keep falling away. Suddenly, the non-believer might be more believing than the believer, the outsider might have something to teach the insider. Suddenly, the difference between Catholic and Protestant, Christian and Buddhist, religious and secular isn't the kind of difference I thought it was.

When I went to Daybreak, my community now, I realized that the difference between handicapped and non-handicapped just wasn't there anymore. I realized that I could love the handicapped only because I was handicapped, that I could be close to people in pain only because somehow they revealed my own pain to me.

The difference between male and female, young and old, married and celibate, White and persons of color—all the distinctions that seemed so important—suddenly the pandemic throws all those differences away—the difference between homosexual and asexual and bisexual people, or between married people and transgender people—I've never heard so many terms!

Henri's audience applauded and cheered.

It seems that these differences aren't that important actually. Married, celibate, single—you can be anything but we are together, the AIDS pandemic brings us together. I tell you that for me personally, and I would guess in some places for you, that when the boundaries are falling away you get anxious sometimes and say "now where do I say stop or here, here, this is it?" And it's no longer there and suddenly you realize that your heart is expanding and there are no boundaries to that expansion.

Henri continued, talking about the paradox he had experienced, that love and intimacy in community can unexpectedly reveal a deeper inner loneliness. But sorrow and joy are not separate, they are always in our flesh, Henri asserted boldly, so *"just start living!"*

Studying the responses of the many new friends he had met over the week, Henri decided to tell them about the Flying Rodleighs. He made it dramatic.

I have a little story to tell at the end of these reflections. A few years ago, my eighty-eight-year-old father came to visit me in Germany. He wanted to do something fun, so I said, "Let's go to the circus."

There were five South African trapeze artists—they left the pedestals and danced in the air and I said to my father, "I think I missed my vocation! That's what I always wanted. That's what I always wanted to do. To fly!"

I said, "You go look to the animals in the break, but I'm going to talk to these artists." And I said, "Hey guys you are absolutely fabulous"—and I was this sixteen-year-old fan looking at these strong and big thirty-year-old guys.

They said, "Well, do you want to come to our practice tomorrow?" And I said, "YES! I want to come to your practice tomorrow!"

Henri's audience whooped as he acted out the scene he was describing. Looking out over people who were daily facing so much death, Henri ached to inspire and encourage them. The spiritual meaning of flying and catching was not just about death, he realized, but about living, about the remarkable community he had experienced that week in the National Catholic HIV/AIDS Ministry conference and saw embodied in front of him. The catcher offered an image for dying, but it was also about the beauty and artistry of flying and catching each other day by day.

There was that moment that he couldn't get out of his mind, when the flyer had to let go of everything and fly in midair, trusting that the catcher would be there at the precise moment when most needed. All that week, Henri had listened to how everybody at the conference was involved in that act, disciplined in their love, risking, letting go, trusting, and catching each other. This was the crucial thing he had learned from Rodleigh.

The only thing I have to do, Rodleigh said, is stretch out my hands. After I've done my thing—stretch out and trust, trust that he will be there, and pull me right back up.

We have to love one another for that kind of trust. You and I are doing a lot of flying and I wish we do a lot more of it, and a lot of jumping and a lot of saltos and I hope we can do a few triples. It's wonderful to see and you will get a lot of applause and it's good. Enjoy it! But finally it's trust—trust, when you come down from your triple, know that the catcher will be there.

The audience was silent for a beat, taking in this image, then applauded for a long time.

28

In a hallway of the Hotel Lapershoek, Henri has lost all sense of time. How long has he been traveling? He realizes that his journey has entered a new phase when his stretcher stops. He can feel a cool breeze.

Through the large, open window, Dennie greets the firefighter standing in the basket handling the controls of the basket and the boom. Henri with his head toward the window cannot see him, so Dennie explains to Henri what will happen next.

"We will rest the stretcher on the window frame. There is someone at the controls of the basket who will help guide the stretcher safely into place. You will go headfirst out of the window."

Headfirst. Henri vaguely wonders if he has always gone headfirst. All his life, his father has liked intelligent people and encouraged Henri to pursue the life of the mind. But in this moment there is no separation between his thinking and his body—like it or not, his whole body is coming out a window. He is well wrapped in his sheet and blanket, with straps now securing him to his stretcher. Dennie's voice and presence comfort him. He is not alone.

The firefighters carefully push his stretcher out over the windowsill toward the basket on the aerial lift. His head is suddenly in the open air. The stretcher slides with a metallic scrape onto the rail along the bottom of the platform in the basket. Dennie stands at his feet, still on the other side of the window opening. Henri looks over and sees the firefighter who is controlling the basket. He nods at Henri, then crouches down to work with Dennie to bring the stretcher into its final position and anchor it. Henri feels it click into place.

"You are attached safely now," says Dennie as he climbs out the window into the basket beside Henri. "There is nothing for you to do." The stretcher feels solid, but the whole situation is unsettling. Dennie seems to guess what Henri is thinking. "I am here with you," he adds reassuringly.

The day is cloudy and the breeze on Henri's face is fresh. He is really in the air now. Henri blinks nearsightedly at the gray clouds overhead. He tries to remember his words about trust in his letter to Bart Gavigan:

One of the parts of the act that deeply moves me is the long jump. In that act the flyer flies across the whole span of the circus, with out-stretched arms and hands, to be caught by the catcher on the moving catch bar. The words that really struck me were the words by Rod-leigh, "When I have done my flying, I have to stretch out my hands, and trust that the catcher will be there for me. The greatest mistake I can make is to try to catch the catcher." I have thought about these words as words that express the human challenge to trust your neigh-bor, to trust your God, to trust love, to trust that finally we will be safe.

He closes his eyes, and his mind floats away again.

.....

By the summer of 1994, Henri decided that the best way to engage an audience would be a filmed documentary with the Flying Rodleighs. Looking back, his excitement had been inspired not by their words, but because he saw them perform. Maybe to understand what he wanted to communicate, an audience would need to see them. *The Flying Rodleighs are a trapeze group that communicates through the body. Their act is wordless, but in the wordless communication they create community. Children, young people, and old people, from all different backgrounds and nationalities can be together in watching their flying and catching.*

Over months, Henri and Bart explored and discussed the film. Jan van den Bosch in Holland was interested in producing it. Bart confirmed that he would direct it, and also write and edit an English-language version.

Of course, Henri also discussed the idea with Rodleigh and the troupe. The Flying Rodleighs were flattered but somewhat bewildered at the prospect of being featured in a film made for a religious channel.

On December 23, 1994, filming began at the Ahoy Sports Centre in Rotterdam. Jan and Bart started the interview with Rodleigh outside, but it was so cold that after a few minutes Rodleigh was unable to enunciate his words. Henri arrived in the afternoon with a big hug and delight beyond words—he just stood grinning at his friends.

Henri's friend Jan interviewed him for the film, asking, "When you describe a situation, if it's faith, or *The Prodigal Son*, or *In the Name of Jesus*, all your best-sellers, you write very intensely about it. What will happen with this story?"

"I don't know," Henri admitted. *"You know I've always tried to write about deep human experiences."*

Jan pressed his point. "Is this too difficult to write about?"

Maybe. I've tried to write about Latin America. I've tried to write about living with the Trappist monks. I have tried to write about intimate things like my mother's death. But I've known the Rodleighs for four years and I still really don't know how to write about it, as if it touches something so deep in me that I'm not yet able to know how to express it. It's even something different than writing about Rembrandt. I mean, this is something totally new for me. Not just that the trapeze is new. What they represent is new. The experience in me of the trapeze—that's new—and I don't even know yet if I ever will be able to give words to it or write a book about it.

Henri became even more animated. How could he communicate his excitement to a viewing audience?

You know, when I got to know the Rodleighs a lot better, I also realized that they are not an ideal family. No family is ideal. They have conflict, they have struggles. They have difficulties—bodily, mentally, spiritually. They are just people like we are. But one of the things they said to me, you know, when you go on the trapeze, forget everything else. Be only there and be totally there.

So here we are, people full of conflicts, difficulties, worries, concerns, guilt feelings, hopes, all that, but somehow the ability to be totally present in the present—that creates kind of a glimpse of eternity, gives you a glimpse of the true life. You certainly know what real beauty is, or real harmony is, or real unity is—something that your heart most desires—for a second.

．••••

PERCHED NOW ATOP THE medical lift in the open air, Henri wonders for a moment how precarious his present situation is. Yet he can't help remembering what he said about risk in the film interview: *We all want to make triples and doubles and layouts and double doubles and all of these things. We like to take risks. We like to be free in the air, in life. But you have to know there's a catcher. We have to know that when we come down from it all, we're going to be caught, we're going to be safe.*

"Henri, trust the catcher!" he reminds himself now.

．••••

THE FILMING WAS COMPLETED and on New Year's Day 1995, Henri came with nearly his entire Dutch family to see the show and bid his friends farewell. He was in a good mood. He gave each of the Flying Rodleighs a heartfelt hug before dancing off along the canals of Rotterdam with his niece Laura. The troupe's final days in Holland were unusually quiet without Henri and they sat after each show reflecting on the whole experience of filming and meeting his family, wondering when they would see him again. Henri had announced that he would be taking a sabbatical later in 1995 to try to complete the book about them.

The Rodleighs received Bart's completed English-language video, titled *Angels Over the Net*, in early July 1995. Its effect surprised them. They listened to Henri's explanation:

> *Now I live and work with people with mental handicaps, and some also have severe physical handicaps. One of the things that has struck me in my life was that the people with a physical and mental handicap are quite often very able to create community.*

I live in a community with people from twenty-one different nations. Some people are married, some people are single, some people are old, some people are young, some people are Japanese, some Brazilian—and normally these people would never form community, but in the middle of them there are people with a weak body who often can't even speak, who can't express themselves in ideas or big discussions yet still these people are able to create a community among people who otherwise would never live well together.

For me, this is a really new discovery. You know, first I taught. I loved to teach in the university. Then I felt I missed something, something of the heart. So I discovered the life of handicapped people. It was a real discovery and the handicapped people became also my teachers, the teachers of the heart. While they can't speak, while they cannot explain, they tell me something. They tell me that being is more important than doing. They tell me that the heart is more important than the mind. They tell me that community is more important than doing things alone. All these great valuable truths these handicapped people taught me without any words.

When I saw the Rodleighs, I saw in a way the same thing. I saw people who don't speak on the trapeze, who do something with their bodies, and who create community first of all among themselves as a little group, and among all these people who come to see them—young people, old people, children, people from all different languages. They all understand—they create family wherever they go. They bring people together.

As Rodleigh watched the video and showed it to others, he began to see their performance and his own responsibility from a new viewpoint. He had never thought of their work as a form of community or even communication with the audience, but now he was touched by the response of people watching the video. He wiped a tear from his cheek. He was not alone; he knew that many others responded in the same way. Henri had confided that he too shed tears each time he watched it.

29

In the summer of 1995, Henri was invited back to speak at the next National Catholic HIV/AIDS Ministry conference. He was surprised by how anxious he felt. He worried about whether he had anything more to offer. But he said yes. His friends Sue Mosteller and Kathy Bruner came with him.

This conference would be bigger, and there had been thousands more deaths in the year since the last conference. Just a month earlier, the American Food and Drug Administration had approved the first antiretroviral treatment for HIV, but there was no treatment for AIDS in sight and the epidemic was exploding. Millions of people had died worldwide.

The gathering began with an interpretive dance. The audience stood in a single large floor space. Many people packed the space, crammed in closely to watch the dancers as they held each other close and let each other go, honoring all those who had died of AIDS. Henri and those around him wept openly.

The dance drew people together into a community like the artistry of the circus, Henri reflected as he dried his eyes. Like the Flying Rodleighs, here were performers who did not speak and had tremendous power to unite people. Living art, in motion and time, creating community.

When Henri got up to speak partway through the conference, he was again both nervous and moved by his audience. He prayed that he would find the right words. This time Henri boldly titled his talk "Befriending Death."

He talked about his friend Peter, who was dying with AIDS. Peter's partner was insisting, *"He won't die—we will fight it!"* while Peter was saying, *"Why me? I have spent my life serving God—I am confused and angry and frustrated."*

Henri explained that he was struck by this: the partner wanted to combat the illness as a warrior, while Peter's voice was the voice of a protester, the voice of resistance. After spending time with them, Henri wondered, *"What is the way here? Is there a way that my friend and his partner can go one more step and embrace the truth of their reality? Can they befriend death that stands in their room and say, 'Yes you are my enemy but I am called to love my enemy and I want to love you. I want to be with you without fear'?"*

"Why was it so hard for them to become lovers of their enemy death?" Henri asked.

He recounted for his audience how he had thought through that question, then realized that his friends were afraid that if they started embracing death, Peter would die sooner. In other words, to start thinking about death would be to give up and no longer resist.

Henri asked the audience, *"Is it possible to love and resist? If we are called to love our enemies, then we must be able to both love and resist at the same time."*

The embodied power of love can make people better resisters,

Henri suggested. *"You must claim your spiritual truth while everything around us suggests disclaimers. It has to come right from your gut, right from your center, right from your heart."*

Describing his own experience in 1989 when he was hit by the van and nearly died, Henri remembered, *"When I was close to death, I experienced one thing: I didn't want to die alone."* But, Henri added, no human being *"can finally give us the spiritual power to make that passage. My deepest conviction is that what allows us to make that passage finally is the communion of saints."* He pointed his listeners to *"that incredible spiritual family that surrounds you and makes your exodus possible,"* and *"that family that reaches out beyond the boundaries of birth and death."*

> *You belong to all the people who went before you. You have to embrace them as saints. Yes, those who were born and died long ago struggled like me and were anguished like me. They had their sexual struggles as I have, and they were lonely and depressed and confused. They went through the black plague. They are part of my human family. I see this crowd of witnesses that I belong to.*

• • • •

SUSPENDED IN MIDAIR OUTSIDE the hotel, for the first time it occurs to Henri that he could die. He hasn't really let that thought enter his mind before. Having survived when the van mirror hit him, he has assumed he will continue living for a long time. His father is well into his nineties. Henri has never imagined the possibility of dying before his father.

But sometimes, thinks Henri, you just have to let go, even if in that moment you are not sure who is your catcher. Maybe it takes a whole lifetime to learn how to fly, and how to fall. He opens his eyes to see the treetops and rooftops of Hilversum, but without his glasses, Dennie and the entire situation feel out of focus. He closes his eyes again.

He is no longer in much pain, but the thoughts swirling in his mind feel urgent and intensely personal. What would allow him to die well? Henri wonders. He has written and spoken a lot about this in the past few years, but the question is now lodged in his own body with shocking immediacy.

> *You were the beloved before you were born, and you will be the beloved after you die. That's the truth of your identity. That's who you are whether you feel bad or not bad, or whatever the world makes you think or experience. You belong to God from eternity to eternity. Life is just an interruption of eternity, just a little opportunity for a few years to say, "I love you, too."*

Dying would be a very understandable reason to leave his trapeze book incomplete, a permanent interruption, he thinks. Maybe he has already learned everything he needs from the trapeze.

> *When I met the Rodleighs and I saw their work and I got to know the trapeze world, again something really new happened. It was suddenly as if I discovered the incredible message the body can give. You know, it was like the university was the mind, L'Arche was the heart, but the trapeze was about the body. And the body tells a spiritual story.*

V

Flying

30

Dennie studies Henri, trying to gauge whether the tension in his body is pain, anxiety, or something else entirely. All he has to work with is what he observes in Henri's physical reactions. Henri's body is certainly telling a story, Dennie thinks, but he wonders how much he is missing of Henri's experience. He notes how inwardly focused Henri seems to be. Henri is a priest, so maybe he is having deep spiritual reflections. Perhaps he is praying. But he needs to stay in his body until they get him to the hospital. Dennie's warm hand cups Henri's shoulder reassuringly.

.••••

HENRI SET THE NEW hardcover journal on the desk in front of him. After admiring the cover's bright detail of Claude Monet's *Bouquet of Sunflowers*, he opened to the first lined page and began: *Oakville, Ontario, Saturday, September 2, 1995. This is the first day of my sabbatical. I am excited and anxious, hopeful and fearful, tired, and full of desire to do a thousand things.*

A year of freedom, *completely open to let something radically new happen,* Henri exulted. *I feel strange! Very happy and very scared at the same time. . . . Free to deepen friendships and explore new ways of loving. Free most of all to fight with the Angel of God and ask for a new blessing.*

On Friday, September 8, he continued, *I have written many essays, reflections, and meditations during the last twenty-five years. But I have seldom written a good story. Why not? Maybe my moralistic nature made me focus more on the uplifting message that I felt compelled to proclaim than on the often ambiguous realities of daily life, from where any uplifting message has to emerge spontaneously. Maybe I have been afraid to touch the wet soil from which new life comes forth and anxious about the outcome of an open-ended story.*

THREE MONTHS LATER IN early December, while staying with friends in Massachusetts, Henri went with his hosts to see the American Repertory Theater's production of *The Tempest.*

By the end of the play I was mesmerized by its magical power, Henri wrote. *Prospero, the exiled Duke of Milan, brooding about revenge, ends up embracing all his enemies.*

Not only that, Henri noted, but Prospero speaks directly to the audience in an epilogue. Henri was so moved by it that he searched out the precise passage and carefully transcribed it into his journal in his graceful handwriting:

> *And my ending is despair,*
> *Unless I be relieved by prayer,*
> *Which pierces so that it assaults*
> *Mercy itself and frees all faults.*

As you from crimes would pardoned be,
Let your indulgence set me free.

Henri stopped to consider why this moved him so much. Maybe because the question of how to turn enemies into friends had been with him his entire life. He had, after all, grown up in Europe during World War II. He remembered those years of political conflict as he considered Prospero's transformation, then turned his thoughts inward to his own lifelong quest to make his tumultuous, passionate interior life into a friend, not an enemy.

Just a few months earlier, Henri had suggested to people at the AIDS conference that in the end, the challenge for every person is to befriend death itself. *The Tempest* was Shakespeare's last play, he noted, and continued writing: *After this he retired to Stratford and died four years later on April 23, 1616. Thus the final words of Prospero get a special meaning: Shakespeare asking his public to free him by their forgiveness.*

There are three old men here, Henri thought: Prospero, Shakespeare, and himself, all looking for forgiveness and the opportunity to launch out and become more free.

He sat with this idea for a while, then finished his journal entry. *For myself, I want to remember the famous words:*

How many goodly creatures are there here!
How beauteous mankind is! O brave new world
that has such people in't.

Less than two weeks later, Henri chuckled to himself, remembering those words as he flew into yet another beauteous new world.

31

A snowstorm was closing in on Signature Aviation in Boston's Logan International Airport as Joan Kroc's private Gulfstream jet, the Impromptu IV, waited to take off. Henri was already on board, roaming around full of excitement, admiring his friend Joan's elegantly equipped plane, touring the cockpit and meeting the crew. Sue Mosteller's flight from Toronto was late, but she arrived in time for a swift deicing of the plane and off they flew to pick up Fred and Joanne Rogers in Pittsburgh, then another friend of Joan's in Minneapolis.

The next morning, Henri and Sue spoke about "a spirituality of care" to about a hundred people gathered at the twenty-four-room hospice in San Diego.

> *A large portrait of Joan in the entrance hall celebrates her as the founder and mega-donor of this remarkable place. The staff is very gentle and friendly and the atmosphere is homey and quite intimate. Both Sue and I spoke about preparing ourselves and others for "dying well." We sang some Taize songs and had a very lively exchange with the audience. We all felt quite uplifted by the event.*

Henri and Joan had met the year before and immediately become friends. They had a lot in common. Joan was a gifted musician who for years had worked as a professional pianist. She intuitively understood Henri's experience of the artistry of the trapeze performance.

Joan's social situation touched Henri. She was the heir of her late husband Ray Kroc's fortune. Over his years at Yale and Harvard then Daybreak, Henri developed a concern for the spiritual struggles of people who were very wealthy. In 1992, he observed, *My experience is that rich people are also poor, but in other ways. Many rich people are very lonely. Many struggle with a sense of being used. Others suffer from feelings of rejection or depression.*

Henri liked how Joan's creative mind was always thinking about how to make life better for all kinds of people, people who lacked adequate housing, people who were dying. He was moved by how she talked about children as the future and wanted every child, no matter their circumstances, to live up to their potential.

Henri also agreed wholeheartedly with Joan's commitment to a more peaceful world, and was intrigued by her insistence that the way to world peace was through education, especially helping women around the world to develop and take up leadership in all levels of society.

Just before 6 p.m., Henri looked in his mirror, smoothed his unruly gray hair, and strolled out to join around ninety guests who had arrived from across the country for a party.

A large tent had been set up with thousands of little lights. All around the pool round tables were placed with splendid bouquets of white flowers. A tree full of lights was floating in the pool. He admired the large stars hung in the biggest trees. Red and white lights adorned the entrance road and hedges. Most dramatic were the sculptures in the garden, illuminated by carefully placed floodlights.

The surroundings were spectacular, the food delicious, the conver-
sations friendly, the music pleasant and everything very, very elegant.
Joan wore an all-gold long dress. She told me that she had bought
that dress long ago and never had a chance to wear it. "So I planned a
party, to have a chance to show my dress," she said jokingly.

By 10 p.m., most guests had left and I went to bed, somewhat
dazzled, puzzled, and intrigued by the life I had been part of.

The next day, after *a lively conversation on the meaning of Advent,* Joan's houseguests toured a homeless shelter that she helped support. Henri was impressed by the scope of the project, but left wondering about the relationships he had seen. *Where and how are the homeless people offering their gifts? Where is there any mutuality between giver and receiver?*

After we had returned to Joan's estate, we celebrated the Eucharist
together in the garden in front of the Mexican creche, with figures
larger than life. We sat around the little table, read the readings,
shared our reflections, prayed and received the sacred gifts of the
Body and Blood of Christ.

At the end of the Eucharist we walked over to the new statue that
Joan had recently acquired. Joan asked me to bless it. It is a huge
bronze sculpture of a seated Cardinal, made by the Italian artist
Giacomo Manzù.

Henri and Joan both loved art. Her new sculpture captivated him, with its clean-shaven, ageless face. The expression was solemn, but the left ear was tucked under the Cardinal's tall miter while the right ear stuck out. It seemed a tender detail, a moment of listening, affirming the humanity of the majestic Cardinal.

Henri packed quickly the next morning, and they all drove back to the airport to board Joan's plane. Henri's friend Robert Jonas picked him up at the airport in Boston.

"How was it?" he asked. I said, "I don't even know how to talk about it. It's like leaving the atmosphere and entering a space where the normal laws of gravity no longer count."

Perhaps, he mused, Joan's world was a bit like the flying trapeze, which also performed seemingly without the limitations of gravity. She and her friends traveled in a world of wealth and power, and yet her situation required its own kind of artistry.

When Henri sat down to write a thank-you letter to Joan, he wanted to offer her something more than just thanks. Thinking of Joan's generosity and social vision, Henri wrote, *Unconditional love is love without conditions, without strings attached, without prerequisites, without demands. It is giving without expecting anything in return.*

He paused and thought about this. Love offered for its own sake. Maybe that too was rather like the trapeze, a performance for its own sake. He thought about something he had said in his taped comments after meeting the Flying Rodleighs. *But when you see these trapeze artists, it becomes a symbol. What do these people do? They fly through the air and they want to do a highly skilled, safe, and entertaining act. They want to do it well and although they're terribly happy when people admire them, there is a kind of "l'art pour l'art."*

Henri carried on with his letter to Joan:

This unconditional love is the love that Jesus calls us to "love your enemies and do good to them and lend without any hope of return. You will have a great reward and you will be children of the Most High, for he himself is kind to the ungrateful and the wicked"

(Luke 6:32–35). Is this a human possibility? It sounds completely unrealistic. Isn't giving without receiving a set-up for burnout?

The answer is quite simple. No, it is not impossible to love unconditionally because we are loved unconditionally! God loved us before we were born, and God will still love us after we have died.

Henri again paused in his writing. He thought about Prospero's swing from decades of plotting revenge to embracing his enemies in mercy. And then Prospero directly engaged the audience, shedding his magical cloak and sharing his vulnerability. Henri recalled his artistic, musical friend Joan in her dazzling gold dress and smiled at the comparison. How could he help a very public, even magical figure like Joan trust enough to give and receive unconditional love?

The Flying Rodleighs had given him an image for the arc of risk and trust that is the shape of each human life, Henri reflected. Ultimately, each person belongs to God and will return to God. But flying is done together, as a troupe of human beings. He chewed his pencil and looked out the window at the cloudy winter sky. Sometimes people are ungrateful or even wicked, as he had just written to Joan. Sometimes people are careless or incompetent or afraid. Everyone makes mistakes. He thought again of Rodleigh's insistence that each member of the troupe honestly assess each performance, criticizing each other, identifying what went wrong, and affirming all that worked well. Then they wrapped themselves in their shiny performance capes to begin the next show with confidence and trust, without carrying resentment or fear. *I was fascinated by their dedication, by their discipline, by the way they worked together, by their kindness to each other, by the whole way in which they did things,* he noted at the time.

He continued his letter, trying to expand for Joan this understanding of unconditional love:

> *It is not a sentimental, all approving, and always agreeing love. It can even be a confronting love. But it is unconditional! Unconditional love, therefore, does not include approval of everything the person we love does.*
>
> *It is not always easy to believe that we can be unconditionally loved even when those who love us disagree with us or disapprove of us. But this is the love with which God loves us and wants us to love each other.*

32

During the first few months of his sabbatical, Henri went to two different circuses. The first was the "Greatest Show on Earth" in the United States.

I was so bombarded with all that was going on in front of me, that I could hardly tolerate it. Glitter, glamour, and excitement! But what to do with it all?

This afternoon I was impressed, overwhelmed, awestruck etc., but never really moved. There was one moment when I got "caught." It was when Vasili Zinoviev performed a one armed handstand on the head of his partner Pavel Karime, who keeps two freestanding stilts in balance on a platform 30 feet above the arena floor.

I could see them so well since our seats were right in front of the act. Vasili's open smile and his beautiful muscular body radiated so much vitality and joyful energy and joy that, for a moment, I felt personally connected with him and would have liked to know him and his partner. But then they vanished in the large anonymity of the show.

It was an important moment for me, short as it was. I recognized within me the same emotions that "caught" me when I first saw the Flying Rodleighs. It was the emotion that made me take the risk of introducing myself to them and that led to a long and rich friendship. Vasili and Pavel were like a flash of light in the darkness, a recognition, a memory, and an inner connection full of melancholy.

In late December, Henri and his father were visiting Freiburg together. Recalling seeing Circus Barum together five years earlier, Henri's father suggested, "There is a circus in town again. Would you like to go?" It was the Christmas Circus Festival featuring the Chinese People's circus with guest artists from Moscow and Paris.

Spectacular as it was, nothing happened to me comparable to what happened five years ago. Then I was "hooked" by the Rodleighs and felt really driven to see them again and again and enter deeply into their world. Now I saw a good show and went home without many after thoughts or after feelings. Then I saw something that opened in me a new inner place. Now I just enjoyed some unusual sights. Then I experienced a personal transformation. Now I had a few hours of good entertainment.

A FEW DAYS LATER, Henri was overjoyed to receive an unexpected phone call from Rodleigh.

"Where are you?" I said.
"We are in Zwolle," he said, "and we have been trying to reach you ever since we came to Holland. Can you come to visit us?"

I was so excited to hear from my friends. The last time I saw them was a year ago when we made the documentary which was shown on Dutch TV.

On Sunday, January 7, I was sitting with Rodleigh and his wife, Jennie, in their caravan. Soon I also saw Jon, Kail, Karlene, and Slava. It felt so good to see them all again. I realized how much I had missed being with them.

Rodleigh told me about their hard times, very complicated problems with their caravans, serious health problems, and most of all the death of Raedawn, Rodleigh's and Karlene's sister, in Italy. Listening to all of it I was amazed that the Flying Rodleighs hadn't canceled any performances and had been able to continue to work on their tricks.

Jennie had stopped working in the acts but Kerri, a sixteen-year-old from South Africa, had been trained to take her place.

The Rodleighs performed poorly. Because of the low ceiling of the hall the whole act had been toned down and the two most spectacular tricks failed. Both Slava and Rodleigh missed their catcher and ended up on the net.

Between the act of the Flying Rodleighs and "the finale," we had tea with Karlene and Jon. Since my last visit Karlene and Jon have fallen in love and become a couple. Karlene's daughter was happy to have a real family now. We had a very good and lively visit.

The reunion was a joy. After the year's absence, Henri had settled in for the short visit as if he had been living with them for the whole year, though Rodleigh noted with concern how exhausted Henri looked, and Henri admitted that his year's sabbatical was more tiring than his usual work.

Driving back to the circus after taking their visitors to the train station, Rodleigh pondered how their five-year friendship had evolved. The year since they had last been together had been painful. When Rodleigh and Karlene's sister died that year, Rodleigh especially missed Henri and wished Henri lived closer to be with him in his grief.

It's strange, thought Rodleigh, he still felt mystified by Henri's desire to write about them. The video helped, but in personal terms, there was something more than the video captured. Thinking about it, Rodleigh tried to puzzle out each element, in the same way that he methodically worked out each move of a complicated new act.

Rodleigh turned back into the fairgrounds and jumped out of the car, wondering if Henri's need for community was satisfied in their troupe because they accepted him without trying to change him. Not that trying to change him would have worked anyway, Rodleigh chuckled, remembering the muddy feet. But something about the flamboyant and marginalized world of the circus felt like home to Henri, as it did to Rodleigh. Every day the troupe dealt with crises and failures, then continued to perform. Perhaps Henri's spiritual life was similar to the daily challenges facing us in our circus life, thought Rodleigh.

Jennie had a pot of tea ready.

"Sometimes I think that Henri desperately wants to be accepted, especially by God. I'm sure it's more than just a boyhood fantasy to perform as a flyer that attracted him to our act," Rodleigh commented. "Maybe we were the ingredients he needed to clarify certain feelings. I think that he sees in us a visual representation of his spiritual feelings, something that he feels within himself."

Jennie poured two cups of tea and handed one to Rodleigh. "What do you think he sees?"

Rodleigh sipped his tea. "We always want to perform a perfect act but we often fail. Do you think that we showed Henri something about overcoming the fear of failure? In a way, he could imagine climbing the ladder with us to try again, even with everyone watching. I think that he learned to identify with us by taking risks and testing his limits."

"Also, all of us have to forget everything else and concentrate on just one thing for a short time. That's how he tried to describe his idea of prayer," Jennie remembered.

Rodleigh grinned. "So we can say that we gave Henri courage as he danced dangerously through the air!"

They gulped back the last of their hot drinks, threw on their track suits, and hurried across the fairgrounds to prepare for the second performance, still wondering why Henri had not been able to begin writing his book.

In Utrecht, Holland, later that evening, Henri completed his journal entry:

> *As I reflected on this short visit I realized how good it had been for me. I am really looking forward to being with them again in June or July—and to realize my long dream to write a book about them. I experienced a new energy to write about the Flying Rodleighs in ways that they themselves could appreciate.*

33

Henri celebrated his sixty-fourth birthday on Wednesday, January 24, with just his father. They watched the *Angels Over the Net* video about the Flying Rodleighs and Henri's father loved it. Because the heating system did not work, they huddled by the open fire, *two old men sitting close to the fireplace warming their hands.*

Henri continued his journal entry:

> *I feel happy today. Grateful to God and my family and friends for all the graces that have come to me during these 64 years. I look forward to the years to come as years to deepen my life with God and my friendship with people.*
>
> *I especially hope that I will have more space and time to write. Deep in myself I feel that something new wants to be born: a book with stories, a novel, a spiritual journal—something quite different from what I have done in the past.*

Meanwhile, Henri and his editor, Bill Barry at Doubleday in New York, had agreed that his "secret journal" from his breakdown in 1987–88 would be published in September 1996. Henri felt both curious and wary diving back into this record of the worst period of his life. How much had he grown through those terrible months? Although he had gained more perspective in the intervening years, he still felt *a certain fear about working on the manuscript. Maybe I am afraid to reenter the extremely painful experience.*

Reviewing his early journal entries from his time of therapy, he came across affirmations spoken to him by his therapists: *Trust, trust that God will give you that all-fulfilling love and will give it to you in a human way. Before you die God will offer you the deepest satisfaction you can desire. Just stop running and start trusting and receiving. You need human hands to hold you there.* That reminded him of discovering the Flying Rodleighs, and growing to understand the trust required between the human hands of flyers and catchers.

The trapeze could become a story of redemption, of resurrection, Henri reflected, but then he stopped. He didn't want to spiritualize it so quickly that the experience became disembodied.

> *The Flying Rodleighs teach me something about being in the body, being incarnate, being enfleshed. You know, the real spiritual life is an enfleshed life. So the Rodleighs are teaching me by who they are something more about what my deepest search really is all about.*

He knew his desire: to tell a true story about the body, and to affirm that story as spiritual, because the spirit is always embodied. But again he was stuck. What story about the body did he want to tell? What was the story of his own body?

As LONG AS HE could remember, Henri had longed to feel physically part of welcoming communities. Writing about the march from Selma, he had claimed that his hitchhiking friend Charles *was turning me into a Black man,* as Henri was shocked to experience a small bit of the exclusion and hatred that Charles lived with daily. The march itself was simultaneously unnerving and joyful.

> *I said to myself, "Yes, yes, I belong; these are my people. They may have differently-coloured skin, a different religion, a different way of life, but they are my brothers and sisters. They love me, and I love them. Their smiles and tears are my smiles and tears; their prayers and prophecies are my prayers and prophecies; their anguish and hope are my anguish and hope. I am one with them."*

Yet some of Henri's most terrifying experiences over the past decades had been when he had literally lost all sense of his own body's boundaries. It happened several times. After giving successful talks to thousands of people he felt himself physically dispersed and scattered. Friends remembered his desperate late-night phone calls or visits, begging them just to hold him until he felt that he was safe in his own body again.

Right from his early days in L'Arche back in 1986, when Henri lived in the Trosly community, he struggled with the very physical foundations of L'Arche relationships. At that time he was not responsible for the physical care of anyone, but the very idea of it unsettled him.

Thursday, March 20, 1986

Until now my whole life has been centered around the word: learning, teaching, reading, writing, speaking. Without the word my life is unthinkable.

L'Arche, however, is not built on words but on the body. Feeding, cleaning, touching, holding—this is what builds the community. Words are secondary. Most handicapped people have few words to speak, many do not speak at all. It is the language of the body that counts most.

"The Word became flesh." That is the center of the Christian message. Jesus confronts us with the word that can be seen, heard, and touched. The body thus becomes the way to know the word and to enter into relationship with the word.

I feel a deep resistance against this way.

When Henri arrived at Daybreak, Henri's friend Sue was amused to notice that he was uncomfortable hugging. It was like hugging a board, she teased him.

Did Henri almost envy Adam? As far as Henri could tell, Adam entrusted his body to Henri's care with no anxiety or self-consciousness.

My closeness to him and to his body was bringing me closer to myself and to my own body. My many words, spoken or written, always tempted me to go up into lofty ideas and perspectives without keeping in touch with the dailiness and beauty of ordinary life. Adam didn't allow this. It was as if he said to me, "Not only do you have a body like I do, Henri, but you are your body. Don't let your words become separated from your flesh. Your words must become and remain flesh."

In the years after Henri's emotional break and his return to Daybreak, he learned to hug. Sue noticed his tense body relaxing, first into trust, then opening out, widening into welcome and blessing.

At the National Catholic HIV/AIDS Ministry conference in the summer of 1994, Henri declared, *"Next I want to talk about the body, which is sort of a scary thing for me to talk about. The body was very much part of this conference."*

His audience laughed at the understatement. Henri continued:

What I have learned is that the body is indeed not just a metaphor, and that I've lived the body very much as a metaphor. I've been increasingly afraid to live in my body as a reality, as a real place of being.

I don't even have the full words to know what this all means but I know somewhere that I have to really discover what it means to be a body, to be in the body, to be incarnate, to be the temple of the Spirit, to be at home in myself and therefore fully intimate with God because of that, at home in my home where God dwells.

I've learned in the conference that there is not only one way, not a thousand ways, but more and more ways to be and live with the body.

When the Flying Rodleighs burst into Henri's life, Henri suddenly found artistic, wordless expression of the body-centered spirituality he had been seeking. And his whole body yearned to participate: *"When I saw the Rodleighs for the first time I said I missed my vocation—I should have become a flyer. On the other hand, my body is as unpractical and unhandy as possible—but interiorly, spiritually, I realize I always would have liked to be a flyer."*

He marveled at how completely at home the Flying Rodleighs were in their physical interactions.

And then there was the intimacy thing. I must say, being caught—the catching is a wonderful image—catching another human being who is coming flying at you—to catch him so he doesn't fall in the net. It has very much of an intimate quality—you're protecting each other from falling.

Rodleigh was making enormous somersaults in the air, then Jon catches him just at the last minute before he goes down. Then suddenly there's this sense of "Wow, he's safe." Somebody is right there at the time you need him.

And Jon, too, hangs by his legs and he's making these swings, getting ready to catch somebody who is flying up to him—he's there to catch them, and they catch each other on the wrists; they don't catch each other on the hands—they sort of slide into each other's arms, but there's a kind of warmth there, a kind of safety, kind of a being held well. And, in fact, Jon and Karlene call their acts that they do right there at the top of the circus, cradling.

So that mutuality, being in touch with each other in that kind of way really speaks to me. And it's a very profound sort of feeling.

In a letter to Bart, Henri tried to express how he saw something spiritual in the bodies of his trapeze friends:

The Flying Rodleighs express some of the deepest human desires. The desire to fly freely, and the desire to be safely caught. The act in a way is an expression of the human spirit, as it is incarnate in the athletic bodies of the trapeze artists.

As Henri became more at home in his body, he raised with several editors the possibility of writing a book that would directly explore questions of sexuality. By the next summer, he mused to a journalist, *"Every human being lives a sexual life, whether you're celibate or married or whatever. Sexual life is life. That sexual life has to be lived as a life that deepens the communion with God and with our fellow human beings. And if it doesn't, then it can be very harmful. I haven't found the right language for it yet and hope I will one day."*

Gradually, Henri began to feel a little more free, even playful. Early in 1996, he amused some of his New York editors over an elegant lunch at the Barbetta restaurant by blurting out happily, *"Don't think that I don't want to have sex with everyone in this restaurant! I have fantasies just like everyone else!"* His editors stared in astonishment, looked speculatively around the restaurant, and then they all burst out laughing together with Henri.

34

Henri's secretary phoned him in New Jersey on February 12, 1996. "You need to come back to Daybreak today, Henri. Adam is dying." Within hours, Henri boarded a plane to Toronto to say goodbye. His words poured out into his journal:

> *Living together with Adam at L'Arche Daybreak has profoundly influenced my prayer, my sense of myself, my spirituality, and my ministry. Adam, the man who suffers from severe epilepsy, and whose life has seemingly been limited because of his many disabilities, has touched the lives of hundreds of L'Arche assistants, visitors, and friends.*

Henri was delayed at Canadian immigration, but finally joined Adam's parents and other Daybreak friends around Adam's hospital bed. Longing to connect with Adam's body, *I kissed him on the forehead and stroked his hair.* Those gathered prayed with Adam, then *after that we just sat with him, following his breathing.*

Adam died peacefully that night. On February 14, 1996, Henri went to the funeral home. *Seeing Adam's body in the casket touched me deeply. He looked so peaceful, like a young man who had just fallen asleep. Tears filled my eyes. I couldn't stop looking at him.*

In his reflections at Adam's funeral, Henri identified how Adam's gentle physical presence had affected everyone who knew him. It was a true story about the body. Henri summed it up later:

> *Adam gave me a sense of belonging. He rooted me in the truth of my physical being, anchored me in my community, and gave me a deep experience of God's presence in our life together. Without having touched Adam, I don't know where I would be today. Those first fourteen months at Daybreak, washing, feeding, and just sitting with Adam, gave me the home I had been yearning for; not just a home with good people but a home in my own body, in the body of my community, in the body of the church, yes, in the body of God. I had heard and read about the life of Jesus, but I was never able to touch or see him. I was able to touch Adam. Each of us who has touched Adam has been made whole somewhere; it has been our common experience.*

A FEW WEEKS AFTER Adam's death, Henri and his friend Frank Hamilton traveled to New Mexico. *"When you go to Santa Fe, be sure to visit my friend Jim,"* Fred Rogers urged them. Jim Smith, a writer and publisher, suggested lunch at his favorite El Dorado Hotel. They enjoyed a leisurely lunch *speaking about our personal histories, spirituality, books, and, of course, Santa Fe.* Delighted with their new acquaintance, Henri and Frank invited him for dinner a few nights later.

It became a quite remarkable evening. After dinner I showed him the video "Angels over the Net" about the Flying Rodleighs, and told him that I always wanted to write a book about them but hadn't found the right form.

Jim responded quite radically: "You must write the book because you have given it so much of your energy and attention. You have to trust your intuition that your friendship with these trapeze artists allows you to say something very important about the meaning of life."

I said: "Yes indeed, that intuition is deep and strong, but I am afraid. When I first saw the Rodleighs, something very deep and intimate within me was touched. They brought back in a very vivid way the longings I had as a seventeen-year old boy for communion, community, and intimacy.

"Much of the longings went underground during my time at the seminary and the university and my many years of teaching. They only manifested themselves in occasional mental wanderings, curiosities, and feelings of anguish. When I went to L'Arche I allowed all these feelings and emotions and passions to reemerge.

"But seeing the Rodleighs catapulted me in a new consciousness. There in the air I saw the artistic realization of my deepest yearnings. It was so intense that even today I do not dare to write about it because it requires a radical new step not only in my writing but also in my life."

Jim said: "I knew all this. The video showed it to me. The Rodleighs are completing something within you that for many years remained uncompleted. It has to do with your sexuality, your search for community, and your deep yearning for completeness. When you do not write the book you will deny yourself an enormous opportunity for growth."

Jim's directness and his challenge amazed Henri. "But what is the book finally about?" he asked.

Jim answered: "About community in the most universal sense. It is the longing of all people that you can express through the Rodleighs' story. It is not just about flying and catching, but about that invisible community that undergirds all that you are seeing in the Rodleighs. You see friendship, family, cooperation, artistic expression, love and commitment, and much more. And that's your final subject."

35

In May 1996, Henri returned to Santa Fe to spend a week writing with Jim's mentorship.

> What I most hope is to learn how to write a good story that engages the reader to the very end. I realize that Jesus told stories and that most spiritual masters told stories. I am busy writing about Adam and plan to write about the Flying Rodleighs. I know what I want said, but I do not know how to say it.

Henri arrived in Santa Fe on May 19, 1996, in time for another lunch together.

> Although I had come to Santa Fe to ask for Jim's help in my writing, our first conversation was focused on what to do with your life between 60 and 80!
>
> For me this is an increasing important and anxiety-provoking question. Over the years I have built up a certain reputation. People

think of me as a Catholic priest, spiritual writer, member of a community with mentally handicapped people, a lover of God, and a lover of people. It is wonderful to have such a reputation.

But lately I have been experiencing it more and more as restricting, because I feel a certain pressure within me to keep living up to that reputation and to do, say, and write things that fit the expectations of those who know me. The Catholic Church, L'Arche, my family, my friends, my readers etc. all have an agenda they want me to follow.

But since I am in my sixties, new thoughts, feelings, emotions, and passions have arisen within me that are not all in line with my previous thoughts, feelings, emotions, and passions.

What is my responsibility to the world around me and what is my responsibility to myself? What does it mean to be faithful to my vocation? Does it require to be consistent with my earlier way of living and thinking or does it ask for the courage to move in new directions even when that will disappoint many?

I am more and more aware that Jesus died when he was in his early thirties. I have already lived more than thirty years longer than Jesus. How would Jesus have lived and thought when he had lived that long? I don't know.

But for me new questions and concerns emerge at my present age that weren't there in the past. They refer to all the levels of life: intimacy, community, prayer, friendship, work, church, God, life, and death.

How can I be free enough not to be afraid of these questions, and to let them emerge whatever the consequences? It feels quite frightening.

IN THE MIDDLE OF the week, Joan Kroc's plane picked up Henri for lunch in San Diego. They had both been reading biographies of artists: Joan was reading about the poet Gerard Manley Hopkins, and Henri had just finished reading an account of painter Georgia O'Keeffe's life. Joan warmly thanked Henri for the boxes of O'Keeffe art cards that he brought her.

> *The more I read about O'Keeffe and look at her paintings, I feel a deep affinity to her. Her struggles in relationships and her struggle to develop her own artform—going back and forth between New York and New Mexico—reveal a person with great needs for love, affection, and personal support but also for independence, freedom, solitude, and space for creativity. Her intense search for intimacy and solitude are part of the art she created.*

After lunch, Joan treated them both to dishes of ice cream. *Driving home, Joan balanced her ice cream cup on the steering wheel with the result that we were zigzagging on the road. I kept shouting, "Be careful—you nearly hit that curve—look out—oh you got real close to that car—" She said, "Oh how funny, you are scared."* But she conceded that they could pull off the road to eat their ice cream.

Henri returned to his writing in New Mexico. He pondered his conversations with Jim about his fears, questions, and longings as he looked ahead in his life. At the end of the week, he carefully gathered up piles of notes and his manuscript, slipping the thick files into his worn leather briefcase. He had been inspired by stimulating time with artistic personalities. He had even drafted most of a book. But it was a book about his friend Adam. He still had written nothing more about the Flying Rodleighs.

36

The hydraulic lift moves, a whirring sound with a slight whine. Henri finds the sound curiously soothing. He is glad that Dennie is with him. He prefers not to travel alone.

·····•

EARLY IN JULY, HENRI jumped off the train in Oberursel, Germany, and looked around eagerly for Rodleigh. They greeted each other with a big hug and hurried back to the circus.

July 9, 1996

I hadn't expected that I would be so moved seeing the Rodleighs again. But I found myself crying as I saw them flying and catching under the circus cupola.

As I watched them in the air I felt some of the same profound emotions that I felt when I saw them for the first time with my father in 1991. It is the emotion hard to describe but it is the emotion coming from the experience of an enfleshed spirituality. Body and spirit are fully united. The body in its beauty and elegance expresses the spirit of love, friendship, family, and community and the spirit never leaves the here and now of the body.

Rodleigh watched Henri. "I wish that I could put Henri into my body to experience the exhilaration of flight to the catcher and our celebration when we return safely," he lamented to Jennie. He really wanted Henri to have the experience of rising, the momentum of leaving the fly bar and going upward, rising into the trick, then being caught by the catcher swinging up from underneath. There was no way Henri's body could do anything like that, but even a limited experience would be better than nothing, Rodleigh figured. The next day, he suggested to Jon that at least they could give Henri a hint of their experience, and so Henri once more tried the trapeze, this time with a catcher.

At the end of the practice session Rodleigh asked me if I would like to make a swing or two. First he helped me to get into the net and showed me how to climb the long ladder to the pedestal. It was my second time since getting to know the Rodleighs that I stood on the pedestal. It is an intimidating place to be. The space below above and around me felt enormously large and awesome. Kerri and Slava put the safety belt around me, held me tight, and handed me the bar. As I held the bar I wondered if I would be able to hold my own weight, but as they lifted me off I felt at ease swinging above the net a few times. I tried to kick a little to get higher but simply didn't have much breath left, so Rodleigh said "hop" and let me drop myself into the net. I repeated the whole sequence once more, with a tiny bit more grace.

Then Rodleigh wanted me to have a sense of the catcher's grip. So

I climbed the ladder at the catcher's side and Jon, who was hanging head down on the catch bar, grabbed me by the wrists and held me hanging there for a while. I looked up at his upside-down face and could imagine how it would be to swing while held by him. Altogether I was happy with the experience. It got me as close as I will ever come to being a trapeze artist!

After the afternoon show Rodleigh invited me to join him in the truck as he put new bandages on the trapeze bar. I didn't know how much care is needed to do this. Practically every week new gauze has to be tightly wrapped around the bar, so that it doesn't move when the flyer grabs it and very even so that it does not cause blisters on the flyers' hands.

Jennie has made a video of the practice session and of the afternoon show. Seeing myself hanging on the trapeze bar made me feel silly. It was a pathetic sight.

But seeing the whole afternoon act in slow motion was a great treat. More than anything else, a slow-motion presentation of the complicated tricks makes you appreciate the highly skillful art of the Rodleighs.

During the evening show I realized how anxious I am when I watch the Rodleighs at work. The more I know about their act, the harder it is to watch it. Knowing the Rodleighs so well and being aware of how much can go wrong, I look at them as a mother who sees her children doing dangerous things. I felt great relief when everything came to a good end. The large audience was ecstatic, stamping their feet and clapping their hands with wild enthusiasm.

At the end of Henri's visit, Rodleigh and Jennie drove him to the Frankfurt rail station. *It was a warm and heartfelt good-bye. I realize how much our friendship has grown over the years and how much we have come to enjoy each other's presence. The two days in Oberursel were very life giving for me and I realize how being with the Rodleighs is one of the best ways for me to really "be away from it all" and to experience relaxation and restoration.*

37

Dennie sighs as he looks down at the parking lot. He is not surprised to see that a small crowd has assembled, attracted by the well-equipped emergency trucks, intrigued by the sight of someone flying out the window. The day is cloudy, a little cool. Probably even more people will be watching from the hotel windows. He can't blame them. It is an unusual sight. It is hard to protect a patient's privacy: you really can't keep a window rescue hidden. Henri's eyes are closed. Dennie hopes that Henri won't feel too exposed when he becomes aware of the spectators.

"I can see our ambulance driver and the other firefighters waiting on the ground for us," Dennie says to Henri. Then he adds somewhat apologetically, "So much unusual activity has drawn an audience. I am afraid it is a bit of a circus."

Henri seems to smile slightly, but he does not answer.

•••••

A FEW DAYS AFTER seeing the Flying Rodleighs, Henri pulled out the final journals he had acquired for his sabbatical, their hard covers featuring art from New York's Metropolitan Museum of Art. These last two journals were identical, with glowing golden covers showing details of the four-thousand-year-old Egyptian sarcophagus of Khnumnakht. Henri studied a journal cover with its painted door between the lands of the living and the dead. Large, pensive eyes painted above the doorway looked from the land of eternity to the land of the living, greeting him each day as he continued his record of his sabbatical year. They reminded him of something he had written in 1992: *I know now that I have to speak from eternity into time, from lasting joy into the passing realities of our short existence in this world. One could call it the "prophetic vision": looking at people and this world through the eyes of God.*

THE RELAXED DAYS WITH Rodleigh and the troupe had been a welcome respite. The spring and summer of 1996 were stressful.

His mind often returned to the questions raised in his conversations with Jim Smith in Santa Fe about how to live the next decades of his life. For years, some friends had urged him to come out as a gay man and be a role model. Aware that his sexual orientation could be revealed without his consent, Henri was often uneasy. By July, he was writing about his *unresolvable struggle* to a friend: *My sexuality will remain a great source of suffering to me until I die. I don't think there is any "solution." The pain is truly "mine" and I have to own it. Any "relational solution" will be a disaster. I feel deeply called by God to live my vows well even when it means a lot of pain. But I trust that the pain will be fruitful.*

On July 31, 1996, Henri sat down and opened his journal. He had confided in his friend Nathan Ball. *I finally felt ready to talk with Nathan about the anxiety that had been plaguing me during the last few months. I felt somewhat embarrassed and ashamed to put my inner burden on my best friend, but I am very glad I did. Nathan felt it hard not so much to listen to my pain but to realize that I had walked with it so long without sharing it with him.*

As he read what he had written, he automatically began to gnaw on his fingernails, then stared at them, surprised to find they were already so well chewed. *I often wonder how I would survive emotionally without his faithful friendship,* he added.

THE NEXT WEEKS OF Henri's sabbatical were full, but the trapeze book was never far from his mind. *Trapeze was my secret door,* he had written earlier that spring to Jim Smith. *But I felt I could not be able to walk through it alone. The trapeze is the place to walk together.* Jim read that several times before writing back. Calling the trapeze a door to walk through together should have been a confusing metaphor, but he liked it. It was an invitation.

38

In August, Joan Kroc invited Henri to visit her in California for the weekend to continue their conversations about the spiritual life. Her jet would again pick him up.

She welcomed me warmly and took me right away to a restaurant. Four of Joan's friends from New York were waiting. Knowing Henri's interest in art, Joan had invited the art consultant who had helped build her art collection. *A very kind and gentle man. But now he is the victim of Alzheimer's disease and needs constant nursing care. A young man who has been his nurse for the past eight months was with him at the table. During the lunch, he was remarkably alert and we were able to have a good conversation.*

Henri enjoyed discussing art, religion, and spirituality over lunch. He and Joan carried on around Lake Hodges, stopping for a drink at a little Mexican restaurant. When they returned to Joan's, Henri settled happily into an afternoon nap before the two of them went out for dinner at Mille Fleurs restaurant.

Over dinner, we talked quite seriously about abortion and the right to life issues. I told her much about Adam. Without Adam, my own life and the lives of many others would not have been so richly blessed.

The next morning, Joan drove Henri in her Jaguar convertible to pick up breakfast: croissants with ham from Burger King. *"This is a special treat. I know I am a naughty girl,"* the heir to the McDonald's fortune told Henri.

Sitting on Joan's terrace, I explained to Joan God's desire to come always closer to us. God is the God-for-us, who protects us, the God-with-us who shares our human struggles, and the God-within-us who dwells in our heart. Three ways of God relating to us in faithfulness.

God does not want to be feared. God wants to be loved. God wants to be as close to us as we are to ourselves, closer even. Joan listened with great attention and we had a very good conversation, quite personal, quite honest, quite sincere.

By lunchtime, Joan decided Henri needed to play.

"Let's go to the races in Del Mar," Joan said. *"I have my own box there and we can have a nice lunch while doing a little betting. After your lesson in spirituality, I will give you a lesson in decadence!"*

It was quite an experience! We sat in a box, which was a lovely lounge with betting machines and a large balcony overlooking the racetrack with a TV to give you close-ups of the races. Joan gave me a voucher for fifty dollars to play with. Soon I wanted to win! I quickly experienced the power of gambling. "Maybe next time I will make a fortune, maybe next time, maybe next time."

Finally, Joan suggested it was time to go. *When we left, I had lost more than won. Joan said, "Why don't you cash your voucher, so you have the feeling you won something?" I cashed the voucher and got thirty-two dollars.*

When we got home again, we celebrated the liturgy in the living room. Joan said, "Why don't we ask Angela, our cook, to join us?" It was Saturday afternoon, but Henri would spend most of Sunday flying back to New Jersey, so he used the Bible readings for the Sunday Mass. "Let the peoples praise you, O God; let all the peoples praise you," they said together at the Psalm.

Joan watched Henri raise his large hands as he had thousands of times in the priestly gesture that he loved so much, lifting the body of Christ in the consecrated bread.

Later, over dinner, Joan had something on her mind. "Henri," she said, then paused. Usually it was Henri who had new insights into God. "You know what you were saying about God, for us, with us, within us? Have you ever thought that when you say Mass and lift the bread and say 'the Body of Christ,' it is like the trapeze act you're always talking about? It's as if Jesus flies to you, and you are the catcher."

Henri stared at Joan, then at his hands, astonished. He had never thought of this. He had written often about his aging hands, about how he stretched out his hands to bless people. But now he imagined that his hands reached for God who is already in motion, catching and holding the body of Jesus in that moment of consecration. Cradling. For almost forty years, he had been catching God.

Joan grinned at his wide eyes. "You know how you are always telling me to trust, trust, trust? Maybe God also has to trust. To trust you. To trust all of us."

She poured Henri another glass of the 1973 Rothschild wine she had opened to drink together. Henri sipped it, savoring both the velvety wine and this new insight.

Joan pressed forward. "Remember that letter you sent to me last year? I remember almost every word. You wrote, *'strange as it may sound, we can become like God for others. It becomes possible to love without demanding love in return. It is a strong, energetic, vital, and very active love.'* The love you described is disciplined, even athletic, like a trapeze artist."

She and Henri had often shared about how hard they found it to believe in God's unconditional love and to trust themselves. "That love sends us out to serve joyously, like you keep saying," Joan added. "If God trusts us, then we can trust ourselves."

39

Lying on the stretcher, Henri concentrates on breathing slowly, the way Dennie had taught him. In, two, three, and out, two, three. In, two, three, and out, two, three.

In, two, three, and out, two, three.

> *Life is a precarious balance. Sometimes I'm out of balance and then writing helps me find it again. I just want to write down the things that occupy my mind so in the end I know more about my own struggle.*

Out of balance. Earlier in the spring, he had confessed in his journal, *I feel quite anxious interiorly. I feel quite powerless in the face of these free-floating emotions of love, hate, rejection, attraction, gratitude, and regret. I realize that I am walking around with some deep, covered-up emotions and that not much is needed to bring that to the surface and throw me off balance.*

Henri takes another breath, then lets it out with a sigh. Off balance indeed. Maybe those disturbing covered-up emotions reveal that his life has been one off-balance failure after another. He tries poking at some of his familiar insecurities, like prodding a sore tooth to see if it still hurts.

What about the book he keeps promising the Rodleighs? They are skilled, magnificent artists. They are bound to be disappointed in whatever he writes.

He tries another question, testing to see how tender it feels: Has his entire life been a pointless story of drifting from place to place like a hungry ghost? Does it look as pathetic as his efforts on the trapeze? He could imagine his life that way. It is like seeing himself in the video, hanging limply before falling.

But strapped onto his stretcher now, his long-running fears are getting no traction. In fact, they seem almost comical. Henri remembers how his embarrassment over the sight of himself haplessly clutching the trapeze quickly turned to amusement in the presence of his cheerful friends. They had chuckled watching the video, and when Henri complained that the video showed that he had two left feet and only thumbs on his hands, their affectionate laughter increased.

In their amusement was unconditional acceptance. As they chortled, Henri could not help laughing, too, joining in the mirth even at his own expense. Rodleigh and Jennie and the others did not judge his effort as sad. They loved offering him that trapeze experience, and they were proud of him for eagerly grasping the opportunity.

Also, he thinks, the sorry sight of his skinny body dangling from the trapeze was the view from the outside. His inner experience was dynamic! He did it. He climbed the swinging rope ladder. With the support of the troupe members, he reached out for the fly bar and launched off the pedestal. Even Rodleigh had been impressed by his eager fearlessness. Hanging for a few moments holding the catcher's hands, looking at Jon's upside-down smiling face was thrilling. Even letting go entirely and dropping into the bouncy net was a joyful experience because it was shared with friends.

No, pathetic would have been refusing that overwhelming physical desire to go to Selma, and missing the experience of offering a ride to Charles, then walking, singing, eating, and sleeping with fear and joy in that extraordinary community. Or staying in his mainly White enclave of people rather than going to be with Martin Luther King Jr.'s people at his funeral. Pathetic would have been staying at Harvard, getting more miserable and lonely by the day. It would have been pathetic to reject the invitation to join the Daybreak community, or to shy away from surprising friendships with Bill, Adam, and so many others. Or to give in to his fear of rejection and not return to Daybreak after his emotional break. Or be too afraid to go to the National Catholic HIV/AIDS Ministry conferences.

And truly pathetic would have been to stay seated in the bleachers at the circus, aching to meet the artists but immobilized by his own self-consciousness.

Instead, he followed his heart, his inner call, even when it meant giving up security, reaching out over and over for something not yet within his grasp.

Of course he has often felt off-balance, he realizes. A flyer needs to lose their balance entirely, reaching out from the platform for the trapeze and committing their body to the forward movement before the trapeze is fully in their grasp. Losing balance is the only way to do it.

It's been a life of trust. And it's not over yet. He can't wait to tell Rodleigh that he flew out a window.

Even with all the monitors on his chest, he feels less anxious than he has in a long time, full of compassion for his fearful, vulnerable self, fumbling to choose a generous life with courage. Many times in his life he has fallen, often not very gracefully.

Just months ago, he had encouraged Joan Kroc: *When we radically claim God's unconditional love for us, we can forgive those who have wounded us and set them free by our forgiveness.* From his aerial act on his stretcher, Henri thinks of the Flying Rodleighs' frank discussion after each performance of their successes and failures together. He sends out a small prayer of contrition and goodwill, forgiving everyone, forgiving himself.

Living means there will be falls. It's life, all of life. How often has he told other people that?

I sometimes have thought, how would it be if I had no desire anymore to judge anyone? I would walk on the earth as a very light person.

Henri glimpses what it would be like also to stop judging himself, to see even his own life *through the eyes of God.* Trapeze artists can't perform by themselves. *A trick is not complete unless it is done from the board, successfully caught by the catcher, and then successfully returned to pedestal board.* Flyers need to trust their catcher not just to safely gather them in, he remembers, but to relaunch them into further flying.

The Rodleighs are saying to me indirectly, don't be afraid to fly a little, don't be afraid to take a few doubles or triples or a few layouts. If you really miss the catcher you fall into the net, so what's the big issue? After all, take a risk and trust, trust, trust. That's how it ap-

plies to my life. You know life is full of new possibilities, full of new adventures, and I just want to keep trying out what life is all about.

He feels lighter and lighter.

THE LIFT REACHES THE bottom with a jolt.

Dennie's voice: "We are here. You don't have to do anything. There are eight firemen to move you into the ambulance!"

Henri opens his eyes, momentarily confused, surprised to find he has fully descended.

He feels like he has been rising.

EPILOGUE

As the three flyers swung away from the pedestal board, they somersaulted and turned freely in the air, only to be safely grasped by their two catchers. I somehow caught a glimpse of the mystery of being the Beloved: the mystery in which complete freedom and complete bonding are one and in which letting go of everything and being connected with everything no longer elude each other.

Henri didn't die. At least, not then. Within minutes, he arrived safely at the hospital.

Henri's father came with his brothers and sister to be with him. Across an ocean, Henri's Daybreak community gathered to pray for him, and put his friend Nathan on an overnight flight to arrive Tuesday morning.

Henri said to Nathan, "I don't think I'm going to die, but if I do please tell everyone that I am grateful. I am so very grateful."

By Thursday morning, the danger had passed and Henri made plans to come home. There was minimal heart damage. At Daybreak, we relaxed and started to joke, "When God closes a door, God opens a window."

On Friday, Henri prayed evening prayer with his friends Jan and Nathan, then walked with them to the front doors of the hospital and waved them off.

Early in the morning of Saturday, September 21, still in the hospital, Henri had a massive heart attack and died.

Henri's family came immediately. After praying beside Henri, his father announced that Henri should be buried with the L'Arche community that he had chosen. All his family would accompany his body to Canada after a funeral in Utrecht.

News of Henri's death reached the Flying Rodleighs after their last show that evening. They had expected to see him after his trip to Russia. They sat for a long time quietly remembering their friend, and the next morning their grief weighed down their practice. But at their afternoon show, after they bounded into the ring swirling their sparkling capes, Rodleigh made a short speech dedicating that performance to the memory of their friend Henri, and they performed flawlessly in his honor. During their final bow, Rodleigh looked at the seat where Henri had last sat watching them, wishing the person sitting there was Henri.

At the funeral in the Netherlands four days later, Rodleigh and Jennie again had the experience of being welcomed like old friends by people they had never met. They already knew Henri's family, and Rodleigh was moved when Henri's brother Laurent insisted that Rodleigh replace him as a pallbearer. "Once again I'm supporting Henri's weight in my hands, but this time not on the other end of a safety harness," thought Rodleigh. He and Jennie sat weeping through the funeral service, and Rodleigh fought back his urge to leap up to tell the assembled mourners their experience of a different Henri: relaxed, curious, a little flamboyant, attentive, hilarious, and fun.

Thus there were two funerals: the one in Utrecht that Rodleigh and Jennie Stevens attended, and then another in Canada that gathered more than a thousand people.

Henri's body flew across the ocean in a beautiful classic coffin of natural honey oak. By the time Henri's body arrived in Canada, there were also two caskets. Years earlier, Henri had told the L'Arche Daybreak woodworking program that he wanted us to make him a casket when he died. During the long week as we waited for Henri's return with his family, I invited community members to draw and paint their feelings. Artwork flooded in, full of life and color, and I used it to create a colorful hand-painted lid. Painted in a radiant rainbow, our work of collaborative art looked like a door. At the funeral home near Daybreak, we moved Henri's body into our homemade rectangular pine casket. His brother Laurent and I gently tugged off his necktie to mark that he had finished traveling, and brought him home to Daybreak.

But he wasn't entirely finished with his travels. Henri's body was buried twice. He had wanted to be buried with other members of his Daybreak community, but fourteen years after Henri was buried in a small Roman Catholic cemetery it became apparent that there would be no space available near him for other Daybreak community members.

His friend Bill Van Buren died in 2009 and was buried at St. John's Anglican cemetery, just north of L'Arche Daybreak. Founded in the mid-1800s, this simple historic cemetery had space for many Daybreak members.

So in 2010, at the request of his brother Laurent, Henri's body made one more journey. A specialized backhoe carefully scooped up all that remained of his body, lifting it through the air then settling it into yet another casket.

Henri's body is buried next to Bill's. Gradually, nearly a dozen other members of the L'Arche Daybreak community have joined them. Even in death, their bodies continue to tell a spiritual story, of the mystery of letting go of everything and being connected with everything.

I suddenly realized that's what life is all about. We are invited to make a lot of triples and jumps but the great thing is to trust the catcher and to know we will be caught when we come down from our special tricks. Do I dare to let go and to say that will happen even when I am a little scared sometimes? I'm grateful that we could be together—let's pray for one another that what we do in the coming years will be full of courage, full of confidence, and full of trust.

ACKNOWLEDGMENTS

Henri was fascinated by the Flying Rodleighs' commitment to each other. Trapeze is not an individual art. Each artist has to expect the best of each other, be swift to forgive, have confidence in themselves, and give each other full support to try again. Every performance is new. This spoke to Henri of the artistry of community. It also speaks to the experience of writing a book! Neither Henri nor I ever wrote a book as an individual endeavor. Writing may be solitary, but creating a book is a communal project.

First, of course, my thanks to Henri Nouwen himself, who was a dear friend to me and my family as well as my fellow member of L'Arche Daybreak. It's been twenty-five years since his sudden death, and his energy and spirit live on.

Enormous thanks to my beloved spouse, Geoff Whitney-Brown, without whom this book would have been less nuanced and the process of writing it much less fun. We spent weeks together in the Nouwen Archives at the University of St. Michael's College's Special Collections in Toronto, where Simon Rogers and Liesl Joson were helpful and patient with our barrage of questions and requests.

Huge thanks to Rodleigh Stevens for letting me use his many vivid memories of Henri during those five years when their lives intersected. I eagerly look forward to Rodleigh's memoir of his own remarkable life.

In those early stages, I confided in my friend Ruth Rakoff that Henri's life was stranger than fiction. Ruth pointed out that key to the story is Henri's relationship with his own body, as well as his attraction to many different communities that are often overlooked or marginalized. Frame the story with Henri looking back during his last and most dramatic flight, out the Hilversum window, she suggested. Thank you, Ruth, for giving this book a shape.

How can a patient in the midst of a heart attack be taken out a window? My thanks to Dennie Wulterkens, emergency medical rescue specialist in the Netherlands. Because of Dennie's careful explanations, all details of Henri's Hilversum rescue are portrayed as accurately as possible, based on the norms and protocols of 1996.

Some gratitude spans many years: my tender thanks and love to Laurent Nouwen and his family for their hospitality, ongoing encouragement, and decades of friendship. My affectionate thanks also to Franz and Reny Johna, and to Robert Jonas.

My special appreciation and respect to Henri's close friends who generously offered their encouragement, wisdom, and good-humored insights, especially Patricia Beall Gavigan and Bart Gavigan, Frank Hamilton, Michael Harank, Peter and Anke Naus, Kathy Bruner, Carl McMillan, and Ron P. van den Bosch. Particular thanks to Robert Morgan for permission to quote his speech at Henri's sixtieth birthday.

I am blessed to have friends and family who read various drafts along the way: David Walsh, Celia McLean, Margaret Ford, Monica

Whitney-Brown, Zachary Brabazon, Jordan Lambeth, Barbara Whitney, Jim Loney, Flavia Silano, Janine Langan, Joanne Hincks, Mary Lou Halferty, Stephanie and Joe Mancini, Jean Crowder, Michael Hryniuk, Janet Burlacu, David Whitney-Brown, Diane Marshall, Jamie Bennett, Spencer Dunn, and Maggie Enwright.

My heartfelt thanks to all who responded generously to my sudden calls for help or advice, including Kathryn Dean, Diana Cafazzo, Kerry Wilkins, Vicentiu Burlacu, Rachel Anderson, Dave and Maureen Carter-Whitney, Joe and Donna Abbey-Colborne, Jonathan Heyman, Mike Blair, Victoria MacKay, Jean Chong, Robert Ellsberg, Michael Higgins, Ian Gwynne-Robson, Joe Mihevc, Rosalee Bender, and all the fabulous staff at Munro's Books in Victoria, BC.

Through the years of writing this book, I have appreciated and benefited from my colleagues at the Centre for Studies in Religion and Society at University of Victoria, British Columbia, and at St. Jerome's University, Waterloo, Ontario.

Like a trapeze performance, a book flies out into the world because of a huge unseen community and team. I thank Sue Mosteller and everyone at the Henri Nouwen Legacy Trust for initiating this project and giving me freedom with Henri's trapeze material, trusting I would "catch" it. Warm thanks especially to Karen Pascal, Gabrielle Earnshaw, Judith Leckie, Sally Keefe Cohen, Stephen Lazarus, and Sean Mulrooney. Thanks also to the Canadian Writers Union, and to Warren Sheffer, the most kindhearted and clear-eyed contract lawyer that any writer could want.

Katy Hamilton at HarperOne has been a supportive and enthusiastic editor from the first time she read my manuscript. Chantal Tom and Mickey Maudlin carried the project forward with friendly competence and commitment. My gratitude also to publisher Judith Curr, and to this book's production, publicity, and marketing experts—in other words, everyone on the great team at HarperOne who helped launch this book into flight.

Finally, I want to acknowledge you, our readers. In many ways, Henri's story is about finding the freedom of flying, falling, and catching with others. Whether in L'Arche or Selma or at Martin Luther King Jr.'s funeral or with people gathered by the AIDS pandemic or in friendship with traveling trapeze artists, Henri's story reveals why it is energizing and spiritually renewing to carry our burdens in companionship and solidarity.

Every time Henri talked about the Flying Rodleighs, his eyes would shine and his face would break into a beaming smile. Just remembering filled his whole body with joy. He was eager to share this experience, hoping it would bring readers to a place of *total absorption, total delight.* We live in times when it is easy to feel discouraged or alone, times when it is more important than ever to reach out to connect with others. May Henri's unlikely story help you to find joy, freedom, and beauty in each of your irreplaceable, imperfect communities.

NOTES

Epigraph

vii **"When I saw the Flying Rodleighs":** Henri Nouwen, interview in English in the unedited footage for the film *Angels Over the Net*, produced by Jan van den Bosch (Hilversum: The Company Media Produkties, 1995). A DVD copy of this unedited footage is held in the Nouwen Archives.

vii **"The ten minutes that followed":** Henri J. M. Nouwen, "Chapter I," 9–10. This unpublished draft typed manuscript is held in the Nouwen Archives.

Prologue

1 **When they received the phone call:** Rodleigh Stevens's accounts of hearing about Henri's death, dedicating their performance to Henri, and attending Henri's funeral are found in his unpublished memoir, "What a Friend We Had in Henri," 1. This memoir is held in the Nouwen Archives.

2 **one speaker described Henri as "anguished" and "wounded":** Many biographies also highlight this side of Henri, with titles like *Wounded Prophet* (Michael Ford), *Genius Born of Anguish* (Michael Higgins and Kevin Burns), and *Lonely Mystic* (Michael Ford).

2 **Henri believed his most important book:** Henri's friends Bart and Patricia Gavigan recall a conversation with Henri: "He wanted the circus story to make the cross-over to a secular audience in a way he had never before attempted. He felt it was the most important thing he would ever

write." Bart Gavigan and Patricia Gavigan, "Collision and Paradox," in *Befriending Life: Encounters with Henri Nouwen*, ed. Beth Porter (New York: Doubleday, 2001), 55–56. This conversation with the Gavigans is included in Chapter 14 of this book.

3 **I lived at L'Arche Daybreak . . . where Henri was also a community member:** See www.larche.org: "L'Arche is a worldwide federation of people, with and without intellectual disabilities, working together for a world where all belong. In L'Arche, each person participates, helps and receives help. L'Arche is founded on mutual relationships." Henri spent 1985–86 in a L'Arche community in France, then in 1986 he moved to L'Arche Daybreak in Richmond Hill, Ontario, Canada.

3 **I wrote an introduction to a new edition:** See "Introduction," Memorial Edition of Henri Nouwen's *The Road to Daybreak* (London: DLT, 1997), reprinted in 2013 edition; "Introduction," *A Spirituality of Homecoming*, Henri J. M. Nouwen (Nashville: Upper Room Books, 2012); "How Not to Comfort a New Orleans Hurricane Survivor," in *Turning the Wheel: Henri Nouwen and Our Search for God*, ed. Jonathan Bengtson and Gabrielle Earnshaw (Ottawa: Novalis, 2007), 135–44; "Henri at Daybreak: Celebration and Hard Work," in *Remembering Henri: The Life and Legacy of Henri Nouwen*, ed. Gerald S. Twomey and Claude Pomerleau (Maryknoll, NY: Orbis Books, 2006), 119–37; "Safe in God's Heart," *Sojourners Magazine* 25, no. 6 (November–December 1996); "Lives Lived—Henri J. M. Nouwen," *Globe and Mail*, October 2, 1996.

4 **My main artistic license:** There is some justification for this fictional framing. In his 1990 book *Beyond the Mirror*, Henri claimed he was able to reflect and think even while he was in a painful medical emergency. See Henri J. M. Nouwen, *Beyond the Mirror: Reflections on Death and Life* (New York: Crossroad, 1990), 23–24, 39. He wrote in his 1993 "Circus Diary–Part I" that in times of crisis life can go into a slow-motion experience of heightened awareness, and *"Some people even say they saw their whole life pass by in a second"*—see his Saturday, May 10, entry in Nouwen, "Circus Diary–Part I: Finding the Trapeze Artist in the Priest," *New Oxford Review* 60, no. 5 (June 1993), quoted in Chapter 17. Further, the droperidol and fentanyl medications that Henri was likely given at Hotel Lapershoek by paramedics would have reduced his pain and anxiety, and could have also made him feel chatty or even garrulous. But with an oxygen mask covering his mouth, he

would have been unable to share his thoughts, so I present Henri chatting internally within himself.

5 **"I wasn't thinking of using the Rodleighs as illustrations":** Sunday, May 17, 1992, entry in "Circus Diary–Part II: Finding a New Way to Get a Glimpse of God," *New Oxford Review* 60, no. 6 (July–August 1993): 10.

Chapter 1

9 **Two paramedics in crisp white uniforms:** Specific details about the paramedics' actions are based upon extensive consultation with Dutch ambulance nurse and emergency medical rescue specialist Dennie Wulterkens.

9 Henri's arrival in Hilversum and call for medical help are described in Michael Ford, *Wounded Prophet: A Portrait of Henri J. M. Nouwen* (New York: Doubleday, 1999), 201; Michael Ford, *Lonely Mystic: A New Portrait of Henri J. M. Nouwen* (New York: Paulist Press, 2018), 143–46. See also Michael O'Laughlin, *Henri Nouwen: His Life and Vision* (Maryknoll, NY: Orbis Books, 2005), 162; and Jurjen Beumer, *Henri Nouwen: A Restless Seeking for God* (New York: Crossroad, 1997), 173.

11 **First he had tried dictating a tape:** Henri dictated his first impressions onto a cassette tape that was subsequently transcribed by Connie Ellis, his secretary back in Canada, and titled "The Flying Rodleighs–The Circus." This unpublished typed transcript is held in the Nouwen Archives.

11 **"What really got to me":** Nouwen, "The Flying Rodleighs–The Circus," 1–3, 4.

Chapter 2

15 **"Develop the story scene by scene":** Theodore A. Rees Cheney, *Writing Creative Non-Fiction: How to Use Fiction Techniques to Make Your Nonfiction More Interesting, Dramatic, and Vivid* (Berkeley, CA: Ten Speed Press, 1991), 33. Henri's own copies of his books about writing are still in the library of the house where he lived at L'Arche Daybreak, with his underlining and marginal notes.

15 **"Visiting the south German city of Freiburg has always been a great pleasure":** Henri J. M. Nouwen, "Chapter I," 1–3. This begins a second attempt by Henri to write about his initial encounters with the Flying Rodleighs, which he simply titled "Chapter I" and "Chapter II." Both

"Chapter I" (as noted above) and "Chapter II" are unpublished typed manuscripts held in the Nouwen Archives. All further quotations from Nouwen in this chapter are from Nouwen's unpublished manuscript, "Chapter I," unless otherwise identified.

16 **"to help myself and others to overcome the deep-seated temptation of self-rejection":** This was a theme in many of Henri's books. He was especially aware of the unique dangers of self-rejection for gay and lesbian people, writing a chapter titled "The Self-Availability of the Homosexual," in *Is Gay Good? Ethics, Theology, and Homosexuality*, ed. W. Dwight Oberholtzer (Philadelphia: Westminster Press, 1971). See Michael Ford's exploration of that essay in *Lonely Mystic*.

16 **"Nonfiction writers limit themselves":** Cheney, *Writing Creative Nonfiction*, 127.

16 **"However, this time in Freiburg was going to become unique":** Nouwen, "Chapter I," 4, 6–9.

17 **"A scene reproduces the motion of life; life is motion":** Henri underlined this passage in Cheney, *Writing Creative Nonfiction*, 49.

20 **"The Flying Rodleighs were stunning":** Henri calls the women's performance costumes "swimsuits" in his dictated text. "The Flying Rodleighs—The Circus," 5.

20 **Henri had always been attracted to men:** See Ford, *Wounded Prophet*, 73, and Ford, *Lonely Mystic*, 56. Henri was cautious in choosing with whom to speak about his sexual orientation. While many readers intuited that he was gay, he never came out. He did not write about his sexuality in any text considered for publication, but he discussed with his publishers the possibility of addressing it in future writings. See Ford, *Wounded Prophet*, 66–67, 141–44, 191–94; Gabrielle Earnshaw, *Love, Henri: Letters on the Spiritual Life* (New York: Convergent, 2016), xiv–xv; Ford, *Lonely Mystic*, 56–72.

Chapter 3

24 **Just nine months ago in Prague he wrote in his journal:** Saturday, January 20, 1996, entry in Henri J. M. Nouwen, original handwritten 1995–96 sabbatical journals, held in the Nouwen Archives. See also Henri J. M. Nouwen, *Sabbatical Journey: The Diary of His Final Year* (New York: Crossroad, 1998), 91.

25 **Even back in his university days, Henri's friends saw him as a social climber:** See Carolyn Whitney-Brown, "Lives Lived: Henri J. M. Nouwen," *Globe and Mail*, October 2, 1996. See also Peter Naus, "A Man of Creative Contradictions," *Befriending Life*, 80–81.

25 **All his life, Henri had wanted a different body:** For a sensitive literary discussion of the complexities of "growing up" as a queer child and adolescent, see Kathryn Bond Stockton, *The Queer Child, or Growing Sideways in the Twentieth Century* (Durham, NC: Duke University Press, 2009). Stockton was one of Henri's students in the 1980s at Yale Divinity School. Interestingly, she names her first experience of kissing a woman as "self-defenestration." *Making Out, Avidly Reads* series (New York: New York University Press, 2019), 15–17.

25 **His mother blamed the strict instructions:** See Ford, *Wounded Prophet*, 72–73. Henri also wrote about Holland's hungry winter of 1944–45 when many people were starving, describing his deep grief as a child when the Nouwen family's hungry gardener stole Walter, Henri's beloved pet goat, to feed his family. Henri J. M. Nouwen, *Here and Now: Living in the Spirit* (New York: Crossroads, 1994), 48–49.

26 **Henri is seized with a desire to tell Dennie more about himself:** Michael Ford writes about Nouwen's "tendency to strike up conversations of great intimacy with strangers" (*Wounded Prophet*, 144; see also 213).

26 **An interviewer in 1995 asked Henri:** Nouwen, interview in English in the unedited footage for the film *Angels Over the Net*.

Chapter 4

27 All Nouwen quotations in this chapter are from Nouwen's unpublished manuscript, "Chapter I," unless otherwise identified.

27 **no one had ever told him that grief felt so much like fear:** This is the first sentence of C. S. Lewis's *A Grief Observed* (first published in 1961). While Henri likely had an earlier edition of Lewis's book, the copy in his library at Daybreak is a 1989 edition. C. S. Lewis, *A Grief Observed* (San Francisco: Harper & Row, 1989), 3.

29 **Karlene was uneasy when the circus owner:** This account draws on Stevens, "What a Friend We Had in Henri," 2.

Chapter 5

32 All Nouwen quotations in this chapter are from Nouwen's unpublished manuscript, "Chapter I," unless otherwise identified.

32 **He has used Ativan for more than seven years:** Henri's use of Ativan and his discussion about it with his doctor, as well as the quotations, come from the unpublished "Thursday March 21, '96" entry in Nouwen, handwritten 1995–96 sabbatical journals.

33 **Writing about shared human experiences:** See Henri J. M. Nouwen, *Our Greatest Gift: A Meditation on Dying and Caring* (New York: HarperCollins, 1994), 4–5.

34 **Rodleigh sighed as he headed backstage:** All details from Rodleigh Stevens's perspective are drawn from Stevens, "What a Friend We Had in Henri," 2–3.

Chapter 6

41 **When Henri had a serious accident in 1988:** Nouwen, *Beyond the Mirror*.

41 **"Everything has changed":** Nouwen, *Beyond the Mirror*, 31.

42 **"as if some strong hand had stopped me":** Nouwen, *Beyond the Mirror*, 31.

42 **"Notwithstanding the severe pain, I had a completely unexpected sense of security":** Nouwen, *Beyond the Mirror*, 39.

42 **"A long time of solitude in a Trappist monastery interrupting a busy life of teaching":** Nouwen, *Beyond the Mirror*, 15–16.

42 **After all:** The Dutch are famously stereotyped as being meticulous and organized. See Henri's description of himself in Nouwen, *Beyond the Mirror*: "Knowing my very impatient disposition and aware of my need to stay in control . . ." (39).

42 **march in Selma that interrupted his studies:** See Chapter 10 notes; Nouwen, "We Shall Overcome: A Pilgrimage to Selma, 1965," in *The Road to Peace: Writings on Peace and Justice*, ed. John Dear (Maryknoll, NY: Orbis Books, 1998), 75–95.

43 **The actual painting is enormous:** For a description of the painting and the chair that Henri was given to view it, see Henri J. M. Nouwen, *The Return of the Prodigal Son: A Meditation on Fathers, Brothers, and Sons* (New York: Doubleday, 1992), 7–10.

44 **"I am here to write, not to go to the circus!":** Nouwen, "Chapter I," 25.

44 **"The next morning while sitting at my desk, I kept looking at my watch":** Nouwen, "Chapter II," 1. The following Nouwen quotations and details in this chapter are from Nouwen's unpublished manuscript, "Chapter II," unless otherwise identified.

45 **Rodleigh was eager to work on his new routine that morning:** Stevens, "What a Friend We Had in Henri," 4.

Chapter 7

50 **"Is this trapeze act perhaps one of the windows in the house of life":** Nouwen, "Chapter II," 8–10. All Nouwen quotations in this chapter are from Nouwen's unpublished manuscript, "Chapter II," unless otherwise identified.

51 **The practice ended:** The account in the rest of this chapter except for Henri's words draws on Stevens, "What a Friend We Had in Henri," 4–6.

Chapter 8

54 **"At the very end, they let themselves fall into the net":** Nouwen, "The Flying Rodleighs–The Circus," 29.

55 **"On one channel a rock concert with Tina Turner":** Unpublished March 6, 1986, entry in Nouwen, 1985–86 journals. These unpublished typed transcripts are held in the Nouwen Archives. Henri simplifies the Tina Turner concert to just Turner and David Bowie, but video footage available on YouTube of Tina Turner's 1985 Birmingham performance shows Bryan Adams singing "It's Only Love" with Turner, then Turner and Bowie sing "Tonight" together.

Chapter 9

58 **"For the next few days, I kept going to the circus as often as possible":** Nouwen, "Chapter II," 14–16. All Nouwen quotations in this chapter are from Nouwen's unpublished manuscript, "Chapter II," unless otherwise identified.

59 **Henri wanted to stay backstage:** Stevens, "What a Friend We Had in Henri," 5–6.

Chapter 10

64 **"Sunday was the last day of the Circus Barum in Freiburg"**: Nouwen, "Chapter II," 21–27.

Chapter 11

68 **"It all began with a feeling of restlessness"**: This account of Henri's journey to Selma, participation in the march, and return home to Topeka draws on Nouwen, "We Shall Overcome," 75–95. All Nouwen quotations and details in this chapter are from "We Shall Overcome" unless otherwise identified.

71 **"Resistance that makes for peace"** and **"Individual people, even the best and strongest"**: Henri J. M. Nouwen, *Peacework: Prayer, Resistance, Community* (Maryknoll, NY: Orbis Books, 2005), 97.

71 **that Martin Luther King Jr. was killed:** This account of Henri's participation in Martin Luther King Jr.'s funeral draws on Henri J. M. Nouwen, "Were You There? The Death of Dr. Martin Luther King Jr., 1968," in *The Road to Peace,* ed. John Dear, 96–105. The following Nouwen quotations and details in this chapter about King's funeral are from "Were You There?" unless otherwise identified.

73 **"You know in this world where there is so much division"**: Nouwen, interview in English in the unedited footage for the film *Angels Over the Net.*

Chapter 12

74 **But just five years earlier:** This account of Henri's move to Daybreak in the autumn of 1986 draws on Sue Mosteller, "Funeral Eulogy for Henri Nouwen," in *Seeds of Hope: A Henri Nouwen Reader*, ed. Robert Durback (New York: Image Books, 1997), 17–18, and Ford, *Wounded Prophet*, 157–58. See also Mary Bastedo, "Henri and Daybreak: A Story of Mutual Transformation," in *Befriending Life*, 27–29.

75 **Longtime community member Sue Mosteller had welcomed:** It is impossible to overstate the importance of Sue Mosteller in Henri Nouwen's life from this point on. See Gabrielle Earnshaw, *Henri Nouwen and the Return of the Prodigal Son: The Making of a Spiritual Classic* (Orleans, MA: Paraclete Press, 2020), 67.

75 **His physical experiences of solidarity:** Henri's journal of his time in

Latin America was published as *Gracias! A Latin American Journal* (Maryknoll, NY: Orbis Books, 1983).

76 **"I was told that L'Arche's mission was to 'live with' core members"**: Henri J. M. Nouwen, *Adam, God's Beloved* (Maryknoll, NY: Orbis Books, 1997), 41.

76 **"I live in a house with six handicapped people and four assistants"**: Henri J. M. Nouwen, "Adam's Story: The Peace That Is Not of This World," in Durback, ed., *Seeds of Hope*, 254–55, which was originally a talk given at Harvard St. Paul's Catholic Church, Cambridge, February 10, 1987.

77 **During the past few months I have developed:** Henri J. M. Nouwen, "L'Arche and the World," in *The Road to Peace*, ed. John Dear, 166–67.

78 **"Adam is the weakest person of our family"**: Nouwen, "Adam's Story," 255–56.

79 **"I was aghast"**: Nouwen, *Adam*, 42.

79 **"It takes me about an hour and a half to wake Adam up"**: Nouwen, "Adam's Story," 256.

80 **"I had to get behind him and support him with my body"**: Nouwen, *Adam*, 43, 46.

Chapter 13

82 **"When I think about Circus Barum and Daybreak"**: Wednesday, May 6, diary entry in Nouwen, "Circus Diary–Part I," 9.

83 **why, Henri wonders:** For Henri's account of his breakdown see *Adam*, 78–80, and Henri J. M. Nouwen, *The Inner Voice of Love: A Journey Through Anguish to Freedom* (New York: Doubleday, 1996), xiii–xvii. See also Ford, *Wounded Prophet*, 168–71.

83 **moving from an "issue-oriented life" to a "person-oriented life"**: Henri asserted that this movement was accomplished by joining L'Arche; see Nouwen, "L'Arche and the World," 168.

83 **"I began to realize that the gentle safety of the New House"**: The following quotations are from Nouwen, *Adam*, 78–80, unless otherwise identified.

86 **"When you find yourself curious about the lives of people"**: "22 Feb '88" entry in Henri J. M Nouwen, handwritten 1987–88 journal. The

journal is held in the Nouwen Archives. Selections from this journal were later published in Nouwen, *The Inner Voice of Love*.

86 **"A new spirituality is being born in you":** "22 Feb '88" entry in Nouwen, handwritten 1987–88 journal.

86 **He now lived in the community retreat house:** Carolyn Whitney-Brown's memories of Henri's home in the L'Arche Daybreak community.

Chapter 14

87 **As Rodleigh drove away from Freiburg:** Stevens, "What a Friend We Had in Henri," 6–7.

88 **"After Circus Barum had left Freiburg and I had returned to To-ronto":** Nouwen, "Circus Diary—Part I," 8. All further quotations from Nouwen are from "Circus Diary—Part I" unless otherwise identified.

88 **"That was wonderful!" were Henri's delighted first words:** Stevens, "What a Friend We Had in Henri," 7–11.

90 **Back in Canada soon afterward:** This account of Henri's conversation with the Gavigans comes from "Collision and Paradox," *Befriending Life*, 55–56, augmented with their further memories in December 2020.

Chapter 15

95 **"Karlene was making these tapes with her camera":** Nouwen, "The Flying Rodleighs—The Circus," 8–10, 14–15.

97 **In the months after Henri returned:** See Whitney-Brown, "Henri at Daybreak," 122–25.

98 **In January, L'Arche Daybreak threw him:** A video made by the community of Henri's sixtieth birthday party at Daybreak is held in the Nouwen Archives. My account of the party comes from this video and from personal memories.

Chapter 16

101 **"What is the risk?" was a key question:** These quotations are selected from Henri's unpublished handwritten notes during the Gavigan workshop, held in the Nouwen Archives.

Chapter 17

104 **"Back in Toronto, when I spoke about my experience":** Nouwen, "Circus Diary—Part I," 9. All Nouwen quotations in this chapter are from "Circus Diary—Part I" unless otherwise identified. I have made some minor adjustments in Henri's technical description following advice given to me by Rodleigh Stevens.

104 **Rodleigh and the troupe were delighted:** This account of Henri's travels and visit with the Flying Rodleighs in May 1992 draws on Stevens, "What a Friend We Had in Henri," 12–14.

Chapter 18

112 All Nouwen quotations in this chapter are from "Circus Diary—Part I" unless otherwise identified.

113 **After three days, Henri looked like he had been with them for years:** This account of Henri's interactions with the troupe draws on Stevens, "What a Friend We Had in Henri," 14–16.

114 **"What you say is incredibly important for life, not just for the trapeze":** Nouwen, interview in English in the unedited footage for the film *Angels Over the Net*. This quotation is also included in the final English version of the film *Angels Over the Net*.

Chapter 19

117 All Nouwen quotations in this chapter are from "Circus Diary—Part I" unless otherwise identified.

118 **Rodleigh and the troupe knew that their trip would be slower with Henri:** Stevens, "What a Friend We Had in Henri," 16.

122 **"The trip on the German roads from Datteln to Kamen last night":** This and the following Nouwen quotations are from "Circus Diary—Part II."

123 **Jennie glanced at Rodleigh and rolled her eyes:** Based on Stevens, "What a Friend We Had in Henri," 16.

Chapter 20

127 **"The longer I am here, the more I find to write about"**: All Nouwen quotations in this chapter are from "Circus Diary—Part II" unless otherwise identified.

129 **"Faced with the search for structure, sit back and sift, shuffle and stack"**: Cheney, *Writing Creative Nonfiction*, 140. Henri drew a line alongside this paragraph.

131 **Rodleigh stayed to do the rigging while Jennie took Henri to the railway station:** Stevens, "What a Friend We Had in Henri," 16–17.

Chapter 21

132 **"I sense that Franz still has some problems with my enthusiasm for the circus"**: All Nouwen quotations in this chapter are from "Circus Diary—Part II" unless otherwise identified.

133 **The apartment on the third floor:** Henri wrote several books during various stays with Franz and Reny, including *Our Greatest Gift*.

136 **"Listen to everyone"**: Henri underlined this passage in Cheney, *Writing Creative Nonfiction*, 127.

137 **After affectionate farewells in the early morning:** Stevens, "What a Friend We Had in Henri," 18.

Chapter 22

139 **"how individualistic and elitist my own spirituality had been"** . . . **"a spirituality for introspective persons"**: Quotations from Henri Nouwen, "Foreword," in Gustavo Gutierrez, *We Drink from Our Own Wells: The Spiritual Journey of a People* (Maryknoll, NY: Orbis Books, 1984), xvi.

140 **"I've seen very clearly that all together form one body, as a whole"**: Interview with Jan van den Bosch, in film *Henri Nouwen: The Passion of a Wounded Healer*, Christian Catalyst Collection, EO Television, available on Amazon Prime (as of January 2021).

140 **Less than two weeks after Henri lurched away in his camper van:** This account of Henri's letter to Rodleigh in June 1992 draws on Stevens, "What a Friend We Had in Henri," 19.

140 **he wrote to John Dear:** Dear, *The Road to Peace*, xxiv.

140 **At the end of November, Henri again wrote to Rodleigh:** Stevens, "What a Friend We Had in Henri," 19.

141 **He could easily imagine using three movements:** This draft outline is in Henri's 1992 unpublished notebook held in the Nouwen Archives. All quotations in this chapter from the outline come from this notebook.

142 **"I don't want to write just another book":** Nouwen, interview in English in the unedited footage for the film *Angels Over the Net*. A condensed version of this quotation is also in the final English version of the film.

143 **"Why should I write about a trapeze act?":** Nouwen, "Circus Diary—Part II," 8.

Chapter 23

144 **The painting illustrated a story Jesus had told:** Jesus's parable of the Prodigal Son is found in the New Testament of the Bible, Luke 15:11–32.

145 **So he meditated on Rembrandt's painting:** Nouwen, *The Return of the Prodigal Son*, 3–15, 19.

145 **In England, his friend Bart Gavigan urged Henry to see himself also in the older son:** Nouwen, *The Return of the Prodigal Son*, 18.

146 **As he began to find some peace in his own body:** Nouwen, *The Return of the Prodigal Son*, 19–20.

146 **When the book was done, he tried a few titles:** These unfortunate titles for Henri's Prodigal Son book are found in his handwriting on the title page of Draft 4 of his manuscript, held in the Nouwen Archives. Gabrielle Earnshaw in *Henri Nouwen and the Return of the Prodigal Son* provides many more details about the writing of Henri's most famous book.

147 **"They were trying to do something new":** Nouwen, "The Flying Rodleighs—The Circus," 8–9.

Chapter 24

149 **"When I saw the Flying Rodleighs for the first time":** Nouwen, "Letter to Bart Gavigan, December 2, 1994," held in the Nouwen Archives.

150 **"To me it's very fascinating that this art":** Nouwen, interview with Jan van den Bosch, in his film *Henri Nouwen: The Passion of a Wounded Healer*.

150 **Henri's friend Frank Hamilton read Henri's 1992 journal:** This

account of Frank Hamilton offering to join Henri in his June 1993 visit to the Flying Rodleighs draws on "Interview with Frank Hamilton," Henri Nouwen Oral History Project, interview by Sue Mosteller, November 1, 2005, transcript page 35. The audio interview and transcript are held in the Nouwen Archives.

151 **Ron sipped his coffee and took his time answering:** Personal email from Ron P. van den Bosch, November 2020.

151 **"I came to know the trapeze life from within":** Nouwen, interview in English in the unedited footage for the film *Angels Over the Net*. Everything in the quotation except the first sentence is also in the final English version of the film.

152 **Henri arrived with Frank in June 1993:** Stevens, "What a Friend We Had in Henri," 19–22.

152 **"What do you think?" Henri asked his friends earnestly:** Adapted from "Interview with Frank Hamilton" by Sue Mosteller, Henri Nouwen Oral History Project, November 1, 2005.

153 **Jennie's lunch the next day:** Stevens, "What a Friend We Had in Henri," 22.

153 **One afternoon, Henri urged Ron to take a photo:** Stevens, "What a Friend We Had in Henri," 22.

Chapter 25

155 **The highlight of the 1993 visit was on June 6:** Nouwen, unpublished handwritten notes in "June 6th '93" entry in his notebook "Flying Rodleighs Technical Description of the Trapeze Act Circus Barum 1992," Nouwen Archives.

156 **Rodleigh enjoyed seeing Henri on the platform:** Stevens, "What a Friend We Had in Henri," 22.

158 **"I really like them, Henri":** Adapted from "Interview with Frank Hamilton," by Sue Mosteller.

158 **"The act is like a Russian icon":** The direct quotations in italics in this scene of brainstorming about Henri's book come from Henri's unpublished handwritten entries titled "Notes by Frank" in a notebook started in 1992 and still being used in 1993, titled on the front cover "Circus Barum, Diary, Notes." This notebook is held in the Nouwen Archives. Henri's notes sometimes identify Ron or Frank as the speaker. Frank Hamilton has confirmed

that my reconstruction of their conversation from Henri's notes accurately depicts what he remembers. In his initial comment, Frank may have been referring to Henri's book about icons, *Behold the Beauty of the Lord: Praying with Icons* (South Bend, IN: Ave Maria Press, 1987).

Chapter 26

160 **Rodleigh did not see Henri again until a brief visit in November 1993:** Stevens, "What a Friend We Had in Henri," 24–25.

160 **When Henri sent him a copy of *Our Greatest Gift*:** Stevens, "What a Friend We Had in Henri," 27.

160 **It was not that he had no religious background:** Henri's unpublished transcript "Interviews with Karlene Stevens and Rodleigh Stevens, November 1991," held in the Nouwen Archives.

161 **"One day, I was sitting with Rodleigh, the leader of the troupe, in his caravan, talking about flying":** Nouwen, *Our Greatest Gift*, 67.

Chapter 27

163 **"I love these trapeze artists a lot!":** On May 3, 1994, at the Dialogue '94: A Call to Partnership conference in Milwaukee, Wisconsin, Henri received the COMISS Medallion (Coalition On Ministry In Specialized Setting), presented to a person who has made an outstanding contribution internationally to the field of pastoral care, counseling, and education. The presentation and his lively talk can be viewed on YouTube: www.youtube .com/watch?v=9hHB0Ph6eKc.

165 **By 1994, AIDS had become the leading cause of death:** For a sense of how the AIDS pandemic grew, see https://www.hiv.gov/hiv-basics /overview/history/hiv-and-aids-timeline. Henri had been grieving the loss of friends, connecting with and supporting people in the AIDS networks since the beginning of the pandemic. See Henri J. M. Nouwen, *Love, Henri: Letters on the Spiritual Life*, ed. Gabrielle Earnshaw (New York: Convergent Books, 2016), 112–13.

165 **"I am really very grateful for being here this whole week":** All quotations of Henri from his talk at the 1994 conference come from the audio recording Henri Nouwen, "As I Have Done So You Are Called to Do," July 26, 1994, at the 1994 Seventh National Catholic HIV/AIDS Min-

istry Conference in Chicago. This audio recording is held in the Nouwen Archives. An abbreviated written version was published as Henri Nouwen, "Our Story, Our Wisdom," in *The Road to Peace*, ed. Dear, 175–83.

Chapter 28

170 **All his life, his father has liked:** Henri often spoke of his father's particular appreciation for intelligent people, books, and analysis.

171 **"One of the parts of the act that deeply moves me":** Nouwen, letter to Bart Gavigan, December 2, 1994.

172 **By the summer of 1994, Henri decided:** This account of preparing for and making the *Angels Over the Net* film draws on Stevens, "What a Friend We Had in Henri," 28–33.

172 **"The Flying Rodleighs are a trapeze group":** Nouwen, letter to Bart Gavigan, December 2, 1994.

172 **Henri's friend Jan interviewed him for the film:** All quotations of Jan van den Bosch and Henri come from the interview in English in the unedited footage for the film *Angels Over the Net*. About a quarter of the quotation here is also included in the final English version of the film.

174 **"We all want to make triples and doubles and layouts and double doubles":** Nouwen, interview in English in the unedited footage for the film *Angels Over the Net*. This quotation is included in the final English version of the film.

174 **"Now I live and work with people with mental handicaps":** Nouwen, interview in English in the unedited footage for the film *Angels Over the Net*. Everything quoted here is also found in the final English version of the film. For clarity, I have put what Henri says about the Rodleighs after what he says about his L'Arche community.

Chapter 29

177 **His friends Sue Mosteller and Kathy Bruner came with him:** Sue Mosteller told me about how anxious Henri was about this second conference. The interpretive dance at the 1995 AIDS conference and Henri's response were described to me by Henri's and my friend Kathy Bruner.

178 **This time Henri boldly titled his talk "Befriending Death":** Henri Nouwen, "Befriending Death," Eighth National Catholic HIV/AIDS Min-

istry Conference, July 1995, in Chicago. A written version of the talk was published by the National Catholic AIDS Network. An audio recording and a copy of the published text of the talk are held in the Nouwen Archives. All further quotations in this chapter are from Nouwen, "Befriending Death," unless otherwise identified.

180 **"When I met the Rodleighs and I saw their work":** Nouwen, unedited footage for the film *Angels Over the Net*. This quotation is included in the final English version of the film.

Chapter 30

183 **After admiring the cover's bright detail:** As Henri began his sabbatical, he was especially delighted with his beautiful hardcover journals. I remember him holding up the bright covers for us to admire at the beginning of his 1995–96 sabbatical.

183 **"Oakville, Ontario, Saturday, September 2, 1995":** "Saturday September 2, 1995" entry in Nouwen, handwritten 1995–96 sabbatical journals. A condensed version of this passage is also in Nouwen, *Sabbatical Journey*, 3.

184 **"I have written many essays, reflections, and meditations":** "Friday September 8, 1995" entry in Nouwen, handwritten 1995–96 sabbatical journals. This passage is also in Nouwen, *Sabbatical Journey*, 10–11.

184 **in early December, while staying with friends in Massachusetts:** "Sunday December 3, 1995" entry in Nouwen, handwritten 1995–96 sabbatical journals.

Chapter 31

186 **A snowstorm was closing in:** "Dec 14–17, 1995" entries in Nouwen, handwritten 1995–96 sabbatical journals. Parts are edited and included in Nouwen, *Sabbatical Journey*, 65–69.

187 **Joan was a gifted musician:** Someone who spent time with Henri and Joan told me that together they were "like peas in a pod." For more information about Joan Kroc's wide-ranging interests, including her career as a pianist, see Lisa Napoli's *Ray & Joan: The Man Who Made the McDonald's Fortune and the Woman Who Gave It All Away* (New York: Dutton Penguin Random House, 2016). Joan's comments about and to children in 1998 can be seen

here: https://www.youtube.com/watch?v=VgLbicSvJxY. In the mid-1980s, Joan established the Kroc Institute for International Peace Studies at the University of Notre Dame (see https://kroc.nd.edu/), and in 2000 began the Joan B. Kroc School of Peace Studies at the University of San Diego (see https://www.sandiego.edu/peace/). For an overview of her contributions to her community and the world, see the 2004 video made when Joan B. Kroc was inducted into the San Diego Women's Hall of Fame: https://www.youtube.com/watch?v=qgA0AMimHBI.

187 **"My experience is that rich people are also poor, but in other ways":** Henri J. M. Nouwen, *Spirituality of Fundraising* (Nashville: Upper Room Books, 2011), 18.

189 **"Unconditional love is love without conditions, without strings attached":** "A Reflection on Unconditional Love for Joan Kroc," in Nouwen, *Love, Henri*, 332.

189 **"But when you see these trapeze artists, it becomes a symbol":** Nouwen, "The Flying Rodleighs—The Circus," 26.

189 **"This unconditional love is the love that Jesus calls us to 'love your enemies'":** Nouwen, *Love, Henri*, 332–33.

190 **"I was fascinated by their dedication, by their discipline":** Nouwen, "The Flying Rodleighs—The Circus," 26.

191 **"It is not a sentimental, all approving, and always agreeing love":** Nouwen, *Love, Henri*, 334.

Chapter 32

192 **"I was so bombarded":** "Friday October 20, 1995" entry in Nouwen, handwritten 1995–96 sabbatical journals. An edited condensed version of this passage is also in Nouwen, *Sabbatical Journey*, 40–41.

193 **"Spectacular as it was, nothing":** "Thursday December 28, 1995" entry in Nouwen, handwritten 1995–96 sabbatical journals. A rephrased version of this passage is also in Nouwen, *Sabbatical Journey*, 74–75.

193 **A few days later, Henri was overjoyed:** "Sunday January 7, 1996" entry in Nouwen, handwritten 1995–96 sabbatical journals. An edited version of this passage is also in Nouwen, *Sabbatical Journey*, 82–83.

194 **Rodleigh noted with concern how exhausted Henri looked:** This

account of Rodleigh reflecting on their friendship with Henri draws on Stevens, "What a Friend We Had in Henri," 37, 41–42.

196 **"As I reflected on this short visit"**: "Sunday January 7, 1996" entry in Nouwen, handwritten 1995–96 sabbatical journals. An edited version of this passage is also in Nouwen, *Sabbatical Journey*, 83.

Chapter 33

197 **Because the heating system did not work, they huddled by the open fire:** "Wednesday January 24, 1996" entry in Nouwen, handwritten 1995–96 sabbatical journals. This passage is also in Nouwen, *Sabbatical Journey*, 94.

198 **his "secret journal":** Passages from his 1987–88 breakdown are quoted from his original handwritten 1987–88 journals. These are held in the Nouwen Archives. Many passages from these journals were edited and included in *The Inner Voice of Love*.

198 **"a certain fear about working on the manuscript":** "Friday January 26, 1996" entry in Nouwen, handwritten 1995–96 sabbatical journals. This passage is also in Nouwen, *Sabbatical Journey*, 94.

198 **"Trust, trust that God will give you that all-fulfilling love":** "Sunday Jan 17" entry in Nouwen, handwritten 1987–88 journals.

198 **"The Flying Rodleighs teach me something about being in the body":** Nouwen, interview in the unedited footage for the film *Angels Over the Net*.

199 **his hitchhiking friend Charles:** Nouwen, "We Shall Overcome," 77.

199 **"I said to myself, 'Yes, yes, I belong; these are my people'":** Nouwen, *Our Greatest Gift*, 25.

199 **Friends remembered his desperate late-night phone calls or visits:** See the accounts by Parker Palmer and Yushi Nomura quoted in Ford, *Wounded Prophet*, 37–38.

200 **"Until now my whole life has been centered around the word":** "Thursday March 20, 1986" journal entry published in Henri J. M. Nouwen, "To Meet the Body Is to Meet the Word," *New Oxford Review* 54, no. 3 (April 1987): 3–4. This quotation was not included in Henri's 1985–86 journal selections published as Nouwen, *The Road to Daybreak*.

200 **"My closeness to him and to his body":** Nouwen, *Adam*, 49.

201 **"Next I want to talk about the body"**: Nouwen, "As I Have Done So You Are Called to Do."

201 **"When I saw the Rodleighs for the first time I said I missed my vocation"**: Nouwen, interview in English in the unedited footage for the film *Angels Over the Net*. This quotation is included in the final English version of the film.

202 **"And then there was the intimacy thing"**: Nouwen, "The Flying Rodleighs—The Circus," 27–28.

202 **"The Flying Rodleighs express"**: Nouwen, letter to Bart Gavigan, December 2, 1994.

203 **"Every human being lives a sexual life"**: Ford, *Lonely Mystic*, 58.

203 **Early in 1996, he amused some of his New York editors**: As recounted by one of the editors who was present.

Chapter 34

204 **Henri's secretary phoned him in New Jersey:** "Monday February 12, 1996" entry in Nouwen, handwritten 1995–96 sabbatical journals.

204 **"Living together with Adam at L'Arche Daybreak"**: "Wednesday February 12, 1996" entry in Nouwen, handwritten 1995–96 sabbatical journals. These passages are also in Nouwen, *Sabbatical Journey*, 103.

205 **"Seeing Adam's body in the casket touched me deeply"**: "Monday February 14, 1996" entry in Nouwen, handwritten 1995–96 sabbatical journals. A version of this passage is also in Nouwen, *Sabbatical Journey*, 107.

205 **"Adam gave me a sense of belonging"**: Nouwen, *Adam*, 126–27.

206 **"It became a quite remarkable evening"**: "March 6, 1996" entry in Nouwen, handwritten 1995–96 sabbatical journals. An edited version of this passage is in Nouwen, *Sabbatical Journey*, 121–22.

Chapter 35

208 **"What I most hope is to learn"**: "Friday May 17, 1996" entry in Nouwen, handwritten 1995–96 sabbatical journals. This passage is also in Nouwen, *Sabbatical Journey*, 167.

208 **"Although I had come to Santa Fe"**: "Sunday May 19, 1996" entry in

Nouwen, handwritten 1995–96 sabbatical journals. An edited version of this passage is also in Nouwen, *Sabbatical Journey*, 168.

210 **In the middle of the week, Joan Kroc's plane:** Henri's lunch with Joan is recorded on "Wednesday May 22, 1996," while his reflections on O'Keeffe are from his "Monday May 20, 1996" entry in Nouwen, handwritten 1995–96 sabbatical journals.

Chapter 36

211 **He prefers not to travel alone:** Henri writes about this in *Here and Now*, 85–86.

211 **"I hadn't expected that I would be so moved":** "Tuesday July 9, 1996" entry in Nouwen, handwritten 1995–96 sabbatical journals. This passage is also in Nouwen, *Sabbatical Journey*, 194–95.

212 **Rodleigh watched Henri:** Stevens, "What a Friend We Had in Henri," 39. The catcher who held Henri on that day was John Vokes, who had replaced Joe. To avoid adding another new name to the story, I have called that catcher by the name of the other catcher, Henri's friend Jon Griggs, who was still with the troupe.

212 **"At the end of the practice session":** "Wednesday July 10, 1996" entry in Nouwen, handwritten 1995–96 sabbatical journals. A slightly edited version of this passage is also in Nouwen, *Sabbatical Journey*, 195–96.

213 **"It was a warm and heartfelt good-bye":** "Thursday July 11, 1996" entry in Nouwen, handwritten 1995–96 sabbatical journals.

Chapter 37

215 **Henri pulled out the final journals he had acquired for his sabbatical:** Henri's journals from his sabbatical year are held in the Nouwen Archives; the cover art is identified by the publishers of the blank journals in printed notes inside the back cover. Online, the Metropolitan Museum of Art describes the images on the front of Henri's last two journals: "On the left side of the coffin box there is an architectural facade with a small doorway in the center at the bottom. This is the equivalent of the Old Kingdom false door, which allowed the spirit of the deceased to move between the land of the dead and the land of the living. In this case, it is painted to

resemble two wooden door leaves secured with two door bolts. Above the door are two eyes that look forth into the land of the living." See "Coffin of Khnumnakht," the Met, https://www.metmuseum.org/art/collection /search/544326.

216 **"I know now that I have to speak from eternity into time":** Nouwen, *The Return of the Prodigal Son*, 15.

216 **some friends had urged him to come out as a gay man:** See *The Essential Henri Nouwen*, ed. Robert A. Jonas (Boulder, CO: Shambhala Publications, 2009), xxviii–xl, and Ford, *Wounded Prophet*, 193–94.

216 **Aware that his sexual orientation could be revealed without his consent, Henri was often uneasy:** This was told to me by Henri's friends.

216 **"unresolvable struggle" and "My sexuality will remain":** From July 1996 letters, quoted by his archivist Gabrielle Earnshaw in *Love, Henri*, xv.

216 **"about the anxiety that had been plaguing me":** "Saturday May 4, 1996" in Nouwen, handwritten 1995–96 sabbatical journals—slightly rephrased in *Sabbatical Journey*, 207.

217 **he automatically began to gnaw on his fingernails:** The Gavigans write, "he himself was spectacularly ill at ease in his body. You had only to watch the way he walked or glance at those bitten-to-the-quick fingernails to recognize the inner battle"; in "Collision and Paradox," *Befriending Life*, 55.

217 **"I often wonder how I would survive emotionally":** "Wednesday July 31, 1996" entry in Nouwen, handwritten 1995–96 sabbatical journals.

217 **"Trapeze was my secret door":** These two sentences about the trapeze are written by Henri and quoted in Jim Smith's unpublished March 25, 1996, letter to Henri Nouwen. Smith's letter is held in the Nouwen Archives, and used with permission from Jim Smith. Smith's letter highlights and repeats these two sentences as part of his response to Henri.

Chapter 38

218 **"She welcomed me warmly and took me right away to a restaurant":** "Fri August 16, 1996" entry in Nouwen, handwritten 1995–96 sabbatical journals.

219 **"Let's go to the races in Del Mar," Joan said:** "Sat August 17, 1996" entry in Nouwen, handwritten 1995–96 sabbatical journals. An abbreviated version is also in Nouwen, *Sabbatical Journey*, 214–15.

220 **For almost forty years, he had been catching God:** Nouwen was ordained a Catholic priest for the Archdiocese of Utrecht on July 21, 1957.

220 **She poured Henri another glass of the 1973 Rothschild wine:** In his handwritten journal, Henri describes their meal: *At 7pm Joan and I had a very nice Mexican dinner with Enchiladas and Rice—with a bottle of Red Wine such as I have never tasted before. Rothschild 1973! Joan said: "It goes down like velvet, don't you think? Ray bought it twenty years ago. It says you have to drink it before the year 2000."* "Sat August 17, 1996" entry in Nouwen, handwritten 1995–96 sabbatical journals. I have invented the conversation over dinner in which Joan suggests to Henri that he is a catcher of God. I owe this insight to Geoffrey Whitney-Brown.

221 **" 'strange as it may sound, we can become like God for others' ":** Nouwen, *Love, Henri*, 333. After the August 1996 weekend with Joan, Henri wrote, "It feels that Joan and I are more relaxed with one another and are indeed becoming friends. A friendship that allows us to speak openly and directly about our real concerns. The great luxury surrounding me seemed less distracting. I felt like our time together had been fruitful and spiritually valuable." "18 August, 1996" entry in Nouwen, handwritten 1995–96 sabbatical journals. Seven years later, as Joan Kroc was dying of cancer, "there was little else she could do but thumb through the leather-bound Bible given her by the late Father Henri Nouwen": Napoli, *Ray & Joan*, 12.

221 **"That love sends us out to serve joyously":** In a letter for her granddaughter Amanda's twenty-first birthday, Joan wrote, "I want you to believe that a life of service is a happy one to lead. Serve others joyously. . . ." A video of Amanda reading Joan's letter aloud can be found at: https://www.youtube.com/watch?v=BQ8znSUilLc.

Chapter 39

222 **"Life is a precarious balance":** From an interview by Jan van den Bosch, in his film *Henri Nouwen: The Passion of a Wounded Healer*.

222 **"I feel quite anxious interiorly":** "Saturday May 4, 1996" entry in

Nouwen, handwritten 1995–96 sabbatical journals. An edited version of this passage is also in Nouwen, *Sabbatical Journey*, 160.

223 **drifting from place to place like a hungry ghost:** Henri wrote about his fascination with the Tibetan Buddhist concept of the hungry ghost in his "6 Feb 1996" entry in Nouwen, handwritten 1995–96 sabbatical journals, then in his "7 Feb 1996" entry he noted with self-aware humor that all day he felt like a hungry ghost. See also Nouwen, *Sabbatical Journey*, 99–100.

223 **Henri remembers how his embarrassment:** "Wednesday July 10, 1996" entry in Nouwen, handwritten 1995–96 sabbatical journals. Rodleigh Stevens also describes this scene in Stevens, "What a Friend We Had in Henri," 22–23.

225 **"When we radically claim God's unconditional love for us, we can forgive":** Nouwen, *Love, Henri*, 333.

225 **"I sometimes have thought, how would it be":** Nouwen, "As I Have Done So You Are Called to Do." See also Nouwen, *Here and Now*, 60–61.

225 **"through the eyes of God":** Nouwen, *The Return of the Prodigal Son*, 15, quoted in Chapter 37.

225 **"A trick is not complete unless":** Henri J. M. Nouwen, "Technicalities of Trapeze Movements: I. the Full-Twisting Double Lay-Out by Rodleigh," May 1992, 9. This typed transcript of Henri's unpublished handwritten notebook is held in the Nouwen Archives.

225 **"The Rodleighs are saying to me indirectly, don't be afraid to fly a little":** Nouwen, interview in English in the unedited footage for the film *Angels Over the Net*. This quotation is also found in the final English version of the film.

226 **He feels like he has been rising:** See Chapter 2 notes: "the trapeze became a dream for me. To be a trapeze artist symbolized for me the realization of the human desire for self-transcendence—rising above oneself, glimpsing the heart of things." The final sentence of the last book published in Henri's lifetime reads: "Together when we drink that cup as Jesus drank it we are transformed into the one body of the living Christ, always dying and always rising for the salvation of the world." Nouwen, *Can You Drink the Cup?* (Notre Dame, IN: Ave Maria Press, 1996), 111.

Epilogue

227 **"As the three flyers swung away from the pedestal board"**: Nouwen, "Chapter I," 9–10.

227 **Henri didn't die:** An account of Henri's last days in the hospital can be found in Nathan Ball's afterword to *Sabbatical Journey,* 223–26. See also Ford, *Wounded Prophet*, 200–207. Ball later wrote, "Henri's heart attack was indeed a gift that helped him to make a passage. . . . He had many struggles and shared them openly with his friends and through his numerous writings. But this I know: Henri died at peace with himself, his family, his own faith community of L'Arche, his friends, his vocation as a priest, and the God whose everlasting love had been Henri's beacon for sixty-four years." Nouwen, *Sabbatical Journey*, 226. Henri ended *The Inner Voice of Love*, which he was working on during his sabbatical and which arrived in bookstores the day of his Canadian funeral, with the words: "I have heard the inner voice of love, deeper and stronger than ever. I want to keep trusting in that voice and be led by it beyond the boundaries of my short life, to where God is all in all" (118).

228 **News of Henri's death reached the Flying Rodleighs:** Stevens, "What a Friend We Had in Henri," 1.

229 **During the long week as we waited for Henri's return:** Details about his two caskets are my own memories as a member of the Daybreak community. At the time, I was working in the Daybreak woodworking shop. I asked community members to create art for Henri, then I painted the community members' images onto the lid of Henri's casket: see Whitney-Brown, "Henri at Daybreak." For a photo and short description, see my Daybreak blog post "The Painted Doors of the Dayspring Chapel," September 1, 2019, https://larchedaybreak.com/the-painted-doors-of-the-dayspring-chapel%EF%BB%BF-by-carrie-whitney-brown/.

229 **Henri's body was buried twice:** Henri's remains were moved to St. John's Anglican Church in November 2010. Details about this second burial were provided by Sue Mosteller. See also Michael Swan, "Famous Catholic Author Nouwen Moved to Anglican Cemetery," *Catholic Register*, November 25, 2010, https://www.catholicregister.org/item/9400-famous-catholic-author-nouwen-moved-to-anglican-cemetery.

230 **"I suddenly realized that's what life is all about":** Transcribed from Henri's talk after receiving the COMISS Medallion in May 1994.

CREDITS AND PERMISSIONS